THE MIDDLE EAST

MILES 100   0   100   200   300 MILES

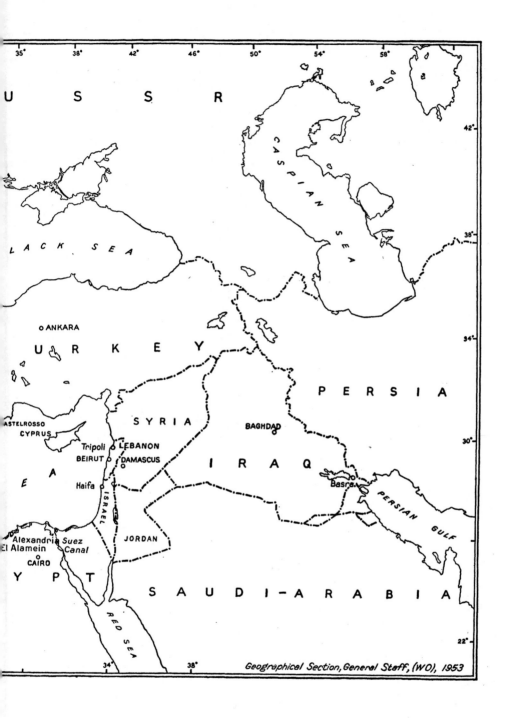

Geographical Section, General Staff, (WO), 1953

THE QUEEN'S OWN ROYAL WEST KENT REGIMENT
1920–1950

from the portrait by Mr. Simon Elwes, V.P.R.P.

H.R.H. THE DUCHESS OF KENT, C.I., G.C.V.O., G.B.E.

COLONEL-IN-CHIEF

THE QUEEN'S OWN
ROYAL WEST KENT
REGIMENT

1920–1950

Lieutenant-Colonel
H. D. CHAPLIN

MARLBOROUGH HOUSE,
S.W.

FOREWORD

This book is the continuation of the story of my Regiment, which began nearly two hundred years ago, and covers the thirty years from 1920 to 1950.

It shows that the tradition and fighting spirit of the Peninsula, Crimea, First World War, and many less important campaigns, have been maintained in peace and war during this eventful period.

I commend it as a record of work well and truly done, and as a guide to those who follow, of what is expected of them in The Queen's Own Royal West Kent Regiment.

Marina

THIS history of The Queen's Own Royal West Kent Regiment is dedicated to the everlasting memory of His Royal Highness The Duke of Kent, K.G., K.T., G.C.M.G., G.C.V.O., Colonel-in-Chief of the Regiment from March 1935 to August 1942, and of the 1,677 other members of the Regiment who gave their lives in the Second World War, 1939–1945.

Their names are inscribed in a Book of Remembrance, which rests on a lectern in All Saints' Church, Maidstone. A page of this Book is turned by a recruit from the Regimental Depot every week.

Roll of Honour
1939–1945

A list of Members of
THE QUEEN'S OWN
*who were killed in action
or died of wounds or disease
in the Second World War*

Ablett, A. W., 6345857, Cpl.
Absalom, L. C., 6467583, Pte.
Acott, J. T. E., 2032649, Pte.
Adams, A. E., 6018777, Pte.
Adams, B. F., 6342044, Sjt.
Adams, F. W., 7537012, Pte.
Adams, J. F., 6097514, Pte.
Adams, R. L., 6355612, Pte.
Adkins, A. C. W., Lt.
Akehurst, C. J., Lt.
Alder, A. J., 7402853, Cpl.
Alderton, B. R., 5829872, L/Cpl.
Aldred, R., 14566010, Pte.
Aldridge, H. C., 6095839, Pte.
Aldridge, W. C., 6348398, L/Sjt.
Alexander, W. E. G., 6348681, Pte.
Allan, J. H., 4859205, Pte.
Allchin, H. V., 6351483, Pte.
Allder, W., 6347244, Pte.
Allen, R. S., Capt.
Ancell, E. C., 6404520, L/Cpl.
Andrewartha, G., 14572160, Pte.
Andrews, F., 6026365, Pte.
Andrews, G. H., 6346660, Pte.
Ansell, D., 6405209, L/Cpl.
Appleton, G. A., 2/Lt.

Archer, A. G., 5571372, Pte.
Archer, D. H., M.C., Maj.
Archer, F. J., 6346932, Cpl.
Archer, T., 14518604, Pte.
Armitage, R. E., 4618186, L/Cpl.
Armitage, R. S., 6345775, Pte.
Armstead, R., M.M., 5345911, Cpl.
Arnell, D., 14394175, Pte.
Arnold, A. H., 6345261, Pte.
Arnott, L. G., 6022746, Pte.
Ashby, B. G., 6345760, Pte.
Ashby, P. F., 5344105, Pte.
Ashcroft, E., 14246262, Pte.
Ashmole, G. W., Lt.
Ashton, R. C., Lt.
Ashworth, W. K. G., 6347543, Pte.
Atkins, A. E., 810128, Pte.
Atkins, H. J., D.C.M., 6346229, W.O.II.
Atkins, T., 6345454, Pte.
Atkinson, G. N., 6348686, Pte.
Auger, F. W., 6106945, Pte.
Austrin, J. P., 5574584, Pte.
Auvray, L., 6354540, Pte.
Avis, J., 14219355, Pte.
Avis, R. F., 5510395, Pte.

Baber, C. J., 6343966, Pte.
Back, D. D., 6346978, Pte.
Back, E. J., 6350629, Pte.
Bacon, P. 5727190, Pte.
Bailey, E., 5727191, Pte.
Bailey, F., 6106586, Pte.
Bailey, H. E., 3976110, Pte.
Baker, G. G., 14026635, Pte.
Baker, G. S., 14216703, Pte.
Baker, R. T., 6289992, Pte.
Balbernie, A. G., M.C., Maj.
Baldwin, P. A., 6347218, Pte.
Baldwin, R. T., 6350378, L/Cpl.
Ball, A. C. J., 14578722, L/Cpl.
Ball, G., 6341584, L/Cpl.
Ball, S. G., 6347969, Pte.
Bampton, S. D., 6349577, Sjt.
Banbury, F., 5678008, Cpl.
Bangle, C., 6339742, Pte.
Barber, N. H., Lt.
Bareham, D. A., 6345759, L/Cpl.
Bargent, A. J., 5512332, Pte.
Barker, D., 5892400, Pte.
Barlow, T., 984292, Pte.
Barnes, D. F., 5509847, L/Cpl.
Barnes, G. L., 6348213, L/Cpl.
Barnes, J. C., 6018662, Pte.
Barnes, P. H., 6348690, Pte.
Barnett, A. S., 6345580, Pte.
Barnett, H. J., 6410481, Pte.
Barnett, V. F., 6346804, L/Cpl.
Baron, J. W., 6350380, Sjt.
Barr, J. W., 6353040, Pte.
Barratt, G. E., 14208439, Pte.
Barrett, H. B., 6097807, L/Sjt.
Barrett, R., 5191997, Pte.
Barrick, G., 14564391, Pte.
Bartlett, A. W. G., 6347135, Pte.
Bartlett, H. E., 6350585, Pte.
Bartlett, P. F., 14361812, Pte.
Barton, C. W., 6345615, Pte.
Barton, S., 6353936, Pte.
Batchelor, C. F., 6354546, Pte.
Batchelor, E. S., 844735, Pte.
Bate, J. M., 6345344, Sjt.
Bates, A., 6463324. Pte.
Bates, J. S., Lt.

Baynes, A. T., 6465647, Pte.
Baynham, E. J., 14574289, Pte.
Beadle, F. J. W., 6341349, W.O.II.
Beasley, K. A., 6344899, Pte.
Beauchamp, P. A., 6350861, Pte.
Beckett, H., 6349827, Pte.
Beeching, K. R., Capt.
Beer, H. G. R., 14551667, Pte.
Bell, T. A., 6350770, Pte.
Bell, W. S., 6198302, L/Cpl.
Benford, E. G., 14568847, Pte.
Benn, F., 6350862, Cpl.
Bennett, D. H., 6351281, Pte.
Bennett, F. E. H., 6403462, Sjt.
Benneworth, C. A., 5727197, Pte.
Benneworth, R., 6346082, Pte.
Berwick, E. J. H., 6346664, Pte.
Billingsley, L. T., 3971841, Pte.
Bingham, H. N., 1548720, Pte.
Binks, K., 4752459, Cpl.
Binstead, J. L., 5572772, Pte.
Birch, H., 6347387, Pte.
Bird, F., 14209992, Pte.
Bird, J. W. J., 5729812, Pte.
Bishop, E. J. R., 6347581, Pte.
Bishop, M. H. E., Lt.
Bishop, P. M., Lt.
Bishop, R. E., 5777304, Pte.
Blackley, T. C., 6349879, Cpl.
Blackman, L. E., 6350386, Cpl.
Bleakley, J. 6345606, Pte.
Blewitt, F., 6347500, Pte.
Blizard, H. S., 5625844, Pte.
Bloomfield, G. P., 6348864, Pte.
Bloomfield, J. W., 6348352, Pte.
Blundell, C. J., 6353757, Pte.
Boakes, J. H., 6346048, Pte.
Boakes, T., 6339924, Sjt.
Boarer, T. G., 6344680, Pte.
Booker, E. V., 6345291, Pte.
Boorman, F. J., 14517075, Pte.
Borrow, J. S. N., 5385346, Pte.
Bosanquet, R. G., Capt.
Botten, B. A., 6355621, Pte.
Botten, L. J., 6343578, Pte.
Botting, C. G., 6341288, W.O.II.
Bottle, E. R., 2/Lt.

Boughton, A. C., Lt.
Bourne, A. H., M.M., 6347155, Sjt.
Bourne, C. W. F., 6344241, Pte.
Bowen, A. W., 6353046, Pte.
Bowen, H. L., 6096127, Pte.
Bowers, J. A., 6104690, Pte.
Bowles, A. C., 6344489, Pte.
Bowles, R. F., 6351547, Cpl.
Bowman, C., 6350389, Sjt.
Boxwell, G. F., 6401983, Sjt.
Boydell, W., 14609242, Pte.
Bradick, F. J., 6410117, Pte.
Bradley, H., 4868083, Pte.
Bradshaw, S., 6107316, Pte.
Bradstreet, J., 6481749, Pte.
Brand, E. G., 6346132, L/Sjt.
Brattman, J. J., 5346620, Pte.
Breeze, R. R., 6348051, Pte.
Brewer, F. W., 6346279, Pte.
Bridges, R. A., 825571, Pte.
Briggs, S., 13001006, Pte.
Bright, G. F., 6023294, Pte.
Brooker, J. H., 6347329, Pte.
Brookes, E. A., 6345991, Pte.
Brophy, B., 14238624, Pte.
Brophy, T. J., M.M., 6405752, Sjt.
Broughton, F. L., 14619040, Pte.
Brown, C., 5827668, Pte.
Brown, E. G., 6350872, Pte.
Brown, J., 5677571, Pte.
Brown, W. J., 5679871, Pte.
Brown, W. R., 6348068, Pte.
Brown, W. R., 6351663, Pte.
Bruun, R. A., 14200370, Pte.
Bryan, D. C. S., D.S.O., Lt.-Col.
Bryer, J. F., 6343831, Pte.
Buck, W. F., 6344924, Cpl.
Buckingham, B. O., Lt.
Buckingham, F. E., 6345494, Pte.
Buckwell, H., 6334019, C/Sjt.
Bulmer, L., 6347448, Cpl.
Bunker, E. J., 14224638, Pte.
Bunnell, D. L., 14428930, Pte.
Bunney, W., 5507702, Pte.
Bunny, A. R. B., 6346388, L/Cpl.
Burden, J. W., 6459422, Pte.
Burden, L. A., M.M., 6104545, Cpl.

Burdett, H., 6022762, Pte.
Burford, K. J., 5193236, Pte.
Burgess, J. W., 6348865, L/Cpl.
Burke, M. A. T., Maj.
Burness, S. R., 6475774, L/Cpl.
Burton, A. D., 6344234, Sjt.
Burton, S., 14531670, Pte.
Bushell, E. T., 6340269, W.O.II
  (C.S.M.)
Butcher, F., 6345788, Pte.
Butchers, R., 5349536, Pte.
Butler, H. G., 6346387, Pte.
Butt, J. A. W., 6022323, Pte.
Buttery, H. D., 4399399, Pte.
Buxton, A. A., 6347398, Pte.
Byhurst, L. H., 6354313, Pte.
Byrne, J., 6344674, L/Cpl.

Caddey, E. A., 14295801, Pte.
Cage, A. W., 6344579, Pte.
Cairns, J. W., 404410, Cpl.
Cairns, T. J., 3254246, Pte.
Calton, S. F., 5572810, Pte.
Campbell, P. A. T. W., Lt.
Cannon, W. T. J., 5385729, Pte.
Capon, G. H., 6347260, Pte.
Carcas, R. C., 6355273, Pte.
Card, A. S., 5577011, L/Cpl.
Carey, D., 6351671, Pte.
Carlisle, A., 6344509, Pte.
Carpenter, D. J., 6347127, Pte.
Carter, F. A., 6101801, Pte.
Carter, F. G., 6345756, Pte.
Carwardine, F. C., 6338194, L/Sjt.
Cashman, J., 14414978, Pte.
Caskie, A. R. N., 6350396, Pte.
Cassidy, G., 6028881, Pte.
Castle, T. W., 6344395, Pte.
Catchpole, 6347855, Cpl.
Catmull, H. E. S., 6348570, Cpl.
Caughlin, L. T., 6340826, Pte.
Causbrook, M. A., 2/Lt.
Cave, W. O., Maj.
Chalkley, G., 6343433, Sjt.
Chalkley, K. A., 14295803, Pte.
Chamberlain, D. H., 6465117,
  L/Cpl.

Chambers, D. W., 1682594, Pte.
Champ, G., 5624218, Cpl.
Chantler, H. G., 6346538, Sjt.
Chapman, D. A., 6346678, Pte.
Chapman, D. T., 6344714, Pte.
Chapman, H. E., 2609532, Sjt.
Chapman, W. H., 6347363, Pte.
Charlton, H. F. D., 6095880, Pte.
Chatfield, F. E., 6346679, Pte.
Chattenton, J. J., 1662626, W.O.II
    (C.S.M.)
Chattenton, W. R., 6354323, Pte.
Cheale, A. G. M., 2/Lt.
Cheeseman, B. H., 6349891, Sjt.
Cheeseman, C. V., 6352502, Pte.
Cheesman, A. L. E., 6470953, Pte.
Cheesman, L., 6353968, Pte.
Cherry, E., 6346257, Pte.
Cherry, N. L., 5393668, Pte.
Child, H. J., 2/Lt.
Chinnery, C. W., 14545229, Pte.
Chudley, J. A., 5620599, Pte.
Chuter, J., 6344386, Pte.
Claringbold, C. E., 6086804, Pte.
Clark, H., 7734223, Sjt.
Clark, J. H., 6348704, Pte.
Clark, L. S., 5730685, Pte.
Clark, R., 3252736, Pte.
Clark, R. G., 6344824, Pte.
Clark, W. D., 6011525, Pte.
Clarke, G. A., 6020836, Pte.
Clay, G. J., 766932, Pte.
Clayton, F. G., 3661813, Pte.
Clayton, R. J., 14648482, Pte.
Clements, A. C., 6343958, Pte.
Clews, A. E., 6350882, Cpl.
Clifford, F. H., 6352117, Pte.
Cohen, E., 6346682, Pte.
Cohen, S. B., Lt.
Cole, J. J., 5730684, Pte.
Coleman, J. D., 14623367, Pte.
Coleman, R. G., 6214523, Pte.
Coleman, W. B., Maj.
Coleman, W. C., 5435453, Pte.
Collins, A. C., 6407209, Pte.
Collins, A. H., 6293905, Pte.
Collins, F. C., 920528, Pte.

Collins, H. A., 6345118, Pte.
Collins, J., 11257832, Pte.
Collins, L. S., 6344443, Pte.
Collins, S. W. J., 6345628, Sjt.
Collins, T. J., 5616078, Sjt.
Collins, W. J. 6350358, Cpl.
Collis, J. T., 6343943, Pte.
Colman, P., 6018686, Pte.
Colyer, R. A., 6348867, Pte.
Combe, G. E., Lt.
Comfort, J. W. A., 6345743, Cpl.
Conolly, L. D., 2/Lt.
Cook, A. F. D., 5617113, Bdsman.
Cook, E., 13092955, Pte.
Cook, E. C. F., 6347351, Pte.
Cook, R., 5733263, Pte.
Cook, R. C., 6017526, Pte.
Cook, T. G., 6341209, L/Cpl.
Cook, W., 3254253, Pte.
Cook, W. L., 6348985, Pte.
Cooper, A., 5349818, Pte.
Cooper, F. L., 6343200, Pte.
Cooper, G. L., 6094636, Pte.
Cooper, G. T., 2/Lt.
Cooper, W. E., 5339781, Pte.
Cooper, W. W., 5389071, Pte.
Corker, P. W., 5346658, Pte.
Cornelius, I. R., 27905, Sjt.
Cottrell, L. W., 14377942, Pte.
Cowburn, H. F., 5727233, Pte.
Cowie, A. C., 14208638, Pte.
Cox, F., 5833794, Pte.
Cox, F. A., 5958591, Pte.
Cox, F. W., 6344646, Pte.
Cox, W. H., 14262212, Pte.
Cracknell, S. J., 6351194, Pte.
Cragen, P. 6346427, Pte.
Crane, C. G. J., 6103540, Pte.
Crathern, A. H., 6014897, Sjt.
Craven, H. W., 14351907, L/Cpl.
Crayford, P. L. 6346013, Pte.
Creasey, D. H., 6345222, L/Cpl.
Crewdson, R. F., 6346893, Pte.
Crisp, C. F., 6345901, Pte.
Crittell, A., 5726418, Pte.
Crook, R. L., Capt.
Crosbie, H. J., 6349907, Pte.

Crosby, M. J., M.M., 6405759, Sjt.
Cross, F. G., 5888338, Pte.
Cross, R. V., 5835480, Pte.
Crossley, J., 4622303, Cpl.
Crossman, J., 14200407, Pte.
Crouch, E., 5777396, Pte.
Crouch, G. W. L., 6347102, Pte.
Crouch, N. L., 5572752, Pte.
Crouch, R. H., 6347194, Pte.
Croucher, S., 6298601, Pte.
Crowther, F., 6348130, Pte.
Crutchfield, L. W., 916231, Pte.
Culy, W. R., 14655758, Pte.
Cummings, W., 5572677, Pte.
Curd, F. C., 14337697, Pte.
Curd, S. J., 6351920, Cpl.
Curley, J. J., 6349908, Cpl.
Curtis, E. G., 6349613, Pte.
Curtis, J. A. T., 6346488, Sjt.
Cutler, R. E., 14216256, Pte.
Cutter, M. A., 6094585, L/Cpl.

Daborn, L. B., 14219837, Pte.
Dadd, A. J., 6295580, Pte.
Dale, G., 3607471, Pte.
Dale, G. E., 6018874, Pte.
Dalley, F. A., 6469734, Pte.
Dalton, F., 5623681, L/Cpl.
Daly, E. A., 14618035, Pte.
Daly, P., 5831954, Pte.
Daniels, H. J., 6345664, Pte.
Daniels, J., 6345022, Pte.
Danks, G. A., 6345172, Sjt.
Danks, W. J., 14207788, Pte.
Dann, E. R., Maj.
Davey, E. C., 6350408, Pte.
Davey, R. W., 6352693, Pte.
Davidge, R. G., 14646569, L/Cpl.
Davidson, J. E., 6347484, Pte.
Davie, W., 5616400, Sjt.
Davies, H., 6013487, Pte.
Davies, K. R., 14270864, Pte.
Davies, L. H., 6345583, L/Cpl.
Davies, R. L., 6346691, Pte.
Davies, T. F., 5348506, Pte.
Davies, W. D., 13078898, Pte.
Davies, W. F., 6339941, Pte.

Davis, G., 5572707, W.O.II
 (C.S.M.)
Davis, N. G., 6344161, Pte.
Daws, E. V., 6354868, Pte.
Dawson, E., 6345697, Pte.
Dawson, E., 4609924, Cpl.
Day, A. F., 6350696, Pte.
Day, A. W., 985313, Pte.
Day, B. J., 6354333, Pte.
Day, H. A., 6346198, Pte.
Day, L. M., 6344772, Cpl.
Daykin, T. B. F., 1658557, Pte.
Dean, A. W., 6398654, Pte.
Dean, J. E., 6410100, Pte.
Debenham, D. M., 5828996, Pte.
Degens, H. J., M.M., 6350412, Sjt.
De Lahay, R. E., 6345070, Pte.
Dell, B. E., 6347309, Pte.
Dempster, J. 6411153, Cpl.
Dench, C. B., 6352676, Pte.
Dench, J. B., 6352991, Pte.
Denholm, J. W., 6410866, Pte.
Dennard, J. A., 6341881, L/Cpl.
De Roode, J., 6339833, Pte.
Devonport, A. E. E., 6345895,
 C.Q.M.S.
Dewe, T. N., 6350413, L/Cpl.
Dewing, E. F., 6352788, Pte.
Dewitt, H. St. C., 6292040, Pte.
Dexter, I. J., M.M., 7668364, Cpl.
Dickens, A., 6474621, Cpl.
Dickenson, H., 6347761, Pte.
Dickie, E. J., 14411418, Pte.
Dillon, M., 6354993, Pte.
Dillon, M. J., 6349003, Cpl.
Diment, B. P., 14579800, Pte.
Dinmore, G. J., 5727244, Pte.
Ditton, J. G., 6346695, Pte.
Divall, J. W., 6347596, Pte.
Dix, W., 6100236, Pte.
Dixey, J. E., 6345948, Pte.
Dolding, J. ,6350640, L/Cpl.
Dorsett, C. P., 6098225, L/Cpl.
Dorsett, R., 6349636, Pte.
Dougan, G., 6350433, Sjt.
Doughty, F., 14742810, Pte.
Dowell, W. J., 1115502, Cpl.

Dowling, G. W., 6410546, L/Cpl.
Dowling, P., 6144871, Pte.
Down, D. V., 841613, Pte.
Downs, C., 6349717, Pte.
Drew, H. S. G., 6344223, Pte.
Drewett, T. H. E., 6348719, Cpl.
Driver, C. G., 6347494, Pte.
Driver, F. J., 6347671, Pte.
Driver, W. W., 6349615, Pte.
Duck, E., 14566917, Pte.
Dudman, K., 14603201, Pte.
Dudman, R. R., 6354583, Pte.
Duffy, P., 6346801, Pte.
Duncan, A. C., 6353627, Pte.
Dunk, S. J., 6101842, Pte.
Dunk, V., 6410818, Pte.
Dunn, E. J., 5349379, Pte.
Dunn, F. C., 5630956, Pte.
Dunning, A. H. T., 6342808, Pte.
Durance, F. F., 6345921, L/Cpl.
Durling, G. W., 6347586, Pte.
Durrant, E. J., 6018177, Pte.
Dwyer, E. J., 6299265, Pte.
Dyas, G. M., M.C., Maj.

Eames, A. D., 14742814, Pte.
Earnshaw, N., 1695568, L/Cpl.
Easten, A. F., 6464194, Pte.
Easterbrook, G. H. V., 14655999, Pte.
Ebsworth-Donkin, D., 885322, Pte.
Ecclestone, G. B., 6346144, L/Cpl.
Edden, N. H., Lt.
Edgell, A., 6095908, Pte.
Edmonds, W. G., 6348327, Pte.
Edwards, E. J., 4035320, Pte.
Edwards, F., 6343382, Pte.
Edwards, H. W., 6346377, Pte.
Edwards, J., 13021662, Pte.
Elcome, A. J., 6348179, Pte.
Ellett, R. F., 6348350, Pte.
Elliott, C., 14391005, Pte.
Elliott, F. H., 6346014, Cpl.
Elliott, L. H., 6345040, Pte.
Ellis, J. H., 6350245, Pte.
Ellis, T., 6344994, Pte.
Ellis, W. H. K., 5624093, L/Sjt.

Elms, E. G., 6198727, Pte.
Emberson, F., 6346190, Pte.
Emmerick, S. H., 6347731, Pte.
Ensinger, W. G., 6349916, Pte.
Ensor, M. H., Capt.
Errington, L. A., 6022336, Pte.
Ettridge, P. C., 6342447, C/Sjt.
Evans, E. H., 6350405, Pte.
Everett, S. H., 6200532, Pte.
Everitt, L. S., 6031285, Pte.
Everson, J., 6349532, Pte.

Facey, T. R. C., Lt.
Fagnoni, R. M., 6102731, Pte.
Fairway, G., 6347505, Pte.
Fall, P. H., 6149336, Pte.
Falwasser, A. G., Lt.
Fancett, D. G., 6346283, Pte.
Fanning, J., 6353828, Pte.
Faram, M. D., 6343599, Sjt.
Farley, C., 5629629, Pte.
Farmer, W. H., 6345148, Pte.
Farrant, B. R., 1828108, Pte.
Farrell, T. J. L., Lt.
Felgate, A. H., 6350421, Sjt.
Fennell, J. G., 6347372, Pte.
Fidler, G., 6354068, Pte.
Fidler, H. D., 6346479, Pte.
Fidler, J. E., 14585611, Pte.
Fineran, G. E., 5511477, Pte.
Firman, W. R., 6350156, Pte.
Fish, G. H., 6019810, Pte.
Fish, L. G., 14204095, Pte.
Fisher, H. J., 6355493, Pte.
Fisher, L. C., 6349924, Pte.
Fitch, J., 14346015, Pte.
Fitzgerald, J., 6346360, Cpl.
Fleming, A. J., 14537938, Pte.
Fletcher, F. C., 6022337, Pte.
Flint, A. G., 6346908, Pte.
Floyd, W. R., 6096123, Pte.
Flynn, J. A., 6351878, L/Cpl.
Flynn, P., 269150, Pte.
Follit, W. R., Capt.
Foord, C. A. V., 6355340, Pte.
Foord, T. G., 6347003, Cpl.
Forbes, D., 6346408, Pte.

Forsyth, W., 14209529, Pte.
Foskett, J. E., 6344721, Pte.
Foster, W., 3652768, Sjt.
Foulkes, T., 3660828, Pte.
Fowler, D. G., 6097132, Pte.
Fowler, H. A. L., 6345518, Pte.
Fox, W. C., 6343889, Pte.
Franklyn, G. M., 6387027, Pte.
Fraser, R. K. J., Lt.
Freail, B., 6018186, Pte.
Freeman, D., 6405495, L/Cpl.
Freeman, V. C., 6350257, Cpl.
Freeman, W., 5510504, Pte.
Frost, W. J., 5727267, Pte.
Fry, J. J., 5617880, Pte.
Fryer, E. C., 6345104, Pte.
Fullerton, G. E., 5346689, Pte.
Funnell, F. G., 6343102, Pte.
Furminger, T. J., 14916093, L/Cpl.
Fynney, B., 6346361, Pte.

Gale, T., 6299644, L/Cpl.
Gallagher, F. W., 14388056, Pte.
Galley, E. H., 6022790, Pte.
Gallop, A. L., 6405195, Pte.
Gallop, H. I., 5677955, L/Cpl.
Galvin, J., 6198942, Pte.
Gammon, H. J., 6345297, W.O.II
  (C.S.M.)
Gantlett, A. S., 5577304, L/Cpl.
Gardner, R. E., 1536065, Pte.
Gartman, L., 6142865, Pte.
Gartrell, R., 14526273, Pte.
Gaston, G. H., 6351211, Pte.
Gaunt, J. A. W., 14646259, Pte.
Gee, J., 6097566, L/Sjt.
Geear, E. J., 6344312, L/Sjt.
Gent, R. A., 6350430, Pte.
George, F. G., 6097567, Pte.
George, J. N., 6345315, Cpl.
Gibbins, J. E., 6757848, Cpl.
Gibbs, F. G., 5832886, Cpl.
Giffen, H. J., 6022792, Pte.
Gigg, A. G., 6196256, Pte.
Gilbert, J. A., 6346570, L/Cpl.
Giles, L., 5623762, Pte.
Giles, P., 6387034, Sjt.

Gilham, E. T., 14559722, Pte.
Gilham, F. J., 6350920, Pte.
Gill, P., 6412477, Pte.
Gillitt, T., 3778961, Pte.
Gilmour, A., 3253148, Pte.
Gipp, W. R. E., 14533777, L/Cpl.
Gipps, F. W., 6351563, Pte.
Goddard, J. S., 14370035, L/Cpl.
Godden, A. W., 14517145, Pte.
Godliman, A. F., 5348997, Pte.
Goggins, T., 3129717, Pte.
Goldfinch, C. T., 6347190, Pte.
Goldsmith, W. C., 6025292, Pte.
Golledge, W. H., 5727274, Sjt.
Gomar, G., 6346823, Sjt.
Gooding, P., 5620901, Pte.
Goodsell, T. A., 14208663, Pte.
Gostinsky, R., 6349589, Pte.
Gough, W. A., 6343594, Pte.
Goulds, J. A., 6347496, Pte.
Goulding, J. H., 5435231, Pte.
Govey, L. A., 6022342, Pte.
Gowing, F. J., 6346336, Pte.
Grace, L. F., 6459235, Pte.
Grant, S. T., 14331629, Pte.
Gray, C., 6017496, Pte.
Gray, F., 5434450, Pte.
Gray, J. E., 4868115, Pte.
Grazier, W., 5113680, Pte.
Green, C. F., 6346866, L/Cpl.
Green, H. F., 6343257, Cpl.
Green, J., 6350434, Pte.
Green, J. A., 14569064, L/Cpl.
Green, R. H., 6348518, Pte.
Green, S. J., 6097581, Pte.
Greenwood, F. G., 5885011, Cpl.
Greenyer, W. R., 804771, W.O.II.
Gregory, A., 6353339, Pte.
Gregory, P. C., 14413927, Pte.
Griffith, K. J., Lt.
Griffiths, C. T., 14205059, Pte.
Griffiths, L. E., 6345169, Pte.
Grigg, A. R., 6352271, Pte.
Grigsby, H. F. J., Lt.
Groeger, G. T., 6347934, Pte.
Groom, D. C., 14407234, Pte.
Grove, F. J., Lt.

Grove, N. C., 6345959, L/Cpl.
Guilford, A. E., 6410503, Pte.
Gully, E. W., 14372280, Pte.
Gurling, A. E., 6292816, L/Sjt.
Gutteridge, C. M., 5391145, Pte.
Gutteridge, W. T., 6347953, Pte.
Guy, C., 6020392, L/Cpl.
Gwilt, I. W., 3909655, Pte.

Hackett, J., 6346147, L/Cpl.
Haddow, W. C., 6406947, Pte.
Hadingham, W. G., 6455292, Pte.
Hadley, G., 5260628, Pte.
Hadnutt, H. A., 6344764, Pte.
Hagger, P. A. W., 6345185, Pte.
Hailstone, G. E., 6097588, Pte.
Haines, W. F., M.M., 6090378, W.O.II (C.S.M.)
Hale, H. C., 5777445, Pte.
Hale, S. F., 5624603, Pte.
Halfpenny, A. C., 6022799, Pte.
Hall, A., 5435309, Cpl.
Hall, E. G., 6465762, Pte.
Hall, E. S., 4209748, Pte.
Hall, F., 5347094, Pte.
Hall, J., 6354351, Pte.
Hall, J. R. J., 6339950, Pte.
Hall, T., 6344977, Pte.
Halliday, M. L., 4189672, W.O.II.
Hammond, E., 6347006, Pte.
Hammond, J. W., 14217097, Pte.
Hammond, R. A. L., 6350928, L/Cpl.
Hance, C. G., 6344947, Pte.
Hancock, W. E., 3654012, Pte.
Hanes, W. C., 6347210, Pte.
Hankinson, A. A., 6348741, Pte.
Hanks, S. J., 6344852, Pte.
Hanks, W. M., 6344825, Pte.
Hansen-Raae, H. W., M.C., Capt.
Hanton, H. E., 6095933, Cpl.
Hardee, M. D., 6348097, Pte.
Harding, A. A., 6089415, Sjt.
Harding, D. E., 14402701, Pte.
Hards, J. A., 6345411, Pte.
Hardy, C. E., 6027936, Pte.
Hardy, W., 6102654, Pte.

Hargreaves, J., 3393904, Pte.
Harman, G. S., 6347843, Pte.
Harman, J. P., V.C., 295822, L/Cpl.
Harris, A. E., 6354353, Pte.
Harris, A. T., 6474116, Pte.
Harris, E., 6355482, Pte.
Harris, F. L., 3657844, Pte.
Harris, J. S., 6355502, Pte.
Harris, R. D., 6347877, Cpl.
Harrold, S. G., 6348745, Cpl.
Harsley, L., 1790176, Pte.
Hart, A. J., 7946642, Pte.
Hartridge, J. W., 6217403, Cpl.
Harvey, B. E., Capt.
Harvey, G. H., 14204201, Pte.
Harwood, G. V., 3965163, Pte.
Haslam, J. G., 3662872, Pte.
Hatton, E. G., 6458566, Cpl.
Hawker, A. T., 6341913, Pte.
Hawkes, G. H., 14208672, Pte.
Hawkes, M., 6097596, Pte.
Hawkes, S. G., 6347615, Pte.
Hawkins, J. E., 6344099, Sjt.
Haxell, C. I., Capt.
Hay, T. E., 6351101, Pte.
Hayden, C., 6354357, Pte.
Haydon, H. J., 14204206, Pte.
Hayes, E., 6341052, Pte.
Haynes, S. K., 5344157, Pte.
Hayter, G., 5727289, Pte.
Hayward, A., 906798, L/Cpl.
Hayward, A. W., 6355349, Pte.
Haywood, G., 4860442, Pte.
Hazell, H., 5507453, Pte.
Hazell, J. A., 6402299, L/Cpl.
Healey, D., 6348746, L/Cpl.
Hearnden, L. W. C., 6348222, Pte.
Heath, F. R., 14417957, Pte.
Heath, T. J., 6398224, Pte.
Heaven, H. J., 14585552, Pte.
Hedger, E. S., 5505166, Pte.
Hedges, H. E. G., 11406807, Pte.
Heley, A. F., 3906591, Pte.
Helmore, D. W., 6344836, W.O.II (C.S.M.)
Hemmington, J. T., 14337778, Pte.

Hemsley, F. B., 6345633, Cpl.
Hemsley, W. O., 6406167, Pte.
Henderson, L. A., 14200501, Pte.
Hendy, G. F., 6029164, Pte.
Henman, L. W., 5350651, Pte.
Henniker, W. J., 6342994, Sjt.
Henson, A. M., 14625281, Pte.
Henson, G. W. T., 6100261, Pte.
Henson, R. P., 5891950, Pte.
Hesketh, J. K., 14408534, Pte.
Hewett, G. H., 6344076, Pte.
Hewett, V. H., Lt.
Hewitt, E. H., 6100262, Pte.
Hewitt, J. L., 6353387, Pte.
Hewitt, W. A., 5260691, Pte.
Hidden, P. 6344743, Pte.
Higgins, A. C., 6343638, Pte.
Higgins, A. T., 6341575, L/Sjt.
Higgins, P. G., 6022347, Pte.
Higgins, R. C., 5681059, Pte.
Hill, C. F., 7946693, Pte.
Hill, E. F., Capt.
Hill, E. G., 6344738, Pte.
Hill, H. C., 14559741, Pte.
Hill, S. J., 6097603, Pte.
Hill, W. H., 2182037, L/Cpl.
Hilliard, L., 6093641, Pte.
Hills, E. R. G., 6346023, Pte.
Hind, J. L., 3598082, Pte.
Hinton, R., 6342915, Pte.
Hitchcock, J. E., 6351447, Pte.
Hocking, D. C. E., 6347374, Pte.
Hodgkiss, J., 5434449, Pte.
Hodson, A. J., 5734023, Pte.
Hole, J. R. T., 6339804, Pte.
Holford, C., 6343628, Pte.
Holland, G. G., 6343858, Cpl.
Hollands, G. E. R., 6346584, Pte.
Hollingsworth, J., 6351745, Pte.
Holloway, G., 5434745, Sjt.
Holman, S. W., 6971009, Pte.
Hook, B. D., 6347580, Pte.
Hooley, H. F., 961330, Pte.
Hooson, S., 14579286, Pte.
Hopkins, H. T., 5126613, Pte.
Hopkins, J. F., 5339047, Pte.
Horton, C., 6347662, Cpl.

Horton, G., 6345781, Pte.
Horton, S., 14322943, Pte.
Horton, V. W. L., 6343589, Pte.
Horwood, F. C., 6354364, Pte.
Houghton, D. W., 14681052, Pte.
Houghton, S. F., 6339554, L/Sjt.
Houlker, D. R., 5346718, Pte.
Houlton, G. H., 4977802, Pte.
Howard, A. E., 849475, Pte.
Howard, A. J., M.M., 6346586, W.O.II.
Howard, N. S., 6347749, Pte.
Howard, S. A., 5775978, Cpl.
Howe, B., 14204247, Pte.
Howe, L. W., 6347626, Pte.
Howell, A., 5434650, Cpl.
Howell, R. H., 6345043, Pte.
Howell, W. K., 6348751, Pte.
Howells, L., 6345484, Pte.
Howes, A. W., 14549692, Pte.
Howes, G. H., 3604177, Pte.
Howlett, B., D.S.O., Brig.
Hoy, C. W., 5889491, Pte.
Hudson, H. F., 6342367, Pte.
Hudson, L. H., 5677432, Pte.
Hughes, F. C., 6147110, Pte.
Hughes, P., 6348752, Pte.
Hughes, W. J., 6199518, Sjt.
Humphries, A. E., 6355275, Pte.
Humphries, C. F., 6342696, Pte.
Humphries, H. T., 6344702, Pte.
Hunt, D. S., 6344473, Cpl.
Hunt, E. C., 6347140, Pte.
Hunt, F. G., 6103455, Pte.
Hunt, J. H., 5349797, Pte.
Hunt, K. H. A., 1789584, Pte.
Hunt, S. C., 6020415, L/Sjt.
Hunt, W. S., 6346026, W.O.II (C.S.M.)
Hunter, W. C., 6411420, Pte.
Hurd, R. F., 6352771, Pte.
Hurley, R. F., 6344521, Pte.
Hurst, W. G., 6022816, L/Cpl.
Huskinson, E., 14406424, Pte.

Inglis, G. E. H., Lt.
Ingrams, H. E., 6352529, Pte.

B

Inward, C. V. M., Maj.
Iontton, E. N., 6347647, Pte.
Ireson, A. H., 14549693, Pte.
Isabel, G. E., 6020546, Pte.
Ison, J., 5346068, Pte.
Isted, H. E., 6345464, Pte.
Ives, R. G., 6479534, Pte.
Ives, T. L. G., 6346099, Cpl.

Jack, D. J., 6346152, Pte.
Jackson, E. W. G., 14215844, Pte.
Jackson, S. D. G., 6410362, Pte.
Jackson, T. C., 6348156, Sjt.
Jackson, W. H. C., 6340531, L/Cpl.
Jaggs, A., 6349954, Pte.
James, A. F., 6344638, Cpl.
James, B. J., 5260243, Pte.
James, G. B., 5572780. Cpl.
James, J., 6345390, Pte.
James, L., 787916, Pte.
Jeal, R., 14337805, Pte.
Jeffrey, W. A., 6466308, Pte.
Jenkins, M. R., 14541622, Pte.
Jenkins, S., 6468264, Pte.
Jenkins, W. J., 6348755, Pte.
Jenner, D. V., 6346172, Pte.
Jennings, D. W., 5339631, Pte.
Jennings, P., 6351542, Pte.
Jessett, E. J., 6341311, Pte.
Jesshope, F. C., 6345961, Pte.
Johncock, T., 14204282, Pte.
Johncock, V. J., 6290542, Pte.
Johnson, E., 5960604, Pte.
Johnson, G. W., 6336978, W.O.III.
Johnson, W., 6354623, L/Cpl.
Johnson, W. J., 6471368, Pte.
Jones, C. J., 6106975, Pte.
Jones, D. B., 3955492, Pte.
Jones, D. H., 14217011, Pte.
Jones, D. S., 14411822, Pte.
Jones, E. C., 6347416, L/Cpl.
Jones, F. J., 6097273, Pte.
Jones, G. O., 4188834, Pte.
Jones, J. C., 6150316, Pte.
Jones, J. J., 6350943, Pte.
Jones, J. O., 6096161, Pte.
Jones, J. P., 6344958, Pte.

Jones, R. A., 14411535, Pte.
Jones, R. C., 6349210, Pte.
Jones, W. G. F., 6343762, Pte.
Jones, W. H., 7896390, Pte.
Judge, A. E., 6296208, Cpl.
Jupp, A. E., 6347914, Pte.

Kay, A. E., 14204295, Pte.
Keane, M. H., Maj.
Keating, C. J., 14216736, Pte.
Keeler, R., 6353173, Pte.
Keene, H. R., 6350169, Pte.
Keep, G. D., 6734751, Pte.
Keith, N. 4271770, Pte.
Kelly, E., 6346727, Pte.
Kemp, W. J., 5727316, Pte.
Kench, G. H., M.M., 6350171, Pte.
Kennard, D. G., 6345395, Pte.
Kennedy, M., 6102626, Pte.
Kennedy, P. L., 14413958, Pte.
Kent, H.R.H. the Duke of, K.G.,
    K.T., G.C.M.G., G.C.V.O.,
    Colonel-in-Chief.
Kent, R. D., 6287135, Pte.
Kenvin, F. J., 5381920, Pte.
Kerr, W. M., Lt.
Kershaw, 3866115, Pte.
Kessell, A. C., 6476386, Pte.
Keyes, S. A. K., Lt.
Kiddell, S. R., 6404438, Cpl.
King, B. G., 6404437, Pte.
King, H. J., B.E.M., 6347577, Sjt.
King, S., 14207859, L/Cpl.
King, S. J., 5727319, Pte.
Kirby, F. 5732696, Pte.
Kirby, R. J., 6350476, Sjt.
Knevett, C. G., 6105896, Pte.
Knight, G. W., 5336083, L/Cpl.
Knight, J. W., 5349833, Pte.
Knight, R. W., 6343585, Cpl.
Konstandenou, D. J., 14335693,
    Pte.

Laddy, M., 6387023, Pte.
Laidlaw, D. R., 6353889, Pte.
Lamb, H. A., 5575035, Pte.
Lamb, J. W. H., 6345589, Pte.
Lambert, S. A., 5777483, Pte.

Lambert, T. F., 5511209, Pte.
Lancaster, F., 5494941, Pte.
Lane, K. J., 14224773, Pte.
Langford, A. E., 6342518, L/Cpl.
Lansdown, H. G., 6146182, Pte.
Lashmar, F. C., 6344285, L/Cpl.
Laver, T., 14317132, Pte.
Lawrence, C., 6346102, Pte.
Lawrence, E. R., 6387016, L/Cpl.
Lawry, E., M.M., 5511086, L/Cpl.
Leach, G. W. H. F., 6344493, W.O.III.
Leagas, T. A., 6410606, Pte.
Lee, A., 6399346, Pte.
Lee, J., 5629582, Pte.
Lee, W. E., 5676031, L/Cpl.
Lee, W. J., 6093678, Pte.
Lees, E., 2182189, Pte.
Len, F. E., 5623669, Pte.
Lendon-Smith, L. J., Lt.
Leonard, P., 5625371, Pte.
Leslie, J. R. L., Lt.
Lewis, L. F. G., 6345525, Pte.
Lewis, L. L., 6353417, Cpl.
Lewis, W. J., 6023186, Pte.
Lewry, J. H., 6411837, Pte.
Lidstone, F. J., 6345571, Pte.
Lihou, R. L., 6102796, Cpl.
Linck, F. W. P. J., Lt.
Lingard, A. A., 6022831, Pte.
Lingham, R. N. G., M.M., 6348273, L/Cpl.
Linstead, T. E., 6153533, Pte.
Lisney, J. F., 6345166, L/Cpl.
Little, W. C., 6143691, Pte.
Littley, E., 1789554, Pte.
Lloyd, E. J., 14604377, L/Cpl.
Lloyd, J. E., 5735078, Pte.
Lockhead, J. J., 6344110, L/Cpl.
Long, G. J., 5620406, Pte.
Longhorn, T. W. S., 14505896, Pte.
Longhurst, H. J., 6345954, L/Cpl.
Longmore, W. F., 2182075, Cpl.
Looker, C., 14400187, Pte.
Lovell, H. G., 13048379, Pte.
Lovelock, B. C., 5577373, Pte.
Lovelock, R. C., 6345233, Pte.

Lucas, G., 6341254, Pte.
Luck, D. E., 6346347, Pte.
Luff, C. D., 5835520, Pte.
Luff, H. H., 6406175, Pte.
Lugg, F. H. G., 5500550, Pte.
Luke, H. R., 6344485, W.O.III (P.S.M.)
Lunnon, H. W., 6353636, Pte.
Lupson, C. G., Capt.
Lusted, G. A., 6345429, Pte.
Lynn, H. W., 6346735, L/Sjt.
Lyons, N. W., 6345917, Pte.

Mabbott, J. W., 4864462, Pte.
Mabbutt, S. F. S., 14405938, Pte.
Mace, E. E. W., 6342096, Pte.
Mace, J. A., 6345873, Pte.
Mace, K. F., 6353687, Pte.
Macgregor, K. G., 14699449, Pte.
Mack, P., 5342953, Pte.
Macvicar, A. F., 5630040, Pte.
Maddy, C. E., 3910113, L/Cpl.
Magee, C. D., 6093683, Pte.
Maguire, J., 6095988, L/Sjt.
Main, T. W., 14528921, Pte.
Makins, A. W., 5777495, L/Cpl.
Males, R. C. D., 6354386, Pte.
Mancey, D. A. A., 6406367, Pte.
Mann, G. E., 6021609, L/Cpl.
Manning, H., 14528184, Pte.
Manning, T. W., 7880997, Sjt.
Mansfield, G. T., 5836846, Pte.
Mantle, R., 5351128, Pte.
Marks, P. C., 799073, Pte.
Marley, C. N., 2/Lt.
Marlow, A. H., 6400633, Pte.
Marsh, C. G., 4032466, Pte.
Marsh, R. H., 6353029, Cpl.
Marshall, I. S., Lt.
Marshall, R., 14337343, Pte.
Marshall, W., 4623730, Cpl.
Martin, A. G., 6353788, Pte.
Martin, A. T., 6351760, Pte.
Martin, C. C., 6347810, Pte.
Martin, E. S., 6344470, Pte.
Martin, E. S., 6347624, Pte.
Martin, F. T., 6347490, Pte.

Martin, G., 5572794, Cpl.
Martin, G. H., 6355036, Pte.
Martin, J., 1695543, Cpl.
Martin, J. H., 2045666, Pte.
Martin, N., 14208521, Pte.
Martin, T. G., 6344491, Pte.
Martin, W. E., 6341001, Pte.
Mason, D. J., 6348558, Pte.
Mason, H., 6351471, Pte.
Mason, J., 6340940, Pte.
Mather, J. F., 3607371, Pte.
Mathieson, W. J., 6349970, L/Cpl.
Matthews, E., 6342249, Pte.
Matthews, G. L., 6343557, Cpl.
Maunder, B. L., 5618820, Cpl.
Maxwell, A. W., 6346935, Pte.
May, F. W., 6346606, Pte.
Maycox, G., 14353575, Pte.
Mayle, J. W., 5932790, Sjt.
Maynard, G. L., 14408274, Pte.
McAvoy, E., 14207026, Pte.
McCarthy, C. F. T., 6354385, Pte.
McClelland, S., 6344536, Pte.
McCrum, A., 13021744, Pte.
McDermott, J. P., 1790450, Pte.
McDonnell, W. M., 4196646, Pte.
McEvoy, M., 14351440, Pte.
McGrath, P., 6353883, Pte.
McHale, M., 5435816, Pte.
McKay, J. D., 6022362, Cpl.
McLean, J. S., 6346063, Pte.
McManus, T., Lt.
McNamee, J., 6093718, Pte.
McQuade, R. G., 14216403, Cpl.
McVitie, H. W. H., 6410545, Pte.
Mead, G., 6350965, Pte.
Mead, L. T., Capt.
Meads, G. E., 6345009, Pte.
Mealing, A. C., 14575978, Pte.
Meardon, T. A., 6097666, Pte.
Mecham, F. C., 6347281, Pte.
Medland, C. J., 6348015, Pte.
Mendoza, E. I., 6396498, Pte.
Metson, T., 6350967, Pte.
Midgley, H., 6457515, Pte.
Mildenhall, W. L., Lt.
Miles, A. E., 6466903, Cpl.

Miles, A. G., 14410796, Pte.
Miles, A. H., 874090, Cpl.
Miles, J. H., 3907297, Pte.
Milham, R. D., 14217787, Pte.
Miller, J. A., 6354392, Pte.
Miller, J. F., 6346512, Pte.
Miller, S., 5348475, Pte.
Millest, C. H., 1076618, Pte.
Millichap, W. G., 6198952, Sjt.
Millington, E. H., 6344986, Pte.
Mills, J. T., 6344402, Pte.
Mills, W. E., 5834144, Pte.
Millward, J. W., 6342725, Sjt.
Mitcham, E. C., 6350969, Pte.
Mitchell, A. G., 6342432, L/Cpl.
Mitchell, H. L., 6355100, Pte.
Mitchem, R. A. J., 6094576, Pte.
Modlock-Vangelder, J., 7956645, Pte.
Mogie, W., 14544530, Pte.
Molloy, M., 14539319, L/Cpl.
Molony, R. H., Maj.
Monaghan, C. J., 5726221, Cpl.
Monahan, D., 2/Lt.
Money, P. S., 5777503, Pte.
Moody, E. A., 14408573, Pte.
Moon, J., 1731614, Pte.
Moore, F., 4978223, Pte.
Moore, H., 14556341, Pte.
Morgan, A., 3660486, L/Cpl.
Morgan, F., 6345031, Pte.
Morgans, G., 14552300, Pte.
Morley, T. H., 5572833, Cpl.
Morris, E. A., 6097669, Pte.
Morris, H. D., 5253337, Cpl.
Morris, H. W., 6346155, Pte.
Morris, J. R., 5630304, Pte.
Morris, R. G., 5513435, Pte.
Morris, S. A., 5888396, Cpl.
Morris, S. S., 6353108, Pte.
Morrish, E. P., 5626143, Cpl.
Morrissey, S., 5777605, Pte.
Mortimore, H. C., 6355521, Pte.
Morton, C. E. J., Capt.
Morton, J., 5382984, Pte.
Moss, F., 6093685, Pte.
Moss, L. D., 6347111, Pte.

Mott, A. E., 14368050, Pte.
Mounger, S. P., 6348229, Pte.
Mousdell, J., 6093686, Pte.
Moxon, C. H. H., 6342058, Cpl.
Moxworthy, W. G. S., 6475588, Cpl.
Moyes, J., 6343367, Sjt.
Muir, W. L., 6345311, Pte.
Muldoon, J., 6022942, Pte.
Mullarkey, M. J., 3965203, Pte.
Mulligan, J., 6348784, Pte.
Mullins, A. D., 6344448, Cpl.
Mullins, E. J., 14660991, Pte.
Munday, F. E., 6353110, Pte.
Murphy, J. H., 6355134, Pte.
Murrant, A. H., 6344555, Pte.
Murray, L. J., 2028398, Pte.
Murrell, H. E., 6340310, Sjt.
Murrells, L., 6342822, Sjt.
Mycock, J., 13021742, Pte.
Myers, M., 6349974, Pte.

Navesey, J., 3393916, Pte.
Neal, A. G., 5727360, Sjt.
Neale, E., 5339131, Pte.
Needham, H. J., 6352681, Pte.
Neil, M., 5388425, Pte.
Nelson, W. H., 6022553, Pte.
Neve, G. E., Maj.
Newitt, H. S., 6020453, Pte.
Newman, J. J., 14567637, Pte.
Newnhan, A., 6345472, Pte.
Newton, A. A., 6347370, Pte.
Newton, C., 5677938, Pte.
Nicholls, S. W., 14208527, Pte.
Nicholls, W. R., 5442051, Pte.
Nicholson, A., 6404449, Pte.
Nickel, W. L., 6411497, Pte.
Nieman, C. C., 6346886, Pte.
Noakes, L. F., 6344636, Pte.
Noakes, R. C., 6342396, W.O.II.
North, H., 6197612, Drummer.
Norton, E., 14574680, Pte.
Norton, E., 6387022, Pte.
Norton, G. R., 5783048, Pte.
Norton, H. A., 6343967, Pte.
Norton, L., 7908419, L/Cpl.

Nottidge, D. R., 6345355, Pte.

Oasgood, J. T., 6343880, Sjt.
O'Brien, J. A. A., Lt.
O'Brien, J. J., 6347995, Pte.
O'Brien, T. J., Lt.
Offen, F. G., 6344603, Pte.
Ogbourne, F. A., 5337140, Pte.
O'Hara, A. T., 6284903, Sjt.
Oliver, D. W., 6348925, Pte.
Olliver, R., 6411955, Pte.
O'Neill, T., 13048429, Pte.
Orpin, H. J., 6339900, Cpl.
Orpwood, A. D., 6342728, C/Sjt.
Orr, A. A., 6387010, Sjt.
Orr, R., 6346156, Pte.
Osborn, G., 6352364, Pte.
Osborne, A. M., 825132, L/Sjt.
Osborne, C. J. J., 6105427, Pte.
Osborne, T. L., 6022841, L/Cpl.
O'Sullivan, P. T., 6343265, Pte.
Ould, A. T., 6347793, L/Cpl.
Outram, S. G., 6345294, Cpl.
Oxford, F. T., Lt.

Pack, R., 5889010, Pte.
Page, A. G., 6020458, Pte.
Page, E. A., 6923778, Pte.
Page, R. S., 6195955, Pte.
Page, S. S., 6097678, Pte.
Pain, G., 6344009, Pte.
Paine, S. B., 6412601, Pte.
Palmer, J., 6348106, Pte.
Palmer, N. C., 6346749, L/Cpl.
Palmer, P., 5106349, Pte.
Palmer, R. V. D., Capt.
Palmer, T., 6353671, Pte.
Palmer, W. J., Lt.
Panton, R. J. J., 6342887, Pte.
Paris, A., 6021643, Pte.
Parker, A. J., 6209530, Pte.
Parker-Bull, R., 14368071, Pte.
Parker, F., 852006, Pte.
Parker, G. W., 4625321, Pte.
Parker, S. H., 6345719, Pte.
Parker, S. W., 6338531, L/Cpl.
Parks, D. H., 6339201, L/Cpl.

Parks, F. E., 6027224, Pte.
Parr, G. A., 14795502, Pte.
Parris, T. A., 6345605, Pte.
Parrott, F. T., 6097682, Cpl.
Parsons, E. A., 6345824, L/Cpl.
Parsons, G. C., Lt.
Partridge, H. D., 6345885, Pte.
Partridge, J. R., 6108244, Pte.
Partridge, L. R., 6463203, Pte.
Pascoe, E., 6022365, Pte.
Pateman, C., 6352942, Pte.
Pateman, W., 6101436, Pte.
Patmore, W., 6352136, Pte.
Pattenden, W. S., 6412474, Pte.
Pattinson, W. M., 4277534, Pte.
Paul, S. M., 6022366, Cpl.
Pauley, T. A., 5833854, Pte.
Pavey, A. W., 6338006, Cpl.
Payne, A. A., 787601, Pte.
Payne, G. H., 14200614, Pte.
Peachey, D. L., 6347369, Pte.
Peacock, A. W., 6340398, Cpl.
Peacock, G. W., 14597398, Pte.
Peacock, J. E. E., 6025562, Pte.
Peacock, L. C., 6350183, L/Sjt.
Peacock, R. H., 6348881, Pte.
Pearce, R. H., 6351533, Pte.
Pearson, C. T., 6097684, Pte.
Peerless, P. M., Capt.
Peerless, T. C., 6349479, Cpl.
Penn, B. A. W., 6826487, Pte.
Pennycook, W., 6348357, Pte.
Pentecost, A., 6349220, Pte.
Perfect, H. G., 6340987, Pte.
Perfect, W. J., 6290481, Cpl.
Perham, J. D., 6347502, Pte.
Perkin, W. J. W., 5618668, Sjt.
Perkins, A. T., 6353116, Pte.
Perkins, E. G., 5730718, Pte.
Perrin, G. R., 14402033, Pte.
Perry, R., 6107353, Pte.
Pert, C. J., 6344643, Pte.
Pert, J., 14214340, Pte.
Peters, G. T., 6344454, Pte.
Phelan, F. E., 6351455, Pte.
Philcox, H. A., 6345270, L/Cpl.
Phillips, H., 5349383, Cpl.

Phillips, R. G., 6346066, Pte.
Phillips, R. J. M., Maj.
Phillips, W. J., 6353117, Pte.
Piesley, W. A., 14872478, L/Cpl.
Pike, G. J., 6097685, Pte.
Pilbrow, R., 5730723, Pte.
Pilcher, J. M., 6140853, Cpl.
Pilgrim, H. J., 5730724, Pte.
Pine, A. T. V., Lt.
Piper, F., 6346755, Pte.
Pitham, P., 6351789, Pte.
Playford, S. A., 6343897, Pte.
Pollard, L. J., 6853763, Pte.
Pooley, R. C., 6346623, Cpl.
Pope, M. H. T., 6347250, Pte.
Porteous, W., 14408079, Pte.
Porter, G. R., 5338003, Cpl.
Povah, H., 6350808, L/Cpl.
Pratt, L. H., 7901440, Pte.
Pressey, S. C., 5510651, Pte.
Preston, L. D., 14316611, Pte.
Prew, E. C., 6348309, Pte.
Price, J. A., 780726, Pte.
Price, P., 4460412, L/Cpl.
Priest, F. T. H., 6347049, Pte.
Prince, R., 7631687, Cpl.
Price, S., 5572693, Pte.
Pritchard, J., 4104575, Pte.
Pullar, K. A., 6345960, Pte.
Punshon, F., 14518703, Pte.
Purland, J., 6341475, Pte.
Pusey, E. H. W., 6345754, Pte.
Pye, S., 6093692, Pte.

Quinn, D., 5346790, L/Cpl.
Quinn, T., 5126811, Pte.
Quy, H. E., 6022369, L/Sjt.

Racine, M., 1584876, Gnr.
Rains, F., 6347173, Pte.
Ralph, W. A. G., 6340623, Pte.
Rand, A. A., 6354666, Pte.
Rapley, A. H., 6345973, Pte.
Rayment, L., 6347921, Pte.
Rayner, C. T., 6022850, Pte.
Rayner, W., 6347827, Pte.
Razzell, T. A., 6097698, Pte.

Read, A. J., 6408768, Pte.
Reader, A. H., 6350185, Pte.
Reason, G. V., 6022852, Pte.
Reed, R. F., 6410881, Pte.
Rees, G. A., 6345844, Pte.
Rees, L., 3972795, Cpl.
Rees, N. C., 3906139, Pte.
Rees, T. J., 6025570, Cpl.
Reeve, H., 6345648, Pte.
Reeves, J. T., 6348798, Pte.
Reeves, V. R., Lt.
Rendell, G., 6344367, Pte.
Reynolds, G. T., 6352387, Pte.
Reynolds, P. J., 6346113, Pte.
Rhoades, K. A., 6347728, Pte.
Rice, R. P., 14413119, L/Cpl.
Richardson, C. J., 14337900, Pte.
Riches, A. L., 6345324, Pte.
Richmond, C. S., 6346950, Pte.
Richmond, N., 6093770, Pte.
Ridley, C. A., 6346466, Pte.
Rigg, T. S., 6473967, Pte.
Riggs, J. W., 5511042, Pte.
Ripley, W. R., 5338615, Cpl.
Robb, W. G., 6406986, Pte.
Roberson, C. E., 6481456, Pte.
Roberts, C. W. H., 6344468, Pte.
Roberts, D., 1624809, Pte.
Roberts, E. A., 5730741, Cpl.
Roberts, E. T. C., 6346899, Pte.
Roberts, L. A., 6095073, L/Cpl.
Roberts, N., 14409901, Pte.
Roberts, R., 5509633, Pte.
Roberts, S. E., 14589101, Pte.
Roberts, T. V., 4460171, Pte.
Robins, A., 5677852, Pte.
Robins, C. J., 5506959, Cpl.
Robins, E. C., 6343372, Pte.
Robinson, P., 6093647, Pte.
Robinson, W., 5126672, Pte.
Robinson, W. F., 6348802, Pte.
Robson, J. C., Lt.
Robson, W. S., 6350810, L/Cpl.
Roche, R. M. J., Capt.
Rockall, A., 5509391, Pte.
Rogan, M., M.M., 6465602, Pte.
Rogers, L. P., 14597419, Pte.

Rogers, R., 6341763, W.O.II.
Rogers, W. H. G., 6340804, Pte.
Rooney, V. G. P., 6350675, Pte.
Rose, A. K., 6341594, Pte.
Rose, E. H., 14585339, Pte.
Rose, H. G., 14525913, Pte.
Rose, J. A., 1589798, Pte.
Rose, L. W., 6020544, Cpl.
Rosen, M., 6350506, Pte.
Rosenburg, W., 5730745, Pte.
Ross, P. G. E., 6350992, L/Cpl.
Rowberry, J. J., 6345884, Sjt.
Rowe, L. J., 6354484, Pte.
Rowe, R. J., 5500161, Pte.
Rowland, E. J., 5727398, Pte.
Rowlings, C. K., 6346431, Pte.
Ruddle, G. W., 4862709, Pte.
Rudling, J. R., 6350994, Cpl.
Runham, J. T., 6290277, Pte.
Russell, A. J., 6346324, L/Cpl.
Russell, S. C., 6354441, Pte.
Rutter, J. V., 6348845, L/Sjt.
Ryan, J. A., 5506126, Pte.
Ryan, T., 6093595, Pte.
Rye, C. F., 6344417, Pte.
Rylands, S. F., 6093696, Pte.
Ryman, F. C., 5680085, Pte.

St. Ledger, F. W., 6089279, Pte.
Sale, J., 11050834, Pte.
Salter, A. W., 6022373, Pte.
Salter, W. C., 5573032, Pte.
Sampson, E. G., 2203354, Sjt.
Sanderson, K. G., Capt.
Sansom, K. W., 5677813, Pte.
Saunders, C. J., 6348292, Cpl.
Saunders, R. T., 14378853, Pte.
Saunders, T. A., 6341601, Pte.
Saunders, T. F. R., 5833642, Pte.
Savage, C. H., 6348361, Cpl.
Sawyer, W. A., 6022858, Pte.
Saxby, E. H. B., 6104108, Pte.
Sayer, J. W., 6351801, Pte.
Sayle, D. B., 5343815, Cpl.
Scales, A. V., 14628061, Pte.
Scales, H., 6347205, Pte.
Scholes, R., 6093771, Pte.

Scott, A. D., 6022583, Pte.
Scott, C. A., 14604947, Pte.
Scott, F. W. H., 6475653, Pte.
Scott, K. B., M.C., Maj.
Scrace, F. N., 6345067, Pte.
Scull, G. A., 6346460, Pte.
Searle, F. C., 6138612, Cpl.
Searle, R. C., 6408432, Cpl.
Sears, A. T., 6354422, Pte.
Secunda, E., 14586859, Pte.
Secunda, H., 6103464, Pte.
Sefton, E. T., 5506129, Pte.
Seymour, J. B., 6283834, Sjt.
Sharp, W. H., 5506392, Pte.
Shaw, W. H., 4688407, Sjt.
Sheehan, P. J., 6344111, Pte.
Sheen, W. C. T., 6199269, L/Cpl.
Shell, B. C., 6352671, Pte.
Shelvey, E. F., 5891553, Pte.
Shemmonds, A. W., 6351892, L/Cpl.
Sheppard, F., 6345966, Pte.
Sheppard, K. A., 5727404, Pte.
Sheppard, P. B., 2/Lt.
Sherrat, W. A., 6345227, Sjt.
Sherwin, A. E. G., 6351428, Pte.
Shilling, E. W., 6345794, Pte.
Shine, C., 5630549, Pte.
Shinnick, W. D., 6464033, Pte.
Shoesmith, J. A., 4696496, Pte.
Shonfield, F. A., 783695, L/Sjt.
Shorter, E., 6346632, Pte.
Shrubb, R. G., 6344081, Cpl.
Shuker, L., 6023228, Cpl.
Sibley, D. C. R., 6021168, Pte.
Sidaway, T. G., 6469056, Pte.
Sillence, R. E., 14592599, Pte.
Simmons, G., 6345211, Pte.
Simmons, J. N., 6355381, Pte.
Simpkin, A. J., 5837441, Pte.
Simpson, B., 6093600, Pte.
Simpson, H., 5730757, Pte.
Simpson, N., 14217558, Pte.
Simpson, R. C., 5347495, Pte.
Simpson, W. A., Lt.
Sims, C., 14594497, Pte.
Sinclair, J., 5125015, Pte.

Sinden, T. W., 14370115, Pte.
Skane, D. J., 6344455, Pte.
Skentlebury, L., 5438369, Pte.
Skryzinsky, A., 6404464, Pte.
Slack, W. V., 6347552, Pte.
Slade, F. I., 6028050, Pte.
Smart, C. K., 6342570, Pte.
Smart, E., 14344177, Pte.
Smart, E. F. W., 6341138, Cpl.
Smith, A., 4209834, Cpl.
Smith, B., 6023042, Pte.
Smith, C. E., 6342117, Sjt.
Smith, D. F. J., 14444760, Pte.
Smith, F. L., 6346750, Pte.
Smith, F. M. H., M.C., 2/Lt.
Smith, F. T., 6344226, L/Cpl.
Smith, F. T., 14752836, Pte.
Smith, G. J., 5346082, Pte.
Smith, G. S., 6404466, Pte.
Smith, G. T., 6346635, Pte.
Smith, G. W. A., 6352773, Pte.
Smith, H. F., 6853488, Pte.
Smith, H. G., 6341108, L/Cpl.
Smith, H. L., 6349993, Pte.
Smith, J. A., 5727409, Pte.
Smith, J. H., 5337680, Pte.
Smith, J. W., 6346770, Pte.
Smith, N. G., 6352864, Pte.
Smith, S. B., M.C., Lt.
Smith, S. G., 5575659, Pte.
Smith, W. E., 6344042, Pte.
Smith, W. H., 6341709, L/Cpl.
Smith, W. T., 6341641, Sjt.
Snell, G., 5338123, Pte.
Sones, F. C., 6022871, Pte.
Soul, T., 5730766, Pte.
South, E. H., 6403546, Pte.
Spencer, L. W., 6346368, Pte.
Spiers, E., 6344028, Sjt.
Spooner, F. C., 6339148, W.O.II.
Spriggs, J. E., 6348023, Pte.
Spurway, D. J., 6014558, Pte.
Squire, F. W., 5509896, Pte.
Squirell, L., 6345968, Cpl.
Stace, W. C., 6279242, Sjt.
Stafford, D. H., 5730772, Pte.
Standerwick, J. H., 6349641, L/Cpl.

Stanford, E. A., 14294097, Pte.
Stanford, L. J., 6348290, Pte.
Starbuck, C., 5730777, Pte.
Stead, R., 4460355, Pte.
Steed, J. A., 6354928, Pte.
Steers, R. E., 6355071, Pte.
Stenner, G. H., 14244322, Pte.
Stephen, E. E., 6096047, L/Cpl.
Stephens, E. D., 143629, Pte.
Stevens, A. C., 6107031, Cpl.
Stevens, A. H., 14625047, Pte.
Stevens, G. D., 6352975, Pte.
Stevens, H. J., 6345632, Pte.
Stevenson, T. F., 6346070, Pte.
Stewart, J., 3252022, Pte.
Stewart, R., 6345946, Sjt.
Stiff, R. A., 14295537, Pte.
Stiles, S. L., 6346039, Pte.
Still, J. L., 14208277, Pte.
Stoter, E., 6344585, Pte.
Strickland, A. T., 6342004, Pte.
Stuart, F. R., 6347820, Pte.
Sullivan, L. R., 6352147, L/Cpl.
Sutcliffe, F., 6343912, L/Sjt.
Suter, A., 6342886, Pte.
Swallow, S. S., 2565362, Sjt.
Swatton, L., 6348854, Pte.
Sweatland, H. E., 5727417, L/Cpl.
Swift, C. M., 6018825, Pte.
Swindell, J. A., 6347593, Pte.
Sydee, R. J., 6355388, L/Cpl.
Symons, E. J., 6341651, Pte.

Tabor, C. R., 5730792, Cpl.
Tadman, E. R., Lt.
Tappenden, S. G., 6348819, Pte.
Taylor, A., 4040072, Pte.
Taylor, A. G., 6354730, Pte.
Taylor, B. S., 6024902, Pte.
Taylor, D., 6022878, Cpl.
Taylor, F. W. P., 6346450, Pte.
Taylor, J. H., 6343595, Pte.
Taylor, J. L., 3907435, Pte.
Taylor, J. S., 5349726, Pte.
Taylor, P. E., 6348294, Pte.
Taylor, R. G., 5352764, Cpl.
Teasdale, G., 3594985, Cpl.

Tee, R. N., 6087861, Pte.
Theobald, E. G., 6344872, Pte.
Theroux, H. J., 6343184, Cpl.
Thomas, F. L., 5340953, Pte.
Thomas, G. J., 14339540, Pte.
Thomas, J. D., Lt.
Thomas, P. W., 5346114, Pte.
Thomas, R., 5126710, Pte.
Thompson, C., 6349991, Pte.
Thomson, J. W. G., 6343846, Pte.
Thorneycroft, L. W., 6354696, Pte.
Thwaites, C. L., 6102054, Pte.
Tibble, A., 14680133, Pte.
Tidy, D. R., 6345334, Pte.
Tillett, E. D., 6347246, Pte.
Tillman, R. V., 14220159, Pte.
Timms, W., 2089833, Pte.
Tobutt, H. G., 6354286, Pte.
Todd, F. J., 6349110, Pte.
Tomsett, A. B., 6347113, Pte.
Tomsett, L. J., 6404607, Pte.
Topham, J. N. O., Capt.
Toy, J. E., 5727424, Pte.
Tranter, A. H., 6482015, Pte.
Traynor, O., 1492907, L/Cpl.
Treleaven, E. A. W., 5727425, Pte.
Tribe, N. E., 6347464, Pte.
Tripp, H. M. H., Lt.
Trodd, R. M., 6410137, Pte.
True, A., 6348085, Pte.
Trussell, A. C., 5730812, Cpl.
Trussler, C. R., 6479554, L/Cpl.
Tucker, J. W. H., 6343286, Pte.
Tucker, L. W. A. G., 5724132, L/Cpl.
Tungate, F. C., 6344873, Cpl.
Turner, C. M. S., Lt.
Turner, G. E. F., Lt.
Turner, J. A., 6410123, Pte.
Turner, L. E., 6340903, L/Cpl.
Turner, P. H., 6344901, Pte.
Turner, R. E., 6354139, Pte.
Turner, W. F., 6348823, Pte.
Turnor, A. H., 6345272, Pte.
Tyrrell, P., 6101455, Pte.

Underhill, F. C., 6346071, Pte.

Underwood, H., 6096063, Pte.
Unwin, E., 4616824, Pte.
Upright, A. E., 6353515, Pte.
Upton, A. J., 6341187, Pte.
Upton, G. L., Lt.
Urquhart, L. S., 6344394, Pte.

Valiant, H. A., 6345062, Pte.
Varney, H. S., 6350011, Cpl.
Varney, T. L., 6474793, Pte.
Venus, S., 6344888, Pte.
Vercoutre, V., 6018272, Pte.
Veron, F. R., M.M., 5502731, Cpl.
Vicary, P., 6346248, Pte.
Vickrage, L. E., 5573325, Pte.
Viles, A. R., 6021736, Pte.
Vincent, C., 6012259, Pte.
Virgo, E. R., 4104863, Pte.
Virgo, R. V., 6352662, L/Cpl.
Virgoe, L. F., 6096067, L/Cpl.

Wackett, J., 6474885, Pte.
Wade, C., 6348320, Pte.
Wade, F. H. A., 6472135, Pte.
Waghorn, F. J., 6340932, Pte.
Wagon, D. W., 6348039, Pte.
Wagstaff, D., 14324516, Pte.
Wagstaff, H. J., 13021797, Cpl.
Wainwright, G. W., 6347427, Pte.
Waite, J. A. D., 6351827, Pte.
Walder, D. F., 6347030, Pte.
Wale, W. H., 7017893, Pte.
Walker, A. C., 6348825, Pte.
Walker, E. F., 6343616, Pte.
Walker, F. J., 14517633, Pte.
Walker, H. G. D., 6096070, L/Cpl.
Walker, R. H., 6350717, Pte.
Walker, W. E., 14203151, Pte.
Walkinshaw, D. W., 6351432, Cadet.
Wallace, M. B., Lt.
Wallis, F. A., 6354450, Pte.
Walsh, J. P., 6348895, Pte.
Walters, R. E., 6348110, Pte.
Walton, S. A., 5677778, Pte.
Wanless, T., 3860547, Pte.

Want, A. W., 6021738, Cpl.
Ward, G., 5725799, Pte.
Ward, J. A., 5724412, Sjt.
Ward, L. J. S., 6460635, Pte.
Ward, L. R., 6296030, L/Sjt.
Warr, V. C., M.C., Capt.
Warren, L. S., 6348014, Pte.
Warren, W. C., 6299604, L/Cpl.
Washford, H. J. G., 6102068, Cpl.
Waters, H. C., 6345774, Pte.
Waters, W., 6339703, Pte.
Watkins, G., 14541733, Pte.
Watkins, R. J., 6355083, Pte.
Watney, C. H., Lt.
Watson, J. H., 6336894, Pte.
Watson, J. H., 6349131, Pte.
Watson, W. E., 6096074, L/Cpl.
Wattis, S., 5349582, Pte.
Watts, A. F., 6345736, Pte.
Watts, L. R., 6346329, Pte.
Watts, R. A., 6345880, Pte.
Weatherly, P. E. J. H., M.C., Capt.
Weavers, G. C., 6344263, Pte.
Webb, C. R., 5336765, L/Cpl.
Webb, G. H., 6299607, Pte.
Webb, H. J., 6411159, Pte.
Webb, J. H., 1679977, L/Cpl.
Webb, L. J. A., M.M., 5625616, Pte.
Webb, R. A. J., 6348032, Pte.
Webley, H. C., 6343890, Pte.
Weeks, R., 6297899, Pte.
Weeks, S., 6474026, Pte.
Weigle, G., 4039645, Cpl.
Welchman, E. R. C., Lt.
Welfare, C. W., 14233956, L/Cpl.
Wells, E. W., 6474237, Pte.
Wells, H. J., 6341954, L/Cpl.
Wells, W. L. B., 7042793, Cpl.
Welsh, E. F., 6516196, Cpl.
West, A., 5628785, L/Cpl.
West, A. J., 6348541, Pte.
West, W. K., 6345251, Pte.
Weston, L., 6354453, Pte.
White, A. J., 6193752, W.O.III.
White, C. R., 6355369, Pte.
White, F., 6345340, Pte.

White, M. E., 6346873, Pte.
White, R. R., 5628225, Pte.
Whitehouse, G. W., 4460273, Pte.
Whitehouse, J., 5435625, Pte.
Whiteside, W. J., 3252066, Pte.
Whitnall, F. G., 6401447, Cpl.
Whittingham, E. B., 3977285, Pte.
Whitty, D. H. N., Lt.
Whitty, J. H. H., D.S.O., M.C.,
 Lt-Col.
Wickens, D. A., 6096080, Pte.
Wickers, C., 6022394, Cpl.
Wickham, A. D., 6347491, L/Sjt.
Wickham, S. F., 6346162, Cpl.
Wicks, W. A., 14858994, Pte.
Wiffen, R., 5512831, L/Cpl.
Wildish, J. T., 6352845, Pte.
Wilkins, C., 14636649, Pte.
Wilkins, H. E., 775356, Sjt.
Wilkinson, J., 14600984, Pte.
Wilkinson, J., 1819552, Pte.
Wilkinson, J. A., 6205422, Cpl.
Williams, A., 14574563, Pte.
Williams, C., 14399733, Pte.
Williams, D., 5572698, L/Cpl.
Williams, J., 6026561, Pte.
Williams, J. E., 5389034, L/Cpl.
Williams, N. S., 6340786, Sjt.
Williams, R. E., 1603170, Pte.
Williams, S. W., 4194090, Pte.
Williams, V. D. G., 5502958, Pte.
Williams, W. D., 5435883, Sjt.
Willmott, C. W. J., 2063544, Pte.
Wills, S. C., 5621204, Cpl.
Wills, W. J., 6022902, Pte.
Wilson, G., 6406337, Pte.
Wilson, J. T., 6340596, Pte.
Wilson, W. B., 6344435, Pte.
Winchester, W. A., 6343870, Sjt.

Windle, D., 14217204, Pte.
Wingrove, R. W., 6404481, L/Cpl.
Wiseman, F. D., 6340934, C/Sjt.
Witchalls, H., 6351554, L/Cpl.
Witherden, J. W., 6347898, L/Cpl.
Wonfor, L. H., 14632281, Pte.
Wood, E. S., 6350545, Pte.
Wood, F. S., 6346180, Sjt.
Woodcock, E. W., 6096087, Pte.
Woodhouse, O. G., Maj.
Woodley, H. C., 5343497, Pte.
Woodman, W. J., 6348363, L/Cpl.
Woods, F. J., 6343268, Pte.
Woollaston, A., M.M., 2564059,
 Pte.
Woollven, N. H., Lt.
Worley, G. H., 6350044, Pte.
Worrell, A. J. H., 6341909, Sjt.
Worsfold, A. A., 6106532, Pte.
Worth, F. W., 6481389, Pte.
Wratten, W. J., 6353563, Pte.
Wren, E., 13290, Pte.
Wren, G. J., 6101458, Pte.
Wrench, B., 6099782, Pte.
Wright, E., 6093706, L/Cpl.
Wright, H., 6348125, Pte.
Wright, H. E., Lt.
Wright, H. S. A., 6022905, Pte.
Wylie, D. V. J., 6464277, Cpl.

Yankovsky, M., 6023064, Pte.
Yates, C. J., 6407803, Pte.
Yates, M. F., 14608383, Pte.
Yeates, J. A., 6405716, Pte.
York, F., 6102088, Pte.
Youens, W. J., 6355402, Pte.
Young, E. H. W., 6348388, Pte.
Young, J., 5727461, Pte.
Young, R. A., 6345770, Pte.

Preface

IN order to contain the history of The Queen's Own Royal West
Kent Regiment through this momentous period in a volume of
moderate length, it has been possible to include only an outline
of the activities of the Regiment and its two Regular and three
Territorial battalions during the years 1920 to 1939, and to give
only a short account of the four battalions which were specially
raised in 1939 and 1940 for the defence of England. The main
bulk of the work is devoted to the deeds of the six battalions
of The Queen's Own which fought in the Second World War.
One chapter gives a brief record of the Affiliated and Allied
Regiments. The last two chapters cover the post-war period,
1945-1950. At the last moment it has been possible to include a short
report, as an appendix, of the achievements of the 1st Battalion in
Malaya in 1951.

The story of the war years has been written almost entirely from
accounts compiled by members of the Regiment and from details obtained during personal interviews. Almost every Commanding Officer
who survived has given information and advice. Many of the descriptions of acts of gallantry have been written from the actual citations.
Thus a real effort has been made to achieve accuracy and to make
this, as far as possible, a true record of events.

In order to save space initials have only been inserted in the text
where they are needed to distinguish between individuals of the
same name and for Commanding Officers and other senior officers.
They can, however, be found in the Index and, where applicable,
in the Roll of Honour, the List of Honours and Awards or Appendix
B. The Index is confined mainly to names of persons, but the reader
can readily find in the text any battle, movement or other important
event by referring to the summaries of the chapters in the Table of
Contents.

In conclusion, I wish to express my pride in having been given
the opportunity of writing the story of the Regiment during one of
the most important periods in its history.

H. D. CHAPLIN

Acknowledgements

THE Battalion War Diaries, on which this history of The
Queen's Own has been based, have been kindly made available by the War Office and the Officer in charge of Records,
Warwick. For the strategic background I have consulted the
following works, to the authors and publishers of which I am
indebted:—

The Second World War by Winston S. Churchill.
Algiers to Austria (78th Division) by Cyril Ray.
The Campaign in Italy by Eric Linklater.
The Fourth Division 1939 to 1945 by Hugh Williamson.
The Tiger Triumphs (8th Indian Division) published by H.M.S.O.
Ball of Fire (5th Indian Division) by Antony Brett-James.

Although a great deal of the detail comes from accounts written
or given to me verbally by members of the Regiment, I have gleaned
much information from the following books:—

Keep the Memory Green by Lt.-Col. Ewan Butler and Major J.
Selby Bradford.
The Green Beret by Hilary St. George Saunders.
The Monastery by Fred Majdalany.
From Kent to Kohima by Majors E. B. S. Clarke and A. T. Tillott.
The Sword in the Scabbard by Michael Joseph.
12th British Infantry Brigade, Italy 1944 by D. O. Henley.

In addition I have obtained valuable assistance from many articles
and descriptions of events which have appeared in the regimental
journal, *The Queen's Own Gazette*.

My thanks are due to the Director of Military Survey, The War
Office, for supplying the maps, from which I was able to trace the
movements of the battalions, and for reproducing my poor sketches
so attractively.

Finally, I would like to express my thanks to all the members of
the Regiment who have given me assistance; to Lieut.-Colonel
H. N. Edwards, who compiled the Roll of Honour and the list of
Honours and Awards; and especially to the late Colonel W. V.
Palmer, who read over and criticised the first draft of this work
and himself wrote Chapter 4 almost in its entirety.

Contents

Hartal: Moves to Bangalore: A 200-mile March: The
Visits of General O'Dowda: Training and Weapon
Training: The Bangalore Memorial.—*2nd Battalion.*
Pleasant Days at Ballykinlar: Tragedy in Dundrum
Bay: Sails for England: Conditions at Woking:
Training in the Aldershot Command: Sails to
Guernsey: Training in Alderney: Visit of General
O'Dowda: Moves back to the Aldershot Command:
The Financial Crisis: Presentation of Colours by The
Duke of Gloucester.—*The Territorial Battalions.* Annual
Camps: The Permanent Staff: A Lean Period: Suc-
cesses at Shooting and Sport.

Captain Upham's two V.C.s: Present Situation.—
Carleton and York Regiment of Canada. Formation of The
Carleton Light Infantry: The 1914–18 War: Alliance
with The Queen's Own: Amalgamation with the
York Regiment: Mobilisation in 1939: Fighting in
Sicily, Italy and Holland: Reorganisation.—*Kent
Regiment of Canada.* Duties during the 1914–18 War:
Alliance with The Queen's Own: Becomes a Machine
Gun Battalion: Home Defence from 1940 to 1945:
Reformation.

PART FOUR

AFTER THE WAR
1945–1950

Becomes 4/5th: Revival of Regimental Institutions: H.R.H. The Duchess of Kent appointed Colonel-in-Chief: Major-General Oliver becomes Colonel of the Regiment.—*1st Battalion* as the Home Counties Training Battalion at Shorncliffe: Wins the Army Team Boxing Championship in 1949 and 1950: Prepares for Operations in Malaya: Farewell Visit of The Duchess of Kent: Embarkation at Liverpool.—*The Regimental Depot* again trains Recruits for the Regiment.—A Bright Prospect.

Illustrations

Acknowledgement is made to the Imperial War Museum and to Mr. Charles Cundall for permission to reproduce his painting 'The Withdrawal from Dunkirk'; and to the Imperial War Museum for permission to reproduce all the photographs except those facing pages 72, 158, 194 (A), 195 (B) and 450.

Maps

Theme

A BRITISH County Regiment is an abiding stronghold of regimental life and traditions. Yet its personnel and the stations in which its battalions serve are constantly changing. The only permanent links are its Regimental Shrine, its Regimental Depot and the customs which are handed down from officer to officer and from man to man.

Kent has two Regiments of the Line: The Buffs (Royal East Kent Regiment) and The Queen's Own Royal West Kent Regiment. The County is divided into two parts by the River Medway; those who dwell east of this river are known as Men of Kent; those who dwell west of it as Kentish Men. But the boundary which divides the recruiting areas of the two regiments is not the River Medway, as will be seen from the accompanying map. While all Buffs may rightly be described as Men of Kent, The Queen's Own, although consisting largely of Kentish Men, has also some Men of Kent in its ranks.

The Queen's Own Royal West Kent Regiment, the 50th Regiment of the Line, has its Regimental Shrine in All Saints' Church, Maidstone, where many of its ancient Colours, shot-torn and tattered, hang like ghostly sentinels of the past. A mile away stands the Regimental Depot, with its entrance on the busy road to Chatham and its tree-lined 'Back Field' sloping peacefully down to the eastern tow-path of the River Medway. Maidstone, the County Town of Kent, is therefore the cradle of The Queen's Own, and the Honorary Freedom of the Borough has been conferred on the Regiment in consideration of the eminent services it has rendered to Britain and the Empire.

And what of the officers and other ranks who have made The Queen's Own so famous? These Kentish Men hale from the urban boroughs of South London as well as from the rural hamlets of Kent. The stubborn alertness of the Londoner is thus merged with the slower solidity of the worker in the Garden of England. The result is a very good blend, which has produced throughout the years the regimental characteristics of fortitude and determination.

On the field of battle these characteristics have developed into a firm tradition not to yield whatever the odds.

In 1914 these men came forth in their thousands from their towns and villages, boroughs and hamlets to fight in the ranks of The Queen's Own against German aggression. That epic has been related in *The Queen's Own Royal West Kent Regiment 1914–1919*. The purpose of this book is to tell the story of the Regiment during the twenty years of recuperation, the six years of global war and the five years of troubled peace which followed.

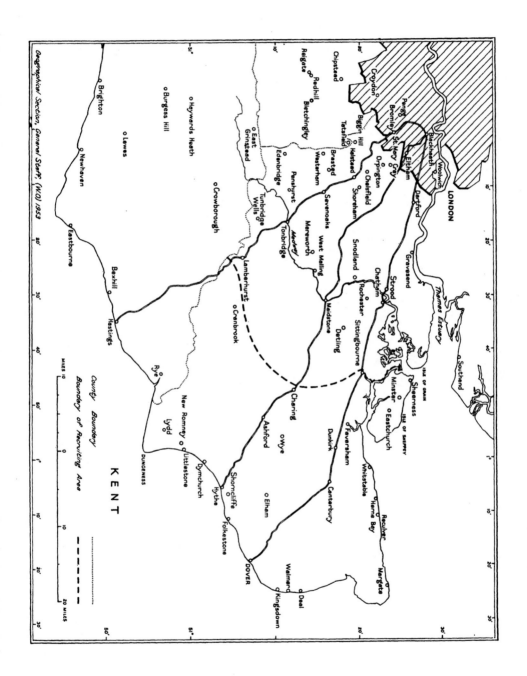

Geographical Section, General Staff, (W.O.) 1953

County Boundary ————
Boundary of Recruiting Area – – – – –

MILES 10 [scale] 20 MILES

K E N T

PART ONE

BETWEEN
THE WARS

1920–1939

CHAPTER 1

The Aftermath of War
1920–1923

1. *Regimental*

AFTER the surrender of Germany in November 1918 the Army Council decided to reconstitute the Regular Army on the same voluntary pattern as the pre-war army. In other words, they considered that an army suitable for garrison duties overseas and for small colonial wars was all that was necessary. This meant a return to the 'Cardwell System,' with one battalion of each infantry regiment at home and one abroad.

By February 1920 The Queen's Own (Royal West Kent Regiment) had returned to its pre-war organisation from its vast expansion during the First World War. At the Depot at Maidstone a few volunteers for the Regular Army were already beginning to enlist. The 1st Battalion, under the command of Lieutenant-Colonel P. M. Robinson, C.B., C.M.G., was stationed at Agra in India.[1] The 2nd Battalion had just moved from Rugeley to Citadel Barracks, Dover, where it was looking forward to a spell of garrison duty in Kent under the command of Brevet-Colonel R. J. Woulfe-Flanagan, D.S.O. The 3rd (Militia) Battalion, with H.R.H. The Duke of Connaught as its Honorary Colonel, was in suspended animation and consisted only of a few officers.[2]

The conditions in the country and in the world did not allow a smooth return to peace-time routine. There were disturbances in India, open rebellion in Ireland, a civil war in Germany and a full-scale war between Poland and Russia, besides discontent amongst the coal-miners at home. All these caused many unusual calls to be made on the Army, and The Queen's Own had its fair share of them. It was not indeed until 1923 that the Regiment can really be said to have returned to normal.

---

[1] The 1st Battalion had sailed for India from Gravesend in the *Kaiser-i-Hind* in October 1919.

[2] Never re-animated, this battalion was disbanded in April 1953.

Before 1914 the life of The Queen's Own had consisted of much more than the flow of events at the Depot and in the various battalions. There had been several institutions which had kept the regimental spirit alive throughout Kent, and, indeed, farther afield; and one by one these traditions were revived. In the summer of 1920 the Regimental Dinner in London for the regular officers of the Regiment was held for the first time since the war. In that year also the Old Comrades' Association came to life again. Several new branches were formed, and the number of members began to increase rapidly. In July 1921 the Kent County Cricket Week was resumed at Mote Park, Maidstone. Many county celebrities and friends were invited to a regimental tent on the ground. This was the restart of The Queen's Own Tent Club, which had held a prominent place in the social life of the county before 1914.

Another important regimental institution was the *Queen's Own Gazette*, the journal which recorded the activities of the Regiment. During the war, when the paper was in danger of having to suspend publication—a fate which befell many similar periodicals—Colonel T. H. Brock had kept it going in spite of many difficulties. For some reason the Adjutant of the Depot had always been the editor, whether or not he was of a literary turn of mind. In 1920 the Regiment was fortunate to have in Captain Palmer a Depot Adjutant who not only wielded a lucid pen but was also a good administrator. Under his editorship the *Q.O.G.* grew from a pamphlet of ten pages in 1920 to a magazine of twenty pages in 1922. Furthermore, he enrolled the *Q.O.G.* as one of the Association of Regimental Papers in October 1921, since when a regular income from advertisements has been assured.

Two important events occurred in those early years after the war. The first of these was that, without reference to the Colonel of the Regiment, the title of the Regiment was changed from The Queen's Own (Royal West Kent Regiment) to the Royal West Kent Regiment (Queen's Own). This aroused a storm of protest, for it had the effect of taking away the cherished name of 'The Queen's Own.' The Colonel of the Regiment, Major-General Sir Edmund Leach, K.C.B., wrote a strong letter to the War Office, and in March 1921 the brackets were removed altogether. The title then became The Queen's Own Royal West Kent Regiment, as it is to-day.

The second event was the burial of the Unknown Warrior in Westminster Abbey. A detachment of 50 men of The Queen's Own was amongst the troops who paraded on November 10, 1920, at Dover Harbour for the ceremony of receiving the body as it was removed from a destroyer. And the Regiment was represented in the funeral procession from Victoria Station, London, to the Abbey on November 11, 1920. On the same day and at the same time a detachment from the Depot attended at Maidstone the first of the Armistice Day ceremonies which afterwards became a permanent annual event in the life of the Depot.

During the strenuous post-war period, while the Service battalions were being demobilised, the Depot at Maidstone was commanded[1] by Major Lister. In December 1920 Brevet-Lieutenant-Colonel Twisleton-Wykeham-Fiennes assumed command. On him therefore fell the work of reviving many of the regimental institutions. By the end of 1920 the Depot was carrying out its normal functions, for it was not only training recruits but was also sending out drafts to replace wastage in both the 1st and 2nd Battalions. In September 1920 the five guns, which had been captured by the 1st Battalion at Goulot Wood in 1917, were placed on the Depot square, where they remained an impressive feature until they were melted down as scrap-metal during the Second World War.

In April 1921 the coal-miners in the United Kingdom came out on strike. On the 8th the Regular Army Reserve was called up because there was a danger that this coal strike might become a general strike. Within a few hours many well-known figures were arriving at the Depot. Scenes reminiscent of the 1914 mobilisation occurred, and many Reservists made their beds on the hard floor of the Gymnasium. This only went on for a few days, however, for on April 14 over 250 of them were sent off to join the 2nd Battalion, then at Dover. The Reserve ultimately stood down in June, when the Reservists returned to the Depot to be dispersed to their homes.

A full description of the unveiling of the Regimental War Memorial[2] and of the Laying Up of the Colours of the Service battalions, which occurred at Maidstone in July 1921, is given on pages 481–483 of *The Queen's Own Royal West Kent Regiment 1914–1919*. There is consequently no need to describe those ceremonies here. They were the last duties to be performed by Major-General Leach before he was compelled to relinquish the appointment of Colonel of the Regiment, through failing health, in November 1921. He was succeeded by Lieutenant-General Sir E. A. H. Alderson, K.C.B., who had retired from the Army in 1920. General Alderson's last appointment had been an Inspector of Infantry.

In March 1923 the Regimental Honours Committee selected the ten Battle Honours which they recommended should be emblazoned

---

[1] A roll of subsequent Depot Commanders is given in Appendix D.

[2] The Book of Remembrance was handed over by the Colonel of the Regiment to the Chaplain in All Saints' Church, Maidstone, in July 1938.

on the King's Colour. They also requested each battalion to compile complete lists of Honours which were to be shown in the Army List. These lists were finally approved by the War Office in March 1924. The ten Battle Honours to be emblazoned on the King's Colour were:

Mons.	Ypres 1914, 1915, 1917, 1918.
Hill 60.	Somme 1916, 1918.
Vimy 1917.	Italy 1917, 1918.
Gallipoli 1915.	Gaza.
Defence of Kut el Amara.	Sharqat.

Fifty-nine other Honours appear in the Army List. The incident selected for inclusion in the *Ypres Book of Valour*, published by the Ypres League, was Hill 60.

Two notable sporting successes were achieved by members of The Queen's Own between 1920 and 1923. Corporal Hoban of the Depot won the Army Featherweight Boxing Championship in 1921 and again in 1922. He was trained by Serjeant Baker, who had been a well-known boxer in the 1st Battalion and indeed in the boxing world before the war. Hoban won this championship again in 1923 when he was attached to the Army Physical Training Staff; he then transferred to that Staff permanently. In 1922 Lieutenant Howlett (Depot) assisted Kent in most of their cricket matches as a fast bowler.

2. *The 1st Battalion at Agra and Calcutta*

At Agra the 1st Battalion was part of a force which was responsible for internal security under the command of Major-General L. C. Dunsterville, the original of Kipling's 'Stalky.' Officers and men quickly settled down to the routine of garrison life in India. Facilities for games were excellent, and we find the battalion playing much football and hockey and holding its first athletic meeting. Many of the officers played polo. When the hot weather came the troops and the families, which had followed the battalion to India, went up, in relays, to the Hill Station at Kailana. The dress in India in those days was: topees, khaki drill jacket and trousers and puttees. The officers wore breeches and puttees (leggings for mounted officers). It was not until later that the cooler and more comfortable shorts were taken into use.

Lieutenant-Colonel P. M. Robinson ended his period in command[1]

---

[1] A roll of Commanding Officers is given in Appendix D.

in March 1920. Major and Brevet-Colonel R. J. T. Hildyard, C.M.G., D.S.O., was appointed to succeed him. Before he could take over he was given command of a brigade, and Lieutenant-Colonel G. D. Lister was appointed instead. Unfortunately Colonel Lister was a sick man and within a few months he had to be sent home. He died in Netley Hospital in November 1921. Lieutenant-Colonel H. D. Buchanan-Dunlop, C.M.G., D.S.O., then assumed command.

The battalion moved to Fort William, Calcutta, in September 1920. Major-General Thomas Astley Cubitt was the District Commander. Both his office and his quarters were in Fort William, so all ranks saw a lot of him. He was well over six feet tall and an imposing figure. The troops admired and respected him, not only because he fully justified his reputation for possessing the finest flow of language in the British Army. There were many guards and other military duties to be done in Calcutta. In December 1921 the Prince of Wales visited the city to unveil the War Memorial. The battalion provided a Guard of Honour, and Colonel Buchanan-Dunlop commanded a combined parade of several units. In the evening fireworks and illuminations made a fine sight while the band of the battalion played a programme of music in Dalhousie Square.

But service in Calcutta had its sterner aspect, for in 1922 the battalion was called out in aid of the civil power to surround an area in which the police had cause to arrest many rioters. Mahatma Gandhi, who later became so well known for his support of self-government for India, was one of those arrested. A little later the battalion assisted in quelling a riot in Alipore gaol.

In December 1920 a draft of some 250 other ranks, who were serving on a war-time short-service engagement, departed for England. These were replaced two months later by a draft of the same number of recruits from the Depot and the 2nd Battalion. This was virtually the restart of the pre-war drafting system. In future one or more drafts were sent out each winter, usually from the 2nd Battalion, to make good the wastage that occurred.

It was during the tour in Calcutta that an invitation to consider themselves permanent Honorary Members of their Mess was received by the officers from the officers of the 2nd Battalion The King's Own Scottish Borderers. It was engraved on a silver plaque and was sent in memory of the close comradeship between the two battalions and the many occasions on which they had attacked alongside each other during the 1914–1918 war. It was decided to return the compliment, and a similar invitation was sent by the officers to the 2nd Battalion The King's Own Scottish Borderers.

During the hot weather in 1921 the Hill Station for the battalion was Darjeeling, and in 1922 it was Lebong. In November 1922 the battalion moved to Poona, which was itself a Hill Station. From then onwards regular peace-time changes of station occurred.

3. *The 2nd Battalion in Germany, Upper Silesia and Ireland*

After it had been only a few weeks at Dover the 2nd Battalion was unexpectedly ordered to join the Army of the Rhine. Lieutenant-Colonel C. E. Kitson, D.S.O., took over command on the day of embarkation (March 5, 1920). The battalion was first of all stationed at Solingen, as part of 'Kitson's Force,' which was occupying a portion of the British bridgehead across the River Rhine. Detachments were at Wermelskirchen, Schaberg, Ohligs and Hilden on railway control duty. A few days after the battalion's arrival the civil war, which had broken out in Germany between the Spartacists, or Communists, and the Government, drew near to the bridgehead, and Kitson's Force was ordered to guard the entrances to Solingen. When the Spartacists defeated the Government troops at Remscheid, a town just across the River Wupper and some three miles from Solingen, about 800 German infantry retreated into the bridgehead. These were disarmed by A and C Companies at Krahenhoe in the outskirts of Solingen. German Government reinforcements then arrived in strength, and the Spartacists, in their turn, sought sanctuary in the British occupied zone. They also had to be disarmed. For this purpose picquets were posted day and night on the main roads leading into Solingen.

The battalion was withdrawn to Rhiel Barracks, Cologne, in June 1920, and for eight months it was stationed alternately either there or in Solingen. There were many entertainments in Cologne in those days, but the battalion remained chiefly interested in football. Towards the end of the season the team was one point behind the leaders in the Rhine Army football league. The final match was never played.

In March 1921 the battalion made a long train journey to Silesia as part of a Force commanded by Major-General A. G. Wauchope. The war between Russia and Poland had just ended in a victory for Poland, and this Force was to supervise a plebiscite to decide whether Upper Silesia should in future form part of Germany or of Poland. Battalion Headquarters and B and C Companies went to Kreuzburg; the remainder of the battalion was scattered. All companies were occupied in passing voters from Poland and Germany

into Upper Silesia. On March 21, the day after polling day, forty
men from Headquarters and C Company broke up a civil disturbance at Kreuzburg, but otherwise there was little trouble.

That duty finished, the battalion was hurriedly despatched to
England in April 1921 because of the coal strike already mentioned.
A few hours after it had marched into Dover Castle 250 Reservists
arrived from the Depot. Fortunately it was not necessary to take
any action in the strike.

No sooner was the coal strike over than the battalion was ordered
to Ireland. That country was now in a turmoil. After the Sinn Fein
rising in Dublin in 1916 the problem of Home Rule for Ireland had
been shelved for three years. But once the war was over disaffection
had spread rapidly. Troops had to be called in to support the Royal
Irish Constabulary. By the middle of 1921 Dublin was almost in a
state of siege, the murder of loyal citizens and police was a frequent
occurrence, and the burning of houses and sabotage of public
services happened every day. Into this the battalion was launched
without its transport, its baggage and a quarter of its personnel.
For the machine-gunners had been left in Upper Silesia, a large
rear party and the transport and baggage were in Cologne, and
details were still at Dover administering the married families.
Having disembarked at Kingstown Harbour on June 16, the battalion
entrained for Dublin. But, in spite of many precautions, the train
was ambushed in a cutting in the Drumcondra area of the city.
Private Saunders was mortally wounded and two serjeants were
slightly wounded. The battalion grimly marched to a barbed-wire
camp in Phoenix Park.

For the next four weeks the battalion was called upon to supply
curfew patrols, whose duty it was to convey curfew-breakers in
lorries to the Bridewell Prison; and street patrols, who had to
search suspicious-looking characters for arms. In addition it found
several guards, two of which were commanded by an officer. Of
these one was in the magazine fort in Phoenix Park, where the
reserve ammunition for the British Army in Ireland was stored, and
the other was at General Headquarters, just outside the Park. An
armistice was declared in July. In September the battalion moved
into North Dublin Union, where it was left in comparative peace.
The peace was not of mind, however, especially for the officers, who
were quartered in disused cells in the lunatic asylum.

There was yet another move when in January 1922 the battalion
went to Ballykinlar Camp, near the Mountains of Mourne in
Northern Ireland. The accommodation was a collection of wooden
huts called 'World's End Camp,' and it was not a misnomer. Even

then the battalion was not to remain undisturbed for long. After only three weeks the headquarters and two companies were sent to Newry, where they were quartered in the barracks of the Royal Ulster Constabulary, and the other two companies moved to the Depot of the Royal Irish Fusiliers at Armagh. The object of this move was to assist the Royal Ulster Constabulary, who were having trouble with the Sinn Feiners on the Ulster border. Small engagements were in fact fought, both at night, at Forkhill and at Fivemiletown; but there were no visible casualties on either side when these skirmishes had been lost or won.

In June 1922 the battalion regathered at Ballykinlar Camp. It was the first time since the war that all companies had been together for long. The surrounding countryside was ideal for minor tactical training, which the troops so badly needed, and full advantage was taken of the fine rifle ranges near the camp to complete the first musketry course that many of the young soldiers had been able to fire. At the end of July three officers and thirty-five other ranks were posted to the battalion from the regiments that had been disbanded or depleted under a scheme for the reduction of the Army. The officers were from The Royal Inniskilling Fusiliers, and the other ranks from the 4th Battalions of the Middlesex Regiment and the Rifle Brigade. In August the band and drums were reissued with red full-dress uniform for wear on ceremonial parades and when playing out. This was taken to be a sure sign that the battalion had settled down to a peace-time routine at last.

4. *The Territorial Battalions*

When the Territorial Force was constituted in 1908 three Territorial Battalions were formed from the 1st, 2nd, 3rd and 4th Volunteer Battalions of The Queen's Own (Royal West Kent Regiment). These were the 4th and 5th Battalions of The Queen's Own and the 20th (County of London) Battalion, The London Regiment. At the end of the 1914–18 war the Territorial Force was disbanded, but was reconstituted in February 1920 as the Territorial Army. The 4th and 5th Battalions remained the same; the 20th Battalion, The London Regiment, regained the name of its parent regiment, for its title was changed to The 20th London Regiment (The Queen's Own).

The 4th and 5th Battalions were re-formed under the command[1] of Lieutenant-Colonels A. R. Cheale and A. E. Hills respectively.

[1] The names of subsequent T.A. Commanding Officers are given in Appendix D.

The headquarters of the 4th were at Bank Street, Tonbridge, and its company drill halls were at Maidstone with a detachment at Snodland, St. Mary Cray with a detachment at Sevenoaks, Westerham with a detachment at Edenbridge, and at Tunbridge Wells. The 5th Battalion had its headquarters and one company at East Street, Bromley, and its other companies at Chatham, Dartford and Penge with a detachment at Beckenham. The 20th London Regiment was re-formed under the command of Lieutenant-Colonel E. Ball. Its headquarters and sole drill hall were at Holly Hedge House, Blackheath.

For annual training in 1920 the 4th and 5th Battalions went to a combined camp at Birchington. In 1921 there was no annual training because the coal strike intervened, but the Government called for volunteers from the T.A. to serve for a maximum of ninety days in a defence force. The response was good. The volunteers from the 4th Battalion were based on the drill hall at Tonbridge; those from the 5th went under canvas at Sundridge Park, Bromley. In 1922 a combined camp for the 4th and 5th Battalions was again held at Birchington. The 20th London went to Aldershot.

CHAPTER 2

The Lean Years
1923–1932

1. Regimental

ALTHOUGH by 1923 the Army had returned to its pre-war footing, there were still serious difficulties to be overcome. In the Regular Army the rates of pay compared unfavourably with those in civilian life, and it was difficult to attract recruits. This shortage of men was felt more by battalions at home than by those abroad, because it was always necessary to keep the overseas garrisons up to strength. Another difficulty was that the slogan, 'No major war for ten years,' caused the Army Estimates to be reduced annually and the production of new equipment and weapons to be postponed. In these circumstances training became something of a farce, with sub-units represented by flags and new weapons by wooden dummies.

In the Territorial Army the situation was even worse. To serve in it often meant financial loss both to officers and men. Indeed at one time it was only the remarkable enthusiasm of a small number of officers and senior N.C.O.s which kept it going at all. After a General Strike, which occurred in 1926, the annual training was cancelled with the consequent withholding of the £5 Bounty; and it was cancelled again in 1932 because of a financial crisis. In spite of this the strength of battalions was maintained at a reasonable level, especially in the country areas where the Volunteer tradition was still very much alive.

In 1926 cuts were made in the pay of both officers and men in the Regular Army, accompanied by reductions in the grants allowed by the Treasury for the training and administration of the Services. In consequence it became even more difficult to obtain recruits. Indeed, but for the widespread unemployment in the country recruiting might have ceased altogether. Nevertheless, all ranks of The Queen's Own faced the adverse conditions with their usual fortitude and determination until, in 1933, the tide turned and all battalions, both Regular and Territorial, emerged virile and keen.

It is significant that fortitude and determination are also necessary if success is to be achieved at the three recreations—boxing, cross-country running and athletics—at which all battalions of The Queen's Own were destined to be above average. Fortitude and determination may be Kentish characteristics, but the root of the matter was probably at the Regimental Depot, where, for lack of adequate playing fields, these three recreations were mainly encouraged. Although the 'Back Field' at the Depot was levelled in 1927 to provide more space for games, the continued predominance of these recreations was assured by the presentation in 1931 of two trophies for inter-squad competition. These were the 'Simpson Cup'[1] for athletics and the 'Durtnell Shield'[2] for boxing. In 1926 boxing received an added interest when Mr. Charles Hardy presented 'The Hardy Cup' for annual competition between recruits of The Queen's Own and recruits of The Buffs.

Before leaving the subject of the Depot two items of modernisation must be recorded. In February 1924 electricity was at last installed throughout the barracks. In 1929 extensive structural alterations were made, including the erection of the existing cookhouse and dining hall.

The organisation of Infantry battalions was changed twice during this period. In 1923 all specialists and employed men, including the band and drums, were taken out of the four companies and collected into a new sub-unit called Headquarter Wing. In 1928 one of the four companies was converted into a machine-gun company and the other three became known as rifle companies. This reorganisation took place a year later in India.

In 1923 the custom began of laying a wreath at the foot of the Nelson Column in London on October 21 each year[3] to perpetuate the memory of the period in 1778 when the 50th Regiment served as Marines. In 1925 a Regimental Cricket Week was inaugurated, matches being played against The Buffs and other Kent teams; but it was not until 1932 that the Regimental Cricket Club was instituted. In 1926 the Regimental Golfing Society was formed, and in 1927 a fund for the acquisition of Queen's Own Relics was launched. In December 1927, to offset the loss of confidence caused by the cuts in the pay of the Army, an order was issued permitting other ranks

---

[1] Presented by Colonel H. Simpson, O.B.E., then M.O. at the Depot.

[2] Presented by H. Durtnell, Esq., whose son, Lieutenant C. S. Durtnell, had won the Army (in India) Officers' Lightweight Championship in 1926.

[3] From 1936 onwards this ceremony has been performed by members of the London Branch of the Past and Present Association.

of good character to wear plain clothes or blue patrol uniform when on leave and when walking out. Paradoxically these clothes had to be provided at the soldier's own expense.

Early in 1927 trouble broke out in China, and Section 'A' of the Army Reserve was called up in March. This affected about sixty men of The Queen's Own, who sailed to China with the 1st Battalions of The Queen's and the Middlesex Regiments. The trouble soon blew over, and the Reservists were back home early in 1928.

The Regiment suffered the loss of its Colonel by the death of Lieutenant-General Alderson in December 1927. Major-General (later Lieutenant-General) J. W. O'Dowda, C.B., C.S.I., C.M.G., who was commanding the Baluchistan District in India, was appointed in his place. General O'Dowda had first been gazetted into The Queen's Own in 1891. During the 1914–1918 war he had commanded the 38th Infantry Brigade in Mesopotamia.

In July 1928 the 1855 Colours of the 3rd (Militia) Battalion of the Regiment were laid up in All Saints' Church, Maidstone. These Colours had been moved from St. Peter's Church, Ightham, to the Depot in 1922.

In July 1932 Brigadier-General E. A. W. S. Grove, who had commanded the 2nd Battalion during the Boer War, gave £500 to the Regiment for the formation of a Trust, which was to be devoted to the promotion of efficiency in the two Regular battalions. Since then two 'Grove Trust' prizes have been presented each year in each Regular battalion; one to the best shot under active service conditions and one to the N.C.O. or man who displays the most intelligence and initiative on training.

During this period the following members of the Regiment won Army or County Championships or represented the Army or a County at sport:

1926. Lieutenant Durtnell (1st Bn.) won the Army (in India) Officers' Lightweight Boxing Championship.

1927. Lieutenant Western (Depot) played rugby for Kent.

1927. C.S.M. Willans (4th Bn.) won the Territorial Army Rifle Championship.

1928. C.S.M. Willans (4th Bn.) won the King's Medal at the Army Rifle Association Meeting.

1928. Captain Howlett (1st Bn.) played cricket for Kent.

1929. Serjeant Aylett (Depot) boxed for the Army.

1931. Captain Howlett (Adj. 4th Bn.) played cricket for the Army.

1932.   2nd Lieutenant Whitty (2nd Bn.) played rugby for the Army.

1932.   Private Archer (2nd Bn.) won the Hampshire Cross-Country Championship and ran for the Army.

2. *The 1st Battalion at Poona, Madras and Bangalore*

When the 1st Battalion arrived at Poona in November 1922 they found that a large detachment would have to be sent periodically to guard the arsenal and ammunition factory at Kirkee, some seven miles away. Another disappointment was that in December 200 men on short service engagements departed to England for discharge. Nevertheless, the drill was excellent when the battalion took part in the annual Proclamation Day Parade on the Racecourse on New Year's Day, 1923; as it was again in November 1923, when the Colour was Trooped on the occasion of the visit of His Excellency the Governor of Bombay.

In November 1925 Lieutenant-Colonel A. K. Grant, D.S.O., assumed command of the battalion. His arrival seemed to herald a spate of ceremonial occasions, including an inspection in April 1926 by the Commander-in-Chief, India, Field-Marshal Sir William Birdwood, and a Guard of Honour and lining the streets when the Viceroy and Lady Irwin visited Poona in July of the same year.

The officers were very active members of the Kirkee Rowing Club, and all ranks took part in sailing and rowing events in the regattas on the river. Within the battalion itself the Cycle Club, which enabled the men to hire cycles cheaply to visit local places of interest, became very popular. The members of the Boxing Club were also enthusiastic, and boxing belts, which were held by the battalion champion at each weight, were introduced in June 1923. This system soon bore fruit, for in 1926 three members of the battalion did very well in the Army in India Boxing Championships. At shooting the traditional trophies were taken into use for the first time since the war at a rifle meeting held in December 1923. Amongst these trophies were the Regimental Bowl, Colonel Harrison's, Colonel Style's and Major Rowe's Cups and the Old Soldiers' Shield. The purchase of a battalion bus, which took teams to matches and troops and families to Kirkee and other places, also added to the contentment of the men.

The battalion moved in March 1927 to Madras, where it was again divided into two parts. Two companies were stationed in the town at Fort George, and the other two were accommodated at

St. Thomas's Mount, some ten miles away. Owing to the lack of amenities, such as electric light and proper *punkas*, at 'The Mount,' companies were changed over every three months, so that, with other moves to camp for weapon and field training, troops and families were constantly changing quarters. Moreover, the climate was very 'sticky' and enervating, though some relief was obtained by bathing in the sea. All ranks were glad when it was their turn to spend a few weeks at the Hill Station at Wellington, near Ootacamund.

There were two outstanding ceremonial occasions at Madras. These were another visit from Field-Marshal Sir W. Birdwood in December 1927; and the battalion found a Guard of Honour for the Governor of Madras in January 1928.

On February 3, 1928, a Hartal, or day of passive resistance, was proclaimed in Madras to boycott the Simon Commission, which was examining the problem of self-government for India. Rioting broke out early in the morning, and picquets were sent from Fort George to guard business premises. The police were unable to control the mob and were forced to open fire. At 1 p.m. the police asked for military assistance. An officer and some twenty men, armed with hockey sticks, toured the troubled area in a lorry. The rioters quickly dispersed, but the picquets remained out that night to keep the streets clear. By the following morning the situation was normal. A Government Order dated February 23 stated that 'The Government wish to place on record their appreciation of the promptness with which the military responded to the application for their assistance.'

Before the battalion left Madras the Governor addressed the men on parade, a hitherto unheard of distinction, and complimented them on their fine record for smartness and good behaviour, and on their good health in the notoriously bad climate.

After a tour of less than two years in Madras the battalion moved to Bangalore in December 1928. The move was carried out by train as far as Gooty, but from there the battalion marched the remaining 200 miles in order to 'show the flag.' Not a man fell out although some, who had blistered heels, cut out the backs of their boots so that they could carry on. The march took approximately two weeks, which included several rest days. One of these was spent near a village called Goddamnazapalli, which turned out to be a much better place than its name implied. At Bangalore the battalion was stationed in Baird Barracks. The men were disappointed to find that the rooms were lit only by oil lamps. It was not in fact until February 1930 that electricity was installed.

In January 1929 the Colonel of the Regiment, General O'Dowda, made the six days' journey from Quetta to visit the battalion. He stayed for a week and was very pleased with the special programme of events that was arranged for him. He made a second similar visit in January 1931. After both visits he wrote very eulogistic reports.

In November 1929 Lieutenant-Colonel O. Y. Hibbert, D.S.O., M.C., assumed command.

Platoon and company training was carried out from a camp at Pinya, and battalion training from a camp at Ranjankunti. The weapon training camp was at Hebbal, where full use was made of the ranges. Indeed in 1930 a platoon of A Company won the Roupell Cup (India), and in 1932 No. 5 Platoon won the Hopton Cup (Abroad) and A Company was second in the Company Shield. All of these were non-central Army Rifle Association matches. The new Commander-in-Chief, India, General Sir Philip Chetwode, inspected the battalion in December 1929.

During this period the battalion was able to field a strong football team, which won the Madras District Football Tournament four times, the All India Football Tournament at Mysore twice, and, greatest success of all, the Rovers Cup at Bombay in 1931. Not to be outdone, the hockey team won the Madras District Hockey Cup twice, and the boxers the Madras District Inter-Unit Competition twice.

Before the battalion left Bangalore in October 1932 a cross of gold was placed on Holy Trinity Church as a memorial to the eight other ranks of the battalion who had died there. Their names were inscribed on a brass tablet within the church.

3. *The 2nd Battalion at Ballykinlar, Woking, Guernsey and Aldershot*

For many of the officers and men of the 2nd Battalion the period they spent at Ballykinlar Camp was very happy. The small village of Dundrum was the only place outside the camp where they could go for entertainment in the evenings, and consequently they had to make their own amusements within the battalion. Gigantic boxing meetings with 200 entries, bayonet-fencing and basket-ball competitions, concerts and dances were all frequently organised. In addition, as the country round the camp was excellent for the purpose, inter-platoon as well as inter-company cross-country races were held every month. There was also plenty of ground for a running track, and in 1923 the battalion was able to hold its first real athletic meeting since the war.

E

As a result of all this activity the battalion won the Northern Ireland District competitions in both boxing and cross-country running in March 1923, and the season ended with its teams being placed 4th in the Army cross-country and 7th in Army boxing competitions at Aldershot. These were no mean achievements at the first attempt. The boxers were trained by Serjeant Sheppard, who had been a member of the battalion team which won the Delhi Durbar Boxing Trophy in 1911. In 1924 the teams again won the N.I.D. boxing and cross-country competitions, but they did not do so well in the Army championships.

On February 4, 1923, a tragedy occurred in Dundrum Bay. It was a stormy night, and the small ferry boat in which a party of troops was returning from Dundrum village was heavy-laden. The waves lapped over the stern, the boat capsized, and six members of the battalion were drowned. They were: F. Bellingham, W. Broom, A. Howe, A. Hunt, A. Hynam and R. Williard.

In September 1923 a mammoth Battalion Rifle Meeting was held, in which were included the traditional competitions for the Eccles, Long, Maunsell and Western Cups. As a result of this, many successes were won in the Northern Ireland District rifle meetings in 1923 and 1924.

In March 1924 Lieutenant-Colonel J. T. Twisleton-Wykeham-Fiennes assumed command of the battalion, which, on the last day of that year, sailed to England once more after a very mixed five years in Europe and Ireland.

The battalion arrived at Inkerman Barracks, Woking, on January 1, 1925. Although Woking is eight miles from Aldershot it was within the boundary of the Aldershot Command, and the battalion not only took part in all the strenuous training exercises of that Command but often had to march the extra eight miles to and from Aldershot in addition. The training was practically continuous throughout the year, beginning with platoon and company exercises on 'local' areas in the spring, then to a camp for battalion training, to other camps for brigade and divisional exercises in the summer, and ending in October, in 1925 only, with army manœuvres. Nor was there very much relaxation in the autumn and winter months, when individual training and shooting on the ranges were carried out. This was very different from Ballykinlar, but the troops saw it through with their usual cheerfulness. Leave was plentiful. Each company went on leave for one month in the winter, and a few days were granted either at Easter or Whitsun and ten days in August.

Besides the training the battalion supplied register-keepers and butt-markers for the Army Rifle Association meeting at Bisley in the summer of 1925 and for the National Rifle Association meeting in 1927. In addition all platoons took part in an arduous competition for the Evelyn Wood Cup, which entailed a forced march followed by a shoot for all the platoon weapons on Ash Ranges. Another similar competition was for the Duke of Connaught's Shield. The Machine Gun Platoons of all battalions in the Command were concentrated at Netheravon, on Salisbury Plain, for two weeks each summer.

In May 1925 the battalion formed part of the funeral procession in London for the Earl of Ypres, formerly Field-Marshal Sir John French. In June it took part in the Royal Review on Laffan's Plain at Aldershot, marching there from a camp at Old Dean Common, Camberley, where it was carrying out training at the time. This was the last Royal Review to be held for ten years.

In its sporting activities the battalion met with far stronger opposition than it had found in Northern Ireland. At boxing the experiment was tried of employing a professional boxer to train the team, but their greatest success was to reach the semi-finals of the Aldershot Command competition in 1925. The barracks were in a built-up area, and consequently it was not possible to train a cross-country team properly. At football the team reached the round before the semi-final in the Army Cup in 1927, but were beaten by the Royal Warwickshire Regiment at Shorncliffe after extra time. In 1925 Lance-Corporal Dyason was second in both the weight and the discus in the Army Individual Athletic Championships at Tidworth.

Before the battalion left Woking, Major-General Sir Edmund Ironside, the Divisional Commander, in a farewell speech complimented the men on their fine record in the Aldershot Command, their excellent reputation for efficiency during training and their splendid behaviour in Woking.

The battalion sailed to Guernsey from Southampton in S.S. *Vera* in November 1927. In Guernsey it was accommodated in Fort George and a Militia camp called Les Beaucamps until June 1928, when the companies were concentrated in Fort George with the Band and Drums in Castle Cornet. The Governor of Guernsey at that time was Major-General Sir Charles Sackville-West, later Lord Sackville of Knole Park, Sevenoaks. In the spring or summer of each year the battalion crossed in two parties in a government vessel to Alderney, where the range courses were fired and a few training exercises were carried out. In Alderney the battalion was quartered in Forts Albert and Tourgie. Some of the families were accommodated in married quarters in Alderney all the year round. Recruits and casuals fired their range courses in Guernsey on a range at Vazon Bay.

Apart from these mild spasms of activity the battalion led a peaceful existence and participated to the full in the social and sporting life of the island. The band gave numerous performances in Candie Gardens and crossed to Jersey at least once each year to give concerts there. Football was immensely popular; the battalion entered teams for all the competitions but found the redoubtable "Northerners" a hard nut to crack. Much cricket was played in the summer. The rugby team assisted the island to revive its interest at that game, and the Siam Cup was resuscitated for competition. Swimming naturally became very popular.

Lieutenant-Colonel E. H. Norman, D.S.O., O.B.E., assumed command in March 1928.

In June 1929 a Guard of Honour was found on the arrival of the new Governor of Guernsey, Lord Ruthven. In July 1930 General O'Dowda, the Colonel of the Regiment, visited the battalion and spent a week with it. A special programme of events was arranged, including the Trooping of the Colour.

The battalion moved back to the Aldershot Command in November 1930, and was stationed in Blenheim Barracks at North Camp. Many of the officers and other ranks had already experienced life in that Command and it held no fears for them. In any case the training was less arduous during this second tour, owing not a little to the fact that lack of money had caused the programme to be curtailed. In 1931 the 1st Division was brought up to strength for training by units of the 2nd Division, and the majority of the battalion was attached to the 3rd Battalion The Coldstream Guards for a few weeks.

The financial crisis of 1931–32 was not without its internal effect on the battalion. As a result of a directive from the War Office economies were made wherever possible, particularly in the Officers' Mess. The Mess waiters ceased to wear livery except on Guest Nights: the long, crested, Irish linen table-cloths were not replaced when they became worn out; and the custom of smoking crested Turkish cigarettes after dinner ceased.

New Colours were presented to the battalion on May 16, 1931, by His Royal Highness The Duke of Gloucester, Earl of Ulster. The Duke was deputising for His Majesty King George V, who was unable to be present on account of ill health. There were four Major-Generals, all former officers of the The Queen's Own, at the ceremony:—J. W. O'Dowda, the Colonel of the Regiment, C. Bonham-Carter, who will be mentioned a great deal later, R. J. T. Hildyard, a future Governor and C.-in-C. of Bermuda, and H. Isacke, who was then commanding 56th (London) Division. The old (1891) Colours were laid up in All Saints' Church, Maidstone, in July.

During 1931 the battalion's interest in cross-country running was renewed and, as a result, the team was third in the Hampshire Cross-country Championships and fourth in the Aldershot Command Team Competition in 1932. What was more significant for the future was that they won the Command Young Soldiers' Competition and were also victorious in the Southern Counties Junior Championships at Beaconsfield that year. Private Archer finished thirty-eighth in the National Cross-country Championship in March 1932.

4. *The Territorial Battalions*

By 1923 the Territorial Army had taken shape. The 4th and 5th Battalions were brigaded together in the Kent and Sussex Brigade of 44th (Home Counties) Division, and The 20th London Regiment (The Queen's Own) was brigaded with the 17th, 18th and 19th London Regiments in 141st Brigade of 47th (London) Division. Every officer and man was obliged to attend twenty 'drills' each year, or forty for recruits, and to fire the Annual Weapon Training Course. In addition voluntary training was often carried out during the Easter and Whitsun week-ends, and Tactical Exercises Without Troops (T.E.W.T.s) were attended by the officers at other week-ends. But the great occasion was the 15 days spent at the annual camp.

The locations selected for these annual camps included Seaford, Arundel Park, Beaulieu and Worthing for the 4th and 5th Battalions; and Aldershot, Falmer, Bordon and Shoreham for the 20th London. Needless to say the camps most enjoyed were those close to the sea. The Easter and Whitsun training was usually carried out at the Depot or with the 2nd Battalion, when it was in England. In 1927 the 5th Battalion was transferred to the Kent and Middlesex Brigade and became separated from the 4th Battalion. That was a lean year for training, as Annual Camp did not take place, the Bounty was withheld, and no pay was granted for the Easter and Whitsun week-ends. In 1932, owing to the financial crisis, recruiting was curtailed, and Annual Training, which was cut down to one week, was carried out by all three battalions at Aldershot with the 2nd Battalion. No Bounty was paid that year either.

The permanent staff of a Territorial battalion included an Adjutant, an R.S.M. and four instructors (two for the 20th London, who had only one Drill Hall) from the Regular battalions. In 1930, owing to the recent reorganisation of the Territorial battalions into three Rifle companies and one Machine Gun Company, several additional Regular officers and N.C.O.s were attached to each

For some time it had been recognised that the existing organisation of three Rifle companies and one Machine Gun Company in an infantry battalion was clumsy from a tactical point of view. The approved plan was to convert some infantry regiments to Machine Gun Regiments and to remove the Vickers guns from the remainder. By the autumn of 1935 enough money was becoming available, and this conversion was very gradually carried out. To the disappointment of many The Queen's Own was not one of the regiments selected for conversion.

Perhaps the greatest proof that the Army's lean time was at an end was the erection of new barracks and the modernisation of some of the old. At the Depot two modern blocks of barrack rooms were built in 1937. These contained sitting rooms, central heating and constant hot water; luxuries undreamed of in 1932. In addition a radio relay system for the Drill Shed and Dining Hall was installed, and by 1938 many of the barrack rooms had been linked to this system.

Relations between The Queen's Own and the people of Kent became close during this period. This was due partly to the arrival of the 2nd Battalion at Shorncliffe in November 1934, but mainly to the fact that in March 1935 His Majesty King George V was graciously pleased to approve the appointment of His Royal Highness The Duke of Kent as Colonel-in-Chief of the Regiment. He was the first Colonel-in-Chief to be appointed to The Queen's Own, and that he should be a son of the King was looked upon as a special honour.

In May 1937 the Association of Men of Kent and Kentish Men and Fair Maids of Kent presented a Silver Bugle to The Queen's Own in commemoration of the Coronation of His Majesty King George VI. The Bugle was handed over by the Duchess of Kent, the patron of the Fair Maids of Kent, and was received on behalf of the Regiment by His Royal Highness The Duke of Kent after a ceremony of Trooping the Colour by the 2nd Battalion at Shorncliffe. People from all countries of the Empire, who were in England for the Coronation, were present at this ceremony.

In April 1933 the name of the Old Comrades' Association was changed to 'The Queen's Own Past and Present Association.' In the summer of that year the first Regimental Reunion was held at the Depot. After assembling on the square the parade marched to the Regimental Memorial in Blenchley Gardens, where a wreath was laid by the Colonel of the Regiment. The parade then returned to the Depot for lunch and various entertainments. This Reunion subsequently became an annual event, a short Memorial Service at All Saints' Church being included in the morning programme from 1934 onwards. The Past and Present Association then began to flourish.

H.R.H. THE DUKE OF KENT, K.G., K.T., G.C.M.G., G.C.V.O.
COLONEL-IN-CHIEF FROM MARCH 1935 TO AUGUST 1942

In 1935 new branches were formed at Tonbridge and Chatham, and at the Regimental Reunion the Colonel of the Regiment presented a Standard to the Maidstone Branch, which was thus the first to own one. In January 1936 new branches[1] were formed at Shorncliffe and London. A social club, as part of the London branch, was formed at Deptford in October 1937.

The Regimental Museum at the Depot was officially opened by Lady Alderson in June 1935. This was inspected by H.R.H. The Duke of Kent when he paid a visit to the Depot in November of that year. On that occasion he also inspected the recruits and members of the Past and Present Association on parade and made a tour of the barrack rooms and institutes.

Thirty-five Section 'A' Reservists of The Queen's Own were called up in August 1936 for service with the East Yorkshire Regiment in Palestine.

General O'Dowda relinquished the appointment of Colonel of the Regiment on August 31, 1936. He was succeeded by Lieutenant-General Sir Charles Bonham-Carter, K.C.B., C.M.G., D.S.O., who was then Governor and C.-in-C. of Malta. Sir Charles had been gazetted into the Regiment in 1896. He was promoted to the rank of General in October 1937.

There were several Royal occasions during this five-year span. For The Queen's Own the highlights were the lining of a portion of the Strand near St. Clement Danes Church by the 20th London for the Silver Jubilee procession of King George V in May 1935; the marching of a strong detachment from the Depot with bayonets fixed to the Town Hall, Maidstone, for the Proclamation of King Edward VIII and of King George VI; and the lining of a portion of Pall Mall from Cockspur Street to Waterloo Place by the 2nd Battalion for the Coronation of King George VI in May 1937. For this occasion the whole of the 2nd and detachments from the 4th and 5th Battalions were accommodated in a camp in Kensington Gardens; detachments from all three battalions marched in the procession. In connection with the Coronation, King George VI reviewed 80,000 members of the ex-Service organisations in Hyde Park in June 1937 and took the salute as they marched past 20 abreast. 250 members of the Past and Present Association with the Standards of six branches were on parade that day.

In January 1938 the change-over from Home to Foreign service of the two Regular battalions occurred. The 1st Battalion came home to Shorncliffe and the 2nd proceeded to Palestine. Thus an eighteen-year cycle in the life of the Regiment was completed. The troopships

[1] The Gravesend Branch was opened early in 1939.

carrying the two battalions passed each other in the night somewhere east of Malta. Both ships called at Malta, where Sir Charles Bonham-Carter had the unique experience of visiting both battalions on board ship in the Grand Harbour and of entertaining the officers at Sant Anton Palace, the official residence of the Governor.

* * *

Two Regimental competitions were inaugurated in 1933. In April the first Regimental Cross-country Race for the Styles Cup[1] was held at Aldershot. Teams from the 2nd, 4th, 5th, and 20th London Battalions and the Depot competed. In October a similar competition at rifle shooting for the Moulton-Barrett Cup[2] was held, also at Aldershot. These two contests subsequently became annual events, each unit in turn acting as hosts. Teams of Regulars and Territorials then began to play each other at cricket and football. There is no doubt that these events were of great value in fostering comradeship within the Regiment. In 1933 there was a Queen's Own officer on each side in the annual rugby match between the Regular and the Territorial Armies; 2nd Lieutenant Whitty (2nd Bn.) played for the Army and Lieutenant Hudson (4th Bn.) played for the T.A.

The 2nd Battalion Cross-country running team won the Army Unit Team Championships at Colchester in March 1937. Two of the team, Lance-Corporal Jordan and Private Hake, received their Army Badges, and the first-named ran for the Army in the Inter-Services race at Bordon.

Other successes gained by members of the Regiment during this period were:—

1933 Drummer Watts (2nd Bn.) was the Kent Javelin Champion.

1934 and 1935 2nd Lieutenant Whitty (2nd Bn.) played rugby for Kent. 2nd Lieutenant Courtney (5th Bn.) won the T. A. Officers' Light Heavyweight Boxing Championship.

1935 Lieutenant Whitty(2nd Bn.) played rugby for the Army. Private Bayliss (2nd Bn.) boxed for the Army. Serjeant White (Depot) played football for Kent.

1936 Lieutenant Whitty (2nd Bn.) was awarded his Army rugby cap and played cricket for the Army. Drummer Watts (2nd Bn.) was the Army Javelin and Discus Champion and the Imperial Services Javelin Champion.

[1] Presented by Captain H. W. Styles of the 4th Battalion.
[2] Presented by Major Moulton-Barrett on his retirement in 1932.

1937 Lieutenant Whitty (2nd Bn.) played in the Army *v* Navy and the Army *v* R.A.F. rugby matches.

Lieutenant Scott (Depot) played cricket for the Army and for Sussex.

2nd Lieutenant Butler (2nd Bn.) was the Kent 440 yards Champion.

Lance-Corporal Watts (2nd Bn.) was the Kent Javelin Champion and the Army Discus Champion.

2. *The 1st Battalion at Secunderabad and Karachi*

The 1st Battalion moved by train to Secunderabad in October 1932 for a four-year tour. It was accommodated in Gough Barracks at Trimulgherry, a military cantonment about three miles outside Secunderabad. The barracks were extensive, with electric light throughout, and there were plenty of grounds for football, hockey and cricket. But the station was notorious for its boredom, known by the troops as 'Deccan Death.' This was somewhat alleviated by the organisation of numerous entertainments such as roller skating, concerts ('Gaffs'), and arts and crafts exhibitions. These, as well as boxing competitions, were held in an open-air theatre or casino. Much use was also made of a small swimming bath in the barracks and of a larger bath at the Secunderabad Club, which was kindly loaned for a few periods each week. A number of officers became members of the sailing club, situated on the Husain Sagar lake near Hyderabad, where the Secunderabad Regatta was held each year. On Thursdays, always a holiday, the troops and sometimes the families often went for outings in the battalion bus to places of interest in the vicinity. The chief of these was Golconda Fort. The Hill Station was still Wellington, and most of the personnel managed to get there at least every other year.

In addition to an infantry brigade there were also two cavalry brigades and several artillery units stationed near Secunderabad. These made an impressive sight when they were all assembled on parade on the *maidan* on occasions such as the Proclamation Day Parade on January 1 each year, the Proclamation of King Edward VIII and of King George VI, and the annual King's Birthday Parade. Other ceremonial occasions included a parade for the visit of His Excellency the Viceroy and Lady Willingdon in November 1933, and the visit of H.E. the Commander-in-Chief, General Sir Robert Cassels, in July 1936.

Range courses were usually fired at Lallaguda, some three miles from Trimulgherry. Company, battalion and brigade training was carried out either from barracks or from camps at Miampur and Ghatkesar, both about 15 miles from Secunderabad. In November 1934 the battalion marched over 100 miles through the Deccan to an area near Homnabad for divisional training. The march there and back entailed an early start each morning so as to reach the next camping site before the heat of the day. The baggage was carried on Army Transport (A.T.) carts, and mules carried the Vickers and Lewis guns and ammunition. A feature of the march was the presence of Mohammed Yassim ('Mister') with the canteen in a very old lorry.

In November 1933 Lieutenant-Colonel G. E. Wingfield-Stratford, M.C., assumed command.

The battalion was issued with Vickers-Berthier guns instead of Lewis guns in September 1936, but it was not till a year later that the Machine Gun Company handed over its Vickers guns to the Royal Scots Fusiliers.

The battalion teams practically 'swept the board' of all the sports trophies in the Area competitions for United Kingdom troops at Secunderabad. They won the boxing, cross-country, swimming, football, cricket and hockey competitions each year, except that the cross-country was lost in 1935, and the boxing was lost in 1936. The hockey team reached the semi-final of the All-India Aga Khan Tournament at Bombay in 1934—a very meritorious achievement—and they won the Fatteh Maidan gymkhana at Hyderabad that year.

At the end of the tour at Secunderabad the District Commander, Major-General O. H. L. Nicholson, complimented the battalion in a farewell speech on its good behaviour and fine record. The final act at Trimulgherry was the unveiling of a tablet in the Garrison Church to the memory of the six members of The Queen's Own who had died in the station.

When the battalion moved to Karachi in November 1936 the first part of the journey was made by train to Bombay with stops for meals at such places as Wadi Junction and Hotgi. The second part of the journey, from Bombay to Karachi, was made by sea in the *Ellora*. At Karachi, after a few weeks in Napier Barracks, the battalion was quartered in Bhurtpore Lines, a collection of temporary hutments which had been erected to house the refugees from the Quetta earthquake. Although the quarters were poor the town of Karachi itself made a pleasant change from the cantonment life at Trimulgherry; the cafés, shops and cinemas were especially attractive. The Union Jack Club, with its large swimming pool and other amenities, was much appreciated, and so was the lido on the sea-shore.

The climate was cooler than the troops had known for sixteen years, though rain, even in the monsoon season, was scarce. When the rain did come it was very heavy and made the ground unfit for training. The Sind Desert, in the hinterland, gave the battalion its first taste of training for desert warfare. Company training was carried out from Drigh Road camp, which was close to the Imperial Airways airport, and battalion and brigade training from a camp at Hab River. In November 1937 a combined Naval, Military and Air Exercise was held and was watched by students from the Staff College, Quetta.

Lieutenant-Colonel P. N. Anstruther, D.S.O., M.C., assumed command in November 1937.

On the last Sunday at Karachi the battalion paraded as strong as possible for Divine Service in the Garrison Church. During the service a memorial tablet to the two other ranks who had died in the station was unveiled.

Before the battalion sailed for England the Khan Bahadur Jan Mohammed, who, as J. M. Kalla, had been associated with The Queen's Own as its contractor since 1911, entertained the officers at a cocktail party and the other ranks at a cinema performance followed by a supper in barracks. When the battalion embarked in H.M.T. *Dilwara* on December 24, 1937, 'Mister' was on the quay, waving farewell with the Malacca walking-stick which had been given to him by all ranks. He had been manager of the canteen since 1926, and had first served the Regiment as a boy in the canteen of the 2nd Battalion at Peshawar in 1912.

Those officers and other ranks whose service was about to expire had been drafted home ahead of the battalion. Eleven officers and 283 other ranks, whose tour of duty overseas had not been completed, left the *Dilwara* at Suez and, having spent one day at Ismailia, proceeded by train and ferry to Kantara East to join the advance party of the 2nd Battalion. The whole detachment then went on by train to Haifa, a ten-hour journey. The main body disembarked at Southampton on January 13, 1938, and proceeded to Napier Barracks, Shorncliffe, which had just been vacated by the 2nd Battalion. For Private 'Nobby' Esplin, the oldest soldier in the Regiment, this was the first time he had been Home for some 34 years. He was interviewed in the British Broadcasting Corporation programme 'In Town To-night' two days later.

In this way the battalion completed its eighteen years' tour of duty overseas, all of which had been spent in India.

3. *The 2nd Battalion at Aldershot and Shorncliffe*

Lieutenant-Colonel N. I. Whitty, D.S.O., had assumed command of the 2nd Battalion in March 1932 and was therefore at the helm during its last two years at Aldershot. The country was still recovering from the financial crisis, and little money was voted to the Army for training. But the battalion took part in a 2nd Division exercise, in which the River Thames was crossed at Pangbourne, in July 1933, and marched to Salisbury Plain for a Corps exercise in September. In the early summer of 1934 much time was devoted to the preparation of a Physical Training Display for the Aldershot Command Tattoo. This military entertainment had become one of the annual events in the South of England and was the chief means of filling the coffers of various Army charitable associations. When the battalion had been stationed at Woking the Band and Drums had taken part regularly—indeed in 1925 Serjeant-Drummer Cousins had been selected to lead the massed Drums of the Command—and in 1932 a detachment had given a Physical Training Display and had portrayed part of the Battle of Inkerman. But in 1934 the whole battalion participated.

In May 1934 the Machine Gun Company won the Army Rifle Association Machine Gun Fire Control Cup, which was fired for at the Machine Gun Concentration at Netheravon, and also won the Smith-Dorrien Cup at the Aldershot Command Rifle Meeting. The A.R.A. Fire Control Cup was again won in 1935.

The battalion cross-country team continued to gain experience by running in the South of the Thames and the Southern Counties Senior races in 1933; and the Aldershot Command Young Soldiers' Race was won for the second time that year. In March 1934, they won the Aldershot Command Inter-Unit Team Competition and were seventh in the Army Championships. At athletics the battalion was third in the Aldershot Command Team Championships in 1933 and won the Young Soldiers' Relay Race in 1933 and 1934.

The battalion moved to Napier Barracks, Shorncliffe, in November 1934. This was the first time it had been stationed in Kent since its short stay at Dover Castle in the spring of 1921, and from the outset every effort was made to strengthen its association with the county. In June 1935, a recruiting march was made through Kent. Having passed through Ashford and Harrietsham the first night was spent at the Depot, where the Colour was Trooped the following evening. Then on to Tonbridge, where the Colour was Trooped again. On the Sunday the battalion marched to Tunbridge Wells for an open-air Church Service and Trooping the Colour on the cricket ground. This ceremony was attended by the Marquess of Camden, Lord Lieutenant of the county. The following night bivouacs were pitched at Cranbrook School. The battalion then broke up and carried out a tactical scheme which ended at Shorncliffe.

In July 1935 His Royal Highness The Duke of Kent, now Colonel-in-Chief of the Regiment, attended a ceremony of Trooping the Colour at Shorncliffe. A gold cigarette case was presented to him by the officers and a silver porringer by the Wives' Club. In October 1936 the Duke again visited the battalion and inspected it on parade at the Stadium, Shorncliffe.

Training in the Eastern Command was more varied but less strenuous than it had been at Aldershot. Shooting was mainly carried out on the ranges at Hythe, and the Machine Gun Company went to Lydd to fire its courses and competitions. In the summer of 1935, battalion, brigade and divisional training was carried out from a camp at Horsebridge in Hampshire. In 1936 the battalion marched to Falmer through Ham Street and Lewes, but training was curtailed owing to an outbreak of foot-and-mouth disease. In that year also it went to Aldershot to take part once more in the Aldershot Command Tattoo. This time it demonstrated 'Infantry Firing Exercises Ancient and Modern,' and portrayed an action during the 'Rangoon River Campaign,' and the 'Music of The Drums.'

Lieutenant-Colonel W. V. Palmer assumed command in March 1936, at the time when the rearmament programme at last began to produce practical results.

Mechanisation started by the attendance of officers and other ranks at driving and maintenance courses; then a few Morris trucks were received; and in July 1937, a Mechanical Transport Section was formed. After that the horse-drawn limbers were not used as transport again, and when the battalion was in camp near Ashford in September for brigade and divisional training the marching was greatly cut down by the use of trucks, lorries and hired civilian buses. In May 1937, the Machine Gun Company carried out 'rifle' training instead of machine gun work for the first time. In July the Vickers guns were handed over to the Royal Fusiliers. By August 1937, the battalion had been reorganised into four Rifle companies.

In July 1937, silver drums, which had been subscribed for by all ranks and by retired officers, were received and taken into use.

While the battalion was at Shorncliffe the cross-country and athletic teams continued their successes. In 1935 and 1936 the cross-country team won the Eastern Command Unit Team Competition, and in 1936 it was fifth in the Army Championships at Tidworth. Then, at last, in 1937, the goal for which the team had been striving since 1931 was achieved. After winning the Eastern Command race for the third time, it won the Army Unit Team Cross-country

Championship at Colchester in March. The team placings were:—

5th	L/Cpl. A. Jordan	7th	Private L. Hake
9th	Private W. Stoner	20th	Private A. Curtis
22nd	Private E. White	23rd	Private F. Wood
26th	Private W. Smith	27th	L/Cpl. E. Stephenson
30th	Private C. Dorman	36th	Private J. Theobold
37th	Private L. Floyd	60th	Private G. W. Davidson

2nd Lieutenant T. T. W. Stanyon and Privates A. Newman and L. Warren were non-counting numbers. The team was trained by Regimental Serjeant-Major Pond.

In 1935 and 1936 the athletic team was third in the Eastern Command Unit Team Competition, and in 1937, determined to emulate the cross-country runners, it won the Eastern Command competition and was third in the Army Unit Team Athletic Championships at Aldershot.

The time was now drawing near for the battalion to begin its overseas tour. In November 1937, the men proceeded on embarkation leave, and there were no absentees when the battalion embarked at Southampton in the *California* on January 4, 1938. A large assembly was on the quay to watch the great ship draw away, carrying the cheering troops to Palestine for special service.

4. *The Territorial Battalions*

The increased popularity of the Army became perhaps more apparent in the Territorial than in the Regular Army. With the resumption of annual training in 1933 recruiting received a boost. The 4th Battalion was not only up to strength but had a waiting list when it went to camp at Shoreham-on-Sea, and the 5th Battalion had its highest strength since the war when it camped at Friston near Eastbourne. In 1934 the annual camps, held for the 4th at Arundel, the 5th at Falmer and the 20th London at Swanage, were also well attended.

The annual range courses were normally fired by all three Territorial battalions at Shoreham in Kent or on the ranges at Milton, Gravesend. Battalion rifle meetings were also held each year. This policy proved to be a good one, for in 1934 both the 4th and 5th did well in the Territorial Army Rifle Association non-central matches, and the 5th won the 44th Division shooting competition. In 1936 the 4th won this competition and also five prizes at Bisley.

The big event of 1935 was the conversion of the 20th London from infantry to an anti-aircraft role. This conversion was explained to the officers at their annual dinner in London by Lieutenant-General Sir Charles Bonham-Carter, who was then Director-General of the Territorial Army. Great disappointment was felt by all ranks when they realised that they would be leaving The Queen's Own to become part of the corps of the Royal Engineers. But the wrench became less when it was known that the Colours, the cap badge and the regimental march would be retained. A Conversion Eve Dinner for the whole battalion was held in the Drill Hall at Holly Hedge House on December 20. The title was at first changed to 20th Battalion London Regiment (The Queen's Own) Anti-Aircraft Battalion Royal Engineers, but in 1936 it became 34th (The Queen's Own Royal West Kent) Anti-Aircraft Battalion Royal Engineers.

By the end of 1937 the public had begun to realise the important part the Territorial Army was taking in the defence of the country. A film called *The Gap*, which depicted the searchlight defence of London, was shown at many cinemas in Kent. The Territorial battalions were invited to see the programme free of charge, and their trophies and weapons were displayed in the foyers of the cinemas. Another step in the right direction was that the payment of one shilling was authorised for each 'drill' a man attended, so that he would not have to pay the fare from his home to the drill hall out of his own pocket.

The pattern of training of the Territorial Battalions was changed by the gradual introduction of mechanisation. In 1936 some of the transport of the 4th Battalion was mechanised for the first time when annual training was carried out at Falmer, and at its annual training at Arundel in 1937 the 5th used trucks and lorries as transport.

The 4th Battalion, with a new team, won the 44th Division Cross-country Championship five times (1933–1937), and in 1936 it was sixth in the Territorial Army Unit Team Cross-country Championships at Northolt, the first time this event was held. At boxing the 5th Battalion won the Munster Cup for the Kent Territorial Group Boxing Competition and were third in the 44th Division Championships in 1933. In 1936 and 1937 the 4th won the Kent Group Competition and the 5th took second place.

F

CHAPTER 4

The Second Battalion in Palestine
January 1938 to March 1939
(Written by Colonel W. V. Palmer)

1. Railway Protection and Curfew Patrols

WHEN in the summer of 1937 the 2nd Battalion received orders to proceed to Palestine, very little was known of the military situation there. So far as could be gathered from the reports in the Press, the battalion was only likely to be called upon to assist in maintaining the internal security of the country. It was known, however, that the Arab rebellion and the Arab-Jewish problem were proving difficult and that the small garrison in Palestine of two brigades of infantry was accordingly being increased.

In August a letter from the Commander of 16th Brigade in Haifa, under whom the battalion was to serve, with a mass of tactical and other instructions applicable to the country, gave the first indication that active operations against Arab gangs were to be expected from the moment of arrival in Haifa. By then it was too late to exercise the battalion in any of the tactical methods peculiar to Palestine, and the battalion reached Haifa with no preliminary training beyond what could be given by lectures at Shorncliffe and on board ship.

The battalion arrived at Haifa on January 14, 1938, under command of Lieutenant-Colonel W. V. Palmer, and, being one of the two foreign service battalions normally stationed in Palestine, took over Peninsula Barracks from a battalion of the Essex Regiment. The barracks consisted of corrugated iron huts pleasantly situated by the sea in a Jewish quarter of Haifa, deep in mud in the winter, and decidedly 'sticky' in the summer. But all ranks very soon came to appreciate the advantage of having the comfort of permanent barracks to return to after days and even weeks spent away on operations or on detachment. Later on, however, Peninsula Barracks became the collecting centre for every vehicle entering or leaving the country, and for hundreds needing repair. A census of vehicles, taken one morning over a period of five hours, disclosed that trucks and lorries of all kinds passed the C.O.'s office at the rate of one a minute, and the peaceful seaside camp became a noisy and dangerous place of residence. It was as well that the families had remained at Shorncliffe.

On arrival the battalion was brought up to Colonial establishment by a draft of some 300 officers and other ranks, which the 1st Battalion had dropped at Suez on its way home from India. This draft formed a valuable nucleus of trained men. But even they had to be refreshed in the handling of the Lewis gun, for they had been using the Vickers-Berthier in India. This draft and the battalion's advanced party had taken over the barracks, and in fact were already providing a temporary static garrison at the village of Mi'ilia in northern Palestine and finding escorts for transport convoys and railway trolleys. Indeed they had already suffered one casualty, Private Harrington having been killed as the result of the accidental discharge of a rifle.

The battalion was allotted the dual role of railway protection, over about 100 miles of railway line, and operational duties within the Haifa area, the boundaries of which included some 600 square miles of coastal plain and hilly country.

The railway protection task included the defence of the Palestine Railway, as far south as Lydda, and of the Hedjaz Railway to the Syrian frontier at El Hamme, from acts of sabotage, and the provision of a special Railway Platoon. This platoon provided the crews of armoured motor trolleys, who had the unenviable task of preceding trains that ran during the hours of darkness. These trolleys were intended, with their strong headlights, to spot any damage to the track, Arab ambushes or landmines and so prevent derailment of the heavy goods trains following behind them. More often than not the first the crew knew of such dark deeds was the sudden derailment of their own trolley, followed by a burst of rifle fire from the darkness. As the trolley always ran one section of the signal system ahead of the train, it was possible for the saboteurs to nip in behind the trolley and explode their mine under the train's heavy locomotive. The Railway Platoon, who called themselves the 'Suicide Squad,' carried out their dangerous task through all kinds of weather with great courage and endurance, and gained much praise.

Four days after landing in Haifa and almost before the baggage had been unpacked, the battalion was ordered to send two companies to occupy four Arab villages some 45 miles south of Haifa, where the inhabitants were strongly suspected of being engaged in sabotage attacks on the railway line. These detachments remained away from Haifa until February 3, when they handed over their duties to companies of the 1st Royal Scots. But two platoons were again in occupation of one of the villages from February 10–16 to enforce a 22-hour curfew laid on the village owing to another sharp outbreak of sabotage. This severe restriction of their daily activities for six days was sufficient to persuade the inhabitants to curb the local night prowlers, which they did by paying the gang leader £80. The detachments at two of the villages were quartered in requisitioned school buildings, both of fairly modern construction and reasonably clean and comfortable. But the detachments at the other two had their first experience of living in Arab houses in small villages, and quickly learnt that, though the inhabitants were removed, they always left a large variety of 'lodgers' behind, which found the white skin of the British soldier more palatable than the tough epidermis of the Arab.

The principal tasks performed by these detachments were night patrolling to enforce a dusk to dawn curfew in the villages, and ambushing railway saboteurs on the main single line. It rained on and off nearly every day they were away from Haifa, and it was very quickly discovered that to proceed on such patrols dressed in battle equipment, greatcoat, boots and puttees, and to wade knee deep in mud in silence was not only almost impossible but most exhausting and very damaging to clothing and equipment. From that time onwards night operations were performed in canvas clothing and P.T. shoes, with a bandolier of ammunition slung across the body.

On January 31 one company was ordered to act under the orders of the Officer Commanding the 2nd Royal Ulster Rifles from Nathanya in an operation against a large gang reported to be in the area of the Musmus Pass. This company, which was moved in reserve, was severely handicapped by appalling weather conditions and lack of experience in Palestine operations, but on February 2, reinforced by three platoons from a company in Haifa, it moved up the Musmus Pass to the village of El Fahm, where on the previous day a company of the Royal Ulster Rifles had only been extricated from a dangerous position by the timely intervention of the R.A.F.

2. Operations against the Arabs

On February 16 the battalion again took over the platoon detachment at Mi'ilia, a small village in the hills near the northern

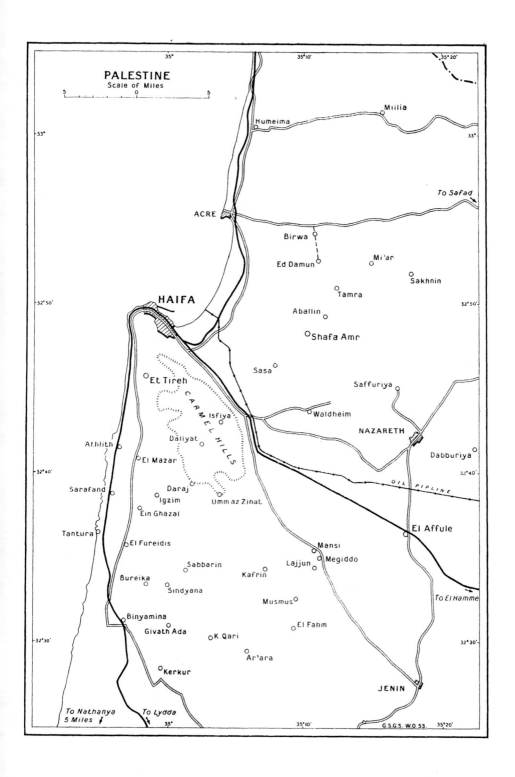

PALESTINE
Scale of Miles
5   0   5

35°   35°10'   35°20'

33°   33°

Humeima

Miilia

To Safad

ACRE

Birwa

Ed Damun   Mi'ar

Sakhnin

Tamra

Aballin   32°50'

Shafa Amr

HAIFA

Sasa

Saffuriya

Et Tireh

Isfiya   Waldheim

NAZARETH

Daliyat

Dabburiya

Athlith   32°40'

El Mazar   OIL PIPELINE

Sarafand   Daraj

Igzim   Umm az Zinat

Ein Ghazal

Tantura   El Affule

El Fureidis   Mansi

Sabbarin   Lajjun   Megiddo

Bureika   Kafrin

Sindyana   Musmus   To El Hamme

Binyamina

Givath Ada   El Fahm

K.Qari   32°30'

Ar'ara

Kerkur

JENIN

To Nathanya
5 Miles   To Lydda   35°

35°10'   G.S.G.S. W.O. 53.   35°20'

CARMEL HILLS

frontier road. This was a popular detached post, from which a magnificent view of the surrounding country was obtainable, and from which also useful patrols and minor operations could be carried out. This post was held at intervals until the summer, when it was handed over to the Royal Ulster Rifles.

On February 18, late in the afternoon, a private car driven by Squadron Leader Alderson was held up by armed gangsters about twelve miles south of Haifa, at a point where the Wadi Mughar from Igzim crosses the coast road. Squadron Leader Alderson was shot and killed and his daughter wounded.

Before dark the police found evidence that at least two gangsters had been in hiding at the culvert crossing the *wadi*, and spent cartridge cases provided a further clue for the use of police tracker dogs. A dog was therefore requisitioned from Jerusalem, and the battalion was ordered to provide the necessary escort for it and its trainer early the next morning.

The trail was expected to lead up the Wadi Mughar to the bad village of Igzim, and B Company, less one platoon, under Major Clay was detailed as dog escort. The fourth platoon was given the task of rounding up 2,300 goats and 200 sheep for confiscation as a punishment on the inhabitants of the area in which the crime was committed. The dog quickly took up the trail and moved rapidly up the Wadi Mughar to Igzim, where it 'marked' a house on the northern end of the village. It was then taken back to the coast road and put on to another clue, again tracking back to the same village, but to a house opposite to the first one. When searched, however, the owners of both houses were absent.

The whole village was then cordoned and searched, while reports were sent to Brigade Headquarters in Haifa on the result of the dog's tracking. Later in the morning orders were received to demolish the two houses marked by the dog, and the troops had to remain in position until a party of Royal Engineers reached the village from Jerusalem late in the afternoon.

* * *

Apart from a three-day Brigade operation in the northern part of the country between Acre and Safed in March, and another two-day operation in the always troublesome area of the Musmus Pass early in April, few incidents were reported, and all companies had an opportunity to get accustomed to the nature of the country, and to learn the many Brigade instructions on the approved methods of dealing with the enemy. But on April 21 the battalion suffered its first casualties from Arab action, when Privates Hayes and Harris were ambushed and killed at El Fahm while acting as escort to the camel drivers, who were drawing water at the local well for the detachment of A Company, which was in camp near the village. This incident led to a two-day search of the district with police dogs and troops, but without success.

*   *   *

Early in May information was received from the Palestine Police, with whom the battalion had a very close liaison, that a well-known Arab gang leader usually spent his nights in the village of Tamra, a fairly large village about fifteen miles east of Haifa. On May 13 a column, consisting of Battalion H.Q. and A and D Companies in thirty-five motor vehicles, left barracks at 11.30 p.m., and by 4.15 a.m. had successfully surrounded and cordoned the village without disturbing the inhabitants. The gang leader was discovered in bed with his rifle beside him, and a number of other wanted men were also picked out in the subsequent search of all the villagers.

This news apparently leaked out to the surrounding villages and even to the town of Safed, whence rebel supporters were despatched on foot and in buses to try and effect a rescue; for as the battalion started to withdraw from Tamra at 12.15 p.m. on the 14th it came under a heavy fire from the high ground above the village. The battalion immediately debussed and was quickly in action on both sides of the track, driving the enemy back towards the hills behind the village. The enemy were judged to be in three parties and to be about fifty in number, and the attack on both sides of the *wadi* was carried on for nearly two hours, the enemy being driven back from ridge to ridge, frequently from close quarters and with several casualties. During this action the transport had been withdrawn from the *wadi* to a more suitable place on the route back to Haifa, and soon after 2 p.m., when all resistance had ceased and the battalion was spread over a very wide front, orders were given for a withdrawal to the convoy.

At 5.30 p.m. the convoy commenced its journey home, but within a few minutes, as it was debouching from the village of Ad Damun to cross a stretch of flat country between that village and the larger village of Birwa, the R.A.F. aeroplane escorting the battalion was seen to be dive-bombing Birwa, and machine gun firing was heard. The battalion at once debussed and deployed to attack the village, being joined at this moment by the Commanding Officer of the Manchester Regiment, who had heard the battalion's wireless call for air cover from a nearby camp at Sakhnin and had hurried to its support with four machine guns mounted in trucks. This party covered the advance of A and D Companies by moving round the foot of a hill firing as they went. A further detachment of the Manchester Regiment arrived from Acre and opened fire on Birwa from the main road. The companies got into the village without difficulty, and here they found a number of enemy dead and captured two more gangsters with rifles, in addition to a number of other rifles and ammunition.

After a quick search of the village in the gathering darkness, the battalion returned to Haifa, reaching barracks just before 9 p.m. very footsore after a great deal of movement over rocky ground in P.T. shoes, but very satisfied at having at last come in contact with the enemy. From various reports it was later estimated that enemy casualties amounted to about thirty killed and about the same number wounded. Eleven suspected gangsters had been captured, and a good supply of arms and ammunition collected. For gallantry in the early part of this action Military Crosses were awarded to Captain Kelleher, R.A.M.C., and Lieutenant Whitty,[1] and the Military Medal to Private Sparkes. Under heavy enemy rifle fire these three went forward to an exposed position where Privates Moyes and Hudson were lying wounded, attended to them and carried them back to cover. Private Moyes died of his wounds.

3. *Static Posts*

In May, owing to the increasing activity of Arab gangs throughout the northern area of Palestine, a system of static posts was introduced, and a large number of Arab villages were occupied by small permanent detachments of troops from the battalions, whose Brigade Headquarters were at Haifa and Nablus. These posts were usually of platoon strength, with a mortar detachment, signallers with wireless equipment and the necessary administrative personnel, all under the command of a subaltern, warrant officer or in some cases a senior N.C.O. Not only did these posts prove a constant source of trouble to the Arabs, but they were undoubtedly a splendid form of training for those in command of them, and in fact for all ranks who served in them. The principal objects of these posts were to supervise and protect road making activities, to enforce the curfew in villages, to lay ambushes and carry out patrols by night and to give protection to friendly villages. The posts were either situated in requisitioned houses suitably situated for the purpose, or in perimeter camps within strongly wired and sandbagged walls.

---

[1] Nephew of Lieutenant-Colonel (later Brigadier) N. I. Whitty.

The first of these posts occupied by the battalion were at Shafa Amr, Kafrin, Daliyat and Suffuriya, but during the ensuing months posts at El Fahm, Sakhnin and Sabbarin were taken over or exchanged with other battalions in 16th Brigade. Though life in these posts was liable to be uncomfortable and at times monotonous, duty in them was, on the whole, popular amongst the troops in whom the spirit of adventure was strong, and the hunting of gangsters with a price on their heads a great incentive. The officers and W.O.s and N.C.O.s who commanded them vied with each other in improving the comfort and security of their posts, and in their efforts to thwart the activities of the gangsters.

4. *The Formation of 'Haicol'*

From June onwards Arab gang leaders increased their activities, roaming the country at night recruiting, drilling, extorting funds from peaceful villages, sniping Jewish colonies and farms and laying ambushes for troops on patrol. Another frequent form of annoyance was to puncture and set fire to the oil pipe-line, which ran from Iraq to Haifa, entering Palestine over the River Jordan a few miles south of the sea of Galilee. The pipe-line stretched for forty miles from the Jordan to Haifa, over country in which no static posts were situated. Special measures had therefore to be taken to deal with the gangs who were attacking it.

About this time there arrived in Haifa from the Sudan an officer with considerable experience in tracking and dealing with night marauders, and a first-class knowledge of Arabic. This officer, Captain O. C. Wingate, later became famous in Burma. A number of picked men from each battalion of the Brigade were formed into Special Night Squads (S.N.S.) and placed under his command for training and operations. The detachment from the battalion was under the command of 2nd Lieutenant Grove, and their activities will be referred to later on.

With so many small detachments away from battalions on static posts, it became clear to the Brigade Commander that steps must be taken to ensure that he had at his immediate disposal sufficient troops to undertake field operations on a large scale. A Brigade 'Field Force' was therefore organised, consisting of seven flying columns from seven different places in the Haifa area. The battalion provided a Battalion H.Q. Flying Column, consisting of 6 officers, 67 other ranks and 10 motor vehicles, and one Flying Column composed of Column H.Q., four platoons and Mortar and Signal detachments, totalling 5 officers, 143 other ranks and 17 motor vehicles. These included two vehicles on which were loaded nine donkeys for carrying ammunition, mortars and Lewis guns. Every man carried on him the unexpired portion of his day's ration and an emergency ration. Seventy-two hours' reserve rations were carried on the transport. The Flying Column was found by the Duty Company and was always on short call, and after a few outings it was remarkable how quickly it could form up ready to move off. Perhaps the hardest-worked people on these occasions were the cooks, who, at very short notice, were required to prepare haversack rations for about two hundred men as well as to ensure that the reserve rations and all the cooking utensils were loaded on to the transport. But under the cheerful and efficient drive of Serjeant Perryman the column was seldom kept waiting.

Later on, when some static posts were withdrawn owing to the menacing situation in Europe and the increasing trouble in Haifa town, the battalion formed a second column, and they then became known as 'Haicol' A and B. These columns frequently went out on raids and searches planned by Battalion H.Q. in conjunction with the Palestine Police, amongst whom was Assistant Superintendent Cohen, a very knowledgeable, efficient and brave man.

When these columns were out without Battalion H.Q. there were usually enough troops left in barracks to deal with an unexpected and generally urgent call for help from a static post or patrol. It often happened that parties were collected together and rushed off in M.T. under the command of the M.T. officer or the Adjutant, and the C.O. found himself the only officer left in barracks, wondering when his chickens would come home to roost, confident that they would have had a good 'party,' and proud of the wonderful offensive spirit that existed amongst all ranks.

*   *   *

From the beginning of June life in Haifa became extremely hectic. Almost every day brought forth some incident, either at a static post or as a result of a column or patrol action.

On June 8 an ambush party under Lieutenant Fawcett was sent to lie up in a house near the previously-mentioned bad village of Igzim. A platoon went with them as escort to bring back their transport. On entering the Wadi Mughar, which leads up to the village, the party was fired on, and a wireless call for air support was duly sent out. This call was passed on to barracks, and two platoons of the Flying Column, under 2nd Lieutenants Butler and Rooke, were immediately despatched to the assistance of the ambush party. On arrival at the *wadi*, they found that Fawcett had pushed on to Igzim and they followed him up. On reaching the village they were fired on, and firing could also be heard from the direction of the house, in which the ambush was to be laid. Butler's platoon remained in Igzim to deal with the enemy there, while Rooke's proceeded to Fawcett's assistance. The action which ensued resulted in the enemy retiring under cover of darkness, having had three of their number killed and their rifles captured, while later information revealed that the gang was probably about fifty strong and their casualties had been a good deal heavier.

The next incident of any importance occurred on July 3, when at 5.30 p.m. the police made an urgent request for the support of a mortar detachment to assist in breaking up an attack being made by a gang on the coast road at El Mazar. This detachment was just leaving barracks under Captain Martyn, the Adjutant, when Lieutenant Fawcett with a platoon returned from escort duty to a police dog. These two set off together, but by the time they reached the rendez-vous firing had ceased, and it was believed the enemy had withdrawn. Lieutenant Fawcett and his Lewis gun section were sent to the top of one of the hills overlooking the road to see if they could bring fire to bear on any retreating bandits, and the mortar was mounted on the roadside to cover them. As this move was being carried out the enemy, who had been hiding on the hillside unseen by the aircraft operating overhead, opened fire. Lieutenant Fawcett and his party got to the top of the hill, and two armed Arabs were bayoneted and three rifles with ammunition were captured. Spasmodic fire went on for a short time, but, as it was now nearly dark, the party returned to barracks.

5. *The Tension Increases*

On July 6 the whole situation in Northern Palestine took a sudden and very serious change for the worse, for on this day a small party of Jews drove a lorry past the Arab fruit and vegetable market in Haifa and hurled a powerful bomb amongst the usual crowd of customers. The immediate result was a casualty list of twenty-five people killed and about one hundred seriously injured, but perhaps the more important result was an increased antagonism between Arabs and Jews, which now spread to the large towns and greatly added to the difficult tasks of the Civil Administration and the Military Forces engaged in trying to restore law and order in the country. Though it must be admitted that the Jews in their farms and colonies had suffered greatly from the attacks of Arab gangs, this dastardly reprisal on Arab men and women, with whom they were living in comparative peace in Haifa, was extremely ill-advised. It brought down on them severe restrictions of their own movements in the town, it inflamed the Arab hostility, lessened British sympathy and, when sufficient troops had been brought into Palestine, caused the introduction of Military Control throughout the country.

The immediate effect on the battalion was the despatch of two platoons to the scene of the bombing, followed by two companies the same night. These remained in the town till late the following night, when they were relieved by parties from H.M.S. *Emerald* which had been ordered to Haifa by urgent signal. This ship was relieved, two days later, by H.M.S. *Repulse*.

From now onwards the Arab gangsters became even more truculent and increased their activities against Jewish colonies and static posts. During the rest of July hardly a day or night passed without some call on the battalion, especially on the Flying Column in barracks. On July 9 the static post at Shafa Amr, which had been evacuated earlier, had to be reoccupied as an Arab gang had surrounded the village, raided the police post and removed a quantity of rifles and revolvers.

On the night of July 10 information was received that a large gang was attacking the Jewish colony at Givath Ada on the coast road south of Haifa. 'Haicol' was immediately despatched there, to be followed early next morning by Battalion H.Q. and another column formed of troops left in barracks. A police dog was used and led the column to the western end of the Musmus Pass, and the village of Ar'ara was well combed, but without any result. The force then returned to Haifa, leaving two platoons in the village of K. Qari for the night. The same night the battalion S.N.S. under 2nd Lieutenant Grove was in action with an armed gang at Dabburiya, near Nazareth. Several casualties were inflicted on the bandits, but unfortunately Privates Suter and Chapman were wounded, the latter dying from the effects of an abdominal wound.

On July 12, another gang being reported in the same area, 'Haicol' moved out to Sabbarin, a static post, and later to Kerkur, near a Jewish colony of that name. They remained there until the 14th, when they returned to barracks, leaving a platoon in occupation. Shortly afterwards this post at Kerkur was converted into a form of concentration camp, in which a large number of active and suspected gangsters were detained for varying periods. This camp required a whole company for guard duty, patrols, defence and administrative duties.

On the night of July 20 a battalion operation across the Carmel Hills was carried out in co-operation with a party of Royal Marines from H.M.S. *Repulse*, with the object of descending on the village of Et Tireh on the coast road. The country traversed was extremely rough and in places very precipitous, but though it was successfully negotiated in the darkness, the village was drawn blank. This was hardly surprising, for it was honeycombed with caves and cellars, in which it was easy for gangsters to hide at the first sign or sound of danger.

About this time a special platoon, known as 'Q' Platoon, was formed under the command of 2nd Lieutenant Rooke. This functioned on much the same lines as the Special Night Squads, only under the orders of the Battalion Commander. This platoon quickly proved its value, and by its skill and courage in laying ambushes and night patrolling inflicted considerable casualties on marauding gangsters. In its first engagement it caused six enemy casualties. On July 26 and 27 it met other gangs, and on July 30 at Daliyat at least seven casualties were inflicted on the bandits.

After the bomb explosion in Haifa on July 6 conditions in the town gradually returned to normal, and the curfew which had been imposed was lessened by degrees and finally raised altogether. But, alas, not for long! On July 26 a second and even larger bomb was thrown in almost the same place as the first one, causing a death roll of about fifty people. Back came the curfew, with still more arduous tasks for the Royal Navy, and additional activities for the battalion against Arab gangs, who sought retribution from the Jews in the rural areas.

*   *   *

On July 28, in response to an urgent appeal for help from a Jewish colony near Haifa, two platoons under 2nd Lieutenants Butler and Rooke went poste-haste to Sasa, where, after a sharp engagement with a gang in the gathering darkness, they inflicted five casualties on the enemy before returning to barracks.

Three days later 2nd Lieutenant Grove with his Special Night Squad and some Jewish supernumaries came across a large armed gang, who were apparently holding a conference. A sharp action ensued in which at least eight of the enemy were killed and fifteen wounded. For his courage and leadership in this and previous actions with Arab gangs, 2nd Lieutenant Grove was awarded the Military Cross.

About this time it became clear to Civil and Military intelligence agents that Arab gang leaders were actively engaged in recruiting for their gangs, either by persuasion or threats, amongst the villages in the Haifa area. To curb these activities, units in the area were ordered to construct camps for the detention of varying numbers of men from villages which had come under suspicion. Accordingly, from July 26 to 30, Battalion H.Q. with 'Haicol' and one company rounded up a large number of the male inhabitants and removed them to the camp at Kerkur, where they were usefully employed on road making and the general improvement of communications at the western end of the Musmus Pass.

Later on, after the introduction of Military Control, a small 'cage' was erected behind the guard room at Peninsula Barracks, where, under the personal supervision of Serjeant Butcher, about fifty of the worst thugs in Palestine were detained pending trial by the Military Courts.

* * *

The month of August opened fairly peacefully, but on the night of the 13th, Battalion H.Q. with two columns and two troops of armoured cars of the 11th Hussars and R.A.F. cover, carried out a search of the villages of Sabbarin and Sindyana. Though no gangs were encountered, one gangster was captured in possession of a rifle, for which crime he was later found guilty by a Military Court.

On August 15 a much more serious incident occurred near the static post of Isfiya, some eight miles south of Haifa. During the morning this post, which was expecting a ration convoy from Haifa, heard distant rifle shots, and, fearing that the convoy was being ambushed, turned out in quick time under Lieutenant Crook. Arriving at the scene of the shooting, they found a lorry containing ten Jews (eight men and two women) all of whom subsequently died as a result of bullet wounds. They also saw a party of ten armed Arabs moving in close formation down a nearby *wadi*, apparently in ignorance that they were under observation. Three Lewis guns were quickly in action. The first burst scattered the gang, and they were then shot down one by one as they tried to escape among the rocks. The escort to the ration convoy had joined in the action, and did good work with rifle fire.

The usual immediate wireless report to Battalion H.Q. brought out two platoons of 'Haicol' under Major Bryan, who arrived in time to assist in clearing up the battlefield. A large landmine was found on the track to Isfiya and was exploded by Lieutenant Whitty by rifle fire. A search of the dense scrub in the *wadi* produced two dead Arabs, two live ones, who were handed over to the Civil Police, five rifles and bandoliers full of ammunition and some valuable documents. It seems likely that this ambush, with the landmine, was intended for the ration convoy, and that the unfortunate party of Jewish workers arrived unexpectedly and were murdered in cold blood. The murderers suffered just retribution.

Two nights later, at about 11 p.m., Battalion H.Q. was informed that a large gang was attacking the civil jail at Athlit, about eight miles south of Haifa, and was releasing the prisoners. This jail encampment was extremely badly sited. It consisted of huts within a high barbed wire enclosure. The coast road ran through it, and it was under close observation from high and very rough ground on the east. Scattered sentry posts in sangars were established in suitable positions. The prison guards were British, Jews and Palestinians. 'Haicol' was immediately turned out and arrived in time to end a dangerous situation, firing a number of mortar bombs on to the high ground to speed the parting raiders. The gang had raided the house of a Jewish police inspector and abducted him, his wife and three children and his brother-in-law.

The following morning 'Haicol' returned to Athlit to escort a police dog, which had been brought to the scene. This involved an arduous and very rough trek across nearly eight miles of hilly country, without finding any trace of the criminals, and the column returned to barracks. On the following day, in a further effort to recover this unfortunate police officer and his family, Battalion H.Q., 'Haicol,' two troops of armoured cars and a column of the Essex Regiment, with R.A.F. cover, carried out a drive across country of roughly six miles. Villages and farms on the way were thoroughly combed, but once more the operation ended unsuccessfully.

On Sunday, August 28, the officers in barracks, hoping to have a few hours' pleasant change from chasing gangsters, had arranged to have a cocktail party in the Mess. Their guests, however, arrived to find most of their hosts rushing around and snatching a quick meal before leaving on another night operation, in an endeavour to capture their most-wanted enemy, Youssef Abu Dorra. This man was the recognised commander of a large gang, which operated over a considerable part of the Haifa area, and was known to every man in the battalion as the prime cause of most of their troubles. He was known to be cunning, ruthless and cruel, and it was even reported that he had been reprimanded by Rebel H.Q. in Damascus for excessive cruelty to Arab villagers, who were unwilling to help him. Nobody knew what he looked like, and, as no village in which he was hiding would dare to give him away, searches for him always started with the betting heavily in his favour. He was eventually killed after the battalion had left Palestine.

The information, which had caused the 'flap' at the cocktail party, was that Abu Dorra was holding a rebel court for the trial of traitors to the Arab cause at Umm Az Zinat. This was a village situated on a fairly prominent feature on the Carmel Hills, approachable from the west across an open stretch of country, and from the east by a track from Isfiya or a steep climb from the Haifa-Jenin road. To arrive there without warning was almost a forlorn hope. However, at 8.30 p.m. that evening, Battalion Headquarters, 'Haicol' and a composite company left barracks, succeeded in quietly surrounding the village in the darkness and closed in at first light to comb that abominable place. But as a correspondent to the *Queen's Own Gazette* so aptly wrote, 'Abu Dorra had evaporated or else turned into a camel. He almost gives one the impression that he is a myth, as solid as Donald Duck and as elusive as Greta Garbo.'

But Abu Dorra was not the only 'wanted' man in northern Palestine, for in May 1938 a secret list was distributed to Battalion Headquarters, giving the names of over three hundred known active rebels, and, as their followers were constantly increasing, the end of the battalion's first seven months in the country did not appear to hold out any hope of a relaxation of its constant and untiring efforts to quell the rebel elements of a people with whom there was a certain amount of sympathy.

6. *Some Lighter Moments*

Lest it be thought that the battalion was permanently engaged on chasing Arab rebels all over northern Palestine, it must be recorded that those who had the fortune to be in barracks frequently had their lighter moments, and even occasional ceremonial parades.

On February 26, 1938, General Sir Arthur Wauchope, the retiring High Commissioner for Palestine, paid a visit to the battalion. He considered it unnecessary to inspect the barrack rooms, preferring to visit the Officers' and Serjeants' Messes to discuss old friends of Mesopotamia days, when Colonel Woulfe-Flanagan was in command. On March 3 the battalion provided a Guard of Honour of fifty files, with the King's Colour and the Band and Drums, under command of Major Clay, to receive the new High Commissioner, H.E. Sir Harold MacMichael, who had arrived in H.M.S. *Enterprise*. Later on General Sir Archibald Wavell, G.O.C.-in-C. the Forces in Palestine, paid two visits to the battalion, one official and one for luncheon in the Officers' Mess, when meeting his son.

On April 14 H.M.S. *Arethusa* arrived in Haifa for a two days' visit, her Commanding Officer being Captain Philip Vian, later to become famous in a convoy to Malta. This visit called for the usual exchanges of hospitalities. A party from the battalion was shown over the ship; contests in football, hockey, tennis and shooting were held in barracks; Captain Vian and some of his officers dined in the Officers' Mess; and the evening concluded with a remarkable dance given by the W.O.s and Serjeants in the Serjeants' Mess, to which not only our Naval visitors were invited but most of the Civil and Military authorities of Haifa as well. The return of our friends to their ship in the early hours of the morning was a hazardous perform-ance, for during the night the wind and sea had risen, the gangway had been put out of action, and the only means of getting aboard was via a derrick.

7. *The Sweep to the Musmus Pass*

To return to more serious matters. Towards the end of August the Brigade Commander, Brigadier J. F. Evetts, decided to send the battalion on a week's trek across the Carmel Hills, not by the usual routes, passable for M.T., but as the gangster moved, straight across country, in the hope that this unusual form of movement might catch Abu Dorra and his followers unawares. This scheme meant that at a certain starting point the M.T. vehicles were discarded, and the troops took to their feet for their own movement and camels for the transport of their baggage and other impedimenta. By the end of the seven-day trek, many of them wondered why feet and camels had ever been invented.

Much could be written about this expedition, but the following brief account, written by an officer who took part in it, must suffice :—

'On September 3 a force under Major Travers, composed of Battalion H.Q., "Haicol" under Major Bryan, Scott Company under Captain Scott, and "Q" Platoon under 2nd Lieutenant Rooke, set out for Isfiya, where motor transport was exchanged for camel trans-port. Then began a journey which lasted a week and took us over the whole length of the Carmel Hills down to the Musmus Pass. The total mileage covered was fifty-two miles, and the country traversed was often very difficult, particularly on the second day, when in one place a path had to be made with picks and shovels through very thick scrub to allow our forty-three camels to pass through.

'During the journey a considerable time was necessarily spent in questioning the local inhabitants, and in searching villages and Bedouin camps. It was disappointing not to have met any gangs, but the battalion was successful in accomplishing one important task, which was to put a stop to all gang activity in the Carmel Hills area for that week at least. Our journey took us from Isfiya to Kafrin, where a day's rest was taken. From there southwards to El Fahm, turning north-eastward for a night march down the Musmus Pass, to surround and search the village of Lajjun at dawn. Finally a very short march to Megiddo, where the night was spent in the Police post and the American Archaeological Expedition's buildings in comfort. On September 10 our transport collected us again and took us back to Haifa.'

Thus ended a novel experiment, which certainly kept the gangsters guessing, for little of importance took place elsewhere during the month, apart from a successful ambush by 'Q' Platoon in the early morning of September 25, when two rebels were killed and a rifle captured.

On September 28 two static posts were withdrawn, and the whole of A company was assembled at Kerkur, in order to keep the coast road open to traffic. The following day D company moved to Acre to take over from the Essex Regiment, who were returning at short notice to Egypt.

8. *The Arab Gangs Grow Bolder*

During the first week of October, Lieutenant-Colonel Palmer, who had been on three months' special leave in England, returned to Haifa and resumed command from Major Travers, who had been acting in command during his absence. From then onwards operations became more serious, for rebel gangs began to act in larger parties and more offensively.

This suited the battalion very well, for during the last nine months almost every operation had been against an enemy who had done his deed and run away. Now they appeared in gangs of anything up to fifty, and were willing to try and shoot it out with the troops. As their tactics were poor they frequently offered very good targets, which caused them many casualties. Their rifles were in the main extremely ancient, dirty and rusty, and the use of the backsight was practically unknown to them. They always tried to conceal their casualties by taking them with them, and considered the loss of a rifle more serious than the loss of a gangster.

The first of these larger operations took place on October 1, when in the afternoon two platoons of C Company with a mortar detachment under Lieutenant Courtney were ordered to proceed to a small

G

village on the road to Shafa Amr, where a store of arms was reported. Just before leaving barracks at 2.30 p.m. a message was received that a police Inspector had been held up on this road by a road block and that a lorry with a Jewish foreman in it was missing in the same area. These two platoons were therefore ordered to move to high ground in the neighbourhood of Sasa, south-east of the scene, and to approach from that direction. An aircraft was also ordered to stand by in readiness to give support if required. Later, D Company at Acre was ordered to send out a force to approach Shafa Amr from the north west, and at 3.45 p.m. one platoon and a mortar detachment left under Captain Heygate.

About 3 p.m. C Company's platoons spotted a band of gangsters just west of Shafa Amr and engaged them, and at 4.15 p.m. the aircraft spotted a gang of about thirty, shot them up and bombed them, claiming about fifteen casualties. Just previous to this episode C Company had run into a party of rebels at fairly close quarters, and claimed ten enemy casualties and the capture of three rifles and a quantity of ammunition. A search of the bombed area made it clear that many casualties had been inflicted, though all bodies had been removed.

The next operation of any importance occurred in the Acre area, giving Captain Heygate and D Company the opportunity of a nice little battle on their home ground, assisted by two platoons of C Company from Haifa. Early on the morning of October 6 Captain Heygate received a report that the police were in action with an armed gang about five miles north of Acre on the coast road. Shortly after 8 a.m., with one platoon, a section and a mortar detachment, he arrived on the scene to find that the enemy had retired eastward, after killing three Jewish lorry drivers and burning their lorries. The party at once turned inland and drove along the road running through Mi'ilia, very quickly coming across an attempt by the enemy to lay a landmine on the road, and soon afterwards spotting a band of about thirty armed men south of the road. This gang scattered directly fire was opened on it by the leading Lewis gun section and a police armoured car. In an effort to round up this gang, Captain Heygate sent two sections northwards to try and cut off their retreat to wooded country, while the remainder went by M.T. to stop movement eastwards. During the move they came under fire from two villages to the east. The mortar quickly had these villages under fire, and a party of enemy was seen retiring from one of them. The other village was then searched and was found to be completely deserted.

At 11 a.m. two platoons of C Company and a mortar detachment, under Lieutenant Fawcett, arrived from Haifa and found the battle in progress about three miles east of the coast road. This party was at once sent further along the road to try and stop the enemy's retreat northward and, after moving about a mile, it came under fire from the north. Debussing, it continued to advance, with one platoon on each side of the road, and then came under fire from the south, where at a long distance a party of about thirty men was seen moving eastward. This party was engaged by the aircraft. At 12.45 p.m. Captain Heygate leap-frogged his platoon through C Company and drove on up the road about six miles, hoping to engage this enemy party. Unfortunately they were seen to be too far ahead and were left to the bombing of the aircraft.

Meanwhile, as the platoons under Lieutenant Fawcett were closing on the road, three isolated armed men had been met, two being killed and two rifles captured. At 3 p.m. the action was broken off, the estimated casualties inflicted on the rebels being ten, which did not include any the aircraft may have caused.

A little later D Company was relieved by the 1st Battalion The Royal Hampshire Regiment and returned to Haifa.

*   *   *

After a few days of comparative peace, activity suddenly shifted to the southern portion of the battalion area, and it fell to A Company under Major Bryan to stage a first-class battle near Bureika, a village about six miles north of the 'cage' camp at Kerkur, where the Company was at the time on duty.

On the morning of October 10, Battalion H.Q. received reliable information that a large gathering of rebels was expected that night at Bureika, and that it was possible that Abu Dorra would be present. A Company, being closest to this village, was obviously the one to do the job, but could only spare one platoon from its guard duties. Consequently a platoon from D Company and a mortar detachment, under Lieutenant Whitty, was despatched from Haifa to Kerkur with secret instructions to Major Bryan, who, with a platoon of A Company under 2nd Lieutenant Rickcord, set off at 4 p.m. so as to approach Bureika from the north east.

Arriving at Bureika about 5.45 p.m. Lieutenant Whitty's platoon occupied the village without incident. But on moving out of it to block a track to the eastward, it came under fire from a small gang. As it was then growing dark, Major Bryan ordered this platoon to withdraw into the village and to occupy houses facing to the north and east. The platoon of A Company became H.Q. protective troops within the village.

During these movements the enemy's fire had considerably increased, and one party advanced close enough to our positions to be dealt with by hand grenades. It was driven off. By 7.30 p.m. it was obvious that the enemy had been reinforced, and heavy firing started from the north of the village, where a number of the gang managed to get within 100 yards of our posts, driving cattle ahead of them and making use of the shadows of the trees in slight moonlight. From 9 p.m. until nearly 11 p.m. the enemy made frequent attempts to get into the village from all sides, their leaders being heard exhorting their men with cries of 'Allah' and 'Abu Dorra,' but all these attacks were successfully beaten off.

During the early part of this action, the Royal Corps of Signals' operator with Company H.Q. had succeeded from a very exposed position in sending out an urgent call to H.Q. in Haifa, whence a mixed force of two platoons, a mortar section under Serjeant Grimshaw, and 'Q' Platoon under Serjeant Hallett of the Orderly Room, was hurriedly despatched under command of Captain Tuffill. An aircraft was also ordered up, and this arrived over the village about 10.50 p.m. and dropped flares, which enabled our troops to see and shoot up enemy on the move. Captain Tuffill's party arrived, after a very rapid journey, at about 11 p.m. by which time all firing had ceased.

Next morning at dawn 'Q' Platoon, covered by a mortar barrage, advanced to the hill from which the enemy's fire had been heaviest, but, although there were many signs of enemy casualties, no further incident occurred. A search of the village disclosed nothing, not even one rifle or round of ammunition.

The following day a police report was received that the road within a mile of Shafa Amr had thirty trenches cut across it and fifty road blocks erected on it. The local inhabitants protested that they had been compelled to do this sabotage by rebel gangs, but this excuse did not relieve them from a fine of £700. Next day Captain Tuffill with D Company went to collect this money, and remained overnight to ensure that the men of the village also repaired the road. A few days later a patrol near this village encountered a gang of about twenty, who, on being fired on, retired in a southerly direction. On the night of October 20, more enemy activity was observed near this village, and one rebel was killed by rifle fire.

9. *The Establishment of Military Control*

About this time Military Control was established in the country, and the port of Haifa became a scene of great activity, the barracks being a collecting centre for hundreds of motor vehicles. No less than ten Infantry Battalions and two Cavalry Regiments, with their horses, had disembarked at Haifa and dispersed to various parts of Palestine. Amongst these units were welcomed the 2nd Royal Irish Fusiliers, who had left England with the battalion on the S.S. *California*, and The Royals, old friends of Shorncliffe days.

At this time, also, Major Clay was appointed Town Major of Haifa, and Major Goater was busily occupied issuing passes, required by all civilians under the emergency regulations controlling road traffic. B Company took over the duties of Town Patrol, a tedious task involving constant patrolling, on foot or in M.T., of some of the more unpleasant and dangerous parts of the town. On more than one occasion patrols were involved in shooting incidents, which caused the deaths of C.I.D. or Jewish policemen, and were frequently under fire themselves. They were also called upon to escort the fire brigade to fires at Jewish-owned buildings. These fires were caused by Arabs who, without the presence of the troops, would stay behind to cut the fire hoses.

Early on the morning of October 25 a Brigade operation started in the Haifa area to search a number of villages where rebel activity was on the increase. For this operation the battalion provided Battalion Headquarters and two columns, 'Haicol' A under Captain Tuffill and 'Haicol' B under Major Bryan. By 5 a.m. these three columns were in their allotted positions at Shafa Amr, Aballin and Tamra. A column of The Royal Ulster Rifles moved eastward from the direction of Acre, and The Hampshire Regiment advanced from a north-easterly direction. At the villages occupied by the battalion's columns the inhabitants were thoroughly checked and the villages and surrounding country searched, but without result.

However, at about 3 p.m. a platoon of 'Haicol' A under Lieutenant Butler, which had been sent on to a hill overlooking Tamra, observed a party of horsemen approaching from high ground to the east. The platoon was ordered to remain motionless, while the Lewis gun section was moved under cover to a spur which overlooked the *wadi* into which the enemy party was moving. This party, consisting of three men on horseback and one on foot, continued to the bottom of the *wadi*, crossed it and then turned northwards across the platoon's front. Fire was opened by the Lewis gun as soon as the party reached fairly open ground, and the band at once ran into the cover of the *wadi* bed. Fearing that they might escape along the bottom of this *wadi* Lieutenant Butler and Corporal Phillips ran down the side of it to cut off their escape. Observing this the party stopped and tried to shoot it out, but two were killed almost at once and a third when trying to get away. Firing having ceased, the platoon moved down to the *wadi* bed and found the fourth man dead also. In addition some ammunition, an assortment of various weapons and a rebel banner were collected. It was later ascertained that the leader of this party was Nur El Ibrahim, a noted Arabic poet and singer and a wanted rebel leader.

That night the three columns took up night dispositions at the same villages, but early the following morning Battalion H.Q. and 'Haicol' A moved to Mi'Ar, and 'Haicol' B to Birwa, further to the north. The C.O. received instructions to supervise the demolition of a large part of Mi'Ar village, as a punishment for fire which had been opened on a column of another unit the previous day. The early work of the demolition party of Royal Engineers was witnessed by the Brigade Commander and a number of Press representatives.

At 3 p.m. a band of armed men was observed in a *wadi* to the south of Mi'Ar and were shelled by one small howitzer, which was with Battalion H.Q. At 4.20 p.m. the troops in the village were heavily sniped from high ground north of the village. The howitzer again came into action and the sniping quickly ceased. The following morning, October 27, 'Haicol' B searched Birwa village and the surrounding country, while 'Haicol' A continued the demolitions at Mi'Ar and made a search of the surrounding country. By then all active rebels had dispersed and the battalion returned to barracks.

Early on the morning of October 29 information was received from the police in Haifa that a rebel court was being held at a small village called Mansi on the main Haifa-Jenin road. 'Haicol' A under Captain Tuffill left barracks at 10 a.m., accompanied by two police officers. The column was sent in vehicles to make it look like an ordinary ration convoy, and one platoon was sent on past the village to the Musmus Pass to occupy high ground overlooking the village and thus stop any escape in that direction. Having collected all the inhabitants of the village for interrogation, the police officers were then informed that the court was sitting in another village, and with one section as escort, they quickly set off for the house which had been named. On arrival there the court was surprised, but there was no sign of prisoners under trial. An armed Arab, seen trying to escape, was shot and killed and a search of the area produced some arms and ammunition and two Underwood typewriters, stolen from Messrs. Thomas Cooks' office in Haifa. Sixty-nine suspects were brought in, including five who were concerned in the rebel court proceedings.

*   *   *

The early part of November did not bring forth any actions

deserving of special mention. But on November 4 one platoon of
A Company, under 2nd Lieutenant Rickcord, had a sharp brush
with a small gang. This platoon, with a section of H.Q. Company,
under Serjeant Parsons, and a mortar detachment, left barracks at
6 p.m. for an all-night patrol on the coastal road. Approaching the
bad village of El Fureidis, P.S.M. Spooner was sent with two sections
to lay up in ambush on high ground overlooking the road, while
the remainder patrolled the road further along. At midnight, as these
two sections started to withdraw to the main road, they came under
heavy fire from a small gang at close range, and one man, Private
Hunt, was seriously wounded and died soon afterwards. The sections
immediately went into action, and by the time the rest of the platoon
arrived on the scene the enemy fire in considerable volume was coming
from the high ground about 500 yards further up the hill. The Lewis
gun and mortar went into action, the platoon advanced up the hill
and the enemy dispersed, leaving behind one dead man with his
rifle and ammunition. Outpost positions were occupied until dawn,
when, after a search of the area, the party returned to barracks. The
following day the C.O. and 'Haicol' and a party of Royal Engineers
visited El Fureidis to demolish some houses, and it was discovered
that efforts had been made to conceal a dead man.

Novel methods were needed to search a village called Tantura, on
the sea coast about 16 miles south of Haifa. It was so situated that
it was almost impossible to surround it without disclosing one's
presence. The nearest and most direct way of approach was via the
railway line, which ran within half a mile of the village. A goods
train was therefore requisitioned, and on the night of November 26,
Battalion H.Q. with 'Haicol' A entrained near barracks, jolted
violently to a stop opposite Tantura, and had surrounded it at first
light before a soul was awake. But they found nothing!

On November 28, soon after breakfast, quite unexpected information and orders were received from Brigade H.Q., which led to the
most successful and effective operation in which the battalion took
part during the months spent in Palestine. It was reported on very
good authority that Abu Dorra was to hold a rebel court at Igzim
and would later move to Ein Ghazal.

Orders were at once issued to Battalion H.Q., 'Haicol' A and 'Q'
Platoon to leave barracks at 11 a.m. and to cordon and search these
two villages. A column of Royal Irish Fusiliers was to proceed from
the east to Umm az Zinat, and aircraft were ordered to be over
these villages in strength to spot and shoot up any gangs seen withdrawing from them. As 'Q' Platoon was moving up to Ein Ghazal
a small gang was surprised leaving the village, one man was killed,

two wounded and three rifles captured. Igzim was quickly surrounded, and during the check of the men an informer stated that
Abu Dorra had left the village early in the morning and had gone to
Daraj. An urgent wireless call was sent to the aircraft to cover Daraj,
and all columns were ordered to converge on this village. The
country between Igzim and Daraj was extremely rough, being
covered in rocks and thick scrub, which slowed up movement when
everyone was anxious to get along as rapidly as possible. But as
Daraj came into sight it was both seen and heard that the planes were
in action, for a number of them were bombing and shooting-up
targets in the direction of the village.

'Haicol' A reached Daraj about 3.30 p.m., at the same time as the
Royal Irish Fusiliers, and while moving through the village to post
protective troops, came under heavy fire from a party of enemy,
who, having escaped the aircraft bombing, were staying to fight it
out. No. 1 platoon, under 2nd Lieutenant Rickcord and No. 2 under
Lieutenant Read, closely followed by Major Bryan and 'Haicol'
H.Q., left the village and located the enemy in a strong position
amongst rocks on higher ground with a very exposed approach.
However, under cover of the fire of the R.Ir.F., these two platoons
began to move across the 300 yards of open ground by short rushes
until they were near enough to throw grenades. They then charged
in with the bayonet to the top of the hill, and the enemy were all
eventually killed.

It was in this fierce attack up the hill that 2nd Lieutenant Rickcord
was slightly wounded and Privates Fluin and Winstein more seriously
wounded. For their gallantry and leadership in this action Lieutenant
Read was awarded the Military Cross and Private Richards the
Military Medal. Other casualties were three killed in the Royal
Irish Fusiliers, and, in the Palestine Police, one Serjeant and one
Constable wounded. Enemy casualties in the whole action amounted
to 40 killed, and 17 rifles, 3 revolvers and over 400 rounds of ammunition were captured.

All troops remained on the ground throughout the night and made
a close search of the scene of the battle next morning. Later the battalion drove home, reaching barracks after dark. A very eventful and
successful two days!

10. *The Arab Gangs break up*

It can safely be said that this battle knocked the stuffing out of
Abu Dorra's gang, for the battalion's records do not disclose any

further incidents of active opposition up to the date of leaving Palestine. This does not mean that the battalion was inactive. On the contrary it was largely because this success was followed up by minor drives and searches on almost every day of December that the rebels hid their rifles and broke up their gangs.

On December 27 the battalion took over Haifa Town duties, and for a month 'Haicols' A and B ceased to exist. On December 31, D Company and one platoon under Captain Tuffill proceeded to camp at Nathanya, where it took over railway protection duties from The Royals, remaining there until January 28, 1939. Next day the battalion was again reassembled in barracks, and at once resumed its searches of suspected villages in all parts of its area. The records show that until February 26, 1939, when it was again called on for duty in Haifa, Battalion H.Q. and one or two columns were operating on eight different occasions. Three of these operations are worth describing.

Late in January the Headman of the village of Sindyana, who was anti-rebel and tired of being compelled to subscribe to rebel funds, appealed to the Commanding Officer for assistance in capturing a well-known gang leader, who used his village rather frequently. His suggestion was that a small party of troops should be hidden in his large house in the village and left there for several days, lying concealed in the daytime, in the hope that they might be able to capture the gang leader on one of his nocturnal visits.

Accordingly, on January 31, Battalion H.Q. and two columns surrounded the village, turned out all the inhabitants, and installed 2nd Lieutenant Rooke and 'Q' Platoon in the Headman's somewhat dirty cellars, complete with wireless equipment and rations until February 4, when they were to be relieved by another party, if their stay had not been fruitful. The battalion then withdrew, and the inhabitants returned to their houses, unaware of their hidden visitors. Unfortunately the wanted gang leader did not choose to pay a visit during the next few nights, so the same routine was repeated. 2nd Lieutenant Rooke's party was released from incarceration, and another party under 2nd Lieutenant Jackson was installed. Four days later this party was released and brought back to barracks, the bird being apparently too wary to walk into the trap. It was no pleasant or easy task for the troops involved, for they had to live in very uncomfortable conditions, in partial darkness and almost complete silence for fear of disclosing their presence to any rebel sympathisers.

On February 17, Battalion H.Q. and two columns took part in a final brigade operation, designed to converge on Shafa Amr from all sides in the hope of capturing a much-wanted rebel leader. Starting from the village of Waldheim at 6 a.m. in torrential rain, the two companies, widely extended and in touch with other units on both flanks, moved across six miles of open country to Shafa Amr, where they arrived soaked to the skin, covered in mud and having found one rifle. Here the Brigade Commander and Unit Commanders were collected, disconsolate at having discovered nothing of importance.

But just as Brigadier Evetts was about to order a withdrawal a secret message from the police was delivered to him, stating that the wanted man was in a convent in the village. This was obviously a job for the battalion, who had so often occupied the static post in this village and knew the layout of the convent. The wet and weary troops very quickly had that convent surrounded, prior to the entrance of a search party. The search was carried out by a platoon under 2nd Lieutenant Butler who, closely followed by the C.O. and Adjutant, cautiously entered by the main entrance to discover Arabs scuttling out of every conceivable hiding-place, while many better-class Arabs were crowded in the lower rooms of the building.

While this search was going on, a sentry posted in the garden saw a man rush up an outside staircase and disappear into an upper room, which the priest in charge stated was the nuns' dormitory. Accompanied by convent officials the whole of the upper storey, including the belfry, was thoroughly searched. But the man had vanished. Reluctantly the hunt was called off, with only a few suspects to show for all the trouble and excitement. Some days later the police informed the C.O. that the wanted man was there all the time, and had climbed to a hiding-place above the bell in the belfry!

A final opportunity to capture an important rebel leader came during the last week in February, when Superintendent Cohen informed the C.O. that he had a very reliable report that a well-known leader would be present in the mosque at Et Tireh at noon on February 24. Owing to the difficulty of getting to this village without disclosing one's approach, it required much guile to transport even a very small party of troops to surround the mosque at the appointed hour. But eventually it was decided to send 2nd Lieutenant Rooke and 12 men of 'Q' Platoon, disguised as Arabs, in two country carts. They, on arrival, were to cast off their disguises and to be followed closely by a platoon in M.T. In spite of mishaps with the drivers and horses, the first party arrived on time, and completely surprised the local inhabitants. But the officer in command was even more surprised to see 300 Arabs emerge from a building in which 100 would have been a crowd. A quick search of the mosque by an Arab policeman and the Headman disclosed a pistol hidden amongst articles of clothing and shoes, and hopes ran high that the 'big noise' was amongst the worshippers. But after an examination which lasted two and a half hours it had to be admitted that he was not present, though several lesser gangsters were recognised and apprehended.

It was distinctly annoying to those responsible for working out and carrying out this operation to learn during the interrogation of the prisoners that there was another mosque in the village, of which they had not been informed.

11. *The Battalion Leaves Palestine*

On Sunday, March 19, 1939, the battalion paraded as strong as possible for a final Church Parade. This was attended by the Divisional Commander, Major-General B. L. Montgomery who, after presenting a number of certificates for distinguished service to officers and other ranks, addressed the battalion in very moving and complimentary terms. During the course of this speech he prophesied that Portsmouth and Wolverhampton would be in the Cup Final and that Portsmouth would win. In this he was correct. But another prophecy of his, that there would be no European War that year, proved, unfortunately, to be wrong.

The battalion sailed from Haifa for Malta in the troopship *Dunera* on March 22, having completed fourteen months in the Holy Land. On board the ship there also travelled the Royal Ulster Rifles and Brigadier J. F. Evetts, who congratulated all ranks on the work they had done in Palestine under his command.

Two months later, on May 21, an oak lectern was unveiled in the Garrison Chapel at Peninsula Barracks, Haifa, in memory of the eleven members of the battalion who had died or been killed in action in Palestine. During the service Major-General Montgomery addressed the congregation. This lectern was brought to England when the British mandate in Palestine ended in 1948 and, at the time of writing,[1] is in the Garrison Church at Shorncliffe. The names engraved on it are: H. C. Harrington, D. Harris, C. G. Hayes, H. Moyes, S. T. Chapman, G. W. Davidson, W. J. Fox, T. J. Hunt, L. Towner, A. E. Jones, and E. C. Rumens.

The following members of the battalion were awarded decorations in Palestine:—Major Travers the O.B.E.; Major Bryan the D.S.O.;

[1] This lectern is now at the Regimental Depot.

Captain Whitty and Lieutenants Read, Rooke and Grove, the M.C.; and Privates Sparkes and Richards the M.M. In addition officers and other ranks were mentioned thirty-seven times in General Orders for acts of distinguished conduct in action and eleven times for devotion to duty. The General Service Medal with the clasp 'Palestine' was issued to all ranks who served with the battalion.

CHAPTER 5

The Sands Run Out
January 1938 to September 1939

1. *Regimental*

WHILE the 2nd Battalion was chasing Arabs in Palestine, Hitler's plans had been unfolding in Europe. As the occupation of the Rhineland by Germany had been resisted only by a storm of protest, he resolved on another adventure. In March 1938 Germany marched into Austria. This further violation of the Peace Treaty also met with no resistance, but it served as a serious warning to the rest of Europe. The British Government decided to press on with the rearmament programme in this country.

One of the results was that the reorganisation of infantry battalions into four rifle companies and a headquarter company was speeded up. The rifle companies contained three platoons, the main weapon of which gradually became the Bren gun instead of the Lewis. Headquarter Company consisted of the Signal, Anti-Aircraft (the Drums), Mortar, Carrier, Pioneer and Administrative Platoons. The vehicle designed for the Carrier Platoon was the Bren gun armoured carrier, which ran on tracks. An M.T. section was included in the Administrative Platoon. Unfortunately the provision of the equipment lagged far behind the organisation.

Other changes in the Army were that all officers with seventeen or more years' service were promoted to the rank of major—this meant that there were eighteen new Regular majors in The Queen's Own in August 1938—and that a new rank, called Platoon Serjeant-Major (P.S.M.) or Warrant Officer Class III, was instituted in order to find commanders for the extra platoons in Headquarter Company. Furthermore the drill of the Army was completely changed; the normal formation for marching became threes instead of fours.

In the summer of 1938, Germany began to exert pressure on Czechoslovakia for the return of the Sudetenland. In September the British Prime Minister, Mr. Neville Chamberlain, held a series of meetings with Hitler which ended with a conference at Munich on

September 30. War was averted only by allowing Germany to assume control of the Sudetenland. While these negotiations were taking place many people in this country thought that a declaration of war was imminent. At the Depot slit-trenches were hurriedly dug round the 'Back Field,' precautions were taken against bombs by blocking the ground-floor windows with sandbags, and a gas-defence centre was organised. Similar precautions were taken by the 1st Battalion at Shorncliffe and at all the drill halls of the 4th and 5th Battalions. The 1st Battalion stood-by at one hour's notice. Sixty members of the 34th A.A. Battalion (the old 20th London), which had been embodied, were billeted at the Depot for one night. When it was all over the slit-trenches were either filled in again or left to collect the rain. Some weeks later at one drill hall a hedgehog was reputed to have been found at the bottom of one very muddy trench.

During this 'Munich Crisis' the mood of the country was reflected by the large number of Territorials who went night after night to their drill halls in case they could be of any use, and by the many recruits who enlisted. The Regular recruiting became so good that the height standard for The Queen's Own was raised to five feet seven inches. Moreover, the women began to lend a hand. The Auxiliary Territorial Service was formed, and the 41st Kent Company A.T.S. began to appear at the Depot in the evenings for training in drill, cooking and clerical duties. The purse strings had also been further loosened, and more modernisation took place at the Depot; the old wooden administrative block was demolished and a new gymnasium as well as a new house for the Depot Commander were erected.

When Germany marched into Czechoslovakia in March 1939 there was an abrupt change in the policy of the Government. Conscription was introduced into the Regular Army and the Territorial Army was expanded to approximately twice its size. Men virtually poured in to the drill halls of the 4th and 5th Battalions, who had already recruited up to their war establishment, and within a few months the numbers had grown sufficiently to form the 6th Battalion from the 4th and the 7th Battalion from the 5th. Another measure to prepare the Army was that the Reservists, both officers and men, were called up to learn about the new weapons and equipment. The first 150 of these arrived at the Depot and were sent on to the 1st Battalion at Shorncliffe in June.

The first batch of conscripts, or Militiamen as they were called, arrived at the Depot on July 15, 1939. To make room for them it was necessary to send the Regular recruits, who were already there, to the 1st Battalion to complete their training. Even then some of the

Militiamen had to be accommodated in some huts which had been erected for them in the 'Back Field.' These young men were from all walks of life, keen and intelligent, and from the first they settled down to the strange military surroundings with cheerfulness and adaptability. There was no sign here of the decadence that was talked about. They were soon moving about the barracks and the town of Maidstone, looking very smart in their new battle dress. The Regular soldiers were surprised to find that this new uniform could be as smart as their own service dress in spite of the ugly side-hat that was worn with it.

As the summer of 1939 passed away Hitler turned his gaze towards Poland, from whom he demanded the return of Danzig. But the British Government had announced in March that Britain would guarantee Poland against aggression. Only a miracle could now avert war. On September 1, Germany invaded Poland, and at 11.15 a.m. on September 3, Mr. Chamberlain told the nation over the radio that Britain was for the second time in twenty-five years at war with Germany. France also declared war.

A few days before the declaration of war the Reservists began to arrive at the Depot quietly and punctually. This was no gay adventure as it had seemed to many in 1914. When they were off duty these men sat in the sun outside the married quarters and listened attentively to the news from the wireless sets inside. The mobilisation stores were in the Drill Shed, and the Quartermaster, Captain Brooks, had arranged that the men should walk in at one door as civilians and stagger out of another weighed down with the full kit of a soldier. They went off in batches, mainly to join the 1st Battalion at Shorncliffe. The 41st Kent Company A.T.S., fifty-five in number, came into barracks each morning to help with the cooking and serving of meals.

2. The 1st Battalion at Shorncliffe

For the first few weeks after its arrival at Shorncliffe in January 1938 the 1st Battalion was occupied with reorganisation and with leave. It then began to practise the new drill in 'threes' in preparation for a War Office demonstration. The actual demonstration was given at the Stadium, Shorncliffe, in April, and was attended by Viscount Gort, who was then C.I.G.S., and other senior commanders.

In May new Colours were presented to the battalion at the Stadium, Shorncliffe, by H.R.H. The Duke of Kent. In spite of heavy rain the parade was carried out faultlessly before a large and distinguished assembly. The old (1909) Colours were laid up in All Saints' Church, Maidstone, on July 17, during the Regimental Reunion.

In June the battalion took part in two displays at the Aldershot Command Tattoo—'The Capture of Fort Moro' and 'The Tudor Rose.' Because of this, training in 1938 was confined to battalion and brigade training and some divisional exercises from a camp at Saxmundham in Suffolk. The year ended with an inspection of the band by the Director of Music, Kneller Hall, who gave it an 'Outstanding' report. In May 1939, the band broadcast for the B.B.C.

The training programme of 1939 was much disturbed by the introduction of conscription into the Regular Army and the doubling of the Territorial Army. Many senior N.C.O.s and other personnel had to be posted away to instruct the Militiamen and the many new Territorial recruits. D Company was in fact closed down for a few weeks until the Regular recruits arrived from the Depot in July to fill it. The great need was for cadre courses to train fresh N.C.O.s. Field training was confined to a few exercises carried out from barracks.

On August 22, 1939, the battalion was recalled from a brigade night exercise because war was imminent. Slit-trenches were dug round barracks, air raid precaution measures were put into effect and anti-aircraft posts were manned. In a few days drafts of Reservist officers and other ranks joined from the Depot. Major Chitty, the second-in-command, went off to be D.A.A.G. of the 1st Anti-Aircraft Division, and the under-age and medically unfit were sent to Maidstone. An Italian Officer, who was attached, made himself quite popular by his tactful good humour.

Orders to mobilize were received at 10 p.m. on September 1. The following day mobilisation stores were issued; an amnesty was granted to men in detention; the mounted officers' chargers, which even then were not quite obsolete, were despatched to the Horse Reception Depot; and the battalion Silver was deposited in a bank at Canterbury. On September 3, the Boys, the Colours and the sealed patterns were sent off to the Depot.

3. The 2nd Battalion in Malta

The 2nd Battalion arrived in the Grand Harbour, Malta, on March 26, 1939, after a very rough voyage from Palestine. Sir Charles Bonham-Carter, the Colonel of the Regiment, who was also Governor and Commander-in-Chief of Malta, was received on board the ship by a Guard of Honour. A small advance party under Majors Chaplin and Knatchbull had previously arrived from England, so the families were already settled in their married quarters. At first the battalion was scattered, with headquarters in St. Paul's Hutments and companies in St. George's and St. Andrew's Barracks; but early in June the whole battalion was concentrated in St. George's.

In April the rear party, under Major Clay, came from Palestine, and Major Pulverman and a draft of 56 men from the 1st Battalion arrived from England. Major Booth-Tucker rejoined from the Staff in Palestine in August. On the debit side several senior N.C.O.s departed to England for duty with the expanding Territorial battalions, and seven officers and a number of P.S.M.s and N.C.O.s went home to train the Militiamen. The battalion was in fact as heavily drawn upon for instructors as the 1st Battalion. The officers to go included Majors Travers, Clay and Bryan. Major Travers was promoted at once to command the Royal Artillery Depot at Taunton.

The operational role of the battalion in Malta was coast defence. It was allotted a sector of the south-east coast,[1] which included much of Marsa Scirocco Bay, and small inlets at Wied Zurriek and Ghar Lapsi. The defences consisted of numerous beach and depth posts. These had been sited by the Brigade Commander, Brigadier L. H. Cox, but many of them had not yet been completed. One of the battalion's first tasks was to erect a number of sandbag posts as temporary substitutes for the permanent posts. In order to practise the men in coast-watching and other duties several manning exercises were held. Whenever possible the Navy would take part in these, and the Royal Marines would make assault landings on various parts of the coast.

On Good Friday, which was always a welcome holiday in the Army, Italy, led by Benito Mussolini, very inconsiderately marched into Albania. This caused a crisis or 'flap,' as the troops aptly called it. All defences were hurriedly manned, and the battalion spent an uncomfortable Easter in, or on the site of, its posts. The Fleet wisely decided that Malta was too close to Italy and set sail for Alexandria, where it remained until the situation seemed to be more healthy.

On Empire Day, May 24, the battalion Trooped the Colour on the Palace Square, Valetta. General Bonham-Carter took the salute and after the ceremony presented decorations won in Palestine. On the King's Birthday the whole garrison assembled on the Floriana Parade Ground and, having carried out the traditional ceremony, marched through Valetta to St. Elmo. During the march as much as possible was made of the few new vehicles and weapons

[1] See map of Malta facing page 180.

H

which had arrived on the island, in order to infuse confidence into the Maltese and awe into the Italians.

In June Lieutenant-Colonel V. S. Clarke, M.C., arrived to assume command. Colonel Palmer was promoted to the appointment of Officer in charge of Records at Hounslow.

The battalion entered fully into the social life of Malta. The band played at numerous functions, notably at Sant Anton Palace, and the dance band, appropriately named 'The Invicta Swingers,' became very popular at the various clubs. Following the example of General Bonham-Carter the relations between the battalion and the Maltese became very cordial. Some Maltese youths were specially enlisted into The Queen's Own. As the summer grew hotter most of the troops spent their leisure hours bathing and boating in St. George's Bay.

Several ships of the French Navy came into the Grand Harbour in July. In order to strengthen the *Entente*, arrangements were made for five officers from each ship to dine on the same night at the officers' messes of the four infantry battalions on the island. Five French naval officers duly arrived at St. George's and were welcomed by the senior major, in a well-rehearsed speech in French, as officers of the the battleship *Provence*. During the speech the faces of the French officers were seen to fall; but it was not until Major Goater took up his glass to propose their health at the end of his oration that it was realised that the wrong five officers had arrived. Hurried telephone calls were made, and it was found that the *Provence* officers had gone to the mess of the Royal Irish Fusiliers by mistake. A hurried exchange was negotiated.

These pleasant pursuits were abruptly ended by the imminence of war. Certain pre-arranged mobilisation instructions were carried out. These included the despatch to the Depot of Bandmaster Jackson with all boys under the age of seventeen, and the conversion of the Band into stretcher-bearers and of the Drums into the Anti-Aircraft Platoon. The Colours and the Silver remained in Malta.

On August 22 the battalion began to erect belts of barbed wire at all possible landing places in its beach sector. The holes for the iron pickets had been previously drilled, refilled with cement and marked with red paint, so that the pickets could be readily driven into the rock. In spite of this the labour of bringing the wire from the R.E. stores and of erecting it in the hot sun was considerable. B Company at Calafrana and C at Birzebbugia spent their intervals of rest bathing in the sea. D Company were more fortunate because their task included the erection of under-water obstacles in the cooling sea at Marsa Scirocco fishing village. For three long days the troops laboured on this task, and then on the evening of August 24, on returning to barracks, the whole battalion was ordered to move out again immediately to occupy its battle positions permanently. The occupation of the beach sector was carried out that night. Thus when war was declared the battalion, with headquarters at Tarxien, was already in its defence positions.

4. *The Territorial Battalions*

The reorganisation of the 4th and 5th Battalions into a Headquarter Company and four rifle companies began in the spring of 1938, but it was not until after annual training that their Vickers guns were actually handed in. In fact the 5th Battalion had the distinction of winning the T.A. Machine Gun Competition when it was in camp at Falmer. The 4th Battalion camp was at Dibgate. Drill at camp was carried out in 'threes' that year, and gas masks were used during training exercises. The *pièce de résistance* was that each battalion had one Bren gun. The year ended with the Permanent Staff Instructors attending a course at the Depot in the Bren gun and anti-tank rifle, both of which had by that time been issued in small numbers.

In October 1938, the 4th Battalion was transferred to 132nd (Kent and Surrey) T.A. Brigade, in which the 5th was already serving. The brigade was then commanded by Brigadier T. T. Waddington; Major Pulverman was Brigade Major. The two Territorial battalions were in this way not only brigaded together again but were serving under a Queen's Own Brigadier with a Queen's Own Brigade Major. Major Howlett became Brigade Major in March 1939.

From the time that it was announced in March 1939, that the Territorial Army was to recruit up to double its strength, a stream of men, as we have seen, began to enlist in both the 4th and 5th Battalions. These recruits could be trained only by draining the Regular battalions of instructors. Another disadvantage was that the Drill Halls became overcrowded, and the overflow had to carry out their 'drills' in car parks, recreation grounds and even in the streets. At the end of May Major W. Nash was selected to command the 6th Battalion and Major A. G. Fuller to command the 7th, when these new battalions should actually come into being. By the end of June the 5th Battalion had doubled its strength and had stopped recruiting.

Both the 4th and 5th Battalions, in the same brigade once more, went to camp very strong at the end of July at Lympne. The emphasis in the training was on defence. In most of the exercises the air played a part. On the last day of camp a parade of the 5th Battalion was held, and the 7th Battalion was separated from it for the first time. This was the official birth of the 7th.

Camp broke up on August 14. On the 24th the key personnel of the 4th, 5th and 7th Battalions were embodied to make preparations for the reception of the remainder of the men. On September 1 the embodiment of these three battalions began. The men assembled steadily and quietly, each company and detachment in its own Drill Hall or at some other place allotted. Guards were then placed on vulnerable points by the 4th and 7th Battalions (most of the 7th were called up before the 5th). The remainder of the personnel were billeted at their mobilisation stations. The 4th, 5th and 7th Battalions had completed their embodiment smoothly and efficiently by the time that war was declared.

PART TWO

WAR: DEFENCE

September 1939 to August 1942

CHAPTER 6

The First Eight Months of War
September 1939 to April 1940

1. *224 Infantry Training Centre*

As soon as war was declared on September 3, 1939, the title of the Regimental Depot was changed to 224 Infantry Training Centre, and its commander, Major E. S. Kerr, became a Lieutenant-Colonel. This I.T.C. then became the basic training establishment for all six battalions of The Queen's Own. Its task was to put up to 2,500 Militiamen at a time through an eighteen weeks' training course, at the end of which they would be fit to take their place in platoons in the field.

To accommodate these additional Militiamen the construction of a hutted camp had already begun on a suitable piece of ground, which had been previously selected at Sandling Park on the Maidstone–Chatham road. This camp later became known as 'Invicta Lines.' While it was being built the personnel for whom there was no room in barracks were billeted in houses in Maidstone. So as not to alarm the householders these billets had been surveyed by officers in plain clothes, who had assessed from the street the number of men each house could take. In the circumstances these officers did remarkably good work, for everything went smoothly and the householders made their enforced guests welcome.

Arrangements had also to be made to feed these additional men in barracks. Every available space indoors was converted into a dining hall, and several temporary alfresco cookhouses were speedily erected. Meals, which seemed to go on all day, were almost entirely in the hands of the A.T.S., whose arrival in barracks every morning had now become routine. These ladies not only served the food but also did most of the cooking of it, and cooking in the open in that severe winter required considerable hardihood. Nevertheless their energy and sense of humour never failed.

The Regimental Comforts Fund, under the patronage of H.R.H. The Duke of Kent, came into being soon after the outbreak of war.

It was administered by a committee of which Mrs. Kerr was the chairman and Lieutenant-Colonel A. Howe the secretary. An appeal, which met with a splendid response, was launched throughout the county, and many voluntary knitting circles were organised. Among the many donations was one of £100 from Khan Bahadur Jan Mohammed, the contractor for the Regiment in India. Of all those who helped the fund none was more indefatigable than Mr. A. W. H. Rickards ('Paddy Doyle'). This old soldier of the Regiment, although in failing health, spared no effort to further the cause. By January 1940 the fund had amassed over £1,000.

2. *The 1st Battalion in France*

When war was declared the 1st Battalion began to move by companies to billets in the village of Elham and its vicinity. The move was completed by September 8, when Headquarters opened at Trelawney Cottage in Elham High Street. By that time all necessary Reservists had joined to bring the battalion up to war establishment plus about one hundred Home Service Details. Stores, equipment and vehicles continued to arrive, and it was not until several days later that mobilisation was completed.

On September 23 the battalion moved as part of 10th Brigade of 4th Division (Major-General D. G. Johnson, V.C.) to Aldershot, where it remained for a week carrying out a few training exercises. During this period some N.C.O.s and men who had been trained in the handling of a new anti-tank gun were posted to 10th Brigade Headquarters to form a Brigade Anti-Tank Company. On September 27 Their Majesties The King and Queen visited the division. This heralded the move to France.

The first to move were the M.T. section and the Carrier Platoon, who drove their vehicles to Avonmouth, their port of embarkation. The main body of the battalion went by train on September 30 to Southampton, where it embarked in T.S.S. *Duke of York* in the early afternoon. That night the *Duke of York* sailed in convoy from Portsmouth. After an uneventful passage the main body disembarked at Cherbourg the following day and went on by train that evening to Le Mans. For the next week the troops were in billets at the village of Noyen, where the transport rejoined.

Before leaving Albuhera Barracks, Aldershot, the Commanding Officer, Lieutenant-Colonel Anstruther, had been taken ill. Major Sharpin had stepped up to command.

With the Germans still committed in Poland there was no likeli-

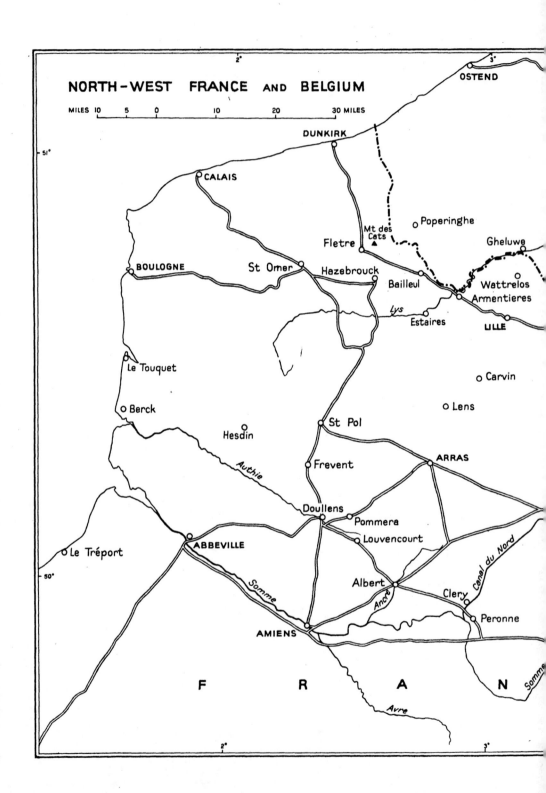

NORTH-WEST FRANCE AND BELGIUM

MILES 10 5 0   10   20   30 MILES

OSTEND

DUNKIRK

CALAIS

Poperinghe

Mt des Cats
Fletre

Gheluwe

BOULOGNE

St Omer

Hazebrouck

Bailleul

Wattrelos
Armentieres

Lys

Estaires

LILLE

Le Touquet

Carvin

Berck

Lens

Hesdin

St Pol

ARRAS

Frevent

Authie

Doullens

Pommera
Louvencourt

Canal du Nord

Le Tréport

ABBEVILLE

Albert

Clery

Peronne

Somme

Ancre

AMIENS

F   R   A   N

Somme

Avre

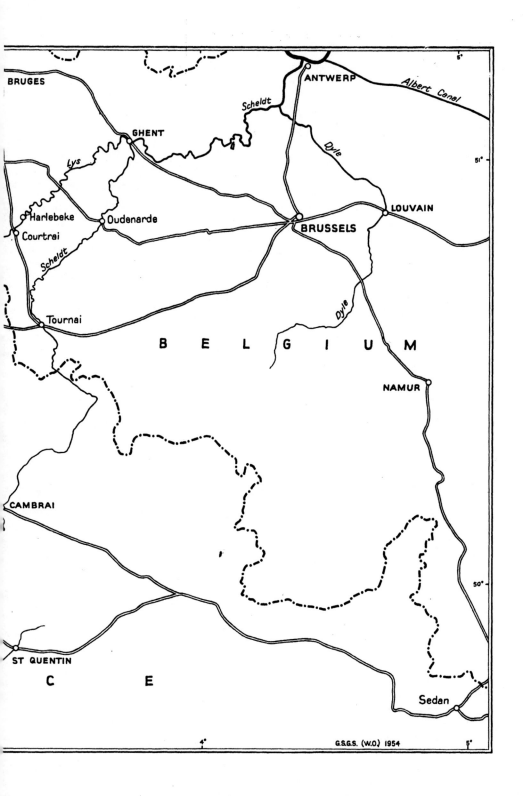

hood of an immediate large-scale offensive against France. But the possibility of an attack through neutral Belgium had to be considered, and the French urged Lord Gort, who was in command of the British Expeditionary Force (B.E.F.), to move his first four divisions, then concentrating in France, to their prescribed positions on the Franco–Belgian frontier as soon as possible. Accordingly the battalion moved north by train to billets at Carvin, between Lens and Lille. 4th Division was in reserve with the role of preventing penetration, and the men were fully employed in digging a defensive position. Life was not all toil, for there were several pleasant sing-songs in the local estaminets in the evenings.

At the end of November the battalion moved forward to Wattrelos, on the Franco-Belgian frontier, where the companies were billeted in factories. The men went each day to work on an extension of the Maginot Line (a series of strong forts which protected France against Germany), which was being constructed along the Belgian frontier to the sea. In addition detachments occupied ten of the frontier pill-boxes, and parties accompanied the French Garde Mobile on their night patrols. Soon after Christmas, which was celebrated in the traditional manner, batches started to go to England on leave. Many of the battalion began to wonder if there really was a war after all. Indeed, had it not been for the intense cold and perpetual labour the troops would have been quite content with their lot.

10th Brigade moved back to the outskirts of Lille on January 22, 1940, for a few weeks' training. The men lived in comfortable billets and entertainments were plentiful. This only lasted until February 18, for the brigade then moved by train to the Saar, where the French Army was in contact with the Germans, in order to obtain battle experience.

Having detrained at Metz the battalion moved up in M.T. to the *Ligne de Receuil*, which was in front of the Maginot Line proper. For ten days it worked on defences, manned a few posts and provided working parties in the *Ligne de Contact*. When off duty, parties visited the immense underground forts rather as if they were going to a museum, except that the guides were given English cigarettes instead of cash as a tip. The battalion then took over a sector in the *Ligne de Contact* itself for about a week. All four rifle companies were forward in a very extended outpost line, but the situation remained quiet and the fighting patrols, which went out in front of the outposts, found no warlike incidents to report. Nevertheless this visit brought home the fact that reality lurked behind the 'phoney' war. On completion of its tour the battalion returned to its former

billets in Wattrelos and continued its work on the extension of the
Maginot Line.

3. The 4th and 5th Battalions in England and France

After embodiment all detachments of the 4th Battalion remained
in billets in the vicinity of their own drill halls until September 7,
when the battalion was divided into two units and the 6th Battalion
came into being. Some of the detachments of the 4th then handed
over their drill halls to the 6th and concentrated at Battalion Headquarters in Tonbridge. There the battalion remained, guarding
vulnerable points and carrying out elementary training, until
October 23, 1939, when it moved to 44th Division's concentration
area in Dorset. It was billeted in Axminster.

The role of the 5th Battalion on embodiment was to support the
civil power in the area of 'P' Division of the Metropolitan Police,
and it moved to billets with Headquarters at Ladywell Police
Station and companies at Lewisham, Bromley, Southend Village
and East Dulwich. Happily the expected bombing and consequent
disorganisation and casualties did not occur; the companies were
able to carry out a certain amount of training in the restricted
suburban surroundings. On October 22 the battalion also moved
to the divisional concentration area. It was billeted at Bridport.

For the next three years the 4th and 5th Battalions were to serve
together in 132nd Brigade of 44th (Home Counties) Division
(Major-General E. A. Osborne). Brigadier J. S. Steele, M.C. (late
Royal Ulster Rifles) had now taken over command of the brigade,
but Major 'Swifty' Howlett was still its Brigade Major. As soon as
they arrived in Dorset both battalions sent a detachment of platoon
strength to form an Anti-tank Company at Brigade Headquarters.
This company was commanded by Captain Sir Derek Watson of
the 4th Battalion and, although its guns were not issued until later,
it carried out its very varied duties in excellent fashion.

On December 4 Lieutenant-Colonel A. A. E. Chitty was posted
from his appointment with the 1st Anti-Aircraft Division to command
the 4th Battalion. The 5th was commanded by Lieutenant-Colonel
H. S. Brown. The Dorset countryside was excellent for training, and
as the weeks went by battalion, brigade and even a few divisional
exercises were carried out in spite of the very cold weather of January
and February 1940. The men found their billets at Axminster and
Bridport very comfortable.

During December and January stores, carriers, mortars, more Bren guns and some ammunition began to come in steadily, until the two battalions were not far short of their full scale of equipment. A move overseas seemed to be indicated. Indeed on February 4 advance parties set off, only to return two days later. On February 7 His Majesty The King inspected 132nd Brigade on the main road leading to Lyme Regis. Departure then seemed to be certain, but it was not until March 18 that advance parties again set off. On the 30th the transport of the brigade left by road, and on April 5 the main body went by train to Southampton. The crossing to France was uneventful.

Having disembarked at Cherbourg both battalions entrained and reached the assembly area near Rousse and Voutre the following morning. Five days later 132nd Brigade moved on again by train to Grand Villiers and Conté. After two days of preparation the march to the Belgian frontier began. This march, of about ninety miles, was completed in four marching days and did much to harden the troops and improve their morale. Bailleul was reached on April 24. Both the 4th and 5th Battalions were billeted in the town or in farms close to it. The billets were good, the people were friendly and the men settled down cheerfully to the work of improving the extension of the Maginot Line—the same task as the 1st Battalion was carrying out at Wattrelos only twenty miles to the east.

4. The Queen's Own Brigade is Formed

Some months earlier the Army Council had decided to introduce one Regular battalion into each Territorial brigade. The battalion selected to transfer to 132nd Brigade was the 1st Battalion of The Queen's Own, which was to replace 1st/6th East Surreys. Its Anti-tank Platoon was to move from 10th Brigade Headquarters at the same time. The short move from Wattrelos to Bailleul was carried out in lorries on May 4.

In this way, for the first time in history, a Queen's Own Brigade was formed. To mark the occasion a Church Parade, attended by all three battalions, was held in the cinema at Bailleul on May 5. Major-General Osborne, Brigadier Steele and Brigadier N. I. Whitty, who was then commanding 133rd Brigade of 44th Division, were present.

At this time the key personnel in the three battalions were:—

1st Battalion

C.O.	Lt.-Col. E. A. Sharpin
2 i/c.	Major I. R. Lovell
Adj.	Capt. J. H. H. Whitty, M.C.
Q.M.	Capt. R. C. E. Mines
R.S.M.	W.O.I R. Benbow
O.C. A	Capt. J. H. Burrows
O.C. B	Capt. E. G. Elliott
O.C. C	Major O. G. Woodhouse
O.C. D	Capt. D. H. Archer
O.C. HQ	Major H. J. S. Brooke

	4th Battalion	5th Battalion
C.O.	Lt.-Col. A. A. E. Chitty	Lt.-Col. H. S. Brown, M.C.
2 i/c.	Major M. M. Ffinch	Major E. B. Loveless
Adj.	Capt. E. B. S. Clarke	Capt. F. K. Theobald
Q.M.	Lieut. F. G. W. Lambkin	Major C. W. Craddock
R.S.M.	W.O.I A. Hennessey	W.O.I S. Terry
O.C. A	Capt. D. H. Andrews	Capt. H. J. D. Combe
O.C. B	Major N. S. C. Elmslie	Capt. E. G. Young
O.C. C	Capt. A. H. Taylor	Capt. T. Kenyon
O.C. D	Capt. P. F. Haynes	Major G. B. Knight
O.C. HQ	Major M. H. Keane	Major E. S. Heygate

A complete list of officers and warrant officers can be found in Appendix B.

5. *The 6th and 7th Battalions*

The 6th Battalion assumed its identity on September 7, 1939, under the command of Lieutenant-Colonel W. Nash, though the officers and men had been embodied on September 1 as part of the 4th Battalion. The battalion, with headquarters at Tonbridge, then became responsible for providing guards at many vulnerable points in such localities as the Isle of Sheppey and the Isle of Grain, at Tatsfield in Surrey and even as far distant as Rye in Sussex.

In the New Year the guards were gradually withdrawn or handed over one by one to the Royal Air Force, the Royal Artillery or the 13th Holding Battalion, Royal Sussex Regiment. By the second week in March the battalion had been relieved of all its guard duties and was concentrated with headquarters at the Drill Hall, Tonbridge, and all four rifle companies at St. Mary Cray—one at the Drill Hall, one at the Rookery and two at the Lagoon Swimming Pool.

*   *   *

Battalion Headquarters of the 7th Battalion opened at Ravenscourt, Pelham Road, Gravesend, on August 26, 1939. Next day 400 men were embodied and were sent under Captain Clout to guard the Royal Ordnance Factory at Woolwich. Four days later the order for complete embodiment was received, and on September 2 the remaining officers and men of the battalion as well as several officers from the Territorial Army Reserve reported and were billeted in Gravesend.

On September 16 the large detachment at Woolwich was withdrawn. A Company then moved to Blackfriars, B to Battersea, C to Croydon and D to Bermondsey to take over guards at vulnerable points. Headquarters remained at Gravesend. This continued until the middle of October, when all four companies were withdrawn to Gravesend and were billeted in the Gordon and Milton Road Schools. Unhappily, after only a few weeks, new guards were taken over at Port Victoria, Dunkirk, Wye and Manston, and B Company moved to Faversham and C to Dover. The battalion retained these guards until April 1940.

On December 14 Lieutenant-Colonel A. G. Fuller was taken ill and Lieutenant-Colonel B. L. Clay, O.B.E., was appointed to command the battalion.

*   *   *

In October 1939, the 6th and 7th Battalions, together with the 5th Buffs, had come under 36th Brigade (Brigadier G. Roupell, V.C.) for administration and training. With the battalions so fully committed on guard duties, however, training had been practically impossible. In any case they had not yet been issued with many weapons to train with. Although every man had a rifle, it was not until the end of January 1940 that the first Bren guns and anti-tank rifles arrived; and even then there were less than four Brens and two A/T rifles for each company. There were still no mortars, no carriers and no signal equipment, and the transport consisted mainly of hired civilian vehicles. Moreover, only twenty rounds of rifle ammunition for each man had been issued for practice. There were as yet only a score of officers in each battalion, and these were mostly Territorial Reservists or young subalterns newly posted from training establishments. The strength in other ranks was approximately only 600. Of these some 200 were Militiamen who had been in the Army only a few weeks and had not yet fired their rifles at all.

There was such a shortage of labour in France in the spring of 1940 that it was decided to send three divisions (12th, 23rd and 46th), which were in a similar state of unpreparedness, to join the B.E.F. Their primary role was to be airfield construction and work on the lines of communication. After three months of this it was intended to send them back to England to complete their training. As theirs was not a fighting role 12th Division, which included 36th Brigade, was to cross to France without artillery or signals and on a much reduced scale of transport and equipment.

So it was that the 6th and 7th Battalions, still without their proper complement of weapons, embarked at Southampton on April 20 and 21 respectively and crossed to Le Havre after nightfall. From there they marched to a hutted camp at Le Manoir near Alizay, some nine miles south of Rouen, where they began work on the railway sidings and marshalling yards for No. 2 Engineer Supply Base Depot.

The principal appointments in the battalions were at this time held by:—

	6th Battalion	7th Battalion
C.O.	Lt.-Col. W. Nash, M.B.E.	Lt-Col. B. L. Clay, O.B.E.
2 i/c.	Major I. Pilditch	Major C. W. Clout, M.B.E.
Adj.	Capt. T. T. W. Stanyon	2/Lt. R. W. H. Brown
Q.M.	Lieut. E. R. Tadman	Lieut. A. E. Watts
R.S.M.	W.O.I F. G. Farrington	W.O.I A. E. Sivers
O.C. A	Capt. H. E. Duff	Capt. G. F. O'B. Newbery
O.C. B	Capt. C. H. Keenlyside	Capt. C. B. Selby-Boothroyd
O.C. C	Capt. J. M. Carr	Capt. S. L. Gibbs
O.C. D	Capt. R. D. Ranking	Capt. E. F. Hill
O.C. HQ	Capt. P. Scott-Martin, M.C.	Capt. H. J. Langdon

A complete list of officers in these battalions can be found in Appendix B.

In this way by the beginning of May 1940, there were five battalions of The Queen's Own in France. The 2nd Battalion was still in Malta (see Chapter 11).

CHAPTER 7

The Retreat to Dunkirk
May 1940

1. *The Queen's Own Brigade at Oudenarde*

IN the spring of 1940 it became clear that the Germans, who had completed the destruction of Poland during the previous autumn, were preparing for an invasion of France. Should the attack be made through Holland and Belgium, the British and the French had agreed on a plan, called Plan D, by which I and II Corps of the B.E.F. would advance into Belgium with the Northern Group of French Armies and take up a defensive position along the River Dyle. The British III Corps (Lieutenant-General Sir Ronald Adam), which included 44th Division, would move forward at the same time and prepare a second line of defence along the River Scheldt.

Although rumours of the impending German offensive were rife, the first few days of May 1940 passed peacefully enough for The Queen's Own Brigade at Bailleul. The days were spent at work on the defences. In the evenings, after listening to the Drums of one or other of the battalions beating Retreat in the square, the men would enjoy a sing-song in the estaminets. On the evening of the 9th the officers of the 5th Battalion gave a memorable cocktail party for the other officers in order to celebrate the formation of The Queen's Own Brigade. The party was somewhat protracted, and many of the officers were rather late getting to bed. Within an hour or so aircraft could be heard zooming overhead, followed by bursts of machine-gun fire. The telephone call from Brigade, to tell the battalions that the German attack had begun, was almost superfluous. It did, however, inform them that Plan D was to be put into operation forthwith.

The Queen's Own Brigade prepared to move at once. Frontier Control Posts were withdrawn. All surplus stores and regimental property, such as band instruments, were dumped in cellars or farms. That afternoon the march across the Belgian frontier began.

Marching mainly during the hours of darkness and on second-class roads, some of them cobbled, 22 miles were covered the first night and 30 the second. The whole of May 12 and 13 were spent in billets at Wortegem, where most of the men managed to get baths. On the afternoon of the 13th the Commanding Officers went to a conference at Brigade Headquarters, during which orders were issued for the occupation of the defensive position along the River Scheldt. That evening the battalion sectors were reconnoitred. There had been much German air activity during the day, and the battalions had turned out several times to deal with false alarms of parachute landings.

The position to be occupied by The Queen's Own Brigade included Eekhout and Oudenarde. On its right was 131st Brigade. To begin with its left flank was in the air, though a regiment of Belgian Chasseurs moved in later. In its rear, in reserve, was 133rd Brigade. Within the brigade the 4th Battalion was on the right, with Oudenarde as its main responsibility; but between it and the 2nd Buffs, who were in positions about the village of Petegem, there was a gap of at least a mile. Depth was given here by the 1st Battalion, which was placed at Eekhout and Mooregem, between but in rear of the 2nd Buffs and the 4th Battalion. The 5th Battalion on the left occupied a frontage of some 3,000 yards, which included the outskirts of Eyne. All three battalions had three companies forward and one in reserve. Brigade Headquarters were at Mooregem.

In front of this position the River Scheldt presented an obstacle some twenty yards wide and ten feet deep. This stretch of it was canalised, with the tow-path ten feet above the level of the water. The forward section posts had thus to be sited on the tow-path itself, and a wire obstacle, to be effective, had to be erected on the enemy side of the river. Even then for the last three hundred yards the approaches to the river were concealed by the opposite bank. From across the river the valley of the Scheldt was overlooked by rising wooded country. To the rear the ground rose gradually to Den Doorn and Knock.

The main points to note in the brigade sector were the villages of Eekhout and Mooregem, which were defended by B and C Companies[1] of the 1st Battalion respectively; the château at Kasteelwijk, where the 4th Battalion's headquarters were situated; the wide plain between Petegem and Oudenarde; and the railway line which ran across this plain just south of Eekhout and Kasteelwijk. Finally there was the town of Oudenarde, the defence of which, by C, B and A Companies of the 4th Battalion, demanded

[1] The names of all Company Commanders are given in Chapter 6, Section 4.

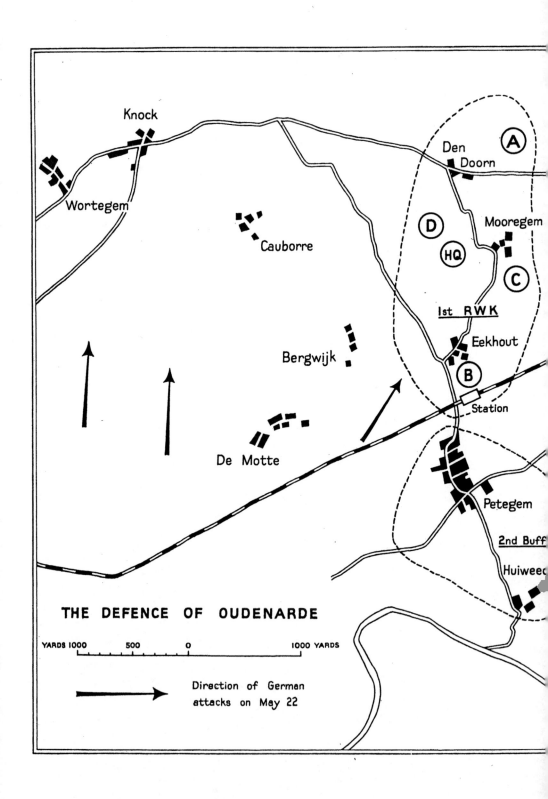

Knock

Wortegem

Den Doorn

Ⓐ

Mooregem

Cauborre

Ⓓ

ⒽⓆ

Ⓒ

Ist RWK

Bergwijk

Eekhout

Ⓑ

Station

De Motte

Petegem

2nd Buff

Huiweeⓓ

THE DEFENCE OF OUDENARDE

YARDS 1000   500   0   1000 YARDS

Direction of German
attacks on May 22

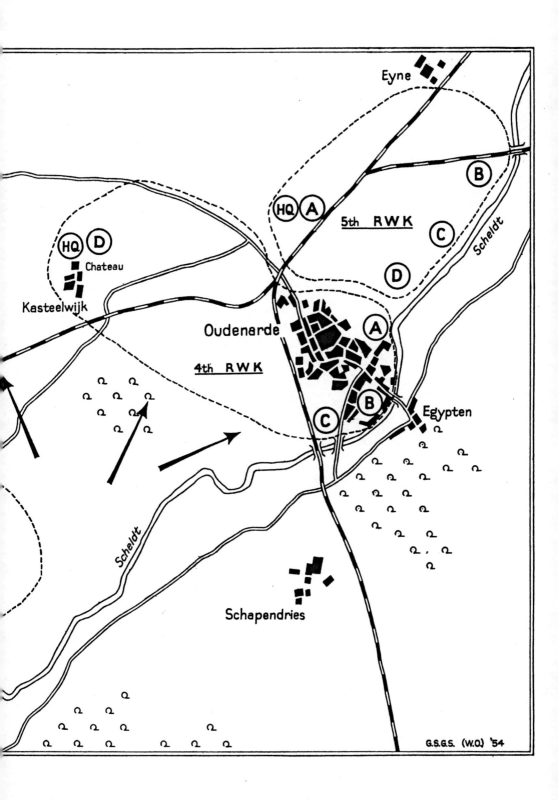

Eyne

⑧ B

HQ Ⓐ

5th R W K

Ⓒ

Ⓓ

HQ Ⓓ

■ Chateau

Scheldt

Kasteelwijk

Ⓐ

Oudenarde

4th R W K

Ⓑ

Ⓒ

Egypten

Scheldt

Schapendries

G.S.G.S. (W.O.) '54

the construction of bomb-proof shelters, road-blocks and sandbag-defences of houses as well as section posts on the river bank.

The battalions moved up to their positions on the River Scheldt on May 14. While the troops were settling into billets near their battle positions the Company Commanders reconnoitred their areas. Section posts were then taped out. Digging and revetting began on May 15. Wire became available on the 17th, when the truck drivers, with little food or sleep, began to ply a ceaseless ferry service between the area and a barbed-wire factory some thirty miles away. By the evening of the 18th the 4th and 5th Battalions were ready to resist attack, and in front of the 1st Battalion only a few yards of tactical wiring had still to be completed.

While the work was in progress bad news had been coming in from the River Dyle. There had been heavy fighting along the whole front from Sedan to Antwerp, and the British 3rd Division, under Major-General Montgomery, had been sharply engaged. But it was between Sedan and Namur—the part of the front which the French had considered to be impassable for a large armoured force, and opposite which they had thought it unnecessary to construct a Maginot Line—that the Germans had flung their heaviest weight. The French front had broken at Sedan, and a wide gap had been pierced through the defences. Once the breach was open, German tanks, with spearheads of motor-cyclists, armoured cars and infantry in armoured lorries, had poured through. By May 16 the right flank of the British I and II Corps had been turned, and they began to fall back to the second line of defence on the River Scheldt.

Ahead of the British troops came a host of Belgian civilians, who crossed the Scheldt and entered Oudenarde. By this time the inhabitants themselves were evacuating the town, and the refugees had to continue their flight westwards. Air-raid warnings were now frequent in Oudenarde, but the only serious raid was on the railway station, round which many houses and shops were damaged. On May 18 units of I and II Corps began to come through. Mingling with them were more refugees and some Belgian troops, who were also withdrawing; there is no doubt that many fifth-columnists were also among the throng. The congestion on the roads was appalling. The Regiment of Belgian Chasseurs now came in on the left of the 5th Battalion, and the two main road bridges over the river were prepared for demolition.

On the morning of Sunday the 19th, Brigadier Steele gave orders for the battle positions to be manned, and all three battalions stood-to. Enemy dive-bombers attacked the road bridge at Eyne and scored a direct hit, causing the first battle casualties—two killed

I

and two wounded of B Company of the 5th Battalion. The forward posts of A and B Companies of the 4th Battalion at the main road bridges at Oudenarde were also bombed, and some twenty casualties were suffered. During the day the level of the water in the river fell considerably, which made it a much less formidable obstacle. This was due to the lock gates being opened so as to flood an area in front of the Belgians. That evening C Company of the 1st Battalion was sent to take up an outpost position east of Egypten until the rearguard of 3rd Division, the last British troops, had passed through. They returned in the early hours of the night, having encountered no enemy. Several parties of troops on traffic control duty east of the river were then withdrawn. Finally, the last bridges were blown and all barges on the river were sunk.

Having retired behind the River Scheldt, II Corps (Lieutenant-General A. F. Brooke) took up a defensive position on the right of 44th Division, with 4th Division adjoining 131st Brigade. To the south four more divisions of the B.E.F. were along the river as far as Tournai, and three were in reserve.

The first Germans appeared early on the 20th, when some patrols approached to reconnoitre the river. Later, a larger group of enemy came forward with floats and bridging material. This move was observed from a windmill south of Oudenarde in the 4th Battalion's sector, and the information was passed back to the artillery by line telephone (wireless was not extensively used in the early days of the war). As a result the guns made a good shoot and checked the advance. This brought retaliation from the Germans, who shelled the river banks. The post held by Corporal Jarvis of the 4th Battalion was hit, but he quickly reorganised his section and gave orders for the reconstruction and rewiring of his position. A few enemy snipers then made their way into some trees just across the river. These were dealt with by C Company of the 4th Battalion. Later, a patrol from this company, led by Lance-Corporal Brooks, crossed the Scheldt and returned with a prisoner. In the evening enemy infantry and armoured vehicles massed opposite Petegem on the front of 131st Brigade, and some of them managed to cross the river and enter the hamlet of Huiweede. Two counter-attacks put in by the 2nd Buffs failed to dislodge them.

During the night the 5th Battalion had two casualties in a patrol which was sent east of the river, but an attack did not develop on the front of The Queen's Own Brigade. Early on May 21 the Germans crossed the Scheldt in strength on 131st Brigade's front, and the left company of the Buffs (C) was forced to withdraw to the railway line south of Kasteelwijk. The headquarters of the 4th Battalion in the château were thus in danger. Fortunately trenches had been dug, and pioneers, cooks and clerks manned the defences. B Company of the 1st Battalion in Eekhout became engaged. The left platoon was temporarily dislodged, and Lieutenant Fraser's platoon was forced out of the area of Petegem station by burning buildings and took up an alternative position in Eekhout. For a time the situation seemed desperate. But Captain Warr, who was second-in-command of the company, rallied the defenders of Eekhout and they stood firm.

Late in the morning Brigadier Steele ordered a counter-attack on Petegem. For this attack the reserve companies of the 1st and 4th Battalions and two sections of carriers of the 4th, under Serjeant Busselle, were placed under the command of Major Ffinch, the second-in-command of the 4th. Some artillery support was arranged. The attack went in under cover of smoke from 2-inch mortars along the railway line from Kasteelwijk to Petegem station. D Company of the 1st was in the van, and Captain Archer led it with great dash. In spite of two or three casualties received from the fire of the defenders of Eekhout, who at first thought it was the enemy attacking, the counter-attack succeeded in recapturing Petegem station but did not link up with the Buffs in Petegem village. Lieutenant Cheale[1] was killed in this action.

The two counter-attack companies then remained as part of the garrison of Eekhout, the defence of which was co-ordinated by Major Lovell, the second-in-command of the 1st Battalion. The village was under mortar and small arms fire for the remainder of the day. It was also shelled a good deal, and several casualties occurred, including Lieutenant Child, who was killed. By the evening the garrison was running out of ammunition. Private Parsons of the 1st Battalion drove his truck through heavy fire into the village and delivered a fresh supply. Moreover, on returning to Mooregem he volunteered to run the gauntlet a second time. During the day the carriers of the 1st Battalion were skilfully manœuvred on this flank by Lieutenant Axford in order to stop the German advance.

The German pressure between the 2nd Buffs and the 4th Battalion had not yet been stemmed, for C Company of the Buffs was still hard pressed on the railway line near Kasteelwijk. Brigadier Steele therefore ordered a second counter-attack. One company of the 1st Battalion was to seize the portion of the railway line immediately left of Petegem station. On the capture of its objective the company was to dig in. Colonel Sharpin detailed A Company for this attack,

[1] Son of Lieut.-Col. A. R. Cheale, who commanded the 4th Battalion 1920–1922.

and the company moved to a wood near Mooregem. While the troops were drawing tools and extra ammunition the area was heavily shelled. This caused some casualties, but after a few minutes delay the company moved off by way of a covered approach through Mooregem. The railway line was reached with little opposition, and the company then dug in on the right of C Company of the Buffs. During the consolidation the company commander, Captain Burrows, was wounded, but he remained with his company.

While this was taking place, and for the remainder of the day, a hostile aircraft was continually in the air over the area directing artillery fire. The transport of all three battalions, which was brigaded at Cauborre, suffered considerably from this fire; two vehicles at the 5th Battalion's headquarters and three of the 1st Battalion's carriers were also hit. The Aid Post of the 1st Battalion in a farm at Mooregem received a direct hit, but the occupants, who were in the cellar, were unhurt. There were also several air raids on Oudenarde that day. During one of them an incendiary bomb came through the roof of the house which Lance-Corporal Culmer and his section were defending. Without hesitation he sprang forward and threw the bomb out of the window, thereby probably saving the lives of his men.

From dusk onwards the enemy made repeated efforts to cross the Scheldt between Oudenarde and Eyne. Although an S O S was put up no artillery support was received, and a few isolated parties of Germans may have got across on the 5th Battalion's very wide front. The main attacks were held off. In the 4th Battalion's sector Lieutenant Smith, whose platoon was defending the river, swam out to one of the barges in full view of enemy snipers to satisfy himself that it had been properly sunk.

This ended the second day's fighting. It was now clear that the bulk of 131st Brigade had been forced to withdraw and that the enemy's bridgehead included De Motte, Petegem and much of the open ground between that village and Oudenarde. Eekhout and the railway line to its left were still in our hands, but Eekhout had now become a salient. The position there was still strong, for its garrison of B and D Companies of the 1st Battalion and D of the 4th still remained practically intact. The position on the western edge of Oudenarde in the 4th Battalion's sector however, was less secure, and B Company of the 5th was moved westwards and placed under Colonel Chitty's orders. He sent them to strengthen his right flank.

By this time the men of all three battalions were very tired after four days' heavy labour and two days' fighting. But there could be little thought of sleep that night, for they were in close contact with the enemy. Food was delivered to all companies except A Company of the 1st Battalion, whom ration parties could not reach owing to enemy fire along the railway line.

On the morning of May 22 the Germans set about enlarging their bridgehead in the direction of Eekhout and the railway line. Eekhout was bombarded by enemy artillery and mortars, and Captain Archer and his company headquarters were trapped in a burning building. They extricated themselves only with difficulty. Captain Archer then withdrew his forward platoon in good order and took up a position in other houses. The garrison of Eekhout maintained this new line intact in spite of numerous casualties, amongst whom were Captains Elliott and Warr, who were wounded, the latter mortally. On the railway line A Company of the 1st Battalion came under heavy enfilade and sniping fire and suffered several casualties. Later, this company was forced to withdraw to the line of a road half a mile back, whence Captain Burrows, who had been wounded the day before, went to the Aid Post. Lieutenant Causbrook assumed command of the company. Touch could not be gained with Lieutenant Elgood's platoon, and it remained forward of the railway line until the following morning, when it was captured. C Company of the Buffs withdrew to the area of the château to conform with this retirement.

By 11.30 a.m. the position on the right flank of the 4th Battalion had become critical. Bold action was required, and Colonel Chitty sent his Carrier Platoon and a mortar detachment to prevent the Germans from advancing across the open plain. Travelling at high speed, and firing their Bren guns as they moved, the carriers charged the enemy and checked their advance. Lieutenant Warner then withdrew his carriers, and the mortars, under Sergeant Roriston, opened fire on a copse and two farms held by the Germans. When the mortars ceased, the carriers again dashed forward and shot down the enemy as they withdrew from the copse and farms. The Germans were surprised by these tactics and were again caught unawares when similar sorties were made from other directions. In these sorties Privates Brooke and Howard drove their carriers with notable skill and gallantry. Eventually the situation was restored; though two posts of C Company near the river were temporarily lost. A Company of the 5th Battalion was then sent to this threatened flank, and the position was held intact until nightfall.

In the evening A Company of the 1st Battalion was pressed back from its position north of the railway line towards Den Doorn. C Company in Mooregem became engaged, and it seemed as if the enemy would penetrate between Eekhout and Mooregem and overrun the headquarters of the 1st Battalion. Eventually accurate fire from a mortar detachment at Den Doorn stopped this advance. During this engagement Private Hughes helped five wounded men to cover and, having dressed their wounds, seized a Bren gun and held the Germans at bay until the wounded men could be moved to safety. One of the guns of the Brigade Anti-Tank Company became surrounded. Before abandoning it Corporal Watts and Private Woollaston dismounted the gun and placed two boxes of ammunition under it. They then crawled back a few yards and rolled a grenade between the two boxes. The explosion destroyed the gun. The 4th Battalion headquarters in the château were now threatened. Operations here were under the command of Major Keane, who inspired the garrison to defend the area at all costs in spite of heavy pressure and intense shell fire. The men fought splendidly, and twenty signallers, the officers' mess cook and sanitary personnel were among the casualties. This was a fine achievement.

Meanwhile very serious news had been coming in. The German armoured spearheads had reached the sea beyond Abbéville and had turned the right flank of the B.E.F. Lord Gort had no alternative but to withdraw his troops to the line of the Franco-Belgian frontier —to the defences they had constructed so laboriously during the winter and spring. The order for 44th Division to retire came at 4 p.m. At 6 p.m. Brigadier Steele ordered The Queen's Own Brigade to retire at nightfall.

The five companies on the river line were the first to withdraw. They broke contact with the enemy without difficulty. Colonel Brown ordered the two companies of the 5th Battalion to assemble by 10.30 p.m. at his Battalion headquarters, whence they withdrew first north and then north-west without casualties. Colonel Chitty ordered his three companies to break contact at about 8 p.m. and withdraw northwards through Oudenarde, while the headquarters personnel of the 4th and the two attached companies of the 5th Battalion, all under the orders of Major Keane, covered the right flank from the area of Kasteelwijk. While conducting this action Major Keane was killed.

By 10 p.m. the Germans had penetrated the Kasteelwijk area, and Captain Young of the 5th Battalion, who was now in command of the flank-guard, decided to break contact. With great coolness he conducted the retirement, the headquarters personnel of the 4th Battalion being skilfully withdrawn by P.S.M. Chapman. By some mischance the orders to retire did not reach A Company of the 5th Battalion, and Captain Combe, having seen from the tower of the château that his company was practically surrounded by

Germans digging in for the night, took a compass bearing on the only gap he could find and extricated his men by marching on this bearing. By that time the only route open was northwards, and the company[1] had of necessity to withdraw with the Belgians, thus becoming separated from the brigade.

The 1st Battalion was the last to retire. Major Woodhouse's C Company in Mooregem denied its positions to the enemy until 10.30 p.m., by which time the troops in Eekhout had got clear. Colonel Sharpin then ordered C Company to retire. Major Lovell disposed the six remaining vehicles of the Carrier Platoon about the cross-roads at Knock to prevent enemy penetration from the right flank. Lieutenant Christofas, the Intelligence Officer, checked each company and detachment as it passed through. Whilst it was at Knock the Carrier Platoon came under shell-fire, and one carrier was damaged so severely that it had to be abandoned.

The Queen's Own Brigade had now drawn clear away from the enemy. But the men were dead-tired. They had fought for three days without rest and with very little food. All transport had previously withdrawn, and the men therefore had to carry the Bren guns, spare ammunition and other heavy equipment. Every effort was made to reach the River Lys before daylight, but the congestion on the roads made this impossible. Nevertheless the bridge at Harlebeke was reached without incident, and the 4th Battalion, the 5th (less A Company) and half of the 1st crossed the river safely. Before A and C Companies of the 1st could cross, however, the bridge was blown. These two companies were therefore forced to continue the march on the east side of the river as far as Courtrai, where they crossed and rejoined the brigade. At Courtrai the whole brigade went into billets. From Oudenarde to Courtrai is some twenty-two miles, yet the weary troops had carried out the march in good order and were still in excellent shape.

The Queen's Own Brigade remained in billets about Courtrai for the remainder of May 23, and the troops took the opportunity o making up a little of the sleep they had lost. Apart from bombing the day was uneventful. At about nine that evening the withdrawal was continued a further twelve miles to Gheluwe, where the brigade embussed. The roads were still very congested, and progress was slow. Consequently it was not until full daylight on the 24th that the brigade reached its billets in farms and villages some miles north of Lille. The brigade was now back behind the Franco-Belgian frontier, and although there was much enemy air activity that

[1] This company subsequently took part in the defence of Dunkirk and was evacuated on June 2 and 3.

morning there was at last nothing to prevent the troops from sleeping very soundly indeed.

2. *The 6th and 7th Battalions at Albert and Doullens*

Momentous events had befallen the 6th and 7th Battalions even before the Battle of Oudenarde was fought. During their first fourteen days at Le Manoir, near Rouen, they had continued their work on the railway sidings unworried by thoughts of battle. On May 9 the 7th Battalion changed over with the 5th Buffs at Fleury, where they hoped to carry out a fortnight's section and platoon training. On the 14th the German armoured spearheads broke through the French defences at Sedan, and at about noon on the 15th Colonel Clay received orders from 36th Brigade that the 7th Battalion was to prepare to move at half-an-hour's notice.

Next day, leaving Lieutenant E. C. F. Brown and fifty other ranks at Fleury as a rear party, the 7th Battalion moved in R.A.S.C. transport to Quevauvilliers, near Amiens, where, together with one troop (four guns) of Field Artillery and one section of Royal Engineers, it became a Mobile Column. This column, which was under the orders of Colonel Clay, was part of 'Petreforce,' an improvised force which was being formed under Major-General R. L. Petre, the Commander of 12th Division, to prevent the German armoured columns from cutting the British lines of communication south of Arras.

By this time the hostile spearheads were nearing St. Quentin, and the situation was so serious that there was no alternative but to confront the German armour with these untrained and ill-armed troops. On May 17 Clay's Column was ordered to move to Clery-sur-Somme, where it was to deny the crossings of the Canal du Nord to the enemy. By 5.30 a.m. on the 18th the column of seventy vehicles and guns had arrived at Clery, where the 7th Battalion took up a defensive position behind the canal with two companies forward and two back. Road-blocks were hastily constructed, and the Sappers demolished all bridges in the vicinity except the main road bridge and another to the north. Later in the day thirty-five Bren guns and a dozen anti-tank rifles arrived from 'Petreforce' to bring the battalion nearly up to establishment in these weapons, though it is doubtful whether there were sufficient trained men to handle them efficiently. The battalion still had only one 3-inch mortar.

In the afternoon some German aircraft bombed and machine-gunned C and B Companies[1] on the canal. To this the troops replied vigorously. Eventually the hostile aircraft were driven off by some British fighters. There was now a continuous stream of refugees moving westwards from Peronne across the two bridges which remained intact. At about 6 p.m. a German motor-cyclist approached the main road bridge. Fire was opened by the section of C Company which was manning the road-block, and the German fell. Soon afterwards three enemy tanks approached this road-block and opened fire with tracer bullets. Clay's Column returned the fire, the 3-inch mortar under Serjeant Drummond doing particularly good work. C.S.M. Glue encouraged the forward platoons to stand firm, while C.S.M. Rawcliffe came forward with a platoon of Headquarter Company and two anti-tank rifles to reinforce the position. The troop of artillery opened fire, and one of their first shots hit a tank, which burst into flames. The other two tanks then withdrew. The night was quiet except for air activity and the dropping of parachute flares.

At 3 a.m. on May 19 Colonel Clay received orders to withdraw and take up a position at Louvencourt, north-west of Albert. C Company were the last to retire. Captain Gibbs and Lieutenant Aldrich's platoon, who remained at the main road-block until the column was clear, lost touch during the withdrawal, but the remainder of the column reached Louvencourt soon after daylight intact. Colonel Clay then issued orders for the defence of the high ground. At that time it was thought that Captain Gibb's party had been captured by the Germans.

*   *   *

Meanwhile the remainder of 36th Brigade at Le Manoir had also been launched into the battle. Early on May 17 Brigadier Roupell ordered the 6th Battalion and the 5th Buffs to prepare to move as a Mobile Column. Vehicles were to be collected from Rouen, and drivers were to be found from within the battalions. At 1 a.m. on the morning of the 18th this column set off for an unknown destination. The road was thick with traffic. French soldiers in lorries, officers in motor-cars, and all manner of vehicles conveying refugees and their pathetic belongings were moving westwards. Progress along the narrow roads was therefore very slow. At about 3 p.m. the column reached Doullens, where orders were issued that the 6th Battalion and the 5th Buffs were to remain in that town, and that road-blocks were to be constructed at all the entrances immediately. After a meal had been hurriedly eaten, work began.

[1] The names of Company Commanders are given in Chapter 6, Section 5.

In this way, by the morning of May 19 both the 6th and the 7th Battalions were confronting the advance of the German spearheads, with the 6th Battalion in Doullens and the 7th at Louvencourt. Although the two battalions were still some ten miles apart, the 7th had come once more under the command of 36th Brigade.

The 7th Battalion was the first to meet with disaster. On May 20, as the situation appeared to have improved, Clay's Column was ordered to move forward and prepare a tank-proof localitity in Albert. By six in the morning the battalion had arrived there, and the transport had been concealed under trees in the main square of the town. There was a great deal of machine-gunning from the air and other hostile air activity, but by seven the companies were getting into position.

Suddenly a strong attack came in by German tanks and lorried infantry. The main weight of the onset fell on the left forward company (D). Captain Hill was killed and casualties were heavy, but Lieutenant Phillips assumed command of the company and organised a strong resistance, while Serjeant Evans conducted the defence by Lieutenant Phillips' platoon with gallantry and skill. As he was dragging some boxes of ammunition from a burning lorry Lieutenant Phillips was wounded and became unconscious. Without hesitation Private Smith ran forward and rescued him. Despite the wound Lieutenant Phillips then organised the defence of a house, and it was not until his small garrison had been shelled out of the upper floors and forced into the cellars that he consented to surrender.

By 7.30 a.m. enemy tanks had penetrated to the main square of Albert, where they began to shell and machine-gun the transport. Captain M. G. M. Archer and R.S.M. Sivers organised the defence of a large school by C Company and battalion headquarters. Lance-Corporal Durance engaged enemy snipers from a very exposed position and shot not less than three of them before he was mortally wounded. But the anti-tank rifles proved to be ineffective against the enemy tanks, and fighting became desperate in the square. By 8 a.m. the right forward company (A) had also become engaged by large numbers of armoured vehicles. Reports came in that the enemy were now north of the town and astride the Albert–Doullens road. Acting on orders previously received, Colonel Clay therefore ordered a withdrawal to the more favourable wooded ground north of Albert. By eleven, having fought their way through the narrow streets of the town, the remnants of the battalion, mainly on foot, had reached a rendezvous in a wood about a mile north of Albert.

By this time, however, the whole countryside was overrun by

German tanks, and Colonel Clay gave orders for the battalion, now approximately only 250 strong, to split into small parties of about twenty, each under an officer or senior N.C.O., and to make their way independently to Doullens, where the remainder of 36th Brigade was in position. The distance to Doullens was some fifteen miles, and these parties were to move through woods and, if necessary, only at night. By noon the battalion had dispersed but, owing to the rapidity of the German advance and the difficulty of finding their way as only two maps had been issued to the unit, very few of the parties managed to make their way to safety. Most of them, including Colonel Clay's, were taken prisoner. Nevertheless Captain Newbery and his company headquarters in a truck managed to reach Brigade Headquarters. Later on they met the party under Captain Gibbs which had lost touch with the battalion during the withdrawal from Clery. Eventually there were about seventy of the battalion assembled under Captain Newbery's command. Meanwhile the Adjutant, Lieutenant R. W. H. Brown, having burned the secret documents, had been sent on a motor-cycle to report the situation to the Brigadier. Whilst dodging Germans he ran out of petrol and, forced to travel to the south, after many adventures reached Fleury on May 27 and joined the rear party which had been left there under his brother's command.

*   *   *

It was not long before the 6th Battalion met with a fate similar to that of the 7th. During the night of May 19, 36th Brigade, less the 7th Battalion, received orders to take up a defensive position along the Doullens–Arras road facing south-east. There were no troops in support. The 6th Battalion, on the right, took over the defence of all the road-blocks in Doullens and was also given a front of about three miles from Doullens to the village of Pommera. On the left of Pommera the 5th Buffs took up a position which extended for over six miles. Within the battalion Headquarter Company held the road-blocks on the eastern and southern edges of Doullens. The road-blocks on the north side of the town were held by A Company, which was also the reserve company. B, C and D Companies took up positions about half a mile in front of the Doullens–Arras road. The second-line transport remained in Doullens. The battalion still had no mortars or carriers, and each of its companies had but four Bren guns and three anti-tank rifles.

At 9.30 a.m. a Gunner officer arrived at Battalion Headquarters with the information that the 7th Battalion had been overrun at Albert by German tanks and had suffered heavy casualties. This information was passed on to the companies, with the warning that they were to expect an early attack. As B, C and D Companies had had no time to construct anti-tank obstacles, Colonel Nash instructed them to lie low if German tanks appeared and to wait for the enemy infantry.

Soon after noon B, C and D Companies came under artillery and machine-gun fire from the direction of the Albert road. During the next hour hostile armoured vehicles and motor-cyclists approached from the direction of both Arras and Albert along the secondary as well as the main roads. At 1 p.m. Brigadier Roupell informed Colonel Nash that the line of withdrawal would be through Frevent to St. Pol; he also said that he would give the order to retire if necessary. A little later a telephone message to Brigade confirmed the impression that the Buffs were retiring on the left, but the Brigadier still required the 6th Battalion to hold on. Soon after this the line to Brigade Headquarters was cut.

By this time attacks had developed on Doullens. The post at the junction of the Albert and Amiens roads was attacked by armoured vehicles, and Lieutenant Pugh, armed with an anti-tank rifle, disabled two of them. This post fought so stubbornly that the hostile column withdrew and by-passed this road-block. At another post Serjeant Ford continued to fire an anti-tank rifle at armoured vehicles until all the other occupants of the post had become casualties; even then he had to be ordered to withdraw. At about 2 p.m. the second-line transport was withdrawn on the orders of Major Fry, the Brigade Major, and made for Frevent. It just got out in time, for at 2.30 p.m. German tanks appeared on the high ground north of Doullens. The houses at the Albert–Amiens road junction were now burning fiercely, and Captain Scott-Martin gradually withdrew Headquarter Company to the western edge of the town. By 3 p.m. an attack on the north side of Doullens had developed. The platoons commanded by Lieutenants Waterhouse and Henchie both came into action against enemy tanks and infantry, but they stood firm.

The position in Doullens was now very grave. Many of the road-blocks had been set on fire by incendiary shells, and the troops had been driven from their positions by gun and machine-gun fire. By 5 p.m. Headquarter Company had been forced to retire to A Company's headquarters in the main square of the town, where fighting continued. About 100 men of these two companies, under Captain Scott-Martin, were defending a building which was being mercilessly shelled by enemy tanks. He considered withdrawing his men through the back of the building, but he found it to be surrounded. Further resistance would have meant much needless loss of life, so at 8 p.m. he surrendered. After this the German armoured columns began to pass through Doullens towards Abbéville. They had been held up by H.Q. and A Companies for eight hours.

Meanwhile B, C and D Companies on the left had been completely encircled by hostile vehicles, and Battalion Headquarters, in the rear of C Company, had been overrun. Several desperate efforts were made to break through, in the course of which Corporal Berwick carried three severely wounded men under machine-gun fire to safety over a railway embankment, and Corporal Hayler returned under heavy fire to retrieve a Bren gun from a position which had been vacated. Patrols were sent to the left, right and rear in fruitless efforts to gain touch with other troops. Eventually Captains Carr and Ranking decided to withdraw their companies southwards under cover of night. Captain Keenlyside split up B Company before ordering similar action.

By the following morning all three companies had separated into small parties, which were scattered over a large area. The whole countryside was being searched by the enemy for any British or French troops capable of offering further resistance, and during the next few days many of the parties, without food and in a country unknown to them, were rounded up and taken prisoner. Three platoons, commanded by Lieutenants Waters, Willis and Bunce, maintained themselves on the country and avoided capture for ten or more days. Lieutenant Waters' platoon actually reached the coast near the mouth of the Somme before being captured. The party commanded by Captain Carr succeeded in reaching Rouen on May 26; they embarked at Cherbourg for Southampton on June 7.

Captain Nixon and Lieutenant Tadman, the Quartermaster, with the second-line transport, together with the 70 men of the 7th Battalion under Captains Newbery and Gibbs, successfully reached Frevent under the orders of Major Fry. From there the column of vehicles moved off for St. Pol. The road was thronged with refugees, but after many delays and by making use of side roads the whole party arrived at Boulogne. The troops were very tired by this time, and they cheered up considerably when they were sent to a rest camp. There was little rest however, for air raids were incessant. After a noisy night they were ordered to assist in the defence of Boulogne. On the evening of May 23 the party embarked in destroyers for Dover and arrived at Maidstone on the 24th. Lieutenant Tadman died of wounds received while he was embarking at Boulogne.

The strength of Captain Carr's party on arriving in England was approximately 25. Captain Nixon's party was about 50 strong. These two groups formed the nucleus of the 6th Battalion when it began to re-form at Gunnerton Camp, Wark-on-Tyne, in the middle of June. The remaining 503 of the battalion were posted as missing.

The 7th Battalion was in similar shape. Except for the rear party of 50, which had been left at Fleury and which arrived at Gunnerton Camp with Captain Carr's party of the 6th Battalion, Captain Newbery's party of approximately 70 were the only personnel to reach England.

From this it will be seen that nearly 1,000 men of the 6th and 7th Battalions, including both Commanding Officers, were killed or captured in the actions at Albert and Doullens. Those who went into captivity were of course far from content with their lot. Many of them made repeated efforts to escape. Of these Captain Keenlyside was twice successful in tunnelling out of his *oflag*, only to be recaptured before he could get across the frontier to Switzerland. Perhaps the most persistent escaper was Lieutenant Pugh, who made seven attempts to escape and helped to dig twelve tunnels. Another notable escaper[1] was C.S.M. Rawcliffe. On the fourth of his six attempts to escape he organised a mass break by 20 men and was at liberty for four days. His fifth attempt gave him two weeks' liberty.

It is now known that it was a full-strength German Armoured Division which swept through Albert and Doullens and destroyed 36th Brigade on May 20, 1940. Against this powerful formation the inadequately-trained and ill-equipped 'Petreforce' pitted its puny strength in vain, for that night the German spearheads reached the sea beyond Abbéville. Although this improvised force failed, it was a gallant failure, and, as Lord Gort wrote: 'It fought and marched and proved, if proof were needed, that it was composed of soldiers who, despite their inexperience and lack of equipment, could hold their own with a better-found and more numerous enemy.'

3. *The Queen's Own Brigade in the Forest of Nieppe*

On its arrival in the billets near Lille on May 24 The Queen's Own Brigade was promised twenty-four hours' rest. But the military situation was too critical to permit this. Having reached the English Channel beyond Abbéville on the night of May 20, the German armoured columns had driven northwards along the coast towards Boulogne with the intention of cutting off the escape by sea of the

---

[1] Captain W. E. Edwards, attached to 12th Division Headquarters, was another Queen's Own escaper. His adventures are described in his book *Escape to the South*.

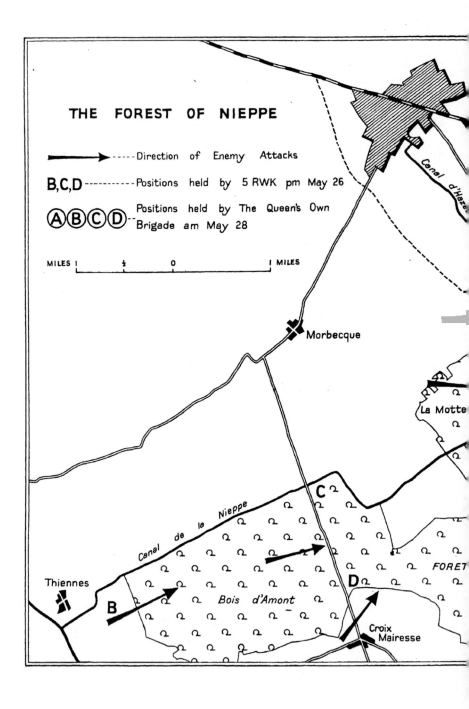

THE FOREST OF NIEPPE

⟶ ----Direction of Enemy Attacks

B,C,D --------Positions held by 5 RWK pm May 26

Ⓐ Ⓑ Ⓒ Ⓓ -- Positions held by The Queen's Own Brigade am May 28

MILES ⌐————————————————————————————————⌐ MILES
½   0   I

Canal d'Haze

Morbecque

La Motte

Canal de la Nieppe

C

Thiennes

B

Bois d'Amont

D

FORET

Croix Mairesse

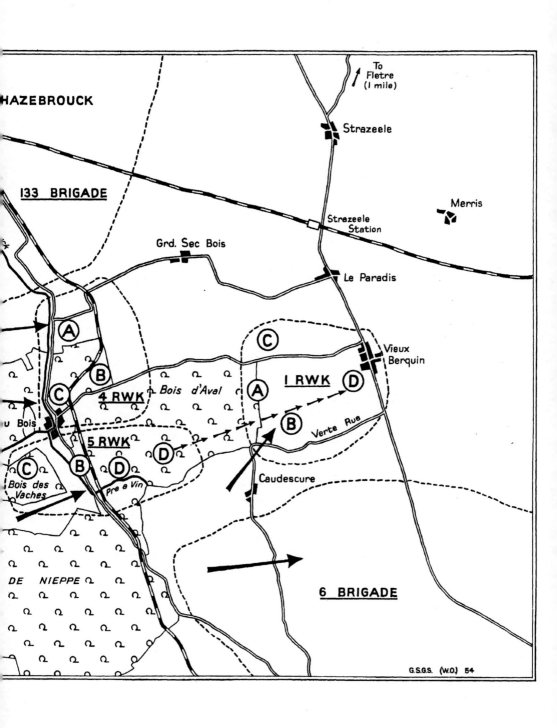

HAZEBROUCK

133 BRIGADE

To
Fletre
(1 mile)

Strazeele

Merris

Grd. Sec Bois

Strazeele
Station

Le Paradis

Ⓐ

Ⓒ

Vieux
Berquin

Ⓑ

4 RWK

Bois d'Aval

Ⓐ

I RWK

Ⓓ

Ⓒ

Ⓑ

Verte Rue

u Bois

5 RWK

Ⓓ

Ⓒ

Ⓑ

Ⓓ

Bois des
Vaches

Pre a Vin

Caudescure

DE NIEPPE

6 BRIGADE

G.S.G.S. (W.O.) 54

B.E.F. Boulogne had been attacked on May 22. After a heroic resistance the garrison, including, as we have seen, some of the remnants of the 6th and 7th Battalions, had been evacuated by the Navy on the night of May 23. The hostile columns had then invested Calais, which was defended by 30th Brigade. Involved in the defence of Calais was Captain Talbot, who was detached from The Queen's Own as Brigade Major of 30th Brigade. When Calais fell on May 26 Captain Talbot was captured with the remainder of this brigade but, after many adventures, he managed to escape and get back to England. The story of his escape is given in Appendix E.

By the morning of May 24 it was plain that Dunkirk was the only Channel port which remained available to the B.E.F. Moreover the British right flank was again in mortal danger. 44th Division was therefore ordered to move at once to the St. Omer area to prevent the Germans from driving north and cutting the lines of communication with Dunkirk. The Queen's Own Brigade was to be in the lead. The troops were consequently hustled out of their billets after only a few hours' rest.

At about 5 p.m., after numerous delays, the brigade set off in R.A.S.C. lorries, with the 5th Battalion (less A Company) leading, and drove through Armentieres, which had been heavily bombed just before. Indeed, as it was still daylight, the column was fortunate not to be bombed itself. Just west of Armentieres the Brigade Major caught up with Colonel Brown and informed him that the enemy were already in the Forest of Nieppe and that the 5th Battalion was to hold the bridges over the River Lys at Estaire. Colonel Brown immediately sent his Carrier Platoon to secure the river crossings; the battalion followed, debussed and deployed. By this time the information about the enemy was thought to be inaccurate, and the other two battalions were ordered to go through. The confusion and congestion on the road were now appalling, delays were frequent and several hours were wasted on the roadside. Eventually the 1st and 4th Battalions arrived just before daylight on May 25 at Vieux Berquin, where orders were given out for the hasty occupation of a delaying position along the Hazebrouck Canal facing west.

The 1st Battalion was on the right in the eastern fringes of Hazebrouck. On the left was the 4th Battalion with its left on the bridge at La Motte au Bois. The 5th came into reserve at Strazeele Station and Le Paradis. The day was spent by the weary troops in preparing the position for defence. During the afternoon the 5th Battalion's area was repeatedly bombed and machine-gunned by hostile low-flying aircraft. In the evening C Company of the 1st, under Major Woodhouse, was sent forward to relieve some armoured troops in an outpost position on high ground north of Morbecque. B Company of the 4th, under Major Elmslie, went out at the same time to a position south-west of Morbecque.

On May 26 the remainder of 44th Division began to arrive to strengthen the position, and orders were received that 133rd Brigade would take over on the canal from the 1st Battalion, which would then move into brigade reserve. The 5th Battalion was to move to the western edge of the Forest of Nieppe with a flank facing north, on the left and forward of the 4th. These moves were carried out during the afternoon and evening. 131st Brigade came into divisional reserve at Strazeele and Fletre. 6th Brigade of 2nd Division was now on the left of The Queen's Own Brigade.

While these moves were taking place the outposts had been attacked by German tanks. These vehicles entered Morbecque, and the left platoon of Major Woodhouse's company was forced to retire to a new position in a wood, from which the further advance of the enemy was delayed until nightfall. During this action Private Waller made three journeys under fire to replenish the ammunition of his post. D Company of the 4th Battalion (commanded by Captain Haynes), which had been sent out to relieve Major Elmslie's company, attacked Morbecque and succeeded in capturing the eastern edge of it. Suddenly German infantry appeared from all sides. D Company, surprised and hard-pressed and having lost many men, split up into small parties, which tried to make their way back to the main position. Only Lieutenant Waring and nine men succeeded in getting clear, however, and they swam back across the canal. The remainder, including Captain Haynes and Lieutenant Smith, went into captivity, where the latter died of his wounds. Meanwhile Major Elmslie's company had been attacked by tanks and infantry in force. Their anti-tank rifles failed to penetrate the armour of the tanks, but Lieutenant Allen boldly withdrew his platoon to the cover of a wood, where the company kept the German infantry at bay until nightfall. Both Major Woodhouse's and Major Elmslie's companies rejoined their battalions the following morning.

At dawn on May 27, B Company of the 5th Battalion, in an isolated outpost position at the forward or western edge of the Bois d'Amont, were strongly attacked by German infantry. P.S.M. Deakins' platoon, which was in a right-angled bend of the Canal de la Nieppe, was overrun. Captain Young succeeded in withdrawing the remainder of the company with few casualties through the wood to the main battalion position. By 10 a.m. the enemy had penetrated to this position, which was along the main road running north-west from Croix Mairesse to the Canal de la Nieppe, and Colonel Brown sent his Carrier Platoon to the aid of C and D Companies, who were holding it. Lieutenant Combe, leading this counter-attack with the gun of his carrier firing, was killed by a bullet, but the Germans were checked for a while. Soon after noon, however, the left flank of the battalion at Croix Mairesse was turned. Brigadier Steele therefore ordered one company of the 1st Battalion to be sent to reinforce the 5th. This company (D), commanded by Captain D. H. Archer, arrived at about 1.30 p.m. and was placed in reserve in the Bois des Vaches.

By about 2 p.m. it had become evident that the 5th Battalion's position in the Forest of Nieppe was untenable. At first Brigadier Steele required a counter-attack to be made, but at 2.30 p.m. he ordered Colonel Brown to withdraw to a position on the left of the 4th Battalion behind the Hazebrouck Canal from La Motte au Bois and then at right angles down the Canal de Pré a Vin. The withdrawal was not carried out without a great deal of fighting in the forest. A counter-attack led by Lieutenant Holland did much to extricate the left flank from a dangerous situation, and by 6 p.m. the battalion was established in its new position.

During the day hostile armoured vehicles had been ubiquitous. Rumours had been many. Some tanks were even said to have penetrated to Strazeele and to have attacked the second-line transport, which was brigaded there. A number of men of other regiments, who were returning from leave or who had become separated from their own units, came under command of the 4th Battalion. C.S.M. Catchpole, who was acting R.S.M., escorted them to positions which were in urgent need of reinforcements, but they could not be very usefully employed as they lacked leaders and equipment.

Although the night of May 27 was uneventful the troops, now dead weary, got little sleep.

On the morning of May 28 the positions held by the three battalions were as follows: The 4th Battalion on the right, with its left flank at La Motte au Bois, was holding a portion of the Hazebrouck Canal with A and C Companies forward and B in reserve. The 5th Battalion, with D Company of the 1st Battalion still in reserve, was holding the left portion of the canal with B and D Companies behind the Canal de Pré a Vin, and C Company forward in the Bois des Vaches. In reserve, the 1st Battalion was in position at the rear or eastern edge of the Bois d'Aval, with C Company at the north-east corner of the wood, A Company, now commanded by Captain Scott, in a clearing to the south of C, and B Company under Captain Whitehead on the left on the Verte Rue road. As the frontages of all companies were very large, patrols had to be sent out to keep touch.

K

The Brigadier expressed doubts about the left flank, and the Anti-Aircraft Platoon of the 1st Battalion was sent to extend that flank towards Vieux Berquin. One platoon of the Brigade Anti-Tank Company was under command of each battalion.

May 28 was a critical day. In the early hours torrential rain fell and continued for some hours. At dawn the enemy began to probe along the whole brigade front, and in several places German infantry crossed the canal and infiltrated into the Bois d'Aval. In the 4th Battalion's sector P.S.M. Gilligan's platoon of C Company was practically surrounded, but he led a counter-attack with great gallantry and extricated his sections. C.S.M. Napier of A Company, intercepted while he was supervising the distribution of ammunition to the forward platoons, twice charged the enemy with his pistol and broke clear. Colonel Chitty restored the situation for a time by sending his Carrier Platoon to cover the rides in the wood. C Company of the 5th Battalion in the Bois des Vaches came under small arms and mortar fire. By noon this company was entirely isolated, and it was withdrawn across the canal. It was now known that 6th Brigade on the left had retired, leaving the left flank of The Queen's Own Brigade in the air.

At about 3 p.m. enemy medium tanks approached the Canal de Pré a Vin opposite the left of the 5th Battalion. These tanks opened fire across the canal with guns and machine guns and caused a number of casualties. One of the guns of the Anti-Tank Platoon was knocked out. Patrols sent to the right failed to locate the 4th Battalion. Another patrol was driven back by enemy fire when it attempted to gain touch with the left-hand company of the 1st. By 3.30 p.m. small arms fire was coming from both the rear and the left flank, and the battalion was in danger of being cut off. As communications with Brigade had now broken down, Colonel Brown gave orders for a withdrawal to a position near Le Paradis which had already been indicated by the Brigadier.

B and C Companies of the 5th Battalion withdrew under Major Loveless in an easterly direction towards Caudescure, and by skilful use of cover reached Le Paradis at about 6 p.m. with only one casualty. D Company covered the withdrawal of the remainder of the battalion. Although under close infantry fire and the fire of two tanks Major Heygate would not leave until he was personally satisfied that the wounded of Headquarter Company had been carried clear. He then made an obverse victory sign and withdrew. The Bois d'Aval was very thick, and after the heavy rain the ground was like a morass, which made the tracks difficult to distinguish. The retirement through the wood was therefore treated as a night operatoin. On debouching from the eastern edge of the wood the detachment was met by artillery and small arms fire. Maps were vigorously waved and the fire, which had been brought down by our own troops, quickly ceased, but not before four men had been wounded. The detachment then went on to Vieux Berquin, where Captain Archer's company reverted to the command of the 1st Battalion. The 5th Battalion took up positions at Le Paradis and Strazeele Station.

While this withdrawal was taking place the second-line transport near Strazeele had been attacked by hostile tanks. One tank put a shell through the lorry driven by Lance-Corporal Peacock and wounded him. Soon afterwards Private Richardson of the 1st Battalion gallantly ran through machine-gun fire to this vehicle and retrieved it.

The withdrawal of 6th Brigade on the left meant that the enemy was free to move against the left flank of the 1st Battalion. B Company, near Verte Rue, was pressed back to Vieux Berquin by attacks supported by tanks, artillery and mortar fire. The gap created allowed the enemy to move round in rear of A Company, at the eastern edge of the Bois d'Aval. C Company at the north-east corner of the wood was also attacked. This was the situation when darkness fell.

With night came orders to withdraw. Calais had now fallen. The Belgian Army had capitulated. A plan to attack southwards in conjunction with the French had failed. With all almost lost, Lord Gort had decided to march for Dunkirk. The organisation of a defensive perimeter round the port of Dunkirk had begun on May 26, and into it the various divisions were withdrawn as they were pressed inwards by the battle.

The Queen's Own Brigade had now been engaged with the enemy or on the move for nine days. This period included three days' fighting at Oudenarde, three days of battle in the Forest of Nieppe and only one night in which the men had been able to sleep. For much of this time the issue of hot meals had been very difficult; in fact many of the companies had lived mainly on dry rations. The men had been wet through by the heavy rain in the early morning, and their boots and socks were still sodden. And now they were faced with a retreat of 50 miles to Dunkirk!

The 4th Battalion found great difficulty in breaking contact with the enemy, who had by this time crossed the canal in large numbers. A Company on the right were twice intercepted when withdrawing through the forest. On the first occasion Captain Andrews led a charge through heavy fire, destroyed two enemy machine-guns with grenades and put the Germans to flight. On the second occasion, with only 19 men remaining, he led an attack which again scattered

the enemy. At about 11 p.m. the remnants of this company reached
Le Paradis, whence they retreated with the 1st Battalion. On the left
C Company managed to get clear only after Captain Taylor had led
a counter-attack and driven the Germans on his front back across the
canal. Lieutenant Yarrow was taken prisoner in this action, while
Lieutenant Allen was captured when withdrawing with B Company
to Le Paradis. By the time that the battalion reached Fletre the mass
of men and vehicles, which was cluttering up the road, made
organised control impossible. Colonel Chitty therefore ordered the
companies to make their way with the stream of traffic to Dunkirk.
During the retreat from Le Paradis it was unfortunately necessary
to leave some of the wounded behind. Captain Cooper, the Medical
Officer, and his staff volunteered to remain with them. They were
taken prisoner.

The companies of the 5th Battalion formed up at Strazeele Station
at about 10 p.m. and set out on the march for Dunkirk. The marching
column remained practically intact until, when passing through
Poperinghe soon after 6 a.m. on the 29th, the congestion of vehicles,
animals and pedestrians became too dense and the men were told
to jump onto such passing vehicles as could carry them. The transport moved with the battalion until the column was well beyond
Fletre. Abandoned lorries then began to block the road, and the
vehicles were left behind with orders to catch up later. Captain
Wonnall and his drivers made a few miles' progress, but at dawn the
road was blocked as far as the eye could see. So, having immobilised
their vehicles, they continued the journey on foot.

The 1st Battalion was the last to retire, Colonel Sharpin receiving
the written orders at about 9.15 p.m. A Company in the centre was
the first to withdraw, followed by B on the left and D in reserve. C
Company and the Carrier Platoon, now reduced to four vehicles,
were ordered to act as rear-guard. There was some delay in delivering
the orders to C Company, but eventually Lieutenant Axford took
them to Major Woodhouse in a carrier. Lieutenant Axford then went
on with a message to Lieutenant Churchill's platoon, which was
holding on in a burning building. Lieutenant Dann's platoon could
not be reached as it was cut off by German armoured vehicles, and
Private Handley volunteered to take a message to it. He succeeded
in getting through and then remained to guide the platoon back to
Vieux Berquin. Ultimately Major Woodhouse managed to extricate
his company and catch up with the remainder of the battalion.

When Colonel Sharpin arrived at Fletre he could find no sign of
any representative from Brigade Headquarters to give him the route
for withdrawal. After some delay he decided to put his battalion on

FRANCE: TYPES OF THE QUEEN'S OWN DURING THE WINTER 1939-1940

FRANCE: MUSICIANS OF THE QUEEN'S OWN IN 'WEEK STREET'

to transport with orders to make northwards for Godewaersvelde, a town about a mile north-west from Mont des Cats. Lieutenant Christofas was sent to lead the column, and Colonel Sharpin travelled in the rear truck. The road was soon blocked by bombed and abandoned vehicles however, and at a level crossing it was found to be completely impassable. As dawn was approaching, Colonel Sharpin decided to take the men off the vehicles and to continue the journey on foot. The men were organised as far as possible by companies, and the process of threading their way through the congestion began. At about daylight the first two parties, with which were Colonel Sharpin and Captain Moss of the 1st Battalion and Captain Andrews and Lieutenants Bensted and Brand of the 4th, were overtaken by the enemy and captured. There was a sharp fight, during which Major Woodhouse was killed; Captain Whitty, although wounded, got away on the pillion of a motor-cycle. The remainder of the battalion went on to Monts des Cats.

It had been intended that 44th Division should make a stand at Mont des Cats, but by 11 a.m. (May 29) the Germans had brought heavy artillery fire on to the hill, and orders were given for the position to be abandoned and for the troops to continue the retreat to Dunkirk. Some remnants of the 1st Battalion set off on foot for the coast while others, under Major Lovell, travelled in a convoy of vehicles as far as Poperinghe. Here the vehicles had to be abandoned owing to the congestion of traffic; this party reached the Dunkirk perimeter on foot early in the evening. Dive-bombing attacks occurred at a number of points on the road, and it is astonishing that there were not many casualties amongst the slow-plodding, weary troops.

On the long beaches round Dunkirk the officers of the three battalions collected what men of The Queen's Own they could find and organised them into parties for embarkation. Many of the men were so tired that they could barely stand on their feet, but their behaviour and discipline were perfect. Though they were quite bewildered by the whirl of events which had befallen them in the last ten days, they could still joke amongst themselves as they shared a tin of 'bully' or sardines with their comrades. They patiently waited in long crocodiles, which stretched out into the sea to reach the many small motorboats, yachts and launches which had been called into service to assist with the embarkation. Occasionally they looked anxiously over their shoulders towards the sand dunes to see whether the German troops were there. Often they fell flat on their faces as German aircraft flew over and dropped bombs and machine-gunned the dunes

THE WITHDRAWAL FROM DUNKIRK

and beaches. But mainly they waited steadily for their turn to climb into the little boats, which plied to and fro between the shore and the destroyers, trawlers, pleasure steamers and other large craft lying-off in deeper water. Miraculously there were no heavy seas to interfere with the process. But bombing attacks on the little boats were continuous, two of the waiting destroyers were hit, and night had come before all of the brigade could be taken off. Throughout the day the troops had been greatly heartened by the presence on the beaches of Brigadier Whitty.

Embarkation began again at dawn on May 30 under cover of a slight mist. Some parties moved along to the mole, where they embarked direct into destroyers. Others continued to wait on the beaches to be taken off by the little boats. About 150 of The Queen's Own crowded into the *Dorien Rose* and reached Folkestone late that night. Most of the remainder were evacuated before dark, but a few had to spend a second night amongst the dunes. On arrival at the ports of England ship-loads of troops were quickly sent by train to various destinations in the southern counties.

44th Division began to concentrate at Oxford between June 3 and 8 and then at Hall Green, Birmingham. By the 19th nearly all of the survivors had rejoined, but it was still difficult to assess the casualties. On that date the 5th Battalion had a strength of 23 officers and 546 other ranks; the strength of the 1st Battalion was 16 officers and 432 other ranks; the 4th had only 381 of all ranks effective. The number of casualties in The Queen's Own Brigade during the last thirteen days of May was thus approximately 1,000 out of the 2,400 who had gone into action.

A list of awards gained by The Queen's Own during the war is given in Appendix A. Amongst them will be found the name of Corporal Bell of the 4th Battalion, who, after being captured in the Forest of Nieppe, escaped by feigning death. He remained in the forest for five days living on rum and leaves, a somewhat unusual diet, and then made his way to Frevent, where he stayed for five months. From there he went south in a goods train to Marseilles, crossed into Spain and reached the British Consulate in Barcelona in February 1941. He was repatriated from Gibraltar in April 1941.

The words of Lord Gort on the conduct of the troops of the B.E.F. will bear more weight than any of mine. He said: 'Most important of all, the campaign has proved beyond doubt that the British soldier has once again deserved well of his country. The troops under my command, whatever their category, displayed those virtues of steadiness, patience, courage and endurance for which their Corps and their Regiments have long been famous.'

Altogether over 338,000 British and French troops were evacuated from Dunkirk Harbour and the beaches round it between May 28 and June 4. For two more weeks it was hoped that the French might by some means continue the struggle. But they were unable to stem the German tide. On June 17 the French asked for an Armistice, ordering all their forces to cease fighting. On June 22 an Armistice between France and Germany was signed.

CHAPTER 8

In Defence of England
June 1940 to August 1942

1. *224 Infantry Training Centre*

During the spring of 1940 the Infantry Training Centre at Maidstone had been busily making soldiers out of civilians, and the 'phoney' war in France had perhaps induced a feeling almost of peace-time routine. The first rush of expansion had subsided, the camp at Sandling Park was still being built, and most of the officers and other ranks continued to live in billets in the town.

This sense of routine was rudely shaken by the evacuation of the B.E.F. from Dunkirk and the defeat of France. The British Commonwealth was left alone in the war against Germany, and invasion seemed to be not only likely but inevitable. Almost overnight the defence of Maidstone became of the utmost importance. The C.O. (still Colonel Kerr) made swift plans. At all approaches to the town defence posts were dug and—as soon as the material became available—camouflaged and wired. One week-end all the pneumatic drills in the town were commandeered and were kept going day and night in the construction of anti-tank obstacles. These defences were manned by such recruits as had fired a rifle and had handled a Bren gun. Later on the Local Defence Volunteers—soon to be known as the Home Guard—became responsible for many of the defences.

In this precarious situation the safe-custody of the Regimental Colours became something of a problem. Before proceeding to France the 1st, 4th and 5th Battalions had obeyed King's Regulations and had sent their Colours to the Depot for safekeeping. The Colours of the old 3rd Battalion were already there. But the I.T.C. was now nearer to the enemy than most of the battalions. An arrangement was therefore made with the Vicar of Maidstone—then Canon A. O. Standen—that on receipt of the signal that the invasion had begun all the Colours would be taken to him at All Saints' Church, where he would lay them on the altar in sanctuary.

On the days immediately following the evacuation from France, several parties of officers and men, who had become separated from the battalions of the Regiment during the retreat, arrived at the I.T.C. tired and hungry. They were all received with the greatest consideration and were fed and accommodated until the various battalions could be located. In this work the Adjutant, Captain Stitt, and the Messing Officer, Major Leigh, gave invaluable help.

Home Office Regulations concerning aliens were now drastically tightened up, and at twenty-four hours' notice a temporary camp for one hundred male internees had to be provided in barracks. The miniature range and the adjoining tennis court were wired in, and mattresses, bedding and other necessities were provided by the Quartermaster, Captain Brooks, with prompt dexterity. The following afternoon, in taxis and buses and escorted by police, the aliens arrived and were ushered into their enclosure by R.S.M. Heath. An officer with some knowledge of German was appointed *Lagerfuehrer*. One of the internees was a key man from an important aircraft factory, and urgent but unavailing telephone calls were made by the manager for his release. The aliens were quiet and well-behaved, but Colonel Kerr was not sorry to see them depart to the Isle of Man after a stay of about two weeks. This had been one more distraction from the task of training recruits; others were to follow.

While the construction of the ground defences was still proceeding, air battles in the skies over Kent—the early stages of the Battle of Britain—were mounting in intensity. Aircraft, our own as well as German, were being shot down in ever-increasing numbers. These crashed aeroplanes attracted souvenir-hunters no matter how inaccessible they might be, and compasses, maps, revolvers and especially clocks disappeared before the overworked R.A.F. Intelligence Officers could arrive. The losses were serious from an Intelligence point of view, and guards had to be provided from the I.T.C. to keep looters away from the wrecked aircraft. These guards, which went out at short notice in lorries, had to remain on the site until the R.A.F. Recovery Section arrived—usually some days later. An effective N.C.O. had to be sent in charge of each guard, and so every guard meant one instructor less for the training of recruits.

On one big day, when nearly twenty aeroplane guards were already out, a further call came through. No more instructors could be spared, and a recruit lance-corporal was sent in charge. The aeroplane—a German one—was not badly wrecked and was lying in a hop-field, where hop-picking was in full progress. The lance-corporal cleared away the hoppers, posted his sentries, and then—contrary to the strict orders in force—climbed into the cockpit and proceeded to try the controls. Inevitably he pressed the firing button, and all the guns fired. Luckily the aeroplane was tilted downwards and the bullets entered the ground just in front of it—but the hop-pickers left the field in record time.

Sometimes the pilots of the crashed aircraft would bale out and land safely in the Maidstone area. When they were German they were brought to the I.T.C. and lodged in the guardroom, and at times the cells were full of them.

For some weeks the I.T.C. was responsible for the ground defence of West Malling[1] and Detling aerodromes, both of which were being bombed by the German Air Force. It is difficult to conceive a worse training area for recruits than an airfield under enemy attack, especially when those recruits are accommodated in section posts scattered round that airfield. These warlike activities —manning defence posts and guarding crashed aircraft, airfields and internees—played havoc with the training syllabus, and it could only be hoped that what the recruits lost in basic training they gained in practical experience.

When, in the autumn of 1940, the R.A.F. had won the Battle of Britain, the Germans changed their tactics to dropping bombs on London and other large towns. Maidstone received less than its expected share of these, but one morning the first of a stick of bombs fell on the barrack square, the remainder coming down in the grounds of the Kent Education Offices just beyond the barrack wall. Apart from making a very large hole, breaking many windows and scaring the band boys of the 1st and 2nd Battalions, who were being paid out, this bomb did little damage; and the lime trees, though shedding some leaves, continued to stand in their sevens round the parade ground.

By this time 'Invicta Lines,' the new hutted camp in Sandling Park, had been completed and occupied. The cookhouses and ablution huts were equipped in a manner of which the older soldiers had never even dreamed, and many were their caustic comments on the decadence of the modern recruit, who had to have hot water to wash and shave in and had to eat his food off a hot plate. The opening of the new camp coincided with a decrease in the number of calls for aeroplane guards and, as the work on defences was now completed, the I.T.C. was able to carry on with its proper task of training recruits with less interference.

In the spring of 1941 Colonel Kerr, who had completed his three years in command, departed to be C.O. of the 5th Battalion, and Major A. A. Eason was promoted to succeed him. But 'Willie' Eason did not command for long. By the autumn of 1941 fewer men

[1] See map of Kent facing page 52.

were available for the Army intake, and it had become impossible to send reinforcements to battalions of their own Regiment just where and when they were wanted. A system of 'linked' Regiments was therefore evolved, by which The Queen's Own was linked with the Queen's Royal Regiment (West Surrey). The I.T.C.s of the two Regiments were amalgamated, that of the Queen's Regiment moving from Guildford to Maidstone. The combined I.T.C. then became 13th Infantry Training Centre at 'Invicta Lines,' with Lieutenant-Colonel D. C. G. Dickenson (The Queen's) commanding. This amalgamation continued until after the war was over. Colonel Eason went to Guildford to command the A.T.S. Training Centre: C. R. Baker went as his R.S.M.

Thereafter the I.T.C. ceased to be a purely regimental concern. A few rooms in the barracks at Maidstone still remained as the Regimental Depot, and in them the Comforts Fund—now called the Prisoners of War Fund—was administered by Captain Love, and the Colours and regimental property were kept in safe-custody.

2. The 4th and 5th Battalions

After its evacuation from Dunkirk, 44th Division completed its concentration at Hall Green, Birmingham, during June 1940, under the command of Major-General F. Mason-MacFarlane. The Queen's Own Brigade was reorganised, the 1st Battalion being replaced by the 2nd Buffs. Reinforcements arrived for the 4th and 5th Battalions from 224 Infantry Training Centre and 50th Holding Battalion at Dover. Colonel Chitty left the 4th Battalion to command the 1st, and Major Ffinch was promoted in his stead.

On June 29, 44th Division moved to the Gainsborough and Epworth area of Lincolnshire, where the 4th and 5th Battalions, now up to strength, were in reserve for the defence of the Wash–Filey sector of the coast of England. For four months they trained hard and long. Many of the troops had only a few weeks' soldiering and, with the country in danger of invasion and thousands of barges waiting to bring the Germans across the Channel, it was essential to get them trained quickly. On September 7 the code word 'Cromwell' was received. This meant that an invasion was imminent, and the two battalions were on their toes ready to move; but the invasion did not occur.

44th Division moved to Kent on November 4, and 132nd Brigade took over the defence of the sector of the coast between Dungeness and Hythe. The 4th Battalion was about Littlestone and the 5th about Dymchurch. The troops were all glad to be in the south, where leave to their home towns was easier, and they put their backs into the reorganisation of the beach defences which was made necessary by the approach of winter. Anti-barge scaffolding had to be erected, wiring renewed, and many new posts made to replace those which had become flooded. For recreation in the evenings the troops went into Hythe and Folkestone on the New Romney–Hythe–Dymchurch Light Railway, which had been requisitioned for the purpose. During this period Brigadier C. B. Robertson relieved Brigadier Steele in command of the brigade.

After a winter on the beaches the brigade pulled out to the Canterbury area at the end of February 1941, and went into reserve. Training in counter-attack and other mobile operations followed. Colonel Brown was promoted to command 219 Brigade; Colonel Kerr was transferred from 224 I.T.C. to replace him in command of the 5th Battalion. A short spell on the beaches about Reculver, Herne Bay and Whitstable then ensued. In reserve once more in May and June, the brigade carried out a strenuous period of training, including a three-day exercise in Ashdown Forest in co-operation with tanks.

In July, 132nd Brigade moved back to the coast in a semi-beach-defence role at Kingsdown, Walmer and Deal. Both the 4th and 5th Battalions were accommodated in billets. The first few weeks were devoted to range-shooting and handling of weapons near the beach sector itself, but after that, the invasion season being over, battalion, brigade, divisional and even corps exercises were held. The brigade, as part of 44th Division, was now in XII Corps, commanded by General B. L. Montgomery, and the corps exercises were consequently hard and lengthy. Only small maintenance parties were left on the coast. The remainder of the troops spent many days and nights away on these exercises, which included 'Binge,' 'More Binge,' and 'Great Binge,' and the Battle of Plucks Gutter. Cultivation sometimes made the exercises lack reality, but 'Monty' never did. He would arrive suddenly at the hottest period of the 'battle' on the pillion of a motor-cycle and 'paint the picture.' The officers of the 4th and 5th Battalions are not likely to forget his 'no smoking and no coughing' lectures in a Maidstone cinema, and all ranks will remember his weekly six-mile cross-country runs in full battle order.

On September 25, 1941, the Prime Minister, Mr. Winston Churchill, who had inspired the country after the fall of France, visited Walmer Castle as the newly-appointed Warden of the Cinque Ports. The 5th Battalion provided the Guard of Honour with the band of the Regiment in attendance. There was another ceremonial day on December 17, when H.R.H. The Duke of Kent, as Colonel-in-Chief, honoured the troops with a visit and inspected them on parade on Coldslow Sports Ground.

The band of the Regiment, mentioned above, consisted of the boys of the 1st and 2nd Battalions under Bandmaster McKenna from the Regimental Depot. Later, this band visited other battalions of the Regiment at home to entertain the troops and to play on ceremonial parades and at regimental functions.

132nd Brigade moved back into reserve again in February 1942, and went into billets in and around Maidstone. New carriers and other equipment had now begun to arrive, and there were rumours of an impending move overseas. Colonel Ffinch left to take up an appointment at Southern Command; Lieutenant-Colonel C. G. S. McAlester (K.O.S.B.) assumed command of the 4th. A New Zealand battalion was also stationed near Maidstone, and the officers of the 4th and 5th Battalions met some of the officers of their allied Canterbury Regiment at a sherry party in the Depot Mess.

On April 4, 1942, 44th Division moved to the Burgh Heath and Chipstead area, near Croydon. This was well known as 'Mobilisation Corner' and was in fact very suitable for it, being close to London and to Kent. Embarkation leave, inoculations and kit inspections followed. On May 14 His Majesty The King visited 132nd Brigade. This meant that departure was imminent. The brigade entrained at Tattenham Corner, on Epsom racecourse, on the 31st for Liverpool, where the 4th Battalion embarked in the *Laconia* and the 5th in the *Orontes*.

3. *The 1st Battalion*

When the 1st Battalion left 132nd Brigade in June 1940, it was accommodated in the premises of the Aston Villa Football Club. The offices were placed at the disposal of the battalion, and the men slept on palliasses under the stands. Although the ground itself could not be used for football, it was very useful for baseball and physical training, and Church Parade was held there on Sunday the 23rd. Colonel Chitty came from the 4th Battalion to assume command, and on the 29th seven officers and 408 other ranks arrived as reinforcements, bringing the strength of the unit to 27 officers and 878 other ranks. The battalion was responsible for the defence of seven aerodromes as well as of a large sector of the Birmingham district. In fact, the area was so extensive that the Commanding Officer had to reconnoitre it in an aeroplane. As the vehicles and much of the equipment of the battalion had been lost during the evacuation from Dunkirk, civilian buses were provided for this mobile role; but an attempt which was made to put into working order four machine-guns, which had stood for years at the entrance to Castle Bromwich fair-ground, was unsuccessful.

On July 7 the battalion moved by rail to Corsham, twenty miles west of Marlborough in Wiltshire, where it was accommodated in Rudloe Camp. Its role was the defence of V Corps Headquarters against air-borne attack, and the companies dug and wired defence positions and co-operated with the Home Guard in defence exercises. At the end of July some vehicles and equipment and a few automatic weapons were received, and the task became easier. Colonel Chitty was then ordered to transfer 13 warrant officers, 11 colour-serjeants, and 25 serjeants to the 6th and 7th Battalions and the newly-raised 9th Battalion of the Regiment to bring them up to establishment. The necessary promotions were made, but this was a heavy demand on the reserve of potential leaders in the battalion. In addition R.S.M. Benbow left to become Quartermaster of the 9th Battalion. C.S.M. Bonwick became R.S.M. By this time the drums and fifes had arrived from 224 I.T.C., and the Corps of Drums had been successfully re-formed when the Colonel of the Regiment, General Sir Charles Bonham-Carter, who had recently returned from Malta on account of ill-health, visited the battalion on August 21. Other visitors were General Sir Edmund Ironside, the C.-in-C. Home Forces, and General Sir Claude Auchinleck, the G.O.C. Southern Command.

At the beginning of September the expected German sea-borne invasion appeared to be imminent, and the battalion was sent to the Isle of Wight to defend the vital sector of the coast from Ventnor to St. Helen's. The journey was made by rail and the Lymington–Yarmouth Ferry. The battalion was billeted in houses and requisitioned buildings at Brading, Lake, Bonchurch and Bembridge. This move brought it into 12th Brigade (Brigadier D. M. W. Beak, V.C.) and back into 4th Division, which it had left in May. The Battle of Britain was now being fought in the air—on one day five enemy and three of our own aircraft crashed on the island— and the troops stood-to morning and evening. On September 23 'Cromwell' was cancelled, and the battalion relaxed to more peaceful occupations.

During this period 117 reinforcements arrived from the Dorset Regiment and 99 from 224 I.T.C., and a Reinforcement Company was formed. In November, thirty-two Bren guns were received to make up deficiencies. On Remembrance Day a service was held in

GENERAL SIR CHARLES BONHAM-CARTER, G.C.B., C.M.G., D.S.O.,
COLONEL OF THE QUEEN'S OWN FROM SEPTEMBER 1936 TO SEPTEMBER 1946

MR. WINSTON CHURCHILL, THE PRIME MINISTER, INSPECTS A GUARD OF HONOUR OF THE 5TH BATTALION AT WALMER CASTLE ON SEPTEMBER 25, 1941

LIEUTENANT-COLONEL J. M. HAYCRAFT SHOWS H.R.H. THE DUKE OF KENT A 2-INCH MORTAR BOMB DURING THE DUKE'S VISIT TO THE 1ST BATTALION AT CAMBERLEY ON MARCH 16, 1942

Brading Church; this was a fitting occasion on which to remember the casualties—10 killed, 18 missing and 167 prisoners—which the battalion had suffered in May. The wounded were also remembered.

The danger of invasion having passed for that season, the battalion moved on December 9 to Highclere, near Newbury, where it had a counter-attack role to deal with enemy air-borne landings in north Hampshire. The troops were accommodated in billets and huts. For the first month the battalion was left mainly to itself and was able to carry out a few local exercises and field firing at Bulford, Netheravon and other places on Salisbury Plain. After Christmas, however, General Montgomery, then commanding V Corps, set three corps exercises, the last of which continued for seven days. As some measure of relaxation, January 16, Corunna Day, was a holiday, and the dance band came from the I.T.C. to give a concert in the N.A.A.F.I. canteen.

In the early months of 1941 there were several changes among the senior officers. Major Lovell, who had been second-in-command for nearly a year, went to command 44th Reconnaissance Battalion. Colonel Chitty left to take over the 70th Battalion of the Regiment; Major Haycraft was promoted from second-in-command of the 9th Battalion to succeed him, and Major Brooke became second-in-command. 'Monty' took over XII Corps in south-east England; Lieutenant-General E. C. A. Schreiber became the Commander of V Corps.

At the beginning of August 1941, the battalion moved to Salisbury Plain, where Headquarters were at Eastover Copse, near Andover, and the companies were deployed in defence of the fighter airfields at Chilbolton, Ibsley, Middle Wallop and Worthy Down. The big event at this time was a seven-day exercise called 'Bumper,' which was in fact described as Army Manœuvres. In October the battalion, now at Chilbolton Camp near Stockbridge, was ordered to mobilise for a move overseas, and the troops were sent on embarkation leave. This order was cancelled however, and the battalion moved by M.T. to huts and billets in Camberley instead. It was there that Brigadier Beak said farewell to the troops before his departure to Malta as G.O.C., and Brigadier R. G. W. Callaghan assumed command of 12th Brigade.

After an absence in Scotland of two weeks, during which it took part in combined operations training at Inverary, the battalion returned to Camberley in time for Christmas. It was now part of the mobile reserve for the south-east of England, with Worplesdon as its concentration area. On March 6, 1942, His Majesty The King inspected 12th Brigade, and on the 16th H.R.H. The Duke of Kent honoured the battalion with a visit. This heralded the departure of 4th Division to Scotland to join Amphibious Force 110, which had assembled there to prepare to launch a sea-borne offensive at some future date.

The move to Scotland began on April 8, when the battalion left Camberley by rail for Catterick. On the 11th the journey was continued by march route, and on the 17th the battalion arrived at Hawick, where it was accommodated in huts and requisitioned wool mills. For the first week of June the battalion went to Castle Toward for combined operations training and co-operation with tanks. At the end of the month 'Rajah' Brooke was promoted to command a battalion of the East Surrey Regiment; Major Archer became second-in-command. During July a course on the new 2-pounder anti-tank gun was organised, and Company Battle Training, including a new battle drill, was carried out. This battle drill greatly speeded up the issue of orders in the field.

Early in August, as a culmination to the training, the mammoth exercise 'Dryshod' was carried out by Force 110. Orders for a move overseas were then expected and, during the lull, 200 men were sent to Kelso to assist the farmers in harvesting their crops. Destiny stepped in however. It was many weeks before the battalion actually sailed.

4. *The 6th and 7th Battalions*

On their return from France the remnants of the 6th and 7th Battalions assembled with 36th Brigade Headquarters and the 5th Buffs at Gunnerton Camp, Wark-on-Tyne. Reinforcements soon began to arrive to bring them up to establishment; for the 6th they came from the 50th Holding Battalion; for the 7th from the 50th Holding Battalion and from the Royal Norfolk Regiment. Captain Nixon's and Captain Newbery's parties rejoined, and new Commanding Officers were posted. Lieutenant-Colonel B. Howlett, whom we have known as Brigade Major of 132nd Brigade, assumed command of the 6th, with Major Knatchbull as his second-in-command. Lieutenant-Colonel D. C. S. Bryan, who had won a D.S.O. whilst serving with the 2nd Battalion in Palestine in 1938, assumed command of the 7th; Captain Newbery was promoted to be his second-in-command. 36th Brigade then became an Independent Brigade under Brigadier A. L. Kent-Lemon, who had obtained his Regular commission in 1914 while serving in the 3rd (Special Reserve) Battalion of The Queen's Own.

On July 11, 1940, the brigade moved and, after one night in billets at Blackburn, arrived at Malvern. There the 7th Battalion went under canvas in Blackmore Park. The remainder of the brigade was billeted in houses, schools and halls in the town. The newly-raised 9th Battalion of the Regiment was also in Malvern at that time, and General Sir Charles Bonham-Carter visited all three battalions on August 13, inspiring the troops to do their utmost in the defence of England should a German invasion occur.

At Malvern the role of 36th Brigade was that of a mobile reserve to deal with any enemy parachutists who might land in the area. For this purpose requisitioned civilian lorries were allotted. There were a few Bren guns in each battalion, and all ranks were armed with a rifle and fifty rounds of ammunition, but there were no other weapons. None of the reinforcements had fired a course on the open range before they arrived, and only five rounds of ammunition for each man was available for practice.

It was essential to get the men fit and efficient as soon as possible and although Cadre Courses to train junior leaders were held, individual training had to be ignored to a large extent in order to devote more time to tactical training. Though some of the exercises were therefore purposely ambitious, they were all carried out with the greatest enthusiasm by the troops. Consequently when the code word 'Cromwell' was received on September 7 both battalions were ready to give a good account of themselves. The brigade stood-to for forty-eight hours, and it was some disappointment to the troops that it was a false alarm. Soon after this the Germans bombed Coventry, and parties were sent to clear away the rubble in the town.

In November, 36th Brigade moved by road to South Wales, the 6th Battalion going into billets at Haverfordwest and the 7th at Pembroke. The billets were empty houses and mills, and the 6th Battalion messed in the Market Hall of Haverfordwest, which was also used for battalion dances. The operational role of the brigade was to prevent enemy landings on the Pembroke peninsula from the sea. Many training exercises up to brigade level were carried out with this in view, including several long marches ending in night counter-attacks. By this time both battalions had received more Bren guns and had been issued with some 3-inch mortars and carriers, and they would have offered considerable resistance to an invading force. With the coming of Spring, 1941, the scope of the exercises expanded, and several divisional schemes were held. The severe bombing of Pembroke Docks occurred on the night of May 12, 1941, and the troops carried out rescue work during the raid itself and clearing up operations after it. Corporal Paterson of the 7th Battalion

L

gallantly rescued two civilians who were buried in the cellar of a burning hotel.

On May 31, 1941, the brigade was ordered to mobilise for the tropics, khaki drill clothing was issued and embarkation leave was granted. This was just eleven months after the battalions had re-formed and spoke well for the standard of efficiency which had been reached in so short a time. The order was eventually cancelled, and the brigade moved to Inverary in Scotland for training in combined operations instead. Before this move General Sir Charles Bonham-Carter paid a second visit, dining with the officers of the 6th Battalion at the Castle Hotel, Haverfordwest, on July 2 and inspecting both battalions on parade on the following day.

The move to Inverary was made on August 15 and 16 by rail to Gourock and thence by sea. 36th Brigade was now part of Amphibious Force 110, which was forming under Lieutenant-General Sir Harold Alexander and which was joined by the 1st Battalion some eight months later. For the first week the 6th Battalion and the 5th Buffs carried out training in assault-landings from the *Ettrick*, while Brigade Headquarters and the 7th Battalion lived in Duke's Camp. These two parties then changed over. During the next month the whole brigade practised assault-landings in co-operation with Royal Marines, Artillery and tanks. In addition the 6th Battalion lived on board the *Winchester Castle* for a week, during which it carried out an intensive toughening up programme.

The 7th Battalion then became separated from 36th Brigade because its shipping space was required for other troops. While the remainder of the brigade sailed on September 30 in the *Winchester Castle* to Byrnes Camp at Pollockshaw, near Glasgow, to continue its training in assault-landings, the 7th Battalion moved to Johnstone, near Paisley, and went under canvas in a picturesque park. There it carried out exercises with the local Home Guard and one called 'Coal,' for the duration of which it linked up with the remainder of the brigade. At the end of November it moved to Pontypool, some twenty miles north of Cardiff, in order to train with pack animals. The battalion was in billets close to an Indian Army Service Corps Animal Transport Company, and *Pakhal* and *Kajawa* replaced the nautical phrases used in assault-landings; Indian mule-leaders replaced naval ratings as training companions.

By January 1942, the 7th Battalion had joined the 6th in the hutted camp at Pollockshaw. The weather was very cold, fuel was scarce and the camp was badly sited. Even a visit by H.R.H. The Duke of Kent failed to cheer up the troops for long. He toured the camp on January 17 and honoured all companies with a visit, a

Guard of Honour being provided by the 6th Battalion. Training was in no way relaxed during the bitterly cold weather, and several strenuous exercises were held, including a particular brute called the 'Englesham Scheme,' which entailed a night advance across the mountains. Colonel 'Dicky' Bryan was taken off to hospital a very sick man, and Lieutenant-Colonel G. Ingham[1] arrived early in February to assume command of the 7th. It is sad to relate that 'Dicky' died of cancer within a few weeks. A brigade memorial service was held for him on April 19 in St. Columba's Church, Crieff.

In April the brigade marched from Pollockshaw to Crieff in Perthshire, a distance of 63 miles, where both battalions were billeted, the whole of the 6th being accommodated in the Hydro Hotel. Toughening and training in combined operations and raids then took place; in May a large-scale assault-landing exercise, known as 'Schuyt,' was held. By this time both battalions had reached a very high standard of efficiency, and the new commander of Force 110, Lieutenant-General E. C. A. Schreiber, referred to them as some of the finest infantry since the Light Brigade at Corunna.

Major H. O. Lovell (cousin of Major I. R. Lovell of the 1st Battalion) took over the duties of second-in-command of the 6th in April from Major Knatchbull, who became Commandant of Force 110 Battle School at Callandar. In May the new battle drill was introduced into the brigade, and an Anti-Tank Platoon, armed with six 2-pounder guns, was formed in the 6th Battalion under Lieutenant Valentine, the Kent cricketer. In August, as we have already seen, the training of Force 110 was brought to an end by exercise 'Dryshod.' By then the 6th and 7th Battalions had been parted.

---

[1] Now recovered from the illness which had caused him to reliquish command of the 9th Battalion.

CHAPTER 9

The New Battalions
November 1939 to March 1943
8th, 9th, 10th and 70th Battalions

1. The 8th (later 30th) Battalion

FOUR new battalions of the Regiment were raised for the defence of England during the Second World War. These were the 8th (later renumbered 30th), the 9th, the 10th and the 70th (Young Soldiers).

The first of these, the 8th Battalion, was formed from No. 2 Kent Group of the National Defence Companies (N.D.C.), the personnel of which were ex-servicemen, mainly between the ages of 50 and 60, who had enrolled in these companies in peace-time[1] and had been embodied some two months before the outbreak of the war in order to guard vulnerable points, such as power stations, aerodromes and ammunition depots.

Soon after the declaration of war the N.D.C. detachments at Tonbridge, Croydon, Westerham, Edenbridge and Sevenoaks were grouped together and became the nucleus of the 8th Battalion, with headquarters at the Drill Hall, Avebury Avenue, Tonbridge. The battalion was actually formed in November 1939, its first Commanding Officer being Lieutenant-Colonel A. Latham. It was a Home Defence unit, and volunteers between the ages of 35 and 50 were invited to enlist into it for home service for the duration of the war.

In February 1940, the headquarters of the battalion moved to Brasted,[2] and its eight companies guarded such important places as Halstead ammunition depot and West Malling, Biggin Hill and Penshurst aerodromes. Boys of 16 to 18 years then became eligible for enlistment into the battalion, and two Young Soldier companies were formed. Lieutenant-Colonel O. M. Fry, who had been Brigade Major of 36th Brigade in France, took over command for the months of July, August and September. He then departed with these

[1] See page 71. [2] For map of Kent see page 52.

Young Soldiers to form the 70th Battalion. Lieutenant-Colonel W. E. Hewett became C.O. Additional commitments at Westerham, Bletchingley and Tatsfield were then taken over, and in January 1941, the battalion became responsible for guards at Chelsfield and at XII Corps Headquarters at Tunbridge Wells in addition.

On August 26, 1941, Battalion Headquarters moved to Chattenden Barracks at Strood, near Rochester, where the 8th Battalion The East Surrey Regiment was absorbed, together with its commitments on the Isle of Grain. Lieutenant-Colonel E. A. Shipton (Rifle Brigade) assumed command of the amalgamated battalion in November, and on December 2 the title of the unit was changed to the 30th Battalion The Queen's Own.

The 30th Battalion moved to Tangmere, near Chichester, on March 27, 1942. Its commitments in Kent were given up, and it became responsible for guarding the Tangmere Group of aerodromes in Sussex. This was an important role and the battalion, in conjunction with the 9th Canadian Infantry Brigade, took part in a series of exercises designed to test the defences of these aerodromes. In May, General Sir Charles Bonham-Carter, the Colonel of the Regiment, visited the battalion. On July 13 it began to march back to Kent.

The new station was Milton Barracks, Gravesend, where the battalion reorganised as a Mobile Defence Unit. Another move occurred on September 25, this time to Napier Barracks, Shorncliffe, so familiar to many of the Regiment. There the battalion came under the orders of 206th Brigade, which was responsible for dealing with enemy raids on the coast from Dymchurch to Folkestone. Its sector included the Sandgate area, which it defended in co-operation with the 8th Kent Battalion of the Home Guard.

The period in a mobile coast-defence role was doomed to be short, for on November 7 the battalion came under War Office control pending disbandment. On December 13 it moved to Herne Bay, and from then onwards officers and other ranks were posted away. Many of the N.C.O.s went to the 7th Battalion. The last batches were transferred at the end of February to 13th I.T.C. at Maidstone and to the Pioneer Corps. On March 10, 1943, the 30th Battalion was officially disbanded.

2. *The 9th Battalion*

'In view of great pressure the Cabinet has decided to increase the size of the Army for Home Defence, interfering as little as possible with Field Army units. A scheme whereby a very great input will be absorbed by Training, Holding and Home Defence units and sixty more battalions created has been evolved. During June 1940, instead of the normal 70,000 Intake, the figure will be 165,000. In July it will rise to 180,000. The new units will be rather in the form of Kitchener Army units, officers being selected and Regimental Associations, the Corps of Commissionaires, etc., being asked to help.'

Such was the letter which was issued by the War Office to announce the steps that were being taken to meet the threat of invasion after Dunkirk, and which launched the 9th Battalion on its career.

The formation of the battalion began on July 1, 1940, in the Drill Hall at the Depot at Maidstone, where a cadre of 17 officers and 150 warrant officers, N.C.O.s and men from 224 I.T.C., 50th Holding Battalion and the battalions of the Regiment recently returned from France began to assemble. Lieutenant Benbow, the Quartermaster, with transport loaned by the I.T.C., began to draw up the necessary arms, equipment and clothing. Lieutenant-Colonel G. Ingham, who had been Assistant Provost-Marshal with I Corps in France and had been evacuated at Dunkirk, was appointed to command. The R.S.M. was H. Hayward.

On July 8 the cadre went by rail to Malvern, where it prepared to receive the remainder of the personnel. These were 800 militiamen straight from civil life, most of them from the 26–27 age groups. Many of these men came from the Regimental recruiting area of Kent and the south-east of London, and their regional pride was strong. Before the end of July the whole intake had arrived and had been clothed, equipped and accommodated in billets or under canvas. The number of weapons available was small owing to the losses at Dunkirk, but no time was lost in getting down to training. The men were excellent material, and when General Sir Charles Bonham-Carter visited the unit on August 13 he was very impressed by the progress that had been made. One of the company commanders was Captain Michael Joseph, author of a history of this battalion entitled *The Sword in the Scabbard*.

On October 11 the battalion moved south by train to take over the operational role of beach-defence. Its sector, from West Lulworth to Swanage, extended over twenty miles, each company being responsible for some five miles of the coast. It consisted largely of vertical cliffs, however, where a large-scale landing from the sea would have been difficult. The sector was wired and there were a few concrete beach posts, but most of the positions were trenches or weapon pits. Battalion Headquarters and its officers' mess were in Bucknowle House, near Corfe Castle, and the four company head-quarters were at Swanage, Kingston, Tyneham and West Lulworth. The Brigade Commander was Brigadier G. W. (later General Sir Gerald) Templer.

During the winter that followed many difficulties had to be overcome. Some of the concrete posts became flooded and new ones had to be built elsewhere; more billets in the shape of bathing huts and bungalows had to be taken over; and the improvement of the trenches and weapon pits usually meant complete reconstruction. There was little to entertain the men in the villages in the evenings, and travelling film shows and dances were organised in the village halls. In addition wireless sets, gramophones and various indoor games were supplied to remote detachments.

Soon after Christmas all N.C.O.s not in the highest physical category were transferred to other units, the first carriers arrived in the battalion, and some of the deficiencies in weapons were made up. These events started rumours that a move was imminent, and sure enough on February 3, 1941, troop-carrying lorries conveyed the battalion through deep snow to Lambourne and Newbury in Berkshire, where most of the men were accommodated in racing stables. The 1st Battalion of the Regiment was in billets at Highclere nearby. The new role was that of Infantry Battalion in the Support Group of the 6th Armoured Division (Major-General J. T. Crocker), and for this the battalion became mechanised.

At the end of February there was another move, this time to Sharnbrook, near Kettering, where headquarters were at Cobb Hall. Companies were quartered in neighbouring villages, all several miles from Battalion Headquarters. The troops were mainly in billets, though some of them were accommodated in the kennels of the local hunt. With several towns in the vicinity they could see some life in the evenings, but there was little time for relaxation. The battalion at last had its full complement of weapons and transport, and training began the day after the move.

On April 26, 1941, the battalion moved to Shepreth camp, near Cambridge, where it was concentrated under canvas. On May 28 Colonel Ingham was obliged to retire to hospital in Cambridge, and Major Fawcett, the second-in-command, answered for him until Lieutenant-Colonel P. H. Macklin arrived on June 12, in time to command the battalion during two important exercises. One of these was the joint Eastern and Southern Command exercise called 'Bumper,' in which the 1st Battalion also took part. At the end of August the battalion was visited by General Sir John Dill, the C.I.G.S., and on September 12 His Majesty The King reviewed

6th Armoured Division at Lakenheath on the first anniversary of its formation.

In October the battalion moved into billets for the winter, headquarters being at St. Neots, near Bedford, and the companies in four villages nearby. Changes were then made in the establishment of armoured divisions, and support battalions were abolished. This was the beginning of the end as far as the battalion's regimental connections were concerned, for at a conference at the War Office on April 27, 1942, Colonel Macklin was informed that it was to be converted into an Armoured Car Regiment. Officers and N.C.O.s were sent on courses at the Armoured Fighting Vehicle School at Tidworth, and some of the personnel were posted to the 4th Battalion, which was then preparing to go overseas. On July 28, 1942, the 9th Battalion officially became the 162nd Regiment, Royal Armoured Corps.

A year later 162nd Regiment was itself disbanded to supply reinforcements for the Reconnaissance Regiments of Infantry Divisions in 21st Army Group. In this way it came about that many of the members of the 9th Battalion took part in the landings in Normandy in June 1944. Colonel Macklin was given command of a battalion of the East Surrey Regiment.

3. *The 10th Battalion*

The 10th Battalion had its origin in the 14th Holding Battalion. This was formed at Tonbridge in January 1940, and consisted of one company of The Buffs, one company of The Royal Fusiliers and one company of The Queen's Own. At the end of May 1940, this battalion was disbanded. The Queen's Own company moved to the Citadel Barracks at Dover, and from it was formed the 50th Holding Battalion The Queen's Own, with Lieutenant-Colonel R. H. Pigou in command. Drafts were received from 224 I.T.C., at Maidstone; but before the end of June upwards of 500 men had been sent to the 4th, 5th, 6th and 7th Battalions as replacements for the casualties they had lost in France.

Owing to the threat of invasion the function of the 50th Holding Battalion was then changed, and it adopted a role similar to that of the 9th Battalion. Three large batches of militiamen, mainly of the twenty-four age group and excellent material, arrived straight from civil life. Officers and Instructors to train them came for the most part from 224 I.T.C. and, as the recruits were mainly from the Kentish suburbs of London, the county associations were strong.

Whilst at Dover this new battalion saw plenty of hostile action. From the beginning it was under cross-Channel artillery fire, and it witnessed the dive-bombing of Dover Harbour on July 12, 1940. Working parties were several times machine-gunned from the air. A detachment carried out rescue work when the Grand Hotel was bombed. At first the recruits manned the entire perimeter of the defences of Dover. Later, while retaining the western sector which included Shakespeare Cliff and the Folkestone Road, they manned some beach posts near the harbour. During the General Alarm, which began on September 7, the battalion remained dressed and under arms for ten days.

In October 1940, the title of the unit was changed to the 10th Battalion The Queen's Own. Organised as a normal rifle battalion, it moved to the Isle of Sheppey in November and had its headquarters at Minster and companies at Sheerness, Eastchurch, King's Ferry Bridge and Pigtail Corner. It was brigaded with the 7th King's Shropshire Light Infantry and the 11th Gloucesters in 221st Brigade with the role of coast defence, and its experiences during that severe winter were similar to those of the 4th and 5th Battalions, which were also defending a sector of the coast of Kent at that time.

Another move was made in February 1941, when the battalion went with 221st Brigade to join the newly formed Yorkshire County Division. Its role was still that of coast defence, and during that spring and summer it defended a sector from Atwick to Auburn Home and later manned defences at Albrough, Mapleton and Hornsea, headquarters being at The Dell, Hornsea. While there it manned a number of 6-pounder naval guns mounted for anti-tank tasks, and was armed with both ·303 and ·300 Vickers guns. From August to November the battalion was relieved of all its duties in order to carry out training from Leven Camp and later from Victoria Barracks at Beverly. Training was much curtailed, owing to many of the troops being away assisting the farmers to harvest the crops. At one time in fact the entire battalion was employed on digging potatoes.

On November 24, 1941, the battalion became responsible for the defence of the aerodromes at Leconfield, Driffield, Lissett, Catfoss and Hutton Cranswick. It was then armed with both types of Vickers gun, some old Lewis guns and some Blacker Bombard Spigot Mortars. Lieutenant-Colonel C. E. P. Craven assumed command in December, but early in the New Year orders were received that the battalion was to be converted. On February 1, 1942, it officially became 119 Light Anti-Aircraft Regiment, as part of the Royal Regiment of Artillery.

For this reorganisation the battalion went to Chester. The initial training over, 119 L.A.A. Regiment defended the coast of East Anglia about Felixstowe and Lowestoft and then the Yorkshire coast about Spurn Head. In January 1943 Colonel Craven was appointed to command 13th I.T.C. at Maidstone and handed over command to Lieutenant-Colonel J. F. Young, a Gunner, who was destined to lead the Regiment to Normandy in June 1944, with 15th Scottish Infantry Division.

4. *The 70th (Young Soldiers) Battalion*

Young Soldier Battalions, all numbered 70th and consisting of volunteers between the ages of 16 and 18, were formed in most Regiments. Their immediate purpose was to take over guards at vulnerable points and so release men for the Field Army; the long term policy was to train boys for service in the Field Army later on. The 70th (Young Soldiers) Battalion of the Regiment was raised by Lieutenant-Colonel O. M. Fry from two young soldier companies, which had been formed in the 8th Battalion. On September 19, 1940, Colonel Fry marched his two companies out of Brasted to billets in Tonbridge, headquarters being in the Drill Hall in Avebury Avenue. Recruits poured in, and by October 31 the battalion was nearly 1,500 strong and organised into six companies.

Gradually, as the boys became trained, guards at vulnerable points were taken over. Guards were also provided for crashed aircraft in the Tunbridge Wells–Sevenoaks area. By the end of February 1941, the battalion was very scattered, with the latest recruits in huts at Maidstone Barracks, one company at each of West Malling, Detling and Gravesend airfields, and two at Biggin Hill aerodrome. The sixth company was at Shirley Hall, Tunbridge Wells. Headquarters remained at Tonbridge.

On April 12, Lieutenant-Colonel Chitty came from the 1st Battalion to assume command.

In May, headquarters moved to Penshurst, and the company at Gravesend aerodrome was withdrawn to Redleaf nearby. Penshurst then became the hub of the battalion. In September, General Sir Charles Bonham-Carter made a two-day visit there, a sports meeting being held on the second day. The first batch of men to come of age for the Field Army was posted to 13th I.T.C. in November.

After six weeks of relaxation and mobile training at Old Park Barracks, Dover, the battalion returned to Penshurst and the aerodrome guards until the end of April 1942. All its commitments were then handed over to the R.A.F., and the whole unit was concentrated

at Mereworth Park, near Wateringbury. Colonel Chitty was promoted to command the Gravesend Sub-area as a full Colonel, and,
on May 18, Lieutenant-Colonel E. S. Heygate assumed command.
Reorganisation into a 'Home Defence and Young Soldiers Battalion'
then took place, with a Headquarter Company and four companies
each of one cycle and three rifle platoons. Wireless sets and a full
complement of carriers and other vehicles were issued, and training
for a mobile role began.

The first large-scale training exercise was held during the last week
in May. This exercise ended at Aldershot, where the battalion
remained for three weeks, headquarters being at Rushmoor Arena
and companies in billets in neighbouring villages. At the end of this
period the battalion marched back to Kent, covering seventy-three
miles in three days, and went into Boxley Camp, near Aylesford, for
four weeks' further training.

Reorganisation and training for its new role were now complete,
and late in July the battalion took over the operational role of counter-
attack troops for Detling aerodrome. In September a similar task
was taken over at Gravesend aerodrome. At the end of that month
the whole unit moved to Milton Barracks, Gravesend, where it
relieved the 30th Battalion of the Regiment.

This was to be the last move. On October 7 the battalion came
under War Office control for disbandment, and a few days later
the posting away of drafts to other units began, some going to the
7th and 30th Battalions. The final parade was taken on October 24
by the Commander North Kent Area and Colonel Chitty, as Commander Gravesend Sub-area. On November 11, 1942, the 70th
Battalion was converted into 28th Primary Training Centre. This
P.T.C. was itself disbanded on February 20, 1943, after an existence
of only three months.

5. *Note on the Home Guard*

Much distress was felt at the time over the conversion and disbandment of these four new battalions, but the reasons for the changes
are now clear and show that the step was made necessary by the
trend of events. Germany invaded Russia on June 22, 1941, and from
that moment an invasion of this country became improbable. This
meant that large numbers of infantry battalions would no longer be
required to guard our coasts, and as Germany became more and
more involved in her struggle with Russia many of these battalions
became redundant. For this reason the 10th Battalion was converted

to a Light Anti-Aircraft Regiment in February 1942, and the 9th Battalion to an Armoured Car Regiment in July 1942.

As the threat of invasion receded so it became possible to place the responsibility for the defence of England more and more on the shoulders of the Home Guard. On February 16, 1942, service in that Force or in the Civil Defence units was made compulsory for men over and boys under conscription age and, as these men became efficient, Home Guard units replaced Home Defence and Young Soldier battalions in the defence of aerodromes and other vulnerable points. These battalions then became redundant. This was the reason for the disbandment of the 70th Battalion in November 1942, and the 30th Battalion in March 1943.

Furthermore, service in the Home Guard was only part time, and men serving in it could continue with their civilian occupations. So, by disbanding the over-age and under-age battalions and compelling the men to serve in the Home Guard, a saving in manpower was achieved.

A list of the Home Guard units which wore the badge of The Queen's Own can be found in Appendix C.

CHAPTER 10

From Defence to Attack

1st, 6th and 7th Battalions

1. Plans to Land in North-West Africa

UP to the middle of 1942 the posture of all battalions of the Regiment, and indeed that of the whole country, had been one of defence. In August 1942, that attitude changed. Unflinching resistance became daring assault. The German attack on Russia in June 1941, had almost removed the threat of an invasion of Britain, and the Japanese assault on Pearl Harbour in December of that year had brought America into the war on our side. With her powerful legions fighting alongside us we could at last switch our armies to the offensive. The theatre selected for invasion was the north-west coast of Africa.

The troops who were to carry out this operation were those who had been undergoing amphibious training in Scotland. Among them were 4th Division, which included the 1st Battalion, and 36th Independent Brigade, which included the 6th and 7th Battalions. In preparation for the expedition Amphibious Force 110 became the 1st Army; 4th Division became a 'mixed division' by shedding 11th Brigade and receiving 21st Army Tank Brigade in its stead; and 36th Independent Brigade became part of the newly-formed 78th Division, whose other two brigades were 1st Guards Brigade and 11th Brigade (from 4th Division).

It was then that the 7th Battalion received a most bitter disappointment. It was ordered to leave 36th Brigade and become a draft-finding unit, its place in the brigade being taken by the 8th Battalion the Argyll and Sutherland Highlanders. This step was necessary because there was no draft-finding unit in The Queen's Own at that time and, with the 2nd Battalion in Malta, the 4th and 5th just gone overseas and the 1st and 6th about to go, such a unit was now essential. Much distress was felt in the 7th Battalion that, after all its strenuous training, it was to be relegated to the status of a non-operational unit. But, now that the 9th and 10th Battalions had been converted, it was the junior Field Army battalion in the Regiment, and it was for that reason alone that it was selected. Thus, in August 1942, Destiny dealt the Regiment a severe blow at the very time when its prospect was bright.

2. *The Death of The Duke of Kent*

That August was indeed a black month, for during it the Regiment suffered the loss of its Colonel-in-Chief. His Royal Highness The Duke of Kent was killed on August 26, 1942, while flying to Iceland on active service in a Sunderland flying-boat. General Sir Charles Bonham-Carter, as Colonel of the Regiment, sent a telegram to Her Royal Highness The Duchess of Kent to express the sympathy of the whole Regiment. Her Royal Highness sent the following reply:

Coppins
Sept. 7th, 1942

DEAR SIR CHARLES BONHAM-CARTER,

I send you and all ranks of The Queen's Own Royal West Kent Regiment my heartfelt thanks for your kind sympathy in my deep sorrow.

Yours sincerely,
MARINA.

3. *The 6th and 1st Battalions Sail*

Now that the decision to invade North-West Africa had been taken the 1st Army made an end to its training, and the planning staffs got busy. 'Torch' was the code word given to the operation. Only a portion of the troops were required for the initial landings and these, including the 6th Battalion, were sent on embarkation leave in September. For several reasons the expedition was delayed for one month, but by the end of October all was ready.

The 6th Battalion embarked in the Dutch liner *Marnix* on October 20 at Gourock. The troops soon found that they were part of a very large convoy, but strict secrecy had been kept and only the Commanding Officer, 'Swifty' Howlett, was aware of the destination. They knew, however, that they were the spearhead of Britain's new armies, and their selection for this task could only mean that they were Britain's best. There was a delay of several days while the remainder of the convoy assembled in the Firth of Clyde, and then at dawn on the 27th they were steaming fast to the west with the Mull of Kintyre immediately to the north. At last the 6th Battalion had been committed.

*   *   *

4th Division, organised as it was with two infantry brigades and one brigade of infantry tanks, was not required for the initial landings but was retained in Scotland as a reserve. It was not called upon for several months and, after their appetite had been whetted for action, the troops of the 1st Battalion returned to the business of training somewhat reluctantly. In October the division went to Inverary for the exercise 'Moss Trooper,' and again in November for further training in combined operations. Whilst at Inverary in October the battalion lived for a week in the trooper *Ettrick*, and everyone was grieved to hear a few weeks later that this ship had been sunk during the landings in North Africa.

At last the long wait came to an end. In January 1943, the 1st Battalion went on embarkation leave in two parties. On February 19, the warning order for the move overseas was received. On March 5 His Majesty The King inspected 12th Brigade at Stobs. On March 14 the battalion went by train to Liverpool, where it embarked in the *Johan van Oldenbarneveldt*. Early on the 16th the convoy of troopships, warships and five aircraft carriers sailed. The quarters on board were very cramped; there was space for little else but lectures on the topography and climate of North Africa. Gibraltar was sighted on the 21st and, after two torpedo attacks from the air, disembarkation took place at Algiers on the 23rd. The battalion then marched 15 miles to a transit camp in a disused brick factory near Cue de Constantine.

4. *The End of the 7th Battalion*

The 7th Battalion moved from Scotland and out of 36th Brigade on August 20, 1942, and its headquarters opened at the delightful village of Dedham, near Dovercourt in Essex, on August 21. The companies were billeted in neighbouring villages. Within a week a draft of 190 other ranks was on its way back to Scotland to join the 6th Battalion. As this was a particularly good draft, a warm letter of appreciation was received from Colonel Howlett. Other drafts began to go almost immediately, and troops were posted in from 13th and other I.T.C.s. A regular routine of 'holding,' training in elementary subjects and posting drafts out then began. In addition a beach-defence role was taken over and assistance was given to the local Home Guard; but this was all very different from fighting in North-West Africa.

Early in October the battalion moved a few miles to Dovercourt, where it became part of the Harwich garrison, and on January 4, 1943, to Blackburn, where it was accommodated in Wellington and Duckworth cotton mills. Draft-finding then became its sole business. On August 6 Colonel Ingham handed over command to Lieutenant-Colonel J. W. E. Blanch and departed to East Africa to assume a full Colonel's appointment on the Command staff. In March 1944, personnel of the 2nd Battalion joined (see Chapter 16, Section 8), and in May these two battalions were amalgamated.

The transfer of all officers and other ranks of the 7th Battalion to the 2nd occurred at Ulverston in the Lake District, whither the 7th moved on April 21. On May 2, Sir Charles Bonham-Carter inspected the 7th Battalion on its last parade, and on May 3, 1944, it officially ceased to exist. In this way the life of a fifth battalion of the Regiment ended.

PART THREE

WAR: ATTACK

M

CHAPTER 11

The Second Battalion in Malta
August 1939 to June 1943

1. *The First Nine Months of War*

WHILE much of the strength of the Regiment—and indeed of the whole country—had been disposed in defence of France and then of Britain, the 2nd Battalion had been serving in the Mediterranean theatre of war, where it was part of the garrison of Malta. When the war began it was at first feared that Italy would come in on the side of Germany, and the immediate danger was that the Italians would attempt a surprise sea-borne invasion of the island. The defence scheme was therefore based mainly on the defence of the coast, especially of the Grand and Marsamuscetto Harbours, the east coast and Marsa Scirocco Bay. The remainder of the coast, except the north, is made secure from large-scale landings by cliffs. In the north there are many open beaches such as Mellieha Bay, St. Paul's Bay and Ghain Tuffieha Bay, which are excellent places for assault landings; but about five miles inland there is a formidable obstacle provided by nature and reinforced by fortifications. This is a precipitous escarpment called the 'Victoria Lines,' which stretches right across the island from east to west. Not only could batteries sited on this escarpment deal with an invading force from the north, but any tanks which might be landed by that force would fail to penetrate it except through the passes, or 'gaps' as they are called.

To defend Malta there were only four trained battalions of infantry —1st Devons, 1st Dorsets, 2nd Royal Irish Fusiliers and the 2nd Battalion—and one as yet ineffective battalion of local Territorials (1st King's Own Malta Regiment). The K.O.M.R. was allotted the northern end of the island, where the training facilities were greater; the Irish Fusiliers defended the east coast north of Valetta; the east coast south of Valetta was allotted to the Dorsets; and most of Marsa Scirocco Bay and several possible landing-places on the south coast, including Wied Zurriek and Ghar Lapsi, were the responsibility of the 2nd Battalion. The Devons were in reserve at Attard. The coast-defence guns as well as the batteries defending the Grand and Marsa-muscetto Harbours were formidable.

Three miles north of Malta lies the smaller island of Gozo, where there are several bays suitable for large-scale landings. It was realised that this island was a potential springboard for an invader, but no troops could be spared to garrison it and it had to be left undefended.

The K.O.M.R. embodied at St. George's Barracks, on St. George's Bay, after the 2nd Battalion had moved out to the coast (Chapter 5). On August 28, 1939, embodiment having been completed, the Maltese unit moved north to Mellieha. Voluntary recruiting continued, and on September 21 a second K.O.M.R. battalion was formed and began training from a camp on the Delimara peninsula. This was followed a few months later by a third battalion. In the meantime the Malta Auxiliary Corps had been formed, and its personnel had joined the various units before the outbreak of war. The M.A.C.s tackled jobs such as despatch rider, motor mechanic and driver, hospital orderly and mess orderly, and a number of them were attached to the 2nd Battalion. Several of them reported with their own lorries and cars, which had been requisitioned, to bring the M.T. section up to establishment.

By this time the majority of the defence posts in the battalion sector had been constructed. They were all section posts made of reinforced concrete. The beach posts were normally of one storey and camouflaged to merge with the coastal background, while the depth posts were of two storeys and constructed so as to resemble the numerous small sandstone buildings which were dotted about the island. The armament of the beach posts usually included a Vickers gun, a Bren gun and an anti-tank rifle, and the fire-plan was to shoot along the coast wire so as to stop the enemy on the beaches. The depth posts were mainly sited to cover re-entrants or other lines of advance inland. All of the beach posts and a few of the depth posts were supplied with a small searchlight, called a Lyon Light, for which a concrete emplacement was provided on or near the post. The power for this light was provided by a small petrol engine, which was often difficult to start and tricky to keep running. The depth posts were numbered L.1, L.2, etc., throughout the south of the island. The beach posts were referred to by distinctive letters and a number according to their position, such as C.5 (Calafrana 5), B.Z.4 (Birzebbugia 4) and S.O.2 (Marsa Scirocco 2). Later on a number of reserve posts were constructed. These were numbered from R.1 to R.34 throughout the island.

*   *   *

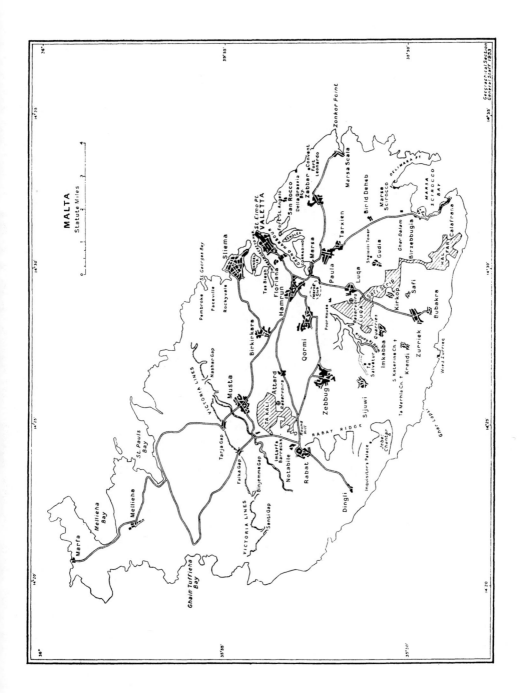

MALTA

Statute Miles

Early in October it was apparent that Italy had no immediate intention of entering the war, and precautions were relaxed on the beaches. Billets were requisitioned for the troops near their battle positions, and the defence posts were manned only for morning and evening stand-to. The headquarters of the battalion moved into a school at Tarxien, with H.Q. Company in various houses nearby. The reserve company moved into billets at Bir id Deheb with its headquarters in the 'Australian Bar.' Near the beaches such places as a block of flats and 'The Tea Pot Hotel' at Marsa Scirocco, Dowdall's Hotel, and a large house called 'Belle Rive' and the 'Smiling Prince Bar' at Birzebbugia were occupied; while the officers of C and D Companies had their Mess in 'Overhills' at Ghar Dalam. At Wied Zurriek the 'Congreve Channel Restaurant' was requisitioned.

On the outbreak of war the Mediterranean had been closed to all British ships not sailing in convoy, and the Fleet had left Malta's Grand Harbour for Alexandria, where it was a thousand miles from Italy instead of a hundred. In October 1939, as things were so peaceful, the Mediterranean was re-opened for British shipping, and convoys were abolished. The larger ships of the Mediterranean Fleet were sent westwards through the Straits of Gibraltar, and Admiral Sir Andrew Cunningham returned to Malta with his destroyers and small craft. This gave the troops a new occupation called 'Contraband Control.' A warship starting off from Malta on patrol took with it a detachment of soldiers. If a ship carrying contraband of war was encountered a party of these soldiers was put on board with orders to take the vessel to Alexandria or Malta for more thorough examination. These detachments were often away from the island for six or seven weeks, and for many of the troops it was a pleasant change from the routine of guards and beach-defence.

In November the status of the Army in Malta was raised to that of a Division. Major-General S. J. B. Scobell arrived as G.O.C. and Lieutenant Flint left the battalion to become his A.D.C. At about the same time a draft of officers and other ranks from the reserve arrived from England.

For the troops, Christmas 1939 was as happy a time as could be expected. The battalion was very dispersed, and Christmas dinners had to be eaten in the most suitable places in the company sectors. The most notable places were the large hall attached to the 'Australian Bar' at Bir id Deheb and Dowdall's Hotel. General Sir Charles Bonham-Carter, as Colonel of the Regiment, and his A.D.C., Lieutenant Buckle, accompanied by Colonel Clarke, visited as many of the troops at dinner as possible. On Christmas night 'Nobby' and

Mrs. Clarke gave a party at their house at St. George's for the officers and their wives. A few nights later the single officers transformed the Mess at 'Overhills' into 'The Bachelors' Arms' and entertained the married officers and their wives in noble style.

After the middle of October a percentage of the troops were able to leave the defence sector each evening for recreation, and married men could visit their families at St. George's or Paceville. There were four cinemas in Valetta for the troops to patronise, and, at Christmas, two special entertainments at the Royal Opera House—a pantomime *The Sleeping Beauty* and the play *French Without Tears*. The latter was produced by the Malta Amateur Dramatic Society. Later, for those who were interested, there was a New Year Race Meeting at the Marsa Racecourse. The battalion team regularly played fixtures in the Rink Hockey League at Rockyvale, and Privates Ludlow and Ovens represented the Army in Malta at football. Those officers who owned cars could still use them so long as they complied with the black-out regulations. Petrol was rationed.

*   *   *

Early in the New Year the battalion moved back to St. George's Barracks and took over the role of Fortress Reserve Battalion from the Devons, who went out to the beach sector at Marsa Scirocco. This was generally looked upon as a good move, because Malta can be very uncomfortable with its cold winds in winter, and fires were available in barracks but not in many of the billets near the beaches. Peace-time routine, including football, boxing and cross-country running, then began, interspersed with training schemes and practices in the new mobile role. As reserve battalion the battle position was at Ta Kali aerodrome, near the centre of the island, from which roads radiated in all directions. These roads were frequently narrow, and considerable knowledge of the island and skill at map-reading were necessary to pilot the whole battalion in M.T. along some of the possible counter-attack routes.

Three of the key personnel left the battalion at this time. Major Pulverman, the Training Officer, went to Egypt for a tactical course. He then took up a Staff appointment there, and two years elapsed before he rejoined. Major Knatchbull, O.C. C Company, departed to England, where he became second-in-command of the 6th Battalion. Captain Martyn, the Adjutant, assumed an appointment at Fortress Headquarters. In September he suffered a severe fall at Lascaris Barracks during the black-out one night and was invalided home. He did not rejoin the battalion until 1945.

On April 2, 1940, Sir Charles Bonham-Carter entered Imtarfa

Hospital suffering from pneumonia. Although he made a rapid recovery, it was apparent that a long convalescence would be necessary. Lieutenant-General W. G. S. Dobbie was appointed Governor of Malta in his stead and arrived by air on April 28. As soon as Sir Charles was fit enough he gave a farewell address to the Malta Council of Government. On May 24 he visited the battalion for the last time, and he left the island with Lady Bonham-Carter in a Sunderland flying-boat from Marsa Scirocco Bay on May 25. Peter Buckle wound up his task as A.D.C. and returned to regimental duty.

*   *   *

Meanwhile, Germany had overrun Holland and Belgium and had invaded France. Anti-British incidents had occurred in Rome, and the possibility of Italy entering the war on the side of Germany had to be faced. The British Fleet returned from the North Sea to the Mediterranean and, with the destroyers from Malta, made its base at Alexandria. Some influential Maltese who had Italian sympathies were interned, and Maltese Bank-notes were issued to replace Bank of England notes so as to limit the consequences of a seizure of currency. On May 21, Count Ciano, the Italian Foreign Minister, announced in a speech in Rome that Italy had decided to fulfil her national aspirations. This could only mean war. In face of this threat a curfew was imposed in Malta from 8.30 p.m. to 5 a.m., air raid precautions were stepped up, and on June 2 the Malta Volunteer Defence Force was formed to deal with enemy parachutists. On June 8 a Maltese named Carlo Mallia made an anti-British speech in Rome, claiming that Malta belonged by right to Italy; in reply an angry Maltese crowd marched through the streets of Valetta on June 9 and broke the marble bust and plaque fixed to the wall of the house in which Dr. Fortunato Mizzi, a former leader of the Italian Party, had lived. This loyalty to Britain undoubtedly sprang from the policy carried out by Sir Charles Bonham-Carter.

With Sicily only sixty miles away, the possibility of an Italian airborne attack on Malta was foreseen. On May 2, wiring of the entire Fortress was ordered, and the battalion began to erect wire round the reserve posts and to block with wire the entrances to Valetta. Two weeks later it was decided to prepare the defence of those areas where parachutists might land in large numbers. The fields of Malta are usually very small. Patches of crops are surrounded by loose, clay-coloured sandstone walls, which criss-cross the island normally in terraces. Because of this the only level and open spaces, on which a large-scale air invasion was probable, were such places as the aerodromes and the extensive playing fields of the United Services Sports Club at Marsa.

There were three airfields. Of these Luqa was the largest but was not quite ready for use. It was situated just over a mile from the base of the Grand Harbour and close to the Marsa Sports Club. Hal Far, in the south of the island near Marsa Scirocco Bay, was small but in running order. Ta Kali, near the centre of the island, was equipped with a reception building and was used by small passenger aircraft, but its perimeter was ill-defined and it was somewhat neglected.

On May 15 the battalion received orders to put Hal Far and Ta Kali airfields and the area of the Marsa Sports Club in a state of defence. That evening three companies hastily left St. George's Barracks, A Company going to the Marsa, B Company to Hal Far and D Company to Ta Kali. Next day these companies began digging and wiring defences in these areas. This was no easy task because Malta is mainly rocky and the earth is shallow, and it is not usually possible to dig down to any appreciable depth. On the 18th, B Company handed over the defence of Hal Far to the Devons and took over the defence of Luqa instead. On the 20th the remainder of the battalion, which had remained at St. George's as a striking force, began to move out to the Marsa. A small rear party was left in St. George's Barracks to safeguard the Colours, silver and other regimental property.

Eventually, Battalion Headquarters and A and C Companies were disposed at the Marsa, with the Officers' Mess in the Club House and the Serjeants' Mess in a pavilion. Posts were dug or erected so that the whole of the levelled area of the playing fields could be covered by fire, and use was made also of a wide ditch that ran through the centre of the grounds. B Company (Major Booth-Tucker) undertook the defence of the aerodrome at Luqa, where they were able to dig down to make slit trenches but had to build up to construct most of their posts. Ta Kali presented a somewhat different picture. There was a large level open space outside the perimeter of the airfield which was also a possible dropping area for parachutists, and the defence of it was a task which D Company (Major Chaplin) could only carry out by the use of Vickers guns. The company headquarters at Ta Kali were in a quaint and massive house called 'Villa Bertrand.' In order to deter enemy aircraft and gliders from landing on all these level areas old lorries, buses and cars as well as all sorts of immobile obstacles were strewn over them.

The defence of Luqa and Ta Kali was a task which extended B and D companies to the utmost. But reinforcements were at hand. On May 21 the 8th Battalion The Manchester Regiment arrived in

Malta and went to the north of the island. The infantry strength in defence of the aerodromes could now be increased, and a company of Royal Irish Fusiliers moved to Ta Kali and a company of Manchesters to Luqa, both coming under command of The Queen's Own Aerodrome Defence Commanders. These companies were made responsible for the static inward defence of both airfields, and The Queen's Own companies assumed responsibility for the outward defence as well as a counter-attack role. At Luqa, B Company occupied positions on the Schinas Reservoirs and others overlooking Kirkop and the Tad Daul Quarries. At Ta Kali, positions were made at 'Round Hill' (beneath the heights of Notabile) and in a clump of bushes near the reservoir west of Attard. Further reinforcements arrived on May 26, when 170 all ranks, who were on their way home on leave from eight regiments in the Far East, were attached to the battalion. These only remained for a week as they were more urgently required in Egypt.

Such was the situation in the battalion when, on the afternoon of June 10, Count Ciano informed the British and French Ambassadors in Rome that Italy would be at war with their countries on the morrow. That evening Mussolini, the Italian Dictator, made a boastful speech to the people of Rome from the balcony of the Palazzo Venezia; in Valetta, General Dobbie broadcast the ill news on the Rediffusion system. Italian air-raids were expected on Malta early the next morning.

2. *At War With Italy*

It was at 6.50 a.m. on June 11, 1940, that the sirens first sounded, and the troops of the 2nd Battalion repaired to their posts and slit trenches wondering how heavy the air attack would be. Ten Italian aircraft were seen flying over the island at about 15,000 feet, chased by white puffs of smoke from anti-aircraft shells. The explosion of bombs was heard. The 'all clear' sounded in half an hour, and it was soon known that Hal Far airfield and Birzebbugia in the Devon's area had been the target. A second raid followed about two hours later, when bombs fell at the Portes des Bombes (the archway at the entrance to Floriana) and at St. Elmo, where an anti-aircraft gun was hit and five soldiers of the Royal Malta Artillery were killed. A motor-launch belonging to Mr. Aveta was also hit and sunk at Pieta. This raid was intended to be an attack on the Grand Harbour, and the Italian radio transformed the launch into a warship. Later in the day attacks were made on Luqa and on Ta Kali, where a stick of bombs just missed the company headquarters. Bombs also fell near the Marsa. Private McKay of the battalion, on guard at Verdala Barracks, was slightly wounded.

There were eight raids altogether on the first day, each of from ten to twenty-five bombers. The bombs were small, 250-pounders, and were very scattered; but each raid was obviously intended as a direct attack on a definite target—either one of the aerodromes or one of the harbours. Seven soldiers and twenty-seven civilians were killed.

To meet this attack Malta's air defences were very weak. There were a few anti-aircraft guns; the newly-formed Dockyard Defence Battery; the Monitor H.M.S. *Terror*, which was moored at Tas Biesh; and three venerable Gladiator fighter aircraft, which were found in packing cases in the Dockyard and were named appropriately 'Faith,' 'Hope' and 'Charity.' In view of this weakness, surprise and gratification were felt when it became known that two enemy aircraft had been destroyed and one damaged on the first day.

In the first week there were thirty similar raids. While the troops were surprised and somewhat relieved at the lightness of the attack, the civilians, thirty-seven of whom had been killed or died in hospital, reacted differently. Men stayed at home to be at hand should their families be bombed. There was a general cessation of routine in the Dockyard; in the towns, shops and businesses were closed. In addition there was a mass movement away from the harbours to remote parts of the island, and the Government scheme for the evacuation of the population from Valetta and the Dockyard area to Attard, Qormi and Zebbug proved to be unnecessary. But bombing did not demoralise the people for long. They soon readjusted their lives, and after a few days normal routine was resumed. When night bombing began they simply took it in their stride. A message of concern from General and Lady Bonham-Carter, who had arrived safely in England, gave the people much gratification.

*   *   *

The news of the Franco-German armistice, which was signed on June 22, was received with agonised interest in Malta. The British were now alone in the Mediterranean, and the nearest British base was a thousand miles away[1] in Egypt. There the British Army was not only five times smaller than that of the Italians but its lines of communication now extended 11,000 miles round the Cape of Good Hope. The anxiety was somewhat relieved by the news that the French Fleet had either been demilitarised and placed under British control or sunk. The situation in England, which was now in danger

[1] See front end-paper map 'The Middle East.'

of invasion, also caused concern, and it was with a feeling of great relief that the words of Mr. Winston Churchill were read in *The Times of Malta:*—'We shall fight on the beaches, we shall fight on the landing grounds . . . We shall never surrender . . .'

At this critical moment General Dobbie, the Governor, issued a message to the garrison: 'The decision of His Majesty's Government to fight on until our enemies are defeated will be heard with the greatest satisfaction by all ranks of the garrison of Malta. It may be that hard times lie ahead of us, but I know that however hard they may be the courage and determination of all ranks will not falter, and that with God's help we will maintain the security of this fortress . . .'

A private soldier, who was defending the aerodrome at Ta Kali, expressed his confidence in different words. 'We are a strong-minded nation' he said, 'and we shall win somehow. We always have before.'

At this time the key personnel in the 2nd Battalion were:

Commanding Officer:	Lieutenant-Colonel V. S. Clarke, M.C.
Second-in-command:	Major W. H. G. Goater, D.S.O., M.C.
Adjutant:	Captain W. E. F. Tuffill.
Quartermaster:	Major A. J. Coe.
Regimental Serjeant-Major:	W.O.I E. P. Flood.
O.C. A Company:	Captain R. M. Allfrey.
O.C. B Company:	Major J. M. D. Booth-Tucker.
O.C. C Company:	Captain R. Butler.
O.C. D Company:	Major H. D. Chaplin.
O.C. HQ Company:	Captain H. E. Scott.

A complete list of officers and warrant officers can be found in Appendix B.

Precautions were now tightened. One platoon of D Company was hastily sent from Ta Kali to Dingli to guard the only radar installation on the island. This detachment was commanded by Captain Buckle and went by the name of 'Bukdet,' being very secret. Another task given to D Company was the closing of three of the 'gaps' through the Victoria Lines in the event of an enemy landing in the north. This meant that the quickest routes to the Falka, Binjemma and Santi Gaps had to be reconnoitred and defence positions constructed there.

The air attacks on Malta continued, and by the end of the first month there had been 65 raids. Eleven Italian bombers had been destroyed. On July 16 one of the Gladiators was shot down and the pilot was killed. This caused great despondency on the island. But four Hurricane fighters then arrived as reinforcements, and on

Sunday, July 28, when most of the people were in church, four enemy bombers were destroyed. Twelve more Hurricanes arrived on August 2, and from then onwards the Italian bombers were always escorted on their raids by fighters. The bombers flew even higher than they had before and, although the air attacks continued, they ceased to be a serious menace. In spite of this the Italian radio announced that H.M.S. *St. Angelo*, the naval shore establishment, had been sunk and that the Maltese coal mine had been destroyed. There is of course no coal mine in Malta.

The troops of the battalion were beginning to feel the strain. Once their defence posts had been constructed there was no more labour, but they had to be constantly on the alert for possible landings by enemy paratroops, and the morning and evening 'stand-to' as well as the frequent night raids deprived them of sufficient sleep. To break the monotony twelve hours' leave was arranged for each man each week. But by this time the expenditure of petrol had been greatly restricted, all private cars had been banned, and buses only ran for a few hours a day and were then greatly overcrowded. Getting to and from Sliema and Valetta was thus something of a problem unless the authorised 'Leave Lorry' was used.

It was about this time that the troops were surprised to find that the names of the streets in Valetta had been changed from Italian to English; Strada Reale becoming 'Kingsway' and Strada Mezzodi 'South Street,' to give two examples. Even the name of the famous Strada Stretta, known by sailors all over the world as 'The Gut,' was changed to Strait Street.

* * *

Meanwhile a second brigade, called the Northern Brigade, had been formed under the command of Brigadier W. H. Oxley. The company at Ta Kali came under its operational control while the remainder of the battalion was in the Southern Brigade under Brigadier L. H. Cox. In order to correct this anomaly D Company was moved on October 14 from Ta Kali to the Marsa. There it became the mobile company and went into billets near the old Tramway Depot, in which the battalion M.T. vehicles were parked. At the same time the Manchester company rejoined its battalion in the Northern Brigade, and E Company, which had been formed from a draft which arrived on September 30, took its place at Luqa. Captain Flint, now returned to the fold, commanded E Company. This meant that the battalion was again responsible for the entire defence of Luqa aerodrome as well as of the Marsa.

At the Marsa, Colonel Clarke was preparing for a siege. He had been through the Siege of Kut in the first World War and he foresaw that supplies of all sorts were bound to be short in Malta before long. He sent parties to scour the area for salvage and organised dumps of wood, corrugated iron and other articles. Serjeant Butcher, the Provost Serjeant, was of great assistance in this work. The polo grounds and spare football and cricket grounds were dug up and planted with potatoes and other vegetables, and the entire bar-stock of the Marsa Club was taken over. These precautions later stood the battalion in good stead when food and fuel for cooking became very scarce.

Preparations had also been made for the autumn rain, which would flood the low-lying area of the Marsa. The temporary posts and the positions in the central ditch had been demolished, and permanent sangars had been built up on the surrounding slopes. These sangars were strongly constructed with Maltese stone, earth and wood, and roofs of corrugated iron had been fixed on them. By mounting Vickers guns and mortars in some of these posts, the whole level area of the Marsa could be swept by fire. Wherever possible, billets had been requisitioned near the posts for the garrisons. Where no billets were available, Elephant Shelters had been constructed.

A new task taken in hand was the training of and co-operation with the Malta Volunteer Defence Force, which later became known as the Malta Home Guard. The Maltese were very keen on this force but, at first, the men were armed only with shotguns and their posts were very flimsy. Later on most of the men were issued with old-pattern rifles, and their posts were made strong with the stone from bombed houses. The first Liaison Officer attached to the battalion was Captain H. Parnis-England, whose area included Luqa, Krendi and Zurriek. But when the battalion became responsible for Hamrun and Marsa instead of Krendi and Zurriek, Captain S. C. Xuereb carried out the liaison duties.

Luqa Aerodrome was now beginning to develop. Concrete posts were erected to replace the temporary posts. The vehicles and obstacles were cleared away from the airfield, and runways were constructed. Wellington bombers began to go out night after night to bomb targets in Sicily and Italy. Reconnaissance aircraft also took off to locate the Italian Fleet and to search for enemy convoys, which were conveying supplies from Italy to Marshal Graziani's army in Libya. Indeed Malta began to retaliate in no small way for the bombs she was receiving from the Italians.

On November 3, three officers of the battalion distinguished themselves in an incident typical of several which occurred on the island at this time. An R.A.F. bomber crashed on a house at Qormi and partly demolished it. The house and aircraft burned fiercely, and frequent explosions of detonated ammunition took place. On hearing cries from the house 2nd Lieutenant Lavington climbed over a wall and entered the burning building. He was joined shortly afterwards by Captains Buckle and Flint and, together with P.C. Camilleri of the Malta Police, they succeeded in rescuing five children from the wreckage. The rescue was carried out in face of considerable danger as the aircraft contained a load of bombs.

Since Italy had come into the war the infantry had been so extended in defence of the airfields and the coast that it had been impossible to find an adequate mobile reserve. This need was at last filled when, on November 10, the 4th Buffs arrived from England in H.M.S. *Barham* and went into a camp at Attard to assume the role of Fortress Reserve Battalion.

Christmas 1940 was a quiet one for the battalion. The troops came from their posts to eat their Christmas dinners in a dining hall which had been erected in a quarry at Luqa and in the club-house, the tramway depot and a garage at the Marsa. Turkeys had been bought some months before and had been fattened up for the occasion, and additional vegetables had been grown at the Marsa to supplement the Army ration. In Valetta the cinemas were still doggedly showing old films, and at the Manoel Theatre the 'Whizz Bangs,' a concert party which had been unable to leave Malta when war was declared and included the well-known personality Christine, presented *Cinderella*. Up to that date there had been some 210 air raids; 200 civilians had been killed; and 40 Italian aircraft had been destroyed and 25 probably destroyed. There had been no casualties in the battalion area, although several buildings had been destroyed by bombs both at the Marsa and Luqa.

A few days after Christmas, A and D Companies moved out to the Rinella beach sector, which was south of the Grand Harbour between Zonkor Point and Fort Rocco. D Company headquarters were in Leonardo Convent (there were no nuns) and A Company headquarters in Della Grazzia Fort. This sector had been unoccupied for some months and, as few billets had been requisitioned, most of the troops lived in their posts.

3. *The Germans Come to the Mediterranean*

Meanwhile important events had been happening in the Middle East. On September 3, 1940, the long-awaited invasion of Egypt by the Italians had occurred, and the British Army, under the command of General Sir Archibald Wavell, had conducted an orderly retreat to Sidi Barrani. The Italians pressed their attack no further. But on October 28 Italy invaded Greece. Britain had guaranteed to give the Greeks all the help in her power, including the sending of supplies from Egypt, and, in order to make the supply route secure, it was important to strike at the Italian Navy. Air photographs taken by aircraft from Malta revealed the fact that the bulk of the Italian Fleet was sheltering in Taranto Harbour. A daring attack was carried out on these ships on November 11 by Fulmar aircraft from the large modern aircraft-carrier *Illustrious*, and photographs taken of the harbour next day showed that three battleships and three cruisers had been sunk. A deadly blow had been dealt the Italian Fleet from which it never recovered.

Nor did the Italians meet with success on land. They found tough opposition in Greece, and early in December the Greeks forced them to retreat into Albania. On December 9, General Wavell, reinforced by formations of the Indian Army and by tanks from Britain, assumed the offensive and quickly drove the Italians out of Egypt. Then, assisted by the Fleet and the R.A.F. based on Egypt and Malta, he forced them to retire to Tobruk and on to Benghazi and El Agheila —halfway to Tripoli—capturing 130,000 prisoners on the way and doing much to even out the difference in numbers between the two armies. These victories caused great rejoicing in Malta.

The satisfaction was short-lived, for on January 2, 1941, it was learned that the German Air Force had arrived in Sicily to bolster up the Italians. This could only mean that the Germans were about to take an interest in Malta. On January 10 there were four alerts in the island after a quiet spell, and a British convoy arriving from the west was dive-bombed by German aircraft. The carrier *Illustrious* was hit and limped into the Grand Harbour with the merchant ships of the convoy, and the destroyer *Gallant*, minus her bows, was towed in past Della Grazzia. The flight deck of the *Illustrious* had been badly damaged; the great ship was berthed in French Creek alongside the peninsula of Senglea and sheltered by Corradino heights. It was realised that the enemy would make every effort to sink this valuable prize while she was in dock, and the work of repair was pushed forward with all speed. At the same time the anti-aircraft defences of the island, which had recently been greatly strengthened, were readjusted to meet the threat.

For five days nothing happened. Then on January 16, as the troops at Leonardo and Della Grazzia were assembling for the afternoon parade, about a hundred aircraft flew overhead in formation at a low height. There was no sound save the roar of their engines, and for some moments it seemed, so confidently did they fly, that these machines must be British. But suddenly, one after the other, they swooped and dived on the Grand Harbour. At the same moment the concentrated barrage of Malta's guns roared out. Fighters from Ta Kali flew straight into the battle. The noise was deafening and continued for some twenty minutes until the last Junkers 87 had dived and dropped its bomb. The *Illustrious*, enveloped in dust, smoke and spray, seemed to have perished; but she had miraculously received only one fresh hit. One of the merchant ships, *The Essex*, was struck in the engine room. There were 38 casualties amongst her crew, but her cargo, mainly ammunition, was undamaged. In order to unload her before the next attack troops of the battalion were called in to help, and the ammunition was removed to safety. The number of enemy aircraft destroyed in this raid was officially given as ten.

On January 17 only one enemy reconnaissance aircraft came over the island. But on that day bombers from Luqa attacked the airfield at Catania in Sicily, and destroyed 60 German aircraft on the ground. This daring feat called for retaliation. On the 18th, formations of enemy aircraft dive-bombed the airfields of Malta for an hour. Ten German aircraft were destroyed.

Next day was Sunday the 19th, and there were two direct attacks on the *Illustrious*, one at 12.40 p.m. and the other in the late afternoon. On both occasions German dive-bombers came in large numbers. They were again met by the deadly barrage and the gallant fighters, and they did not dive so low as they had in the first attack. The ship was hit again but not vitally. 19 enemy bombers were certainly destroyed, making a total of 39 for the three days. It is probable that many more were so badly damaged that they failed to reach Sicily because, for the next few days, enemy aircraft were seen searching the sea for missing comrades.

The town of Senglea was in ruins. Most of the buildings and houses had been hit, and stone and rubble filled the streets. Nearly a hundred civilians had been killed; many more had to be dug out of the debris. Those that survived sought shelter with their relations in the remote parts of the island, and flat carts bearing pathetic little loads of household goods made their way out of the stricken area. Troops of the battalion assisted in the rescue work. For ten days Colonel Clarke, from a headquarters in Senglea Police Station, directed operations day and night, while the men cleared away the debris and the lorries of the M.T. section carried the rubble out of the battered streets. Speed was essential because everybody expected that the Germans would try again.

The enemy had had enough however. There were no more attacks on the *Illustrious*, and on January 23 at dusk she left the Grand Harbour under her own steam for Alexandria. Later on she went to America, where she was fully repaired.

*   *   *

Early in February information was received that German parachutists were in Sicily. It was feared that a large undefended strip of country about Krendi might be selected by them as a suitable landing area. So on the 5th, D Company was hurriedly moved from Leonardo to Krendi, where their platoons were dispersed over a wide area with observation posts at Ta Merhla Church, San Katerina Church and Bubakra. A Company took over D Company's portion of the Rinella sector.

The danger soon passed, for on February 21 the 1st Hampshires and the 2nd Cheshires arrived from Alexandria. The Cheshires became responsible for the ground defence of the Grand Harbour and part of the Rinella sector. The Hampshires took over the Krendi area with three companies, their battalion headquarters being established at Sheleili Tower near Gudia. D Company then moved to the Marsa, where Major Chaplin became second-in-command in relief of Major Goater, who went to open up an O.C.T.U. for Maltese officer cadets at Ghain Tuffieha. Later on 'Jimmy' Goater took over command of the 1st K.O.M.R. Soon after this A and B Companies changed over, A going to Luqa and B to Rinella. From then onwards companies frequently changed places.

At the end of February a Conscription Act was passed in the Malta Council of Government. This Act made all males between 16 and 56 liable for National Service and men between 18 and 41 for service in the armed forces. The first call-up was of the 20 and 21 age groups, and instructors were sent away from the battalion to train them. Later on, in the absence of a training establishment for the infantry, squads of Maltese recruits were attached for ten weeks to the Regular U.K. battalions and were trained by them.

*   *   *

Meanwhile the Germans had been concentrating their attacks on the aerodromes of Malta. Many of these attacks were at night, when the raids were usually preceded by the dropping of parachute flares. All the light anti-aircraft guns and sometimes even the machine-guns of the garrison would open fire at these parachutes until, at times, the sky was full of flares and tracer bullets. Parachute mines, aimed

N

at the harbours, were also dropped in large numbers, and many fell in Valetta, Floriana and Sliema. The main streets became blocked with rubble, and the troops on 24 hours' leave often preferred to spend the night in their posts rather than in the towns. Even so, amidst all this destruction a new cinema, the 'Coliseum,' was opened in Valetta, its first film being *Pygmalion*.

Luqa was bearing the brunt of this onslaught. A barrack hut was demolished, luckily when no troops were in it, and on February 26, 94 enemy aircraft dive-bombed the airfield, damaged three of the infantry posts and wounded six other ranks of C Company. There was a very heavy raid on the night of April 29, when one of A Company's shelters was partially demolished. On May 3, two Elephant Shelters were damaged. So the raids went on, and Aerodrome Defence Headquarters were moved into an excavation in the side of a quarry. This was a bad period for the troops at the Marsa also, for, situated between the Grand Harbour and Luqa, they received many of the bombs which were aimed at those targets. The bombs fell mainly in the vicinity of the Abattoir and Marsa Creek, but there were no casualties. Battalion Battle Headquarters were now in an ancient underground burial place near the Abattoir, and one signaller slept snugly night after night in the hollow hewn for a corpse many hundreds of years before. For most of the troops the loss of sleep caused by the noise of bombs and guns at night was the greatest strain.

The civilians also were getting plenty of bombs. During the period January to May, 1941, over 300 of them were killed. The smallness of this number was mainly due to the excellence of the shelters, which were either existing subterranean vaults and passages or cavities hewn out of the limestone rock. Shelters were also constructed above ground at intervals on the sides of the main roads. One of the worst raids for the civilians occurred on April 30, when many bombs and mines fell in Valetta during an attack on the Grand Harbour. So great was the destruction that fifty men of the battalion were required for several days to assist in clearing the rubble from Kingsway.

The Germans had a distinct advantage in the air over Malta at this time because the machine guns of the Hurricane fighters could not pierce the armour of the Junkers 88s. Nothing but the cannon of Spitfires could do that, and as yet there were no Spitfires on the island. But in spite of its pounding Malta carried on as an offensive base. Wellington bombers went out night after night from Luqa to attack aerodromes in Sicily and Italy; and submarines from Marsamuscetto Harbour took their toll on enemy convoys bound for Libya,

MALTA : B.Z.3, A BEACH POST AT BIRZEBBUGIA OCCUPIED
BY C COMPANY OF THE 2ND BATTALION IN 1939

MALTA : THE MAIN STREET OF SENGLEA—VICTORY STREET—FROM WHICH MEN
OF THE 2ND BATTALION CLEARED AWAY THE DEBRIS AFTER THE RAIDS
ON THE 'ILLUSTRIOUS' IN JANUARY 1941. THE WHOLE STREET WAS IN RUINS,
EVERY BUILDING WAS SHATTERED, AND NOT A SINGLE PERSON LIVED THERE

MALTA: OWING TO THE SHORTAGE OF
PETROL THE INFANTRY TAKE TO BICYCLES

MALTA: THE AID POST IN A QUARRY AT LUQA
WITH A DEFENCE POST IN THE BACKGROUND

where the Germans were now building up a force to assist the Italians.

4. *A Lull in the Air Attacks*

In May 1941, the Germans suspended their onslaught on Malta. The climax came on May 5, when there were very heavy raids. After that the *Luftwaffe* left Sicily, the Italians again took over the air attack on the island, and a period of raids by Italian Savoia bombers escorted by Macchi fighters followed. These raids were comparatively ineffective, for the Hurricane fighters found these Italian machines a very different proposition from the Junkers 88s. The enemy definitely lost air superiority over Malta during this period.

The Germans had gone to the assistance of the Italians in Greece. In reply, troops and supplies had been hurriedly sent from General Wavell's Desert Army to assist the Greeks who, with this help, withstood the German invasion for seven weeks. Their heroic resistance saved Iraq, where a German-inspired revolt fizzled out because it began too early. Baulked in Iraq, the Germans invaded Russia on June 22. This had the desirable effect of prolonging the absence of the *Luftwaffe* from Malta. Coinciding with the invasion of Greece was a renewed enemy attack in Libya, where the German Afrika Korps, under General Rommel, had now arrived to assist the Italians. Weakened by the loss of the men and supplies they had sent to Greece, the British were driven back, and once again the enemy crossed the frontier of Egypt. Tobruk stood firm however, and the German advance was halted.

The return of the enemy to Egypt and the loss of Greece and more especially of Crete meant that convoys to Malta from Alexandria had to run the gauntlet the full length of the channel between Crete and Africa. From Gibraltar to Malta was no better because of the narrow passage, 90 miles wide, between Sicily and Tunisia. Consequently the passing of convoys to Malta now became a dangerous operation. It was fortunate therefore that food rationing had begun in the island on April 7.

On July 25 a convoy entered the Grand Harbour. That night and again the following morning at about dawn the air raid sirens sounded, guns began to fire, and the troops at the Marsa inspected the sky. No air battle developed though the firing continued, and the troops realised that something unusual was afoot. The Italians had launched two sea-borne attacks! Seventeen Italian E-boats and one-man submarines had attacked the Grand Harbour in an attempt to destroy the convoy. But the fire of the harbour batteries and of the Cheshires' machine guns was so accurate that only one of the Italian boats reached the breakwater, where it blew up and destroyed one of the bridges of the outer mole. The other boats were sunk by the guns or the R.A.F. fighters.

By this time petrol was very short on the island, and instead of carrying out the numerous training exercises in M.T. every officer and man was issued with a bicycle, on which his weapons, equipment and ammunition had to be carried. An anti-tank rifle or even a Bren gun is no mean load on a bicycle. The worst point about these bicycles was that so many of them were lost. Should one be left outside a billet or a shop for a few minutes it would be stolen. Eventually every man was issued with a padlock and chain, the bicycles were kept under guard, and when on leave the men had to park them in selected safe places. These precautions had the desired effect. Other innovations were that all steel helmets and vehicles were camouflaged with a zig-zag pattern of grey and brown paint so that they would merge with the irregular stone walls on the island; and patches of yellow cloth were sewn into the flap of the respirator as a means of identifying our own troops.

At the end of July the Central Brigade was formed under the command of Brigadier I. De la Bere; the battalion was included in it. As the Rinella sector was not in the new brigade's area the company was withdrawn from there to the Marsa, where it was billeted in the Poor House.

Malta-based aircraft now began to hit hard at enemy convoys bound from Italy and Sicily to Libya with reinforcements and supplies. Luqa was the bomber base, Ta Kali the fighter aerodrome, and Hal Far the landing ground for the torpedo-carrying aircraft of the Fleet Air Arm. The three airfields had been greatly enlarged, but so many aircraft had been destroyed on the ground that even wider dispersal was sought. At Luqa two reservoirs to the north, the Wied Ta Kandia to the west (*wied* means valley) and quarries to the south meant that dispersal areas could only be constructed to the east and then south, between Gudia and Kirkop, towards Safi. Taxi tracks and dispersal points from Hal Far were at the same time spreading northwards. Before long the dispersal areas of the two aerodromes met and became one. Thereafter the whole locality was dotted with aircraft.

The Navy also was playing its part in the destruction of enemy Libya-bound convoys. Force K, consisting of the light cruisers *Aurora* and *Penelope* and two destroyers, arrived in the Grand Harbour and sallied forth, usually at week-ends, on offensive operations. In their first encounter ten supply ships and two destroyers were sunk.

The small force of submarines based on Marsamuscetto Harbour also created havoc amongst enemy convoys, and Lieutenant-Commander M. D. Wanklyn, in command of the submarine *Upholder*, was awarded the V.C. for his gallantry in numerous attacks.

So many enemy reinforcements were destroyed by these air and sea attacks that the British were able to advance once more in Egypt at the end of November. Before the end of the year Benghazi had again been captured. Early in January 1942, the Desert Army, now called the 8th Army, was at El Agheila for the second time, and the garrison and people of Malta felt that they had played a small part in this victory.

In spite of this success the year 1941 ended on a gloomy note in Malta. Convoys were now few and far between, stocks of most commodities were low, and the shops were practically empty. The shortage of fuel for cooking and heating was especially felt in that cold winter, and the brewing of beer had to be curtailed. In Valetta and Sliema cinema performances became fewer because the electricity was cut off periodically to conserve fuel in the power station. To make matters worse German bombers began to reappear in the sky. Furthermore, Japan was now in the war. Hongkong fell on Christmas day, and Malaya and Singapore were threatened. News came that Major Neve, a stalwart rugby player for the battalion in former years, had died of wounds he had received whilst carrying out his duties as G.S.O.2 Operations in Hongkong.

At the turn of the year Colonel Clarke left on promotion to command a sub-area at Suez; Major Chaplin took over the battalion temporarily. 'Bosun' Pulverman, who had been appointed to command, was still in Egypt, and it was nearly two months before he was able to get through to Malta.

5. *The German Air Force Returns*

At the beginning of 1942 the interrelation between Malta and the campaign in Libya once more became apparent. In this campaign the outcome of each phase depended on the rate at which supplies could reach the two armies by sea. For the enemy this only meant the two or three days' passage across the Mediterranean from Italy or Sicily to Tripoli. But Malta lay across this route, and we have seen how for months past the British air and naval forces based on Malta had been striking at enemy shipping and had enabled the 8th Army to resume the offensive and to recapture Benghazi. In order to subdue Malta, German air squadrons now returned to

Sicily and resumed their heavy raids both by day and night. The number of night attacks especially increased, until there were normally six or eight a night.

Many of these raids were aimed at Luqa aerodrome. The runways there became pitted by bombs, and large working parties were required from the battalion to repair them. Crater-filling parties, at platoon strength with lorries ready-filled with stone and rubble, stood by night and day to fill in craters on the airfield. For the troops it was a time of perpetual strain without the relief of movement or change of scene. Although they had permanent quarters, sanitation and ablutions and regular supplies and rations, their quarters were mostly uncomfortable defence posts, the rations were small and there was no possibility of retiring to positions secure from bombing. Sentry posts and O.P.s had to be manned continuously, and the heavy work on the aerodrome was relieved only by blazing away with twin Lewis guns at an attacking dive-bomber or by a turn at driving a steam roller. Work was continued through the raids unless bombs were actually falling in the near vicinity. Sometimes lone enemy raiders would surprise the working parties in the centre of the aerodrome. Privates Holford and Panton were killed during this period, all the huts and a store in the defence headquarters quarry at Luqa were destroyed, and the officers' and serjeants' messes there were damaged.

During a heavy raid one night several bombs fell on the Abattoir at Marsa, and a large boiler was blown from the furnace and came to rest alongside a post near Battalion Headquarters. Next morning, when the C.O. visited the post, the corporal in command met him, saluted smartly and, indicating the boiler, said nonchalantly, 'This arrived last night, sir.'

In January 1942, Major-General D. M. W. Beak arrived from England, where the 1st Battalion had been in his brigade, to assume the duties of G.O.C.

In February there were ninety-seven night bombing attacks, mainly by single aircraft, and fifty-six daylight raids, mainly high-level bombing of aerodromes, dispersal areas and the Dockyard by small formations of Ju. 88s. On February 11 the destroyer *Sikh* was hit in the Grand Harbour and burnt out, its ammunition exploding. On Sunday the 15th the 'Regent' Cinema in Valetta was hit during a packed performance, and there was heavy loss of life. This occurred during the arrival of a convoy, the first for some time. Many of the ships of the convoy had been sunk on the way, and restrictions were tightened. Bread was rationed at 14 ounces a head a day and was later reduced to 10½ ounces, the ration of sugar and of animal fodder was cut, and buses were allowed to run only in the morning and evening to take people to and from work. 'Victory' or community kitchens were opened, to which the people could take a portion of their rations and receive a hot meal in return.

This continuous battering of Malta had the effect that the Germans desired. Supplies had begun to reach Libya more freely, and Rommel had been able to attack. The British had again lost Benghazi together with all the supplies which General Auchinleck, who had taken over from General Wavell, had been gathering there. And now, in order to keep up Rommel's rate of supplies, the Germans intensified the attacks on Malta's airfields. The raids came in regularly after breakfast, before lunch and at tea time. Sometimes there was one for supper as well. First of all an advance guard of Messerschmitt fighters would arrive, followed by up to a hundred Junkers bombers. Then would come a rearguard of fighters, which would circle round until the bombers were headed for Sicily and would then shoot up any target which presented itself—a fishing boat, a Gozo boat or even an R.A.F. 'mercy' launch. The two boats which ran as ferries between Malta and Gozo, the *Royal Lady* and the *Franco*, were attacked in this way, the former becoming disabled in the harbour at Imjar, Gozo.

By this time our fighter strength was seriously depleted, and the need for Spitfires to shoot down the Ju. 88s was acute. On March 7, thirty-four Spitfires flew in from the aircraft carrier *Eagle*, sixty miles out. The situation improved for a while, and in less than three weeks the enemy lost fifty-two bombers and seven fighters. But by that time most of the Spitfires had also been destroyed.

Grim starvation now faced the garrison of Malta. It was estimated that by May the island would be in danger of famine, and the Royal Navy was ready to take all risks to carry in supplies. On March 20 four merchant ships left Alexandria with a strong escort commanded by Admiral Vian. On March 23 this convoy reached Malta after day-long battles against mass attacks by the *Luftwaffe* and a successful action against the Italian fleet. One merchant ship had been sunk. Two others, the *Pampas* and *Talabot*, entered the Grand Harbour, but the *Breconshire* was disabled and was towed round to Marsa Scirocco Bay. The warships could not refuel in Malta and they turned away, but Force K went out to act as escort to the incoming convoy. This force then dispersed, with the exception of *Penelope*, which had been holed by a near miss and was left behind in dry dock.

The enemy then began intensive dive-bombing attacks on the ships in the harbours. For eight days the battle raged. The *Breconshire* was sunk before any of her cargo could be unloaded. The *Pampas*, damaged on the 23rd, was hit again on the 26th, and little over half of her cargo was unloaded before she sank. The *Talabot* was hit on the 26th and started to burn. Strenuous efforts were made to put the fire out, but her cargo included a quantity of ammunition and, in order to avoid destruction in Valetta, the ship was scuttled on the 29th when only about 1,000 of her 9,000 tons of cargo had been unloaded. Thus the very great majority of the cargo from these ships was lost after they had reached Malta, and there was much criticism of the slowness with which the cargo had been handled. As a result of this loss the rations had to be cut again.

Meanwhile *Penelope* had been enduring all these attacks. Her crew remained on board to fight her guns. The workers rushed out of their shelters after each raid to continue her repairs. The ship became pitted with over 2,000 holes, and the troops gave her the name 'H.M.S. Pepperpot.' The smaller holes were stopped up with pegs of wood, patches were welded over the larger holes, and in two weeks she was repaired, leaving the Grand Harbour under the cover of darkness.

*   *   *

By the end of March 1942, there had been 2,000 raids on Malta. In that month the alerts totalled 372 hours, the equivalent of fifteen days and nights, and 177 enemy aircraft were destroyed or damaged. Amid the din and destruction of these raids Lieutenant-Colonel R. O. Pulverman arrived by air from Egypt to take over command of the battalion. Major Chaplin went to open up a Training Establishment for the King's Own Malta Regiment and later to command a battalion of that Regiment. At about the same time Major Booth-Tucker left to form the Malta Pioneer Group. Major Scott became second-in-command temporarily.

The battalion was at this time disposed with B Company defending Luqa airfield; D Company as mobile company near Imkabba; E Company at the Poor House; and the remainder of the battalion at the Marsa. The company at Luqa undoubtedly had the toughest task. Commanded by Captain Flood, it was bombed every day, except when flying was impossible owing to the weather, and was harassed nightly by nuisance raids. Twin Lewis and Bren gun positions had to be manned continuously for anti-aircraft defence, and the gun teams had no chance of taking cover. Near misses on the posts were a common occurrence, but though there were 804 tons of bombs on the airfield in April the total casualties were only three wounded. On more than one occasion this company had to rush out at night to fill in bomb craters on the runways with a ticking unexploded bomb a few yards away, or to wheel away a blazing aeroplane from the vicinity of a post. One of the most famous and most bombed posts at Luqa was L.Q.9. This post was a fortified windmill, and it accommodated a platoon headquarters as well as a section. The Platoon Commander was Lieutenant Clark and the Section Commander was Lance-Corporal North. On the roof of the post were mounted two Bren guns for anti-aircraft defence, and many were the gallant deeds performed by the crews of these guns against low-flying enemy aircraft. This post received several near misses, but no casualties occurred in it. Eventually it was razed to the ground in order to make space to extend a runway.

The remaining companies now took on a new task. In spite of wide dispersal many aircraft were still being destroyed on the ground, and in order to give them protection from bomb splinters and blast, if not from a direct hit, the next step was to build protective pens into which the aircraft could be wheeled as into a garage. These three-sided pens were constructed with stone from the ruins of nearby villages or with four-gallon petrol tins filled with rubble and earth. The stone and rubble had to be foraged and brought to the site, and the pens were then built up until the walls were five or six feet in height. Colonel Pulverman was in charge of the pen building in the Luqa area; Captain Butler was his staff officer. The labour was arduous and it was considerably slowed down by raids, so it soon became necessary to work at night during moonlight periods as well as to increase the strength of the working parties. The night work was especially tiring, and the troops looked forward to the sound of the bell on the donkey-cart on which the cooks, led by Serjeant Perryman, brought round tea and sandwiches in the early mornings.

Still there was no easing up of the bombing. The attacks increased in severity as Rommel's preparations for a further advance were completed. On April 7 the island had its largest raid. The target appeared to be Valetta, for the Royal Opera House and several other large buildings were destroyed and the Palace, which was the seat of Government, and the Auberge de Castille were badly damaged. So great was the destruction that the terminus for the buses was changed from Valetta to Floriana. During another raid on Valetta, Private Urquhart was killed whilst on leave.

Towards the end of April the enemy turned his attention to infantry accommodation, and on the 25th the Poor House at Marsa received a direct hit. In it the Mortar Platoon of the battalion was sleeping, after working at Luqa aerodrome during the night.

Lance-Corporal O'Sullivan and Privates Edwards and Walker were killed, and Corporal Green died of his wounds two days later. The Poor House was evacuated. During the same attack the barracks at St. George's and St. Andrew's, near Pembroke, were practically destroyed. Most of the families of the battalion were in quarters there and many of them became homeless. Their household possessions were lost, and some of them only had the clothes they were wearing at the time. As there was no alternative accommodation, some of the families were forced to live in shelters, while others made their home in an underground tunnel beneath Pembroke Fort—not a pleasant prospect for the married men when they went home on leave. Serjeant Ellis had previously been wounded at St. George's whilst visiting his family, and Captain Read, now Adjutant, was injured during a raid on Sliema.

When St. George's Barracks were destroyed the rooms in which the Regimental silver and other property were stored were badly damaged. The rooms were therefore vacated, and all the property was moved into an empty building at Paceville. The Colours were taken to Command Headquarters for safe-custody.

The Marsa Basin now became a much-bombed area. Battalion Headquarters, its neighbouring posts, the M.T. lines in the Tramway Depot and several billets were destroyed. Battalion Headquarters, Headquarter Company and the mobile company then moved to the slopes near the Poor House, where some caverns had been excavated in the cliff's face in readiness for such an emergency. Battalion Headquarters itself was in some slit-trenches and had a look-out sangar built of stones with a wooden roof covered with rubble. In here the whole of headquarters were bombed for over an hour. The lips of the bomb craters touched the sangar but, although all communications were destroyed and the personnel were severely shaken, nobody was hurt. After that raid was over R.S.M. Swann magically produced an undamaged bottle of whisky. It was greatly appreciated.

The words of a private soldier, who returned to the battalion after a period of detachment in comparatively peaceful Gozo, show the spirit in the battalion at this time. 'A battalion is a funny thing,' he said. 'It doesn't matter what happens; you can put up with anything when you're with it.'

On April 15 His Majesty The King awarded the George Cross to Malta. The citation read:—'To honour a brave people I award the George Cross to the island fortress of Malta to bear witness to a heroism and devotion that will long be famous in history.' The troops felt that they had some small share in this.

*   *   *

By the middle of April the Germans had complete mastery in the air over Malta. The few Spitfires which had arrived earlier in the month had been destroyed, some of them being knocked out on the ground immediately after they had landed. At one time there were no fighters up for eleven days, and the A.A. gunners took on the defence of the island on their own. They were once in action for sixty-six hours out of seventy-two. Both the Bofors (light A.A.) and the heavy guns then began to run out of ammunition, and their expenditure was restricted. This left the German fighters free to dive low and shoot up working parties and gun-sites. But the gunners stuck it out, and they shot down 101 enemy machines during April. To assist the Bofors, the battalion mounted all available Bren guns about Luqa airfield to fire at diving aircraft. Some Me.s were shot down, others were riddled with bullets, and one crashed at the Marsa, the pilot being taken prisoner. Serjeant Bidmead and Privates Mitchell and Wynne were conspicuous for their gallantry when manning these guns.

General Dobbie resigned as Governor and Commander-in-Chief, and Lord Gort arrived on May 7 to replace him.

And then on May 9 large reinforcements of Spitfires flew in from the American carrier *Wasp*. Elaborate arrangements had been made to receive them at Luqa and Hal Far as well as Ta Kali, so that they would be able to take off again before a raid could come in and destroy them on the ground. As the Royal Air Force was short of ground staff, infantry volunteers had been called for to help to wheel these Spitfires into pens as soon as they arrived, to refuel them and to fit in their guns and ammunition. There was an immediate raid and a few of these precious Spitfires were destroyed on the ground, but most of them were in the air again within ten minutes. On May 10, in the first attack, sixty Spitfires were air-borne, and sixty-three enemy aircraft were destroyed or damaged. Soldiers and civilians stood in the open to cheer as they watched the battle. Air superiority had been regained in one raid, and the Germans lost 200 aircraft in the next week. Moreover, the fast mine-layer *Welshman* steamed into the Grand Harbour on May 10, bringing much-needed supplies and Bofors ammunition. She was met by Spitfires and was unloaded by infantry very quickly. The blockade had been proved to be not impenetrable.

The battalion virtually took control at Luqa during this period. Colonel Pulverman was in the control tower directing operations, and four subalterns—Clark, James, King and Matthewman—regularly 'scrambled' aircraft by firing Very lights when they received orders to do so from the control tower. Eight signallers, under Lieutenant Thatcher and Serjeant Newman, carried on their work amid bombs and dust and never failed to maintain contact between the operations room and the dispersal pens; and despatch riders were always at hand to take messages to the dispersal areas even though a raid on the airfield was actually in progress. The troops refuelled, rearmed and refilled the ammunition belts of the Spitfires, bombed up the bombers, acted as armourer's assistants, filled in craters on the runways, drove steam rollers and dragged away with carriers the wreckage of burnt-out aircraft. It was a welcome change from the routine of air raids.

6. *The Siege*

Although superiority in the air had been gained the trials of Malta were not over. The passage of convoys to the island was still a hazardous undertaking; she could still be starved out. Malta was now in dire need, and the attempt was made in the middle of June to pass convoys from both the east and the west at the same time. The eastern convoy was forced to turn back by heavy attacks. Only two ships from the west got through, a cruiser and five destroyers being lost in the process. The destruction of the convoy in harbour in March had shown the need for speed in unloading those ships which managed to get through, and an elaborate organisation, including working parties from the battalion, was set up. For the first time a smoke screen was in action over the Grand Harbour, and the cargo was discharged by the troops in record time. Later on the submarine *Porpoise* arrived with some aviation spirit and a few other essentials. This was a help but it was not enough.

Rationing now became tighter. Flour was permitted to be used only for making bread. There was no cheese or butter, little margarine and sugar, and eggs (at 2/6 each) were very scarce. The troops had no fresh meat at all, and only a few ounces of 'bully' and a third of a sardine a few times a week. Amenities became scarce also. There was no beer; cigarettes were severely rationed. There was no food in clubs and hostels such as the Vernon, the Knights of St. Columba and the Connaught Homes. Water was short. There was no electric light, which meant that all cinemas had to close altogether; and there was a lack of other entertainments. Leave, up to five days, was still possible in Malta, but the Rest Camp at St. Paul's Bay was closed and food could only be obtained at the Command Fair in Valetta, where the troops could draw their Army rations. It was impossible to get leave out of the island.

In the face of all these difficulties it was refreshing to read in the local paper that 'The Drums of The Queen's Own will play on the square at Luqa at 7.45 p.m. on June 10.' In fact the Band and Drums played at various villages in the island as a morale-raiser for the local population. As every member of the Band and the Corps of Drums was fully employed in his war-time role and many were by this time senior N.C.O.s, this meant considerable extra work, and great credit is due to Colour-Serjeant Watts, who acted in his old role of Drum Major, and to C.S.M. Dunton, who acted as Bandmaster. They produced really fine parades, which earned the praise of Lord Gort, who was a frequent spectator.

The air attack on the island was now confined to raids by fighter-bombers, which dropped armour-piercing and incendiary bombs. Although the raids were light they were dangerous. On June 24 Lance-Corporal Byrne was killed and two other ranks were wounded at Luqa; on July 3 the ablution hut there was demolished, luckily when it was empty. On July 24, D Company headquarters at Imkabba received a direct hit, and Private Kent, the youngest of four brothers to serve in the Regiment, was killed. Six others in the post were injured, including Captain Duffield and Captain MacFarlane. The latter, who was detailed from The Queen's, had to have his leg amputated.

*   *   *

Meanwhile Rommel had been slowly building up his supplies, and on May 26 he had been able to resume his attack in Libya. Tobruk fell on June 21. By July 1 the 8th Army had retreated to El Alamein, 200 miles within the frontiers of Egypt. This success caused the German leaders to revise their plans. They had intended that their next major effort should be the capture of Malta, and the details of an air- and sea-borne invasion had been worked out. But Rommel now requested approval for a pursuit into the heart of Egypt in order to force that country to capitulate. The invasion of Malta was accordingly postponed until the conquest of Egypt was complete. In the meantime the Germans determined to intensify their efforts to starve out the island.

With the enemy once more in possession of the whole of the Libyan coast, it was not until August that another convoy fought its way through to Malta. During the passage from Gibraltar the aircraft-carrier *Eagle*, the two cruisers *Manchester* and *Cairo* and the destroyer *Foresight* were sunk. Four merchant ships entered the Grand Harbour on August 13 amid cheers from the people; the tanker *Ohio* arrived on the night of the 15th with a destroyer and a mine-sweeper lashed to either side and another destroyer towing her in.

Prodigious efforts were made to unload these ships quickly, and the organisation tried out in June was again set in motion. As soon as the cargo was unloaded it was rushed in lorries away from the Grand Harbour to open spaces, which were used as 'clearing houses' where the supplies were sorted. Commodities were then despatched in vehicles to various dumps—called Red, White, Blue and Pink, like the car parks at the Aldershot Tattoo—which were dispersed throughout the island. Some unperishable goods were even spread out alongside the main roads. Traffic was organised so as to leave the important roads clear, and parties were detailed to free these roads of obstacles. Over four hundred men of the battalion worked on these tasks in shifts, day and night. The troops were employed as winchmen, hatchwaymen, stevedores and tally-clerks as well as M.T. drivers, traffic controllers and lorry-loaders. Unloading was completed by August 21.

The arrival of this convoy meant very little increase in rations, for stocks had to be built up for the future and it might be months before another convoy could get through. The ration scale was now 2,000 calories a day instead of the 4,000 which a soldier should get. For a time the civilian scale was as low as 1,200. Not only did the troops begin to lose weight but there was also a danger that they might go stale for want of recreation. There were no cricket balls, no boots or balls for football, and no transport to take players to the playing fields. Indeed petrol was so short that the battalion had to make do on ten gallons a week. Most of this was used up by the C.O. and the Medical Officer in visiting the companies. Numerous flat carts had to be requisitioned for taking water, rations and stores to outlying posts and detachments. These carts would arrive each morning with a Maltese driver and depart in the early evening after eight hours' work.

In an effort to provide colour and entertainment, public investitures and ceremonies of guard mounting and Beating Retreat were organised in Valetta. The Band and Drums of the battalion beat Retreat three times at Castille Place, on the last occasion wearing white uniform. The dance band began playing again at the Vernon Club. Entertainments were organised at the Command Fair, and the R.A.F. and the Royal Artillery presented concert parties at the Vernon Club and the Manoel Theatre. On August 26 a concert party from the battalion presented 'In the Mood' at the Vernon Club. This was organised by the Quartermaster, now Captain Pond, and several of the wives and daughters of the battalion took part.

MALTA : TROOPS CLEAR BOMB-DAMAGE IN VALETTA

MALTA : MEN OF THE 2ND BATTALION AND THE R.A.F.
REFUEL A SPITFIRE IN A PEN AT LUQA AERODROME

MALTA : TROOPS UNLOAD A CONVOY

MALTA : THE BAND AND DRUMS OF THE 2ND BATTALION BEAT RETREAT ON THE PALACE SQUARE, VALETTA, DURING THE WEEK IN OCTOBER 1942 WHEN THE GERMANS FLUNG IN THEIR LAST AIR ONSLAUGHT ON THE ISLAND

On August 9 Major-General R. MacK. Scobie became G.O.C. Malta, in relief of Major-General Beak.

During September the battalion at last moved from the Marsa and Luqa areas, after a stay there of two years and four months. It was relieved company by company by 11th Lancashire Fusiliers, whose billets and posts it took over. The new role was partly mobile and partly beach defence. Battalion Headquarters were at Birkirkara, the beach sector was along the Sliema front to Pembroke, and the mobile companies were C at Zebbug, E at the Cowsheds east of Qormi, and D at L'Imsierah, west of Sliema.

7. The Siege is Raised

Events then moved swiftly in Malta's favour. On August 31, 1942, Rommel began his drive for Cairo, but the 8th Army, now commanded by General Montgomery, stood firm at Alam Halfa (see Chapter 12). In an effort to ensure the safe arrival of their convoys, which were now urgently required to restore their strength, the Germans flung in a desperate air onslaught on Malta. On October 10 the sirens sounded in the island after a quiet period—making 3,000 alerts—and a big raid developed. Air battles and heavy bombings continued for a week, during which 1,400 bombers came over and 114 were destroyed. On the 17th the raids slackened off as suddenly as they had begun, and the enemy resorted to tip and run tactics. Presumably he had had enough. Since June 1940 he had lost 1,000 aircraft.

The date on which Malta's supplies would run out was now estimated as early November. All eyes were turned towards the 8th Army in Egypt for deliverance. 'Monty' struck at Alamein on October 24 and, victory being ours, the 8th Army drove westwards to Benghazi. Help was also on its way from the west. On November 9 British and American Armies landed in North Africa, and the British 1st Army began to advance eastwards from Algiers (see Chapter 13).

Convoys could at last reach Malta in comparative safety. On November 19 the siege was raised when a convoy steamed in unmolested under an umbrella of fighters. The machinery for unloading the ships was put in motion again, and commodities were quickly moved to R.A.S.C. and civilian stores from the dumps. A succession of convoys followed. Rations were increased on December 21. That year the troops had a full-sized Christmas dinner, though not all on Christmas Day itself as the work of unloading ships continued uninterrupted. The major commitment of the battalion was now the new central 'Pink' Dump at Floriana Parade Ground, where the troops worked for three months in twelve-hour shifts day and night, with only short intervals of rest between convoys.

The siege of Malta was indeed over. The mail which had been piling up in Alexandria was delivered, and the troops received parcels which had been sent to them one or even two years before. Many of these parcels contained food for the previous Christmas. It goes without saying that much of it was tantalisingly unfit for human consumption.

Malta now began to hit back in earnest. Not only did the R.A.F. strike at Tunis, Tripoli and other enemy bases in North Africa and shoot down Junkers 52 troop-carrying aircraft on their way to Tunisia but submarines, based in Marsamuscetto Harbour, took their toll. A new 'K' Force came to stay in the Grand Harbour, and its cruisers and destroyers went out on numerous occasions to attack enemy convoys. In addition the R.A.F. began the new game of attacking the railways in Sicily and Italy, and many locomotives were hit and destroyed. Tripoli fell to the 8th Army on January 22, 1943. Next day there were demonstrations of enthusiasm in Valetta, where crowds marched through the streets and Union Jacks and Allied flags were hung from the windows. The tide had really turned at last. The only fly in the ointment was an epidemic of infantile paralysis, which caused all cinemas, bars and dances to be closed to the troops. There were some cases in the battalion, but luckily the disease was quickly under control. This was the only epidemic of any sort in Malta during the war years.

On March 3, 1943, the bulk of the battalion's commitments were handed over to the 11th Lancashire Fusiliers, and a period of training began. Two companies went to Gozo for a week at a time, and a platoon of C Company under Lieutenant Rickcord went to Manoel Island for training in combined operations. E Company was disbanded to bring the other four rifle companies up to strength. Many saw in this a welcome sign that the battalion would soon be leaving the island. It was therefore with a certain amount of envy that the troops heard that the 1st Malta or 231st Brigade, with Major Tuffill as Brigade Major, had left the island on March 30, and that the Band of the battalion had played the regimental marches of the Devons, Dorsets and Hampshires as the ships sailed past the Customs House out of the Grand Harbour.

It was with greater envy that the remainder of the battalion heard that Lieutenant Rickcord's platoon had helped to capture the Kerkenna Islands near Sousse. On April 4 this platoon, as part of a composite force of ten officers and eighty-six other ranks, left Marsa-muscetto Harbour in naval craft and, after a few days at Tripoli, arrived at Sfax on April 13. Leaving there at night they reached the two Kerkenna Islands, Rhabi and Chergui, and landed without opposition to find that the Italian garrison had been evacuated two days before. The force arrived back in Malta on April 19 after an excellent holiday.

Awards for their work at Luqa, including the O.B.E. to Colonel Pulverman, were presented to five members of the battalion by Lord Gort on the Palace Square, Valetta, on April 24. Another big ceremonial occasion was on April 15, the anniversary of the award of the George Cross to Malta, when the Band and Drums, in white uniform, beat Retreat on the Palace Square. The Archbishop of New York, Monseigneur Spellman, watched this ceremony from the Palace balcony.

*　　　*　　　*

At the beginning of April 1943, the battalion said farewell to 233rd (Central) Brigade and moved into the 234th or Western Brigade, which was commanded by Brigadier F. Brittorous, M.C. The other two battalions in the brigade were 2nd Royal Irish Fusiliers and 1st Durham Light Infantry. Battalion Headquarters were at Ta Salvatur, near Sijuwi, two companies were on the Rabat Ridge at The Inquisitor's Palace and Jebel Chantar, and two in billets at Zebbug and Sijuwi. It was confidently believed that this brigade would be the next to leave the island, and this belief grew when the new G.O.C., Major-General W. H. Oxley, visited the battalion on April 22 and Lord Gort inspected the brigade at Rabat on April 25.

On May 9 Colonel Pulverman, who had injured his back, departed by air to Egypt to receive specialist treatment. Lieutenant-Colonel B. D. Tarleton (R.N.F.), who had been second-in-command since January, assumed command. Preparations for departure then began, and on June 11 the battalion embarked with the remainder of the brigade in H.M.T. *Neuralia*. At four that afternoon the ship steamed slowly out of the Grand Harbour, and the battalion saw the last of the island that had been its home for over four memorable years.

Before the battalion sailed the Regimental property was moved from the house at Paceville, where it had been stored since the spring of 1942, and was placed in two rooms hewn into the sides of a tunnel under Pembroke Fort. One of these rooms was accessible from the moat, and much of the battalion sports kit and the property of some individuals were rifled. The band instruments and silver, locked in

o

the other room, remained intact however. These were sent home after the war. The Colours, safe at Command Headquarters, were despatched at the same time. A shield bearing the Regimental crest was left in a prominent position at the Marsa Club, as a memento of the battalion's long tenancy there.

Lord Gort's farewell message to the brigade commander included the following words :— 'We have come now to the end of the chapter which records the part you and the three famous battalions under your command have played in the siege of Malta. When you sail our good wishes will go with you all, and with these wishes we also give the assurance that Malta will not forget you . . . and later history will show how the troops of this garrison added fresh lustre to the traditions of the great Regiments to which they belong. Farewell.'

The dominant feeling amongst the troops was pleasure at the prospect of a change of scenery and operations. But many of them were leaving behind wives and sweethearts, who waved farewell from the barraccas and bastions of battered Malta. They left behind also in the peaceful cemeteries below Notabile Hill, at Pembroke and amid the cypress trees at Pieta, nineteen of their comrades—a miraculously small number under those grim conditions of 'blitz' and siege.

CHAPTER 12

The Fourth and Fifth Battalions
in Egypt and Iraq
July 1942 to September 1943

1. *Arrival at Alam Nayil*

WHEN the *Laconia* and *Orontes*, with the 4th and 5th Battalions on board, left Liverpool on June 1, 1942 (Chapter 8, Section 2) their destination was unknown to the troops. Conditions seemed peaceful enough, but the crowded mess-decks and cabins, the black-out and the possibility of submarine attacks made the voyage far from comfortable. For reasons which are explained in Chapter 11 the Mediterranean was virtually closed, and the convoy of some thirty vessels had perforce to make the long voyage round the Cape of Good Hope. After a few days at Capetown, where the hospitality of the people was so outstanding that the troops were reluctant to leave, the convoy steamed up the east coast of Africa. It became certain that Egypt was to be the destination.

The news from Egypt was bad, and the convoy increased its speed. The *Laconia*, with the 4th Battalion on board, became a lame duck and was forced to loiter unescorted in dangerous waters until she was joined by a slower convoy. Consequently the 5th disembarked at Suez on July 21, two days before the 4th, only to find that they were not expected at Khatatba camp. Nevertheless, the Quartermaster, Lieutenant Blake, believed in self-help, and by the time that the 4th Battalion arrived everything was prepared.

The situation in Egypt in July 1942 was critical. Early in the month the British 8th Army, forced to retreat, had taken up a defensive position extending from the railway station at Alamein on the coast to the impassable Qattara Depression thirty-five miles to the south. Having reorganised, the 8th Army made a series of counter-attacks. The Germans and Italians, under Rommel, took up the challenge and renewed their attempts to break through to Alexandria. By the end of July both sides had fought themselves to a standstill. The 8th Army had weathered the storm, and for a time Egypt was safe.

It was in this atmosphere of urgency that the 4th and 5th Battalions began to learn the technique of desert fighting, how to be sparing in the use of water and, above all, how to navigate in the desert. Anti-tank platoons were formed in both battalions, and the Mortar Platoons were issued with carriers. Topees were gradually put away or lost; the troops began to turn up the end of their shorts and the officers to wear corduroy trousers; and all ranks took to wearing a handkerchief round their neck as a sweat rag. In other words they became warriors of the 8th Army.

The two battalions still belonged to 132nd Brigade of 44th (Home Counties) Division. The 2nd Buffs completed the brigade, which was commanded by Brigadier C. B. Robertson. The key personnel in the battalions were:

	4th Battalion	*5th Battalion*
C.O.	Lt.-Col. C. G. S. McAlester (K.O.S.B.)	Lt.-Col. E. S. Kerr
2 i/c	Major J. A. E. Mulgan (Oxf. Bucks.)	Major J. H. H. Whitty, M.C.
Adjt.	Captain H. B. H. Waring	Captain A. A. Faulkner
Q.M.	Captain F. G. W. Lambkin	Lieut. A. G. Blake
R.S.M.	W.O.I W. Bowler	W.O.I E. H. Creed
O.C. A	Captain C. B. E. Williams	Captain J. D. Stocker
O.C. B	Captain J. H. Winstanley	Major E. G. Young, M.C.
O.C. C	Major P. E. M. Shaw	Captain G. M. Dyas
O.C. D	Captain S. H. J. Roth (R. Sussex)	Captain R. J. M. Phillips

A complete lists of officers in the battalions can be found in Appendix B.

*   *   *

It soon became apparent that Rommel's preparations for a renewal of his offensive were nearing completion, and General Montgomery, who had just taken over command of the 8th Army, inspired all in Egypt to stem the expected attack. The training of 132nd Brigade was suddenly cut short. On August 16 it moved up to the desert to form a defensive flank at the southern edge of the New Zealand Box (defended area) which was under the command of General Freyberg. This Box was at Alam Nayil, just south of the Ruweisat Ridge and some five miles in front of the Alam Halfa Ridge, which was held by the remainder of 44th Division. It was

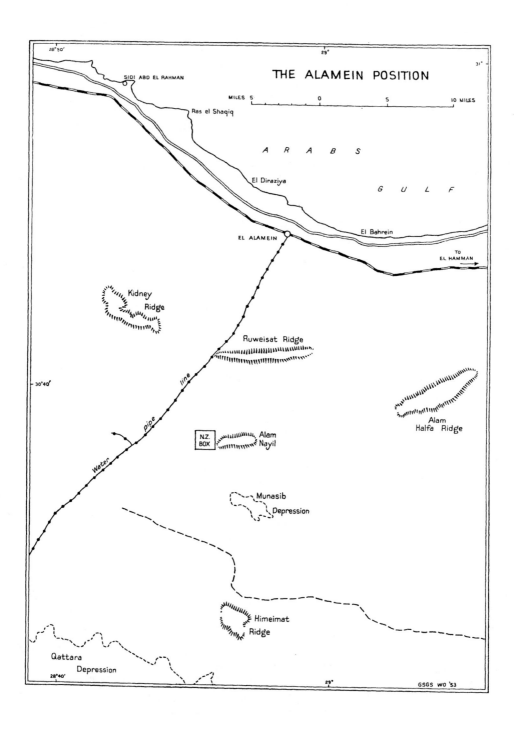

THE ALAMEIN POSITION

MILES 5   0   5   10 MILES

28° 50'

29°

31°

SIDI ABD EL RAHMAN

Ras el Shaqiq

A R A B S

G U L F

El Diraziya

El Bahrein

EL ALAMEIN

TO
EL HAMMAN

Kidney
Ridge

Ruweisat Ridge

Alam
Halfa Ridge

30° 40'

N.Z.
BOX

Alam
Nayil

pipe line

Munasib

Depression

Water

Himeimat
Ridge

Qattara
Depression

28° 40'

29°

GSGS WO '53

virtually the left flank of the Alamein position, for farther south there were only minefields and light motorised units. The 5th Battalion was given the south-east corner of the Box with the 4th on its right.

The positions occupied by the two battalions contained no weapon pits, and the utmost difficulty was experienced in digging them in the rocky ground. Many of the pits had in fact to be drilled with compressors or blasted with gelignite. An attack was known to be imminent, and the troops worked in shifts, night and day. In spite of the heat, the flies, desert sores and the ravages of 'Gyppy Tummy' the position was quickly completed. Water was rationed at one bottle a day. This had to suffice for all purposes except tea at meals. The New Zealanders gave the battalions every assistance, and officers and N.C.O.s were sent to them in turn for a day's attachment to learn about living, patrolling and fighting in the desert. 'Monty' paid a visit to the brigade in a jeep and an Australian hat smothered with regimental badges, including that of The Queen's Own; the new Corps Commander, Lieutenant-General Brian Horrocks, also visited the brigade.

On August 29 the brigade was unexpectedly ordered to take over positions from a New Zealand brigade on the forward edge of the Box. The relief was barely completed on the 30th when, at about midnight, the enemy opened a steady artillery and mortar fire on the positions of both the 4th and 5th Battalions. Fortunately the casualties were very light.

2. *The Battle of Alam Halfa*

This bombardment proved to be the prelude to Rommel's expected advance on Cairo. Under cover of it he made a feint attack against 5th Indian Division on the Ruweisat Ridge. But his main thrust went in, as General Montgomery hoped it would, against the deliberately-weak British left flank. Rommel's armour quickly penetrated the lightly-defended minefield south of the New Zealand Box, and it then swung northwards. It came, again as 'Monty' had planned, against the well-defended Alam Halfa Ridge and was rolled back. Next morning, September 1, Rommel tried again. But the sand was much deeper than he had been led to believe and the resistance far stronger. This attack also failed. Rommel's petrol was now running short, and he took up a defensive position and waited for the British to attack. 'Monty' declined the invitation.

The British plan was to extend the New Zealand Box southwards so as to threaten Rommel's main supply route. This was a track which ran from west to east along the southern edge of the Munasib Depression. The operation was to be carried out by two brigades, 132nd Brigade on the right and 5th New Zealand Brigade on the left, and was to take place on the night of September 3. A New Zealand battalion was given an intermediate objective on the right of 132nd Brigade.

Late in the afternoon of September 2 the 4th and 5th Battalions were relieved in their positions on the forward edge of the New Zealand Box and moved back to 132nd Brigade's concentration area in the north-east corner of the Box. It was dark before some of the companies got back to this area, but their rest was undisturbed. During the night New Zealand patrols probed southwards to the Munasib Depression. Some enemy posts were encountered and, although their strength was not discovered, it was evident that the forthcoming operation would be opposed.

Brigadier Robertson issued his final orders at about 2 p.m. on September 3. 132nd Brigade was to move under cover of darkness to the northern lip of the Munasib Depression, where the battalions would dig in. The brigade would advance with all three battalions forward, the 5th Battalion on the right, the 4th in the centre and the Buffs on the left. Owing to a minefield a mile in width the Buffs would be separated from the remainder of the brigade, and theirs would be a more or less independent advance. There would be no artillery support, but a squadron of tanks would be under brigade command. The direction of the advance would be maintained by the Brigade Intelligence Officer, who would be in the centre between the 4th and 5th Battalions. He was to have a jeep with a red lamp fixed to a pole and shining backwards. Each battalion would have under command two troops of anti-tank guns, a platoon of medium machine-guns of the Cheshire Regiment and a section of Royal Engineers. The latter were to bring large quantities of anti-tank mines and also some compressors for making anti-tank pits during consolidation. Tools for digging in would be taken in vehicles. The carriers of the Mortar and Carrier Platoons were also to move with their battalions, thus bringing the number of vehicles with each battalion to forty. It was realised that, with all these vehicles moving in bottom gear at a slow walking pace, the noise would be considerable.

The issue of these verbal orders ended shortly after 4 p.m. and, as the marching parties had to move off to the assembly area at 6 p.m., there was very little time for the battalion commanders to prepare and issue their own orders. Consequently some company and platoon commanders were forced to give out their orders whilst on the move to the assembly area. A last-minute complication was that the Sappers had not had sufficient time to clear a gap wide enough for vehicles through the minefield south of the New Zealand Box, and in consequence all vehicles had to move off at new timings.

During the move to the assembly area, which was near the southern edge of the New Zealand Box, information was received that the enemy had begun to withdraw from the Alam Halfa area and that the track south of the Munasib Depression was packed with enemy vehicles moving westwards. This news was immediately passed to the troops as they marched along in small groups. Unhappily two enemy fighter aircraft flew over the area soon after this, and there can be little doubt that their pilots saw the numerous little parties of men and vehicles all moving south towards the track which was now the enemy's escape route.

On arriving in the assembly area the troops were issued with a hot meal. Owing to the companies being dispersed, some of the troops did not get their food before it was time to move off to the starting point. From this point two tracks led through the minefield to the Forming Up Position (F.U.P.). These tracks were lit by coloured lamps placed 200 yards apart, white for the Buffs and green for the remainder of the brigade. The Mortar Platoon of the 5th Battalion followed the white lamps in error and eventually took part in the battle with the Buffs.

The advance to the F.U.P. was carried out under cover of darkness, the column threading its way through the minefield along the green lamp lane. Progress was constantly delayed because the mine-lifting parties had not yet completed their work. Eventually the southern edge of the minefield was reached. 800 yards beyond was the F.U.P. This had been marked by white tape, and as each company arrived guides led them to their correct positions. The troops were moving well without any unnecessary sound.

The 4th and 5th Battalions deployed on the F.U.P. into platoon columns fifty yards apart. The 5th Battalion had two companies in front and two about two hundred yards in rear. The 4th had three companies in front and one in rear. When the companies had deployed bayonets were fixed, and the troops sat down to rest. By this time the vehicles were coming up, and the fighting vehicles were directed to positions between the forward and rear companies. The administrative trucks and the tanks remained in rear of the battalions. The noise made by the vehicles had obviously reached the enemy, for he opened a steady mortar fire. But he had over-estimated the range, and most of the bombs went harmlessly overhead.

The advance from the F.U.P. began at 11 p.m. at the pre-arranged pace of 100 yards every two minutes. The going was hard and firm, and there was no check as the platoons moved forward. When the advance had continued for some 2,000 yards the northern lip of the Munasib Depression was reached, and the forward companies halted. So far there had been no sign or sound from the enemy. Suddenly there was a babel of voices. The silence was shattered by a roar of automatic fire, and showers of Italian grenades burst amongst the forward companies. Many of the men were hit, but the leading platoons charged the enemy positions. Colonel Kerr was wounded at the head of one of these charges. Lance-Corporal Eakins of the 5th Battalion silenced an enemy post with his Tommy-gun. Serjeant Jenkinson and Corporal Gallon of the 4th were conspicuous in leading their men forward. Some of the enemy's trenches were cleared and a number of Italian prisoners were taken. By now the heavy machine guns and anti-tank guns of the enemy had opened fire, and the night was lit by bands of green tracer-bullets. Many of the British vehicles were hit and began to burn brightly. The attacking troops were silhouetted against the burning trucks. Casualties began to mount quickly. Further gallant attempts to work forward were of no avail, and for the most part the troops were forced to find what cover they could on the rocky ground.

Efforts were then made to consolidate the positions which had been gained. But to dig in thoroughly in the hard ground was impossible without a large quantity of tools, and most of those which had been brought were burning in the vehicles. The troops therefore lay out in the open exposed to the enemy's fire. To make matters worse, practically all the vehicles of both battalions were now burning and hostile aircraft began to drop parachute flares, which lit up the whole area. Lieutenant Watts of the 4th Battalion and Serjeant March of the 5th distinguished themselves at this critical time by moving amongst their men and encouraging them to remain firm. But, in the circumstances, the only course that could be taken was to withdraw before daylight came.

Casualties amongst the senior officers had been so heavy—in the 5th Battalion alone Colonel Kerr and two of the company commanders, Major Young and Captain Lupson, had become casualties —that the organisation of a withdrawal was difficult. But Captain Dyas, on whom the task of collecting the remnants of the 5th Battalion fell, showed great presence of mind. He first of all led his 150 men, many of whom were wounded, back to a ridge and formed a defensive laager with the tanks. He then went for orders to Brigade Headquarters, where he found that the Brigadier had been seriously wounded. Finally, acting on the orders of the Brigade Major, he took his men and the tanks back to Brigade Headquarters and organised a defensive position there. Eventually the remnants of both battalions reached a ridge some 2,000 yards north of the Munasib Depression. There they reorganised and prepared to withstand a counter-attack.

* * *

The operation as a whole had been partially successful. Although the Buffs had been held up before they had reached the Munasib Depression, 5th New Zealand Brigade on the left had captured their objective. In spite of this most of the German armour escaped the trap and made its way out into the desert. There, however, the Royal Air Force found it in daylight and took a heavy toll. In this way Rommel's much vaunted thrust for Cairo ended not only in a decisive defeat but almost in a rout, and the Battle of Alam Halfa will be known in history as a notable victory.

After an anxious day in their hastily-organised defensive position, the 4th and 5th Battalions and Brigade Headquarters threaded their way in darkness back through the minefield to their bivouac in the New Zealand Box, where the 'left out of battle' had a hot meal ready for them. The losses in both battalions had been grievous, more than half of the troops engaged becoming casualties. Two hundred and fifty of the 4th Battalion were killed, wounded or missing, and of the 5th only eight officers and 225 other ranks remained. The officers killed were Captain Ferguson[1] and Lieutenant Watney of the 4th, Captain Lupson, Lieutenants Bishop and Upton of the 5th and Lieutenant Venning, the medical officer of the 5th.

When a battle ends in victory it is perhaps unwise to criticise adversely. But it will seem to some who read this account of the action, as it seemed then to many who took part in it, that 132nd Brigade had been thrown away in a suicidal attempt to cut off the retreat of the enemy. Others will consider that the risk was justifiable. Whatever the verdict, the operation will remain as a ghastly memory for the survivors.

3. *The Battle of Alamein*

After this bitter experience 132nd Brigade was withdrawn for a short period to the coast to re-equip and to receive reinforcements.

[1] Detached from The Middlesex Regiment.

Brigadier L. G. Whistler took over command of the brigade, Lieutenant-Colonel W. H. Lambert (E. Lancs.) of the 4th Battalion, and Lieutenant-Colonel R. H. Senior (The Queen's) replaced Colonel Kerr, who was in hospital recovering from his wounds, in command of the 5th.

The brigade then returned to the desert and took over positions on Ruweisat Ridge, where life was reasonably peaceful. A little later it moved to the southern end of the Alamein position, relieving first of all the newly-formed Greek Brigade and then 131st Brigade near the Munasib Depression. There it was in close contact with the enemy, and both battalions had periods of patrolling and mine-laying alternating with spells of rest and training.

During the second week of October, the 8th Army began to regroup in preparation for the Battle of Alamein. The attack was to begin on October 23 during a full moon period. General Montgomery's plan was to deceive Rommel into thinking that the blow would fall in the south, while the main attack actually went in to the north near the coast at Alamein. As part of this plan of deception the 4th and 5th Battalions were called upon to make long journeys in lorries eastwards down the desert during the hours of darkness, returning in extended formation when the sun was well up. This heavy movement of transport deceived the enemy into the belief that large concentrations of troops were taking place south of the Alam Halfa ridge, while in reality the bulk of the armour was assembling farther north. Thus occupied, the effects of the disastrous battle of September 3–4 gradually wore off, and the large numbers of reinforcements were assimilated into both battalions.

During the last few days before the battle every man in the 4th and 5th Battalions was told exactly what the plan was, and what part he was to play in it. This time there was no hurried preparation. 44th Division was to support a feint attack by 7th Armoured Division in the south, and to occupy bridgeheads on the forward edge of the minefields when gaps had been made in them by the flail tanks.

In the full moon of the 23rd of October the British barrage of nearly a thousand guns opened, and under this concentration of fire XXX and X Corps advanced to attack in the north. 4th Indian Division launched raids from the Ruweisat Ridge, and 7th Armoured Division broke into the enemy defences south of it, thus achieving the object of inducing Rommel to retain his two armoured divisions on the southern part of the front. For the first two days of the battle 132nd Brigade was not required, and the troops remained in their slit-trenches, waiting. It then became known that 7th Armoured Division had met determined opposition in the broken ground in front of Himeimat Ridge and that its losses in tanks had been considerable. 'Monty' therefore decided to withdraw it in readiness for the climax of the battle. Its place in front of the minefields was to be taken by the 4th and 5th Battalions, who were to move through the gaps which had been made and take over the defence of the bridgehead. This change over was successfully accomplished in bright moonlight on the night of October 25.

When dawn broke on the 26th the two battalions found themselves in positions on a bare, rocky ridge which was completely overlooked by the enemy from Himeimat. Later in the day the Buffs joined them, and the whole brigade consolidated on this exposed position. There was little cover from the intermittent artillery and mortar fire of the enemy, but the troops remained steady. During the next few days the armour moved away to the north and, at night, gramophones with amplifiers, playing 'tank track' music, were carried about in lorries to make the enemy believe that our tanks were still there. This had the effect of bringing unpleasantly accurate enemy mortar fire on to the area, and the losses were heavy. In all the two battalions suffered nearly 100 casualties during the seven days that they held the bridgehead.

Only continuous offensive patrolling at night prevented the enemy from launching a counter-attack, and both battalions took part in several of these successful enterprises. One of them was a fighting patrol of the 4th Battalion, which attacked a strongly-defended enemy post near Himeimat on the night of October 28. The post was successfully destroyed. During the withdrawal Corporal Gilbert, who was commanding one of the sections, was the last to retire through a gap in a minefield. When half-way through he heard a cry for help. The enemy's mortar and machine-gun fire was now heavy, but he returned and found Lance-Corporal Mercer lying badly wounded about 100 yards on the enemy side of the minefield. He carried him to the edge of the minefield and laid him on the ground while he went for assistance. Finding none, he was returning to the wounded man when he heard voices and realised that Mercer had been taken prisoner. It was only this which prevented Corporal Gilbert from carrying his wounded comrade to safety.

During the period spent in these positions north of Himeimat Major Whitty, who had been wounded in May 1940, when he was adjutant of the 1st Battalion, was promoted from second-in-command to command the 5th Battalion.

Meanwhile, to the north, the British and German armour had been fighting a fierce conflict at Kidney Ridge. The British had won this decisive tank engagement, and it was believed that the enemy were about to withdraw. On the night of November 3 patrols from the 5th Battalion probed forward and found that the German positions in front of 132nd Brigade's bridgehead had been vacated. Similar reports came from other parts of the line. Next day 44th Division began to advance.

Rommel was now in full retreat. The 4th and 5th Battalions were formed into motorised columns and drove right through the Himeimat area. It was completely clear of enemy. The columns were then directed to an objective fifty miles ahead, and for the next few days they made a victorious drive through what had recently been enemy territory. Thousands of prisoners were rounded up, and much equipment was captured. Although their part in the battle had been unspectacular, the troops felt that these sweets of victory were some measure of retribution for the losses that had been suffered at Alam Halfa.

*   *   *

Only a limited number of infantry was required in the pursuit of Rommel's defeated army, and 132nd Brigade was withdrawn to Amiriyia, near Alexandria, where it was engaged in guarding prisoners-of-war. On November 30 information was received that 44th (Home Counties) Division was to be disbanded. 131st and 133rd Brigades were to become lorried infantry, and 132nd Brigade was to join another Division. This news was the cause of much regret to the troops, whose loyalty to 44th Division had been very strong. But worse was to follow. 132nd Brigade was also to be broken up, each of the three battalions going to separate Indian Brigades. The Buffs were to join 26th Brigade in Syria; the 4th Battalion were to go to 161st at Qassassin; and the 5th to 21st at Tahag. While the 8th Army sped westwards in pursuit of the enemy to Tripoli and, ultimately, to Tunisia, the 4th and 5th Battalions were destined to go eastwards to a backwater of the war.

4. *Iraq*

Qassassin and Tahag are near Ismailia on the Suez Canal. Both the 4th and 5th Battalions were in fact in camps near the battlefield of Tel-el-Kebir, where the Regiment had fought some sixty years previously. But, as the two battalions were now in different divisions, it was generally expected that their destinies would at last be separate. It was not to be, however. Both battalions were ordered to move to Iraq.

Although the situation in Iraq was quiet at this time, the German offensive against Russia had brought German armies to the Caucasus, and it was considered desirable to reinforce the small British garrison in Iraq in order to safeguard the oilfields and pipelines in that country. Both 5th and 8th Indian Divisions, in which the 4th and 5th Battalions were now serving, were therefore ordered to join the British force in Iraq, known officially as the Persia-Iraq Force (Paiforce). The opening of the New Year, 1943, found both battalions bound for Baghdad.

The journey to Iraq was made by road through the Sinai Desert, Palestine and Syria as far as Rutba. There the heavy rains had made the road impassable, and a wide detour had perforce to be made through the desert. The 4th Battalion accomplished the whole journey of over a thousand miles in ten days, and went into Quetta Camp on the outskirts of Baghdad. The 5th had farther to go and, having been delayed at Tuz Khumatli by the rains for seven days, did not arrive in their camp at Qara Tepe until the twentieth day.

Both battalions remained in Iraq for about four months. The situation remained peaceful, and every opportunity was taken of the lull to get down to recreational training, concerts, rifle meetings and demonstrations. Operational training was greatly interrupted by heavy rains, but it was found possible to carry out a few battalion and brigade exercises. At the end of February 1943 Colonel Lambert left to take up a staff appointment, and Lieutenant-Colonel S. F. Saville came from Egypt to assume command of 4th Battalion. By this time the successful defence of Stalingrad by the Russians had removed the threat of a German advance on Iraq, and in May 1943 it was decided that the size of Paiforce could safely be reduced. This meant that the 4th and 5th Battalions were at last to part, for 5th Indian Division was to go east to India and 8th Indian Division west to Syria.

The 4th Battalion embarked at Basra in the *Empire Trooper* and had an uneventful voyage to Bombay. There it entrained and, after a five-day journey, arrived at Chas, 150 miles north-west of Calcutta, where, living in a tented camp, it had its first taste of the Indian monsoon. Early in September the battalion moved fifty miles south to the Ranchi area. In October Lieutenant-Colonel H. J. Laverty (Essex) assumed command in relief of Colonel Saville, who was posted to a Staff appointment at G.H.Q., Delhi. Soon after this the battalion moved to Burma.

Meanwhile the 5th Battalion had moved by road to Syria, where it trained intensively for four months. The training included 'dry-shod' combined operations, mountain warfare, and a journey by rail to Kabrit, Egypt, for 'wetshod' combined operations training. In August the battalion went again to Egypt by rail, this time to Suez, where it embarked in the troopships *Dilwara* and *Dunera* for exercise 'Outcry.' In September orders were received for a move to Italy, and on the 20th the battalion embarked at Alexandria in three parties in the *Monarch of Bermuda*, the *Empress of Australia* and the *Arundel Castle*.

CHAPTER 13

North-West Africa
November 1942 to June 1943
1st and 6th Battalions

1. *The 6th Battalion Lands in Algeria*

ONE night in October 1942 Captain Courtney of The Queen's Own, with two other members of the Special Boat Section, was cruising off the coast of French North Africa in a submarine. Their orders were to put ashore five members of the American General Staff, including Major-General Mark Clark, at a spot where a white light would be burning. This they accomplished by each launching a collapsible rubber boat from the deck of the submarine. On touching the beach they leaped out and were preparing to get the boats into the shadow of some bushes when a man appeared. A brief conversation followed, and the General decided that a conference must be held next day. Thereupon Captain Courtney got into touch with the submarine by radio and arranged for the party to be taken off the following night.

After this the rubber canoes were carried up to the courtyard of a villa, where the boats were manhandled inside and locked in. The party then adjourned to a small room, where glasses of whisky were 'forced' upon them. Introductions to other Frenchmen followed. The French were clearly on edge and explained that all traffic had been stopped on that stretch of coast so as to keep the meeting secret.

The Americans began their conference with French staff officers early next morning, while the British officers remained hidden in the villa. When the talks were over and all the important Frenchmen had gone, it was decided to leave as soon as it was dark. A strong northerly breeze had sprung up, and there was a deal of surf on the open beach, but it was hoped that the evening shore wind would damp it down.

At dusk, when the party began to get the rubber boats out, the caretaker of the villa rushed up with the news that the police were arriving. The boats were hurriedly bundled back, and the party descended a wobbling ladder into the cobwebby wine cellar. The trapdoor was lowered, barrels were rolled on top and dust was scattered over the boards. This last action was somewhat unfortunate because the dust percolated through and caused one of the party to sneeze frequently and very loudly.

The party remained in the cellar in darkness for two long hours, listening to the Frenchmen above whistling and talking cheerfully to give the impression that they had nothing to conceal. At one point the General could be heard clicking the mechanism of his carbine, until someone whispered 'For heaven's sake put it down,' in a tone not normally used to generals. Eventually the barrels were rolled away, and everyone lent a hand to haul out the boats and carry them to the beach.

On the shore the surf was still nasty, but the whole party cheered up when the submarine appeared in its pre-arranged position. The first boat was immediately floated, waist deep; but just as it was almost clear of the surf an extra large wave arrived and rolled it over. In an instant British and Americans were struggling in the waves, and it was some minutes before everything was rescued, including the all-important paddles. Someone was heard to say: 'Never mind the General; get the paddles.'

Remembering how the natives of the Gold Coast landed their canoes, 'Jumbo' Courtney then decided on a new method. With the help of the shore party, who stripped off their clothes, the boat was carried beyond the first line of surf, which was the worst. The General and his rower scrambled in while the shore party heaved the boat up and, paddling furiously, they managed to surmount a series of waves and get clear. Then Courtney and an American staff officer tried and came to grief. But the shore party hauled them out, shook the water out of them and launched them once more. For a moment it was touch and go, but after furious paddling they won through. Eventually the whole party reached the submarine in safety, handed up their kit and scrambled on to the casing.

Next morning a Catalina flying-boat came out from Gibraltar and settled on the sea close to the submarine. The Americans and their baggage were ferried across to her, and she took them away northwards.[1]

*   *   *

The object of this adventure had been to ascertain how the local French administration was likely to react to the landing of a large force of British and American troops in French North Africa. A firm answer had not been obtained, but it had been apparent that

[1] This episode is more fully described in H. St. G. Saunders' *The Green Beret.*

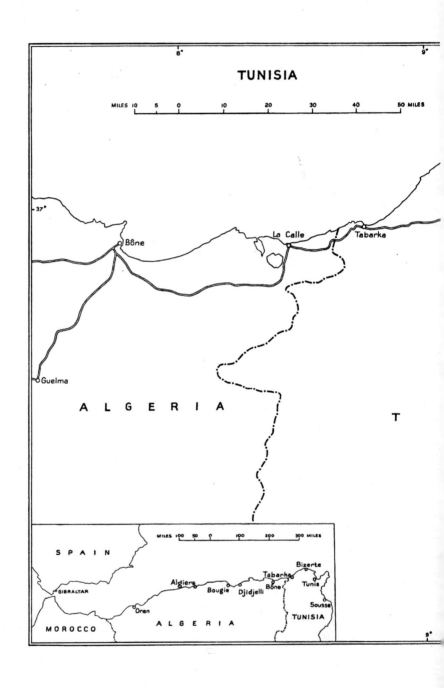

TUNISIA

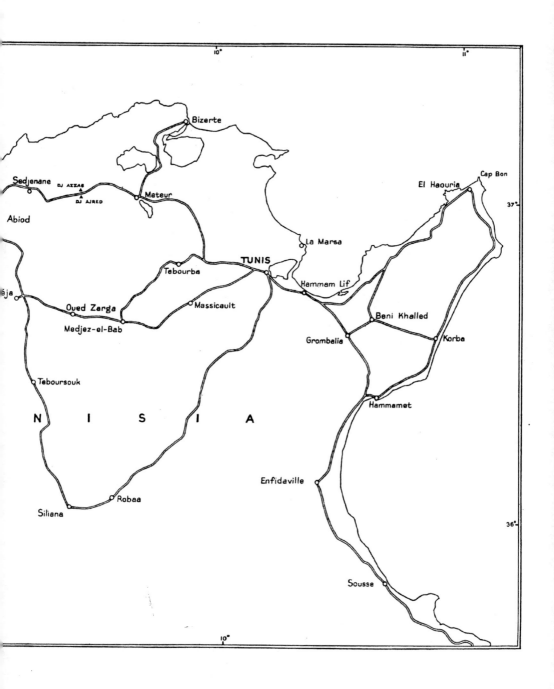

bitterness towards the British was strong in many French hearts for the part they had played in the subjugation of the French fleet in July 1940. It was therefore decided to conduct the landings as an all-American operation under the supreme command of General Dwight Eisenhower of the U.S. Army.

The landings were to be focused on three points: Casablanca, Oran and Algiers. British and American troops, under Major-General C. W. Ryder of the U.S. Army, were to co-operate at Algiers, and the two western landings were to be carried out entirely by the Americans. Algiers had been selected as the most easterly point at which to land, because allied air support from Gibraltar could reach no farther. Major-General Ryder had under his command 34th U.S. Division; 78th Division (Major-General V. Evelegh) less one brigade; a British armoured regiment; Nos. 1 and 6 British Commandos and some U.S. Rangers.

If all went well with the allied landings at Algiers the British 1st Army (Lieutenant-General K. A. N. Anderson), consisting of only 78th Division, the armoured regiment and the two Commandos, was to strike eastwards along the African coast with Tunis as the objective. The distance from Algiers to Tunis is over 400 miles, but there were as yet no Germans or Italians in Tunisia and, if the French did not resist, it was hoped to seize ports and airfields in quick succession and capture the city of Tunis before the enemy could organise effective opposition.

All this was explained by Colonel Howlett to the troops of the 6th Battalion on board the *Marnix* on November 1, 1942, as they steamed in convoy southwards towards Gibraltar. He also issued orders concerning the landings at Algiers, during which 36th Brigade, of which the battalion formed part, was to act as a floating reserve. If the landing was successfully accomplished, the battalion was to go on by sea to capture the port of Bougie. The company commanders then explained to the troops in detail by means of models, air photographs and large-scale maps the part they were to play.

On November 5 the invasion convoy was joined by a large escort of warships, and that night the whole armada passed through the Straits of Gibraltar. The following morning the first enemy aircraft flew over and were fired at by anti-aircraft guns and pursued by fighters from the escorting aircraft-carriers. On the 7th frequent bombing attacks were made on the convoy, but only one ship was hit and that was astern of the *Marnix*.

The landings at Algiers began at 1.15 on the morning of November 8, when 11th Brigade of 78th Division disembarked and moved towards the town. They met some opposition from the French in

P

the area of the naval fortress, and at five in the evening the companies of the 6th Battalion were ordered to land and assist them in the capture of the airfield. The landing was carried out with great difficulty on account of the rough sea, but no sooner had the companies begun to march inland than counter orders were received. They were to re-embark, as the French garrison had surrendered and had agreed to give the Allies harbour facilities. Re-embarkation was completed by dawn on the 10th. For the remainder of the day the *Marnix* was heavily attacked by enemy aircraft, but no damage was sustained.

* * *

When Algiers had been secured, Major-General Evelegh directed Brigadier A. L. Kent-Lemon to carry out with his 36th Brigade the pre-arranged plan for the capture of the port of Bougie and the airfield at Djidjelli. Besides the 6th Battalion, 36th Brigade consisted of the 5th Buffs and the 8th Argyll and Sutherland Highlanders. The state of the 6th Battalion at that time was:—

Commanding Officer	Lieut.-Colonel B. Howlett
Second-in-command	Major H. O. Lovell
Adjutant	Captain D. B. Burne
Quartermaster	Lieutenant H. Huskisson[1]
Regtl. Serjeant-Major	W.O.I W. J. Napier
O.C. A Company	Captain B. E. Harvey
O.C. B Company	Major A. H. Miskin
O.C. C Company	Captain R. K. Murphy
O.C. D Company	Major P. E. O. Bryan

A complete list of officers in the battalion can be found in Appendix B.

The voyage to Bougie began on the evening of November 10, and the *Marnix* arrived off the beaches south of that port soon after midnight. While the troops were descending into the landing craft a message was flashed from the harbour saying that the town had surrendered. The landing on the beaches was carried out as arranged, however, and the 6th Battalion began to advance on the town itself. There was no opposition. Before long a French naval officer arrived in a car with a white flag on it and informed 'Swifty' Howlett that the French did not wish to fight. The battalion then marched through Bougie, where it received a great welcome from the inhabitants, and took up positions in the hills north of the town. Meanwhile the *Marnix* and the escorting vessels had steamed into the harbour, where the disembarkation of the transport had just begun when the

---

[1] Detached from The Bedfordshire and Hertfordshire Regiment.

ships were fiercely dive-bombed by German aircraft. Some of the vessels were hit and burned all day.

The enemy air attacks on the shipping were continued on November 12. During one of them the *Cathay* was hit and set on fire. Later both she and the *Karanja* sank. Our losses in equipment were heavy, and for some time to come the only clothes the troops of 36th Brigade had were those they wore when coming ashore. The loss of the greatcoats was particularly felt, because the nights were already cold.

During the afternoon of the 12th orders were received for the 6th Battalion to continue the progress eastwards to Bone, where No. 6 Commando would have already landed. The move was carried out in two destroyers. These accommodated only 500 men between them, the remainder of the battalion, including the transport, proceeding by road. After a precarious voyage and a disembarkation which was hastened by bombs from Italian aircraft, the battalion landed at Bone without casualties at 7 a.m. on the 13th. They then marched 25 kilometres south to Lake Fetzara, where defensive positions were taken up. That night patrols made contact with No. 6 Commando on Bone aerodrome. On the 14th, after an uneventful journey, the road party arrived from Bougie, and the battalion was at last all together ashore with its weapons and transport.

Although the French administration in Algeria had agreed not to oppose the allied advance, it was still not known what the attitude of the authorities in Tunisia would be. Consequently, on November 15 the second-in-command, Henry Lovell, was sent by Major-General Evelegh to find General Barré, the Commander of the French forces in Tunisia. He set forth in a French taxi, accompanied by an American interpreter, and found General Barré in a farm near Beja. At the outset of the conference the French did not feel that they were strong enough to take any part in the campaign, but at the end they had become convinced of the strength of the allied force and offered to take up positions on the right flank to support the advance.

Eleven French charcoal-burning lorries were now commandeered to complete the transport of the battalion. They were very smelly and difficult to start, but the battalion covered the 80 miles to Tabarka by road and reached a wood on the east of the town by noon on November 16. No sooner had the troops debussed in the wood than a bridge, on which some of the empty vehicles were standing, was dive-bombed by Ju. 87s. Two trucks were destroyed and several casualties—the first in the battalion—were suffered. Two Bren gunners, Corporal Boarer and Private Babbs, remained with their truck and met the dive-bombers with well-directed fire.

One Ju. 87 was brought down, the bridge was hit only once and the road was kept open to traffic.

2. The 6th Battalion at Djebel Abiod

Although the Allied landings in Algeria had taken the German and Italian Commanders by surprise, their reaction was swift. The German Air Force occupied the airfield at El Aouina, near Tunis, on November 9, only a day after the landings, and German and Italian troops began to arrive in large numbers in Tunisia by air and sea. By November 16 their advanced elements were known to be in Mateur.

Forty miles west of Mateur, 78th Division, still only two brigades strong, was concentrating its artillery, tanks and administrative troops near Tabarka. Its orders now were to advance on Tunis and Bizerta with all speed. The French were to cover the right flank of the advance, which was to be along two roads. 11th Brigade on the right was directed from Beja along the road that runs through Medjez to Tunis. On the left 36th Brigade was to advance along the road that runs parallel with the coast from Tabarka, through Djebel Abiod and Mateur, to Bizerta. A small column, known as Hartforce, was to operate ahead on this northern road.

The first task of 36th Brigade was to seize and hold the important road junction at Djebel Abiod. To achieve this the 6th Battalion less D Company, who remained to protect Brigade Headquarters, left Tabarka soon after dark on November 16 and marched a distance of 21 miles to Djebel Abiod. Arriving before dawn on the 17th the battalion took up defensive positions about the road junction and began to dig in. Control of this road junction was of great importance because it ensured lateral communication with 11th Brigade on the right, and the intention was that it should be held at all costs. To assist in this defence eight 25-pounders arrived during the morning and took up anti-tank positions in the village.

In the early afternoon the Reconnaissance Unit ahead reported that a column of enemy tanks and motorised infantry was advancing towards Djebel Abiod from Mateur. Some fifteen minutes later eleven enemy tanks followed by lorries of infantry were seen on the road approaching the village. Fire was held until the tanks were less than 250 yards away and had passed Lieutenant Maling's platoon, who were concealed in some houses in front of the village. The battalion's two-pounder anti-tank guns then opened up. Serjeant Povey, who commanded one of the guns, waited till the leading tank was within

100 yards before he opened fire, and Captain Valentine moved from gun to gun encouraging the crews. Eventually all eleven tanks were disabled. Then, as the German crews descended from their tanks, Lieutenant Maling directed the fire of his platoon on to them, inflicting some 40 casualties. Private Bingham was killed as he attempted to destroy one of the disabled tanks. The German infantry now jumped down from their lorries to attack; but under heavy fire they took cover on both sides of the road while the lorries withdrew. More tanks and some self-propelled guns then began to bombard our positions, and under cover of this fire the enemy infantry tried to cross a shallow river. They did not succeed. A steady fire was kept up by the enemy until dusk, but no more attacks were attempted.

When the action broke off at about five in the evening all of our positions were still intact. Lieutenant Maling's platoon was then withdrawn into the village. A determined attack by a strong German armoured column had been repulsed, and the important road junction was still in our hands. Our casualties had been very light, but two of our anti-tank guns had been destroyed. The Germans had lost eleven tanks and many casualties. They withdrew discomfited to a position north-east of the village under cover of darkness.

During the night the battalion was strengthened by the arrival of D Company but, although the enemy shelled the positions for most of the morning, no attack developed on the 18th. In the afternoon German aircraft dive-bombed and destroyed two Bofors guns, which had arrived to protect the battalion, and caused several casualties, including Lieutenant Edden, who was the first Queen's Own officer to be killed in the campaign. All through the 19th the enemy shelled and mortared the positions intermittently, but he still held off his attacks. Eventually on the 20th, after holding the road junction for four days, orders were received that the battalion would be relieved by the 8th Argylls. The relief was carried out that night, and the battalion, leaving D Company at Djebel Abiod, marched back to Tabarka.

Before D Company rejoined the remainder of the battalion they took a major part in beating off a strong enemy attack. In addition, on November 22, Lieutenant Shaun Stewart led a patrol to destroy a disabled enemy tank in a river bed 300 yards from the enemy positions. On setting out they met a strong enemy patrol but, though outnumbered, they attacked, killed four of the enemy and captured their machine-gun. Later on Lance-Corporal Donnelly and Privates Clews and Kench returned to this tank. A sticky grenade having failed to explode, they then poured petrol over the tank, set it alight and remained until it was completely destroyed.

3. *The 6th Battalion at Green Hill*

By this time the concentration of 78th Division was complete, and 36th Brigade was ready to begin its advance on Bizerta. Now that the enemy had been met, the advance was bound to be slower than had been hoped. Furthermore, the Germans were still building up their forces, several units originally destined to reinforce Rommel in the desert having been landed by air in Tunisia. Advanced elements of a Panzer Division and nearly a dozen Italian infantry battalions had also arrived. Before the end of November, 15,000 fighting troops with 100 tanks were advancing to battle, and German dive-bombers, based on good airfields in Tunisia, were there to support them. The delay caused by the vacillation of the French leaders had robbed us of the quick success we had hoped for.

In these circumstances 36th Brigade would have to fight for further gains. The immediate task was to attack and drive out the enemy who were entrenched on the high ground north of Djebel Abiod. It was to be a brigade attack, and the 6th Battalion moved up from Tabarka on November 25 to an area west of Djebel Abiod, where they found the 5th Buffs and No. 6 Commando already assembled. The 6th Battalion was to make a wide turning movement to the left, and they formed up on a start-line three miles west of the village.

The battle opened at dawn on November 26 with a heavy artillery bombardment of the enemy positions. The battalion's attack went in supported by a troop of General Grant tanks. Very little resistance was met. By mid-day all objectives had been seized, and 14 Italian paratroops had been captured. After a short rest the battalion carried out a further attack on Tamera, which was captured with little fighting by 3 p.m. Defensive positions were then taken up for the night. Although battledress had been issued the previous day to replace the denims that had been worn since disembarkation, the troops still had no greatcoats or blankets and the night was uncomfortably cold and wet.

Next day the battalion consolidated its defensive positions to withstand a counter-attack. None came in, but the heavy enemy air attacks on the road from Tabarka continued. During one of these attacks Lieutenant Huskisson, the Quartermaster, was killed as he was bringing up a convoy of ammunition and rations. R.Q.M.S. Landman was promoted to take his place.

The advance of 36th Brigade towards Bizerta was resumed at dawn on November 28 with the 8th Argylls as advance guard. At Sedjenane D Company again left the battalion, this time on a fruitless mission to the coast. The march was notable because, for the

EGYPT: A SECTION OF THE QUEEN'S
OWN ON ITS WAY TO THE ASSEMBLY
AREA BEFORE THE NIGHT ADVANCE
TO THE MUNASIB DEPRESSION,
SEPTEMBER 1942

EGYPT: TROOPS DIG A SLIT-
TRENCH IN THE DESERT
BEFORE THE BATTLE OF
ALAMEIN

N.W. AFRICA: BALD HILL, WHICH WAS THE 6TH BATTALION'S
OBJECTIVE ON NOVEMBER 30, 1942

N.W. AFRICA: BREN GUNNERS IN POSITION WEST OF MATEUR

first time since the opening of the campaign, the column had fighter protection overhead. In spite of this, towards evening, the vanguard ran into an ambush at a spot where the road passed between high hills, and 8th Argylls lost eight carriers and all except six men of their leading company. The Buffs and the 6th Battalion immediately took up positions astride the road to cover the withdrawal of the remainder of the Argylls.

Next morning, after reconnaissance, the enemy were located in strong positions on Djebel Ajred (Bald Hill) to the south of the road and Djebel Azzag (Green Hill) to the north. A valley some 1,200 yards wide separated these two hills, of which Bald Hill was by far the larger. It was a great rolling hill, and as the name implies, bare of cover. The plan of attack was for the 6th Battalion on the right to attack Bald Hill, with the Argylls in support. At the same time No. 6 Commando was to attack Green Hill. If this was captured 5th Buffs were to move round the left flank on a wide encircling movement. As it was essential that an attack should be launched that night, company and platoon commanders had only a few minutes in which to view the ground before darkness fell.

The companies of the 6th Battalion formed up at 1 a.m. on November 30 and moved up the slopes of Bald Hill under cover of darkness. Good progress was made in spite of enemy defensive fire on fixed lines until, as dawn broke, the leading companies reached the summit. There they were met by the vicious fire of enemy medium machine guns sited on the reverse slope. On the right A Company, now commanded by Captain Crook, cleared the crest, and Lieutenant Kerr rushed on and destroyed at least two of these guns before he was mortally wounded. A Company was then overrun by a counter-attack. On the left C Company also cleared the crest and nearly reached their objective before they were pinned down by fire. A similar fate befell B Company. Owing to the fact that the wireless had broken down it was impossible to get artillery support, and in their efforts to get forward almost incredible feats of bravery were performed by the junior leaders. The fighting became confused, but by mid-afternoon, owing to the intense fire, the attack had come to a standstill. No better success had been gained on Green Hill; and in the evening when the light had faded, orders were received to withdraw to positions astride the road in rear of the Buffs. D Company rejoined the battalion during the night.

Casualties had been very heavy in this action, 11 officers and some 150 other ranks of the 6th Battalion being killed, wounded or missing. The officers killed were Captains Crook and Harvey and Lieutenants Adkins, Akehurst, Kerr, and W. J. Palr _r (a son of Colonel W. V.

Palmer). Captain Murphy had been very seriously wounded. Colonel Howlett, although slightly wounded, remained at his headquarters.

*   *   *

It was now evident that the Germans were in too strong a position for 36th Brigade to have any hope of dislodging them until reinforcements were received. Moreover, since landing at Bone most of the troops had had no real respite. They had had no proper sleep, had existed on emergency rations and had very rarely had a chance even to remove their boots. It was therefore decided to hold the ground already won and to take up a hedgehog position with all-round defence astride the main road. The troops dug deep trenches in the small hills at the entrance to the valley, and in them they warmed up their 'compo.' rations and found some protection from the heavy rain.

The Germans made no attempt to attack and remained conveniently inactive until December 11 when, having apparently been reinforced by artillery, they began to shell our positions. A shell fell on the native hut in which Serjeant Bucksey was working the battalion telephone exchange, and one of the occupants was wounded and the remainder were buried. Serjeant Bucksey extricated the wounded man and, while shells were still falling, carried him to safety. Then, calling for medical aid, he returned to his post.

At about this time the first reinforcements, consisting of six officers and 150 other ranks, arrived, and the spare stores and baggage came up with the rear party from Bougie. These stores included such things as razor blades and soap, and the troops were able to resume their erstwhile clean appearance. In addition, eight Vickers machine guns were received. An effort was then made to give the troops some rest, and parties were sent back to Sedjenane for 48 hours at a time. There, shower baths were available and unserviceable kit could be replaced. But the troops had little respite, for the tobacco factory in which they were intended to rest was frequently bombed. On Christmas Day the first mail arrived and, by a feat of organisation, cold pork and a bottle of beer were provided with the rations. These were not very appetising when consumed huddled up in a gas-cape in pouring rain, but the effort was appreciated.

On December 16 'Swifty' Howlett received orders to take over command of the brigade. Henry Lovell assumed temporary command of the battalion with Major Paul Bryan as second-in-command.

During this period many patrols were sent out at night to gain information about the dispositions of the enemy and his intentions for the future. On December 4 Lieutenant Shaun Stewart led a patrol to the rear of the German positions. This patrol marched for nine hours and, after lying up all day, returned with important information. On December 22 Lance-Corporal Kench took a patrol five miles into enemy country. Although heavy rain and mud made the going very difficult, this patrol ambushed a motor-cycle combination, killed both the occupants and returned with the information required.

*   *   *

The second battle for Bald Hill and Green Hill was fought on January 5, 1943. The role of the 6th Battalion was mainly to hold its present positions and to give close Vickers gun support to the attack. One section of Vickers guns under Serjeant Kendall went forward with No. 6 Commando, however, and did excellent work. Soon after dawn the attackers gained a footing on Green Hill, but later in the day the Germans counter-attacked and regained their positions. Another attempt was made on the 6th, but this also failed. It was then decided to call the operation off. As wireless communication had broken down, Lieutenant Howard of the 6th Battalion set out with two men to carry the order to withdraw to two detachments which had become isolated. He reached the first unit, but then ran into German positions. After several attempts to get round, he ordered his escort to return and began to work his way alone through the enemy lines. He was chased four times, escaped once by feigning to be wounded, and got through eventually only by hiding in a bush while a German patrol passed by. It was then almost dawn, but he returned in daylight through the enemy lines and arrived back after an absence of eighteen hours.

After this battle the battalion began offensive patrolling. Every night fighting patrols harassed the enemy, often penetrating several miles into their territory. On January 15 two patrols, led by Lieutenants Beall and Howard, met strong enemy opposition and inflicted a number of casualties before withdrawing. The following night Lance-Corporal Lipscombe, when returning with a patrol, destroyed a German post by throwing a grenade over the parapet.

By these patrols 36th Brigade was gradually regaining the initiative. But it was to put in no more attacks on Green Hill. During the nights of January 17 and 18 it was relieved by a brigade of the newly-arrived 46th Division and withdrew to an area near Beja.

Meanwhile to the south, after the capture of Medjez on November 26, 11th Brigade had pressed on along the southerly road to Tebourba. But there the Germans were encountered in strength. Although reinforced, 11th Brigade was forced to fall back. On Christmas Day, further German counter-attacks recaptured Djebel el Ahmera (Longstop Hill), a hill which dominated the entrance to the plains of Tunis. Torrential rain then fell and, on account of the incredibly deep mud, the feature had to be left in enemy hands. The southern prong of 78th Division's advance had been brought to a halt.

A pause in the fighting was now necessary for the Allies so that they could build up and reorganise their forces. To the north the ground won by 78th Division had to be consolidated. Farther south the long sector held by the French and the Americans was very lightly defended and had to be strengthened. Now, too, came the heartening news that the British 8th Army, pursuing the enemy along the north coast of Africa, had entered Tunisia from the east. This Army was placed under General Eisenhower's supreme command, and General Alexander took charge of all land operations.

But the Germans had no intention of allowing the Allies to re-organise in peace. On January 18, 1943, newly-landed German troops supported by Mark VI Tiger tanks swung in from Tunis to drive a wedge between the British and the French at Robaa. The French were overrun, and reinforcements had to be found to go to their assistance. So it came about that the 6th Battalion's rest near Beja was cut short. On the evening of January 22 it was placed at one hour's notice to proceed to Robaa and, arriving there next day with 36th Brigade, it immediately took up defensive positions in very hilly country. The following night C Company (now commanded by Captain Taylor) carried out a local counter-attack and drove some Italians from a hill which overlooked the battalion's right flank. This extended the frontage so that the battalion was defending some six miles of country. But although the Italians were extremely nervous and the slightest movement in the area brought forth tremendous bursts of fire, no further contact was made with the enemy.

This state of affairs continued until January 31, when the Germans launched another attack. At dawn a dozen tanks headed by two Tiger tanks approached down the main road. These were forced by a battery of 6-pounder anti-tank guns to turn off the road into cover. Some tracked vehicles and lorries full of infantry then appeared, and by 9.30 a.m. an infantry attack had developed. The brunt of this was borne by the Buffs, who held their positions and repulsed repeated attempts to break through. On the right flank, however, the French positions were overrun, and D Company of the 6th Battalion (Captain Scott) counter-attacked, drove the enemy back and captured a large number of prisoners. The following morning D Company put in a second counter-attack, cleared some small hills in which the enemy were still lurking, and completely restored the position.

After this the enemy was quiet except for some shelling in the daytime. A battalion of French Moroccan troops (Goums) now came under Henry Lovell's command, and he became responsible for ten miles of front. By February 21, however, when Lieutenant-Colonel E. S. Heygate arrived from the 70th Battalion to take over command, the sector had been reduced to a mere two miles.

The Germans then switched their attacks farther north. 78th Division held an assault on Medjez, and 46th Division, which was now holding the coastal sector, bore the brunt of an attack on Beja. 36th Brigade took a small part in both of these actions. First of all it moved on March 1 to Teboursouk and took over a reserve position there. Secondly, on March 19, the brigade returned to the familiar Djebel Abiod, to which place 46th Division had been driven back by the enemy's assaults. The 6th Battalion's defensive position was on high ground to the south of the village, and it held this without any difficulty for ten days.

5. *The 6th Battalion at Djebel Bou Diss*

Spring had now arrived, and orders were issued for local operations which were to lead up to a major assault on Tunis and Bizerta. In the northern sector 46th Division was to drive the enemy back beyond Sedjenane; and 36th Brigade, still under command of that division, took part in this attack. The 6th Battalion, moving across hilly country to the south of the road, had an exhausting time. But the enemy did not resist strongly, and by March 31 Sedjenane had been retaken and positions on the high ground west of Bald Hill had been consolidated.

36th Brigade was now free to return to 78th Division in the Teboursouk area where, for the first time, the division was assembling as a complete formation, with 38th (Irish) Brigade as its third brigade and the North Irish Horse, with their Churchill tanks, as its armoured regiment. 78th Division's immediate task was to clear the enemy from the mountainous area to the north of the Medjez-Beja road. This vast tract of country, where every hill was a brigade objective and the steep slopes were too rocky for digging in, was unsuitable for tanks except in small numbers. The movement of vehicles was also restricted, and the division had to rely on pack mules to carry its supplies, mortars, wireless sets and tools. This Battle of The Peaks, as it was called, was therefore to be essentially an infantry battle.

The plan was to advance with all three brigades at once, with 36th Brigade in the centre; and the 6th Battalion moved to Oued Zarga on April 6 and prepared to attack a hill to the east of that village. Lieutenant Bernau, the Intelligence Officer, was wounded early in the advance, but by the evening of the 7th the battalion had captured its objective. A number of other casualties had been suffered from artillery, and enemy aircraft had dive-bombed the advancing troops. On the 8th the battalion reached the village of Chaouach. Several similar piecemeal attacks on features held by the enemy were successfully made during the next three days. Resistance was slight, but progress was much impeded by the many booby traps which had been laid in all the approaches.

On April 12 the last of the peaks, the dominating feature of Djebel el Ang, reared up ahead. Intervening was the lower Djebel Bou Diss, and strong patrols were sent out to probe the enemy positions on it. One of these patrols was attacked three times by the enemy. When it finally withdrew, part of Serjeant Lenihan's platoon was cut off. Ordering his men to remain hidden, he eventually brought them back by crawling through the enemy's lines. Another patrol was attacked when in a position of observation. Serjeant Benge coolly stood up in full view and threw grenades and fired his Tommy-gun at the charging enemy. He then covered his section as they withdrew. From the information brought back by these patrols the enemy positions were found to be strong and skilfully sited.

In the evening Major Miskin was ordered to occupy a minor feature with two platoons of B Company, but to withdraw if the hill was found to be strongly held. When they reached the top a counter-attack came in which was repulsed only after determined close-quarter fighting. During the night a second attack developed, but Major Miskin refused to withdraw until his men were driven off the hill by a bayonet charge; and even then he led an unsuccessful flanking movement to regain it.

The battle for Djebel Bou Diss began on the night of April 13 with an artillery programme. The leading companies, A (Captain Clarke)

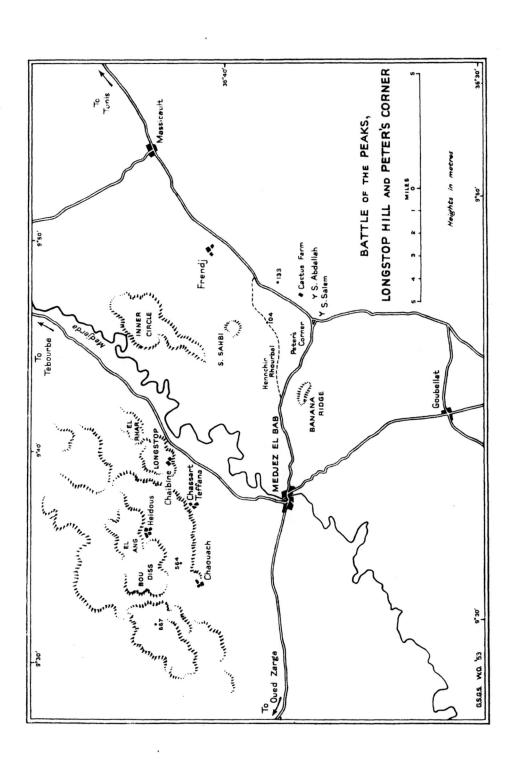

BATTLE of the PEAKS,
LONGSTOP HILL and PETER'S CORNER

MILES
5   4   3   2   1   0   5

Heights in metres

G.S.G.S. W.O. '53

and D (Captain Scott), moved forward, but when half-way to the objective they came under mortar and machine-gun fire. Captain Scott immediately moved to the front of his company and, closely followed by Private Rogan's section, led his men to the top of the hill. There the advance was checked by heavy fire from two machine-gun posts. Serjeant Bryant took his platoon through and wiped out the post on the left flank. At the same time Private Bullock rushed over the crest firing his Bren gun from the hip and forced the crew of the other gun to withdraw. To reinforce this success the men of the Carrier Platoon, whose vehicles were not required in the battle, moved to the top of the hill, where their commander, Lieutenant Fuller, was wounded. Ultimately the feature was captured after fierce hand-to-hand fighting, in which C.S.M. Dean of D Company was conspicuous. By this time B Company had been sent forward as reinforcements, and under the direction of Major Miskin the position was consolidated at dawn. Many of the enemy gave themselves up and were taken prisoner.

The following afternoon a German counter-attack came in. This was preceded by heavy mortar fire, which fell mainly on our machine-gun positions. Serjeant Kendall immediately ordered the crews of his two Vickers guns to take cover but, staying with one gun himself, he fired continuously at the advancing enemy and broke up the assault. Artillery fire finally halted the attack, and the enemy withdrew having suffered a large number of casualties.

By April 16 Djebel el Ang had been captured by the Irish Brigade, and on the 17th the 6th Battalion was relieved on Djebel Bou Diss by the Argylls and moved back in reserve for rest. This was the end of the Battle of The Peaks, of which General Anderson wrote in his dispatch: 'I consider that 78th Division deserves the highest praise for as tough and prolonged a bit of fighting as has ever been undertaken by the British soldier.'

6. *The 1st Battalion Moves In*

Meanwhile the 1st Battalion had arrived in the Oued Zarga area with 4th Division (Major-General J. L. I. Hawkesworth). Having spent ten days in the transit camp at Algiers (see Chapter 10, Section 3) it had embarked in the *Princess Beatrix* for Bone. Thence it had moved by road to Beja and then to Oued Zarga, near which place it took over positions from the 2nd Hampshires on April 9.

On arrival in Africa the key positions in the battalion were held by:—

Commanding Officer	Lieut.-Colonel J. M. Haycraft
Second-in-command	Major D. H. Archer, M.C.
Adjutant	Captain B. I. Royal-Dawson
Quartermaster	Captain R. C. E. Mines
Regtl. Serjeant-Major	W.O.I. A. J. Hayley
O.C. A Company	Captain M. H. Ensor
O.C. B Company	Major E. R. Dann
O.C. C Company	Major H. P. Braithwaite
O.C. D Company	Captain W. R. Follit

A complete list of officers serving in the battalion can be found in Appendix B.

12th Brigade (commanded by Brigadier R. A. Hull and consisting of the 1st Battalion, 2nd Royal Fusiliers and 6th Black Watch) received orders to follow up 78th Division as it moved forward in the Battle of The Peaks; and the 1st Battalion actually occupied positions which had just been vacated by the 6th Battalion. These positions were on a high feature and, although the enemy were some distance away, shelling was frequent and some casualties were suffered. The battalion soon came to realise the value of the 'reverse slope' position—a lesson which the 6th Battalion had learned at Djebel Abiod in November. The troops dug weapon pits on the rear slope from 50 to 150 yards below the crest and so obtained freedom of movement out of enemy observation for distributing, brewing up and eating their 'compo.' rations, washing and shaving and other items of personal hygiene.

When the Battle of The Peaks was over, the battalion was relieved by an American unit and moved on the night of April 19 to Banana Ridge, near Medjez, where 12th Brigade went into divisional reserve. In the large-scale offensive which was about to begin, 4th Division's role, in the early stages, was to secure the right flank. Until 12th Brigade was required to assist in this task, the battalion had a few days' respite in which to send the 'left out of battle' to B echelon and generally prepare for attack.

7. *The 6th Battalion at Longstop Hill*

The British First Army, reinforced by divisions from Britain and America and by troops from the 8th Army (now nearing Enfidaville) was at last strong enough to mount an attack on Tunis. The route selected was down the valley of the River Medjerda and thence, through Massicault, to the plain of Tunis, where the country was very suitable for tanks. Dominating the Medjerda valley was Longstop Hill. The first phase of the battle was therefore the completion of 78th Division's advance to the Medjerda and the capture of Longstop.

The task of taking this famous hill was given to 36th Brigade. During the night of April 21 the 6th Battalion moved to a gully east of Chaouach, in which area the brigade was assembling. Casualties had been heavy at Djebel Bou Diss, and the battalion was obliged to bring up all the cooks, storemen and administrative personnel. Even then the rifle companies were less than sixty strong. The following day, the 22nd, the approaches to Longstop were reconnoitred, and in the evening the battalion moved forward to Chassart Teffana, where it formed up on its start-line with the Buffs on the left. The Argylls were in reserve.

After four hundred guns had bombarded the enemy positions, the 6th Battalion attacked that night with C and D Companies leading. The opposing machine-gun and mortar fire was considerable, and progress was also impeded by barbed wire and booby traps. In spite of this the village of Chaibine was reached. There the advance was checked. Private Lingham, with all his section casualties, personally dragged his wounded men clear of the wire and sent them back to the Aid Post. Eventually, D Company reached their objective but were then driven back. C Company were unable to get beyond Chaibine. A footing had been secured at the base of the hill however, and a second attempt after dawn made further progress. On the left the Buffs had been more successful and had advanced farther up the slopes. Brigadier Howlett then brought forward the Argylls, who put in a fierce and heroic attack supported by the tanks of The North Irish Horse and reached the crest of Longstop. That evening the 6th Battalion moved up, joined the Argylls and began to dig in. At that moment Colonel Heygate was wounded by a shell, and Captain Defrates, now Adjutant, coolly reorganised the battalion and consolidated under heavy fire. Major Lovell later assumed command.

The morning of April 24 opened with heavy shell and mortar fire from the enemy on the whole of the summit of Longstop. In the afternoon the 6th Battalion was ordered to take Djebel el Rhar, which was a distinct feature separated from Longstop by a deep gully. B and C Companies formed up on a start-line on the reverse slope of the main feature, and our artillery opened up on the el Rhar position. But the German guns immediately retaliated and so saturated the forming-up position with shells that the troops were checked. C Company moved forward after some delay, and in face of heavy machine-gun fire nearly reached the objective. Private Sullivan's section charged and actually destroyed an enemy post. But too many casualties were being sustained, and the Brigadier, who was closely watching the battle, called the attack off. During the action a shell landed on an anti-tank gun on the southern slopes of the hill and killed one and wounded one of the crew. Serjeant Bourne, who was in charge of the stretcher-bearers, immediately left his slit-trench and made his way across shell-swept ground to the gun, tended the wounded man and carried him to safety. When the battalion reorganised it was found that there were only eighty men left in the four rifle companies. These were formed into two companies of forty.

For the remainder of April 24 and for the whole of the 25th the battalion, thus depleted, held on to its positions in spite of continuous and intensive artillery and mortar fire. More casualties were suffered. One of the wounded men, lying on the exposed slope of the hill, called out for help, and Private Cooper left his mortar detachment, crawled forward and eased his position. Cooper then went back for assistance but, finding none, crawled out again and dragged the wounded man a distance of seventy yards to safety. In this situation not only the evacuation of the wounded but also the replenishment of the companies with ammunition, food and water was extremely difficult. This was in the hands of Major Bryan, who time after time personally led carrying parties across the heavily-shelled area. In this work he was greatly assisted by Lance-Corporal Lambourne of the Signal Platoon, who was in charge of a small column of mules.

It was not till mid-day on April 26 that the situation was relieved by an attack on Djebel el Rhar by the Buffs, who, sweeping wide round the left flank and well supported by the tanks of The North Irish Horse, took the Germans by surprise. The hill was seized, and more than 300 enemy surrendered. The whole of Longstop was now ours. After the battle it was found that the Germans had tunnelled right through the hill in several places and were thus able to obtain complete security from our artillery and mortar fire.

That night the remnants of the 6th Battalion were relieved on Longstop and marched back to Chassart Teffana, where they were able to rest and refit. The following day Brigadier 'Swifty' Howlett was informed that he had been awarded an immediate D.S.O. for his brigade's success. Fittingly, he celebrated the occasion in the 6th Battalion's mess that evening. Three days later upwards of

200 reinforcements arrived to replace the casualties, and the battalion prepared for further action.

8. *The 1st Battalion at Peter's Corner*

While the attack on Longstop Hill was still in progress 4th Division, fulfilling its role of securing the right flank, began to drive the enemy from positions which dominated the Medjez-Massicault road at Peter's Corner. For this purpose 12th Brigade was brought up from reserve. The Germans were found to be in strong positions on a series of small features well protected by minefields. For two days the 2nd Royal Fusiliers and the 6th Black Watch hammered away at them with piecemeal attacks. Brigadier Hull then decided to call forward the 1st Battalion, which was on Banana Ridge, and ordered Colonel Haycraft to put in two company attacks on the night of April 26. A Company was given Sidi Salem as an objective, and B Company Sidi Abdallah. The remainder of the battalion was to attack Point 133 later.

A Company, from a start-line in front of Banana Ridge, had almost reached its objective before it was fired on by enemy machine guns. Very confused fighting followed, and the situation became critical owing to a shortage of ammunition. But the objective was reached and consolidated as dawn came. Meanwhile B Company, from its start-line along the Massicault road, had moved off towards Sidi Abdallah. Soon after the start the compasses were influenced by a minefield, and it was impossible to keep direction. Major Dann therefore decided to halt and continue the attack in daylight. The presence of the company was now known, however, and when they moved on at first light the leading sections were held up by heavy machine-gun fire. Corporal Burden stripped off his equipment and, armed with grenade and bayonet, rushed a machine-gun post single-handed. He reached the post, threw the grenade, silenced the gun and enabled the advance to continue. Groups of men, still opposed by fire, succeeded in reaching the crest of Sidi Abdallah, where they held on. By this time a gap had been cleared in the minefield, and some tanks managed to come through. But on reaching the ridge they too came under severe enemy fire; many of them were knocked out. As casualties were still occurring amongst the infantry the position was considered to be untenable, and the remaining troops and tanks were withdrawn to the start-line. The cost in casualties had been heavy. They included Major Dann and Lieutenant Ashton killed and Lieutenant Besley wounded.

Q

During this fighting A Company remained on Sidi Salem, beating off several counter-attacks. Although isolated, they held on staunchly there for the whole of the 27th and 28th and till the morning of the 29th, when they were relieved by a company of the Black Watch. In this defence a detachment of mortars under Serjeant Rogers gave particularly good support.

The battalion, less A Company, put in the attack on Point 133 at dusk on April 28. Under cover of a formidable artillery barrage C Company on the right reached its objective; but on the left D Company was unable to do so owing to heavy machine-gun fire, which was made effective by the use of flares. Three hours later the enemy counter-attacked strongly and C Company was surrounded, almost every man becoming a casualty or being taken prisoner. Major Braithwaite, the company commander, was severely wounded. After daybreak B and D Companies went in with a rush and re-took C Company's objective. But while consolidating, these companies came under intense and accurate shelling and mortar fire and, as the ground was mainly rock and digging in was impossible, it was decided to withdraw them under cover of smoke from our artillery.

That morning, the 29th, A Company, having been relieved on Sidi Salem, came under command of 2nd Royal Fusiliers for an attack on Cactus Farm, a cluster of ruined white buildings surrounded by a cactus hedge on the left of Sidi Abdallah. The enemy held his small arms fire until the last moment. It was only when the leading platoons had reached the cactus that machine-gun fire broke up the assault. The right platoon of A Company received the full force of this fire, and Lieutenant Whitty (son of Brigadier N. I. Whitty) was killed as he tried to force a way through the hedge. The left platoon and Company Headquarters were pinned down in the open and suffered severely, Captain Ensor and C.S.M. Chattenton being killed. The third platoon was extricated with great skill by Lieutenant Sharpe. As evening approached, all that remained of A Company, some thirty-five unwounded men, rejoined the 1st Battalion at Peter's Corner.

The battalion, hastily reorganised into three companies of two platoons each, then prepared for an attack on Cactus Farm. This was to begin as soon as an attack on Point 133 by a battalion of 10th Brigade was well under way. Without delay the depleted companies formed up on their start-line on the Massicault road. It was to be a silent attack and, except for some harassing fire during the early part of the night, there was to be no artillery preparation. News came that the attack on Point 133 was not going well but, at 3.35 a.m., the companies crossed the start-line as planned. B

Company was in the lead with D following, while A Company was given the role of protecting the left flank. When the leading troops were close to the farm buildings an intense fire was opened on them, and many were shot down. Major Archer, who was in command of the operation, was mortally wounded. Lieutenant Turner, the Intelligence Officer, was killed. The impetus of the attack was lost. Nevertheless, small groups of men managed to get up to the farm buildings, where they found that, concealed by the cactus hedge, the enemy positions were protected by concrete. D Company then moved forward in an attempt to turn the right flank, but they too were met by heavy fire and could not enter the buildings. By dawn it was clear that the attack had failed. The attack on Point 133 had also been unsuccessful.

Communication with the assaulting companies had now been lost, and the artillery put down a smoke screen in the hope that it would be understood as a signal for withdrawal. It was in fact so understood. Some of the survivors of these two companies got back under cover of the smoke to the Massicault road, where they joined A Company. The remainder withdrew as best they could. Six men of B Company under Captain Hansen-Raae stayed out all day attempting to locate other groups of the battalion. It was not until they were sure that none remained that they withdrew in good order in the evening with valuable information about the enemy.

The casualties in the battalion during these four days' fighting numbered 16 officers and 317 other ranks. It had fought continuously and well but with little success. Sidi Abdallah, Cactus Farm and Point 133 were still in German hands, and it was with heavy hearts and weary limbs that the troops trudged back to Banana Ridge for reorganisation and sleep.

9. *Victory in Tunis*

Although 12th Brigade's attacks at Peter's Corner had not been successful, 4th Division had fulfilled its role of securing the right flank for the attack. Moreover, farther north, all positions necessary for the launching of an offensive had now been captured. General Alexander decided therefore that the time to deliver the final blow had come. While 78th Division stood firm on the high ground about Longstop Hill, 4th Division was to attack north of Peter's Corner towards Massicault with Frendj as its objective. When this was taken, 6th Armoured Division was to go through for Tunis.

Supported by massive concentrations of artillery, this offensive went forward in the darkness of the early hours of May 6. Neither the 1st nor the 6th Battalion had any serious fighting. The 6th Battalion, on the previous night, captured and held the start-line for the main attack; and the 1st, in support on the left flank of 4th Division, occupied Frendj on the evening of the 6th. The offensive was completely successful, and on May 7 British troops entered Tunis.

May 8 was a great day for the 6th Battalion. Passing thousands of Germans and Italians, many of whom were driving their own vehicles to the prison cages, they drove into Tunis in lorries at about midday. The population gave them a wonderful welcome, waving flags and giving flowers and wine to the troops. Billets were allotted in the town, and some of the men had the pleasure of sleeping under a roof for the first time for six months. The following day the battalion moved out of Tunis and, on the 11th, settled down at La Marsa, where it enjoyed a spell of well-earned relaxation.

Meanwhile the 1st Battalion moved forward with 4th Division to cut off as many enemy as possible in the Cape Bon Peninsula. On entering the peninsula at Hammam Lif the battalion, as advance guard to 12th Brigade, began to meet slight, disorganised resistance. The enemy were rounded up, however, and lorries full of German troops and senior German officers in large staff cars drove up and surrendered. One lorry carried a complete military band which, later, rendered melodious concerts to the troops. All this gave a very different picture from the retreat to Dunkirk, where our troops had had no thought of surrender. By dawn on May 11 the brigade had reached the east coast of the peninsula at Korba. It then turned north up the coast and met an armoured car of 10th Brigade coming from Cape Bon. The encirclement of the peninsula was complete. Very few enemy troops escaped, and large quantities of material were captured. Africa was at last clear of all foes.

In England the bells of all churches were rung for this great triumph, and in Tunisia on May 20 Generals Eisenhower and Alexander and the French Commander, General Giraud, took the salute at a victory march of the Allied troops through Tunis. All arms participated, marching nine abreast. Detachments of some 150 all ranks from both the 1st and 6th Battalions marched in the procession. It was a magnificent spectacle, and none enjoyed it more than the civilian population.

*　　　*　　　*

After some three weeks at La Marsa, where football matches, bathing parades, concert parties, film shows and even garden parties were organised, the 6th Battalion moved at the end of May to Guelma, near Bone. On June 17 His Majesty the King visited 78th Division, and the battalion lined the Bone–Guelma road to cheer him as he drove past. Then, after a month of reorganisation and training, the battalion moved to Hammamet, on the east coast of Tunisia, to prepare for the invasion of Europe.

But the 1st Battalion, who moved to the neighbourhood of Bougie to prepare for the same task, suffered a grievous blow. 4th Division, with its one tank and two infantry brigades, was deemed to be an unsuitable formation for making an assault landing and for holding a sector of ground, and was reduced to an administrative formation. Drafts were posted away, and the battalion was given such tasks as escorting prisoners-of-war to the ports and moving dumps of ammunition. Further drafts left. Eventually the battalion became responsible for running a transit camp. For those who remained—some 12 officers and 150 other ranks—there seemed to be no future.

CHAPTER 14

The Sixth Battalion in Sicily
July to September 1943

1. *The Vital Reserve*

THE 6th Battalion moved from Hammamet (see Chapter 13, Section 9) to Sousse on July 8, 1943, in readiness for the invasion of Sicily. The actual invasion took place on July 10, but the battalion with 78th Division was in reserve for the initial landings and was not required till the second phase of the operation. This entailed a somewhat protracted wait on the shores of the Mediterranean, during which Colonel Lovell, who had been suffering from severe headaches since he had been blown up in a carrier in February, was sent home. When he was examined there it was found that he had a fractured skull, and he was posted as a Chief Instructor to the Home Guard. The Ministry of Food intervened, and he returned to his pre-war occupation in the Argentine. Major P. E. O. Bryan was promoted to succeed him in command of the battalion.

Meanwhile operations in Sicily had been going well. The seaborne invasion had been preceded by air-borne attacks south of Syracuse and north of Gela, and it was in those localities that the main landings—the British 8th Army on the right and the American 7th Army on the left—were made before dawn on July 10. The rough sea had persuaded the enemy that no attack would be made that night. Resistance was, therefore, slight. Swift advances north and west were made. On the right the British 5th Division entered Syracuse without difficulty that evening; the Americans advanced rapidly inland; and all day our bombers attacked the enemy airfields, and our fighters from Malta and Gozo maintained cover over the beaches. The 8th Army, still commanded by 'Monty,' then began to advance north and north-west. By the morning of July 13 the 5th and 50th Divisions had reached Augusta and Lentini, and on the left 51st Division (which had sailed from Malta) and 231st (Malta) Brigade (which had sailed from Egypt) had entered Vizzini.

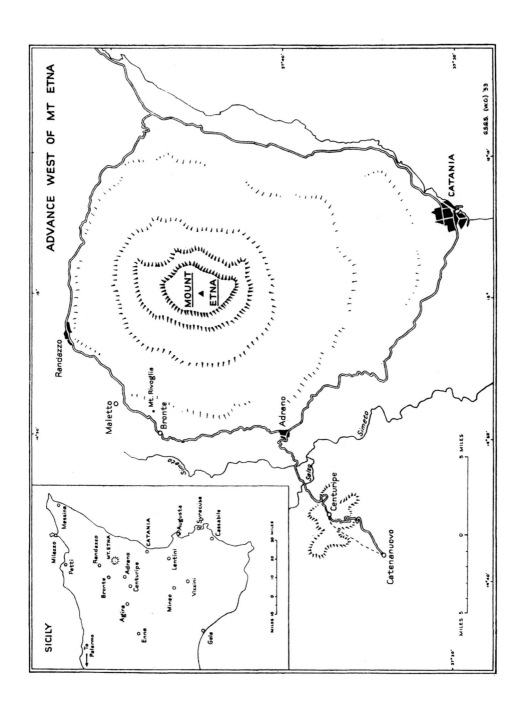

German resistance then stiffened. By the 22nd the advance of 8th Army had been stopped south of Catania on the coast and at Agira some thirty miles inland. On the left the American advance, continuing satisfactorily, had reached Enna to the north; while westwards it was thrusting to the western corner of Sicily before turning north for a drive on Palermo.

The enemy had now concentrated his main forces in the north-east of the island and was preparing to fight a stubborn delaying action in country very suitable for defence. High mountains and narrow valleys gave many positions that could be held by a few machine guns and mortars against an army. To attempt to advance up the coastal plain would be very expensive in men and material, and 'Monty' decided to outflank the enemy positions based on Mount Etna with an attack through Centuripe on Adrano. Another division was required for this vital attack, and 78th Division was brought from Sousse for this very purpose.

2. *The Battle of Centuripe and the Capture of Adrano*

The 6th Battalion embarked in landing craft in Sousse harbour on the afternoon of July 25. After a smooth and uneventful crossing the troops landed on the beaches at Cassabile, south of Syracuse, on the evening of July 26 and marched to 36th Brigade's concentration area. Next morning the battalion embussed and arrived at Mineo, north of Vizzini, in the afternoon. The heat and the heavy white dust had made conditions very uncomfortable, but in the several towns that had been passed the civilians had given the troops a rousing welcome. That evening the march north began, and by dawn on July 28 the battalion was arriving at the assembly area in some gullies four miles south of Catenanuova. That day Colonel Bryan and the Company Commanders viewed the ground ahead from an O.P., and on the 29th the battalion was bombed from the air and shelled from the Centuripe area. The battle was obviously close at hand.

The attack against the enemy defensive positions on the south-western flank of Mount Etna was to begin on August 1. These positions were of great natural strength, for between Catenanuova and Etna rises a series of steep hills separated from each other by deep gorges. On one of the steepest and highest of these hills stands the town of Centuripe, known by the troops as 'Cherry Ripe.' This was the formidable feature which was to be 36th Brigade's first objective. Not only was it defended by the best German troops in

Sicily but the approach to it was a narrow road which, running along the edge of a precipitous gorge, was commanded from the slopes above. Near the town the hillside was terraced for cultivation, but farther away it was covered with slippery grass and loose stones. The scaling of these slopes would be arduous, and, to make matters worse, the sulphur fumes from Etna were making the troops incredibly thirsty. It was fortunate therefore that many of the men who had been wounded in Tunisia had now returned to the 6th Battalion to give it a good leavening of troops experienced in fighting in mountains.

On the afternoon of July 31 the battalion marched through Catenanuova to a forming-up position north of that town. During the move enemy fighter-bombers dived low and dropped bombs amongst the transport and on either side of the marching column, but there were no casualties. Before midnight the battalion began to move to the start-line, which was about four miles south-west of Centuripe and was being held by 11th Brigade. The advance from there was to be made with the 6th Battalion moving over the hills on the left, the Buffs moving up the line of the road on the right, and the Argylls in reserve. It was to be a silent attack, and for the battalion the objective was the high ground west of Centuripe.

The night was very hot. There were no mules, and, because of the doubt as to whether there would be any wells to quench their sulphurous thirst, the troops were each carrying two full water-bottles besides the burden of tools and rations and ammunition for forty-eight hours. A Company (Major Defrates) was in the lead, and their scouts moved forward to gain contact with the troops of 11th Brigade on the start-line. But some German parachute troops, who had been hiding in rear of 11th Brigade's forward positions and had now come out of their caves, caught A Company in a vicious cross-fire before the start-line was even reached. These Germans were on a steep hill, and when A Company attempted to move round behind them they fired rifle grenades from the top of it. C Company (Major Taylor) came forward, and the two companies moved up the hill against heavy automatic fire. Major Taylor was wounded, the troops checked, and Gordon Defrates, assuming command of both companies, shouted encouragement to the men and led them up the rocky slope. This assault was greatly assisted by the supporting fire of two Bren guns, which were personally placed in position by Serjeant Obbard. The enemy were driven off the hill, but casualties in the assault were numerous, including Major Defrates and Lieutenants Restall and Tyler, who were wounded.

Before dawn the start-line had been cleared, and the whole

battalion moved forward. But soon after daylight considerable sniping from an enemy outpost on a feature in front held up the advance. C Company was launched against it. The enemy fire was too strong, and the company went to ground about half-way up the hill. D Company then went forward and, after a tough fight, the enemy withdrew to his main positions about Centuripe. Meanwhile, on the line of the road, the Buffs had been pinned down by devastating fire, and 'Swifty' Howlett, still commanding 36th Brigade, ordered the Argylls to assault Centuripe straight up the hill, while the Buffs followed and the 6th Battalion continued its advance on the left. It was now intensely hot, the overloaded men were tired as well as thirsty, and the ground was so broken that the use of tanks was impossible. Nevertheless the troops of the battalion scrambled forward over the jumble of loose rocks and gorges under mortar and machine-gun fire from the peaks above. Most of the fire was coming from high ground to the left of the town, and the advance in that direction continued slowly for the remainder of the day.

That night, August 1, the East Surreys from 11th Brigade were thrown into the battle between the Argylls and the 6th Battalion with orders to advance up a mule track. At 11.30 p.m. the attack was resumed after a heavy bombardment by our guns, and A and B Companies of the 6th Battalion succeeded in capturing two steep features after a brisk battle with German snipers. Up to this time casualties in the battalion had been twelve killed and thirty-three wounded. There was still no sign of the enemy withdrawing, and all next day the fight continued across the gorges. That evening, August 2, B Company put in an attack on yet another hill. This also was successful, though the supporting bombardment for this attack caused five casualties in C Company through one gun firing short. By this time the brigade had been on the move and fighting continuously for nearly forty-eight hours against a determined enemy and, although it had been unable to capture Centuripe, General Evelegh decided that it had done enough. The Irish Brigade passed through the positions held by 36th Brigade and captured the town that night.

After three nights' and two days' bitter fighting the Battle of Centuripe had ended in a notable victory for 78th Division. In General Montgomery's opinion no other division in his army could have carried out the operation successfully. In the division itself the general belief was that it had been worse than Longstop.

*   *   *

By the morning of August 5 the Irish Brigade had secured crossings over the rivers Salso and Simeto, and plans were made for an attack on Adrano by 36th Brigade. The Argylls were to lead the attack and gain a footing on the plateau overlooking the town. The 6th Battalion, following through, was then to take the town itself. The Buffs were to protect the right flank.

After two quiet days south of Centuripe, the battalion marched through the town on the evening of August 5 to a harbour area north of the River Salso. The route was difficult to find in the darkness, and the boulders and lava which covered the track made the going very rough. As the battalion was about to cross the river enemy guns opened fire on the waiting troops, and a number of casualties were suffered. In their efforts to find cover the companies became dispersed, but by 3 a.m. on the 6th all had arrived in the harbour area just off the main road and were digging in. Cover was plentiful, and the battalion remained comparatively undisturbed throughout the day while the Argylls went forward to the high ground overlooking Adrano.

At ten that night, soon after darkness had fallen, the battalion moved off towards Adrano. Our guns put down an intensive barrage on the enemy positions in front of the town and five minutes' concentrated fire as the troops neared the objective. As soon as the guns stopped the leading companies moved in. No opposition was met. The enemy had withdrawn. By 4.30 a.m. on August 7 the battalion was in Adrano. The town had been badly damaged by bombs and shell fire, and it was some hours after the battalion's entry before the civilians began to appear from their houses in ones and twos. No Germans were to be found. Patrols in carriers, probing forward, encountered only Italians, some of whom hastily surrendered. Some billets were found for the troops, and the remainder of the day and the night passed uneventfully.

3. *Bronte and Monte Rivoglia*

By the capture of Adrano the British had gained possession of the only lateral road south of Mount Etna. The enemy's positions about Catania thus became untenable, and he began to thin out everywhere, holding delaying positions as he retreated. In pursuit 11th Brigade pressed on slowly northwards along the narrow road to Bronte and, after fierce fighting, captured that town on the afternoon of August 8. That evening 36th Brigade moved forward to relieve 11th Brigade, the 6th Battalion travelling in troop-carrying vehicles from Adrano to a copse about a mile south of Bronte. Just after

N.W. AFRICA: A 3-INCH MORTAR OF THE 6TH BATTALION IN ACTION IN
THE ROBAA AREA DURING THE ENEMY ATTACK ON JANUARY 31, 1943

N.W. AFRICA: INFANTRY MOVE UP FOR THE ATTACK ON
LONGSTOP HILL, APRIL 1943. WITH THEM IS A CHURCHILL TANK

SICILY: INFANTRY LEAVE CATENANUOVA FOR THE ATTACK ON CENTURIPE

SICILY: BREN-GUN CARRIERS MOVE INTO CENTURIPE ON AUGUST 3, 1943

debussing they came under shell and mortar fire from the enemy, but there were no casualties. Colonel Bryan was then ordered to take the battalion through Bronte and establish a firm base on the western slope of Mount Etna. With this as an O.P. the Gunners would be able to bring fire to bear on to the enemy as he withdrew along the road to Randazzo.

Before midnight the 6th Battalion marched off up the road and into Bronte. Going through the town was very difficult. Enemy snipers were still active, and heaps of rubble caused by bombing and shelling blocked the streets. Indeed, for the mules carrying the mortars and machine guns progress was nearly impossible, and the battalion had to press on without them. Once through the town progress was but little easier because the track petered out and the lava beds had a disturbing effect on the compass of the Intelligence Officer, who had difficulty in finding the route. Eventually, on the approach of daylight, the battalion was forced to establish the firm base where it was, on a large outcrop of lava. As dawn broke shots began to ring out, and it was discovered that the leading troops were less than 100 yards from an enemy outpost. A sharp, exciting engagement then took place before the enemy withdrew; fifteen prisoners were taken. Soon afterwards the enemy began to shell and mortar the area, but with no effect. This was the situation when Brigadier Howlett arrived at ten o'clock.

'Swifty' brought the information that the Buffs had reached Monte Rivoglia, north-east of Bronte, but had been unable to overcome the enemy's resistance on that feature. The 6th Battalion was, therefore, to seize Mt. Rivoglia and would cross the start-line, about half-a-mile south-west of that hill, at three that afternoon. Accordingly the battalion moved off at midday. While on the move the troops were mortared for the first time by *nebelwerfers*, the unnerving German multiple mortars, which caused a number of casualties. These included Major K. B. Scott, the brother of Major H. E. Scott of the 2nd Battalion and a Walker Cup golfer, who was fatally wounded. In spite of this the start-line was reached, and the companies prepared to go forward. The Gunners then reported that they would not be ready in time, and zero-hour was postponed until 5.30 p.m. This also allowed three tanks, which had managed to find a way through Bronte, to come up. Unfortunately these were of no assistance owing to the unsuitability of the ground. The mortars and machine guns of the battalion had still not arrived.

As the attack began the enemy artillery put down a heavy concentration, which put our Gunners' wireless out of action and caused numerous casualties in the battalion. With great bravery

Corporal Armstead treated these casualties and made several journeys with wounded men to the Aid Post across ground exposed to close-range machine-gun fire. This fire caused the leading troops to pause, and Colonel Bryan moved up among them and encouraged them to press forward. The two forward companies then moved on until, when about five hundred yards from Mt. Rivoglia, C Company on the right suffered heavy casualties, including Lieutenant Wood, from shell and mortar fire and went to ground. At the same time B Company on the left were completely pinned down by machine-gun fire. A Company (Captain R. L. Clarke) then came through and, advancing up a gully which gave some protection from the fierce fire of the enemy, swept on with C Company. For the next hour Captain Clarke, followed by Serjeant Richardson, who took over command of the leading platoon when Lieutenant Falwasser was killed, led this party up the steep slope of Rivoglia under heavy fire. Ultimately he reached the summit with forty men and quickly organised the defence on the left part of the hill. On the right D Company, led by Captain Wakefield, also made use of a gully for cover and seized their part of the objective despite strong opposition. The battalion then consolidated on Mt. Rivoglia. This attack was a fine example of courage and cool leadership, and many deeds of gallantry were performed.

It was now late in the evening. On account of the continued mortar and sniper fire of the enemy, Paul Bryan expected a counter-attack to be launched. He therefore asked for reinforcements to help in the defence of the large feature. Two companies of the Buffs soon arrived. Before dark some machine guns and mortars also came up, and the position was made secure. No attack came in, however, and early next morning, August 10, patrols went forward. One of these found a well-concealed enemy machine-gun post, and a mortar 'stonk' was directed on to it during the morning. There was spasmodic hostile shelling for the remainder of the day, but no other aggressive action was taken by the enemy.

The following day the Irish Brigade went forward to attack enemy positions in the area of Maletto, which was captured on the night of August 12. The Irish then moved on towards Randazzo, where they joined hands with the Americans, who had been advancing along the north coast from Palermo. For 36th Brigade the campaign was over. Brigadier Howlett was awarded a bar to his D.S.O. for his inspiring leadership of the brigade at Centuripe and in the Bronte area.

4. *The End of the Campaign*

The enemy had begun to withdraw his forces from Sicily after the fall of Adrano, and when the Irish Brigade and the Americans joined hands at Randazzo he broke contact all along the front. Every effort was made to check the German evacuation, but the Straits of Messina are only two miles wide, and this way of escape could not be stopped at night. From August 14 there was a stream of small craft crossing the narrow sea to Italy during the hours of darkness, and all efforts of the Allied air and naval forces failed to prevent it. Much German equipment was left behind in Sicily.

The losses of the 6th Battalion had not been unduly heavy in the campaign—two officers and thirty-three other ranks had been killed—and the fighting had not been prolonged. But the physical strain had been great while it lasted, with rough marching, hard lying and little sleep. Such was the morale and happy spirit in the battalion, that these hardships meant little to it.

The battalion remained on Monte Rivoglia for two more days, during which some 120 reinforcements joined, and then moved to an area north of Bronte on the evening of August 13. In a few days parties began to go to a rest camp near Patti on the north coast of the island for five days at a time, and on the 29th the whole battalion moved there. After a period of training by day and concerts and films at night, the warm days of ease and wonderful bathing came to an end when the battalion moved on the night of September 22 to some woods near Milazzo. At ten next morning the troops marched to the beach and embarked in the *Royal Scotsman*. At midday the ship steamed out towards the Straits of Messina for Italy and another campaign.

CHAPTER 15

Italy: Termoli to the Arielli
October to December 1943
5th and 6th Battalions

1. *The Initial Landings in Italy*

THE Fascist régime in Italy had crumbled even before the fall of Sicily. Mussolini had been arrested on July 25, 1943, and Marshal Badoglio had at once begun secret negotiations for an armistice with the Allies. On September 9 the fact that Italy had surrendered was made public; but by that time two Allied armies had landed in Italy.

The first of these was the British 8th Army, which invaded the toe of Italy[1] across the Straits of Messina from Sicily on September 3, 1943. Taking San Giovanni and Reggio against little opposition the 5th Division and the 1st Canadian Division immediately thrust northwards. On the 9th the 1st Airborne Division made an un-opposed sea-borne landing at Taranto, and columns promptly drove east and north to capture the ports of Brindisi and Bari. 11th Brigade of 78th Division and 4th Armoured Brigade then landed at Bari. From them a mobile force, known as Force 'A,' was formed and was sent in pursuit of the German rearguards up the Adriatic coast. By September 27 the airfields at Foggia had been seized. Meanwhile the other army—the 5th—under General Mark Clark and consisting of the British X and the American VI Corps, had landed on the Salerno beaches. The Germans put up strong opposition there, and it was not until October 1 that Naples was captured.

The advance up the leg of Italy by these two armies then began. Communications across the Apennine mountains, which occupy the centre of Italy, are very difficult, and these two forces operated entirely separately. The 5th Army, using Naples as its base, began to advance up the Tyrrhenian coast. The 8th Army, still commanded by General Montgomery, used the triangle of Bari, Taranto and Brindisi as a base and pressed on along the shores of the Adriatic Sea.

By October 2 the forward troops of Force 'A' had reached the

---

[1] See rear end-paper map.

River Biferno, five miles south of Termoli. The bridge over the river had been demolished by the Germans, but 2nd Lancashire Fusiliers waded across and established a bridgehead. The remainder of 11th Brigade then turned inland east of the river to seize Larino. The next step was the capture of Termoli, and it was decided that this should be done by two Marine commandos and the other two brigades of 78th Division. The commandos landed at Termoli in the small hours of October 3, quickly overcame the weak German garrison, took possession of the town and made contact with the Lancashire Fusiliers. 36th Brigade was to be the next to land, with the 6th Battalion in the van.

2. *The 6th Battalion at Termoli*

Having landed at Taranto on September 24, the 6th Battalion moved four days later to Trani. On October 2 it moved by road to Barletta, and the troops embarked at midday on October 3 in Infantry Landing Craft, being seen off by 'Monty.' Before midnight the ships were lying off Termoli. At 1 a.m. on October 4 the first party, consisting of Brigadier Howlett, part of 36th Brigade Headquarters, Battalion Headquarters and B and D Companies, disembarked and went into some buildings in the town. Soon after dawn enemy aircraft dropped bombs on the quay, but by eight the second party had disembarked and the whole battalion was having breakfast in Termoli. The Buffs and the Argylls, with the remainder of Brigade Headquarters, also disembarked safely.

The key personnel of the 6th Battalion now were:—

Commanding Officer	Lieut.-Colonel P. E. O. Bryan, D.S.O., M.C.
Second-in-command	Major W. L. R. Benyon (R.W.F.)
Adjutant	Captain B. J. Goodenough
Quartermaster	Lieutenant T. Landman
Regtl. Serjeant-Major	W.O.I P. Byrne
O.C. A Company	Major R. L. Clarke, M.C.
O.C. B Company	Captain P. H. Austin
O.C. C Company	Major I. H. Roper
O.C. D Company	Captain D. J. Wakefield
O.C. Support Company[1]	Captain J. L. Williams (D.L.I.)

A complete list of officers is in Appendix B.

[1] A Support Company was formed in each infantry battalion at about this time. It contained all the supporting weapons of the battalion, including the Carrier, Mortar, Anti-tank and Assault Pioneer Platoons, leaving only the administrative personnel in Headquarter Company.

The battalion moved off without delay. At 9 a.m. Colonel Bryan made a reconnaissance with Brigadier Howlett, and at ten the battalion marched south behind an advance guard and reached its assembly area in a wood in the Lancashire Fusiliers' bridgehead west of the River Biferno. The Company Commanders then made their reconnaissance, while the troops had dinner. 36th Brigade's intention was to advance inland to the town of Guglionesi. The move was to be made with the Argylls on the right directed on the village of San Giacomo and the 6th Battalion on the left. The Buffs were in reserve. Paul Bryan was given a wood and a farm at Point 193 as his objective. He selected another farm about 1,200 yards nearer than this as an intermediate objective. This was named Chocolate Farm by the troops.

The advance began at 3.15 p.m., when the artillery fired a short programme. D Company broke cover and moved forward on a front of one platoon towards Chocolate Farm, with the mortar platoon and machine guns following up. When the leading platoon, commanded by 2nd Lieutenant Jarrett, was within fifty yards of Chocolate Farm some enemy were seen in it. The platoon immediately opened fire on them. This fire was returned; but the platoon assaulted, covered by fire from their own Bren guns, and the enemy fled. One prisoner was taken. Continuing its advance from Chocolate Farm this platoon then came under fire from Point 193. The other two platoons of D Company were committed and, overrunning some machine-gun positions near the wood at Point 193, they put the enemy to flight with the bayonet. This action aided C Company, who worked their way round the right flank and prepared to clear the area of the farm. The final assault was made by the platoon commanded by Lieutenant Desmond, who was severely wounded by a grenade as he approached the objective. Serjeant S. G. Smith at once assumed command of the platoon, led a bayonet charge in face of heavy fire, captured the farm and directed fire effectively on to the retreating enemy.

The whole objective was now in our hands. But the area was still under fire from enemy machine guns on a spur to the right flank. Lieutenant Morris's platoon was ordered to silence these guns. On emerging into the open it came under heavy fire, and two mortar detachments under Serjeant Dyke and the machine-gun section commanded by Serjeant Youens were brought up to cover its advance. But the ground was too open and, after the platoon had received severe casualties and Lieutenant Morris and Serjeant Youens had been wounded, it was decided not to press home the assault. B Company was then brought up on that flank, the battalion con-

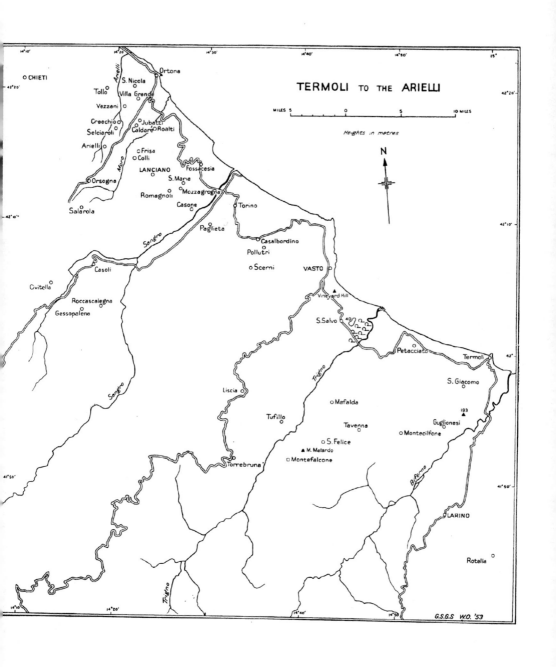

TERMOLI TO THE ARIELLI

MILES 5   0   5   10 MILES

Heights in metres

N

O CHIETI

Ortona
S. Nicola
Tollo
Villa Grande
Vezzani
Creechio
Jubatti
Selciaroli
Caldaro
Roalti
Arielli
Frisa
Colli
Fossacesia
LANCIANO
S. Maria
Orsogna
Romagnoli
Mozzagrogna
Casone
Salarola
Torino
Paglieta
Casalbordino
Pollutri
Scerni
VASTO
Casoli
Vineyard Hill
Civitella
Roccascalegna
Gessopalena
S. Salvo
Petacciato
Termoli
S. Giacomo
Liscia
Mafalda
193
Tufillo
Tavenna
Guglionesi
S. Felice
Montecilfone
M. Matardo
Torrebruna
Montefalcone
Sangro
Trigno
Biferno
Trigno
LARINO
Rotella

G.S.G.S W.O. '53

solidated about Point 193, and all companies dug in for the night. Meanwhile, on the right, the Argylls had not been so successful. They had met stronger opposition and had not been able to capture San Giacomo.

During the night patrols were sent out, and two farms in front were found to be clear of enemy. Later, however, one of the forward platoons clearly heard the approach of German tanks. This was a serious matter, because the heavy rain which had been falling had made the ground so soft that it had been impossible to bring up the anti-tank guns. Moreover, the rain had made the River Biferno impassable, and our own tanks would be unable to cross until a Bailey bridge could be built. The gravity of the situation was fully realised at Brigade Headquarters, for at dawn on the 5th 'Swifty' Howlett arrived and gave orders that the battalion was to withdraw to a wood near Chocolate Farm if it was attacked by tanks. He also said that arrangements would be made to send up some anti-tank guns; but the fields were still too sodden and these did not arrive.

At about 10.30 a.m. machine-gun fire was heard and six enemy tanks approached from the right. Heavy fire was opened by all weapons, but these naturally failed to stop the tanks, which came on at speed. Colonel Bryan therefore reluctantly ordered the withdrawal to the wood. To disengage the troops proved to be difficult. Although the mortar detachment under Serjeant Meade remained in action until the tanks were less than 100 yards away, some of the personnel in the forward companies were taken prisoner by the German infantry which followed the tanks. As the companies withdrew the guns of the tanks caused severe casualties, including Captain Peerless, who was killed. Nevertheless the battalion reorganised in rear of the wood at Chocolate Farm and ultimately took up anti-tank defence positions near the main road to Larino.

The situation in 36th Brigade was now serious. On the right the Argylls had also been forced to withdraw, and in the centre the enemy tanks had overrun two companies of the Buffs. Brigade Headquarters itself was under fire from the German tanks, and Captain Shaun Stewart, who was detached from the battalion as Brigade Intelligence Officer, collected stragglers and organised the defence of the headquarters' area with inspiring coolness and gallantry. At 1 p.m. all available men at Rear Battalion Headquarters in Termoli were sent forward in trucks under Major Clarke and Captain Beall. These were ordered to occupy a farm in advance of Brigade Headquarters, while Major Roper with a force of some 40 men seized another farm on the left flank. These farms were both

R

successfully occupied. Captain Beall then moved across some open ground to an anti-tank gun to see if it could be brought into action. In doing so he was hit in both arms by machine-gun bullets, but he would not give up his attempt until his leg was smashed by a shell from a tank. Without hesitation Serjeant Obbard walked across to attend to him. Peter Beall's leg had to be amputated later.

At 2.40 p.m. the situation was at last relieved when a Bailey bridge over the Biferno was completed and the Sherman tanks of Force 'A' were able to cross. They were led straight up to the ridge in front of Brigade Headquarters, where they engaged the enemy tanks. Then, with the Buffs, they moved forward to positions little short of Point 193, while the 6th Battalion reorganised to protect the left flank. On the right, in the Argylls' sector, the situation was more precarious, and it was not until the evening that the Germans were finally checked. That night the Irish Brigade landed at Termoli and, moving into the attack early next morning, they captured San Giacomo. By the evening of October 6 the Battle of Termoli was won; but it had been 'a close-run thing.'

*   *   *

While the Buffs advanced south-westwards to capture Guglionesi and the Irish Brigade advanced steadily up the coast towards the River Trigno, the 6th Battalion went into billets in Termoli. There it remained for the next week, during which five officers and seventy other ranks arrived to replace the casualties. Then on October 17 the battalion moved to Guglionesi for an advance on Montecilfone, some four miles farther south-west. This town had already been seized by a squadron of 56th Reconnaissance Battalion but, as it was uncertain whether the enemy were still in the vicinity, the advance was made after nightfall with the battalion deployed as for an attack. Montecilfone proved to be clear of enemy, and by two in the morning its occupation was complete.

That afternoon, October 18, B Company's defence position on a wooded hill on the outskirts of the town was attacked strongly, and the two forward platoons and Company Headquarters were forced to fall back. But Lance-Corporal Hunt with the other two signallers remained in their slit-trench with the telephone until the enemy were only thirty yards away. Grenades thrown by the Germans rolled almost into the trench, but they hung on. After a few minutes a message came over the telephone, and Hunt crossed ground which was under fire and in full view of the enemy and delivered it to the Company Commander. A brisk engagement then ensued, the position was reoccupied, and the enemy retired under machine-gun fire.

After five more days of intermittent shelling and patrol clashes at Montecilfone, the battalion moved back to Guglionesi, where it was at six hours' notice. It was not, however, until October 29 that the call came, and the battalion moved in M.T. to Petacciato in readiness to cross the River Trigno.

3. *The 5th Battalion Arrives on the Trigno*

By this time it was apparent that the Germans intended to oppose the advance of the 8th Army up the Adriatic coast by more than mere rearguard actions, and that more divisions would be required to drive them back. The 8th Indian Division was brought from Egypt to Italy and began to come into the line at Larino, on the left of 78th Division, towards the middle of October. With this division came the 5th Battalion.

8th Indian Division, commanded by Major-General D. Russell, consisted of 17th, 19th and 21st Indian Infantry Brigades. The 5th Battalion was part of 21st Indian Brigade, which was commanded by Brigadier B. S. Mould and contained in addition the 1/5 Mahratta Light Infantry and the 3/15 Punjaub Regiment. The key personnel in the 5th Battalion at that time were:

Commanding Officer	Lieutenant-Colonel J. H. H. Whitty, M.C.
Second-in-command	Major D. W. Jackson
Adjutant	Captain J. M. Wollaston
Quartermaster	Lieutenant A. G. Blake
Regtl. Serjeant-Major	W.O.I E. H. Creed
O.C. H.Q. Company	Major M. H. Wonnall
O.C. A Company	Captain R. A. Abbott (Devon)
O.C. B Company	Major J. D. Stocker
O.C. C Company	Captain D. H. Gwilliam
O.C. D Company	Captain E. L. Hill (Wilts.)
O.C. Support Company	Captain D. W. J. Wood

A complete list of officers can be found in Appendix B.

Having arrived at Taranto on September 24 (see Chapter 12, Section 4), the battalion had remained there until October 16, when its transport arrived from Egypt. It had then moved by rail to Trani and thence by march route to a concentration area close to Barletta. Colonel Whitty then took some of his officers and N.C.O. specialists to stay for three days with the 6th Battalion, then at Montecilfone, in order to learn the local methods of waging war. This visit was such a success that Major Jackson took up the remaining officers and more specialists a few days later.

The battalion moved into the line with 21st Indian Brigade on October 25, and first contact was made with the enemy at Mafalda, just short of the River Trigno. On November 1 a patrol to the river suffered four casualties, including the Intelligence Officer, Lieutenant Marshall, who was killed. On the same morning the battalion's transport was shelled in Tavenna and three men were killed and Major Jackson was wounded in the head. Major Wonnall became second-in-command temporarily. This was the only action the battalion was to see for some weeks, for when 8th Indian Division crossed the Trigno the following day, 21st Brigade was in reserve, and the battalion was not committed at all during the battle.

4. *The 6th Battalion at San Salvo and 'Vineyard Hill'*

The Germans were now to fight their first stubborn delaying action. The position they had taken up on the River Trigno was typical of many which they were to defend throughout the campaign. From the Apennines mountain ramparts fall down to either coast, and between these ridges run streams which rain and snow may swell into raging torrents. The Germans used these rivers merely as obstacles, and defended them only with light forces to oppose the approach and crossing. Any reinforcement of the bridgehead, especially with anti-tank guns and armour, would be strenuously opposed. But it was beyond the river, on the commanding ground overlooking it, that their main positions would be constructed. Thus the River Trigno was only lightly defended, and the Germans' main positions were on the San Salvo Ridge, some two miles beyond it.

On the right flank 78th Division opened the attack on October 27, when the Irish Brigade, having already established a bridgehead over the Trigno, attacked the town of San Salvo. The German defensive fire was formidable, the attack was halted and, to save needless casualties, the Irish were withdrawn to their bridgehead, which by now had been turned by heavy rain into a quagmire.

36th Brigade was then ordered forward, and the 6th Battalion left Petacciato on November 2, crossed the river and arrived at its assembly area in a wood east of the coast road before midnight. The area was being shelled spasmodically, and slit-trenches were dug. Next morning the brigade attacked after elaborate artillery preparation and air bombing. The ground was still sodden, but tanks managed to cross the river and attack the enemy machine-gun nests. By ten the Buffs were in the outskirts of San Salvo and, having beaten off a counter-attack, they then cleared the town and took up positions 700 yards beyond it. Meanwhile the 6th Battalion, in reserve, had moved forward from the wood on to higher ground at ring contour 40, about a mile south-east of San Salvo.

The 6th Battalion was then ordered to pass through the Buffs and attack the enemy on 'Vineyard Hill,' a feature on the right of the coast road midway between San Salvo and Vasto. It was to be a night attack, and Colonel Bryan took his company commanders forward to the Buffs' positions to view the ground in daylight. While he was giving out his orders a heavy German attack with infantry and tanks developed. The Buffs were compelled to fall back to the outskirts of San Salvo. Consequently Paul Bryan's orders were cut short, and when the 6th Battalion moved forward after dark that evening there were several miles of un-reconnoitred and enemy-held country between San Salvo and 'Vineyard Hill'.

At nine that evening the battalion began to advance astride the coast road. It passed through San Salvo safely, but about a mile north of the town enemy tanks were heard. Almost immediately these tanks opened rapid fire with machine guns, and the whole battalion went to ground. The leading troops had blundered into an enemy tank harbour. There was temporary confusion while Colonel Bryan attempted to manœuvre the battalion in pitch darkness. An artillery concentration was called for, and the troops opened rapid fire with their own weapons; but it was impossible to continue the advance, and the battalion fell back to San Salvo and later to ring contour 40.

*   *   *

The Germans had apparently sent these tanks forward to cover the withdrawal of their main forces, for during the night, November 3, they pulled them back. When, at dawn, 78th Division's attack was resumed the way was at first clear. Unopposed the 6th Battalion moved forward through San Salvo and up the line of the coast road until 'Vineyard Hill' was reached. Here, as had been expected, the enemy was encountered, and B Company, supported by tanks, was ordered to assault the hill. As the leading platoon neared the summit it came under machine-gun fire which checked the impetus and forced the men to cover. But Serjeant Crosby, disregarding the fire, strode up to the crest of the hill, rallied his platoon and placed each section in its fire position. During the fire-fight which followed Private Wearn showed great coolness in firing his Bren gun from an exposed position, and it was mainly due to his courage that the enemy was forced to withdraw. The battalion then consolidated about 'Vineyard Hill,' while 11th Brigade went through to capture Vasto.

Next morning, November 5, the battalion moved on again up the coast road and passed through Vasto. On leaving the town the leading troops were fired on by German snipers, and soon afterwards enemy infantry and armoured cars were met. The advanced guard failed to brush aside this opposition, and at 3 p.m. some tanks came up to support a battalion attack. For two hours confused fighting continued against small groups of evasive enemy, but at dusk the resistance had still not been overcome and defensive positions were taken up for the night just east of the coast road. That evening Major Tuffill, who had been Brigade Major of 231st (Malta) Brigade during the invasion of Sicily and Italy, joined the battalion as second-in-command. His stay was short, for he contracted jaundice and was evacuated after a few days. He did not return to the Regiment but took up an appointment on the planning staff in England. It is sad to relate that he was killed in a riding accident in Iraq after the war.

Early next morning, November 6, the advance was continued. The enemy had withdrawn during the night and no opposition was met, but progress was slow because the bridges had been demolished by the retreating enemy. That night 11th Brigade went through again, and by the evening of November 8 their leading troops had reached the River Sangro. A march that day up the coast road to Casalbordino and thence across country to Torino brought the 6th Battalion to the river also. That evening the companies took up positions on high ground overlooking the Sangro.

* * *

Meanwhile on the left flank 8th Indian Division had been equally successful. Its leading brigade, the 19th, had crossed the Trigno on November 2 and captured the village of Tufillo on the 5th. This brigade was then joined by the 17th, and together they advanced with little opposition, captured Atessa and reached the River Sangro. The attack had been successful all along the front, and both 78th and 8th Indian Divisions began to assemble their troops in preparation for the next battle.

5. *The 6th Battalion on the Sangro*

The Italian winter had now set in with snow on the hills, grey skies, strong winds and heavy rain. North of Torino near the coast the River Sangro, swollen with rain and snow, ran five feet deep and a hundred yards wide between steep banks. Across the river, level farm-land extended for over a mile. Then there rose an escarpment 150 feet high, and beyond that an upward slope to a ridge on which stood the villages of Fossacesia, Santa Maria and Mozzagrogna. On this ridge the Germans had prepared their main defensive positions, which included machine-gun nests connected by tunnels, pill-boxes, houses reinforced by concrete and deep shelters. Anti-tank and anti-personnel minefields covered all approaches; one of the most troublesome of the mines for the infantry was the small schu-mine, which would blow off the foot of anyone who trod on it. This immensely strong position, called the Gustav or Winter-Line, extended the whole width of Italy and was designed to stop the Allied advance once and for all.

When the 6th Battalion led 36th Brigade to the River Sangro on the evening of November 8 it was raining hard. Snow fell on the 10th, and on that day the Commander of V Corps, Lieutenant-General C. W. Allfrey, visited the battalion's positions and viewed the ground across the river with Major-General V. Evelegh, who still commanded 78th Division. Patrols had already discovered that the river was only lightly defended in accordance with German custom. It was now decided to extend the patrolling across the river in order to find out as much as possible about the enemy; to deny the Germans access to the river; and at the same time to protect reconnaissance parties of Sappers and armoured formations.

Major J. D. Forman, who was now second-in-command, was placed in charge of patrolling in the battalion. As 'Patrol Master' he established his headquarters in a farmhouse on the Torino Ridge with a magnificent view across the river. From this he briefed patrols to clear the mines; reconnaissance patrols to discover what positions the enemy were occupying; patrols to draw fire from these positions and thus find out their strength; fighting patrols to destroy these positions when their strength was known; and patrols to protect R.E. and tank reconnaissance parties. An average of ten patrols or 60 men were in this way sent across the river every twenty-four hours. A patrol diary was kept, and each patrol was carefully cross-examined on its return. The information obtained was collated by the Intelligence Section and shown on a large panoramic sketch of the area.

The first task was to lift the mines which the Germans had carefully laid on all the tracks across the level farm-land and in all the possible approaches to the escarpment. Even a worse obstacle than these was the River Sangro. Indeed, after the first few days the river presented greater difficulties than the enemy. For, to begin with, the Germans attempted to contest the control of the river area by fire by day and by patrolling at night; but they soon gave this up and were content merely to defend their positions on the escarpment. On the other hand the river was at first not very difficult to cross, but later it was often necessary to swim it. In fact to cross it became a most precarious undertaking, because it varied in depth and rate of flow according to the amount of rain and snow that had fallen in the hills. Several men were drowned because of an unexpected rise of the river, and it thus became necessary to re-test each crossing-place before it was used a second time. It was found that the best way to cross was for a patrol to wade out to the middle of the river, each man firmly gripping the man in front of him, and then to turn upstream to face the flood until a shelf of firm shingle was reached. The troops would invariably be wet through at the outset of every patrol, with a consequent loss in fighting efficiency.

In spite of these difficulties, at the end of nine days all the mines had been lifted; tank crossings and routes had been reconnoitred; the enemy had lost numerous casualties and had withdrawn from his forward positions to the escarpment; and above all the Germans had been reduced to a state of nervous tension. It was, however, a great strain on the battalion, which, in those nine days, lost more casualties than any unit which took part in the subsequent attack.

The most ambitious patrol was led by Major Forman himself. It consisted of some sixty men and was divided into two parties. One party went forward to the escarpment and took up positions on it while the other assaulted enemy posts near a farm. The assaulting party was seen by the Germans and was caught between two fires, which caused numerous casualties. But the troops rallied, scaled a wire obstacle and charged the enemy posts. They reached the main trench, cleared it and killed at least six Germans and captured two others. Our own casualties had been two killed and four seriously wounded. The patrol then withdrew, taking three enemy machine guns and one mortar with it. A less dramatic but equally important patrol was that carried out by Serjeant Knight and Lance-Corporal Lingham. On the way out they located four enemy machine-gun posts, and all next day they lay up and observed movements on the Fossacesia-Santa Maria road. On the way back that evening rain fell heavily. Several crossings over the Sangro were found to be impassable. Eventually Lingham, who had won an M.M. at Longstop Hill, was dragged away by the current and swept out of sight. Serjeant Knight reached the east bank exhausted but rushed down the river and continued his search for him till early morning. No trace of Lingham was ever found. Another outstanding patrol was that led by Serjeant Obbard and Lance-Corporal Andrews on the moonlit night of November 13. It was a fighting patrol to destroy enemy positions on the escarpment. Threading its way through a minefield this patrol moved up a covered approach, advanced swiftly on the nearest slit-trench and wiped out the garrison. Surprise was now lost, but Obbard, switching the direction of his attack twice, led his men against all trenches and diggings in the area and put the enemy to flight. Altogether the fighting lasted twenty minutes before the patrol withdrew successfully.

*　　*　　*

While this patrolling had been going on all the apparatus for the main attack in the coastal sector had been gathered behind the Torino Ridge. The time had come for the battle to open, and General Montgomery held a conference at Vasto to explain his plans. It was attended by Commanding Officers and above. As Colonel Bryan made his way to it he wondered how our attack was ever going to succeed against the river and the formidable mine and concrete obstacles. When he came away, having listened to 'Monty' for an hour, he felt quite sorry for the Germans. The plan was for 78th Division to establish a bridgehead across the Sangro and seize and hold a start-line on the escarpment. 8th Indian Division would then capture the enemy's main defensive positions on the ridge about Santa Maria and Mozzagrogna, and 78th Division would pass through and sweep right-handed to Fossacesia and the coast.

The start-line was to be seized by 36th Brigade, with the Argylls on the left and one composite company each from the Buffs and the 6th Battalion on either side of the main road. The company from the 6th Battalion consisted of one strong platoon from each of the four rifle companies; it was commanded by Major Roper. This company crossed the river at 2 a.m. on November 20 under cover of darkness and lay up below the escarpment waiting for the pre-arranged barrage. At 4.15 a.m. the guns opened fire, and the troops moved forward. Almost immediately the leading platoons encountered a field of schu-mines, which had been newly laid by the Germans, and the best part of one platoon was killed or wounded. The other two platoons reached the escarpment with only slight opposition, and the start-line was seized. It was then necessary to evacuate the wounded. Corporal Pickford, who was commanding a section of Pioneers at company headquarters, took charge of the task and worked untiringly under enemy fire until a lane had been cleared through the minefield. He then led the stretcher-bearers with the wounded back through the mines. Later some reinforcements were sent over the river with more mine-detectors, and the whole mine-field was lifted.

While the start-line was being seized, the rain had been pouring down and had made it impossible to complete any of the bridges across the river. The main attack, which had been timed to begin that morning, was therefore postponed. This meant that the start-line would have to be held for a longer period than had been expected and that Major Roper's force would have to be relieved. Major Defrates, who had now recovered from the wound he had received at Centuripe, took another company across the river that night, and Ian Roper's force returned to the Torino Ridge early next morning. The Germans now became aggressive. They attacked the Buffs' company in considerable strength and by degrees forced them to fall back across the river. In spite of this Gordon Defrates' force held on for the whole of the 21st, and that evening Colonel Bryan, with a skeleton Battalion Headquarters, took two more companies across the river to reinforce them. At the same time 11th Brigade also began to reinforce the troops on the escarpment. By the 22nd a reasonably secure bridgehead had been formed.

Meanwhile the rains continued, the mud became deeper and the river flowed faster than ever, and the troops in the bridgehead, who were shelled all the time and were forced to fight a series of minor actions against the enemy, crouched in water-logged slit-trenches with their clothes perpetually wet. They were very short of support-ing weapons, and the only way their stock of ammunition could be replenished was by DUKWs ferrying a supply across the river mouth. After two days a few tanks succeeded in fording the river. Later some anti-tank guns arrived on the escarpment. The very presence of these tanks had the desired effect. The enemy ceased his aggressive raids and withdrew to his main positions on the Fossa-cesia-Mozzagrogna Ridge. Before dawn on November 24 the troops of the battalion on the escarpment were relieved by the Buffs, and the whole battalion went into 36th Brigade reserve.

*   *   *

The 6th Battalion was not called upon to take any further part in the Sangro battle, but remained on the Torino Ridge watching the efforts of our Sappers to throw Bailey bridges across the river, and the enemy artillery and aircraft trying to destroy them. By Novem-ber 28 our Sappers had won the contest. 8th Indian Division crossed the river and went into the assault on Mozzagrogna. The only brigade of 78th Division to take part in this attack was the Irish—

the other two had been fully committed to hold the start-line—and this brigade captured Fossacesia on the 30th.

The success on the Sangro was marred for the 6th Battalion, and indeed for the whole of 36th Brigade, by the death of Brigadier Howlett on November 29. On that evening there was intensive enemy shelling on the area of the lateral road in front of the brigade positions, and the brigadier was killed by a shell while he was visiting posts. This was a great loss to the Regiment. During the year in which he had commanded a brigade 'Swifty' had led it with an inspiring confidence which had won for him the D.S.O. and bar and had made promotion to high rank assured. By an ill chance the shell that killed him wounded Lieutenant Ronald Palmer, who was acting as Brigade Intelligence Officer and had previously been commended by 'Swifty' for making his way through the German lines with a message. Ronald was a son of Colonel W. V. Palmer and twin brother of John, who had been killed at Green Hill in N.W. Africa.

Early in December, 78th Division handed over its place on the right of the 8th Army to the Canadian Division and went back for rest to the Campobasso area on the mountain slopes north of Foggia. The 6th Battalion moved back with it and went into billets in Baranello.

6. *The 5th Battalion at Romagnoli*

Let us now trace the part played by the 5th Battalion in the Sangro battle. After the battalion had crossed the River Trigno it was occupied for a few days in repairing roads and other maintenance tasks at Torrebruna. Thence, on November 9, it moved to Pollutri, and preparations began for the attack across the Sangro. Air photographs were studied, and the company and platoon commanders went forward to view the ground from an O.P. in the 6th Battalion's area on the Torino Ridge. On November 18 Lieutenant Bland, covered by a patrol of the 6th Battalion, crossed the river to reconnoitre the route to the start-line. Finally, on the evening of the 19th the battalion marched to 21st Indian Brigade's assembly area near Torino, where it arrived next morning and set up headquarters next to those of the 6th Battalion. Heavy rain fell all that day, and the troops bivouacked miserably in boggy fields. It was then that the attack was postponed. The battalion was able to find cover in some buildings.

The River Sangro, swollen by this rain, did not subside sufficiently for a crossing to be made for several days. Eventually the plan of attack had to be modified. 21st Brigade was moved back in reserve to Paglieta, where the 5th Battalion remained until the evening of November 27. That night the attack began, and the battalion, in brigade reserve, suffered fifteen casualties from enemy mortar fire as it crossed the river. The attack went well at first. 17th Brigade, leading 8th Indian Division, penetrated to the outskirts of Mozzagrogna. The German resistance then stiffened, and it was not till the night of the 28th that Mozzagrogna was captured.

21st Brigade now moved up the slope to Mozzagrogna, and on the afternoon of November 30 the 5th Battalion, leading the brigade, turned west along the ridge towards Romagnoli, which was the next enemy stronghold. As the leading troops approached the village they came under fire, and the battalion deployed for attack with D Company on the right, A Company on the left and B and C in support. Since the axis of the attack passed in front of the German reserve positions, the weight of fire was coming from the right. Arrangements were therefore made for tanks to give supporting fire on that flank.

After artillery concentrations had been fired on the German positions for ten minutes the attack went in at 3.15 p.m. For 800 yards the leading troops advanced quickly, but first D and later A Company were then held up by machine-gun fire from the right flank. During the fire-fight which followed the crew of a 2-inch mortar were seriously wounded, and Lance-Corporal Longhurst, although under heavy fire, assisted them to cover, fetched the mortar and brought it into action again in another place. One of the Bren gunners, Private Webb, located an enemy Spandau post 200 yards away. Moving his gun from position to position until he was within 100 yards of the post, he killed all its occupants. No headway could be made, however, and Colonel Whitty went forward across bullet-swept ground to co-ordinate the supporting fire. This gallant action set an example which put new heart into the men.

Colonel Whitty found that D Company had suffered severe casualties, including Captain Hill, who had been killed, and that there was little hope of gaining ground on the right flank. He therefore ordered B Company (Major Stocker) to come forward on the left. When Major Stocker reached A Company he found that Captain Abbott had been wounded and was unconscious. He at once took command of both companies himself and organised a further attack. He gave orders for most of the Bren guns and all of the 2-inch mortars of the attacking platoons to be collected, and he formed these into a support group under C.S.M. Atkins of B Company. By this time the enemy had been located in a cluster of trenches concealed by hedges. The fire of the support group as well as that of the battalion's 3-inch mortars was directed on to this strong-point. Under cover of this fire, and moving to the left below the crest of the ridge so as to get into dead ground, A and B Companies pressed on and stormed the strong-point from the rear. The trenches were found to be reinforced with concrete and linked by tunnels, but the troops rolled up these positions and the village was captured with the loss of only one man killed. Total casualties for the whole battle were one officer (Captain Hill) and seventeen killed, and two officers and thirty-three wounded. The two officers, Captain Abbott and Lieutenant Leslie, died the following day. Thirty Germans were taken prisoner. John Stocker's handling of the reserve company was a model tactical feat which made the battalion's first battle in Italy a notable victory.

That night the Germans launched a counter-attack with tanks and infantry. For a time it looked as if it would be successful. But Colonel Whitty, again exposing himself to the enemy's fire, went to the scene of the possible break-in and restored the situation. The enemy made no further attacks, and the battalion was relieved in Romagnoli the following afternoon by a battalion of 17th Indian Brigade. It then moved on, with tanks in support, to Lanciano.

7. The 5th Battalion on the River Moro

The Gustav Line had now been completely breached, and the enemy had withdrawn behind the River Moro. After a few days in reserve 21st Indian Brigade continued its advance and reached the river. As usual the river was only lightly defended by the Germans, and a Canadian battalion had already established a bridgehead on the far side at Roalti. On December 7 the 5th Battalion crossed the Moro and took over the defence of this bridgehead.

On the right near the coast the Canadian Division had begun to attack the German positions west of the River Moro. But they had been able to make little headway in the difficult country, and 21st Brigade was now ordered to employ deception tactics so as to draw German reserves from the Canadian front. As part of the deception plan the Sappers began to build the 'Impossible Bridge' backwards from the bridgehead on the enemy's side of the river. This caused the Germans to become extremely active in this area. Shelling became intense, and fighting patrols began to attack the positions held by the 5th Battalion in the bridgehead. Before daylight on the

8th there was a raid on B Company's positions which was driven off without loss, but soon afterwards a large body of troops was heard approaching. Serjeant Degens crawled out to ascertain whether they were friend or foe. They were within 20 yards of him before he discovered that they were enemy, and he gave the alarm by firing his Bren gun at point-blank range. Surprise having been lost, the enemy tried to work round to the rear of the battalion, but defensive fire was brought down and, after a brisk engagement, they withdrew, leaving a dozen dead and six prisoners. Our losses were three killed and ten wounded.

That afternoon artillery fire and smoke was put down on the left of Roalti in order to persuade the enemy that 21st Brigade was about to attack. The Germans reacted at once. They shelled and mortared the village for ninety minutes, destroyed B Company's Headquarters and killed six and wounded a dozen of the battalion. In this ordeal the fortitude of the troops was excellent. Next day a message of congratulation on the behaviour of the battalion during the deception and subsequent shelling was received from the Army Commander.

For four more nights the battalion remained isolated in the bridgehead fighting minor engagements. And then, on December 12, the 'Impossible Bridge' was opened, and that night the Mahrattas crossed the river and reinforced the bridgehead. The Canadian attack was still going badly. In order to assist them it was now decided that 17th Indian Brigade should attack on their left and capture Caldare. With this in view a patrol from the battalion was sent forward under cover of darkness to find out if Caldare was strongly held by the enemy. On approaching the village it came under heavy mortar fire, and Lieutenant Reeves died from wounds received in this action. The necessary information had, however, been obtained. On another patrol Captain Van Beek was taken prisoner, but with great ingenuity he managed to escape and rejoin the battalion after three weeks in German hands at Tollo.

The attack by 17th Indian Brigade was successful. By the evening of December 14 it had seized positions on the Ortona-Orsogna lateral road. The 5th Battalion was then ordered to attack and occupy Point 239, a feature on the lateral road to the left of the positions already captured.

The battalion was relieved in the bridgehead on the evening of the 15th. At 2 a.m. next morning the companies moved off to the forming up position. At 5 a.m. the artillery programme began, and B Company (Major Stocker) and C Company (Captain Gwilliam) crossed the start-line. It was a damp, misty morning and the smoke from the shells produced a fog effect which caused the companies to

SICILY : THE ITALIAN MAINLAND FROM MESSINA

ITALY : THE RIVER SANGRO AND THE ESCARPMENT

ITALY: THE BAILEY BRIDGE OVER THE RIVER MORO AS SEEN FROM
THE BRIDGEHEAD HELD BY THE 5TH BATTALION, DECEMBER 1943

ITALY: MEN OF THE 5TH BATTALION PREPARE TO MAKE TEA IN VILLA
GRANDE DURING A LULL IN THE GERMAN SHELLING ON DECEMBER 29, 1943

cross over and arrive on reverse ends of the objective. Nevertheless, by 6 a.m. the leading platoons had reached the lateral road and had begun to occupy Point 239. It was then found that, in the artificial fog, they had failed to see two enemy tanks which were stationary on the road. C.S.M. Atkins immediately went back to a reserve platoon, led it to these tanks and captured them intact together with their crews. A few minutes later a third tank, a flame-thrower, approached and began firing at 100 yards range. Private Godden, who was covering the road with his P.I.A.T.,[1] hit the turret of this tank with a bomb which failed to explode. Undeterred, he calmly reloaded and fired again when the tank was 20 yards past him. This time the bomb exploded on the turret, and three of the crew baled out. The tank went on at reduced speed. Later it was destroyed by our tanks, which managed to come forward in daylight in spite of the softness of the ground. During the action some forty enemy prisoners were taken. Our casualties were ten killed and about forty wounded and missing.

Next day, December 17, a strong enemy patrol approached Point 239. Lance-Corporal Enever waited till the enemy scouts were within 15 yards of his section post before he ordered his Bren gunner to open fire. He then left his pit, ran 50 yards across bullet-swept ground, and directed the fire of another section on to the enemy. On his return his own Bren gun broke down, and he ran across under fire to his Platoon Headquarters to obtain another. It was largely due to his courage and initiative that this raid was beaten off. As a counter-measure a raiding party of D Company attacked the village of Selciaroli on December 18. But the enemy had already gone, and the village was occupied without opposition. Two days later 19th Indian Brigade went through to attack Villa Grande. The battalion moved back across the River Moro to Frisa for rest.

While the battalion was on the lateral road much of the transport was at Lanciano, where it was dive-bombed by enemy aircraft on December 16. An anti-tank portee, which was loaded with 6-pounder shells, was hit by a bomb and began to burn. Private Drew jumped into the driving seat of this vehicle and, after several attempts, succeeded in driving it away although two shells exploded and ripped the seat covers and damaged the superstructure. Then, undaunted, he returned and drove several other vehicles to cover.

[1] Projector Infantry Anti-Tank. This must have been one of the first enemy tanks to be disabled by this comparatively new weapon.

8. *The 5th Battalion at Villa Grande*

At Frisa Major B. J. F. Malcolmson[1] arrived to be second-in-command. With him came a much-needed draft of 90 Cameronians. But the battalion was still so much under strength that, even with 60 more reinforcements which arrived just before the next battle, it could only muster three full-strength rifle companies. A re-distribution of key personnel and some promotions were then carried out, clean clothing was issued and baths were arranged at a Mobile Bath Unit. On the morning of December 22, after only two days' rest, the battalion marched back to Point 239 on the lateral road, where it remained for Christmas. The battalion was in reserve, and on Christmas morning itself Colonel Whitty and the Padre visited the forward company and platoon areas and held a short service in each. Later, John Whitty visited each company at dinner, which consisted of composite rations, pork and a large measure of local *vino*.

Meanwhile the attack on Villa Grande by 19th Indian Brigade had been only partially successful. The Germans were still holding on to the northern outskirts of the village, which was the key to their defences in that sector, and Colonel Whitty received orders to carry out an attack on this northern edge on December 28. Air photographs were studied, the objective was viewed from an O.P., the route to the start-line was reconnoitred and, on December 27, the final co-ordinating conference was held with the tank and gunner commanders. This conference was also attended by the commander of a Mahratta company, which was to be under command. Most of these careful preparations were destined to be wasted.

The battalion moved off from the lateral road at 4 a.m. on December 28, reached the start-line at 4.45, and formed up with B and D Companies forward, C in support and the Mahratta company in reserve. A disaster then occurred. When the barrage opened at 5.25 many of the shells fell on, and even behind, the start-line instead of 160 yards beyond it. The troops scattered and went to ground, but casualties were numerous and included Captain Wollaston and Lieutenant Washbourne, who were wounded. Control was impossible under these conditions in the darkness, and when, at about 5.50, the barrage lifted sufficiently for the troops to move forward, the whole battalion advanced, assaulting and reserve companies together. Even then further casualties were suffered from our own guns. Nevertheless, the troops stubbornly pressed forward.

---

[1] Detached from the Bedfordshire and Hertfordshire Regiment. Originally he was a Regular officer in the Royal Leicestershire Regiment, but he retired early. At the end of the war he transferred to The Queen's Own.

When the barrage finally ceased there were no sounds of small arms fire ahead, and the advance continued unchecked. The Germans were found to have fled. By 7.15 a.m. the whole battalion was on its objective and the Mahratta company began to clear the north end of Villa Grande. The destruction caused by our guns had been appalling. The whole village was a shambles, with dead Germans strewn on heaps of rubble and floating in their flooded trenches. Casualties in the battalion were 11 killed and 50 wounded.

All the remainder of that day and for the whole of the 29th the battalion was under spasmodic shelling and mortaring, which caused several casualties. There was no counter-attack. On the evening of the 29th the Mahratta battalion came forward and occupied positions some distance ahead. This gave the troops a chance of some slight relaxation. But not for long, for on the evening of December 31, after dark, the battalion went forward and took over the forward positions which the Mahrattas had occupied. During the move rain began to fall heavily and it became very cold. The rain turned into snow. By midnight a blizzard was at its height. It was so bad that C and D Companies had to evacuate their trenches because they became full of slush, and large fires were lit in the forward positions. The Germans did the same. Next day all companies were moved into buildings, but even then the conditions were appalling, and it was with relief that the battalion marched back to an area astride the lateral road on January 3. Next day it went into divisional reserve at Jubatti.

*   *   *

The bad weather continued. The blizzards made controlled movement impossible, and the advance came to a standstill all along the front. The prospect of the weather improving was remote, and as the prolonged enemy resistance had caused an unexpectedly large number of casualties General Alexander, who was in command of all the Allied ground forces in Italy, decided to halt the offensive in the Adriatic sector for the winter.

The end of the year saw the departure of General Montgomery from Italy. He had been appointed to command the 21st Army Group in England in preparation for the invasion of Normandy, and on December 30 he handed over command of the 8th Army to General Sir Oliver Leese.

S

CHAPTER 16

The Second Battalion in the Aegean and England

June to November 1943, and continuing to August 1945

1. *Training in the Middle East*

IN order to maintain the correct chronological sequence of events, the story of the campaign in Italy must now be interrupted to describe the adventures of the 2nd Battalion on the Aegean Islands.

Having spent two days at Tripoli the *Neuralia*, with the battalion on board, sailed for Alexandria on June 14, 1943, in a convoy of twelve ships. When south of Crete one of these ships, the *Palma*, carrying enemy prisoners-of-war and their escort, was sunk by a torpedo. Boat stations were manned for the remainder of the day, but there were no further attacks. After that the voyage was uneventful, and the battalion, under the command of Lieutenant-Colonel B. D. Tarleton (R.N.F.), disembarked at Alexandria on June 19 and went into a transit camp at Sidi Bishr. Four days' leave was then granted to half the battalion at a time, and the troops were able to taste the dubious delights of an Egyptian city in war-time.

At the end of June a party of officers and N.C.O.s left by M.T. to attend a Mountain Warfare Course at Amioun in the Lebanon. This finished on July 8. The party then went on to Arde in Syria, whither the remainder of the battalion had already moved. A short period of training in mountain warfare followed, interspersed with evening leave to Tripoli. The battalion then moved to Zirin (Jezreel) in Palestine, where it carried out 'Dryshod' combined operations training. The usual 'Wetshod' training at Kabrit in Egypt ensued, during which personnel of the 5th Battalion, which was in Egypt at that time for Exercise 'Outcry,' were met for an hour or two. The orthodox training having now been completed, the battalion moved by rail on August 22 to Insariyah, south of Sidon in the Lebanon.

On September 11 a detachment under the command of Major Shaw (Welch), who was now second-in-command, and consisting of B Company (Captain Flood), was sent to Castelrosso, a small island off the south-west coast of Turkey. Their task was to defend the island against a possible German landing; happily the Italian garrison gave them every assistance. Two days later the remainder of the battalion moved to Haifa and went under canvas in a sandfly-ridden olive grove at Et Tireh, two miles south of the town. A draft of about 100 reinforcements then arrived from the Infantry Base Depot at Geniefa. These were all posted to rifle companies, which had already been made nearly up to establishment by the disband-ment of the Anti-tank and Carrier Platoons and the M.T. section. The battalion was under orders to move to an unknown destination, and the days were spent in packing and weighing stores. In the evenings most of the troops went into Haifa on pleasure bent.

On the evening of September 19 the battalion moved by M.T. to Haifa docks, where the troops worked all night under arc-lamps loading kit in two destroyers. They finally embarked early the next morning, H.Q. and D Companies in the *Frobisher* and A and C Companies in the *Faulkner*. A rear party of some 50 all ranks under Captain Plewman, the M.T.O., was left behind to look after the heavy baggage and the vehicles. The equipment of the battalion consisted of the normal small arms and 3-inch mortars, double the normal scale of ammunition, 'compo.' rations for seven days, and 1,000 gallons of water in 2-gallon cans. The men had no kitbags; spare clothing was carried in the pack.

The two destroyers were loaded to capacity, the decks being crowded with stores; but the crews looked after the troops with maternal care and pressed large quantities of naval rations on them when the voyage was over. Early on September 21 the two ships steamed into the bay of Portolago, the port of Leros, and the troops and stores were disembarked by lighter. It was then revealed that the battalion was to go on to Samos in a small cargo boat called the *Eolo*. So the afternoon was spent in reloading stores, and at about eight that evening the troops again embarked. As the ship would not hold the whole unit, C Company had to remain behind and come on three days later. The *Eolo* sailed at midnight, arriving at Vathy Harbour, Samos, at about seven next morning.

2. *Samos*

Samos is a Greek island in the Aegean Sea, one mile off the coast of Turkey and sixty miles south of Smyrna. To the south lie the Italian Dodecanese Islands, the most important of which are Leros, thirty miles south of Samos, Cos, 25 miles south of Leros and, largest of all,

Rhodes. Farther south still, Crete stretches across the entrance to the Aegean. After Greece fell in 1941 an Italian force had occupied Samos, the Italian garrisons on Leros and Cos had been strengthened, and some 6,000 Germans had reinforced the Italian garrison on Rhodes. A strong German force had also been established in Crete. In fact all the Aegean islands were under the control of the enemy.

The surrender of Italy on September 8, 1943, gave us the chance of gaining the Dodecanese islands and Samos at very small cost. The Italian garrisons would probably fight for us if we could reach them before they were overawed by the Germans. The command of the Aegean was thus within our reach, and this might turn the scales in wooing Turkey to our side. Rhodes was the key to the group of islands because it had good airfields from which our own Air Force could operate in defence of the remainder. The 8th Indian Division, including the 5th Battalion, was accordingly made ready to sail for an attack on Rhodes. But the shipping arranged for it was despatched for an operation elsewhere, and the expedition did not sail. Later on another division, which had also been earmarked for the task, was taken to participate in the campaign in Italy instead, and the invasion of Rhodes never took place. So the chance was missed, and the Italians submitted to the authority of the Germans in Rhodes.

These changes of plan meant that we were forced to occupy and hold the remaining islands with insufficient troops. The 234th (Malta) Brigade was selected for this operation (perhaps because it was thought that the brigade had a liking for islands), and the 1st Durham Light Infantry went to Cos, 2nd Royal Irish Fusiliers to Leros and the 2nd Battalion to Samos. Brigade headquarters, renamed G.H.Q. Aegean with Brigadier Brittorous promoted overnight to the rank of Major-General, was established in Leros. There was one airfield in Cos, and a flight of Spitfires was established on it.

With Crete and Rhodes in enemy hands between our bases and these Aegean islands, the task of supplying 234th Brigade was difficult and dangerous. The situation was made even more precarious when Cos was captured by an air- and sea-borne German force on October 3, for this deprived the brigade of the only fighter airfield available. From then onwards there would be no air cover at all should Leros or Samos be attacked. In face of this the garrison of Leros was reinforced by the 1st King's Own, and also by the 4th Buffs, one company of which was lost by the sinking of a ship en route from Malta. In addition, B Company of the 2nd Battalion, having been relieved in Castelrosso at the end of October, was retained in Leros and came under command of the 2nd Royal Irish Fusiliers.

*   *   *

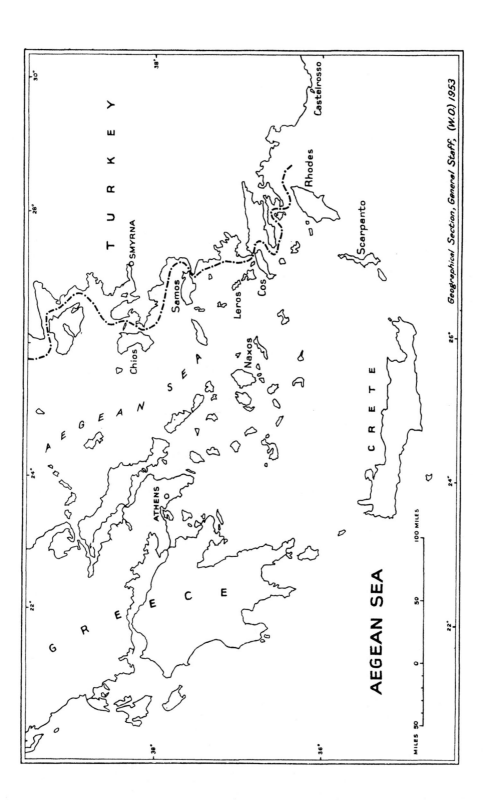

AEGEAN SEA

MILES 50   0   50   100 MILES

Geographical Section, General Staff, (W.O.) 1953

The 2nd Battalion spent a very pleasant week at Vathy, the capital of Samos. Having unloaded the stores from the *Eolo*, the battalion marched off at about midday on September 22, 1943, to its billets, which were in a large and modern tobacco factory on the far side of Vathy Bay. The island had already surrendered to the British Military Mission in Turkey, and the street was lined with cheering people, and flags were waved from the windows and the roof-tops. In the evening, when the troops had leave to visit the town, the welcome was repeated. The Military Governor, Brigadier I. R. Baird, who had arrived with the battalion, was installed with his staff in a house at Vathy next day.

The battalion settled down quickly. The billets were very comfortable and their closeness to the sea gave many opportunities for bathing. The Italian garrison was friendly, and the policy agreed to was that the British and Italians would combine to prevent the Germans from occupying Samos. The battalion was to be the mobile reserve. This was more difficult than it sounds, because it had no vehicles. But after some discussion the Italians agreed to hand over twenty large lorries and two cars. Reconnaissance of the island then began. The officers were agreeably surprised to find that the British maps which had been issued to them were dated September 1943, and were very good.

At the end of September the battalion moved to Mytilene, which was in a more central position from which to carry out its mobile role. Only headquarters and some administrative personnel were in billets in the village, for, in order to provide some local defence for Mytilene, the companies prepared and occupied defensive positions in the fields outside it. For bivouacs the troops used some rubber sheets supplied by the Italians. These made excellent little tents. Water was rationed, and baths could only be had at Vathy. The troops were kept fit by frequent route marches, mountain-climbing exercises and bathing, as well as practice counter-attacks on key positions on the island.

It was not easy to keep Samos supplied. There were two main methods. First, small naval vessels and *caiques* maintained communications with Leros; and secondly, stores of all kinds were dropped by British aircraft at night into dropping zones lit by flares. The achievements of the Royal Navy during this period were notable. At least two German convoys were sunk, and the enemy bases on Cos were harassed. Owing to the complete mastery of the air by the Germans, these activities could be only carried out after dark. During the day our vessels lay up out of harm's way. Even so, many heavy losses were suffered in men and ships.

After the fall of Cos on October 3 the tension on Samos increased.
The rumble of German bombs falling on Leros grew louder each
day, and some familiar Ju. 88s flew over Mytilene. A few days later
some of these aircraft dive-bombed Triganion Harbour and sank a
few small ships. They also machine-gunned Vathy and killed some
Italian troops. Reports then began to arrive of enemy convoys
assembling at other islands and of preparations for large-scale enemy
operations. Although G.H.Q. Aegean maintained a dignified silence,
these alarming reports led to the battalion moving to a position on
the Dhimitrios Ridge, a dominating feature in the eastern sector of
the island. Once more the companies were living in battle positions,
but this time they were widely dispersed. In spite of their many discomforts, the troops remained in good heart.

On November 11 Major-General H. R. Hall, the new G.O.C.
Aegean, arrived at Samos with his complete staff. Billets and offices
had already been made ready for them in Vathy, and it was assumed
that their arrival was the prelude to a new phase of operations. This
assumption proved to be correct.

3. *The Move to Leros*

At 6.30 a.m. on November 12 an observer on the highest feature
in the battalion area reported that he could see Leros being invaded.
The rumble of bombs from that island then grew louder and more
frequent, and a large column of smoke was seen rising from it.
Information was scanty, the B.B.C. being the most fruitful—though
somewhat unreliable—source of news. Hopes were unduly raised
by hearing over the air that British fighters were making sweeps
over Leros; whereas in actual fact Beaufighters flew near, not over,
the island on one occasion only.

That evening Battalion Headquarters with A and D Companies
were ordered to embark for Leros at Triganion Harbour. The troops
left Dhimitrios Ridge at about eight wearing battledress, which had
been issued only that afternoon, and before midnight embarkation
in two minesweepers was complete. The Naval Commander then
decided that, because of rough seas, it would be impossible for the
landing on Leros to be accomplished and for the ships to reach
safety before dawn. The troops therefore disembarked and returned
to Dhimitrios.

Late next afternoon, November 13, it was decided to embark the
troops at Vathy, where the harbour was more protected from the
wind. The same companies drove straight to the quay, but only one

minesweeper managed to get into the harbour because of heavy seas. A Company (Major Butler) embarked in this vessel and sailed. The remainder of the troops were billeted for the night in the tobacco factory at Vathy. A Company did not reach Leros that night, as their ship was forced to shelter off the Turkish coast and lay up all next day. The company eventually landed in Leros at about 11 p.m. on the 14th.

The remainder of the battalion (less a small rear party under Captain White, Lieutenant Matthewman and some other ranks on the staff of the Military Governor, and Lieutenant Pollock and a few men in hospital) embarked in two destroyers on the evening of the 14th and sailed. Even then only one destroyer, with Battalion Head-quarters, the Signal Platoon and C Company (Major Read) on board, was successful, arriving at Portolago in Leros some five hours after A Company. The other destroyer, with D Company (Major Flint) and the remainder of H.Q. Company on board, developed engine trouble, due to a near miss from a German bomb, and they eventually reached Leros on the night of the 15th in a minesweeper and five Motor Torpedo Boats (M.T.B.s).

The result of these misfortunes was that the 2nd Battalion did not fight in Leros as a complete unit. B Company (Captain Flood) was already there, and the other three rifle companies reached the island at three different times over a period of twenty-four hours and went into battle in separate actions. What is more, this series of false starts meant that Leros was not reinforced by troops fresh from billets but by men who were already tired.

A list of officers and warrant officers who were in Leros with the battalion is in Appendix B.

4. The Situation in Leros

The island of Leros is divided by two narrow necks of land into three hilly sectors. The garrison was initially disposed with 4th Buffs defending the northern sector, 2nd Royal Irish Fusiliers the central, and the 1st King's Own the southern sector. B Company of the 2nd Battalion was on the west coast in the central sector. In addition to the infantry there were one British Light Anti-Aircraft Regiment and one troop of British 25-pounders. The coastal defence and heavy anti-aircraft guns were manned by Italians. Fortress Headquarters was in a tunnel in the highest hill in the central sector. The policy was to stop the enemy on the beaches, and the island reserve was only one company of the King's Own, which was in the northern sector.

The most prominent feature on the island is Mt. Meraviglia in the central sector. A continuation of this feature, called Rachi Ridge, runs northwards into the northern neck. On either side of this ridge are deep bays, Alinda Bay to the east and Gurna Bay to the west. The main harbour is Portolago at the base of Portolago Bay on the west coast. Midway down the east coast is Pandeli Bay. The terrain is rocky, and the lower slopes of the hills are covered with prickly scrub seldom more than knee-high. The tops of the hills are bare. Olive groves grow in the valleys.

Since October 2, Leros had been constantly bombed by enemy aircraft, the weight of the attack being mainly against Mt. Meraviglia, on which was Fortress Headquarters, and Portolago. During this period no British aircraft had come over the island except to drop stores at night. There is no doubt that this constant bombing was a tremendous strain on the garrison.

The battle started at 6.30 on the morning of November 12, when the Germans landed from the sea at three points on the east coast. It was a clear, calm morning but, although the enemy craft had been visible from six onwards, the Italian batteries did not open fire until they were well inshore. Enemy bombing began soon after these landings and continued all day. The Germans established a beach-head on the northern shore of Alinda Bay and, in spite of action by the company in island reserve, captured an Italian battery on Mt. Clide. After another landing at Pandeli Bay the enemy climbed Mt. Appetici and captured one gun of an Italian coastal battery there. The reserve company of the Royal Irish Fusiliers then counter-attacked and forced the enemy to withdraw to the narrow beach, where they were pinned down but not destroyed.

Then came a most unpleasant shock for the garrison. It had been thought that the island was unsuitable for paratroop landings; but soon after four in the afternoon about 700 German parachutists dropped between Alinda Bay and Gurna Bay. Many were destroyed, not a few of them by the medium machine guns of B Company of the 2nd Battalion from the north-western slopes of Mt. Giovanni. These four guns were switched on to the Ju. 52s, as they passed low overhead, by C.S.M. Greenyer, who himself took a gun and raked the targets with belt after belt of ammunition. In spite of this reception the parachutists succeeded in establishing themselves at Point 100 on Rachi, thus cutting the island in two. During the night a counter-attack on Pt. 100 was organised but was later cancelled, and the enemy was able to consolidate his gains undisturbed. These gains were a beachhead on Mt. Clide, a foothold below Mt. Appetici, and a strong position on Pt. 100.

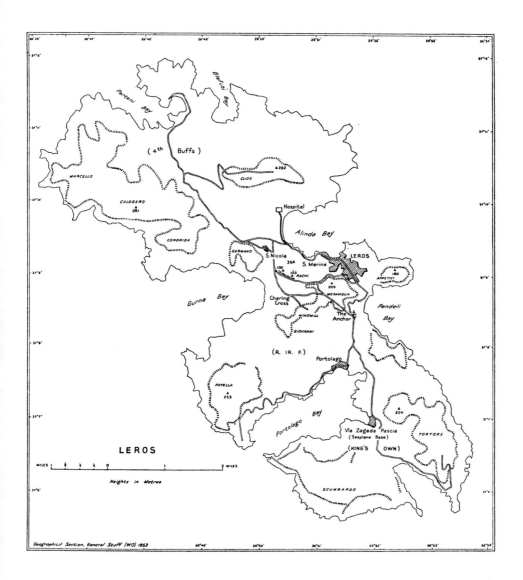

LEROS

MILES | 1 ½ ¼ 0 | 1 | 2 MILES

Heights in Metres

On November 13, enemy bombing began again at dawn and again continued all day. In the early morning German reinforcements and supplies were dropped from the air in the same place as before. Heavy casualties were again inflicted on them, but the survivors reached Pt. 100. The remainder of the day was spent by the garrison in preparing attacks on Rachi Ridge and Mt. Clide. In the evening, however, the Germans attacked the crest of Mt. Appetici from below, drove off the company of Royal Irish Fusiliers which was defending it, and occupied Leros village. The decision was then made to recapture Mt. Appetici before attempting to take Rachi and Clide.

The attack on Mt. Appetici was made before dawn on the 14th by two companies of King's Own and one company of Royal Irish Fusiliers. The attacking troops suffered heavy casualties, including Colonel Maurice French of the Royal Irish Fusiliers, who was killed. The attack failed. After daylight, assaults were launched on Mt. Clide and Pt. 100. Both operations were partially successful. In the north the 4th Buffs gained a footing on Mt. Clide; and a composite battalion of two companies of King's Own and two of the Royal Irish Fusiliers managed to reach Pt. 103 on the southern slopes of Rachi Ridge.

B Company of the 2nd Battalion, who had all this time been in their positions on the northern slopes of Mt. Giovanni, were then ordered to attack Mt. Germano, which had been occupied by German parachutists. This meant that they had to pass right below Rachi Ridge and, as they crossed flat ground, they came under heavy machine-gun fire. About a dozen men were hit. These included Captain Flood, who, though wounded in the leg, rallied his men and led them forward. Mt. Germano was then assaulted and captured. On Germano, B Company linked up with a company of the 4th Buffs and came under command of that battalion. These two companies were then directed on St. Nicola. Fighting was intense, but they were unable to make much progress because the enemy were found to be in every house in the village. Both companies were withdrawn after dark for food and rest.

At dusk three British destroyers bombarded the enemy positions on Rachi Ridge with every possible weapon from close inshore. This retaliated in some measure for the intense air attacks which had been made on our troops by German Stukas and Ju. 88s, and raised British morale considerably.

November 14 ended with a British gain at Germano and with a footing won on Clide and Rachi. Moreover, before midnight, companies of the 2nd Battalion began to arrive at Portolago to reinforce the garrison.

5. *The Fight for Leros*

A Company of the 2nd Battalion was the first to arrive, and Major Butler immediately made his way to Fortress Headquarters on Mt. Meraviglia for orders. At about 3.30 a.m. on November 15 he rejoined his company in an assembly area west of Portolago and gave warning orders for a company attack on the Rachi feature. The company then moved off to the forming-up position, which was at a road junction called Charing Cross. The Colour-Serjeant and the cooks were directed to the Anchor Monument.

At about this time (4.30 a.m. on November 15) Battalion Headquarters and C Company arrived at Portolago and disembarked rapidly. They were met by a liaison officer, and the troops moved off to an assembly area near the Anchor, where Battalion Headquarters were established, slit-trenches were dug, and breakfast was prepared. Meanwhile Colonel Tarleton had gone to Fortress Headquarters, where he was informed of A Company's impending battle and received orders to attack the eastern slopes of Rachi Ridge with C Company from the south. C Company (Major Read) then moved off to their assembly area south of Leros village, where they awaited further orders.

Enemy aircraft had by this time arrived over the island again, and Mt. Meraviglia, the assembly area near the Anchor, and Charing Cross were constantly bombed. After 9 a.m. these air attacks were intensified, and several members of Battalion Headquarters were killed. These included the Intelligence Serjeant (Williams), the Signal Corporal (Pilcher) and Corporal Robins of the officers' mess.

*   *   *

The last platoon of A Company arrived at Charing Cross soon after 7 a.m. Major Butler then went to Mt. Meraviglia to receive his final orders from the Fortress Commander (Brigadier R. Tilney). This gave his troops their first chance of viewing the ground which they had to cross. The plan was for the company to advance northwards, pass through the positions held by the King's Own on the southern end of Rachi and capture and hold Pt. 100. No supporting fire could be expected except from the small arms of the King's Own on Pt. 103 (Searchlight Hill); but until this feature was reached the troops would be in dead ground. Zero hour was to be 8.30 a.m.

Until the leading platoons of A Company were slightly north of Pt. 103 their advance was unhindered. They then came under sniping fire, mortar concentrations and dive-bombing attacks from the air. Soon after this they met aimed automatic fire from Pt. 100 and from a strong-point about a concrete gun emplacement, and were held up. By this time all three platoon commanders had become casualties. Making use of all available cover, Robert Butler then led the left forward platoon to within fifty yards of the concrete emplacement, but they were unable to assault it. As the wireless sets were not working, Robert returned to his other two platoons and, having asked by orderly for some close mortar support and smoke from the 25-pounders, issued orders for another attack. Up till now the company had lost some twenty-five casualties, including Lieutenant Hewett and C.S.M. Spooner killed. Private Reynolds, one of the stretcher-bearers, had shown great gallantry in tending the wounded under fire.

The second attack was carried out by two composite platoons made up from all available men of A Company. The Bren guns were grouped under Lieutenant Groom to give covering fire. One detachment of mortars of the Royal Irish Fusiliers arrived to support the attack. At 2.30 p.m. the smoke from the 25-pounders began to burst over the enemy positions, and the troops started off. They were met by heavy automatic and mortar fire, but by making use of ground the advance continued slowly. Eventually Pt. 100 was assaulted and cleared. The troops were now much dispersed. Casualties had been heavy and it is doubtful if there were more than a dozen men on the objective. Major Butler, who had himself been badly wounded in the knee in the final assault, realised that he had insufficient men to hold the position and, as his requests for reinforcements were unanswered, he ordered a withdrawal at dusk to Pt. 103. There the remnants of the company (three serjeants and twenty-five men) were reorganised by Colour-Sjt. Watts, who was now the senior rank, and came under command of the King's Own. Most of the company's wounded were evacuated that night in a destroyer.

*   *   *

During the morning C Company had moved up to a position south of the village of Santa Marina on the southern shore of Alinda Bay. In the early afternoon Battalion Headquarters followed, coming under machine-gun fire from the Germans on Mt. Appetici and in Leros village on the way. At about 2.30 p.m. (the time at which A Company began its second attack) Colonel Tarleton gave Major Read his orders for an attack on the eastern slopes of Rachi Ridge. The intention was to clear the enemy from Pt. 36 and then to capture the road junction north of it. All possible coastal batteries and 25-pounders, together with the mortars and machine guns of the

Royal Irish Fusiliers, were to support this attack. One composite company of the Royal Irish Fusiliers was to follow up C Company and mop up. This company eventually failed to muster more than forty men and, owing to its late arrival, the attack had to be postponed. Thus most of the benefit of the supporting fire was lost.

C Company's attack started at 3.30 p.m. A spur jutting out from Rachi towards the coast was quickly reached, but during this advance Major Read was severely wounded. Captain Newbald assumed command of the company, and the attack continued. The left forward platoon lost direction in the difficult country, but the right platoon, although its commander, Lieutenant Jode, had been wounded on the start-line, pressed forward. Success depended on speed and the passage of the coast road, which was lined with houses full of snipers. Serjeant Wallington took command and, by using ground, avoided the fire of the snipers and led the platoon with great dash through heavy automatic and mortar fire to within assaulting distance of Pt. 36. He was then wounded. Heavy fire prevented the platoon from advancing further.

Meanwhile the German snipers in the houses lining the road were still active, and the Battalion Reconnaissance Group, which was following up the attack, was held up by their fire. Lieutenant James and Drummer Brown of the Intelligence Section ran forward under this fire and found a secure position from which the 'R' Group could watch the progress of the attack. They then entered several of the houses and cleared them. By this time the composite company of Royal Irish Fusiliers had also begun to clear the houses, and the German snipers were prevented from interfering further with the troops in front.

The reserve platoon then moved forward. Taking advantage of a sunken road, Lieutenant Browne quickly brought them up on the left of Serjeant Wallington's platoon, picked up some of that platoon and, in spite of small arms fire at close range, assaulted the objective. Many enemy were killed on the position, upwards of twenty-five prisoners were taken and Pt. 36 was captured. At this moment, however, a most effective enemy mortar and machine-gun concentration came down on Pt. 36, and many of the attackers, including John Browne, became casualties. With no reinforcements at hand they were unable to consolidate. The remnants of the platoon withdrew to the coast road.

It was soon after this that A Company, only 300 yards away at Pt. 100 on the crest of Rachi, was also forced to withdraw because of the lack of reinforcements. In both of these attacks, therefore, only the absence of reserves prevented the companies from consolidating and holding the ground that had been won. The faint hope of a link up between A and C Companies now vanished.

After dark Captain Newbald patrolled the area and picked up several small groups of effectives of C Company. He also directed the walking wounded to a chapel on the coast road, where Captains Young and Seddon (the Padre and the M.O.) were organising the collection of the stretcher cases. While this was going on, the stretcher party bearing Major Read to the chapel met the head of a column of Germans moving south. The Germans challenged the party, but Private Bett immediately opened rapid fire on the column, which broke and took cover. Private Bett then ran off and reported the presence of this column to Captain Newbald who, realising that the Germans were probably advancing to make an attack southwards, sent details of this force to Battalion Headquarters by wireless. Captain Newbald then withdrew his men to Battalion Headquarters. The Padre and the M.O. as well as the wounded of C Company were taken prisoner.

*   *   *

All available troops were now organised to defend the Battalion Headquarters' position astride the coast road near Santa Marina. Small groups of men were disposed in houses and on a spur of Mt. Meraviglia, and a few Royal Irish Fusiliers, who arrived with three Bren guns, were included in the defences. The first Germans approached down the road at about 9 p.m. They were in close order and were ambushed at about thirty yards by Bren gun and rifle fire. They withdrew. About an hour later a heavier attack came in. This time the enemy managed to infiltrate round both flanks and, to avoid encirclement, a withdrawal was made to a position farther up the slopes of Mt. Meraviglia, where the Germans were stopped by grenades thrown by a party of signallers under Captain Thatcher. The fighting then became confused, and a further withdrawal was made to a machine-gun position manned by a small party of Royal Irish Fusiliers. At about eleven this position came under mortar or rifle-grenade fire, and the Adjutant (Captain Cropper) realised that a counter-attack was imperative.

Every available man was required for this counter-attack and Lieutenant Jode, who had been wounded in the foot during C Company's attack that afternoon, came from the Regimental Aid Post, picked up a Bren gun and gave covering fire. The counter-attack started, but the Germans met it with a shower of grenades. Captain Cropper and several others became casualties. No progress could be made, and the remnants regrouped at a house farther up the

hill. The enemy made no attempt to follow up. Later on, Colonel
Tarleton ordered all available troops of the battalion to rendezvous
at the Anchor.

Thus ended that fateful November 15. It had seen the virtual
destruction of A and C Companies, who had been sent piecemeal
into hastily-prepared attacks. Battalion Headquarters and the
Signal Platoon had also suffered many casualties. The remnants of
the battalion were now much dispersed, with some twenty-five men
of A Company fighting under command of the King's Own at
Pt. 103, with B Company still on Mt. Germano under command
of the Buffs, and with the remainder on their way to the Anchor.
D Company had not yet arrived. The Germans had lost no ground
that day, but they had suffered heavy casualties. It is probable that
enemy reinforcements landed at Alinda Bay during the night.

*   *   *

At about midnight on November 15, D Company (Major Flint)
and part of Headquarter Company, having disembarked at Portolago, arrived at the assembly area at the Anchor, where Captain
Pond, the Quartermaster, was preparing a meal for all and sundry.
D Company was ordered to occupy some deep trenches in order to
give the troops cover from the bombing which was sure to start again
at daylight, the Mortar Platoon (Lieutenant Cruickshank) was
dispersed in three detachments and ordered to dig in, and the A.A.
Platoon (Captain Rickcord) was sent as a fighting patrol north
towards Alinda Bay to watch for signs of enemy movements southwards.

There was patrol activity during the early hours of the morning,
after which breakfasts were issued and the troops stood-to. Enemy
automatic fire began to harass the assembly area and make movement in it difficult, and at daylight enemy aircraft appeared overhead and began their usual bombing. It was apparent that enemy
ground troops indicated the British positions to their aircraft with
light signals, and several casualties occurred in the assembly area.
Suddenly the Germans made a determined attack on the Anchor
position. Some of the forward troops were captured, but the Germans
did not exploit their success. The remnants of C Company, who had
just arrived in the area, were then withdrawn to a position in rear
of D Company, where they were formed into a composite platoon
under Captain Newbald.

About an hour later orders were received for D Company to
attack Leros village. They deployed and moved off to a start-line,
suffering some casualties from bombing as they did so. Soon after

9 a.m., however, the Fortress Commander arrived at Battalion Headquarters and cancelled this order. He informed Colonel Tarleton
that Fortress H.Q. on Mt. Meraviglia was being evacuated because
of the proximity of the enemy, and ordered him to collect all available
men of the battalion and move them along the west coast to the
north end of the island, where they would come under command of
the 4th Buffs for an attack on Rachi Ridge. It appears that Fortress
Headquarters did not actually vacate their position.

*   *   *

The depleted 2nd Battalion immediately began the difficult
process of disengaging while under enemy observation and bombing.
There were no vehicles to carry the stores, and it was with heavy
hearts that the Mortar Platoon disabled their mortars. The reserve
rations and extra bandoliers of ammunition were issued to the troops.
B Echelon moved first at about 10.30 a.m., followed by the remnants
of C Company, H.Q. Company and Battalion Headquarters. D
Company brought up the rear. As concealment from the air was of
paramount importance, each detachment was split up into small
groups under an officer or senior N.C.O., with orders to take a
certain general route and to assemble at a given rendezvous in the
northern sector of the island. The direction of the move was westwards to the south of Mt. Giovanni, and then northwards along the
coast on the west of Rachi Ridge. The Germans made no attempt to
follow.

Throughout this precarious move enemy aircraft were constantly
overhead in large numbers. Progress was slow, as the troops had to
stop and take cover frequently in order to avoid casualties from
bombs. While passing below Rachi sniping was intense, and Major
Shaw was mortally wounded. All the way up the coast small parties
of troops and individual stragglers from other units were met. Many
of these went on with the battalion. One of the first groups to arrive
in the Buffs' area was the small party of B Echelon under Captain
Pond. When they arrived they found that the troops there were
forming up for an attack southwards, and they were ordered to
follow up with the reserve company. The consequence was that, to
their astonishment and annoyance, they found themselves moving
back towards the Anchor. This does not appear to have happened to
any of the other groups.

By sunset most of the small groups of the 2nd Battalion, about
160 all ranks, had arrived at the foot of Mt. Germano. No other
British troops were in the vicinity and, as the position of the Buffs
was not known, it was decided to make for Mt. Conrida. Positions

were taken up on that hill after dark. Later on a patrol made contact
with a platoon of the Buffs, which was on its way south. As there
were no fresh orders for Colonel Tarleton, the night was spent on
Conrida. Thus November 16 passed without an engagement being
fought by D and Headquarter Companies.

6. *The Surrender of Leros*

It is now necessary to consider briefly what had happened to the
remainder of the garrison on November 16. Soon after daylight,
patrols sent out by B Company of the 2nd Battalion from Mt.
Germano found that St. Nicola village had been abandoned by the
Germans. B Company, still led by Captain Flood in spite of his
wounds, was then sent forward with one company of the Buffs on its
left. These two companies advanced practically unopposed, prisoners
came in, and Pt. 100 was captured. From there it could be seen that
the Germans were launching a large-scale attack on Mt. Meraviglia,
and that our troops were holding on there with difficulty. In spite
of this, the two companies were ordered to withdraw. The reason for
this is not clear.

By this time the units of the garrison were much intermingled,
there was little control, and the situation was very confused. In
the northern sector of the island the Buffs were mainly dispersed
in defence positions; some of the King's Own were in the St. Nicola
area. In the centre the Royal Irish Fusiliers and a company of the
King's Own were scattered in small groups endeavouring to defend
Mt. Meraviglia; a conglomeration of troops was about Portolago,
which was being continuously bombed. In the south the remainder
of the King's Own still occupied some of the static defence posts.
The remnants of the 2nd Battalion were moving slowly northwards
along the west coast. And all the time in large numbers overhead
were enemy aircraft ready to dive-bomb any suitable target.

At about 3 p.m. the Fortress Commander arrived at St. Nicola
and issued orders for all available British troops to attack southwards.
If successful in driving the enemy from Rachi Ridge they were to
make for the Anchor and await orders. These instructions did not
reach Colonel Tarleton, who was threading his way up the west
coast with the remnants of the 2nd Battalion; but it was this attack
which took Captain Pond's party southwards with it. B Company
also took part.

This last all-out effort was too late. Soon after the Fortress Commander arrived back at his Headquarters the Germans overran it

and captured him and what remained of his staff. In face of this disaster the island was surrendered unconditionally at about 5.30 p.m.

The progress of the battle had been anxiously followed by the General Staff in the Middle East, and when reporting the surrender of the island General Sir Henry Maitland Wilson (G.O.C-in-C. Middle East) wrote: 'Leros has fallen after a very gallant struggle against overwhelming air attack. It was a near thing between success and failure. . . . When we took the risk in September it was with our eyes open, and all would have been well if we had been able to take Rhodes. . . .'

*   *   *

Information that the island had been surrendered did not reach the remnants of the 2nd Battalion on Mt. Conrida until 7 a.m. on November 17. The troops were astonished by the news, but all maps and papers other than means of identification were at once destroyed. Food was then gathered from various food dumps and a meal prepared. Thoughts next turned to escape. Several parties went out in search of a boat, but none could be found on the coast near Conrida, and most of the officers and other ranks resolved to wait for a more suitable opportunity for escape on the mainland.

B Company of the 2nd Battalion knew of the surrender of the island on the previous evening. They had joined in the final attack southwards and had been in position near Leros village when the news reached them. Captain Flood quickly marched his company back to their original area on Mt. Giovanni, south of Gurna Bay, and there they had a good meal and much-needed sleep. They also collected what winter clothing there was available and destroyed all articles of value.

All unwounded and walking wounded British prisoners were eventually assembled at the barracks of the Italian seaplane base south of Portolago Bay, and most of the officers and some of the men were evacuated in two Italian destroyers on November 19. The remainder followed as soon as ships were available. The destination was Piraeus, the port of Athens. During the voyage some of the officers were invited to the ward-room of one of the destroyers to join the Commander in a drink. This was only lemonade, but it was a courteous gesture which was appreciated. The German officers said that the British had fought well against heavy odds.

After disembarkation at Piraeus the British prisoners were marched through the streets of Athens to a disused aircraft factory some miles from the city. During the march of one of the columns a German

T

Serjeant-Major, whom the troops called 'Puss in Boots' because of the huge jackboots he wore, threatened to shoot those prisoners who were whistling. He was also very brutal to the many Greeks who gave the troops fruit and cigarettes as they plodded past. But the morale of the Greeks was wonderfully high, and they were not in the least intimidated by this treatment.

Some three weeks were spent in the aircraft factory near Athens. The prisoners were then divided into two parties, the officers and a small number of other ranks being the first to continue the journey. On the way north through Greece some of the officers of the 2nd Battalion made an effort to escape. They had managed to conceal some jack-knives when they were captured, and near Larissa they began to cut through a wooden panel of the goods wagon in which they were travelling. They worked by candle-light during the night and had cut through and were knocking out the panel, when the German guards opened fire on them from the next carriage. The officers lay flat on the floor while the bullets ripped through the wagon. Captain Newbald was wounded in the head, but miraculously none of the others was injured. The train came to a halt and they were pushed by the guards at the point of the bayonet into another wagon already containing twenty officers. They finished that night wedged in the wagon in a standing position. Eventually this party arrived at Luchenwalde, where the officers were thrown into solitary confinement pending interrogation.

The second party of prisoners was taken by train from Athens a few days later. They travelled through Greece and were then dispersed to several working camps in Germany and southern Europe, where they spent the remainder of the war in captivity.

7. *Escapes*

But not all of the unwounded personnel of the 2nd Battalion were put 'in the bag.' First of all Lieutenant Huckle, C.S.M. Greenyer and Privates Crowhurst and Hose of B Company were given a *caique* by some Greeks at Gurna Bay. Setting out at midnight on November 16 in this leaky boat, they lay up next day in an inlet and rounded the northern tip of Leros during the night of the 17th. They kept afloat by constant bailing until, at 4 p.m. on the 18th, when within a mile of the Turkish coast, they were taken on board by an M.T.B. Next, Captain Turner and Lance-Corporal Honey gathered some food from a dump at Conrida and remained hidden all day on the 17th. After dark they crossed the island to Alinda Bay.

They were stopped on the way by a party of Germans, but managed to persuade them that they were Greeks. At Alinda Bay they hid by day and reconnoitred by night until the evening of the 19th, when they met two Italian sailors who were repairing a damaged *caique* with a view to attempting to escape. These Italians agreed to take them and, taking it in turns to row, they arrived off the Turkish coast at about noon next day. They were then taken in tow by a Turkish fishing boat to a small village. The following day they went by sea to Bordrum and thence by R.A.F. launch to Cyprus, arriving in Cairo on November 23. Lastly, some sixteen others managed to get away from the island by various means after its surrender. This number included Lieutenant Clark, C.S.M. Dunton, Colour-Serjeants Hayward and Cook and Corporal Ready, who were taken off in M.T.B.s.

Captain Cropper and Lieutenant Browne, who had been wounded and captured in the fighting on November 15, were taken to a hospital at Alinda Bay. When they were convalescent they made several attempts to escape and finally got away in a *caique* on the night of December 2 with Private Hodges, who was acting as an orderly in the Hospital. These three eventually reached Cairo.

Another party of wounded to escape imprisonment included Major Read, Lieutenant Jode and sixteen other ranks of The Queen's Own. This party, which was also in the Alinda Bay hospital, was evacuated at the beginning of December in a German hospital ship. On its way to Greece this ship was captured by a British destroyer, and the party was taken to Italy and from there sent direct to England.

*   *   *

The record of escapes would not be complete without some mention of the notable adventures of four privates of the Signal Platoon—H. Atkins, Gardener, Hunt and Chander—and an account written from the diary kept by Atkins follows:—

'Officers were quickly separated from other ranks by the Goons (Germans), and the following day we were sent by Italian destroyer (manned by Germans) to Piraeus, the port of Athens. Here we were thoroughly searched and kept in an old factory. The sanitary conditions were foul, and with little food we felt rather pessimistic as to the future but, seeing how cheerful the Greeks were under the jackboot of the enemy, our morale improved and we were wondering what the next move would be.

'After a few days we were bundled into cattle trucks with a thin layer of straw on the floor, and the train steamed out of Athens for the north, as we guessed. Once outside Greece we knew that our chances of escape were practically nil, and we four decided to escape as the train was travelling slowly through Greece, possibly north of Larissa. We pooled our odd pieces of food, arranged a code word, and agreed that if we became separated we would endeavour to reach the high ground round Mt. Olympus.

'Various ways were suggested as to how we should get out of the cattle truck. This had four unglazed windows two feet by eighteen inches, which had been criss-crossed with barbed wire. Fortunately I had managed to secrete on my body a service jack-knife, so quickly got to work on the barbed wire. This obstacle removed, we climbed through the aperture, and as the train slowly made its way up a gradient we managed to bale out and lie at the side of the track until the rear compartment (containing the armed guards) was out of sight.

'The time was about 6 p.m. and quite dark, but we made our way from the line towards the foothills. We were now free but in an enemy-occupied country, and life was going to be hectic from now on. Our first fright was to hear a German sentry singing quietly to himself. He must have been near his guard detachment for we also heard a field telephone ringing. At nine we carefully approached a Greek village. A villager came up but, as we could not understand him, we told him in Army language to "keep his mouth shut and to buzz off"—which he did.

'At about 9.30 p.m. we saw a light in a house, but on approaching it we saw a man armed with a Sten gun standing at a corner. We moved towards him and found ourselves surrounded by local Andarti (Greek partisans) armed to the teeth. We were interrogated by the Andarti captain, and by means of signs we were able to convey to him that we were British soldiers who had escaped from the train, and that we were very hungry.

'We were given bread and beans, which we proceeded to devour like wolves. The meal over, we were hurriedly moved from the village and headed north. Two hours' forced march brought us to a large building in a village called Castania. Here we were given cigarettes, and once again marched northwards. At 4 a.m. we arrived at another small village, where we were given sheepskin rugs and managed to sleep until eight. After a hearty breakfast of bread and dripping made from goat's fat, we headed N.W. into very mountainous country. Marching all day, with a few minutes' rest after each four hours, we reached a partisan stronghold, where we were at once interrogated by an Andarti leader.

'By now it was December 10 and we had reached the village of

Moskopaomus, headquarters of the Greek partisans. We were told that we would meet an Englishman when we reached Scuterna in the heart of Mt. Olympus. We had great pleasure in meeting Captain S —— of the Allied Military Mission, who had been dropped in the country some months before. A tin of meat and veg. was issued to us (what a come down after living on the fat of the land!), and we were taken to a house and told to sleep. Next day we managed to de-louse ourselves and take a rough bath. As we had no spare underclothing our change meant turning them inside out, but it was good to be free.

'The Mission, including us, marched for five days to a safer destination at Diskata, where a delightful Greek family took the whole nine of us for the night. On Xmas Day we managed to get a good dinner prepared, and my pal made what he called a Xmas cake (or was it a pudding?? No one knows, but it went down very well). Toasts to the folks at home were drunk in local wine. On Boxing Day we were chased out of Diskata by the advancing Germans.

'At Koupuri we visited a Greek theatre. This was very impromptu and, as we could understand very little of the language, we had to restrain our laughter and only applauded with the remainder of the audience.

'On December 31 we were introduced to Colonel A —— (C.O. of the Mission). His only escort was a wireless operator with a set capable of working to H.Q. in Egypt. Our final lap led us into western Macedonia, and our guide, known as "Pilly," was a muleteer employed by the Mission.

'On January 4 we reached the Mission headquarters in western Macedonia, where British officers and other ranks were enjoying a party. Here we were given food, a bath and clean clothing (the first for some three months). The meal was cooked by an Austrian who was a deserter from the German Army. After the meal we were given pyjamas and told to sleep.

'The following morning one of my pals left for another area as wireless operator, and I began to attend school to learn the art of sabotage and demolition. The next four months I spent in training Greeks in the art of soldiering. We were out continuously on sabotage schemes, which were successful, and it was great fun to blow up railway lines, trains, etc. I began to become quite a "Lawrence of Macedonia" in a small way.

'My next task was at Grevena, forty miles away and near to a German H.Q. I was placed in charge of 800 Greek labourers and my role was to construct an aerodrome. On August 12, 1944, an

Allied aircraft circled and landed on our aerodrome, and the cheering from the workmen and locals was terrific. I carried on with work at the airfield for a while, and eventually was flown home.'

8. *The War Ends for the 2nd Battalion*

The remnants of the 2nd Battalion assembled at the Home Counties' Reinforcement Depot at Fayid in the Suez Canal area. By January 1944, the strength was about 160, consisting of eight officers and thirty-five other ranks who had escaped or been evacuated from Leros; four officers and about sixty other ranks who had been evacuated through Turkey from Samos; and two officers and fifty other ranks who had been with the rear party in Haifa. A regimental *enclave* was formed with Major Turner in command, and the regimental flag was bravely flown outside the tent of the detachment's headquarters.

At first the policy was that the battalion should gradually be brought up to strength, but this had to be changed owing to the fact that there were not at that time sufficient reinforcements in the Middle East. It was then decided that those men with four and a half years' unbroken service overseas should be repatriated and that the remainder should be sent to reinforce other units in the Mediterranean Zone. So on February 23, five officers and eighty-five other ranks embarked at Suez in the *Strathaird* for home.

This party was met at Glasgow on March 19 by Colonel Blanch, the Commanding Officer of the 7th Battalion, and by Major Buckle, who had left the 2nd Battalion only a few months earlier. The troops had hoped to be stationed in the South of England after so many years overseas, and it was with some disappointment that they found that they were to go to Blackburn, where they were to be 'held' by the 7th Battalion. They were, however, immediately granted a well-earned and much-desired twenty-eight days' leave.

*   *   *

When these men returned from leave they found that they were in 80th Division, which was commanded by Major-General L. H. ('Bouncer') Cox, who had been a brigadier in Malta and was therefore well known to most of them. During their absence on leave it had been announced that the 2nd and 7th Battalions were to be amalgamated with a view to the 2nd Battalion being reconstituted as a Field Army unit. In the meantime they were to continue to carry out the role of the 7th Battalion, which was to train reinforcements for drafting overseas, mainly to other battalions of the Regiment but also to the Royal Hampshires.

On April 21 the composite battalion moved to Ulverston in the Lake District, and it was there that all the officers and other ranks of the 7th Battalion were transferred to the 2nd. On May 3, 1944, Sir Charles Bonham-Carter, Colonel of the Regiment, inspected the new 2nd Battalion on its first parade. On that day the amalgamation officially occurred.

The first step towards the 2nd Battalion becoming an operational unit took place in July, when all men under training were gradually transferred to other draft-finding units. Officers and other ranks who had been employed in administering and training these men went with them. At the same time the drafting overseas of trained personnel continued.

One of those to leave the battalion at this time was C.S.M. Greenyer. He went to the 7th Battalion Royal Hampshire Regiment, which was at that time commanded by Lieutenant-Colonel Talbot of The Queen's Own and formed part of the 43rd (Wessex) Division on the Dutch-German frontier. Later on, in January 1945, Greenyer won the D.C.M. for conducting two fine patrols into the 'Siegfried Line.' The first was a daylight reconnaissance patrol through several minefields and across two streams. Leaving the patrol under cover Greenyer worked his way forward to each of three forts in turn and, failing to draw fire by exposing himself, entered and found them unoccupied. The following day he volunteered to lead another daylight reconnaissance patrol, the purpose of which was to draw fire from the enemy's forward defended localities and thus assess their strength. Safely negotiating some minefields, he led his patrol across the River Wurm to within shouting distance of the enemy positions. At this point the patrol came under heavy fire and one man was wounded. Having remained under fire long enough to locate the enemy positions accurately, Greenyer skilfully withdrew his patrol over open ground and sent his Bren group and the wounded man back over a bridge across the river. He then found it impossible to cross with the remaining three men because of heavy enemy fire. He therefore led them by a different route to the river, waded four hundred yards upstream to the safety of dead ground, and returned with very valuable information. Three months later, during the last major action in which the battalion took part—the capture of Cloppenburg—C.S.M. Greenyer was mortally wounded by a sniper's bullet.

Two other awards were won by members of The Queen's Own while they were serving with this Hampshire battalion. Colonel

Talbot won the D.S.O. for planning the part to be played by 130th Brigade and successfully commanding it in operation 'Blackcock' during the temporary absence of the Brigadier. Major Rooke, who was second-in-command to Dennis Talbot and commanded the battalion during his absence, won a bar to the M.C. he had won in Palestine for his drive and careful planning during the capture of the villages Putt and Waldenrath.

Two other Regular officers of The Queen's Own, who served in North-West Europe with battalions of other regiments, were Major R. H. Molony and Major G. G. Elliott. Major Molony had been Adjutant of the 1st Battalion just before the war and was then attached to The King's Own Scottish Borderers. It is sad to record that 'Pat,' as he was affectionately called, was killed while commanding a company of their 6th Battalion after the capture of Goch. Major Elliott, who had been for a short time second-in-command of the 7th Battalion at Blackburn, won the D.S.O. while commanding the 2nd Battalion The Essex Regiment.

*   *   *

The 2nd Battalion moved on July 23, 1944, to Hatch Park near Ashford, where the troops were at last among the orchards and hop-fields of Kent. Officers and other ranks then began to join. These included Colonel Macklin, who returned to the Regiment from commanding an East Surrey battalion and took over command from Colonel Blanch on September 12. At that time Major Annadale was second-in-command and Captain Cropper, having recovered from his wound, was Adjutant.

Unhappily the sojourn of the battalion at Ashford was very short, for by the middle of September it was at Lerwick, in the Shetland Islands—far more remote even than Blackburn—where it was em-ployed as garrison troops. A start was made, however, in training for an operational role, and a Support Company was formed and Cadre courses began. But once more the process was interrupted. By the middle of November the battalion was on its way south to Hastings, where all hope of proceeding overseas in the near future vanished when nearly a thousand Gunners arrived for eight weeks' training to convert them into Infantrymen. This heralded a return to the role of draft-finding. The process of intake and departure was once more resumed, and the war had ended before the battalion became opera-tional.

So it came about that, although many of its officers and other ranks served with 21st Army Group in North-West Europe, there was no battalion of The Queen's Own fighting in the final campaign against Germany.

CHAPTER 17

Italy: The Switch to the West
January to April 1944
1st, 5th and 6th Battalions

1. Winter in the Adriatic Sector—5th Battalion

At the beginning of 1944 the German line in the Adriatic sector of Italy[1] ran from the coast, two miles north-west of Ortona, across the River Arielli to the villages of Creechio and Arielli. It then passed east of Orsogna and climbed into the foothills of the Apennines towards Civitella and the upper reaches of the River Sangro. Opposite this line the British 8th Army stood halted, and in its centre 8th Indian Division occupied positions on a two-brigade front.

Both sides had settled down to static warfare for the winter, and in 8th Indian Division a regular routine of relief in and out of the line had begun. For the first days of January, 21st Indian Brigade was in divisional reserve at Jubatti, and we find the troops of the 5th Battalion having baths at a Mobile Bath Unit, cleaning up, checking weapons and making up deficiencies of kit. For entertainment there was a cinema show at Roalti. Then on January 10 the brigade moved up into the line after dark to take over from 17th Indian Brigade, the 5th Battalion relieving 1st Royal Fusiliers at San Nicola. Here the enemy posts were only a few hundred yards away, and there was much patrol activity by both sides at night. Otherwise, except for some enemy shelling and mortaring, the area remained comparatively quiet by day until January 13, when the brigade handed over the sector and moved back to Lanciano.

For the next twelve days the 5th Battalion remained at Lanciano, where the troops were billeted in houses in the town and were able to find some rest and a little recreation. The opportunity was also taken to absorb two officers and ninety-three other ranks, who had arrived as reinforcements a few days before, and to conduct the officers and senior N.C.O.s over the battlefield at Romagnoli. On

[1] See map 'Termoli to the Arielli.'

Sunday, January 23, Divine Service was taken in the Canadian cinema by Rev. V. J. Pike, the former Irish rugby international whom Colonel Whitty had known so well at Aldershot before the war.

The second period in the line began on January 25, when the battalion relieved the Frontier Force Regiment of 17th Indian Brigade near Vezzani. In this sector our troops were in touch with the enemy on the River Arielli, and there was much patrolling at night to the river and sometimes beyond it. On January 30 and 31 the Canadian Division on the right carried out several raids to clear the east bank of the Arielli on their front, and the Mortar Platoon of the battalion put down concentrations to support them. When this tour in the line came to an end on February 5, the battalion marched back across country to billets in Jubatti once more, the support company being billeted in Caldari. These constant reliefs in and out of the line gave the senior N.C.O.s a great deal of administrative work, and none was busier than R.S.M. Creed, who was always on the last lorry to leave after satisfying himself that the battalion's posts or billets had been left clean and tidy.

*   *   *

The 8th Indian Division then side-stepped to the left to take over a sector between Orsogna and the mountains, and, after only two days at Jubatti, the battalion moved on the night of February 7 to Salarola, where it was on the extreme left of the division's front. It would be difficult to exaggerate the discomfort in which the troops had to live and fight in this sector. They bivouacked in blizzards, snow-drifts were five feet deep, gales blew, the cold was bitter, and weapon pits in the frozen ground became filled with icy slush. Few days passed without considerable artillery and mortar activity and consequent casualties. Sleep was disturbed at night by the noise of vehicles or battle or by being sent out on patrol. There was also always the possibility of an enemy raid to 'snatch' a prisoner, and sentries had to be numerous and alert. To make matters worse the positions on the left flank were isolated. When these were raided by the enemy after dark on February 8 seven casualties were lost, of whom five were missing. Here also on the night of the 19th a patrol of C Company was ambushed and suffered three casualties. And so the nerve-racking contest went on among the snow-covered ridges and valleys, until, on the nights of the 25th and 26th, the battalion was relieved and moved back to positions midway between Lanciano and Orsogna. Even here there was not much relief; but a percentage of the weary men were allowed to visit Lanciano for baths and recreation.

When the battalion returned to Salarola on March 15, Major Malcolmson was in command, for Colonel Whitty had fallen sick while he was on leave in Egypt and had been admitted to 19th General Hospital in Cairo. This second tour at Salarola, which lasted for three weeks, differed little from the first, and the battalion began once again the routine of patrols and raids on houses occupied by the enemy by night and the quenching of fires caused by enemy shelling by day. No outstanding event occurred. The battalion was relieved on April 3 and moved back through Lanciano to Colli, where it was accommodated in billets and a few tents. In this reserve area the battalion was at five hours' notice in a counter-attack role, and days were spent in minor tactical training. For recreation a percentage of the troops were again allowed to visit Lanciano. Some dozen officers of the 8th Manchesters from Malta, including Colonel George French,[1] were attached for a few days. These were the fore-runners of 10th Indian Division, which was about to move up into the line.

On April 7 the 8th Indian Division began to move from the Adriatic sector for rest and training. 21st Brigade was the first to go, and the 5th Battalion marched out of its billets at Colli and set off in M.T. for Rotella, away back east of the River Biferno. En route, however, Major Malcolmson was issued with fresh maps and different orders. To his surprise the new rendezvous was only a few miles south of Cassino, near the west coast of Italy, where the battalion arrived on April 15. That night positions were taken over at Cassino Station. So, while the remainder of the division went to a training area on the River Volturno, 20 miles south of Cassino, 21st Brigade went straight into action again without any rest. This meant that the 5th Battalion, which had been fighting more or less continuously since November 1943, began the spring campaign of 1944 tired, under-trained and without having had the chance to absorb properly several drafts of reinforcements which had arrived.

2. *Winter in the Adriatic Sector—6th Battalion*

After the Battle of the Sangro the 6th Battalion went back for rest and recuperation to Baranello, where it arrived on December 4, 1943. Baranello is a fair-sized town on the mountain slopes east of the River Biferno, and the billets for the troops were very comfortable. One of them was specially selected and was turned into a bar, which was called 'The White Horse Inn.' Another innovation, not so popular

[1] Colonel French's regiment was The Royal Irish Fusiliers. He was a brother of Maurice (see p. 281).

with the troops, was the mounting of a guard at Battalion Head-quarters. During the first few days congratulatory messages were received from 'Monty' and the Corps Commander on the success of the Sangro battle, but thoughts were now turned more towards sleep and recreation than fighting. At Christmas the festivities were a great success. The troops sat down to a very appetising meal in their company areas, and Brigadier J. L. Spencer, the new Brigade Commander, visited them and made a short speech to each company. New officers and other reinforcements then joined, and much re-organisation was carried out. Snow fell and a snow-plough, hitched to two carriers, had to be used to clear the roads. Even with this the road from Baranello was only just cleared in time for the battalion to move out. Colonel Bryan was away visiting hospitals and reinforcement centres, and in his absence Major Forman took the battalion back to the battle area.

On January 3 the battalion embussed in troop-carrying vehicles (T.C.V.s), and after a long and very cold journey through Termoli, Vasto and Atessa the column reached Casoli on the morning of January 5. The companies were sent out straight away to take over their positions. 78th Division (now commanded by Major-General C. F. Keightley) was holding a sector overlooking the upper Sangro, and the battalion was widely dispersed between Casoli, Rocca-scalegna and Gessopalena. The forward positions were in the foothills of the Apennines. Although the companies were not in contact with the enemy, conditions were unpleasant. Snow still fell intermittently and, with the roads blocked, it was difficult to get supplies through and contact with the scattered companies was at times impossible. Some of the troops lived in ruined houses, but most of them had only bivouacs or slit-trenches.

The forward companies of the battalion carried out a policy of aggressive patrolling to the neighbouring villages in the mountains, and if any enemy were found in a village it would be earmarked for a raid on another day. In this way much valuable information was gained. As a result one company was moved farther into the hills and made Civitella its patrol base. Three of the most notable patrols were carried out on consecutive days. On January 27 Corporal Ingram took a small reconnaissance patrol to Corpisanti. While it lay up in the outskirts of the village a score of Germans approached from the rear. Ordering the patrol to escape down a gully, Ingram held the Germans at bay with his Tommy-gun until his men were clear and then led them back to safety, having obtained valuable information. Next day Serjeant Edmeads set out with one man to find out whether Torricella was occupied by the enemy. After lying up in observation all day, they entered the village at dusk and ascertained that it was occupied by about thirty Germans. As they were withdrawing they were fired on by a sentry in the outskirts of the village, but they got away safely after finding out the positions of two more sentries and of the German headquarters. On the night of January 29 Serjeant Brophy took a patrol to raid an enemy O.P. at Madonna del Rosetta. The O.P. was defended by a minefield, and Brophy went forward alone, felt for the mines with his hands and guided his men through. At dawn five Germans came out and lounged in the porch of the church. The patrol shot them all; the O.P. was not re-occupied by the Germans. There is no doubt that by the end of January the battalion had obtained patrol superiority on its front.

The sympathy of the Italian civilians was with the British, and the battalion was helped a great deal in this patrolling by a band of Italian partisans. Contact had been made with this band in the mountains as soon as the battalion arrived in the area. Its leader, 'Nick Williams,' had asked for arms and ammunition. More details of the guerrilla force were naturally required before these could be supplied, and a representative of the band was taken to Brigade Headquarters. The consequence was that on January 10 a Guerrilla Force was formed under Major L. Wigram (Royal Fusiliers), who had joined the battalion immediately after the Battle of Termoli. This force was organised into platoons by localities. Volunteers flocked in although as yet the only arms available were an assortment of antiquated Greek, Albanian, Spanish, German and Italian weapons. A conference, attended by 'Nick Williams' himself, was then held, and a working policy was agreed on. The force was to have its headquarters in Casoli with a mixed staff of British and Italian clerks. Representations were again to be made to higher authority on the subjects of feeding and arming the guerrillas.

The first foray of this band was on January 15, when a mixed patrol of guerrillas and troops from the battalion attacked a German post and captured much equipment, including two machine guns and a field telephone. This success gave a distinct boost to the guerrilla recruiting. It also gained the required interest of higher authority, for on the 17th the Corps Commander, Lieutenant-General M. C. Dempsey, visited the battalion to find out more about the partisans. It also brought reprisals from the enemy, for on the 19th the Germans shelled the village of Gessopalena and on the 21st news came that they had totally destroyed Agata, a small cluster of houses to the north, and had massacred about thirty men, women and children. Undeterred by this, Major Wigram's guerrillas, who had now become a mobile column called 'Wigforce' operating from a base in the mountains across the River Sangro, caught a small German detachment in enemy-held territory on January 25, destroyed it and captured four prisoners. A similar success was gained on the following night. By this time 'Wigforce' had obtained information that the Germans were withdrawing from many places in the mountains, and the guerrillas made corresponding incursions. These culminated in an attempt by them on the night of February 2 to destroy a German headquarters at Pizzoferrato, ten miles south of Casoli. This was the last adventure of 'Wigforce,' for the raid ended in disaster and in it Major Wigram was killed.

Meanwhile, entertainment had not been lacking for the troops. A percentage of them were allowed to visit Casoli every day, and there they could attend cinema shows or performances given by a concert party called *Stars in Battle Dress*. Some of the lucky ones also went to Lanciano to see a show given by Leslie Henson, the famous comedian. In addition small parties of men proceeded for a few days at a time to the Corps Rest Camp at Paglieta and the 8th Army Rest Camp at Bari. It was unfortunate that Lieutenant G. E. F. Turner, who had only recently arrived from the 2nd Battalion, should be fatally injured by a mine while he was out on reconnaissance on January 29.

The battalion had now been in the sector for over a month, and on February 7 the outlying companies handed over their positions and concentrated in Casoli. Snow then fell so heavily that it appeared that a further move would be impossible. But orders had been received for 78th Division to transfer to the western sector of Italy, and the battalion motored south in T.C.V.s over icy roads. On the 16th the road ahead was blocked by snow, and two nights had to be spent in barns at the roadside or in the T.C.V.s themselves. On the 18th the journey was continued. On the following day the battalion arrived at Villa Volturno, just north of Capua and some thirty miles from Cassino.

3. *The 1st Battalion Arrives on the Garigliano*

By January 1, 1944, the 5th Army in the Tyrrhenian sector had not progressed so well as the 8th, for it was still confronted by the Gustav Line. On the right the 5th Army had crossed the River Rapido and had seized positions in advance of Cairo village; in the centre it had reached Cassino and the River Gari; and on the left, except for a bridgehead west of San Martino, its positions extended along the River Garigliano to the coast near Minturno. With the

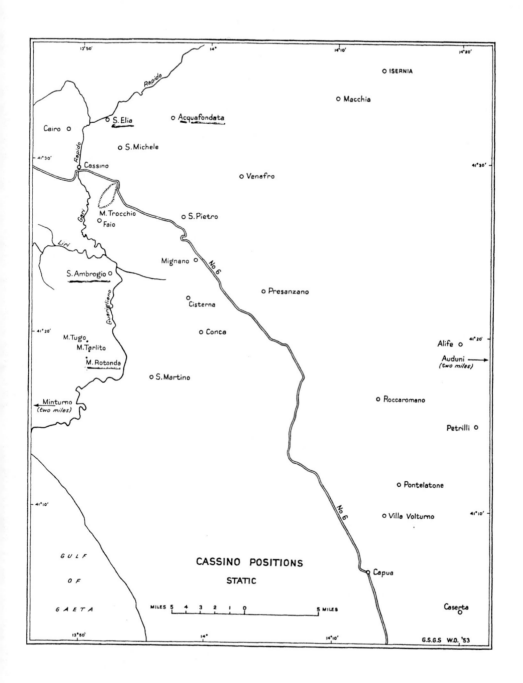

O ISERNIA

O Macchia

Rapido

O Acquafondata

Cairo O   O S.Elia

O S.Michele

Cassino

O Venafro

M.Trocchio

O Faio

O S.Pietro

Mignano O

No 6

S.Ambrogio O

O Cisterna

O Presanzano

Alife O

Auduni →
(two miles)

M.Tugo
M.Tarlito
M.Rotonda

O Conca

O S.Martino

O Roccaromano

Minturno →
(two miles)

Petrilli O

O Pontelatone

GULF

O F

No 6

O Villa Volturno

CASSINO POSITIONS

STATIC

GAETA

MILES 5 4 3 2 1 0   5 MILES

O Capua

Caserta
O

G.S.G.S W.D. '53

object of easing the 5th Army's task by threatening the Germans' rear and cutting their communications with Rome, an Allied landing was made at Anzio on January 22. As luck would have it, severe gales delayed the disembarkation of tanks and other heavy equipment and the Allies failed to break out from the beachhead. Another plan was therefore prepared which entailed the transfer of the main strength of the 8th Army to reinforce the 5th Army; and we have already seen how 78th and 8th Indian Divisions were switched from the Adriatic coast for this purpose. More divisions were also transferred from other theatres. One of these was 4th Division, which included the 1st Battalion.

This battalion, which we left near Bougie in North-West Africa (Chapter 13, Section 9), had sailed from Algiers on December 26, 1943, had disembarked at Suez a few days later and had proceeded to the Combined Training Centre at Kabrit for two months' vigorous training. It had then embarked at Port Said in the *Sobieski*, and on March 5, 1944, the battalion disembarked at Naples. There, somewhat overawed by the sight of Mount Vesuvius in eruption, the troops climbed into T.C.V.s and were driven to the divisional assembly area. Two days later the battalion moved north-west in M.T. to San Martino and thence by march route into the line south of San Ambrogio, where it took over defensive positions from the 2nd Hampshires at Monte Rotondo.

The 1st Battalion still formed part of 12th Brigade (Brigadier F. M. Elliot) in 4th Division (Major-General Hayman Joyce). The other two battalions in the brigade were still 2nd Royal Fusiliers and 6th Black Watch. The third brigade in the division was now the 28th, which had recently joined from Gibraltar, making 4th Division up to three Infantry brigades[1] with no armoured formation. The key personnel in the 1st Battalion at this time were:

> Commanding Officer: Lieutenant-Colonel J. M. Haycraft.
> Second-in-command: Major H. P. Braithwaite.
> Adjutant: Captain B. I. Royal-Dawson.
> Quartermaster: Captain R. C. E. Mines.
> Regimental Serjeant-Major: W.O.I A. J. Hayley.
> O.C. Support Company: Captain S. F. H. Glynn.
> O.C. HQ Company: Major E. G. Reeves.
> O.C. A Company: Captain P. H. N. Jeffery (R. Hamps.)
> O.C. B Company: Major H. W. Hansen-Raae, M.C.
> O.C. C Company: Major J. H. Brock.
> O.C. D Company: Major W. B. Coleman.

A complete list of officers and warrant officers is in Appendix B.

[1] The other brigade was the 10th.

The positions which the battalion now occupied were part of the bridgehead west of the River Garigliano, some dozen miles south of Cassino. The bridgehead was quiet except for some enemy shelling and patrolling, but on the night of March 11, Major Coleman was killed in an ambush whilst visiting an outlying platoon. A short move on the night of the 12th took the battalion to the area of Monte Tugo and Monte Tarlito, where mortar and artillery harassing fire was more frequent and several casualties occurred, including R.S.M. Hayley, who was wounded. The troops were practically confined to their sangars, which were roofed with bivouac sheets and wooden beams covered with boulders, as protection against rain and missiles. The weather was still cold and the troops, just arrived from a warm climate, made full use of the leather jerkin, thick underwear, four pairs of socks and at least two blankets with which they had been issued. The water ration of two pints a day could be increased by melting snow, and brewing up in tommy-cookers was possible. Supplies were brought up by mules. This was just the kind of toughening up that was required by the young soldiers who had joined the battalion at Bougie and had seen no fighting at all.

There was plenty of patrolling at night, when the troops laid booby-traps in all the approaches to their posts. On one occasion an enemy patrol was encountered, and a short fight followed in which Lieutenant Hogg was wounded. On the night of March 22, 2nd Lieutenant S. B. Smith led a fighting patrol to destroy an enemy post. When challenged, he replied with coolness to deceive the enemy, rushed in with his patrol and silenced the post with grenades. At this moment Lance-Corporal Lawry saw that one of the enemy was about to fire a signal flare to call for defensive fire, and he swung quickly round and killed the German with his Bren gun. The patrol then attacked other enemy sangars with grenades, seized three prisoners and returned without loss. This was the first successful patrol of 4th Division in Italy and brought a congratulatory message from the divisional commander.

*　　　*　　　*

After a rest in the Venafro area from March 23 to April 1, the 4th Division took over the Sant Elia sector north of Cassino, and the battalion moved to Aquafondata, where it was in 12th Brigade reserve. On arrival the battalion came under heavy artillery fire and there were more than a dozen casualties, but otherwise the tour was uneventful. On April 10 the battalion relieved the 6th Black Watch in the line just north of the village of Sant Elia. The positions were in wild and mountainous country and had been sited to block the valley of a tributary of the River Rapido. They were overlooked from mountains held by the Germans, who could thus direct their artillery fire from observation posts as they pleased. Shelling and mortaring were consequently more frequent, and more casualties were suffered. At night patrols were sent out to gain information about the enemy's strength, but there were no clashes. This was only a short tour, for on April 14 the battalion moved back to Alife in the valley of the River Volturno, where 4th Division was promised a period of rest and training.

This period lasted, in fact, for ten days only, but during it there were changes in the higher commanders, Major-General A. D. Ward assuming command of 4th Division, and Brigadier A. G. W. Heber-Percy of 12th Brigade. Meanwhile 4th Division had received fresh orders, and on the night of April 23 the battalion moved to Cassino, where 12th Brigade was relieving 1st Guards Brigade in the town.

CHAPTER 18

Italy: Cassino
February to June 1944
1st, 5th and 6th Battalions

1. *The 6th Battalion at Cassino Castle*

THE 1st, 5th and 6th Battalions of the Regiment had now converged on the Cassino sector, where the valley of the River Liri runs parallel to the coast to within a few miles of Rome. The entrance to this valley is strongly protected by nature, for the first few miles of it lie between high mountains and the entrance is closed by the swift-flowing River Gari. On the northern side of the entrance Monte Cassino, topped by a great monastery, looks down from a height of 1,700 feet and completely overlooks the valley. At the eastern base of Monastery Hill, as Monte Cassino is usually called, lies the town of Cassino, and to the north of it rises Castle Hill. Highway Six, the main road which joins Naples and Rome, runs into Cassino town, swings round the foot of Monastery Hill and then turns along the northern side of the valley.

The Germans were still in possession of the entrance to the Liri Valley, and the far bank of the River Gari was heavily mined and was also guarded by wire and concrete posts. The hub of their defensive system was Monastery Hill; so long as they held it nothing could enter the valley without their consent. They had reinforced the natural strength of the position by well-hidden machine-gun emplacements and mortars on the reverse slopes. They were also still in Cassino town, which was strongly fortified. Its narrow streets and thick walls were well suited for defence, and its defenders were supported by machine guns on the steep slopes behind. Ten German battalions were deployed on Monastery Hill and in Cassino town, and, although they had few tanks and less than two hundred guns, they had many mortars and machine guns as well as the advantage of excellent observation. What is more, the Allied bombing attacks had reduced the town to a heap of ruins and rubble, which made it an impassable obstacle for our tanks and nullified our superiority in

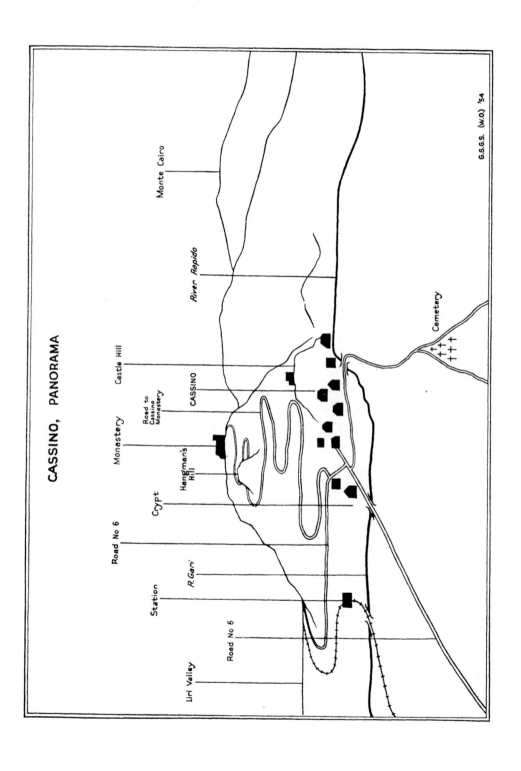

CASSINO, PANORAMA

Liri Valley Station Road No 6 Crypt Monastery Castle Hill River Rapido Monte Cairo

R. Gari Hangman's Hill Road to Cassino Monastery CASSINO

Road No 6

Cemetery

G.S.G.S. (W.O.) '54

armour. In addition, at this time of the year the flat and low-lying expanse of farm-land in the Liri valley was too sodden to be suitable for tanks.

The 6th was the first battalion of the Regiment to reach this sector. Arriving as we have seen at Villa Volturno on February 19, it passed with 78th Division under command of the New Zealand Corps. The New Zealanders had taken over the whole of the Cassino sector and were about to attempt a task which the Americans had already failed to achieve—the capture of Monastery Hill and the establishment of a bridgehead over the river south of it. 78th Division was not to be launched into the battle until it was possible to exploit success.

After a week in the concentration area at Villa Volturno the 6th Battalion moved through thick mud and heavy rain to a very boggy camp at Cisterna, some ten miles south-east of Cassino. The troops were mainly accommodated in tents, but a few caves and barns gave additional shelter from the rain which continued to fall for the best part of five days. The evenings were particularly miserable, although they were made a little more pleasant by visits to a Y.M.C.A. hall in a neighbouring village. A rum issue also helped. Later on a company football league was started, and some of the troops attended E.N.S.A. shows at Capua. By this time Colonel Bryan had resumed command of the battalion, and he made final preparations for the battle. Owing to a great shortage of reinforcements in this theatre of war A Company was disbanded, and its personnel were posted to the other three rifle companies to make them up to strength. The surplus N.C.O.s were put into an R Company, which would be strengthened by the Left out of Battle (L.O.B.s) when the battalion went into action.

The New Zealand Corps opened its offensive against Cassino on the morning of March 15. After four hours' intensive bombing of the enemy positions the 4th Indian and 2nd New Zealand Divisions advanced to the attack. The first objectives were Castle Hill and that part of the town north of Highway Six. By the evening these had been captured. Rain then slowed down the attack, and it was not until the 17th that further progress was made and Hangman's Hill and Cassino Station were taken. By this time casualties had been severe, and the 6th Battalion was loaned to 4th Indian Division, which was short of infantry. The task given to the battalion was to take over Cassino Castle and positions on Castle Hill. The troops moved off in M.T. on the morning of the 19th to a harbour at San Michele, while Colonel Bryan and the Company Commanders went forward to Castle Hill to view the ground. As they were doing so the C.O. of the 1/4th Essex, who was handing over the positions to them, was sniped and badly wounded. Ten minutes later, as they walked back down the hill, Major Birch[1] and Captain Weatherly were killed. The loss of these two Company Commanders at this stage was a severe blow. In the evening the battalion moved forward behind an advanced guard to the Cairo area, and after dark one company took over the Castle while the remainder of the battalion took over positions on the hill.

Cassino Castle consisted merely of a strong tower and a courtyard, which were surrounded by a thick wall some ten feet high. It was perched on a rocky crag behind and 300 feet above the German-held part of Cassino town, and some of the enemy positions to the west and south were within a hundred yards of the wall. Moreover the Germans looked straight down into the courtyard from Cassino Monastery so that movement was virtually impossible in daylight except under a smoke-screen. In fact during the day the defenders lay up in two cellars beneath the tower. The only approach to the Castle was from the town up a steep rocky incline, up which supplies had to be brought by porters after dark. The defenders were thus rather like rats in a trap. The other positions held by the battalion were on a steep spur called Point 175, which was across a narrow ravine to the north of the Castle. These positions were under constant artillery and mortar fire, and the men lay low in holes and hastily-built sangars during the day. After dark there was less danger, and rations and ammunition could be taken up the slope and issued. This meant that the mule-train, under Captain Nixon, had to bring forward the supplies from San Michele by day and run the gauntlet of a long stretch of open road under enemy fire. On arrival, the mules were unloaded in a quarry at the foot of the slope near Battalion Head-quarters, where R.S.M. Byrne organised carrying parties to take the supplies up to Point 175 after dark.

*   *   *

All day on March 20 the positions held by the battalion were shelled and mortared spasmodically. That night, to assist the renewed New Zealand attack on the Monastery, Colonel Bryan received orders to assault a yellow house some 120 yards away from the Castle walls. In order to do this the troops had to debouch from one of the Castle entrances, which was covered by German fixed lines of fire, and then deploy on the rocky slope of the hill. The space in which to deploy was so small that only one company could be used. D Company (Major Wakefield) was selected to carry out the attack. The first platoon succeeded in leaving the Castle, and it was approaching the yellow house when a mine exploded and killed four men and wounded

[1] Detached from The King's Regiment.

the platoon commander. Undeterred by this, Serjeant Norman, who had also been wounded, remained at the head of his platoon and led it up to the objective. Major Wakefield then brought the other two platoons forward, but just as they reached the area of the yellow house more electrically-detonated mines exploded and caused more casualties. By this time machine-gun and mortar fire was sweeping the confined area. There was considerable confusion, and Major Wakefield moved about amongst the men encouraging them to press home the assault. But the enemy's fire was too heavy. As dawn broke the troops were ordered back to the Castle to reorganise. A counter-attack came in immediately and, although it was beaten off, the attempt to capture the yellow house was abandoned.

At dawn on the 22nd another counter-attack came in and the Germans, who had worked their way up a gully in the darkness, threw grenades over the Castle wall. Hand-to-hand fighting took place. Major Roper calmly went from one threatened point to another to conduct the defence. For a time the situation looked black, but Colonel Bryan had arranged for this gully to be carefully registered, and such a hail of fire from the artillery and from Serjeant Brindley's 3-inch mortars swept the attackers that they went to ground. When the fire ceased, nearly forty Germans rose from cover behind the rocks and walked with their hands up into the Castle to surrender. The approach to the Castle wall was littered with enemy dead and wounded, and many more Germans must have perished in the gully. Not only was the counter-attack not renewed, but for some hours afterwards German stretcher-bearers under the Red Cross flag were evacuating their wounded up Monastery Hill. As a result of this action a message of congratulation was received from General Freyberg, who was commanding the New Zealand Corps.

For the remainder of the morning the battalion endured heavy mortar and artillery fire. During the afternoon a number of officer reinforcements joined. Their arrival was timely, for some of our smoke canisters fell near Battalion Headquarters and smashed the foot of Major Forman, the second-in-command, and Major Roper was wounded by a shell which fell in the Castle courtyard. In fact the enemy shelling caused a constant drain on the strength of the battalion, and on the 24th all administrative personnel who could be spared were sent forward to man the positions.

By this time the New Zealand attack had been abandoned, and it had been decided to defer further attacks against Cassino until the spring, when firmer ground would enable the armour of the Allies to move through the low-lying Liri Valley. This meant that the small band of Gurkhas, who had captured Hangman's Hill and were now isolated, had to be extricated. On the evening of March 24 their withdrawal was covered by a heavy artillery barrage and by a feint attack on the yellow house from the Castle. At nine that night the weary Gurkhas began to come down the hill, and the last of them had passed through the battalion's positions by midnight. The enemy were not slow to retaliate. Before dawn a bout of shelling on the Castle killed sixteen and wounded seventeen of the garrison. One shell destroyed a 3-inch mortar and set alight the reserve ammunition for it. The bombs began to explode but Serjeant Dyke ran to them and moved them away, thereby saving the lives of several men. Another shell fell on the garrison headquarters and killed most of the staff and all of the stretcher-bearers except Private Shiplee. He carried the wounded to shelter and dressed their wounds, although shells were still falling, it was snowing and he had no light. At dawn he was still tending them, and he continued to do so until they had all been evacuated under a Red Cross flag in daylight. The Red Cross flag was always strictly respected by the Germans.

The battalion handed over its positions on Castle Hill on the night of March 26. While the relief was in progress a dump of mortar bombs in the quarry near Battalion Headquarters was set alight by a shell. Many of the bombs exploded and R.S.M. Byrne, setting an excellent example of coolness, organised the evacuation of the wounded. This ended the grim period on Castle Hill, during which the battalion had lost ten officers and over a hundred men. But the many gallant deeds that had been performed had proved that the fighting spirit of the troops had in no way diminished. Nor were the achievements unrecognised, for on the 30th the Divisional Commander addressed the whole battalion and congratulated them on 'a magnificent performance.'

For the next three weeks the battalion was in the San Michele area, where it was dug in amongst the olive groves. Although in reserve, the proximity of Monastery Hill made it necessary to sleep in or near slit-trenches, but life was somewhat eased by parties going off to rest camps and by fifty men being allowed to visit Naples each day. Six officers and some hundred and fifty other reinforcements joined in the course of a few days, and the battalion was reorganised again into four rifle companies. Between April 15 and April 20, two companies at a time went to Presanzano to practise co-operation with tanks. On the night of the 21st the battalion moved forward once more to the positions on Castle Hill, with one company in the Castle.

Both sides had now settled down again to static warfare, and the battalion was glad to find that Castle Hill was a much quieter place than it had been before. Indeed, except for occasional enemy harassing fire and danger from our own smoke canisters, life was almost peaceful. So much so that the only casualties were two tins of salmon and three of herrings, which occurred when spent bullets fell in the area from an air battle overhead. After a week on the hill the battalion was relieved, and before dawn on April 28 was on its way to a reserve area at Pontelatone.

2. *The 5th Battalion at Cassino Station*

The second battalion of the Regiment to arrive in the Cassino sector was the 5th, who took over positions at Cassino Station from a New Zealand battalion on April 15. This area, like the Castle, was overlooked by the Germans from Monastery Hill, and as movement in daylight was impossible except under a smoke-screen Colonel Whitty, who had rejoined from hospital that day, was unable to reconnoitre the area and the relief was carried out in darkness. The positions taken over were in the railway station itself and on some slag heaps nearby. The nearest Germans were only twenty yards away. At night, standing patrols were sent out to protect two Bailey bridges over the river. These positions were occupied by one company, which was relieved every six days. This was not too short a period, for by the end of it the men were completely exhausted owing to the impossibility of sleeping at night or of moving from their weapon pits by day. The company had to be maintained at a strength of 132, for if the numbers dropped below this there was a risk that the Germans would occupy the vacant weapon pits.

The company at the railway station was the only one in close contact with the enemy. Another company was about a mile back at the end of a railway embankment; the remainder of the battalion was some distance farther back still. The embankment was covered by the fixed lines of fire of the enemy, so that reliefs for the railway station had to be carried out man by man; even then casualties occurred. Because of this, rations were taken up on tanks and then only every third night. The rations were placed in sandbags—one bag for each two-man weapon pit—and the sandbags were slung round the tanks, which drove along the embankment and round the station positions. A solid petrol cooker was included in each sandbag, and the men did whatever cooking was possible in their pits.

Except for spasmodic shelling and mortaring by the enemy, usually in the afternoons and evenings, the situation was quiet and there were no casualties for eight days. Then on the afternoon of April 24 a post of D Company (which was at the station at that

time) was hit by a shell and seven men were killed and fourteen
wounded. The evacuation of the casualties was organised by C.S.M.
Mott, who went to the post under fire and arranged a dressing station
there. Within an hour the wounded had all been carried back under
the Red Cross flag. On the night of May 4, enemy shelling set off a
dump of smoke generators, which was very close to the two Bailey
bridges, and the picquets had to be withdrawn until the smoke subsided. That evening several mortar bombs fell near the slag heaps
and wounded eight men. These were the last casualties at the railway
station. That night the battalion was relieved and moved back in
M.T. to Petrilli to refit.

3. *The 1st Battalion in Cassino Town*

The 1st Battalion moved into Cassino Town on the night of April
23. The Germans were still holding the western fringe of the town
nearest to Monastery Hill, and 12th Brigade had taken over the eastern
part with the Royal Fusiliers on the northern edge, the Black Watch
in the centre about Highway Six, and the 1st Battalion in the more
open southern outskirts adjoining the railway station. The 1st and
5th Battalions were in fact shoulder to shoulder. The town had been
smashed by bombing into heaps of rubble, among which stood bare
walls and archways, and the only suitable place for Battalion Headquarters was the crypt under the church, which the 1st Battalion
shared with the Black Watch. There all members of both headquarters lived and slept in one underground vault. The forward positions
held by the battalion faced a lateral stretch of Highway Six and were
separated from the enemy by the River Rapido which, formerly
passing under the town in a conduit, had now been opened up by
the bursting of bombs. These positions were either loopholes pierced
through the base of those walls which still remained, basement windows or open weapon pits dug amongst the rubble. Some of the posts
were out of sight from each other, and some sections were thus
virtually isolated.

The troops lived an unhealthy life in their pits or in cellars below
the ruins. Some of the bomb-craters were used for washing, others
as latrines. Corpses lay everywhere. In fact conditions in the forward
positions were so bad that the defenders had to be relieved every
few days. As movement was impossible in daylight the reliefs could
be carried out only at night, and the wounded had to wait until
darkness fell before they could be evacuated. Rations likewise were
brought up by carrying-parties only at night. Cooking and 'brewing-

LEROS : ALINDA BAY LOOKING NORTH

ITALY : MARCH 1944. SIGNALLERS OF THE 6TH BATTALION ON CASTLE HILL KEEP TOUCH WITH TROOPS IN CASSINO BY RADIO

ITALY: A PATROL OF THE 6TH BATTALION SEARCHES
ALATRI FOR STRAY GERMANS ON JUNE 3, 1944

ITALY: THE RUINED SQUARE OF CASSINO WITH CASTLE HILL IN THE BACKGROUND

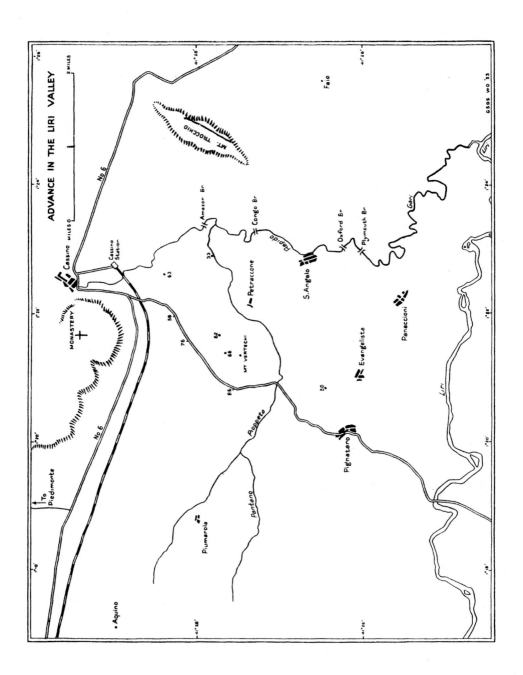

ADVANCE IN THE LIRI VALLEY

up' had to be done in all sorts of odd corners. There was little patrol activity in the battalion's area, but shelling and mortaring was considerable, and sometimes the grenade-throwing and grenade-firing by the enemy would be most unpleasant. Casualties were surprisingly few. In the early part of the night the guns were usually silent while the rations of both sides were being delivered by men in rubber-soled shoes, but after midnight the guns and mortars would become noisy, the ruined town would become deserted, and walking amid the maze of rubble, masonry and craters would be a somewhat eerie business.

When the battalion was relieved on the night of May 5 by a battalion of the Grenadier Guards, after eleven days in these macabre surroundings, three men were wounded by shell-fire as the companies proceeded independently to the main road. There they embussed and went into reserve at Roccaromano.

4. *A Lull Before the Battle*

From the foregoing sections it will be seen that for the period from April 23 to April 28 there were three battalions of the Regiment, although in three different divisions, alongside each other at Cassino —at the Castle, Town and Station. This must surely be a unique occurrence. But what made the coincidence even more remarkable was that all three battalions then went for a period of rest to localities within a few miles of each other—the 1st Battalion to Roccaromano, the 5th to Petrilli and the 6th to Pontelatone—and that they were all in reserve in the early stages of the final battle for Cassino which followed. Furthermore, the command of two battalions changed hands during the period of rest. Colonel Haycraft, after three years in command, handed over the 1st Battalion to his second-in-command, Major H. P. Braithwaite, and went to be G.S.O.I. of a General Headquarters Training Team in the Middle East and later to be Commandant of the Middle East Weapon Training School. Major Shipley (Royal Fusiliers) was appointed second-in-command. Colonel Bryan, who had been with the 6th Battalion without a break for sickness or wounds since its formation in 1939 and had commanded it through ten months of very active campaigning, went to England to be Commandant of 164 O.C.T.U. at Barmouth. Major R. A. Fyffe came from the Rifle Brigade to command the 6th Battalion.

The period of rest for the 1st and 5th Battalions was only six and seven days respectively. On May 11 they both moved forward to be ready to enter the battle—the 1st Battalion moving to Monte

Trocchio and the 5th to Mignano. The 6th Battalion had a longer period at Pontelatone, and during it co-operation with tanks and river crossings in assault boats were practised. Then on May 14 they moved up to 78th Division's concentration area and thence, on the 15th, to Monte Trocchio. By this time the final battle for Cassino had begun.

5. *The 1st and 5th Battalions in the Final Battle for Cassino*

The Battle for Cassino was designed to culminate in the fall of Rome. The plan was simple. On the right the Polish Corps was to assault Monastery Hill from the north-west; in the centre XIII Corps, which included 4th, 78th and 8th Indian Divisions, would attack south of Cassino and break into the Liri Valley; and on the left near the coast the 5th Army, containing the French and American Corps, would advance from the Garigliano. At the appropriate moment the Allies were to break out from the beach-head at Anzio, cut off the enemy's retreat and make for Rome.

At Cassino the intention was that XIII Corps (Lieutenant-General S. C. Kirkman) should force a crossing over the River Gari[1] south of the town and join hands with the Poles on Highway Six, thus encircling the Germans who were on Monastery Hill. XIII Corps was to attack with 4th Division on the right and 8th Indian Division on the left. 4th Division was to seize a bridgehead across the Gari between Cassino and Sant Angelo and then push on and swing right for Highway Six. 8th Indian Division was to cross the river at and south of Sant Angelo, clear the tongue of land between the Gari and the Liri, and press straight on. 78th Division, in reserve, would be held for the break-through and pursuit.

The River Gari, which bars the entrance to the Liri Valley, is some sixty feet wide, and the farm-land on the far side of it is covered with hillocks and undulations which provide good defensive positions. These had been improved by the Germans by skilfully placed machine-gun posts and wire. Moreover, from Monastery Hill the whole area can be overlooked, and every move of XIII Corps could be carefully observed by the Germans. Efforts were made by the artillery to cover Monastery Hill with a pall of smoke in order to conceal the movements of the troops, and these were frequently helped by a heavy ground mist or heat haze. But winter had now turned to spring, the mud had become a white dust, and the presence of vehicles, tanks and even of marching troops was therefore

[1] The River Gari is sometimes called the Rapido as far south as Sant Angelo.

difficult to hide. The one factor in the attackers' favour was that the olive trees and grape vines were now in full leaf, and the corn and grass were also high enough to provide some concealment.

At eleven on the night of May 11 all the guns of XIII Corps opened fire on the German positions. At a quarter to twelve the infantry of the two divisions advanced. In 4th Division's sector the 10th and 28th Brigades crossed the River Gari in assault boats and, after desperate fighting, established bridgeheads. In 8th Indian Division's sector 17th and 19th Brigades also crossed the river and, in mist and smoke, formed bridgeheads. In both divisions the Sappers began to erect Bailey bridges as soon as the infantry were across the river, while bulldozers shifted the earth to make ramps for the launching sites. When daylight came the men working on the banks of the river in 4th Division's sector were forced to withdraw by furious shelling, and work was held up all day. In 8th Indian Division's sector however, 'Oxford' bridge was completed by 9 a.m. A few minutes later tanks began to cross, nearly 24 hours before they were able to do so on 4th Division's front.

At first therefore the Indians made better progress than 4th Division, and on May 13 the assaulting troops of 17th Indian Brigade, with tanks firing into the German machine-gun nests, dashed into Sant Angelo. After sixty minutes of fierce fighting the village was captured. Soon afterwards the attack of 19th Brigade on the left was equally successful, Panaccioni was captured and one battalion began to clear the area where the Gari and the Liri join. Both flanks were now firm, and 21st Brigade was brought forward to act as reserve for an attack on Pignataro. With it came the 5th Battalion, which had spent the whole of May 12 and 13 lying up in the Mignano area at three hours' notice to move. Just before midnight on May 13 the battalion embussed in troop-carrying vehicles and was carried to within thirty minutes' march of the rendezvous at Faio. At 4.30 a.m. Colonel Whitty received a warning order to move, and at 5.40 the fighting vehicles crossed the River Gari by 'Oxford' bridge. As dawn broke a smoke-screen was put down on the area. The companies were thus concealed as they marched across 'Plymouth' bridge, which had now been built. By ten they were moving into position half a mile north-east of Panaccioni, where they dug in so as to obtain some protection from the intermittent mortar and shell fire.

17th and 19th Brigades had opened the attack on Pignataro at dawn, but the Germans resisted strongly and it was not until the late afternoon that Colonel Whitty received orders to pass through 17th Brigade on the right and advance to Point 50 north of Evangelista. At nightfall A and B Companies, with four detachments of mortars and supported by tanks, crossed the start-line while C and D Companies remained in reserve in a convenient re-entrant. B Company (still commanded by Major Stocker) soon encountered enemy opposition, but they pressed on and occupied Point 50, capturing 17 prisoners on the way. D Company then moved forward to protect the left flank and C Company took up a position in rear of B. By this time 19th Brigade had captured Pignataro and, except for taking five more prisoners next morning, the 5th Battalion took no further part in the battle.

8th Indian Division had in fact completed its task, the battle had rolled forward and the division was withdrawn into reserve. On the evening of the 16th the 5th Battalion was relieved by a battalion of its allied Carleton and York Regiment of Canada and marched back to Faio. On the 17th it moved in M.T. to an area close to Presanzano.

*　　*　　*

We must now return to 10th and 28th Brigades of 4th Division, which had been clinging to their bridgeheads for the whole of May 12 while the Sappers attempted to erect Bailey bridges across the River Gari. By the evening the situation in the bridgeheads was desperate, and it was decided to finish 'Amazon' bridge at all costs so as to allow the reserve brigade to cross. Work went on through the night. By 8 a.m. on the 13th, infantry and tanks were crossing the river. The leading battalions of 12th Brigade then pressed forward through 10th Brigade's bridgehead on the right, and by noon they had advanced some 1,000 yards.

It was now the turn of the 1st Battalion to attack. Before daylight that morning the troops had moved forward from Monte Trocchio into an assembly area just east of 'Amazon' bridge. At eleven the battalion crossed the bridge, which was being heavily shelled, and rode forward on the tanks of the Lothian and Border Horse part of the way to the start-line at Point 33. There was little time for orders or reconnaissance. The attack went in at 2 p.m. under cover of smoke with A Company (Captain Jeffery) leading on the right and B Company (Major Hansen-Raae) on the left and the small river Piopetto as the axis of advance. The forward troops came under mortar and machine-gun fire as they moved through fields of high corn, but the fire was not very effective and Casa Petraccone was reached without much difficulty. Several Germans gave themselves up during the advance. As the battalion was consolidating, B Company was troubled by bursts of fire from an enemy machine-gun post on the left, and Private Gridgeman was sent forward to reconnoitre. As he approached the post he was fired on, but he continued to crawl forward until he was within 40 yards of it. He then rushed the post, silenced the gun and returned to his company with seven prisoners. B Company then exploited towards Point 66, but at dusk it was withdrawn so that its left flank was resting on Casa Petraccone.

At dawn on the 14th the advance of 12th Brigade was resumed in a mist that was so thick that visibility was less than ten yards. This greatly hampered the movements of the supporting tanks. On the right 6th Black Watch massed infantry and tanks together in a square formation and succeeded in reaching Point 76, across the Cassino-Pignataro road, where they dug in and beat off several counter-attacks during the day. On the left the 1st Battalion, in much closer country, came under fire from German machine-guns from Monte Vertechi and were held up for several hours in a maze of walls, hedges and ditches about Point 62. There was much confused fighting. At times the enemy were only a few yards away, but counter-attacks were averted by calling for artillery concentrations. At 6.15 p.m. a fresh attack was mounted with 2/4th Hampshires, who were temporarily attached to 12th Brigade, advancing simultaneously on the left. The battalion's objective was a stretch of the Cassino-Pignataro road 1,000 yards in length between Point 76 and Point 86, and, as by this time the battalion could only muster three weak rifle companies, Colonel Braithwaite decided to cut the road at a single point on a one-company frontage. Once again fighting was confused, and the battalion suffered a steady drain of casualties, including Major Hansen-Raae and Captain Jeffery, who were both killed. Nevertheless the road was cut on the left of the Black Watch by A Company. The remainder of the battalion reached Point 66. The 2/4th Hampshires were also successful, for they stormed and captured Monte Vertechi. By midnight on May 14, therefore, 4th Division had extended its bridgehead to a depth of 3,000 yards and was precariously on the Pignataro road.

Next morning the 1st Battalion strove to extend its gains to the left to Point 86. As the other companies were already deployed on that stretch of the Pignataro road which had been captured, D Company, now reduced to some twenty men, was ordered to carry out this task, with Sherman tanks of 19th New Zealand Armoured Regiment to support them. There were still several enemy machine gun posts on Point 86 and these offered stiff opposition, but the remnants of D Company, led by Major Towers-Minors, advanced under the covering fire of the battalion's machine-guns and 3-inch mortars and reached a position from which they could control, and the tanks could bombard, the feature. This position also overlooked the area to the left, and it was with grim satisfaction that the men of

D Company watched 11th Brigade of 78th Division fighting its way forward. By the evening the 5th Northamptons had captured Point 86. The 1st Battalion was withdrawn into brigade reserve near Casa Petraccone after dark.

With 78th Division on its left, 4th Division now changed direction half-right to cut Highway Six. As a preliminary move the 1st Battalion was brought forward from reserve on the evening of May 16 to close a gap on the right of the Black Watch, who were still on Point 76. The advance was led by tanks, but as the troops passed between Point 63 and Point 76 they were stopped by German machine guns. Owing to the height of the crops the tanks could not locate these guns, and Corporal Dexter mounted the turret of one of the tanks and directed their fire. Although he was sniped at continuously he clung to his position on the tank until the advance was able to continue. Wireless communication with one of the leading companies then failed, and Private Jennings, who was C Company's runner, maintained contact by making the dangerous journey between it and Battalion Headquarters several times. He then guided his own company, which was in reserve, round the left flank to overcome renewed enemy resistance. By nightfall the battalion had not got as far as had been intended, and the companies were forced to dig in about Point 58, from which contact was gained with the Black Watch. During the night the Germans withdrew their troops northwards. When a company of the battalion moved forward with tanks next morning, the only enemy found were those who intended to surrender. Long-range machine-gun and mortar fire was the only opposition. Highway Six had been reached by noon, and by the evening the whole battalion was astride the road and railway which led to Rome. The Black Watch on the left had also moved up to Highway Six and had made contact there with 78th Division, who had reached the road still farther to the left.

The life-line to Cassino had now been severed, and the Germans on Monastery Hill were in danger of being hemmed in from all sides. It was expected that they would attempt to make an organised breakout that night, and the 1st Battalion was ordered to intercept any enemy traffic which attempted to escape from Cassino. The troops therefore dug in astride Highway Six and the railway. The anti-tank guns and machine-guns were sited to fire east along these and other likely escape routes. Sure enough, soon after eleven that night a party of Germans approached the battalion positions. There was a roar of automatic fire, and the enemy fled leaving twelve dead. Later on, a number of Germans were taken prisoner on the railway. There did not appear to be any attempt at a mass break-out.

Next day, the 18th, the Polish Corps captured Monastery Hill from the north, and a Polish patrol met troops of 78th Division on Highway Six to the left of 12th Brigade. The Germans had lost the Monastery at last, and with its loss they abandoned all hope of prolonging the defence of the Liri Valley. They had no alternative now but to fall back to their next prepared position. The task of 4th Division was thus completed. Although 12th Brigade, with the 1st Battalion in reserve, remained on Highway Six until May 20, the whole division ultimately went back for a well-earned rest to Auduni. The 1st Battalion had indeed acquitted itself well in its first major action in Italy. Its casualties had been: Officers—four killed[1] and nine wounded; Other Ranks—forty-six killed[2] and a hundred and sixty-two wounded.

6. *The 5th Battalion at Piedimonte*

Similar successes to those achieved by the Poles at Cassino and XIII Corps in the Liri Valley had also been gained by the French Corps from the Garigliano bridgehead and by the Americans nearer the coast. Rome was the prize. The Germans were to be harried by all possible means and followed up before they had a chance to reorganise. The pivot of their retreat was at Piedimonte, on a spur north of Highway Six, and the Poles pressed on to storm it. Unexpectedly the resistance was strong, and 8th Indian Division was suddenly recalled into the battle area on the right flank of XIII Corps.

The rest period of the 5th Battalion near Presanzano was accordingly cut short. Before dawn on May 19 Colonel Whitty received orders to move the battalion in M.T. Within a few hours they were on their way to an area west of Cassino. After an uneventful night there, the battalion moved off with 21st Brigade astride Highway Six to a position south-east of Piedimonte, where there was now a gap between the Poles in the hills and 78th Division near Aquino. The Poles were still meeting with tough resistance at Piedimonte, and the 5th Battalion was ordered to advance westwards so as to provide an infantry screen for Polish tanks, which were to support a Polish assault against the village from the north. Two points on a sunken road between Piedimonte and Highway Six were given to Colonel

---

[1] Major Hansen-Raae, Captain Jeffery, Lieutenant Wallace and Second-Lieutenant S. B. Smith.

[2] These included C.S.M. Beadle and Colour-Serjeant Ettridge.

Whitty as objectives. The lack of an interpreter prevented any proper liaison with the Poles.

The operation began at 12.30 p.m. on May 20. The advance was across open cornfields swept by enemy fire from the hillside on the right, and the companies went forward by platoons in short, controlled rushes. Major Wollaston and Lieutenant Sainsbury of D Company were both wounded, but the company went on under the command of C.S.M. Mott. Casualties were numerous. Nevertheless, the battalion swept over the objective with great dash and dug in along the sunken road, having captured thirty-one prisoners. This sunken road was only 200 yards below the enemy's main bastion and was an almost impossible position to hold. Consequently, when the Germans concentrated their fire on the area of this road, it became touch and go whether the forward troops could hold on, and Captain Harmer, who was now adjutant, went forward through a hail of bullets and walked amongst the men steadying them and exhorting them to stand firm. By this time wireless touch had been lost, and Private Powell was sent back with a message to Battalion Headquarters. He crossed the sunken road, which was enfiladed by machine-gun fire and in full view of the enemy, but was unable to find the headquarters in the locality which had been pointed out to him. He then searched the area, although it was also under fire, found the headquarters at last and delivered the message. The darkness of night provided a cloak of concealment under which the battalion could consolidate.

Next morning the Polish tanks came close to the battalion's positions during another Polish attack on Piedimonte and attracted heavy mortar fire from the enemy. In consequence the troops near the sunken road suffered badly. Great difficulty was experienced in persuading the tanks to move away because nobody spoke Polish, and the fire continued for most of that day and the next. Indeed, to make matters worse, on the second day the Polish artillery actually shelled C Company. Nevertheless, for two more days the battalion hung staunchly on in these trying circumstances, the Signal Officer (Lieutenant Buckingham) and nine other ranks being killed and forty-two being wounded during the four days. Ultimately the Poles captured Piedimonte, and the Germans fell right back. May 25 was so quiet that a mobile N.A.A.F.I. canteen was able to come up from Highway Six. That evening 19th Indian Brigade came through. The 5th Battalion went into reserve, after an ordeal second only to that experienced by the battalion at Villa Grande.

7. *The 6th Battalion in the Advance on Rome*

The enemy was in full retreat. His last stronghold in the mountains north-west of Cassino had fallen, and on May 23 the Allies had broken out from the Anzio beach-head to cut his lines of communication. The advance on Rome could now begin in earnest. In the van drove 78th Division. This division, as we have seen, had come through between 4th and 8th Indian Divisions in the Liri Valley and had cut Highway Six. It had then turned west towards Aquino to overcome German resistance there. Now it was to press on through Arce and Frosinone[1] as the right wing of the advance on Rome.

The 6th Battalion had been in reserve with 36th Brigade for the whole of 78th Division's advance to Highway Six. It had left Monte Trocchio and crossed the River Gari by 'Congo' bridge on May 18, and had spent that night in an area south of Aquino aerodrome. On the 19th the battalion had been in 36th Brigade reserve for an attack on Aquino, but the attack had later been abandoned and the battalion had been withdrawn to Piumarola. After six quiet days there in reserve and two more at Aquino, the battalion was at last brought forward on May 29 to take part in the pursuit. That night was spent by the troops in a wood at Macchia di Ripi. The axis of advance was along Highway Six towards Frosinone, with the Irish Brigade on the right and 36th Brigade, now commanded by Brigadier J. G. James, on the line of the road itself.

Next morning, the 30th, the brigade set off with 5th Buffs on the right, directed on Ripi, and the 6th Battalion on the left. Each battalion had a squadron of Sherman tanks in support, but the country was most difficult for tanks, as they were apt to lose their tracks in the numerous ditches and streams, and it was mainly an infantry advance. The Germans were withdrawing very skilfully from one good position to another. They had left mines and booby-traps in all avenues of advance, which were also covered by observed artillery and mortar fire. Consequently progress was extremely slow, and it was not until the afternoon that A Company, which was leading the 6th Battalion, gained contact with the enemy. The Germans were in a rearguard position on high ground in front, and the leading platoon was pinned down by fire from tanks and infantry. The platoon commander and several others became casualties, but Corporal O'Flynn quickly took command and moved the sections under cover. He then wirelessed accurate information of the German position to Company Headquarters, thus enabling the artillery to put down concentrations and the tanks to come up and outflank it. This

[1] See map 'Pursuit to Lake Trasimene.'

caused the enemy to withdraw, and the battalion moved forward unopposed to the high ground and dug in for the night, the only other casualties being one man killed and one wounded when the C.O.'s carrier struck a mine. The Buffs on the right had also captured their objective—the village of Ripi.

The pursuit was resumed next morning, May 31, with B Company leading. Soon after the start another carrier was blown up by a mine and again two casualties were suffered. Shells and mortar bombs then began to slow down the pace, but the advance continued across open ground until five enemy tanks were met. These opened rapid fire, and the whole company went to ground. Thereupon Lance-Corporal Mitchell, who was a signaller at Company Headquarters, crawled forward to the Company Commander and, although exposed to the fire of the tanks, communicated the enemy's position by wireless to Battalion Headquarters. Once again the required artillery support was forthcoming, the enemy tanks withdrew, and the village of Torrice was occupied by B Company. That evening Frosinone was captured by a Canadian formation, which was fighting on the left of 36th Brigade. The battalion dug in astride a secondary road east of that town for the night.

After a day in reserve 36th Brigade was directed north on June 2 along the axis of the road to Guarcino. The Argylls took the lead, and the 6th Battalion moved behind them to an area south of Alatri. Having deployed in the hills on either side of the town the Argylls were then held up by machine-gun fire from a German rearguard position. In the afternoon the 6th Battalion was ordered forward to clear Alatri. The Germans did not wait for the assault, however. The rearguard slipped away to the west, and before nine that evening the battalion had passed through the town and had consolidated north of it. The following morning 6th Armoured Division went through. On June 4 the battalion moved back to an area east of Frosinone, where 78th Division was to enjoy a spell in reserve.

Meanwhile the Americans had been advancing more rapidly near the coast, and Rome was entered by them on June 4. For days the advantages of Rome over Naples as a leave-centre had been discussed, and there was much disappointment amongst the troops of XIII Corps when they were told that they were not to taste the pleasures of that city. The hard battles of the Liri Valley were over, but their duty led them still to the north in pursuit of the beaten enemy. A great victory had been won, but the time to relax was not yet.

CHAPTER 19

Italy: The Pursuit to Florence
June to August 1944
1st, 5th and 6th Battalions

1. The 1st and 6th Battalions Pursue to Lake Trasimene

THE conquest of the Germans in southern Italy and the capture of Rome was a major victory for the Allies, but it was over-shadowed by the successful landing of the Allied Armies in Normandy two days later. More than ever now the requirements of the Army in France took precedence over the needs of General Alexander in Italy, and the already-inadequate supply of reinforcements for the 8th Army was still further restricted. Furthermore, an invasion of the French Riviera was also about to occur, and an American Corps and the French Corps were soon to be withdrawn from the battle in order to prepare for that operation. Nevertheless, the policy of the Allies was to force the Germans to retain as many troops in Italy as possible. The pursuit to the north was therefore continued with relentless vigour.

In XIII Corps the pursuit began with 4th Division on the right and 6th Armoured Division on the left. 4th Division was directed on Tivoli and, to begin with, the 1st Battalion was in reserve with 12th Brigade. This battalion had been enjoying a spell of relaxation at Audini, whence parties of troops had gone to a rest camp at Bari for seven days' leave and day passes had been granted for others to go into Naples. Reinforcements had arrived, and Major Gwilliam had come from the 5th Battalion to be second-in-command in place of Major Shipley, who went to command a battalion of his own Regiment. For fourteen days this period of ease and sunshine had continued till, on June 4, the day that Rome fell, the battalion had embussed in troop-carrying vehicles (T.C.V.s) and had driven through Cassino to the 4th Division concentration area at Arce. On the 6th the battalion moved forward with 12th Brigade to a bivouac near Capanelle. 10th Brigade, which was leading the pursuit, was already north of Tivoli. Up to now there had been no enemy resistance, and only bad road surfaces, demolished bridges, and mines had delayed the advance.

12th Brigade then moved up on the right of 10th Brigade with the Black Watch leading. At the approaches to Palombara the Black Watch debussed to clear the town, but it was soon evident that the Germans had gone. About a mile beyond Palombara a demolished culvert blocked the road, and as the column reached it the enemy began to shell the area accurately. At the same time the Black Watch, who were deployed astride the road, met close-range machine-gun fire from an enemy rearguard position. The 1st Battalion, which had debussed at Palombara, now moved up on the left of the road and advanced through the orchards and hedges. As they went forward they were continually engaged at close range by enemy machine-guns, which were carefully concealed amongst the undulations, and Major Bosanquet was killed by a machine-gun bullet as he was bringing up B Company. There was much confused fighting, but the battalion pressed on to the west of Moricone and occupied Monte Libretti by nightfall. That night patrols found that the enemy rearguard had slipped away.

On June 10, two days after this brief engagement, 4th Division was drawn into Corps reserve, and the 1st Battalion moved westwards to the divisional concentration area on the west bank of the River Tiber, some fifteen miles north of Rome. The city itself, at that time, was out of bounds to the troops of the 8th Army.

*   *   *

78th Division had already joined in the pursuit. With it had come the 6th Battalion which, after Rome fell, had enjoyed only a short period of rest near Frosinone. On June 8 a warning order had been received to move next day to 78th Division's concentration area north of Rome but, owing to the debris of the retreating Germans which littered the roads, it was not until midnight on June 10 that the battalion had finally moved off in M.T., passed through Rome the next morning and gone into billets at Fabrica. There it remained, with the delights of Rome tantalisingly near, until June 17, when it moved forward in T.C.V.s to an area north of Ficulle.

11th Brigade was already in touch with an enemy rearguard at Citta della Pieve, and 36th Brigade was sent forward on June 18 to by-pass that town. While the Buffs engaged the enemy the 6th Battalion advanced with the Argylls and, after a sharp fight, both battalions were well north of Citta della Pieve by dark. Early next morning the 6th Battalion took the lead and quickly encountered another rearguard astride the road. Here again there was a brisk

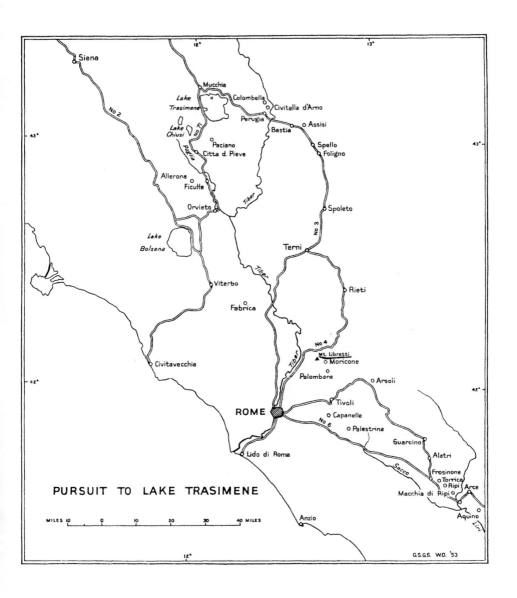

Siena

No 2

Mucchia

Lake Trasimene

Colombella

Civitella d'Arno

Perugia

Bastia

Assisi

No 71

Lake Chiusi

Paciano

Spello

Foligno

Citta d. Pieve

Paglia

Allerona

Ficulle

Orvieto

Tiber

Spoleto

No 3

Lake Bolsena

Terni

Viterbo

Tiber

Rieti

Fabrica

No 4

Civitavecchia

Mt. Libretti

Moricone

Palombara

Arsoli

ROME

Tivoli

Capanelle

No 6

Palestrina

Guarcino

Alatri

Lido di Roma

Sacco

Frosinone

Torrice

Ripi

Arce

Macchia di Ripi

Anzio

Aquino

Liri

PURSUIT TO LAKE TRASIMENE

MILES 10   0   10   20   30   40 MILES

G.S.G.S. W.O. '53

12°

13°

43°

43°

42°

42°

12°

engagement. Casualties were caused by enemy snipers and shells, but the battalion pressed on through the village of Palazzolo (see map 'The Battle of Lake Trasimene') to the Moiano stream. The advance was then halted by shell fire. It was apparent that the enemy were holding a strong position on the high ground north of the stream, and a brigade attack was prepared.

After a preliminary barrage the attack went in at 7.30 that evening through rain and mist, with the 6th Battalion on the right and the Buffs on the left. Although tanks could not come forward in the darkness, the leading troops were on their objectives by ten. The battalion consolidated at Point 356. At dawn, patrols from the battalion went forward and found the vicinity clear of enemy. But when the advance was continued that afternoon the leading companies were delayed by snipers, and they could get no further than Point 336, which overlooked Lake Chiusi. As night fell the Argylls went through and attacked Vaiano. The town was held by a strong German battalion, and the attack failed.

All next morning, June 21, patrols of B Company probed forward to reconnoitre the enemy's positions. One of these patrols found some Germans in a farm and killed three and wounded one for the loss of two casualties. This quickly brought retaliation, for the forward platoons of the company were shelled and suffered fourteen casualties. At noon the Buffs passed through the village of Strada and put in a fresh attack on Vaiano. This too was unsuccessful. It was now clear that opposition stronger than the usual rearguard had been encountered and that reinforcements would be required to overcome it. That night a unit of 28th Brigade of 4th Division moved up to Point 336 to relieve the battalion, which was withdrawn with 36th Brigade to a reserve area at Paciano.

2. *The 5th Battalion at Colombella*

Since the fall of Rome, 8th Indian Division, now part of X Corps, had been pursuing the enemy to the east of Lake Trasimene. Their route had been through Arsoli and Terni, and the historic town of Assisi had been captured on June 17. Next day 17th Indian Brigade drove an enemy rearguard from positions on an escarpment east of Perugia, but—as to the west of the lake—enemy resistance was stiffening, and it was not long before 21st Indian Brigade was brought forward to lend a hand.

During this period of continual pursuit the 5th Battalion had been following up in reserve with 21st Indian Brigade. Days had been occupied by false starts and sudden moves, triumphant drives through cheering crowds in villages, and the capture of numerous straggling prisoners. Sometimes the roads would be congested with traffic, and demolitions would cause delays. At other times the way would be clear for a speedy advance. Most of the nights were spent near villages with pleasant names, Cantelupo and Piano Lotrafe being perhaps the most delightful, and in the warm weather the tired troops slept quite comfortably. At Terni a platoon of A Company acted as Town Guard for a few days. On the 20th the troops were allowed to visit Assisi to see the birthplace of Saint Francis, and that evening the battalion supplied the Town Picquet for Bastia. Finally, on the night of the 24th, the battalion took over positions at Civitella D'Arno, where the Gurkhas of 17th Brigade had been in touch with the enemy and had been subjected to considerable shelling and mortaring.

The Germans were believed to be holding positions at Colombella, which was a large house with several farm buildings girdled by clumps of trees. A patrol sent out after dark on June 26 clashed with an enemy patrol, and it was decided to seize and occupy Colombella that night. At 2.40 a.m. C Company (Captain Harper) went forward after artillery concentrations had been fired on the buildings. There was no resistance from the enemy. The company entered the fringe of trees and began to put the buildings in a state of defence. Before this could be completed the Germans counter-attacked from all sides. The three platoons of C Company were soon hotly engaged. The trees interfered with their field of fire, and Serjeant Healing went out in front of his platoon in full view of the enemy and calmly directed the fire of his sections. At another threatened point Lance-Corporal Haigh, who had been wounded in his right arm, also went forward and, holding his Tommy-gun in one hand, accounted for several of the enemy. Serjeant Marsh, whose platoon was under fire from positions which overlooked it, moved it section by section to better cover. These efforts were unavailing. The Germans still pressed in.

As C Company was now in danger of being cut off, Colonel Whitty ordered them to withdraw under cover of artillery and machine-gun fire to a triangle of roads south of Colombella, where A Company had established a firm base. The withdrawal was conducted with great skill by Captain Harper, and Lieutenant White, who was last away from Colombella, stood up and defied the enemy while he thinned out his platoon. At one point some high corn prevented aimed fire, and Private Cockle, armed with his own and another Tommy-gun which he had taken from a wounded man, went forward to a suitable position and kept the enemy at bay until his platoon had withdrawn.

Eventually the firm base was reached successfully, although the Germans were now mortaring the triangle of roads. Casualties in C Company had been six killed and some forty wounded, and A Company had lost twelve casualties from mortar fire. The Germans made no attempt to follow up. During the morning, while our artillery and mortars 'stonked' the enemy positions, light tanks took up rations and ammunition to the triangle of roads. The situation remained unaltered until the evening, when C Company was withdrawn into reserve.

Next day representatives of the 1st King's Own (10th Indian Division) reconnoitred the area, and on the night of June 29 that battalion took over the positions south of Colombella. Before dawn the 5th Battalion was on its way twenty miles south to Foligno, whither 8th Indian Division, having completed nine months of continuous campaigning, was being withdrawn for a period of rest.

3. *The 1st and 6th Battalions at Lake Trasimene*

Meanwhile, on the west of Lake Trasimene the Germans had found a good defensive position between Lake Trasimene and Lake Chiusi. Moreover, a break in the fine weather had given them an opportunity to organise their resistance in depth and to bring up a heavy weight of artillery. To assail this position 4th Division had come forward from reserve to reinforce 78th Division; 28th Brigade having taken over the sector between the village of Strada and Lake Chiusi from 36th Brigade in order to narrow the front of 78th Division, and 12th Brigade having moved up from the concentration area at Viterbo to a reserve area at Citta della Pieve. When the Battle of Lake Trasimene opened, therefore, the 6th Battalion was in reserve with 36th Brigade at Paciano and the 1st Battalion was in reserve at Citta della Pieve.

The battle began at dawn on June 24 with an attempt by 78th Division to punch a hole in the German defences near the shores of Lake Trasimene. After slow and hard fighting the village of Pescia was captured and the enemy were cleared from the south bank of the River Pescia by the 11th and Irish Brigades. The actual crossing of the river was to be made by 36th Brigade, which moved forward from Paciano through Pucciarelli that evening. The River Pescia was normally little more than a stream, but the recent heavy rain had made it an effective anti-tank obstacle. Two companies of the Buffs crossed the river and formed a small bridgehead, while the remainder of the brigade waited on the south bank for a Bailey bridge to be erected.

By the time that the 6th Battalion had moved up to the river a considerable area on the south bank, as well as the site of the Bailey bridge, was under accurate and effective enemy artillery fire. One of the forward platoons of C Company suffered severe casualties, and Serjeant England volunteered to cross the shell-swept ground to his Company Headquarters to report the incident. When he arrived he found that all the personnel at Company Headquarters had become casualties. He immediately assumed command, manned the wireless set and passed the information to Battalion Headquarters. On hearing the news Corporal Dickenson, who was in charge of the company stretcher-bearers but had been wounded in the foot by a shell earlier in the evening, left the Aid Post to tend the wounded and assist Serjeant England to organise their evacuation. The prompt and brave actions of these two N.C.O.s undoubtedly saved several lives.

In spite of the shelling and the heavy rain, which was now falling, the Bailey bridge was completed. At 7 a.m. on June 25 the 6th Battalion crossed the river and passed through the Buffs. The Argylls followed an hour later and came up to the 6th Battalion's left. The actual crossing was made extremely hazardous by enemy shelling, which was now apparently being directed from O.P.s on tall buildings in Castiglione del Lago, and any movement north of the river was also immediately punished by a salvo of shells. In this way one of the forward platoons of B Company suffered a number of casualties. With great courage Private Cull set out alone to tend them and, having dressed their wounds, he remained with them until they could be moved out of the shelled area. Casualties were also suffered at Battalion Headquarters.

The battalion now pressed forward along the shores of Lake Trasimene with the road from Castiglione del Lago to Casamaggiore as the objective. Tanks could not join in the attack because the ground near the lake was marshy and further west there were numerous deep ditches. From the start the leading companies suffered heavily from mortar and machine-gun fire; amongst those killed being Serjeant Manning, who was hit while gallantly bringing forward a section of anti-tank guns into an exposed position. The heavy shelling continued also, and by the afternoon the whole battalion had been pinned down some 300 yards short of its objective. It was subsequently found that some of the leading troops were no more than 25 yards from two German self-propelled guns. Further efforts were made to get forward next morning, but there was still strong opposition. In

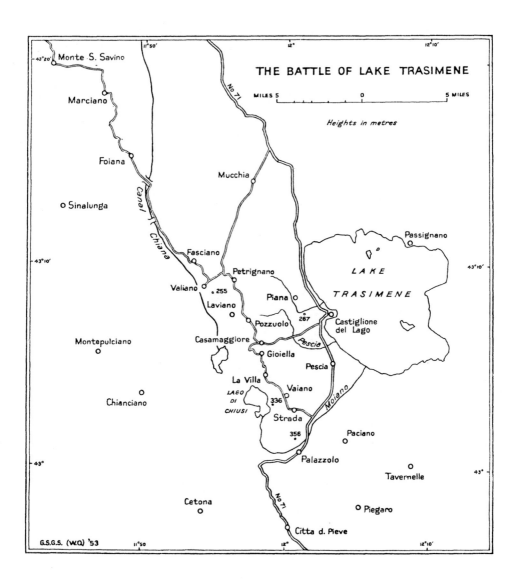

THE BATTLE OF LAKE TRASIMENE

MILES 5   0   5 MILES

Heights in metres

Monte S. Savino

Marciano

Foiana

O Sinalunga

Mucchia

Fasciano

Valiano

Petrignano

255

Laviano

Piana

Pozzuolo

267

Castiglione
del Lago

Casamaggiore

Gioiella

Pescia

Montepulciano

La Villa

Vaiano

Chianciano

LAGO
DI
CHIUSI

336

Strada

356

Paciano

Palazzolo

Tavernelle

Cetona

Piegaro

Citta d. Pieve

LAKE

TRASIMENE

Passignano

Pescia

Canal

Chiana

No 71

No 71

Noiano

G.S.G.S. (W.O.) '53

43°20'

43°10'

43°10'

43°

43°

11°50'

12°

12°10'

11°50'

12°

12°10'

the close country the leading companies could not locate the enemy machine guns, and Serjeant Sisley, who was in charge of a section of mortars, went to the top storey of a house to use it as an O.P. The windows were covered by snipers, and the house was hit more than once by shells, but he remained at his O.P., although twice wounded, and scored several hits. At 9.30 a.m. Brigadier James drove up in an armoured car to find out the situation. He went too far forward and was killed by a shell from one of the German self-propelled guns.

No further progress could be made that day. In the evening 56th Reconnaissance Regiment came up between the lake and Highway 71 to relieve the right-hand company. This gave the battalion an opportunity to reorganise and to prepare to repel counter-attacks against the salient which they had made in the enemy's position. But the German resistance had been loosened by X Corps, which was making an encircling movement on the east of Lake Trasimene, and by 4th Division, which was coming up on the left. Indeed, when the attack was renewed at 8.30 next morning, June 27, there was little opposition other than shelling, and by midday the road from Castiglione del Lago to Casamaggiore had been reached and contact had been made with the Argylls on the left. Both battalions then consolidated.

The first signs that the Germans were withdrawing were found by 56th Reconnaissance Regiment on June 28. That night patrols sent out by the 6th Battalion to woods in front encountered no enemy. At first light on the 29th, Serjeant Villette took a patrol of three men to confirm this information; an enemy patrol was met, two Germans were shot and Serjeant Villette closed with the remainder and returned with two prisoners. These confirmed the fact that a general withdrawal was taking place. Shortly afterwards A Company patrolled to Point 267 and found this feature clear, and at 10 a.m. 56th Reconnaissance Regiment entered Castiglione del Lago and found it free of enemy also. At dusk the battalion moved into the town and spent the night in comfortable billets. For them the battle was over. Mention must be made of the good work done by Serjeant Lambourne, the Signal Serjeant, during this battle. During the heavy shelling, line communication was frequently broken, and on one day he spent nine hours under shell fire repairing the cable. Late in the day he was wounded in the face, but he completed his task before reporting to the Aid Post.

The 6th Battalion was to advance but little further, for on July 3 they were withdrawn out of the battle to Paciano, where 78th Division was concentrating. It was from there that Colonel Fyffe departed to command a battalion of his own Regiment, and Major

Defrates, who had returned from a Senior Officers' Course in England six weeks previously, took over from him. Major Roper became second-in-command. 78th Division was now leaving Italy for a long period of rest in Egypt. After an interesting journey, mostly by rail, through Cassino and Benevento, the battalion embarked at Taranto on July 17 in the Polish liner *Batory*. There was no bombing during the voyage, even from Crete, and the ship arrived at Alexandria on July 22.

*   *   *

While 78th Division had been forcing back the enemy near Lake Trasimene, 10th and 28th Brigades of 4th Division had simultaneously been advancing along the shore of Lake Chiusi to the Casamaggiore Ridge. Here they had met stiff opposition, and 12th Brigade had been brought into the battle to carry out an enflanking move on 4th Division's left flank. At the head of 12th Brigade was the 1st Battalion, who moved from Citta della Pieve to an area south of La Villa on June 28. At dawn next morning the battalion, with tanks in support, passed through Goiella and struck off north-westwards across country to Laviano. The Germans had retired during the night to conform with their withdrawal on the shores of Lake Trasimene, and by dusk the only opposition had been from harassing machine-gun and artillery fire. At nightfall the battalion consolidated some two miles north of Laviano and gained touch with 10th Brigade at Pozzuolo.

Patrols sent out during the night made contact with the enemy and found that the Germans were holding a delaying position from Petrignano to Valiano. 10th Brigade began an attack on Petrignano at 10 a.m. and, with the Royal Fusiliers on its right, the 1st Battalion again moved across country to the north-west to outflank the German positions. When they approached Valiano the leading company came under fire from enemy mortars and machine guns grouped in that village and at Point 255. The resistance was determined, and a battalion attack was prepared. There was to be no major action here, however. As night fell the fire slackened and finally ceased, and during the night lorries could be heard moving away to the north. In the early hours of July 1, when the battalion moved forward, there was no opposition, and Valiano was entered by six. The local inhabitants gave the troops a rousing welcome as they marched through the village to clear the high ground to the north. But the enemy had got well away.

4. *The 1st Battalion at San Pancrazio*

After the Battle of Lake Trasimene the pursuit was continued by 4th Division. The enemy had withdrawn in sudden haste and the 1st Battalion, leading the pursuit, advanced from Valiano to Fasciano and sped on to the crossings over the Chiana Canal. Both bridges had been demolished but, leaving the supporting tanks to search for a place to cross, the infantry hurried on and occupied Foiano. Shelling and mortar fire then delayed the advance for a time, but on July 3 the battalion made a left flanking movement towards Marciano. Progress was slow through cornfields which concealed snipers, and it was some hours before that village was reached. On rounding a bend in the road the leading carrier, commanded by Serjeant Turner, saw three Germans. Two were killed and the other fled. At dusk the battalion consolidated for the night short of Monte San Savino. The morning of July 4 found them in reserve and resting.

This continuous pursuit had not been without its difficulties. At every defile and road junction small rearguards of snipers, machine guns and self-propelled guns had been met. Every bridge had been demolished and every obstacle had been sown with mines. This meant that most of the advance had to be carried out on foot without the support of the tanks of 14th Canadian Armoured Regiment. The Germans usually held their fire until the last moment, so that positions which appeared to have been evacuated were often held in strength. Having once been deceived, Colonel Braithwaite planned the advance as if each feature ahead were strongly held and, having attacked it and occupied it, used it as a firm base from which to resume the pursuit. This method undoubtedly saved many casualties. But after a few days of continual advance under a hot sun, consolidating at night and standing-to at dawn, the troops became very weary and a short rest was desirable.

4th Division now encountered a strong German defensive position in the steep hills to the south-west of Arezzo, and 12th Brigade was directed to that portion of it to the left of Civitella. After a day of rest the 1st Battalion again took the lead and moved towards the village of San Pancrazio in the early hours of July 5. Progress through steep and rough country was difficult. Shelling and mortar fire were met also, but in the evening the battalion was ordered to press on, to capture San Pancrazio that night and to consolidate on a hill called Poggio al'Olmo (Point 539) immediately west of it. The men were weary after the day's advance, yet after confused fighting in the darkness and the thickly wooded country the village and the hill were both occupied. At dawn tanks came up to assist in the consolidation.

Unhappily, as the light brightened, the Germans put down prolonged concentrations of artillery and mortar fire on to Poggio al'Olmo. Casualties were numerous and a counter-attack appeared to be imminent. At this critical moment Colonel Braithwaite moved up the hill amongst the forward companies. Though exposed to the shell-fire, he personally organised the work of the stretcher-bearers and did not leave the position until the wounded had all been evacuated and the shelling had ceased. His personal example put new heart into the troops.

The rapid advance of 4th Division had at last been checked, and there was a period of almost static warfare while XIII Corps re-grouped for an attack. During the first few days the 1st Battalion, in its salient at San Pancrazio, sent out many patrols to gain information about the positions held by the Germans, improved its own defences, and laid on defensive fire tasks in readiness to repel counter-attacks. There were frequent bouts of enemy shelling. One of them took several N.C.O.s of the Support Company unawares in the yard of a small house. Serjeant Foster was killed outright, and Serjeants Turner and Dunn were both severely wounded. The first counter-attack occurred in the early hours of July 9, when enemy infantry approached in two waves. They were effectively engaged by small arms fire as well as by artillery and mortars firing on fixed lines. By 3 a.m. all was quiet again. Another strong raid came in at dawn on the 10th. After a heavy mortar concentration the Germans were seen approaching through wooded country on the left. This time they were met by fire from all the infantry weapons, and the machine guns of the tanks also lent a hand. The attack was beaten off with few casualties.

A few days later the town of Arezzo was captured by 6th Armoured Division. This success turned the enemy's flank and forced him to resume his retreat. 4th Division quickly took up the pursuit again with 10th and 28th Brigades in the van, while 12th Brigade went into reserve. On July 16 the 1st Battalion vacated its positions at San Pancrazio and moved back to Monte San Savino for ten days' rest. Since entering the Battle of Lake Trasimene on June 29 its losses had been: Officers—one killed[1] and seven wounded; other ranks—thirty-eight killed and approximately one hundred and forty wounded and missing.

5. *The 5th Battalion Moves up to the River Arno*

While the 1st Battalion was resting at Monte San Savino the French

[1] Lieutenant A. Mitchell (R. Warwick).

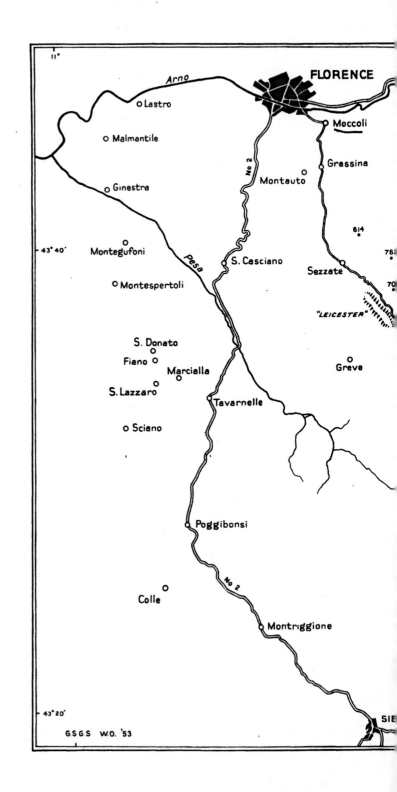

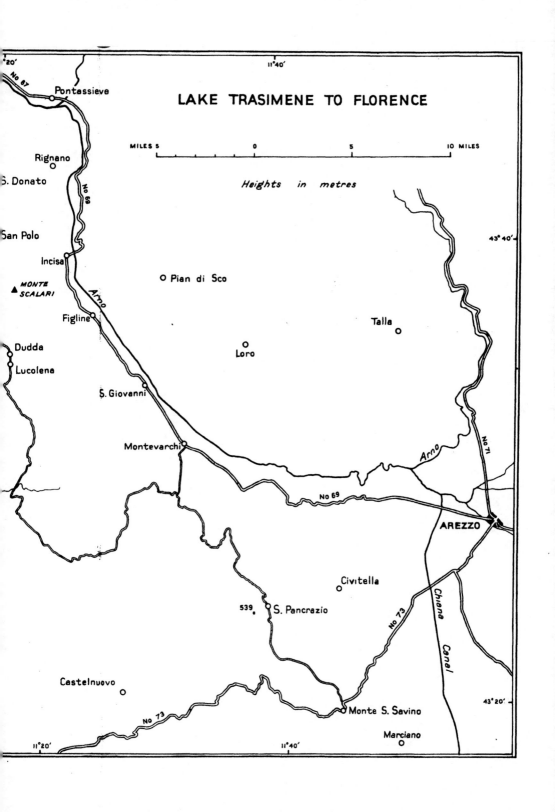

LAKE TRASIMENE TO FLORENCE

MILES 5   0   5   10 MILES

Heights in metres

Expeditionary Force was transferred from Italy for the invasion of
the South of France, and 8th Indian Division came in on the left of
the advance on Florence in its stead. With the Indians came the 5th
Battalion, which had spent one week at Foligno, during which twenty-
four hours' leave had been granted to Rome and evening passes to
Assisi, and two weeks near Spoleto, where clubs were handy for an
evening's recreation. Then on July 18 the battalion had moved westwards in T.C.V.s through Siena on Highway Two to 8th Indian
Division's concentration area at Monteriggione. Two days later the
battalion drove through Poggibonsi, and the relief of a French unit
was completed that night in the vicinity of Sciano. This was on the
right flank of 8th Indian Division's sector. The enemy were close in
front.

The advance of 21st Indian Brigade began on the evening of July
23, when the 5th Battalion moved across country with mule transport
and occupied San Lazzaro before dawn. Only a few rounds of harassing artillery fire opposed the advance. The pursuit was continued the
following night, again without opposition, and a strong-point was
established at San Donato. On the 25th, while the battalion stood
firm, the remainder of 21st Brigade sped on to Montespertoli. Still no
enemy was encountered. On July 27 the battalion once more went to
the front. A mobile column was formed with B and D Companies,
tanks, anti-tank guns and mortars, under the command of Major
Stocker, and this force advanced on foot across country until, in the
late afternoon, the River Pesa was reached opposite the village of
Ginestra. So far there had again been no opposition. But at dawn
next morning the Germans mortared B Company's area and killed
Lieutenant Farrell and two other ranks and wounded fifteen others.
And when an attempt was made to cross the river such strong resistance was met that the remainder of the battalion moved up and
prepared to force a crossing. Colonel Whitty then received orders to
go no further until the remainder of the brigade arrived.

By August 1 the brigade was ready to launch an attack across the
River Pesa. The battalion was ordered to establish a bridgehead, and
that night two companies crossed the river unopposed. Patrols probing forward in daylight found no enemy. After dark that night the
remainder of the battalion crossed. The enemy seemed to have withdrawn; but as the leading troops entered Malmantile, shelling and
mortaring caused several casualties, and while the Castle was being
occupied, German rocket projectiles blew in a portion of the walls and
wounded fifteen men. Florence was now in sight. Italian Partisans
from Lastra came in to Malmantile with a report that the Germans
were in full retreat across the River Arno. But the battalion was not

to follow. 17th Indian Brigade passed through on August 5 on its way to Florence, and on the 6th the battalion was withdrawn with 21st Brigade to Greve.

6. *The 1st Battalion at Monte Scalari*

By the time that 12th Brigade was recalled into the pursuit the remainder of 4th Division had advanced through Montevarchi and San Giovanni and had reached the Chianti Hills, a stretch of mountainous country about twelve miles south of Florence. The 1st Battalion was ordered forward from Monte San Savino on July 24, and on the 26th they were shelled as they were dismounting from their lorries in the village of Lucolena. This is barely fifteen miles east of San Donato, where the 5th Battalion was on that day holding a strong-point. But instead of bounding forward as the 5th was able to do, the 1st Battalion was forced to fight.

Leaving the lorries at Lucolena, the 1st Battalion passed through the Black Watch and advanced on foot through the tiny village of Dudda, with a miniature fort nicknamed 'Leicester' as its objective. Demolitions and snipers made progress very slow, but tanks of 142nd Regiment R.A.C. gave covering fire as the troops climbed the terraces of the hill and occupied the fort. During the day Colonel Braithwaite was taken ill; Major Gwilliam assumed command. The next stage was the capture of Point 706, known as 'Conn.' Delayed only by mines, the leading troops were carried forward by tanks on July 27 and reached Point 706. From there they were directed on Point 770 with Monte Scalari (Point 778) as the ultimate objective. Almost immediately the leading companies were met by fierce mortar and machine-gun fire from all the hills in the area. Progress up the steep slope of Point 770 was very difficult, but with the support of the mortars and machine-guns of the battalion the forward platoons got within four hundred yards of the summit, mainly owing to the gallantry of Serjeant Webb of B Company, who led his platoon across a stretch of open ground with great dash. After dark the feature was captured. Casualties had been thirty-two killed, including Major Preston,[1] Lieutenants Wilson[2] and Boughton and C.S.M. Rogers, and seventy-nine wounded.

The fighting strength of the battalion had now been reduced to approximately two hundred, so the Brigade Commander decided to leave it on Point 770 while the Black Watch captured Monte Scalari.

[1] Detached from the Oxfordshire and Buckinghamshire Light Infantry.
[2] Detached from the Union Defence Force of South Africa.

Consequently July 29 found the companies with two troops of tanks consolidating on Point 770. During the next three days the Germans made many attempts to dislodge them by intensive artillery and mortar fire, but they held on with the tenacity and fortitude which are typical of the men of the Regiment, until, after heavy fighting, the Black Watch had captured Monte Scalari. At last light on July 31 a strong fighting patrol from the 1st Battalion went forward to Point 762 and found it to be clear of enemy. Next day the other hills in the vicinity were also found to be unoccupied. The Germans had again withdrawn, and 12th Brigade concentrated at Sezzate to prepare for a renewal of the pursuit.

After a night and a day of rest the battalion moved north in T.C.V.s on the evening of August 3 to Montauto, where it debussed and marched a short distance to the Grassina area. There was no enemy in the vicinity. The following afternoon the battalion again moved forward on foot and reached Moccoli. This village is on high ground overlooking the River Arno and the historic city of Florence beyond. The troops were anxious to enter the city, but the immediate task of the battalion was to ensure that there was no enemy south of the river. Patrols searched the locality, and from information received from them and from Italian Partisans it was firmly established that the south bank was clear. Across the river the streets of Florence were deserted. It had been declared an 'open' city, which meant that only small arms could be fired into it, and nothing but occasional bursts of fire, caused by clashes between patrols of Germans and Partisans, was heard from the centre of the city. No attempt was made by either side to cross the river. The battalion therefore remained in its positions, unworried except by occasional bouts of enemy shelling.

On August 11 the battalion handed over to the 1st Buffs of 1st Division. Before dawn on the 12th it had begun the long road journey back to the rest area near Foligno, so recently visited by the 5th Battalion.[1] Led by Colonel Braithwaite, now recovered from his illness, a search was made for billets in Spello. By the 15th the whole battalion was comfortably settled. Leave was started, four days at a time, either to Rome or to the shores of Lake Trasimene, and the 8th Army clubs at Assisi were frequently visited. Some of the working hours were devoted to the absorption of a large number of reinforcements, amongst whom were a number of officers and men who had previously been wounded in action with the battalion, and the re-organisation of the rifle companies. So the rest period slipped quietly away.

[1] See map "Pursuit to Lake Trasimene."

By August 12 the main German forces had withdrawn from Florence, and patrols of 17th Indian Brigade had forded the River Arno and penetrated to the centre of the city. The Florentines were in dire need. Large areas of the city had been without food, water and light for five days, and many of the people were threatened with famine and disease. To add to their troubles booby-traps had been left everywhere. Germans would suddenly appear from unexpected hideouts and clash with Italian Partisans, who were scouring the streets for them. Mêlées between pro-Fascist and anti-Mussolini gangs were frequent also. 21st Indian Brigade was therefore ordered into the city with instructions to assist the civilian police to restore law and order.

The 5th Battalion moved with 21st Indian Brigade from Greve in T.C.V.s. By the afternoon of August 12 the companies were on the south bank of the Arno at the entrances to the four bridges leading from Highway Two—Ponte Vecchio, Ponte Alle Grazie, Ponte Alle Carraia and Ponte San Trinita. These bridges had all been blown except the Ponte Vecchio, and both ends of that bridge were blocked by debris from demolished buildings. Later that afternoon one platoon of A Company crossed the river on a weir, over which the water was flowing shallow and slow, and took up a position at the northern end of the Ponte San Trinita. Next morning C and D Companies crossed the river in single file on the weir and a breakwater. The trucks and carriers crossed later in the same way. By seven both companies had reached the centre of Florence, with C in the Cathedral Square and D in the vicinity of the Railway Station. During the day the remainder of the battalion crossed the river and moved to the centre of the city, Battalion Headquarters being set up in the Savoy Hotel. The magnificent cathedral was found to be undamaged.

After a quiet night the carriers and anti-tank guns were dispersed to points of vantage, and the companies began a house to house search to clear away booby-traps and other signs of the German occupation. The sound of shots exchanged by Germans and Partisans was often heard, but the battalion area remained comparatively quiet until the evening of August 15, when a German tank suddenly appeared and engaged one of the battalion's anti-tank guns. The gun crew replied with several well-placed shots, and the tank made off at speed. At the same time the headquarters of A.M.G.O.T., which were in a street nearby, were attacked, one of the Partisan guards being hit. But the marauders quickly withdrew when C Company arrived on the scene. Early next morning a dozen German infantry accompanied by an armoured car entered the area looking for trouble. This group was engaged and dispersed by a platoon of A Company. Casualties occurred on both sides.

Such incidents as these had now become rare in the city. Law and order had been restored. On the evening of August 16 the battalion moved to a bivouac in the outskirts of Florence, where the next two days were devoted to rest and cleaning up. On the 19th they marched out of the city to San Polo, eight miles south-east of Florence, and remained there in reserve until September 2.

CHAPTER 20

Italy: The Gothic Line
September 1944 to February 1945
1st, 5th and 6th Battalions

1. *The 5th Battalion at Monte Romano*

AFTER the capture of Florence a new phase of the campaign began. The retreat of the Germans had at last brought them to their prepared defensive positions across the northern neck of Italy. These positions, which were called the Gothic Line, extended from Rimini on the Adriatic coast to the Gulf of Genoa. Designed to deny the Allies entrance into the valley of the River Po, they were formidable and well-constructed, and the Allied forces were regrouped to attack them. The bulk of the 8th Army was once more concentrated near the Adriatic coast for a drive north-westwards on Faenza. The 5th Army was directed northwards against the mountain barrier south of Bologna. XIII Corps, which was on the right of the 5th Army, was to attack north-eastwards from Florence and converge on 8th Army's thrust for Faenza.

8th Indian Division, which remained in XIII Corps, was accordingly concentrated about Pontassieve, east of Florence, and it was to this area that the 5th Battalion moved in T.C.V.s from San Polo on the evening of September 2. As the advance was to take the division into the heart of the Apennine mountains, a change over to mule transport was then made. On September 11 the battalion entered the battle area with 21st Indian Brigade and took over a sector at San Martino. 17th and 19th Indian Brigades had already moved up to the River Sieve, and 21st Brigade had been brought forward on the right to lead an attack which was about to be launched on Monte Femmine Morte, Monte Vitigliano and Monte Veruca. The countryside was mountainous and wild. The steep slopes of the hills seemed to be unscarred by man. Yet the summits were studded with carefully-concealed enemy trenches and strong-points; concrete machine-gun posts were roofed over and camouflaged; and all approaches were wired and sown with mines. The spurs of the hills

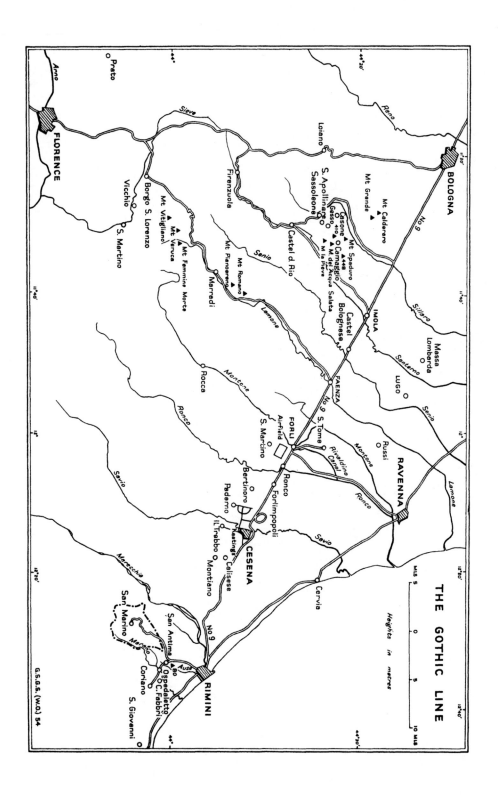

THE GOTHIC LINE

were bare and rocky. The crests had no means of communication except narrow, winding footpaths.

The attack by 21st Brigade began at dusk on September 12 with the 5th Battalion in reserve. The resistance was not so strong as had been expected. Monte Vitigliano was captured by the Punjabis early next morning, and by the evening the Mahrattas were on Monte Veruca. The 5th Battalion then prepared to move forward for an attack on the right flank. At the critical moment, however, the enemy resistance suddenly collapsed, and Colonel Whitty was ordered to consolidate on Monte Vitigliano instead and to send out patrols from there to keep in touch with the enemy's movements. No Germans could be found in the vicinity, but on the 20th a patrol found some enemy in positions near the Marradi- Borgo San Lorenzo road. Even these were evacuated after the Gunners had brought down concentrations on them. The ease with which this strong and well-fortified position had been pierced surprised everyone. The Germans appeared to be very thin on the ground, but the decisive factor was probably the Allied Air Forces, which bombed and blasted the enemy positions all day and even most of the night.

With no enemy confronting them, 17th and 19th Indian Brigades now took on the task of flank-guard to XIII Corps along the axis of the Borgo San Lorenzo-Marradi road, while 21st Brigade remained in reserve at Monte Vitigliano. By October 6 the first steep bastions of the Apennines had been reached, and it was here that the Germans began to resist further progress strongly. 21st Brigade was therefore again required to lend a hand. On the 7th, the 5th Battalion passed through Marradi and took over a sector just north-west of it, where the Germans were content to remain on the defensive. But the company areas were occasionally shelled, and during a bout of mortaring on the 9th Lieutenant Oxford was killed. Four days later the battalion was relieved and became responsible for the defence of Marradi; while the Punjabis and the Mahrattas attacked and captured Monte Pianoereno, a hill 2,300 feet high which dominated the main road. Beyond Monte Pianoereno was Monte Romano. This was the next objective; but in front of it the Germans continued to hold a ridge on which were groups of farm buildings at Valle Nuova and Valle Sopra. The capture of this ridge and then of Monte Romano was assigned to the 5th Battalion.

At 3 a.m. on October 20, B and C Companies went forward, with the ridge from Point 711 to Valle Nuova as their objective. The first part of the advance was down a bare hillside, and at the bottom of it the leading troops encountered the German defensive fire. Once through this, B Company (Major Stocker) reached an intervening ridge, which was found to be unoccupied, and dug in under heavy fire. C Company (Captain Balleine) then moved off to the left flank, only to be quickly pinned down by mortar and machine-gun fire. Both companies made several attempts to get forward, but when dawn broke Colonel Whitty ordered them to withdraw under an artillery smoke screen. There had been fourteen casualties, including Lieutenant A. D. Morgan[1] who was killed. This failure was a severe blow to the battalion.

Another attack on Valle Nuova and Valle Sopra was prepared for that evening, while a smaller force was to capture Point 711 before dawn. After an artillery programme, D Company (Major Grimsey), reinforced by two platoons from other companies, moved forward as soon as darkness had fallen. They immediately ran into heavy machine-gun fire and mortar and artillery defensive fire, which dispersed the leading platoons in the darkness and put the wireless sets out of action. Private Fry, a platoon orderly, gallantly carried a number of messages to the scattered sections in order to collect the company, and Major Grimsey, rallying the equivalent of two platoons, dashed for the group of houses at Valle Nuova. The impetus of this bold charge was such that with only 40 men he reached the buildings. On the right flank Serjeant Moore arrived with only one man of his platoon behind him, yet he dashed on, firing his Tommy-gun, reached the pit of a Spandau and pulled the gun out by the barrel. This so surprised the crew that all seven of them surrendered. Private Carson, who had led his section on to the objective after his section commander had been killed, went forward alone with a Bren gun and captured six prisoners in a building. Altogether thirty prisoners were captured, nearly all of whom were officers and N.C.O.s. The remainder of the enemy fled. Having organised the evacuation of the wounded and consolidated the defence of the buildings at Valle Nuova, Major Grimsey then collected the equivalent of a platoon, led them round to the rear and occupied Valle Sopra. This was his final objective; but he now learned that the attack on Point 711 had failed, which meant that his position would be untenable in daylight. He therefore led another attack on Point 711 with his own weary troops, overcame the enemy on it and organised the consolidation of the whole ridge. By his courage and skill Major Grimsey undoubtedly turned what was nearly a second failure into a complete success.

The capture of Monte Romano itself, a steep hill which towered above the Valle Nuova ridge, had now to be achieved. This task was given to one company of Punjabis, which had been placed under

[1] Detached from the Devonshire Regiment.

Colonel Whitty's command. A smoke screen was laid over the hill by the artillery, and under cover of it the Indians began the ascent. But the fire of the enemy's machine-guns was too skilfully placed, and they were held up well short of the crest. At nightfall the Punjabis were relieved by A Company with the intention of renewing the attack. As luck would have it, however, the night was dark and misty, rain fell, and the bad visibility limited movement to patrolling. In the early morning a reconnaissance patrol climbed the steep slope to the top and found it to be clear. The enemy had slipped away in the night. One platoon of A Company then occupied the hill, and the position on Monte Romano was later consolidated. Next day patrols found that the enemy had withdrawn from all the hills in the vicinity.

The battle was at last successfully over and arrangements were made for the battalion's relief. During the morning of October 23, Colonel Whitty went back on foot with Lieutenant Robson, the Mortar Platoon Commander, and his orderly to meet some of the Mahratta officers. As they were taking a short cut through a field one of the three trod on an 'S' mine. Colonel Whitty was killed instantly; the other two were seriously wounded and died later. They were buried in the village cemetery at Vicchio,[1] north of Florence, with full military honours, and Lieutenant-General S. C. Kirkman, the Corps Commander, and other senior officers attended the funeral. The death of Colonel Whitty was a great shock to the battalion. He had commanded it since 1942 and had led it through all its battles in Italy. His vigorous personality, his cheerfulness, and his determination in face of difficulties were greatly missed. As it happened he would not have remained with the battalion even if he had not been killed, for soon after he had left his headquarters for the last time a message came through to say that he had been appointed to command a brigade. Major Malcolmson stepped up to command; Major R. d'A. Mullins was later attached from The Queen's Regiment to be second-in-command.

The battalion was now much below strength. No fresh reinforcements had arrived in Italy for six months, and those few which had joined the battalion had been of poor quality and practically untrained in the handling of infantry weapons. Moreover, many of the key personnel of the battalion had been fighting too long without an adequate rest. In short, the battalion was in need of a long spell out of the battle in order to receive and train reinforcements, train more N.C.O.s, and recuperate generally. This it was at last able to do. After ten days in reserve at Vicchio the battalion was withdrawn

[1] These three now lie in the British Military Cemetery on the Florence–Pontassieve road. Lieut. Robson was detached from The Royal Berkshire Regiment.

from 21st Indian Brigade and moved back to San Donato, six miles south-east of Florence, where it came under command of the Florence Garrison.

2. *The 1st Battalion at Ospedaletto and the River Ausa*

When Florence had fallen, 4th Division was transferred to the Adriatic coast to join 8th Army's thrust north-westwards on Faenza. For the 1st Battalion the journey from Spello, near Lake Trasimene, began on September 4. After an all-night drive the battalion arrived at 4th Division's concentration area at Senigallia on the east coast, whence, after 48 hours, it moved north towards Rimini along secondary roads and arrived at San Giovanni on September 12, ready to enter the battle. At this time the Germans were holding the line of the River Marecchia in strength, and 4th Division was ordered to fight towards this objective through country broken by steep ridges and wide valleys, through which ran numerous small streams. The Germans overlooked the valleys from positions on the ridges. The only cover for the attackers were plough, vegetable patches and low vines.

The first task given to 12th Brigade by Major-General Ward was to attack north-west from Coriano and capture the ridge on which Casa Fabbri stands. The attack began soon after dawn on September 14, when the Black Watch and the Royal Fusiliers went forward. By the afternoon the Casa Fabbri ridge was firmly in our hands, and the 1st Battalion, which had been in reserve, moved up to a re-entrant in rear of it.

The battalion was now ordered to pass through and force a crossing over the River Marano that night. Shortly before midnight A Company (Major Raisin), B Company (Major Towers-Minors) and C Company (Major Marsh) set out across country on independent compass bearings towards Ospedaletto. They met no Germans south of the river, though track vehicles could be heard pulling out ahead and the bridge over the river was actually blown up as B Company approached it. When crossing the river, however, C Company was fired on from close range by a heavy machine gun. There was a moment's confusion, but they pressed on and met no other opposition. Before dawn a bridgehead had been successfully established about Ospedaletto. Several prisoners were captured, and the Germans seem to have been taken by surprise. This operation was a fine example of the efficient use of the compass in a silent night attack.

Next morning, September 16, 28th Brigade passed through for an attack on the next ridge, and the troops in the bridgehead remained in their slit-trenches enduring continuous mortaring and shelling. In the evening two direct hits on a platoon of C Company caused the first casualties in the battalion, eight being killed and eleven wounded. That night A, B and C Companies returned to the area of Casa Fabbri, and the battalion went into reserve.

The attack by 28th Brigade was successful and took it on to the ridge overlooking the River Ausa, which at that time was merely a shallow trickle of water. On the far bank the ground rose again to another ridge on which were Point 80 and the small village of San Antima. This ridge was to be the 1st Battalion's next objective, for they were ordered to cross the Ausa and establish and hold a bridge-head. Nothing was known of the German dispositions, and there was no opportunity to view the ground. But excellent air photographs were available, and these showed that some houses at the river cross-ing, some buildings below Point 80, and the village of San Antima were likely to be strong-points. The total distance from the start-line to Point 80 was nearly a mile. As most of the route was a bare slope with no vestige of cover Colonel Braithwaite decided to carry out the attack silently without any supporting fire and at night. Searchlights were to provide artificial moonlight by projecting their beams motionless into the sky.

The approach march from Casa Fabbri began before midnight on September 17, and the battalion crossed the start-line (the crest of the ridge held by 28th Brigade) at 2.30 a.m. on the 18th with three companies forward and C in reserve. A Company on the left im-mediately ran into trouble from enemy machine guns in the houses at the river crossing, Lieutenant Folkard[1] being killed and several others in the leading platoon becoming casualties. Serjeant Austin then crawled forward, took control of this platoon as well as his own and led a bayonet charge down the hill. Yelling fiercely as they ran they cleared the houses successfully, but more machine-guns opened fire on them and they could make no further progress. There were now several wounded men lying out in the open under machine-gun fire and, as the stretcher-bearers had not yet come up, Corporal Goffee ran out to assist them. He found that one of them was badly hit and returned for some dressings. He then made four more journeys under fire, bringing in a wounded man each time and saving their lives. The total number of casualties in A Company was eighteen.

The noise of this engagement must have distracted the attention of the enemy, for B and D Companies moved down the bare slope, crossed the stream dry-shod and scrambled up the far bank without opposition. The routes of these two companies then diverged; B

---

[1] Detached from The Dorsetshire Regiment.

veered towards San Antima while D (Major Brock) bore right, with the buildings below Point 80 as their first objective. The leading platoon of D Company reached and entered these buildings successfully, and the other two platoons went on towards Point 80. There they met considerable opposition, Serjeant Hughes being killed at close range. Lieutenant Archdeacon, although wounded in the wrist and leg, was able to rally both platoons, lead them on to the objective and organise their consolidation. At first light it was found that this assault had cut a wedge into the enemy's position, and when a counter-attack came in these two platoons were in danger of being surrounded. Serjeant Shepherd, who had taken command of Serjeant Hughes's platoon but was unable to walk on account of a wound, crawled from section to section to move them to better fire positions. The enemy were driven back. The buildings farther down the slope were also counter-attacked by about thirty of the enemy. The brunt of this was borne by Major Brock and C.S.M. Thomas, who had now moved up. These two dashed from house to house with their Tommy-guns, killed four and wounded three Germans, and forced the remainder to flee into the arms of B Company's stretcher-bearers, to whom they surrendered. The situation at Point 80 was finally stabilised when a troop of tanks arrived and, after a brisk action, cleared the whole feature.

The attack by B Company against San Antima encountered strong opposition. The leading platoons were halted short of the village, and Company Headquarters went into a house about 300 yards south-east of San Antima. The enemy must have been taken completely by surprise, for this house became almost a receiving centre for astonished Germans, who walked unsuspectingly into the front door in the belief that the house was still in German hands. At daylight a troop of tanks came up, and with them the company went forward again and cleared San Antima. Movement farther forward drew heavy fire from a ridge beyond. The leading platoons therefore moved back and consolidated on the reverse slope in readiness for a counter-attack. None was attempted. Instead, at about eleven, the enemy withdrew. Altogether, B Company captured some thirty prisoners.

Shortly after dawn C Company came down the hill and took over the positions on the river crossing, while A Company moved up in rear of San Antima. The bridgehead was now firm. The whole action had been another example of a neat and efficient night attack, rounded off this time by supporting tanks in daylight. The total number of prisoners captured in the battle was forty-nine. Our casualties were eleven killed and thirty-nine wounded.

3. *The 1st Battalion at Cesena*

12th Brigade remained in reserve in its battle positions on the River Ausa for nearly a month, during which the remainder of 4th Division fought its way to the River Marecchia and other divisions then continued the thrust towards Faenza. Although the brigade had to maintain a continuous state of readiness, there was plenty of time in the evenings for recreation and concerts. At the beginning of October the establishment of infantry battalions in 4th Division was reduced owing to the shortage of reinforcements in Italy. Each battalion was reorganised as three Rifle companies and a Carrier Platoon at full strength; the Anti-tank Platoon was disbanded and the Vickers machine-gun detachments were replaced by a machine-gun platoon of the 2nd Royal Northumberland Fusiliers. So, when the 1st Battalion moved forward in pouring rain on October 17 to scattered billets between Montiano and Calisese, A Company had been disbanded.

By this time the Germans had retreated to the River Savio, and the first tasks given to 12th Brigade were to force a crossing over that river south of Cesena and to clear the built-up area on the west bank. The first move was to the ridge overlooking the Savio, from which the Royal Fusiliers and the 1st Battalion sent forward patrols to investigate the river. These patrols reported that the river would be difficult to cross because the two bridges had been demolished, the banks were either steep or made soft by rain, the width was some forty yards, and the depth was nowhere less than five feet. Moreover, the Germans, from high ground west of the Savio, overlooked the area, and any movement in daylight drew their artillery fire. Before dawn on October 20, however, the Royal Fusiliers crossed the river by a ford they had found, took the enemy by surprise and established a small bridgehead.

Brigadier Heber-Percy now ordered the Black Watch and the 1st Battalion to cross the river that night and enlarge the bridgehead, so as to enable the Sappers to repair the demolished bridge south of Cesena. This bridge was given the code name 'Keatings.' The Black Watch were to cross north of this bridge, and the 1st Battalion was to wade over at the ford used by the Royal Fusiliers, which was some 500 yards south of 'Keatings.' But when Captain Dunmall reconnoitred the ford that evening he found it to be under heavy fire. By wading the river several times he eventually found another crossing place. The battalion began to wade over at 1.30 a.m. The water was chest-deep, apart from pot-holes, and in order to assist the heavily-loaded troops Captain Dunmall tied a rope to a tree on the home bank, swam with the other end across the river, and held on to it

while the whole battalion filed across. Throughout this perilous undertaking the slope down from the ridge and both banks of the river
were under shell-fire, yet by good fortune the two leading companies
crossed safely. B Company were less fortunate, for they sustained
several casualties as they approached the river.

D Company on the right and C on the left then began to enlarge
the bridgehead. They passed through the Royal Fusiliers without
mishap, but the leading platoon of D Company then encountered a
strong wire fence and drew heavy fire from the enemy. While this
platoon dug in, the remainder of the company reached its first objective, having taken five prisoners. C Company met less opposition and
reached their objective after capturing seven prisoners. But before
they could consolidate the enemy counter-attacked with a tank and
infantry. They were forced to withdraw slightly, and eventually dug
in about a quarry. By daylight these two companies were some 200
yards forward of the Royal Fusiliers; B Company were dug in in a
reserve position just west of the river; and Battalion Headquarters
were established in the same building as the Fusiliers' headquarters.
On the right nearer Cesena the Black Watch had consolidated a
perimeter some 400 yards west of the river. The bridgehead was now
large enough to allow the Sappers to begin the repairs to 'Keatings'
bridge. They found that only the centre span had been demolished,
and by midday an Ark tank had been driven into this gap so that
tanks were able to cross.

12th Brigade then began its second task. With tanks to support
them the two battalions were ordered to resume the advance, the
Black Watch along Highway Nine and the 1st Battalion on the axis
of the road leading west from 'Keatings.' As soon as the tanks arrived,
D Company of the 1st Battalion diverged to the north and gained
contact with the Black Watch. C Company, with a troop of tanks in
support, began to make their way westwards through a semi-built-
up area which consisted of gardens, isolated blocks of buildings, single
houses, hedges and an occasional narrow country lane. This type of
close country was far from ideal for tanks. Before long the advance
was held up by fire from a group of houses, which the tanks could
not locate. As wireless communication with the tanks had failed
Private Groves, a platoon orderly, ran across an open stretch of
ground, climbed on to one of the tanks and directed their fire on to
the enemy positions. Under cover of this fire his platoon rushed
forward and captured the houses, together with 17 prisoners. Meanwhile B Company, supported also by a troop of tanks, had moved
up on the left of C Company. They made considerable progress,
clearing several blocks of houses as they went, before darkness and

increased enemy opposition brought their advance to a halt. This ended the fighting for October 21.

The next problem was to supply the troops in the bridgehead. Late in the afternoon, before any vehicles had been able to cross the river, the Ark at 'Keatings' bridge had been put out of use by a direct hit from a shell. Rations and ammunition had therefore to be brought across the Savio on assault boats and taken to the various strong-points by carrying parties. This was a dangerous task, for there were pockets of enemy resistance all round. Eleven of the porters were wounded, and these and the casualties which had occurred during the day were taken back across the river to the dressing station in Cesena.

By daylight it had still been impossible to get any wheeled vehicles or carriers across the river, and the companies were still without anti-tank guns. It was therefore decided not to attempt a further advance that day, but merely to make minor adjustments in the perimeter. While these moves were taking place the whole area was continuously shelled by the Germans. One of the tanks with the battalion was hit by a long-range shell and burst into flames. C Company Headquarters was in a farm nearby, and Lance-Corporal Marchant, who was a stretcher-bearer there, immediately rushed to the tank, pulled the tank commander from the turret, beat out the flames from his burning clothes and carried him the fifty yards to the farm. He then returned to the tank, tore off the burning clothes of another member of the crew with his bare hands and carried him to safety. The tank was now burning furiously, but Marchant made yet another journey to it, in order to satisfy himself that no more of the crew were alive, before he sought treatment for his own injuries. By the end of the day there had been a total of thirty-four casualties in the battalion since leaving Calisese. Thirty-nine Germans had been taken prisoner.

During the night of October 22 a new Ark was placed at 'Keatings' bridge so that more tanks were able to join the infantry. Reinforced by these additional tanks, though still without carriers or anti-tank guns, the brigade was ready to undertake a further attack. Plans were prepared next morning, and while the Brigade Commander was giving out his orders in the building which was shared by the Royal Fusiliers and the 1st Battalion as a headquarters, the wall of the house was hit by a shell. Miraculously no one was killed, but Colonel Braithwaite received numerous abrasions on the head and eventually consented to be evacuated. Major Gwilliam was in command for the attack next day. But the Germans were already in the process of withdrawing. When the battalion advanced at dawn on October 24 the only opposition was from long-range fire and from a few Germans who were found hiding in cellars. By nightfall the battalion had reached a ridge some six miles west of Cesena. During the advance Major Marsh[1] was killed by a shell, and as the other officers of C Company were deployed with their platoons, C.S.M. Worsley assumed command of the company. Before long Worsley was himself wounded in the back, but he continued to send back wireless reports of the company's progress and would not be evacuated until consolidation was complete. Casualties in this advance were one officer and nine other ranks.

That night the battalion handed over its positions and marched back to billets in Cesena, where the troops had their first real sleep for five days and nights.

4. *The 1st Battalion at Forli and San Tome*

The 1st Battalion remained in Cesena until November 8, when it moved up in T.C.V.s to a concentration area south of Forlimpopoli. The enemy had already retreated across the River Ronco, and 10th Brigade had formed a bridgehead between Ronco Village, Forli airfield and San Martino. The new plan was for 12th and 28th Brigades to resume the attack and clear the town of Forli. 12th Brigade, with the 1st Battalion on the right and the Black Watch on the left, was to advance from the airfield to Highway Nine and then wheel left towards the northern part of Forli.

On the evening of November 8 the 1st Battalion made a quick move forward, crossed the Ronco by a pontoon bridge and formed up on the airfield south of Forli without incident. At 6 a.m. on the 9th the forward companies moved slowly northwards across ground much pitted by bomb craters. No opposition was met, although numerous hastily-sown mines, which had been laid on the roadside, had to be cleared by Serjeant Nicholls and a section of his pioneers. Soon after first light Highway Nine was reached, and the barracks on the outskirts of Forli were then quickly cleared. It now became apparent that the enemy did not intend to fight for the town itself. The battalion therefore passed to the north of Forli and turned westwards again towards the Canal di Rivaldino. At this stage the Black Watch were also approaching the western exits of the town without having met any Germans.

Contact was first made with the enemy in the evening, when they

---

[1] Detached from the Lancashire Fusiliers.

were found to be holding a strong-point in some buildings on the banks of the canal. At this point a culvert carrying the road over the canal had been demolished, thus presenting an obstacle over which tanks could not cross. The leading platoon of B Company attempted to cross the canal, but several Spandaus opened fire from the windows of a factory and two enemy tanks came up. Major Waring, who was now commanding B Company, therefore ordered the leading platoon to take cover in some buildings while an attack was prepared. But Colonel Braithwaite decided to pass another company through, and the attack was put in by D Company supported by artillery and mortar fire at 11.30 that night. The canal was crossed and some buildings were captured, but the factory with its high walls proved to be very formidable. During the assault against it one of the leading sections was stopped by Spandau fire; three men were killed and a fourth, wounded in the hip, lay out in the open. Lance-Corporal Hermitage, a stretcher-bearer, at once crawled out to reach him. He was fired at whenever he attempted to move, but he slowly got to within thirty yards of the wounded man, waited till the attention of the Spandau crew was distracted, and then rushed to his side and dressed the wound. Seeing this brave action another section dashed across the open space and silenced the gun. But the two enemy tanks then re-appeared, and further assaults were postponed until carriers could bring up some P.I.A.T.s to deal with them. During this pause Serjeant Nicholls crossed the canal and began to clear mines from the road, so that tanks would be able to move forward rapidly once a bridge had been built. This road was under fire from enemy snipers, and Nicholls was badly wounded in the arm; but he continued to lift the mines until the task was finished.

Brigadier Heber-Percy now decided to pass the Royal Fusiliers through to continue the attack towards San Tome, while the 1st Battalion made contact on the left with the Black Watch, who were still fighting hard at the western exits of Forli. This attack was to take place as soon as an Ark had been placed at the demolished culvert and tanks had been able to cross the canal. By the afternoon the Ark had been placed in position, and soon after dark the leading companies of the Fusiliers passed through. C Company then attempted to gain contact with the Black Watch by leap-frogging their platoons across the open spaces between buildings. But they were soon held up by fire from tanks and Spandaus, and it was apparent that no headway would be made without the aid of tanks. The company therefore consolidated to await them. Eventually at midday on the 11th a troop of tanks came up, the advance was resumed, and touch was gained with the Black Watch at dusk. By this time the Royal

Fusiliers were well clear of Forli, and the 1st Battalion had come into brigade reserve.

By dawn on the 13th the leading troops of 12th Brigade had fought their way to within 1,000 yards of the village of San Tome, and the battalion was ordered to pass through the Black Watch and seize San Tome as its first objective. After the scattered houses in the village had been heavily bombarded by our guns, B and C Companies started off at 8.30 a.m. with tanks in support. C Company on the right were at once opposed by machine-gun fire from a farm, but Serjeant Whittick located the gun in a haystack, quickly stalked it and rushed it single-handed with his Tommy-gun. The crew of four Germans surrendered. The company objective was then seized successfully without further opposition, four more prisoners being taken. B Company's advance on the left was opposed only by slight mortar fire. By midday both companies had consolidated about San Tome.

In the afternoon the attack was resumed across a stretch of flat low-lying fields towards the River Montone with D Company in the lead. Wide ditches caused the supporting tanks a deal of trouble, visibility was limited by numerous hedges, and Spandau fire from individual houses slowed up the advance. One of these Spandaus was a particular nuisance, but the reserve platoon worked its way round to a flank under cover of a smoke-screen put down by the 2-inch mortars of C Company, and the Spandau crew withdrew hastily. At dusk D Company had advanced to within a mile of the River Montone. B Company then passed through and began to move cautiously forward towards the river. There was no opposition at all, but the process of clearing the houses was slow. As the darkness deepened sounds of the enemy withdrawing were heard, and a fighting patrol, sent forward to investigate, reported that the enemy were retreating across the river. This ended the battle for the battalion. The total casualties in the actions at Forli and San Tome had been nine other ranks killed and two officers and 37 other ranks wounded.

After dark on the 14th the battalion marched back to Forli. The guns of the enemy frequently harassed the town. Shells fell around their billets; but the men were too tired to care. Rest was what they needed now, and rest they were promised. 4th Division was due to proceed to Palestine to recuperate for the offensive in the coming spring. The journey south began on November 24, when the battalion moved in T.C.V.s through Chieti to Ortona, and thence by train to Taranto. There they went under canvas to await the ships which were to take them to Palestine.

Trouble had flared up in Greece, however, and plans were suddenly changed. 4th Division was ordered to proceed to Athens forthwith to reinforce the British troops already there. On December 12 the battalion, less an advance party which had already proceeded to Palestine, a rear party left in Taranto and all its transport and drivers, embarked in the *Bergensfjord* bound for Greece. Thus the 1st Battalion took no part in the final battles in Italy.

5. *The 6th Battalion at Monte del Acqua Salata and Casone*

The 6th Battalion returned to Italy after only six weeks' rest in Egypt. These weeks were spent at Qassassin camp, which was now almost a town with shops, cinemas, hospitals and an officers' club. While it was there the battalion was brought up to full strength by drafts from reinforcement depots and other units in Egypt. The return voyage was made in our old friend the *Johan van Oldenbarneveldt*, which had transported the 1st Battalion to Algiers from Scotland, and disembarkation took place at Taranto on September 15, 1944. Training of the newcomers then began in earnest, with the emphasis on platoon and section work. The Company Commanders now were: Major Austin (A), Major Kennedy (B), Major Hartland (C), Major Wakefield (D) and Major Clarke (Support). Colonel Defrates' adjutant was Captain Wheater.

At first 78th Division (now commanded by Major-General R. K. Arbuthnott) was ordered to Rimini to join the 8th Army. But these orders were changed, and the division was sent to XIII Corps, on the right of the American 5th Army. At this time the Americans were attempting to break through the mountains to the plains of Bologna before winter came, and XIII Corps was pressing north-eastwards along the axis of the Firenzuola-Castel del Rio-Imola road to safe-guard their right flank. But the attack was petering out as much because of lack of stores and ammunition as the fire of the enemy. Attempts were now to be made to probe northwards through the hills so as to outflank the German positions west of Imola. 78th Division had been brought in to give more strength to this outflanking manœuvre.

The 6th Battalion arrived on October 13 at Sassoleone, some fifteen miles north of Marradi, which the 5th Battalion was then defending. Having sent a tenth of its personnel to the 'Left out of Battle' area, the battalion moved forward to the village of San Apollinare, where 36th Brigade, now commanded by Brigadier C. D. Packard, was taking over positions. Its stay there was brief, for 36th Brigade had been ordered to seize Monte la Pieve, which 11th Brigade had already failed to capture. The 6th Battalion's part in the attack was to be an assault on a feature called Castellaro, which towered up less than a mile to the north-east. To reach it the troops had to descend seven hundred feet down a bare hillside, ford a narrow stream, and climb nine hundred feet to the objective. At nightfall on October 18 a platoon of C Company secured the crossing over the stream and taped the difficult portions of the descent. D Company followed at 1.45 a.m., taking with them ammunition, tools and other necessary apparatus on mules. 138 Field Regiment then put down a barrage, and the leading troops ascended the rocky slope of Castellaro. But there was no fire from the enemy. At 3.30 some empty slit-trenches were occupied, and by 4.30 the whole feature had been overrun without finding any Germans willing to fight. A few prisoners were collected. For some reason the enemy had decided not to withstand another assault, and the whole brigade objective was occupied without resistance.

This was a good start; but it was not long before intense shelling began, particularly of Battalion Headquarters. Another problem was that of supply, for ammunition and rations had to be carried forward along the battalion axis from San Apollinare. No sooner had this been organised than orders were received for another night operation. This time the battalion was to pass through Monte del Acqua Salata (The Hill of Dirty Water), which had now been captured by the Argylls, and seize a feature farther north. But when the column set off, with C Company in the van, at 9 p.m. on October 21, the track had been turned into a treacherous sea of mud by steady rain. Darkness and fog covered the valley like a blanket, and artificial moonlight improved the visibility very little. A guide was picked up at the correct place, but soon afterwards the track petered out and he became hopelessly lost. Out of the darkness came the Brigadier, also lost. After a rapid calculation it was decided that it was now too late to launch a night attack. The battalion was back on Castellaro by dawn.

The attack was then shelved, and the battalion was ordered to relieve the Argylls at Acqua Salata instead. Before the troops could move off, Serjeant Waterhouse, single-handed, had to clear the track of glassmines, a variety of mine which had not been previously encountered. Nevertheless a start was made at the proper time. By nine that night the battalion was beginning to cross the causeway which led to Acqua Salata. This causeway was barely ten yards wide, its sides dropped away down 300 feet of wet clay, and the only protection from German shells which fell on it accurately and heavily every night was a series of tiny hummocks. The battalion crossed

ITALY: ONE OF THE DEMOLISHED BRIDGES OVER THE RIVER ARNO IN THE CITY OF FLORENCE. THE PONTE VECCHIO IS IN THE BACKGROUND. THE BAILEY BRIDGE IN THE FOREGROUND WAS ERECTED AFTER THE 5TH BATTALION HAD CROSSED THE RIVER

ITALY: A PLATOON OF THE 1ST BATTALION MOVING FORWARD FROM CASA FABBRI ON SEPTEMBER 17, 1944

ITALY: A 'FANTAIL' ENTERING THE WATER

GREECE: A DETACHMENT OF THE IST BATTALION MARCH-
ING THROUGH MISSOLONGHI ON MARCH 24, 1945, DURING
THE CELEBRATION OF GREEK INDEPENDENCE DAY

safely. By 2.30 a.m. on the 23rd it was moving into position with three companies forward and one in support. The whole of Acqua Salata was overlooked by German O.P.s, and all that day the battalion was shelled and mortared. But the Argylls had dug well down. Casualties were limited to seventeen, of whom five were killed. By nightfall the firing had ceased.

That evening the problem was to get the supplies from San Apollinare, which was some five miles back. Exceptionally heavy rain had turned the track, where it existed, into deep mud, and much of the route, especially the causeway, was under shell-fire. The problem could be solved only by the use of mules. A mule-train was formed at San Apollinare under Colour-Serjeants Smith and Gilbert. Corporal Veron was sent from Acqua Salata to meet it. Shells were falling frequently, and one blew him off his feet; but he went on, met the mule-train and began to guide it to the causeway. Before long one of the leading mules was blown up on a mine; Colour-Serjeant Smith was wounded and knocked unconscious by the blast, and the mule-train was dispersed. It took the three N.C.O.s several hours to get the mules back on to the track. The column eventually reached Acqua Salata eight hours after leaving San Apollinare. Subsequently the normal time taken by the mule-train was three hours each way. On the third night the hooves of the mules, digging deep into the mud, detonated three glassmines. Our detectors could not locate this new type of mine and the causeway was never in fact really clear of them.

Colonel Defrates' orders were to push forward as soon as the opportunity occurred to Monte Verro (Point 410), a hill about 700 yards away from Acqua Salata. Taking advantage of a mist, Serjeant Hammett led a patrol forward at dawn on October 24, and disarmed and captured the occupants of a house half-way up this hill without a shot being fired. Two men then moved farther up the slope and captured seven more Germans. The bag of prisoners was now nineteen, and two Tommy-gunners started back with them while the remainder of the patrol covered their retreat. One of the prisoners was killed on the way by a German machine-gun, but eventually the patrol and eighteen prisoners arrived safely. Serjeant Hammett was captured by the enemy during the withdrawal.

Colonel Defrates at once decided to take advantage of this success and ordered C Company to capture Monte Verro. After the Gunners had fired a few rounds to soften up the enemy, the leading platoon moved forward to the lower ground out of sight of the Germans. The next step was to blind the enemy with a smoke-screen. For once the Gunners failed to produce this. When the assault was eventually made at seven that evening, some of the Germans were determined

z

and were killed on the hillside, but the majority fled and the objective was seized. A further half-dozen prisoners were taken. Some hours later a small counter-attack came in and threw one of the platoons into some confusion; but Private Dyer, the platoon runner, took command of a Bren-gun group and kept it in action until the situation had been restored. At dawn next morning the enemy retaliated with an attack on the right flank of the main Acqua Salata position. But A Company was prepared. After a brisk flurry of shots the Germans went to ground. Serjeant Lee then led out a sortie of eight men, put the enemy to flight and brought back seventeen more prisoners, making a total of nearly fifty in twenty-four hours. This success was very encouraging.

Next day icy rain poured down incessantly, trenches caved in, tracks became water-logged and the mule supply route was turned into a morass. To make matters worse the Germans resumed their heavy bombardment of Acqua Salata, and the number of casualties in the battalion rose to nearly one hundred and thirty for the six days from October 23–28. Amongst the twenty-three killed was Major Kennedy.[1] Lance-Corporal Cull[2] was again conspicuous for his gallantry while caring for the wounded under fire. He was awarded a bar to his M.M. There was also such an alarming wastage on account of sickness that a contraction to three rifle companies became necessary, B and C Companies being merged into Z Company under the command of Major Hartland. Eventually, on the night of October 28, the battalion was relieved by the Argylls and went back to an area near Castel del Rio for rest.

The weather was now so bad that plans for further aggressive action were postponed, and 36th Brigade settled down to a spell of static warfare and a system of routine reliefs. On the night of October 31 the battalion moved back again to Acqua Salata. In the meantime Gully House, made famous for the number of times it was counter-attacked, had been captured by the Buffs and was now included in the sector, and the contraction to three companies meant that one company had to be borrowed from the Argylls to garrison it. This period in the line was uneventful. Six days' rest followed. During a third and final spell on Acqua Salata the Germans twice attacked Gully House unsuccessfully, and they frequently brought heavy fire down on to the area. Although a number of casualties were suffered, our guns and mortars were now in a position to retaliate with good measure. Serjeant Meade in particular obtained good results from his mortar shoots. On numerous occasions Serjeant Lancelotte, the

[1] Detached from The Buffs.
[2] Cull won the M.M. for gallantry as a stretcher-bearer at Lake Trasimene.

Signal Serjeant, went out himself under shell-fire to repair lines which had been broken, and Private Coleman crawled out five times on one moonlit night to repair the line to Gully House.

Towards the end of November the battalion carried out two tours of duty in a new sector near Casone. In this area the Germans were quiet enough, but Brigade required a prisoner for identification and C.S.M. Obbard was selected to lead a patrol to capture one. The patrol of ten men set out just before midnight on November 24 and made straight across open ground with little effort at concealment. Suddenly Obbard saw a German sentry a few yards ahead. He fired first, and the patrol rushed in. Obbard destroyed a machine-gun with a grenade, three of the enemy were killed in their trenches and five were taken prisoner. The entire operation only took thirty-five minutes. The next night a large party of Germans suddenly charged up the slope and took our troops by surprise. But wire and mines prevented penetration, and after a few bursts of fire the enemy withdrew.

There had now been some improvement in the weather. As a preliminary to another advance by 78th Division, 36th Brigade was ordered to capture Monte Maggiore (Point 448) on the Camaggio ridge. This attack was to be carried out from Acqua Salata, and on December 9 the battalion crossed the causeway once more and took over the accustomed positions. The only possible route for the attack entailed an approach march of about a mile down the slope of Acqua Salata and along a narrow saddle which led to the top of the Camaggio ridge. The Buffs were to attack alongside on the right, and arrangements were made for plenty of support from the guns and mortars.

At 11.15 on the night of December 13, after forty-five minutes' softening up by the Gunners, Z Company moved in pouring rain through the mud down the slope and on to the saddle. There they came under mortar fire and lost several casualties. On the way up the ridge the mud was in places thigh deep. During the ascent the right forward platoon came under fire from a machine-gun. There were more casualties, but Serjeant Jones led a charge and silenced the gun. His platoon then struggled on to within a hundred yards of Camaggio. The other platoons were suffering heavily from the German defensive fire, however, and the company was ordered back. The Gunners now arranged a second fire plan of ten minutes' intense fire from all available guns. As soon as this got under way D Company, who had been frozen by the icy wind while waiting on the reverse slope, took the route across the saddle. By the time the Gunners' fire had stopped, the leading platoons had reached a steep bank surmounted by a thick hedge. This formidable obstacle was covered by enfilade fire from enemy machine-guns. Many casualties were suffered here, but, splendidly led by Major Shaun Stewart,[1] some of the company got through the hedge. Firing as they went they gathered their strength and charged uphill through the mud. The Germans bolted and the summit was reached.

While the remainder of D Company reorganised on Point 448, one platoon was sent to occupy a farm on the lower slopes. But the enemy retaliated with such accurate machine-gun fire that it was impossible to secure the entire ridge without assistance. Major Stewart therefore asked for a flank attack by the follow-up company. By this time the Brigade Commander had decided on a withdrawal, however, and both D Company and the Buffs fell back under a smoke-screen before dawn. Stretcher parties at once set about the task of bringing in the wounded, who were lying in large numbers on the hillside near Camaggio. At the worst places it took ten men to move one stretcher through the mud, and some of the wounded were on stretchers for ten or eleven hours. In all, the battalion lost over seventy casualties in this last attempt to resume the offensive before winter.

After this unhappy affair the battalion rested for a few days at San Apollinare and then moved off once more to Casone. Much of the time there was spent in reorganising the companies. Otherwise the tour was uneventful. By December 23 the battalion was back at San Apollinare collecting kit, for the exciting news had been received that it was moving out of the battle area for a rest. Christmas Eve was spent in travelling to Rignano, seven miles south-east of Florence and only two miles from the 5th Battalion at San Donato. In order to give time to make the necessary preparations it was arranged that Christmas should be celebrated on December 26. This revision of the calendar worked admirably, and the Quartermaster's secret and probably illicit accumulation of livestock was eaten with appropriate speed on that day.

6. *The 5th Battalion at Bagni di Lucca and Pisa*

A few days after the 5th Battalion arrived at San Donato Colonel Malcolmson went to Benevento to obtain reinforcements. Most of the men at the Reinforcement Depot were from artillery regiments which had been disbanded, but he selected one hundred and forty of them, all volunteers and of good physique. After suitable individual training they fell into the role of infantrymen exceptionally well. On his return Colonel Malcolmson made several changes in the key

[1] Major Stewart had just rejoined from Brigade Headquarters.

personnel of the battalion. Captain Wood was appointed Military Manager of the Savoy Hotel in Florence, and Major Wonnall took over command of the Support Company from him; Major Stocker became second-in-command of the rest camp in Florence. For recreation two *vino* bars, called 'The Rising Sun' and 'The White Horse,' were opened in the battalion area, a dance band was formed and on Christmas Day the troops enjoyed a good dinner in comfortable surroundings.

Meanwhile a dangerous situation had developed on the west coast of Italy near the Gulf of Genoa. This area was vital to the American 5th Army because the bulk of its supplies were drawn from the port of Leghorn,[1] which was merely forty miles behind the weakly-held front. A comparatively limited advance by the Germans would disrupt the 5th Army's communications, and recent Intelligence reports had revealed that the Germans were mustering a large force in the vicinity. On Boxing Day the enemy did in fact launch an attack which succeeded beyond all expectations. The danger point was Lucca, and it was to this area that the 5th Battalion made a quick move in T.C.V.s on December 27 and arrived at Bagni di Lucca that evening.

The battalion was placed in reserve to 19th Indian Brigade, which deployed to meet the German attack. But the attack did not develop. There were no signs of war. Perhaps the operation had been no more than a German bluff. Whatever the explanation, British armoured cars probing forward next day encountered no enemy, and in a few days the scare was over. The battalion therefore settled down in comfortable billets with electric light and resumed its training. At Bagni Caldi nearby was a hot water spring running down into marble baths. This was greatly enjoyed by the troops.

Early in January 1945, the whole of 8th Indian Division (including 21st Indian Brigade, which the battalion now rejoined) was withdrawn to the Pisa area to train for the spring offensive. The battalion's billets at Rezzano were overcrowded owing to the large number of Italian refugees. But within a few days better billets were found at Calci, some half-dozen miles from Pisa. The companies were then able to get down to platoon and company training as well as exercises in the use of assault boats on the River Arno. On February 11 the move back to the battle area began. This time it was to be the Adriatic sector and, after staying the night near Perugia, the battalion went into billets at San Bendetto del Tronto, close to Ancona.

[1] See rear end-paper map.

7. *The 6th Battalion at Monte Grande*

When the 6th Battalion left the Florence area on December 29, it returned to a sector in the mountains south of Bologna where the physical conditions caused more discomfort than the fighting. The positions were on Monte Calderaro, north of Monte Grande, and were 1,800 feet above sea-level. By day the temperature was below freezing point and at night it descended fifteen degrees lower. As a result it was found necessary to fire a few rounds through the Bren guns every fifteen minutes in order to keep the mechanism from freezing. Otherwise, owing to the difficulty of supply, the expenditure of ammunition was strictly controlled. Snow began to fall, and patrols were issued with white smocks, which did much to conceal their movements. Daylight patrols consequently became more popular than usual; indeed the consensus of opinion was that it was better to go on patrol than to freeze in the trenches. As a matter of fact there was an issue of Mountain Warfare kit, which included thick sweaters, windproof blouses, extra socks and string vests, so the troops kept fairly warm. But it was with more than usual pleasure that the sector was handed over on January 11, 1945. The battalion returned to Rignano. In a few hours the discomforts of the mountains were forgotten. Day-leave to Florence did much to restore a feeling of well-being, and the Argylls were soundly defeated at football.

Towards the end of January 1945, the battalion drove forward to the mountains once more, to a sector south of Monte Grande. The companies were dispersed to cover a frontage of over 2,000 yards; D Company in particular was very isolated. For several days the sector was quiet. Then unexpectedly on the afternoon of February 9 the enemy began to shell a house called Casa di Sopra, in which was a complete platoon at rest. In a few minutes the house was a shambles and many of the platoon were lying badly hurt under the debris. Stretcher-bearers at once set out from D Company Headquarters, and the Medical Officer, Captain Jackson, left the Aid Post with more rescuers. A platoon from the reserve company soon followed. The task of evacuating the casualties then began. All that evening and night and until dawn the following morning the work went on, frequently made dangerous by the collapse of another part of the building. At last nobody alive remained inside. Of the garrison of twenty-five, seven were killed, nine were evacuated to hospital, five were 'walking wounded,' and only four escaped unhurt.

Two days later the battalion was relieved in pouring rain and drove back south of Florence. 78th Division was being transferred to the main 8th Army front near the Adriatic coast, and next day the battalion travelled east to the village of Bertinoro, between Cesena and Forli, where it was to recuperate and prepare for action in the spring.

CHAPTER 21

Italy: The Last Battles
February to August 1945
5th and 6th Battalions

1. *The 5th and 6th Battalions on the River Senio*

THE 8th Army had established its winter line along the River Senio, and it was there that the 5th and 6th Battalions came together again in March 1945. The 5th Battalion only remained for twelve days in its comfortable billets near Ancona, for on February 24 it moved to Bagnacavallo and took over a sector on the Senio, south of San Potito. The 6th Battalion remained for a longer period at Bertinoro, where the town hall, the school and a number of houses were requisitioned as billets. They had a cinema and a reading-room, and a new venture called the 'Queen's Own Parlour,' as well as another 'White Horse Inn.' The nearest leave town was the bomb-scarred Ravenna. On March 11 the battalion moved up to the River Senio to a sector north of Cotignola, less than three miles south of the 5th Battalion.

The River Senio was strongly held by the Germans, who had complete control of the river bed. In some places the 8th Army had reached the banks of the river; in others vineyards and orchards intervened. In still other places the 8th Army positions were on an open plain a few hundred yards back from the Senio. But in general the forward troops on both sides were dug in opposite each other on the river banks. The river itself did not exceed thirty feet in width and five feet in depth, but the banks were built twenty feet high and six feet wide at the top so as to contain the river when it was in spate. Usually our troops were on the reverse slope of the east floodbank, with the enemy on the opposite bank twenty yards away. But here and there the Germans actually held positions on the river side of our floodbank, within a few feet of our troops.

In these circumstances reliefs could only be carried out and supplies brought up under the cover of darkness, and, once in position, the forward platoons had to be constantly on the alert to deal with

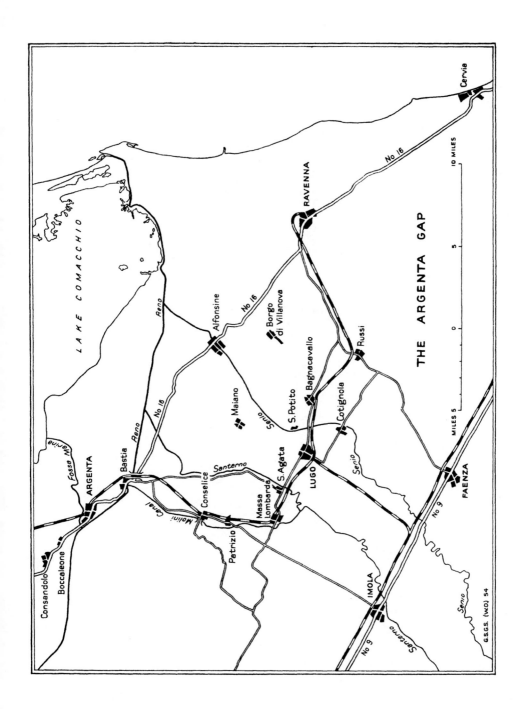

THE ARGENTA GAP

an enemy foray. These platoons were mostly dug well into the home side of the floodbank, with fire positions on the top and crawl-trenches to reach them. Mines and wire gave a certain amount of protection, but at night the top of the floodbank was always manned. In order to obtain observation of the river by day both sides had dug tunnels eight or ten feet long through the floodbanks. P.I.A.T.s were splendid weapons with which to destroy these tunnels, and they were all employed on the river. The most frightening of the enemy's weapons were the powerful short-range rockets, which were brought up at night on half-track vehicles and fired electrically.

During their first period on the Senio the tension in both the 5th and 6th Battalions was extreme, though Battalion Headquarters and the rear companies could relax somewhat. The nights were particularly hideous with the noise of machine guns, mortars, grenades and rockets. On the night of March 1 the 5th Battalion staged a diversion to assist a neighbouring battalion to advance its positions to the river, and on the following night a retaliatory raid had to be beaten off. On the night of the 8th a strong enemy fighting patrol on the left of the battalion's sector was stopped only with difficulty; on the 12th the Germans fired propaganda leaflets into the area. The 6th Battalion were having similar troubles. Soon after their arrival they had to deal with an attempt by the enemy to establish a strong-point on their side of the river. One night the Argylls on the right were so heavily smoked and shelled that it was thought that a full-scale enemy attack was about to start. And one morning, in order to discover more exactly the location of the enemy's guns and mortars, a mammoth weight of fire was let loose on to the forward German positions. For twenty minutes every available gun and mortar fired against every known enemy position within five hundred yards of the river. In reply the German defensive fire-plan was put into operation; and as a result a dozen new machine-gun posts were located as well as more battery and mortar positions. The expenditure of ammunition was enormous.

The 5th Battalion was relieved on the night of March 14, when the troops marched back to Bagnacavallo and went in T.C.V.s to Russi for ten days' rest and training with 'Kangaroos.'[1] The following night the 6th Battalion also moved back to Russi for a spell of rest. The two battalions actually occupied houses on opposite sides of the main street, and as a natural consequence they met at football at Russi Stadium. The result was a victory for the 5th Battalion. The exact score is still disputable because one battalion's War Diary

[1] A 'kangaroo' was a Sherman tank de-turretted and adapted to carry a section of infantry.

gives it as 9–0 and the other (you can guess which) as 7–1. The 5th must in fact have had a team well above the average because it got into the final of 8th Indian Division's knock-out competition soon afterwards.

After this the 5th Battalion moved to the 21st Brigade reserve area at Borgo di Villanova, while the 6th Battalion returned to the Senio. The new sector was slightly south of the old, but conditions in it were similar. D Company was unpleasantly surprised before dawn one morning by a sudden enemy raid which came in over the floodbank; but after five confusing minutes the raiders withdrew. Almost at once another patrol attacked. Our troops were very wide-awake and touchy by now. They flung so many grenades that this second band of Germans beat a hasty retreat. The remainder of that tour on the river line and another in the former sector passed uneventfully, and on April 7 the battalion was withdrawn to Russi to await the spring offensive. Meanwhile the 5th Battalion had again moved up to the river for a few days; but on April 4 it was relieved by a regiment of the Italian Cremona Group and went back to Bagnacavallo. There it carried out training in river crossings in preparation for the forth-coming battle.

2. *The 5th Battalion Crosses the Senio*

Everything was now ready for the promised offensive. The attack was mainly to be carried out by 8th Indian, New Zealand and 78th Divisions, and they were rested as much as possible and were shown the many new weapons and vehicles which had arrived for the battle. There were flame-throwing tanks known as 'Wasps' and 'Crocodiles'; new Sherman tanks with heavier guns than before; bull-dozing tanks; Ark tanks, which these divisions had not yet met; and the 'Kangaroos' which they had already used. In addition there were the tracked amphibians called Fantails. All these made a formidable array and gave a great boost to morale. The troops felt that they were no longer the 'poor relations' in the war, but that they were at last getting as good equipment as the armies in France were receiving.

The offensive was designed to bring the war in Italy to an end. The intention was to destroy the enemy forces south of the River Po, to force crossings over that river and to capture Verona. The plan was for 8th Indian Division on the right and the New Zealanders on the left to smash the German defences on the Rivers Senio and Santerno. These divisions were then to establish a bridgehead across the San-terno, through which 78th Division would advance, thrust through the Argenta Gap—a strip of land four miles wide between Lake Comacchio and the marshlands of the River Reno—and make straight for Ferrara and the River Po.

April 9 dawned bright and clear. In the early afternoon, while the infantry rested under a warm sun, wave after wave of heavy bombers flew over and dropped their bombs on the enemy areas. This continued for ninety minutes. At 3 p.m. the forward troops retired for several hundred yards from the River Senio, and twenty minutes later a tremendous artillery concentration pounded the German positions near the river. This bombardment continued for four hours, until a vast cloud of dust hung in the air. Then, in order to occupy the attention of the enemy, fighter bombers dived low in dummy attacks. At the same time long lines of tanks and flame-throwers followed by infantry moved forward to the river. As the aircraft swooped for the last time the 'Crocodiles' spurted sheets of flame and the guns of the tanks pounded the German posts. A few minutes later the leading infantry climbed the floodbank of the river and plunged into the stream. After a fierce fight the opposite bank was cleared, and the infantry swept on.

Just north of Lugo, 21st Brigade was on the left of 8th Indian Division's attack. Farther to the left, south of Lugo, there was a two-mile gap between it and the New Zealanders. The 5th Battalion, in 21st Brigade reserve for the initial assault, had assembled in a concentration area west of Bagnacavallo on the afternoon of the 9th. In the evening it moved towards San Potito and, led by guides, crossed the River Senio at about 8.40 p.m., soon after the leading troops. C Company, who had already crossed the river as a reserve for the Punjabis, had ten casualties while crossing, but the remainder of the battalion only had one. The whole battalion then assembled in an area just west of San Potito.

While the remainder of 21st Brigade fought its way forward to the River Santerno, the 5th Battalion's role was to mop up any isolated pockets of resistance which remained on the west bank of the Senio. The artillery plan to support the battalion went awry because many of the Gunners' wireless sets had become wet during the crossing of the river. But the battalion, after its long rest, was fighting fit again, and the rather complicated night operation went with a swing. Using C Company as a firm base, Colonel Malcolmson sent two companies to sweep southwards along the bank of the river. As each strong-point was located it was quickly outflanked, Corporal Munday in particular displaying courage and skill in leading his section to the enemy's rear. At Casa Mazzerini, the main stronghold, the fire of Serjeant Wrycraft's Bren-gun group was so effective that the resistance crumbled almost immediately. Some of the other posts fought for a time, but many of them surrendered willingly enough. Altogether one hundred and twenty-seven prisoners were taken. By noon on the 10th the task had been completed with a loss of only a few wounded.

The battle was everywhere going according to plan. During the night tanks had crossed the Senio on Bailey bridges and had swept forward with the infantry towards the Santerno in daylight. The gap between 8th Indian and the New Zealand Divisions still existed, and in order to block it the 5th Battalion was ordered to move into Lugo and put that town in a state of defence. Before dark on the 10th, therefore, Battalion Headquarters had been established in the square at Lugo with the companies disposed round the perimeter. In the evening a few enemy shells fell in the town and caused two casualties, but otherwise that night and all day on the 11th were surprisingly uneventful. On the night of the 11th there was another bout of shelling, which caused no casualties. Nothing else disturbed the quiet.

By this time the bridgehead west of the River Santerno had been established, and on the afternoon of April 12 the battalion marched out of Lugo and took over a sector of the bridgehead about a mile north-west of San Agata. The relief was completed by 9.30 that evening. In carrying it out C Company suffered some casualties from enemy mortars, and B Company, while assembling, were fired on in error by a battalion[1] of 78th Division, which was now passing through. Tragedy was averted by the unusual spectacle of one British battalion displaying a white flag to another, and only two men were wounded. Next morning the battalion was relieved of all operational commitments. 78th Division had swept on towards the Argenta Gap.

3. *The 6th Battalion at Conselice and Boccaleone*

During the first three days of the Senio battle the 6th Battalion had been stripped for action in Russi at four hours' notice to move. Late on April 11 Colonel Defrates received a warning order, and early next morning the battalion moved in M.T. across the River Senio by a Bailey bridge to an area near Lugo, where 36th Brigade (now commanded by Brigadier G. R. D. Musson) was concentrating. After a day of cat-naps a surprise order came for the battalion to set off again within the hour. At 1.45 a.m. on the 13th the column of seventy or eighty vehicles was on its way to San Patrizio, on the

[1] Fortunately this was not the 6th Battalion.

Imola-Argenta road. The Argylls, leading 36th Brigade and 78th Division, had already passed through 8th Indian Division's bridgehead at San Agata and were a mile north of San Patrizio. The 6th Battalion was to pass through the Argylls and capture Conselice. Little was known of the German defences; but just to the west of Conselice was a bridge over the Molini Canal, and it was certain that the enemy would defend this escape route until the last possible moment.

The battalion began to move northwards from San Patrizio at first light on April 13 with a squadron of Churchill tanks of 48th Royal Tank Regiment in support. By 6.30 a.m. the two forward companies were within 500 yards of Conselice. On the left, A Company (Major Austin), with a troop of tanks, were astride the road in sight of the town when bursts of fire came from well-hidden machine guns. The tanks attempted an outflanking move to the left, but the area was intersected by ditches and they could make no progress. The forward platoon had by now suffered a number of casualties, and Major Austin ordered them to dig in and locate the enemy positions more exactly while he prepared a company attack. On the right D Company (Major Jarrett) were also in trouble. At first a railway embankment and a tongue of vineyards had given them a covered approach. But after that the ground was open and any attempt to advance across it drew fire from enemy self-propelled guns. In one attempt to cross Lieutenant Grove was shot dead. The troop of tanks with the company then made a wide swing in an effort to reach a group of farm buildings close to the town. These aggressive tactics at first met with success, and the tanks knocked out two self-propelled guns. Nevertheless, it was apparent that this side of the town would be no easier to approach than the other. Colonel Defrates therefore ordered the two forward companies to halt until he had prepared a new attack.

While plans were being made with the artillery and tank commanders, an air-strike dived low and destroyed a group of German mortars and a self-propelled gun, which were sited north of Conselice. One small bomb hit the bridge over the Molini Canal with a pleasing crump. Before the Germans could recover from the effects of this raid, two sections of A Company filtered forward to a small house within a hundred yards of the town. The success was short-lived. At about 5 p.m. this isolated house was attacked by a strong party of Germans. Although three or four men were on watch, some of the enemy managed to enter the yard. A hand-to-hand fight took place, and it was only after a fierce mêlée that the Germans were driven off, leaving three dead. As the house was now a shambles the garrison was withdrawn to the main company area. Our losses included Serjeants Brophy and Maguire, who were both killed. Major Austin, who had gone forward to investigate, was wounded in a leg which had to be amputated later. C.S.M. Obbard was also wounded in this skirmish. He was a great loss, for he had won a D.C.M. and bar as well as an M.M. while serving with the battalion (see Appendix A).

The battalion was now ready to put in its fresh assault. After this latest indication that the Germans were still determined to hold their ground, however, Brigadier Musson decided to launch a co-ordinated brigade attack instead. His plan was for the Argylls to clear the marshland to the south-west of Conselice; the Buffs were then to pass through, attack north-westwards and block the Germans' escape route over the Molini Canal. The role of the 6th Battalion was to turn the right flank and clear Conselice.

At dusk C Company (Major Stewart) began a long encircling movement round the right flank with a troop of tanks under command. As the forward platoon drew up to Conselice it came under mortar fire, and C.S.M. Groves, who had located the enemy position, dashed across the open to the leading tank and directed its fire from the turret. He then joined the forward platoon in a successful assault. Meanwhile A and D Companies had moved forward to the southern outskirts of the town. As all three companies pressed inwards the Germans withdrew, leaving their wounded in the hospital and a good deal of damaged equipment in the town. Altogether fifty prisoners were captured. On the left the Argylls and the Buffs had been equally successful.

*　　　*　　　*

The Argenta Gap was now but a few miles ahead. To the east lay Lake Comacchio, to the west flooded marshlands; and between these a funnel of firm land. This was a vital defile in the strategic plan. April 14, 15 and 16 were days of great triumph for 78th Division. By the evening of the 16th its Sappers had bridged the River Reno. That night 11th Brigade thrust right through the defences and by midday on the 17th had a foothold in the town of Argenta. In the town itself the Germans made a desperate stand, but by nightfall the Irish Brigade had pressed on and established a bridgehead across the Fossa Marina north-east of Argenta.

It was now time to bring 36th Brigade back into the battle. Brigadier Musson was ordered to pass through the bridgehead over the Fossa Marina, advance quickly up Highway 16, and capture Boccaleone. The 6th Battalion, which was to take the lead, therefore left Conselice on the afternoon of April 17. The first move was to

Bastia, where the battalion was assembled in a large field by 7 p.m. The troops then brewed-up under cover of the hedges in preparation for a night attack. The march to the Forming-Up Position began at 10.30 p.m. To the left strong German forces were still fighting, and heavy fire from that direction threatened a counter-attack in the rear. By 2 a.m. all the men, trucks and tanks had arrived at the F.U.P. without a hitch, however, and last orders had been given out. These were for C Company, with one troop of tanks, to advance northwards along a lane for about two miles and then turn west and attack Boccaleone. B Company, also with tanks in support, were to follow and be prepared to pass through. The other two companies were held back.

At 2.30 a.m. on April 18, C Company passed through the bridge-head across the Fossa Marina and began to move cautiously along the moonlit lane. After brushing aside slight resistance and capturing ten prisoners, the place was reached where the company was to turn westwards for the assault on Boccaleone. It was now dawn, the ground was open, and the two leading platoons were very exposed as they moved towards the village. Machine-gun fire from a group of buildings threatened to stop the advance, but Serjeant Statham led his platoon forward at great speed and silenced the post with his Tommy-gun. The impetus was maintained by Major Stewart, who charged with the other platoon and captured an anti-tank gun and its crew without a shot being fired. The clearing of the houses then began. When the main street was reached, German machine guns opened fire from a farmhouse. Major Stewart was wounded in the leg. While he lay helpless in the open, Lance-Corporal Sharp, a signaller who had remained with his Company Commander although his wireless set was an obvious target, ran to him and helped him to safety. The whole area had abruptly blazed into life, and Major Stewart continued to direct operations from a house nearby in spite of his wound. He immediately called for smoke from the artillery and sent a platoon to deal with the enemy in the farmhouse. This platoon was led by Lieutenant Cooke with such dash that it quickly overran the post and captured ten prisoners. Another platoon and two tanks then moved up the main street. Within an hour fifty more Germans had surrendered.

Nevertheless the Germans were still in considerable strength in Boccaleone. B Company (commanded by Captain Joubert, a South African) had already thrust forward northwards three-quarters of a mile to a lateral road and were fully committed. In consequence A Company (now commanded by Captain Court) were sent to sweep the south-western corner of the village. But they were met by a combination of mortar and machine-gun fire which held them up 200 yards short of their objective. At 9.30 a.m., when Colonel Defrates was about to commit D Company, the Brigade Commander arrived with the comforting news that the Argylls were on their way round the right flank to attack Consandolo. This would relieve the pressure on the battalion. The leading company of the Argylls, turning west too soon, became heavily involved with the enemy in Boccaleone. But they were soon redirected and went on to a notable victory at Consandolo.

For the remainder of the day A and C Companies were occupied in clearing the south-western part of Boccaleone. That night D Company went out to comb the banks of the River Reno. There was very little opposition, and before dawn on the 19th, with the co-operation of other units, Highway 16 from Argenta to Consandolo had been secured. During the whole battle the battalion had captured 143 prisoners, while its losses had been five killed and fifteen wounded. Major Shaun Stewart was awarded a second bar to his M.C. for his stirring leadership (see Appendix A).

4. *The 6th Battalion advances to Ferrara*

78th Division was now right through the Argenta Gap. The 6th Battalion was allowed a breathing space of two days in Boccaleone, and then on the evening of April 21 the column of vehicles was again on its way. Colonel Defrates' orders were to follow up the Argylls as far as Chiusa and then to strike north-west, capture Agascello and exploit northwards. This entailed a long night drive through country made dangerous by pockets of Germans, but all went well. By 2 a.m. the troops were debussing at Chiusa, where Colonel Defrates gave a final briefing to his Company Commanders. An hour later B Company, supported by a troop of tanks, moved off along the road towards Agascello to secure the southern entrances to the village. Behind them moved D Company and three more tanks directed on the northern part of Agascello. A Company gave flank protection to the Chiusa area; C Company remained in reserve.

B Company advanced up the road with only one disturbing incident. This was when a German self-propelled gun and a machine-gun raked part of the road for a few minutes. After a pause the company continued on its way and reached the outskirts of Agascello just before dawn. The leading platoon then encountered some enemy armoured cars hidden in a small wood; one car was knocked out by a P.I.A.T., and the tanks came up and successfully ended a short

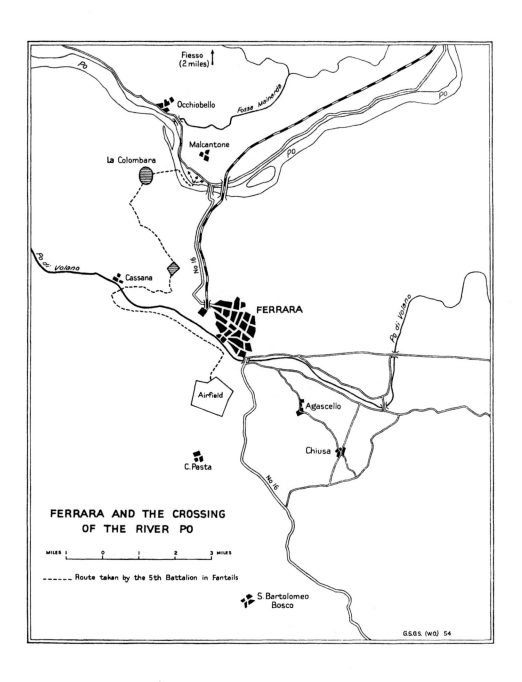

Fiesso
(2 miles)↑

Po

Occhiobello

Fossa Mainarda

Malcantone

La Colombara

Po

No. 16

Po di Volano

Cassana

FERRARA

Po di Volano

Airfield

Agascello

Chiusa

C. Pasta

No. 16

FERRARA AND THE CROSSING
OF THE RIVER PO

MILES 1   0   1   2   3 MILES

------ Route taken by the 5th Battalion in Fantails

S. Bartolomeo
Bosco

G.S.G.S. (W.O.) 54

but brisk engagement. On entering the village the company was met by bursts of fire from several directions, but the tanks disabled a German half-track vehicle, which was causing much of the trouble, and a foothold was gained in the southern end of Agascello. D Company then moved through to the northern part of the village, searching houses and winkling out Germans on the way. No major action developed. Sniping went on until ten, when the village was clear.

This rapid success caused a change of plan. A and C Companies pressed on northwards, capturing a few prisoners on the way. They discovered that all the bridges over the Po di Volano had been destroyed, and patrols of C Company, probing westwards, reached Highway 16 just south of Ferrara. They met no Germans, but the whole of this area was overlooked by the churches and tall buildings in the town, so that any movement brought mortar fire and sniping from the enemy. The battalion had now completed its task. Later in the day 8th Indian Division passed along Highway 16 to clear Ferrara, but for the battalion the night passed peacefully. The following evening, April 23, the companies concentrated in Agascello, where, free of all commitments, they went into billets.

5. *The 5th Battalion Crosses the River Po*

The 5th Battalion came forward into the battle with 8th Indian Division. After four days near San Agata it had marched a few miles north-east to a concentration area at Maiano. On April 22, when the division began to advance towards the River Po, the battalion moved in M.T. to San Bartolomeo Bosco, and at five that evening began a long sweep on foot across country through Casa Pasta to Cassana on the Po di Volano, where two bridges were captured intact. This sweep was carried out on two different routes, mostly in darkness, over a distance of some fifteen miles. Enemy strong-points were avoided, and the thrust successfully split the German resistance in two.

After only a short rest the battalion set off again at six next morning, April 23, with two companies forward and a squadron of tanks of the North Irish Horse in support. The advance continued smoothly, with but slight resistance from the enemy. In fact many groups of Germans surrendered without firing a shot. At 10.45 a.m. a patrol of D Company, led by Lieutenant Morgan, reached the River Po one mile west of Occhiobello, and the forward companies then moved up to the south bank. During this advance the battalion

AA

suffered no casualties. By four in the afternoon 156 prisoners, fifty horses and several vehicles in running order had been captured. That night was uneventful.

The following day, as the battalion was so far the only unit of the 8th Army to have reached the river, the troops lay low so as not to disclose their presence to the enemy. On the morning of the 25th the battalion was relieved by the Mahrattas and moved back eight miles to the area of Ferrara aerodrome.

Preparations then began for the crossing of the River Po. Thirty-six transporters, each carrying a Fantail, arrived and parked in neat rows on the aerodrome. A hectic hour followed, during which details of how to load stores, embark troops and lower ramps were learned. Each Fantail was to carry one whole platoon, and some rude comments were made by the troops when they found out that these amphibious vehicles were not bullet-proof. By 4 p.m. air and artillery programmes had been arranged; the Sappers had prepared the approaches to the river; the route had been marked by the military police; all the Fantails had been loaded, down to the last jeep and anti-tank gun; and the column was on its way to the assembly area about a mile east of Cassana. During the day small arms fire from the enemy had beaten back several attempts by the Mahrattas to launch assault boats. Colonel Malcolmson therefore decided not to make the crossing in daylight. 'H' hour was fixed at 9.15 p.m. Before dark the R.A.F. gave an impressive display of dive-bombing, and at last light the column of Fantails moved to the forward assembly area near La Colombara, about 1,000 yards from the south bank of the river. The artillery programme of H.E. and smoke on to the enemy positions on the far bank then began. The Germans replied with a little inaccurate shelling.

At 'H' hour the first wave of Fantails moved off to the river. The place selected for the crossing was some two miles south of Occhiobello, on the west side of a wide loop of the river. At this point the river was 400 yards wide with steep banks. When the leading Fantail reached the water's edge a vertical drop of eight feet presented an unexpected problem. The Sappers immediately got busy with a Sherman-dozer and an ordinary bulldozer and, after a call for more smoke from the artillery, a slipway into the water was constructed. At 10.10 p.m. the first Fantail entered the river. The only resistance offered by the Germans was a little ill-aimed small arms fire, some inaccurate mortar fire and quantities of Very lights of every colour, which fortunately failed to bring down their defensive fire—at any rate in the right place.

The first and succeeding waves of Fantails were carried some hundreds of yards down stream by the strong current, and they landed on a mudbank. This somewhat disorganised the disembarkation, but by 10.30 p.m. the two leading companies had penetrated the thick scrub on the north bank and had reached the first objective, which was a lateral road some 300 yards north of the river. As the companies advanced the Germans withdrew rapidly, leaving some dead and wounded and a score of prisoners. These companies therefore pressed on, practically unopposed, north to the Fossa Mainarda and east to a railway embankment, which were the final objectives. By 4.30 a.m. on April 26 the whole fighting echelon of the battalion was firmly established in the bridgehead, with headquarters at Malcantone, A Company (Captain Harmer) and C Company (Major Harper) on the eastern perimeter, and B Company (Major Huckson) and D Company (Major Grimsey) along the northern. Before dawn other units of 21st Indian Brigade were also over the river.

With very little time for preparation the 5th Battalion had crossed one of the major river obstacles in Western Europe with no casualties. The enemy, it is true, were by now completely demoralised. The remains of their transport and equipment, which lay discarded in fields, lanes, farmyards and ditches, bore witness to this fact. But this unexpectedly rapid crossing of the River Po enabled the pursuit to be continued twenty-four hours sooner than had been hoped, and undoubtedly did much to undermine the German resistance. 8th Indian Division sped on. On the night of April 27 the leading brigade crossed the river Adige, fifteen miles beyond the Po. On April 30 Padua fell. This was virtually the end, for on May 2 the unconditional surrender of the German Armies in Italy was announced.

The 5th Battalion did not cross the River Adige. Having concentrated in its bridgehead over the River Po while the remainder of 8th Indian Division went through, the battalion moved four miles north to Fiesso on April 30. There the troops enjoyed the long rest which they had hoped for. The war in Europe had ended before they moved again.

6. *The War Ends for the 5th and 6th Battalions*

Nor was the 6th Battalion called upon to do any more fighting. Officers and men rested luxuriously in the peaceful oasis of Agascello while the din of war rolled northwards. Another 'White Horse Inn' was organised, and leave into nearby Ferrara began. In fact, when the news of the capitulation of the Germans in Italy was received some of the troops were on day pass in that town; but after nightfall they all trickled back to the battalion area, where much of the tracer ammunition and all the flares were being expended in a gigantic *feu de joie*. There were indeed sounds of revelry that night.

It was perhaps just as well that the battalion left Agascello the following afternoon. A long drive northwards across the River Po and north-eastwards past Venice ended at midnight at Sacile in the foothills of the Alps. Next day the collection and sorting out of prisoners of war began. The Italians were very friendly, the billets were comfortable and it was unfortunate that the stay at Sacile was short. Early on May 7 the battalion moved on into the mountains. The task given to Colonel Defrates was to seek out a group of Germans who had refused to surrender and were planning to continue resistance in the hills some seventy miles away. On arriving at San Stefano the battalion split into two parties and began to scour the roads. But, although some Italian partisans, a group of Georgians and a band of marauding Cossacks were encountered, no hostile parties were found. That evening, personnel at Battalion Headquarters, peacefully listening to the B.B.C., were scarcely prepared for the shattering news that Germany had everywhere surrendered unconditionally to the Allies. The war in Europe was over! Without delay a party was organised in the hotel at Forni Avoltri, with the local Italians enthusiastically joining in the dance and song.

The following evening the battalion moved on across the Austrian border to Griefenburg. Into the area were streaming the remnants of several armies in trucks, on mules, on bicycles and on foot; and the battalion was given the tasks first of supervising several of their camps, and then of repatriating the personnel. The latter was an unpleasant and distressing duty, for many of the refugees had a growing terror of falling into the hands of the Russians. In July, after these tasks had been completed, the battalion was engaged in the normal routine of garrison duties, with plenty of time for riding and swimming, seven days' leave at a mountain lake in the neighbourhood, and, for some, even leave to England.

At Griefenburg a Remembrance Service was held. During the service a great Cross, rough-hewn from a stout Austrian pine, was dedicated as a memorial to the men of the battalion who had been killed between October 1942 and May 1945. Their names were inscribed on it.

*   *   *

For the 5th Battalion the war ended very differently. It was still at Fiesso when Germany capitulated, and Victory in Europe or V.E. Day (May 8) was celebrated by each company individually. After that, trips to Venice were organised each day. On May 22 a move to Spoleto, near Lake Trasimene, was made by road and rail. There, on the 28th, a Guard of Honour was found for General Sir Claude Auchinleck, who congratulated the battalion on its fine record of service.

A complete reorganisation of the battalion then took place. War was still being waged against Japan, and the intention was that all infantry personnel with less than one year and nine months' continuous service overseas should have a short spell in England and then be sent to the Far East. The 5th Battalion was one of the units earmarked to proceed. All ranks ineligible for service in the Far East were posted away from the battalion to other units, and drafts of eligible personnel arrived to replace them. When this had been done, the reorganised 5th Battalion moved by rail to Lammie, near Naples. Embarkation took place on June 27, and next day the battalion sailed, forty-four officers and 966 other ranks strong, in the *Georgic* for England.

CHAPTER 22

The First Battalion in Greece
December 1944 to August 1945

1. *Street Fighting in Athens*

WHEN the 1st Battalion arrived in the Bay of Piraeus on December 15, 1944, it was at first thought that the troops might have to fight their way ashore. But a reconnaissance party landed without incident and, by nightfall, the companies were in billets in tactical positions in a beach-head south-west of Athens. Although the arrival of the battalion had not been opposed, numerous rifle shots were heard in the area during the night, and it was clear that difficult operations lay ahead.

The cause of the trouble in Greece was a political schism which had torn her for many years. Even the subjugation of the country by the Germans in the spring of 1941 had failed to unite the various political parties, and active hostility had divided the partisan guerrilla bands in their camps in the mountains. In spite of the efforts of British liaison officers, who were dropped by parachute to train them, some of the bands had actually aligned themselves with the Germans. As the years passed the rival groups had merged into two main parties, which became known as ELAS (the Greek People's Liberation Army) and EDES, the right-wing party.

When the Germans had begun to withdraw their forces from Greece in the summer of 1944, a conference had been held by the Allied High Command at Caserta. At this conference both ELAS and EDES had agreed that British troops should be given the task of reoccupying Greece. British air-borne troops had landed near Athens in mid-October 1944, and had received a great welcome from the population. On October 19 Lieutenant-General R. MacK. Scobie, who had been G.O.C. in Malta eighteen months earlier, had arrived to command the Land Forces in Greece and had entered Athens with the Greek Prime Minister and his Government. For a time all had gone well. But on December 2 the ELAS members of the Greek Government had resigned. A general strike had then been declared. ELAS troops had attacked the Naval Headquarters and had attempted to seize the reins of government. To prevent this General Scobie had ordered all ELAS formations to leave Athens by December 7, under penalty of being declared hostile. Instead they tried to seize the capital by force, and 4th Division had been hurriedly despatched from Italy to deal with the situation.

When the 1st Battalion landed, key appointments were held as follows:—

Commanding Officer	Lt.-Col. H. P. Braithwaite, D.S.O.
Second-in-command	Major D. H. Gwilliam
Adjutant	Capt. D. S. Scull
Quartermaster	Capt. R. C. E. Mines
O.C. HQ Company	Major E. G. Reeves
O.C. S Company	Capt. S. F. H. Glynn
O.C. B Company	Major H. B. H. Waring
O.C. C Company	Major H. P. Towers-Minors
O.C. D Company	Major H. N. Raisin

A Company, which had been disbanded in Italy, had not yet been re-formed.

The situation ashore was very confused, but it appeared that two British brigades were holding a narrow strip of the coast and a small portion of Athens. In the capital itself the British were having a lively engagement with ELAS troops, who were difficult to identify because as a rule they wore no uniform. The immediate task of the battalion was to defend a sector of the beach-head, and this was manned on December 16.

Two days passed quietly enough. As the ELAS troops could readily slip through the lines as civilians, the Greeks were only allowed out of their homes between midday and four in the afternoon, and they then had to be checked and searched in company areas before they were allowed to proceed. There were no incidents. On the evening of the 17th the sector of the beach-head was handed over, and the battalion was placed in brigade reserve, remaining in the same billets. Later that evening the original advance party rejoined from Palestine.

During the night British troops began to clear the way to Athens. 28th Brigade of 4th Division advanced up Singros Avenue from the coast and, creeping along with rubber-soled shoes, were two miles inland by dawn on the 18th and had captured the Brewery by ten.

On December 19 the 1st Battalion, with 144th Battalion of the Greek National Guard (G.N.G.) under command, began the task

of clearing the suburbs on the left of Singros Avenue. The advance
began at eight in the morning with C and D Companies leading
and S in support; B Company was away operating with another
unit. One company of the G.N.G. was placed under command of
each of the leading companies to follow up and carry out a methodical
search of every house and building for arms, ammunition and
ELAS troops. The leading companies soon came under small arms
fire, but the opposition, although troublesome, was not organised.
The advance from room to room, house to house and street to street
against an enemy in civilian clothes was very slow, and the same
neighbourhood always had to be searched twice. By noon the
opposition had slackened to long-range sniping. At two in the
afternoon the leading companies were firmly established on a lateral
road about a mile inland, and S Company passed through in order
to clear the area of a school. There was no opposition, but from the
ammunition and equipment found in the school it was apparent that
it had only recently been evacuated by ELAS troops. At four all
companies consolidated without interference from the enemy. During
the evening and night the area occupied by D Company came under
mortar fire, and direct hits on some houses caused several casualties.
B Company had by now rejoined the battalion.

Consolidation required careful organisation. It was dangerous
to occupy a house with anything less than a platoon unless two
houses actually adjoined, and each building occupied had to be
made a strongly defended post. One section normally manned
positions outside the building in order to prevent the enemy from
creeping up to it. Another section manned posts inside the house.
The third rested in a reserve role. The G.N.G. assembled within the
battalion area. Their knowledge of the language and of the people
had proved to be invaluable, and to their thorough searching must
be attributed the fact that no casualties were suffered from the enemy
in rear. Hot meals were brought up on trucks by the cooks to companies soon after the battalion had consolidated, though the troops
had carried a twenty-four hour man pack in case of emergency.
In order to avoid mistaking the enemy for our own troops, movement
at night was kept down to a minimum, but patrols between platoons
and Company Headquarters were maintained.

On December 20 the battalion continued the advance with three
companies leading. Determined resistance was quickly met on the
left, and four tanks were called up to help by engaging numerous
sniper positions. By noon fair progress had been made on both
flanks, but in the centre our troops were still locked in a battle for
a house. A tank then put twelve rounds gun fire straight into the

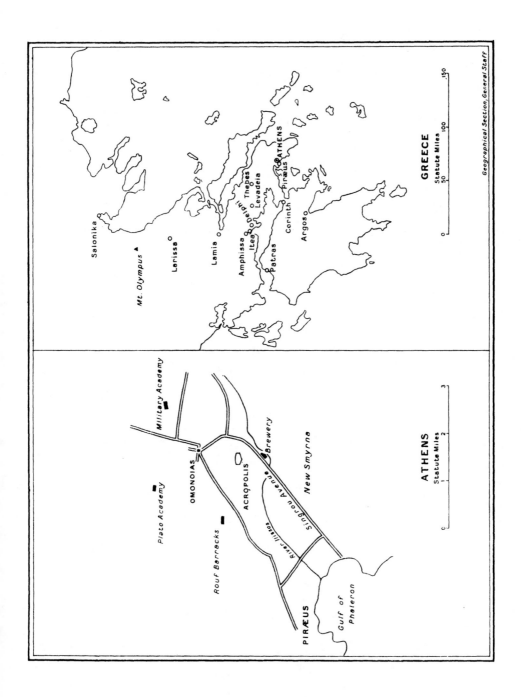

GREECE

Statute Miles

0   50   100   150

Geographical Section, General Staff

Salonika

Mt. Olympus ▲

Larissa ○

Lamia ○

Amphissa ○ Delphi ○ Thebes ○
Itea ○   Levadeia ○

Patras ○

Corinth ○ Piraeus ● ATHENS
Argos ○

ATHENS

Statute Miles

0   1   2   3

Military Academy

Plato Academy

OMONOIAS

Rouf Barracks

ACROPOLIS

River Ilissos

Singrou Avenue

Brewery

New Smyrna

PIRÆUS

Gulf of Phaleron

building. Despite this, attempts to enter brought grenades and rifle fire from the windows, and the storming party was forced to withdraw. A repeat shoot was then called for from the tank and, under cover of a screen produced by smoke grenades, 15 Platoon (Lieutenant Matthews) entered the house and captured seven ELAS youths on the top floor. By two in the afternoon all three companies were level and again moving forward. At four the battalion consolidated on a lateral road, having advanced another mile during the course of the day. There was spasmodic shelling of the battalion area until midnight, but after that all was quiet.

The battalion made no move forward on the 21st, and the opportunity was taken to search the company areas again for suspects, arms and ammunition. On the 22nd a different method of advancing was employed. Two companies, with tanks under command, moved forward as quickly as possible, leaving the mopping up to the other two. The G.N.G. continued the search in the rear. Apart from long-range and inaccurate sniping, progress was unmolested, and the method worked well. In the early afternoon the bend of the River Ilissos was reached. Soon afterwards the battalion consolidated for the night. Progress of another mile had been made that day.

That was the end of the battalion's advance for the time being. Other British formations were steadily closing in on each side, and a strip of safe ground soon joined Piraeus and Athens. For the next three days the battalion area was thoroughly re-searched for warlike stores and any fanatical ELAS troops who might have infiltrated back into it, and a considerable quantity of food, ammunition and dynamite was collected by the companies.

On Christmas Eve and again on Christmas Day companies were placed under command of the 2nd Royal Fusiliers to help clear their area. During these operations 18 Platoon (Lieutenant McLelland) captured a bridge over the Ilissos and found it to be prepared for demolition. A quantity of gelignite and some telermines were removed together with eighty gallons of petrol. Next day a fighting patrol found a large ELAS food dump in a house. Attempts to load the food on to trucks were hindered by enemy fire, but after dark six tons of food were brought away.

The celebration of Christmas Day was officially postponed by order of General Scobie. The day itself was certainly no festival for the battalion. In addition to the operations mentioned above, the house to house search went on as usual. The weather was bitterly cold, cigarettes were in short supply, and rations were limited to bully beef, M. and V., and biscuits.

By December 26 the battalion area was considered to be free

from enemy, and the next few days passed quietly enough. The night of the 28th was somewhat disturbed by a clash between a band of ELAS youths and a patrol of the Greek National Guard. The troops stood-to, but the din soon ceased and Colonel Braithwaite gave stand-down after half an hour. On the 30th the whole battalion moved to Rouf Barracks in defence of that area.

During the fourteen days of street fighting the battalion had suffered twenty-seven casualties, of whom three had been killed and twenty-four, including Lieutenant Archdeacon and Lance-Serjeant Shaw, wounded. The majority of the casualties had been in D Company.

*   *   *

The next task was to clear the central part of Athens. The battalion was to attack north-eastwards from Rouf Barracks towards Plato Academy. The troops were restrained by strict orders from any action that could possibly damage the historic parts of the city, and wide safety circles were drawn on the officers' maps round every building of importance.

After some sharp shelling of the battalion area on the night of January 2, 1945, B Company left the barracks on the afternoon of the 3rd and secured the start-line for the attack without incident. Early next morning C Company joined B on the start-line, and at 8.30 both companies began to advance, each with two tanks and a section of Sappers or Pioneers under command. C Company quickly encountered a road block made of stones and bricks and an old car, but, after the Sappers had searched it for mines, one of the tanks smashed through it. Except for slight mortar and machine-gun fire the advance then continued unopposed, with the usual search of rooms and cellars. A large factory was reached by four in the afternoon. It was another hour before C Company, who had become engaged in close fighting for a block of buildings containing an ELAS headquarters, were able to consolidate.

After a quiet night the advance continued, opposed only by spasmodic sniping. The ELAS headquarters, which had held up the advance on the previous day, was . captured together with numerous maps and files, some rifles, ammunition and explosive. By the evening the battalion had reached Plato Academy, having captured sixty-one rifles and 35,000 rounds of ammunition during the day, and the companies consolidated on their final objective. The night was again quiet.

Southern and central Athens had now been occupied and cleared by British forces and the Greek National Guard, and the ELAS troops began to stream out of the northern part of the city, closely followed by mobile British columns. The battalion could thus turn to the more peaceful occupation of feeding the local inhabitants. On January 6 a 'Soup Kitchen' under Captain Galilee opened for business in a block of buildings. During the day 2,000 people were given a free issue of soup and beans. The Greeks' idea of lining up for rations was to fight their way in, and it was some time before they could be persuaded to form an orderly queue. Even then two queues had to be formed, for Greek men and women do not mingle on such occasions. All sorts of tricks were tried by the women in order to 'jump' the queue. Expectant mothers were allowed to the front, and several ladies with cushions under their dresses had to be sent back.

On January 7 the battalion handed over its positions and the pathetic task of feeding the people, and moved back to the New Smyrna area for rest in comfortable billets. The operational side could not be relaxed entirely, for strong guards had to be mounted; but for two days the troops rested, took shower baths and cleaned up generally.

The first phase of the reoccupation of Greece had been completed, and General Scobie issued a congratulatory message to the troops. Extracts from it are:

'I send my warm congratulations to all ranks on the successful outcome of the operations in Athens and Piraeus.

'The prolonged street fighting in the heart of a friendly city has been a sad and most difficult operation of war. In these exceptional and testing circumstances, you have done your duty without fear or favour. Your discomforts have been severe. . . .

'Despite great provocation you have fought with a self-restraint and self-control truly worthy of the British Empire; the minimum of harm was caused to civil life and property, although this sometimes caused you to suffer avoidable casualties. . . .'

2. *The Truce*

ELAS troops had now been driven into the hills, and 4th Division moved north to follow them up. At the head of 12th Brigade the battalion passed through Athens in lorries on January 10 bound for Levadeia, where it received a very subdued welcome from the population. It soon became evident that the citizens were supporters of ELAS, and the companies took up tactical positions in order to defend the town in case of trouble. The dangerous calm prevailed, however, and for the next three days mobile columns at company strength, with machine guns and mortars under command, carried out a systematic search of neighbouring villages. There was no opposition. In fact in most of the villages the inhabitants gave these columns an enthusiastic welcome. In none were any warlike stores found.

Meanwhile a difficult situation had developed in Levadeia. On the evening of January 13, crowds of singing youths and children paraded through the streets. At the same time it was reported that some hundreds of armed ELAS troops were infiltrating back into the town from the mountains. Colonel Braithwaite, who was responsible for the defence of Levadeia, therefore decided to carry out a surprise search of the town next morning. Except for some dynamite hidden in a chimney, nothing was found, but one company of the Royal Fusiliers was sent by Brigade as reinforcements. In the evening reports were received that the power station was to be blown up that night, and the Carrier Platoon was sent to guard it. Nothing occurred.

In Athens General Scobie and the ELAS Central Committee had by this time worked out the terms of a truce to bring the conflict to an end. Fighting was to cease at midnight on January 14, 1945, and all ELAS troops were to withdraw to the northern parts of Greece during the following three days. So, from early on the 15th numerous small parties of ELAS began to pass through Levadeia on their way to the demarcation line, some of them spending a few hours with their friends in the town. Everything went well until the afternoon of the 16th, when part of a unit of the Greek National Guard arrived and came under command of the battalion. This caused another lively demonstration by the Youth League, but there were no serious consequences.

On January 18 the search of neighbouring villages was renewed with varying results. The largest haul of warlike stores was sixty-one shells and seven sticks of dynamite, which were found in a church. On the 25th the battalion began to evacuate non-combatant refugees to Athens for interrogation and disposal, great care being taken that all political parties received identical treatment. These efforts at impartiality obtained the co-operation of the people, and calm prevailed in the town.

The battalion returned in M.T. at the end of January to Athens, where the troops were accommodated in comfortable billets in the town. The festival of Christmas was celebrated on February 3 and, appropriately enough, it was known as 'Scobiemas.' During this rest period the battalion received a visit from Brigadier R. A.

Riddell, who had last served with it at Karachi in 1937. At the beginning of the war he had been D.A.Q.M.G. of 4th Corps, and had then been Commandant of the Administrative Staff School and later the Junior Staff School at Oxford. After a period with the planning staff at the War Office for the invasion of Normandy, he had been head of a British Mission in Australia. At the time of his visit he was on the A/Q Staff of Land Forces Greece.

3. Civil Relief

After three weeks in Athens the battalion moved north on February 19 to Thebes and then, a week later, to Amphissa, Delphi and Itea. Everywhere the troops were given a warm welcome. The people now realised that the sole aim of the British was to help to restore their country to order and prosperity, and there was no lack of co-operation.

The battalion had two tasks to perform at Amphissa. The first was to take over the arms, ammunition and transport of the 2nd ELAS Division which had been surrendered by a final agreement with the ELAS commanders. Once these arms dumps had been taken over, the arms and ammunition had to be collected in the battalion vehicles, and the ELAS troops had to be evacuated to their homes in Athens, Corinth and Thebes.

The second task was to carry out a systematic survey of all the villages in the district. This survey revealed that many of these villages were in a desperate plight. The Germans had done their best to destroy the houses and had driven away the cattle, without which the people could produce no food. The villagers now lacked clothes and medicine as well as food and shelter, and, with the assistance of Red Cross teams, the battalion was called upon to convey these commodities to them.

The relief work in the extensive district of Phokis continued until the end of May. Some of the mountain villages were situated on mule or goat paths and were almost impossible to reach. Before the battalion vehicles could make their way to them, detours had to be constructed and the paths converted into jeep-tracks. This work, which often required a considerable amount of explosive, was carried out excellently by Corporal Henson and the Pioneers; and the M.T. drivers demonstrated their skill in driving their vehicles over appalling roads. Eventually every village in the area was visited and supplied with food, clothing and medical stores. Fuel was also lacking, and the village people were organised into working parties to hew and carry timber from the hills to the sides of the roads, where it was sawn up by a mobile saw bench.

Meanwhile several events of domestic interest had occurred in the battalion. On March 6 the fourth Rifle Company (A), which had been re-forming from reinforcements, arrived from Athens. A few weeks later the vehicles of the Carrier Platoon and most of the remainder of the vehicles of the battalion arrived with the rear party from Italy. On March 24 a detachment of five officers and 120 other ranks took part in the traditional celebration of Greek Independence Day at Missolonghi. Finally May 8, which was Victory in Europe (V.E.) Day, and May 9 were observed as holidays—though there was very little entertainment for the troops in the poverty-stricken villages—and a Thanksgiving Service and Victory Parade were held in Amphissa on May 13.

4. *The End of the War*

As soon as the war in Europe was over the younger soldiers, as in Italy, were to be posted to the Far East. Two officers and 217 other ranks below the rank of serjeant were eligible for posting there, and these were sent as the 'Minerva' Draft at the end of May to join the 5th Battalion. To offset this loss in some measure forty-nine reinforcements were posted in, and in July a draft of 150, including men from the 5th Battalion, arrived.

The battalion had by now handed over many of its tasks to the Greek National Guard and had settled down to more or less normal routine duties. Captain Glynn became Town Major of Amphissa; Major Gwilliam and other personnel went to open a Greek Battle School. A Battalion Rifle Meeting (including the Grove Trust Competition) was held on June 14, and a Battalion Athletic Meeting a few days later. E.N.S.A. shows, concert parties, dances and even water polo matches then became frequent. To complete the return to near peace-time conditions, the battalion moved on August 19 to Larissa, where it was accommodated in barracks.

CHAPTER 23

The Fourth Battalion in Burma
October 1943 to August 1945

1. *Arrival in the Arakan*

SOON after the invasion of Italy by the Allies in September 1943, the 4th Battalion moved to the Arakan, on the west coast of Burma, and became part of General Sir William Slim's 'forgotten' 14th Army. At this time the battalion was commanded by Lieutenant-Colonel H. J. Laverty of the Essex Regiment, and Major T. Kenyon was second-in-command. The Company Commanders were Captain H. C. Smith (HQ), Major P. E. M. Shaw (A) Major J. H. Winstanley (B) and Major C. B. E. Williams (C). Captain L. A. Carey (then Adjutant) took command of D Company when it was re-formed shortly after entering the Arakan; Captain J. D. K. Short then became Adjutant. The battalion still belonged to 161st Brigade of 5th Indian Division (Major-General H. R. Briggs). The other two brigades in the division were 9th and 123rd. 161st Brigade was commanded by Brigadier D. F. W. Warren, and the other two battalions in the brigade were the 1st/1st Punjabis and the 4th/7th Rajputs.

In order to obtain a clear picture of the campaign in the Arakan in the autumn of 1943, it is necessary to recall the course of events in Burma since it was invaded from Siam by the Japanese in January 1942. The invasion was opposed by 17th Indian Division, but, after a fortnight of fighting against superior Japanese forces, this division was forced to fall back to the River Salween. By February 20 a retreat to the Sittang River was imperative and, with the one bridge demolished prematurely, only a portion of the division contrived to cross and join the British forces about Rangoon.

On March 5 General Alexander took command of the British forces. Although he could not save Rangoon, he organised an orderly retreat with his whole force, including transport and artillery, to Prome and linked up with the 1st Burma Division at Toungoo. There was no hope of reinforcements, because there was no port at which to land them, and a grim race with the Japanese followed. For our troops and a mass of civilians there was no way out but a six-hundred mile march through jungle and mountains. On March 24 the Japanese resumed their offensive and captured both Prome and Toungoo. At the end of April they stood before Mandalay, and the retreat continued. The routes were little more than jungle paths, and thousands of refugees encumbered them. But by May 17 Alexander's force and this mass of humanity was concentrated at Imphal, where the troops stood on the defensive while the refugees plodded on to safety. The way to India was barred.

The monsoon rain then intervened, and five months passed, during which both sides built up their forces. At the end of this period the British launched a small-scale offensive in the Arakan. The intention was to attack south from Chittagong, which port was still in our hands, and capture Akyab, itself a useful port. Bad weather delayed the operation, and it was not till December 1942 that the British advance began. Movement was slow owing to the difficulty of bringing forward supplies along bad roads, and when an attack was made on Rathedaung on January 6, 1943, the Japanese had been reinforced and were well dug in. Four successive attacks were launched in vain. The Japanese then carried out an out-flanking movement and, in order to avoid encirclement, the British withdrew. On May 12 Maungdaw, which had been built up as an advanced base, was evacuated. The operation had failed.

The Japanese advanced no farther than Maungdaw and stayed there during the monsoon period that summer. Several months of static warfare and active patrolling then followed, and it was not till the end of December 1943 that the British made another advance in the Arakan. By that time the whole of 5th Indian Division was disposed north of Maungdaw and was ready to do battle against the Japanese for the first time.

The 4th Battalion had arrived at Chittagong on October 29 after an uneventful four days' voyage from Calcutta in the *Ethiopia*. From there the journey had been continued for some fifty miles by train to rail-head at Dohazari and thence on foot. The heat had been intense and the road thick with dust, which was thrown into the faces of the marching troops by passing vehicles; and after the first day it had been decided to march only at night. This was cooler and less dusty, but the mosquitoes were more unpleasant. After seven days' marching the battalion had rested and trained for a few days and had then moved forward to Chota Maunghnama, where 161st Indian Brigade was in reserve. This last move had involved the crossing of a *chaung* (river) which had not yet been bridged, and ferrying across it in *sampans* had been very slow.

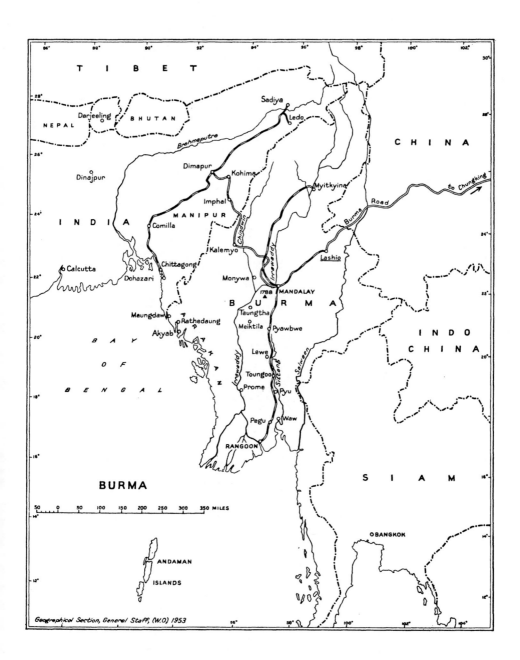

BURMA

50 0 50 100 150 200 250 300 350 MILES

ANDAMAN
ISLANDS

Geographical Section, General Staff, (W.O.) 1953

At Chota Maunghnama the battalion carried out patrols east across the Mayu range of hills and west into the swampy ground on the banks of the Naf River. There were no important incidents, but much knowledge was gained of the difficult country. A Company was on a feature in the centre of the Ngakyedauk Pass, and the troops soon simplified the name of this gap through the hills to the 'Okidoke' Pass. The main difficulty for A Company was that all their supplies, including rations and water, had to be taken up to them by mule transport. Later on a jeep track was made through the Pass; later still this was widened into a road.

On December 14, 1943, an open jeep brought a V.I.P. to visit the division. This was Lord Louis Mountbatten, who had just taken over the new appointment of Supreme Allied Commander South East Asia. The 'Supremo,' in Naval uniform, had a profound effect on the morale of the troops when he addressed them, and, in turn, their cheerfulness and enthusiasm did much to dispel any misgivings he might have had about their confidence and will to win.

A few days before Christmas, 161st Brigade moved forward a little and took over part of the defensive line. The Punjabis were on the left in some scrub-covered hills, and the 4th Battalion was on the right in some small hills overlooking the Naf River. The surrounding landscape was a series of tangled, narrow ridges separated by mountain streams and covered with dense scrub. Between the ridges were many small and isolated paddy fields. This country was ideal for defence, for movement across it was difficult for infantry as well as tanks.

In front of the battalion's position was the Hathipauk *chaung*, across which, and four hundred yards away, was Point 124. The enemy was on Point 124 and in its vicinity, but the policy was to leave him in peace while reconnaissance patrols found out as much as possible about his strength and positions in readiness for the forthcoming attack. As a result Christmas passed quietly. With the arrival of a draft of reinforcements, D Company was re-formed. This draft had only a short period of training before the attack began.

2. *The Advance to the Maungdaw-Buthidaung Road*

The object of the offensive was to capture the metalled road which ran laterally from the port of Maungdaw through tunnels in the Mayu Range to Buthidaung. This lateral road was vital, for so long as the Japanese controlled it they were able to move troops speedily from one side of the hills to the other, while our forces lacked a suitable means of lateral communication. The great obstacle that barred the

BB

way to the capture of this road was the so-called fortress of Razabil. Here, on a series of hillocks about the cross-roads, the Japanese had dug skilfully-selected positions. Before these positions could be assaulted the low hills in front of them had to be secured. This task was given to 161st Brigade.

The first of these hills was Point 124, which lay on the west of the main road. The plan for the capture of it involved all three battalions of the brigade. The Rajputs were to carry out the main attack from the north-west; the 4th Battalion, less two companies, was to move round from the east behind Point 124 on the previous day to act as a stop; and the Punjabis were to advance and occupy positions on the east of the road to conform with the main advance.

On the night of December 30 the 4th Battalion, less A and D Companies, moved in single file along a route previously taped by the Intelligence Officer, Lieutenant Dungay, and occupied positions in rear of Point 124 to prevent any large parties of enemy from approaching or withdrawing from that feature. This difficult night march was carried out exactly as planned and was uneventful. All platoons were in position by first light. The troops then lay low with the intention of not making their presence known to the enemy, while the Rajputs began their attack.

The Japanese positions had been so well chosen that the Rajputs were forced to attack continuously for six days before they were successful. Each scrub-covered hillock had a ring of trenches round the summit with little tunnels leading to a cave inside the hill, and each was covered by the fire of machine guns on fixed lines from other hillocks. When a particular hill was attacked the defenders would fire a Very light and take cover in the cave. All posts giving covering fire would then open up with their machine guns on the post being attacked. If the assaulting troops managed to get close to the post in spite of this fire, the defenders would lob showers of grenades over the parapet. Thus opposed, the attacks proved too costly, and it was eventually decided to adopt a policy of starvation and attrition.

Under the impression that the operation would be short, the troops of the 4th Battalion had travelled light, wearing only canvas patrol boots instead of ammunition boots and carrying only light rations. By the second day their feet were getting soft through wading in the paddy fields and their rations were running out. It was therefore decided to send forward rations and the men's packs, which contained a blanket and groundsheet, on carriers. Because of streams and obstacles the only route for the carriers was down the road, and because the matter was urgent the task was carried out in daylight.

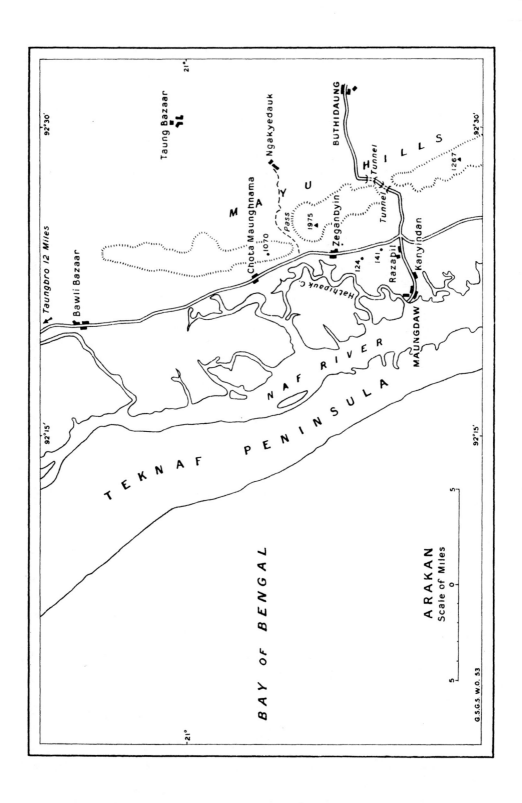

BAY OF BENGAL

NAF RIVER

TEKNAF PENINSULA

ARAKAN
Scale of Miles

G.S.G.S. W.O. 53

Taungbro 12 Miles

Bawli Bazaar

Taung Bazaar

Chota Maunghnama

Ngakyedauk

M A Y U

Pass

·1070

·1975

Zeganbyin

BUTHIDAUNG

H I L L S

Tunnel

Tunnel

·1267

124·

141·

Razabil

Kanyindan

Hatligauk C.

MAUNGDAW

21°

92°30'

92°15'

92°30'

92°15'

21°

Under cover of smoke put down by the artillery the carriers arrived safely. But the movement was observed by the Japanese. The carriers were shelled while they were being unloaded at Battalion Head-quarters, and casualties were three killed, including C.S.M. Gammon of HQ Company and Provost Serjeant King, and three wounded, including R.S.M. Bowler. These were the first casualties in the battalion in Burma. The carriers made a second journey that evening without enemy interference.

It is probable that the Japanese thought that these moves by the carriers were either patrols or part of the scheme for the attack, for they still did not know of the presence of the battalion in the area. That night a Japanese patrol, some twenty strong, tried to get through to their friends on Point 124. It was quite unprepared for a fight, and three of the enemy were killed. The next day, January 2, was quiet and uneventful. During the night A and D Companies joined the remainder of the battalion in order to close some of the gaps through which the enemy might slip. Later that night another enemy patrol tried to get through, but it ran off after gaining contact.

Two more quiet days followed. On the night of the 4th, C Company began to infiltrate towards Point 124 from the south in conjunction with renewed action by the Rajputs from the north-west. Some opposition was met from snipers and machine guns. Next day the probing attacks continued, and that afternoon A Company moved forward to a feature closer to Point 124 and dug in. During the night a wind sprang up and there was heavy rain. On the morning of January 7, A Company as well as C began to advance northwards, and both companies reached the area of Point 124 without opposition. The Japanese had slipped away during the night under cover of the rain and wind.

During the whole operation the battalion's casualties had been one warrant officer and seven others killed, and one warrant officer and nine others wounded. The Japanese casualties were difficult to assess because their positions had been badly damaged by shell-fire. Many bodies must have been buried in their ruined trenches.

*   *   *

At dawn on January 9, 1944, the 4th Battalion began to advance southwards towards Point 141, the next hill that intervened before the fortress of Razabil. The leading companies, B and D, went forward under the assumption that the hill was held by the enemy, but, on receiving a report that it was clear, D Company on the left closed in and moved down the main road. In the tangle of hills they passed Point 141. Suddenly they were fired on from all sides. The whole company was in the open and was thrown into confusion. One platoon managed to get to some sort of cover on a feature and return the fire, and this gave the remainder of the company an opportunity to collect the wounded and get to cover. The mules were some distance to the rear under C.S.M. Haines who, hearing the firing, came up with a small party of mule-leaders. He then rallied another platoon and led it up the slopes of a feature, where it dug in. At dusk the remainder of the company, carrying the wounded, assembled on this feature and consolidated. In this way D Company were saved from disaster, but their casualties had been heavy.

In the meantime B Company had been moving south on a parallel route on the right of D Company. Their advance was along ridges and was therefore slow, and when that company was fired on they had not yet reached Point 141. When the sounds of conflict were heard a platoon was sent towards that feature to create a diversion, but it came under heavy fire and was ordered to return. B Company then consolidated. That ended the day's advance. During the night both companies were able to evacuate their casualties.

Next morning, January 10, B Company moved on southwards and, at the expense of some casualties, turned east round the rear of the enemy before they came under fire and were held up. C Company had in the meantime taken up a position north of Point 141 and had engaged the enemy. With D Company in position to the east, the Japanese were now encircled, and the fire of all weapons was directed on them. Their position became untenable. That night they pulled out, leaving a large quantity of ammunition and four flags in our hands. Thus the action, which had begun with a setback, ended in triumph.

That night B and C Companies moved into positions so that they could watch, if not dominate, the Razabil Fortress. In daylight A Company pushed farther to the south and took up a position on a feature astride the road to Maungdaw. These positions were maintained for five days until January 15, when the companies began to concentrate back north of Razabil. On the 17th the whole battalion was withdrawn to an area north of Point 124 for a few days' rest. The total casualties since December 30 had been twenty-three killed and fifty wounded.

3. *The Capture of Razabil*

A full-scale offensive against the Japanese-held hillocks round the cross-roads at Razabil was now prepared. The plan was that our

Air Force should bomb targets in the area, and that the battalions of 161st Brigade should then attack through the foot-hills to the cross-roads. In support of these battalions would be the 25th Dragoons (General Lee tanks), which had now come forward secretly in darkness.

The 4th Battalion moved eastwards from Point 124 on the night of January 24 and took over the positions then occupied by the Punjabis, who were to clear a series of hillocks to the north-east of the Razabil cross-roads as a preliminary to the main attack. Next morning the Punjabis began their attack. Several Japanese posts were overrun, but heavy and skilful cross-fire prevented further advances. The hoped-for break through on this flank was unsuccessful.

On January 26, dive-bombers roared overhead, and a pall of dust and smoke soon hung over Razabil. But the bombing was not effective owing to the depth of the enemy bunkers, and the Rajputs only managed to gain a footing in the Japanese positions west of the road, where they dug in. The attack on this flank had also failed.

Meanwhile patrols from the 4th Battalion had found that two hillocks to the east of the road were clear of enemy. These were occupied on the night of January 27. Next morning C Company, supported by tanks, attacked a third hillock. The tanks engaged the neighbouring enemy positions with machine guns, and under cover of this fire C Company moved up the hill and had nearly reached the top when a shower of grenades forced them back. Further fire from the tanks enabled our troops to move forward again and, coming within throwing range, they hurled grenades into the enemy trenches and drove the Japanese from the hill. Our casualties in this action were two killed and four, including Lieutenant Rogers, wounded. Corporal Hay and his stretcher-bearers did gallant work in carrying back the wounded under fire.

After this minor success the battalion moved westwards again and took over positions from the Rajputs west of the main road. The attack was not resumed. The main task of the infantry was to locate the Japanese bunkers, which were very cunningly concealed, and to report their position to the artillery. The 'bunker-busting' medium guns would then open fire and with their fifth round they would often destroy a bunker. The Japanese would then build up the bunker again during the night, only for it to be destroyed a few days later. That the enemy was using large quantities of timber on the reconstruction of bunkers was confirmed by Serjeant Brooks, who led a patrol through a Japanese outpost and established it on a position from which it could observe the movements of the enemy.

*   *   *

After the failure of this attack it was decided to switch our main offensive further to the east. This offensive—an attack on Buthidaung by 7th Indian Division—was due to start on February 8. But the preparations were not yet complete when the enemy, who had passed the better part of a division through the jungle round the left flank of 7th Indian Division, attacked first. This Japanese force captured Taung Bazaar on February 5 and, swinging south-west, struck at the 'Okidoke' Pass. Within a short time 7th Indian Division was completely encircled. The Japanese expected that it would withdraw. But they reckoned without one factor—supply by air. 7th Indian Division grouped into perimeters and stood their ground, and for two weeks food, water and ammunition were delivered to them from above. The enemy, on the other hand, had only supplies for ten days. Unable to overwhelm our troops, they broke up into small parties to fight their way back through the jungle, leaving five thousand dead behind them.

During this battle for the 'Okidoke' Pass 161st Brigade was required to extend its front facing Razabil and to contain the enemy there, while the remainder of 5th Indian Division took on the task of opening up the Pass. The 4th Battalion became responsible for an area previously held by two battalions, and several adjustments were required in the company commitments. But neither side had more than a holding force on this front. Except for patrolling, harassing fire and sniping, the period was comparatively inactive. Many of our patrols infiltrated through the enemy lines by night and, lying up by day, brought back valuable information of the enemy's movements. From this information the plans for a second assault on the Razabil Fortress were made; and 161st Brigade moved back to a concentration area near the 'Okidoke' Pass on March 4 in order to prepare for this operation. The troops were at last able to bathe and make up some lost sleep.

*   *   *

Frontal assaults having failed, the new plan was to attack the group of defended hillocks known as the Razabil Fortress from the rear. 161st Brigade was to move round to the west of Razabil and, taking the Japanese by surprise, attack from the south. At the same time 123rd Brigade was to simulate a major attack against Razabil from the north. 9th Brigade would remain in reserve.

161st Brigade began its move forward on the night of March 8 with an approach march to Maungdaw, which was now in our hands. This march of nine miles through country held by us was uneventful. The troops lay up in the Maungdaw area next day. In the evening the brigade moved on through Kanyindan and then south-east across paddy fields to the main road. The 4th Battalion was at the rear of the brigade, and the march was slow and tedious through a night so quiet that it seemed that the slightest noise would make the Japanese aware of our advance across his line of retreat. Each battalion was stretched in single file, and weapons were carried unloaded to eliminate the risk of their use. In spite of inevitable halts in order to check positions, and other concertina-like movements, all went well with the winding column. There was neither noise nor confusion, and before daylight the brigade began to enter the foothills, where the track was no more than a yard wide. Had there been any enemy in these hills the column could never have passed through this defile, but by dawn the tail of the column was clear. How completely the Japanese were taken by surprise was revealed when six of them were found washing in a stream.

By this time the Punjabis were in their allotted positions astride the road east of the Razabil road-junction, and the Rajputs were climbing the hills to their position south of the fortress. There was a ground mist that morning, through which the leading companies of the 4th Battalion turned north and began to feel their way through the features the Rajputs were occupying. As they moved forward the mist suddenly cleared, and they became visible to the Japanese. The mules, loaded with heavy stores and rations, were disclosed in a mass and presented an ideal artillery target. The enemy were quick to seize the chance, and casualties to men and mules were caused before they could get under cover. Positions were then occupied. Four men had been killed and some thirty wounded.

The remainder of that day and the 11th were spent by the battalion in reconnaissance and in consolidating its positions. On the 11th, shelling caused the dry scrub and undergrowth in the area to catch fire, and there were anxious moments when some ammunition might have been set off. That night 123rd Brigade began its attack from the north. At first light next morning, after an exceptionally heavy artillery bombardment, the attack of 161st Brigade went in. The 4th Battalion's axis of attack was from east to west, and all companies advanced without opposition. The Japanese had realised that their position was untenable and had slipped away in small parties during the night. All objectives were occupied without casualties. Quantities of ammunition, equipment and documents were seized.

4. The Battle for the Tunnels

As soon as Razabil was in our hands Brigadier Warren sent patrols

eastwards along the road that led to Buthidaung. The next objective
was 'The Tunnels.' The road from Maungdaw to Buthidaung was
originally built as a railway, and these two tunnels had been constructed for it. After a few years the railway lines had been torn up,
and the railway became a road, the tunnels remaining in use. Should
these tunnels be destroyed the road would be impassable. It was
therefore imperative that they should be captured before the Japanese
had time to demolish them.

The road ran through a gorge, and the ground on either side was
high and rocky. The Punjabis advanced south of the road, the
Rajputs on the north, and Brigade Headquarters and the 4th Battalion along the axis of the road itself. By the evening of March 13 the
leading battalions, having outflanked or brushed aside slight opposition, were nearing the first of the tunnels. D Company of the 4th
Battalion had reached a spur from which this tunnel was visible and,
trying to push forward, came under fire and suffered some casualties.
The wounded were assisted down the bullet-swept slope by Private
Nelson, one of the platoon orderlies. That evening Colonel Laverty
sent A Company to the top of the hill above D Company (now
commanded by Captain Easten). This was a fortunate move, because
that night a party of enemy tried to occupy the hill. In driving them
off, A Company took the battalion's first Japanese prisoner.

It was now apparent that the enemy was in a stronger position
than had been expected. The brigade could make little headway,
and by the 16th the whole of the 4th Battalion had been concentrated
forward. That day D Company put in an attack supported by
Sherman tanks, which shelled the enemy positions on top of the
tunnel. The Japanese held on staunchly amidst the thick bamboo
undergrowth, and although Captain Easten fearlessly moved about
in the open encouraging his men forward, the attack was driven off
with heavy casualties.

The next day C Company moved round to the north through the
Rajputs in order to outflank the enemy. The going was very difficult,
but they eventually reached a position above the tunnel and began
to move southwards. All went well until the officer commanding
the leading platoon saw a Japanese sentry and shot him. The enemy
position then came to life, and a hail of fire struck this platoon. The
only approach was narrow, wide enough for only one man, and
although the enemy's fire was answered the company was forced to
withdraw.

On the 18th, B Company moved along a similar route to C Company's to attack the main Japanese position on the tunnel. This move,
through thick undergrowth, was very slow. The bamboo-covered

slopes were difficult to climb. B Company reached their start-line, however, and called for the artillery support which had been arranged for the attack. The fire came down, but it fell on the very place where B Company were waiting. The first salvo put the company's wireless set out of action, and the guns had to be stopped by word of mouth. Before this could be done seventeen men had been killed and some forty-five wounded. Had the enemy attacked at that time the plight of the company would have been serious indeed. But Major Winstanley and Lieutenant King rallied their men and, by gallant leadership, quickly consolidated and succeeded in holding the valuable ground which had been gained.

The evacuation of the casualties then began. The company stretcher-bearers had been killed but, in any case, it would have been too slow a journey to attempt to carry the wounded back by the same route as the company had taken. The medical officer, Captain Wattison, guided by Private Murrell who, as company runner, had gone back to Battalion Headquarters to report the situation, came up with a stretcher party by a shorter route along a *chaung* below the tunnel. At the same time C Company moved forward to protect them. All the wounded were evacuated. Eventually B and C Companies changed places in order to give B Company a better chance to reorganise.

This disaster caused a pause in the operations, but on the 20th, D Company pushed forward a little with the aid of tanks. Meanwhile A Company, on their hill overlooking the tunnel, had beaten off another attack and had taken another prisoner—but not before they had been shelled by the enemy and had themselves lost some casualties.

This ended the Battle for the Tunnels for the 4th Battalion. On March 22 it was relieved and moved back to the Kanyindan area, where the troops began to check their kit and to clean up. They also hoped to have their first thorough rest for several months. But this was not to be, for 5th Indian Division had been unexpectedly ordered to the Imphal area. The move was to be carried out mainly by air, and there were many preparations to be made. As the jeeps, mules and ammunition were to accompany the troops, the load-tables had to be carefully checked. The heavier transport, including the carriers, was to travel the seven hundred miles by road.

The move began on March 27, when the 4th Battalion marched to Maungdaw, where it embarked in three river-craft, reaching Taungbro about noon. From there it moved by lorry that evening, and arrived in a staging camp at Dohazari early on the morning of the 28th. Next day the battalion flew from Dohazari airfield to

Dimapur, being the last unit of the division to leave the Arakan. No one was sorry to leave that area, where the battalion's casualties had been sixty-three killed, one hundred and forty-six wounded and two missing. Of the wounded, over ninety rejoined the battalion later.

5. *Dimapur and Kohima*

The reason for the hurried move to the Imphal area was that the Japanese had attacked heavily on that front. They intended to capture our stores at Imphal in order to feed themselves, and to cut the road to Dimapur, which was our rail-head. Important issues were therefore at stake. By the end of March the Japanese were pressing towards the Imphal plain from three sides, and 5th Indian Division, less 161st Brigade, was flown from the Arakan to reinforce Imphal, while 161st Brigade was flown to Dimapur. Thither, later on, came also 2nd British Division by rail and 7th Indian Division by air.

On March 29 the Japanese 31st Division cut the road between Imphal and Kohima, and 161st Brigade, which was then arriving at Dimapur, was given the task of keeping the road north of Kohima clear of enemy raiding parties. Speed was essential, so when the 4th Battalion arrived on the flooded airfield at Dimapur it immediately embussed and moved along the main road in lorries towards Kohima. On arriving at the 42 Milestone, just north of Kohima, the battalion debussed. The main body spent the night in the vacated buildings of 53rd Indian General Hospital. The remainder of the brigade had already arrived at Kohima.

Next day the battalion moved into the area of the town. Reconnaissance was then carried out for the defence of Kohima, and plans were actually made. By the following morning the situation had changed, however, and it was decided that the existing garrison was sufficient. Consequently, on April 2, the battalion drove back the forty-six miles to Dimapur with the remainder of the brigade and set about preparing the defences of that town instead. This move of the brigade had all the appearances of a retirement, and it probably had an adverse effect on the morale of the garrison of Kohima.

During those three days in Kohima eighty reinforcements had arrived to replace in part the casualties which had been suffered in the Arakan; but the battalion was still well under strength. A list of officers can be found in Appendix B.

This short stay in Kohima had given the battalion a glimpse of the town and its garrison. The town is situated on two ridges. The native part of the town, a collection of native huts, is on the eastern

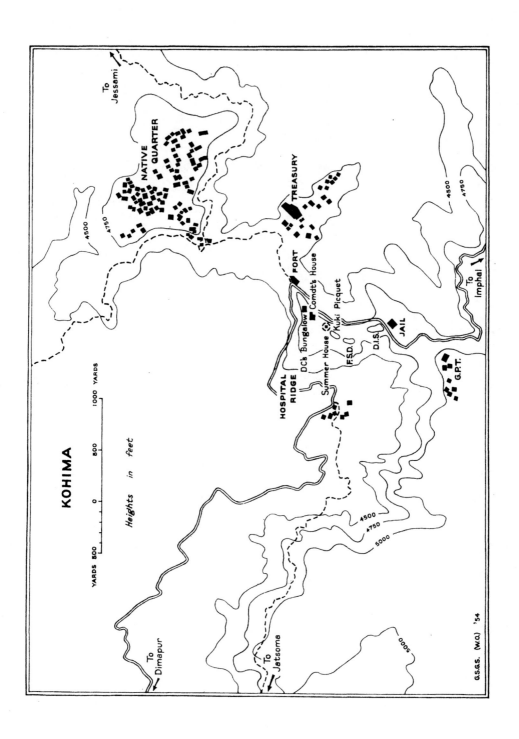

KOHIMA

YARDS 500   0   500   1000 YARDS

Heights in Feet

To Jessami

NATIVE QUARTER

TREASURY

FORT

Comdt's House

DC's Bungalow

Kuki Picquet

Summer House

HOSPITAL RIDGE

F.S.D.

D.I.S.

JAIL

G.P.T.

To Imphal

To Dimapur

To Jotsoma

G.S.G.S. (W.O.) '54

ridge, and the European community lives on the western ridge. The main road from Imphal to Dimapur runs between them and winds round the base of Summer House Hill. To the east a track leads to Jessami and the Chindwin River; to the west a jungle path winds to Jatsoma. In peace-time Kohima was a hill station with a General Hospital, a Convalescent Depot and a Reinforcement Centre. In order to maintain these it contained a Field Supply Depot (F.S.D.), a Daily Issue Store (D.I.S.) and a General Purpose Transport Company (G.P.T.). Two of the largest houses on the western ridge were the Commandant's house and the District Commissioner's (D.C.'s) bungalow.

The garrison of Kohima consisted of untried Indian troops of the Assam Regiment and Assam Rifles, who had already marched from the Chindwin River and were weary and under strength from hard fighting at Jessami. In addition, there was a handful of British troops at the Convalescent Depot and Reinforcement Centre, which were situated in the Fort, and the non-combatant Indian administrative staffs of the F.S.D., D.I.S., and G.P.T. The total number of heads in the garrison was some 2,500 all ranks, but for Colonel H. V. Richards, the Garrison Commander, many of them were only hungry mouths which had to be fed and bodies which had to be protected.

Late on April 4 an armoured carrier patrol brought bad news to Dimapur from Kohima. The Japanese had attacked strongly from the south; some of the outlying defences had been abandoned, as the untried Indian troops had been unable to withstand the heavy mortar fire; and the Garrison Commander urgently required reinforcements. That night 161st Brigade received orders to advance again to Kohima. At first light next day the 4th Battalion, one Battery of the 24th Indian Mountain Regiment, one section of an Indian Field Company and one detachment of an Indian Field Ambulance were on their way south. For this move the strength of the battalion was less than 500, for the Administrative Company and fifteen carriers were left behind. At intervals, stragglers were met coming from Kohima, some walking, others packed in speeding lorries. This gave such an impression of disorganisation within the garrison that Colonel Laverty hoped that the entire defence would not have collapsed before his force arrived.

The fifty troop-carrying vehicles went on with all speed to the road junction near the D.C.'s bungalow, where the leading companies debussed under spasmodic machine-gun fire from the north. There was no time to unload the kit and some of the stores. B Company immediately rushed forward and occupied Kuki Picquet. C Company went on past them to the D.I.S. Hill. Both companies suffered a few casualties whilst moving into position. Meanwhile Battalion Headquarters and A Company had gone to the main feature known as Summer House Hill, and D Company to the spur between this feature and Hospital Ridge. The debussing was only just completed in time as the lorries, which had no space in which to disperse, came under artillery fire a few minutes after the troops had left them. Many vehicles, some of the men's kit and some stores were destroyed. That evening the Japanese shelled the whole area for half an hour, but under cover of darkness the undamaged lorries returned to Dimapur.

6. The Defence of Kohima

'When you go home, tell them of us and say
For your tomorrow we gave our today.'

The night of April 5 was quiet and gave time for Colonel Laverty, who had virtually assumed command of the defenders of Kohima, to assess the situation. To the south the Japanese had gained a footing on Jail Hill, but G.P.T. Ridge was still in our hands. To the north the enemy were in the native village and probably also in the Fort. From these positions they could overlook the garrison, making the task of the defenders more difficult and dangerous. The positions occupied by the 4th Battalion have already been described. The Assam Regiment was entrusted with the defence of Hospital Ridge. The troops from the Convalescent Depot, reinforced by a portion of the R.W.K. Carrier Platoon, were defending the area of the D.C.'s bungalow. Some Indian troops were still holding out on Jail Hill and G.P.T. Ridge. The battery of 24th Indian Mountain Regiment was in a wooded area near the D.C.'s bungalow, but the guns were in full view of the enemy and soon had to be abandoned.

Administratively, the situation was fraught with difficulties. Although ammunition and food supplies were ample, the water reservoir was near the Rifle Range, outside the perimeter, and soon fell into enemy hands. Canvas tanks were available, but it was too late now to fill them with water as a reserve. Facilities for tending the wounded were lacking, as the Hospital was already mainly in ruins and the Aid Posts were not dug in. Communication trenches had yet to be dug.

The remainder of 161st Brigade had set out from Dimapur some time after the 4th Battalion and had been unable to reach Kohima. Brigadier Warren therefore decided to form a defensive box near Jatsoma, some two miles west of Kohima. This was established by nightfall on April 5th. From this box 24th Mountain Regiment was able to give valuable support to the troops in Kohima by answering their calls for defensive fire, and the box also relieved some of the pressure on the garrison by drawing upon itself attacks from the enemy.

On April 6 the enemy began his main attack on Kohima from the south. During the morning the Indian troops were forced to withdraw from G.P.T. Ridge to Jail Hill. Half an hour later Jail Hill itself was evacuated. D Company (Captain Easten) was ordered up from near the hospital to retake this position, but it was then seen that the Japanese were too firmly established. An attack would have caused unnecessary casualties, so D Company was sent to occupy F.S.D. Hill instead. During the morning a company of Rajputs managed to reach the garrison from Jatsoma and took over D Company's former positions near the hospital. Later in the day the road west of Kohima was cut, and further communications by this route became impossible.

That night Lieutenant-Colonel J. Young, who commanded the Field Ambulance, arrived from Jatsoma by the jungle path, which was still open. He at once organised the centralisation of medical stores and set parties of non-combatant Indians to dig trenches in the hospital area to protect our wounded from shell-fire. On the following night about eighty walking wounded and one hundred non-combatants, escorted by a Rajput platoon, left the garrison by the jungle path and reached Jatsoma in safety. This relieved some of the strain on the administrative system.

Meanwhile the enemy had resumed his attacks from the south. When night fell on April 6 a full-scale frontal attack came in from Jail Hill, the Japanese attempting to cross the main road to storm D.I.S. Hill, which was held by C Company (Major Shaw). Mortar fire caused some casualties to the enemy in their forming-up areas, but fire was then held until the Japanese were on the main road and within thirty yards of our forward positions. Bren guns and grenades then killed scores of them in the open. Serjeant Stammers, who was in command of one of the forward platoons, constantly visited his section posts during this action, taking them ammunition and keeping the men steady. This strong attack was repulsed, but in the darkness some thirty or forty Japanese infiltrated round the west flank into some *bashas* and pits between the D.I.S. and the F.S.D. Major Shaw was seriously wounded and Captain Watts, his second-in-command, was also hit. Captain Coath later assumed command of C Company.

When dawn broke on the 7th the situation was serious, and Colonel Laverty ordered D Company to destroy the enemy who had infiltrated during the night. This counter-attack was made hazardous by an enemy gun which fired over open sights from G.P.T. Ridge, but Captain Easten, by skilful leadership, carried out this task successfully with complete disregard for his own safety. Second-Lieutenant Doresa's platoon was directed against an enemy bunker near an ammunition dump. Ordering his platoon to give covering fire, he led a small party forward and personally bombed this position, thereby driving the occupants into the open, where they were killed. During this engagement the ammunition dump was set on fire, and the Japanese were shot down as they bolted from it. Two prisoners were captured in this counter-attack, one, an officer, being brought in by Lance-Corporal Harman. At least forty-four Japanese were killed. Donald Easten then led his men on to the D.I.S. Hill to reinforce C Company, who had suffered heavy casualties, and took command of the area. The Rajput Company moved from the hospital area to the F.S.D.

Before dawn on the 8th the enemy was heard forming up for another assault on the D.I.S., but defensive fire was called for by wireless from the mountain guns in the brigade box and the assault did not develop. Many small attacks had been made during the night, and in the morning it was found that the Japanese had established a machine-gun post in a position which overlooked the whole area. Lance-Corporal Harman was in command of a forward section which was within fifty yards of this gun but, owing to the lie of the ground, could not bring fire to bear on it. 'Without hesitation,' states the official citation, 'he went forward by himself, and using a 4-second grenade, which he held on to for at least two seconds to get immediate effect, threw it into the post and followed up immediately. He annihilated the post and returned to his section with the machine gun.' This saved the situation for a time.

The remainder of the 8th was comparatively quiet in the D.I.S. area, but at dusk a heavy attack came in which was repulsed with difficulty. Serjeant Tacon, who was in command of one of the forward platoons, caused heavy losses to the enemy by skilful fire control of his platoon. Later, although severely wounded, he attempted to recover one of his section commanders who was lying wounded in a bullet-swept area. Although two other attacks were beaten off during the night, the Japanese succeeded in penetrating one of the forward platoon areas; and the following morning Lance-Corporal Harman's section was ordered to reinforce this platoon by occupying a position 150 yards away from the enemy on a forward slope.

'On occupying this position Lance-Corporal Harman discovered a party of enemy digging in under cover of machine-gun fire and

BURMA: AN OBLIQUE AIR PHOTOGRAPH OF THE KOHIMA AREA

1. D.C.'s bungalow and tennis court
2. Summer House Hill
3. Kuki Picquet
4. The F.S.D. (Field Supply Depot)
5. The D.I.S. (Daily Issue Store)
6. Jail Hill
7. G.P.T. (General Purpose Transport) Ridge
8. Rifle Range.

LANCE-CORPORAL JOHN PENNINGTON HARMAN, V.C.

snipers. Ordering his Bren gunner to give him covering fire, he fixed his bayonet and alone charged the post, shooting four and bayoneting one and thereby wiping out the post. While walking back calmly he received a burst of machine-gun fire in his side.' So runs the official citation, but more followed. Lance-Corporal Harman reached his section, lay down behind cover and said 'I got the lot. It was worth it.' Five minutes later he died. For his deeds on these two days Lance-Corporal John Pennington Harman, whose home was on the island of Lundy and who had begun his soldiering as a volunteer in the 70th (Young Soldiers') Battalion of the Regiment in the autumn of 1940, received a posthumous award of the Victoria Cross. He had joined the 4th Battalion in December 1943, in the Arakan.

During the night of the 9th the Japanese made a further heavy attack on the D.I.S. Hill and gained a dangerous hold on the feature by occupying some trenches, which could not be manned owing to lack of numbers. On the following night, 10th-11th, having burned the *bashas* on the D.I.S. Hill and booby-trapped the approaches to their new positions, what remained of C and D Companies withdrew to the F.S.D. Thus, after five days of fighting, the perimeter had to be shortened, mainly on account of the large number of casualties which had been suffered. For the next few days the enemy concentrated his main attack on the D.C.'s bungalow area.

*   *   *

By this time the enemy had established artillery in the hills north of Kohima, and his gun on G.P.T. Ridge had been reinforced, so that the garrison was under direct fire from all sides except the west. Moreover, both the medical and water problems had become serious. Attacks on the hospital area had prevented the further evacuation of walking wounded, and the number of stretcher cases was now so great that only the more severely wounded could be sheltered in trenches from the worst of the fire. Many of the wounded in the Advance Dressing Station (A.D.S.) were wounded again or killed. As for the water, the only supply now in our hands was a spring near the D.C.'s bungalow. This was only thirty yards from the enemy, and men had to crawl forward singly at night to fill their containers. Later on, another water point, a mere trickle, was found near the hospital; but this, too, could be reached only at night. Water was therefore rationed to half a mug a day for each man, and even then there was barely enough for urgent medical purposes.

The situation in the D.C.'s bungalow area now became critical. During the morning of the 9th the enemy had strengthened his hold there, and many bunkers and trenches had been blown in at point blank range by his artillery fire. Enemy troops had then burrowed into the space beneath the bungalow itself, where they could not be reached by grenades. A counter-attack by the Assam Rifles had failed to dislodge the Japanese, and late in the afternoon A Company (Major Kenyon) had been sent forward from Summer House Hill to prevent further enemy gains in this area. No sooner were they established than a fierce enemy charge had come in. This had only been beaten off with the aid of defensive fire from the Mountain Gunners in the brigade box, who took a heavy toll.

From the morning of April 10 onwards this area became the scene of fierce fighting. There was no wire round the positions, and every night grenade battles were waged round the ruined bungalow and across the width of the tennis court. On the night of the 10th, one of the forward sections of A Company was knocked out by a direct hit. Realising the importance of the position, Serjeant Bennett collected some men of his Platoon Headquarters, led them forward under heavy fire, reoccupied the position and held it against frequent attacks until relieved by a section of the reserve platoon. On several occasions the forward posts of A Company ran out of ammunition, and Serjeant Williams, who was acting C.S.M., repeatedly carried forward boxes of grenades to the foremost pits in spite of heavy fire and, when there, helped to reorganise the defence. Under these conditions, with all the platoon positions constantly under fire, it was difficult to keep the men fed. But Colour-Serjeant Eves always managed to get rations to them, generally by crawling forward himself with a container of food.

Two days at a time in this area was thought to be long enough, and on the night of April 11, B Company (Major Winstanley) moved from Kuki Picquet and relieved A Company successfully. B Company was still under strength from casualties lost in the Arakan, but a further attack on this area on the following night was thrown back, heavy casualties being inflicted on the enemy.

*   *   *

Although there were no enemy gains on April 11 and 12, constant mortaring and shelling of the restricted area within the perimeter caused many fresh casualties. Enemy sniping was also intensified, and there was no position entirely safe from this, the journey up Summer House Hill from the north being extremely hazardous. This fire caused additional casualties, although our own counter sniping was not without effect. All these casualties made the need for more medical supplies so great that an airdrop of medical stores, water and ammunition was called for by wireless.

The Mortar Platoon performed particularly valuable work during this period. The various detachments were widely separated and in exposed positions, which could not be concealed from the enemy. In spite of this Serjeant King, who was commanding the platoon, constantly visited the detachments while they were under fire. When communications were destroyed he went from pit to pit to bring down close and accurate defensive fire for our hard-pressed positions, doing much to break up enemy attacks before they developed. In the task of keeping vital communications open the garrison was greatly assisted by the Signal Platoon, of which Private Archer was conspicuous in his devotion to duty. The Signal Officer, Captain Topham, was seriously wounded by mortar fire, and, later, died of his wounds.

The Japanese attempted to undermine the morale of the garrison by shouting propaganda in Urdu and English. Calling out that the garrison was surrounded and without water, they urged them to throw down their arms and surrender; adding that in a recent attack over a hundred Japanese had been killed. They requested, somewhat quaintly, that such bloodshed should cease. Morale among the fighting troops of the garrison remained high, however, and the only reply was a shower of grenades. This nightly entertainment was brought to an abrupt and proper end by a couple of howitzer shells, which caught the Japanese 'Lord Haw-Haw' unawares.

In reality the nights were made horrible by a feeling of isolation. There was often no means of communicating with adjoining positions, and attention became concentrated on the slope in front, which ended in a patch of darkness. Suddenly frenzied shrieks told that an attack was coming in elsewhere on the perimeter. For a time the night would be full of commotion. This would at last die down, and silence and the sense of isolation would return. Welcome though daylight was, it was far more dangerous than darkness. As the branches of the trees were broken down by shells and mortar bombs our troops became more and more exposed. Even the cover of crawl trenches gave little safety.

*   *   *

April 13 was a bad day. First, the enemy resumed his attacks on the F.S.D. and succeeded in occupying some forward trenches there. Although a platoon of A Company restored the situation, the whole of the F.S.D. area remained under constant machine-gun fire and it was only precariously held. Secondly, mortaring and shelling were

cc

unusually heavy during the day, and two direct hits on the A.D.S. killed two medical officers and wounded two others. Finally, yet another attack on B Company in the D.C.'s bungalow area was hurled back only by hand-to-hand fighting, Lieutenant King personally throwing grenades, and one Bren gunner, Private Williams, whose weapon had jammed, killing his assailant with a shovel. At dawn on the 14th, a further fierce attack came in against this area. Preceded by a shower of grenades and grenade-discharger bombs, it also was only beaten off with difficulty. Enemy casualties were very heavy. At dusk B Company was relieved by men of the Assam Regiment, and the weary troops were at last able to get some rest.

For two days sounds of heavy firing on the road to Jatsoma had indicated that a relieving force was on its way. But hopes of an early relief were dashed when it was learned that the force was meeting with strong opposition and was making very slow progress. Another disappointment was that the dropping of the required supplies from the air had not been an entire success. Although the much-needed medical stores had come down safely inside the perimeter, by some error quantities of mortar ammunition and grenades had dropped on enemy positions in the Treasury area. On the 16th the airdrop was more successful, bringing the now urgently-required grenades as well as water, rum and a further supply of medical stores.

During the night of the 16th, having inflicted severe casualties on our troops in the area by artillery fire during the day, the Japanese resumed their heavy attacks on the F.S.D. In mist and darkness they gained a footing on the hill. Early next day our troops there were relieved by the Assam Rifles, D Company withdrawing to Kuki Picquet. During the night calamity befell the garrison. The Indian troops on F.S.D. Hill abandoned their positions and streamed back through D Company on Kuki Picquet. Captain Easten was wounded, C.S.M. Haines was killed and, having only a handful of men left, the company was forced to withdraw to Summer House Hill. This meant that the enemy was now only 100 yards from Battalion Headquarters, and only heavy defensive fire prevented him from advancing further. Once more the perimeter had been shortened.

That was the 13th night of the siege, and the whole battalion, having had no sleep since April 3, was extremely weary. The outlook was black indeed. Over 200 casualties had been suffered, including eight officers, and Brigade was warned of the gravity of the situation. The 18th brought some relief. Two companies of Punjabis, supported by tanks, cleared the road as far as the hospital and joined the garrison. One of these companies took over the area of the D.C.'s

BURMA: INFANTRY OCCUPYING A HILL NEAR RAZABIL IN THE ARAKAN

BURMA: MULES TOIL UP A STEEP HILLSIDE IN THE JUNGLE WITH SUPPLIES

BURMA : THE RUINED D.C.'S BUNGALOW AND TENNIS COURT AT KOHIMA

BURMA : THE CROSSING OF THE MANIPUR RIVER

bungalow, while the other strengthened the western flank of Summer House Hill. Three hundred wounded and some non-combatants were safely evacuated under slight enemy fire. This greatly eased the administrative situation.

That night the enemy returned to the attack on the D.C.'s bungalow area. Although the main assault was repulsed by the Punjabis, the Japanese managed to occupy some vacant positions within forty yards of Battalion Headquarters on Summer House Hill. At first light next morning 2nd Lieutenant Faulkner of A Company personally directed the fire of the 2-inch mortar of his platoon on to these positions and set fire to the roof of the main bunker. This forced the Japanese to run out into the open, where they were shot down by Bren-gun fire. By this action, and his well-directed supporting fire from his platoon, John Faulkner enabled a counter-attack by the Punjabis on the whole position to be successful, with minimum loss to our own troops. During the night of the 19th, two more heavy attacks supported by grenade-discharger fire came in. They were beaten off with great difficulty, and during them two more company commanders were wounded—Captains Smith and Coath.

Relief was now at hand. A cipher message was received that the battalion would be relieved next morning.

Sure enough, on the morning of April 20 the battalion and attached troops, still in good heart but very battle-weary, were relieved by the 1st Royal Berkshires of 2nd Division. On relief, companies moved separately and at intervals down past the hospital on to the main road, where they climbed wearily into lorries and were taken direct to Dimapur. A few casualties were suffered from sniping and mortar fire during the relief. Near Jatsoma the battalion was met by Brigadier Warren, who congratulated them on being the first to 'bend' a complete Japanese division and get away with it.

Thus ended a fine episode. During those fifteen long days, out of the 500 who went into the battle the 4th Battalion had lost 61 killed in action, 125 wounded and 13 missing. 25 major enemy attacks had been repulsed, and well over 1,000 casualties had been inflicted on the Japanese. This staunch defence had also averted a catastrophe. By denying the route to Dimapur to the 31st Japanese Division for fifteen days, the advance of the enemy had been held up long enough to allow 2nd British and 7th Indian Divisions to arrive in the battle area and prevent the invasion of India. For the conduct of this gallant defence against enormous odds Colonel Laverty was awarded the D.S.O.

Much of the praise for the successful outcome of this siege must, as often in the story of the British Army, be given to the private

soldiers and the junior leaders. This was indeed a 'soldiers' battle.'
Hand-to-hand skirmishes were fought practically every night, and
time after time the brave and skilful deed of a section or platoon
commander prevented disaster. Many of the troops who were not
counted as casualties had in fact been slightly wounded or concussed
by blast, and a number of the less seriously wounded had returned
to their posts because the A.D.S. was already full. As the days passed
the platoons and sections grew smaller and smaller. At the end, one
platoon consisted of a single private. He asked, with a grin, if he
could put a 'pip' up.

*   *   *

This was not the end of the battle for Kohima. It was not till May
11 that our troops were in sufficient strength there to begin a full-
scale attack against the main positions still held by the Japanese.
The 6th Brigade of 2nd Division and 33rd Brigade of 7th Indian
Division then attacked Kuki Picquet and F.S.D., D.I.S., and Jail
Hills. Two days later the ruins of the D.C.'s bungalow were recaptured, and by the evening of May 13 the whole of Kohima was in
our hands. So ended one of the bitterest periods of fighting on any
front.

7.   The Relief of Imphal

On arriving at Dimapur the remnants of the 4th Battalion found
that the Administrative Company had prepared a comfortable camp.
What they needed was rest and sleep and a chance to recuperate.
April 23 was Easter Sunday, and a service of thanksgiving and
remembrance, held in the canteen, was attended voluntarily by
every available man. This was a memorable occasion.

Meanwhile more troops of the 2nd Division were fighting their
way into Kohima and driving the Japanese from the hills north of
that town. 161st Brigade was ordered to keep the road between
Dimapur and Kohima open, and, the Punjabis being still in the
Kohima box, a company was required from the 4th Battalion to
form a base from which the Rajputs could operate. On April 23
therefore B and D Companies, acting as a composite company under
Major Winstanley, moved back towards Kohima to Milestone 32.
This meant that, although they were still very weary, these troops
were to have the further strain of guards and loss of sleep. Happily,
on the day they moved up, the enemy was driven from the hills
nearby, and this combined company moved on to the Zubza box

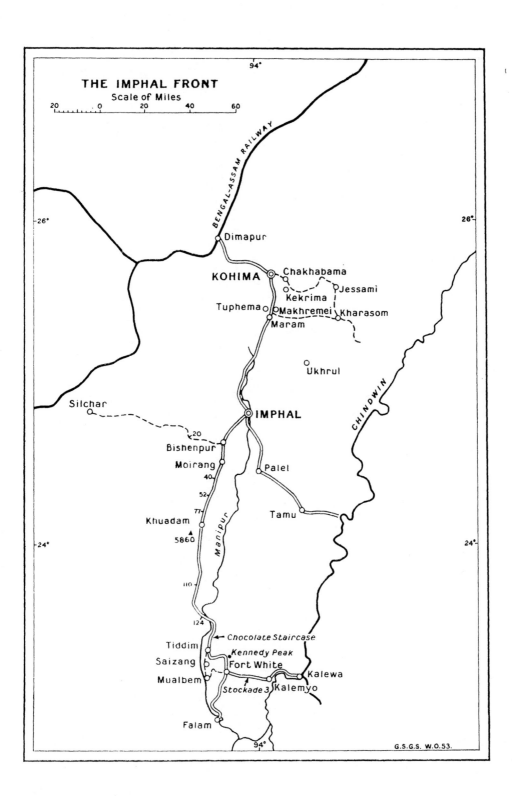

THE IMPHAL FRONT
Scale of Miles

BENGAL-ASSAM RAILWAY

Dimapur

KOHIMA   Chakhabama
Kekrima   Jessami
Tuphema   Makhremei   Kharasom
Maram

Ukhrul

Silchar

IMPHAL

20
Bishenpur
Moirang   Palel
40
52
77
Khuadam   Tamu
▲
5860

Manipur

Chindwin

110

124
Chocolate Staircase
Tiddim   Kennedy Peak
Saizang   Fort White
Mualbem   Kalewa
Stockade 3   Kalemyo

Falam

G.S.G.S. W.O.53.

at Milestone 37, which was the administrative base of 2nd Division. The Zubza area was comparatively quiet.

On May 4 the whole battalion moved up to the Jatsoma box where, in addition to defending various features, the troops kept the road clear and escorted casualties back to Dimapur. Reinforcements began to arrive, and leave parties were able to go for a few days at a time to a Rest Centre on the Brahmaputra. On May 17, Kohima being in our hands, the battalion moved back to Dimapur to reorganise and refit. Cadre courses, the rearrangement of key personnel, recreation and rest were the main requirements. It was then decided that 161st Brigade should come under command of 7th Indian Division (Major-General F. W. Messervy), whose 33rd and 114th Brigades had now arrived at Dimapur from the Arakan. Its third brigade was operating in the Imphal area.

Everything was now ready for an advance southwards to the relief of Imphal. While 2nd Division pressed down the road, 7th Indian Division was to clear the hills to the left of it. The task given to 161st Brigade was the clearance of the area immediately east of Kohima, and on May 30 the 4th Battalion moved to that town and concentrated in the area of the Fort, where the litter of battered buildings, broken household utensils and dead bodies was appalling.

The clearing of the hills began on June 5. It was on this day that Colonel Laverty departed for a lecture tour in India, command being assumed by Major P. H. A. L. Franklin during his six weeks' absence. The monsoon had broken, and the teeming rain, wet clothes, lack of shelter and the leeches made the operations very uncomfortable. There was only slight opposition from small parties of Japanese but, had they stopped to resist from their deep bunkers covered with thick timber, the fighting would have been severe. On several occasions there were signs that the Japanese had withdrawn only on the approach of our troops. The one track available for transport was that which led to Jessami. It was now a sea of mud, and could not be used by vehicles heavier than jeeps. It was therefore necessary for the troops to carry their own personal kit as well as two days' reserve rations; only essential stores and one blanket per man were carried by the mules. The jeeps were used to bring up the rations, which were distributed by the second-in-command.

Progress was slow in the thick jungle. On June 10 the main body of the battalion bivouacked at Chakhabama. On the 12th it moved on to Kekrima. On the 16th it became known that the Japanese were withdrawing eastwards along the track from Tuphema to Kharasom, and the battalion was ordered to move southwards across country as quickly as possible to block that track. Blankets were left behind, and only bivouacs were carried by the mules. On the morning of the 18th the track was reached by patrols, which found that Japanese positions near it had only just been vacated. By the afternoon the track had been blocked but, because of a land-slide, contact could not be made with the Rajputs on the right. It was then found that the enemy had escaped from the trap, and, on the 20th, a diversion having been made round the landslide, the troops moved off westwards. The following afternoon the 4th Battalion settled into the brigade concentration area at Makhremei.

By this time 2nd Division had captured Tuphema on the main road, and 5th Indian Division, which was besieged with three other divisions in the Imphal plain, was fighting its way northward. On June 22 these two forces met, and the road to Imphal was opened. On the same day the 4th Battalion moved south to Maram to ensure that no Japanese crossed the Imphal road in that area. Many patrols were sent out, but the enemy could not be found. Full use was there-fore made of a Mobile Bath Unit, and every man had a change of clothes—the first for nearly four weeks. On the 26th the battalion, with 161st Brigade, rejoined 5th Indian Division in the Imphal area.

8. *The Pursuit to Tiddim*

As soon as the garrison of Imphal was relieved the pursuit of the Japanese began. 7th Indian Division, travelling light, turned to the east and converged on Ukhrul. Surprising the enemy there, they pressed on towards the Chindwin River and threatened the Japanese lines of communication in that area. The enemy was forced to with-draw.

Nor was 5th Indian Division idle. It was immediately directed to the west side of the Imphal plain to harry the enemy in the Bishenpur and Palel areas; and it was amongst the hills to the north of the track to Silchar that the 4th Battalion spent the first few days of July. Patrols failed to find any Japanese. On July 5 the battalion began a steady advance southwards. No enemy was met; but the rain continued to fall, and, with only bivouacs and capes for protec-tion, the troops' clothes were continuously damp.

On July 8 the battalion began to take over positions about Mile-stone 20 on the Silchar track. These positions in the hills were blanketed by clouds for most of the time, and the plain below was invisible. The track was impassable to wheeled transport because of mud. Contact between posts was therefore difficult. Moreover the posts were scattered and crumbling, and it was as well that the enemy was not on the offensive. Frequent patrols were carried out to keep contact with other units and to ensure that the track was clear, but, apart from capturing two prisoners, there were no incidents.

Colonel Laverty returned from his lecture tour on July 17, and the opportunity was taken to reorganise the battalion on to a new war establishment. Headquarter Company lost the Carrier Platoon, which had not been used since leaving the Arakan, and gained a Headquarter Platoon. The Transport Section was greatly reduced, the surplus drivers being posted to one platoon of D Company. The only vehicles that remained were a water cart, four jeeps and four 15-cwt trucks. Forty-one mules also remained. A few P.I.A.T.s were issued to the battalion. Reinforcements were also arriving, and the battalion began to approach full strength. Morale was high in spite of some stomach disorders due to chills and polluted water.

*   *   *

Meanwhile to the east the Japanese, driven back in the Tamu area, were withdrawing down the Chindwin valley to Kalewa. On the Bishenpur front they were carrying out a fighting withdrawal down the road to Tiddim; and 5th Indian Division was now ordered to take over the pursuit on this axis. The Tiddim road runs over the mountains and is narrow and winding. In some places it is actually hacked out of the hillside. This meant that the division would be operating in the monsoon season on an unmetalled road which would be liable to landslides. During wet weather the dirt surface would become deep mud, and the transport driver's task would be made difficult and dangerous.

On July 29 the 4th Battalion moved into divisional reserve at Moirang. Ten days later the troops marched forward to Milestone 40 (Milestones were numbered from Imphal), and then on August 15 to Milestone 52, where 161st Brigade was preparing to take over the pursuit from 9th Brigade. Brigadier Warren's plan was that each battalion in turn should carry out an outflanking movement against the enemy, while the remainder of the brigade moved along the axis of the road, clearing it as they advanced. The 4th Battalion was to carry out the first 'hook.'

Sending a patrol ahead the 4th Battalion moved up to Milestone 77, where some mountain gunners and sappers joined it. By the evening of August 23 the Punjabis had met opposition at Milestone 86, and at dawn next day the battalion moved off south-westwards on its outflanking movement. The tracks along which the battalion moved through thick jungle were overgrown and difficult to find.

Men and mules were heavily laden, three days' 'compo.' rations being carried. The first obstacle was a river in flood, waist-deep and fast flowing, with the bottom covered with boulders. This was followed by a long, steep hill up which the track wound uncertainly for two miles. The mules had great difficulty in climbing this and, as it was now late in the afternoon, the battalion bivouacked for the night. That evening news came over the wireless that the Punjabis were still fighting in the area of Milestone 86.

At first light on the 25th the battalion moved off again and began a steep climb up to the main ridge in the area. The mules again found the going very difficult. The track was narrow, and over-hanging bushes sometimes forced a mule outwards over the hillside, down which it would roll two hundred feet. There it would lie quietly until a rescue party reached it. In spite of these checks the top of the ridge was reached soon after midday, and a firm base was then formed for the night, while C Company went forward to a hill above the village of Khuadam.

When C Company approached this village they were fired on, and it was with difficulty that they climbed up the hill through thick undergrowth. Next morning B Company, and later D, were sent forward to take over the positions on the hill, while C Company went on to a feature overlooking the road. In spite of some enemy resistance, by the early afternoon both B and D Companies had reached Khuadam hill, C Company had blocked the road at Milestone 90, and the mountain guns were engaging the enemy who were still holding up the Punjabis on the road near Milestone 86. The battalion had expected an airdrop of rations that day but, although aircraft circled overhead, they could not find a suitable dropping zone. Consequently the battalion went hungry.

At first light on August 28, patrols found that the enemy had withdrawn during the night, and C Company immediately started off along the road in pursuit while the battalion concentrated on the road. Better still, rations came up during the afternoon in addition to a partially-successful airdrop. That evening C Company regained touch with the enemy, but that night, after they and the artillery had harassed them for a while, the Japanese withdrew. The first 'hook' had been completed. The Rajputs in their turn then began an outflanking movement, while the 4th Battalion, followed by the Punjabis, continued the pursuit along the road.

*   *   *

It soon became apparent that, although progress on the road was somewhat easier than along jungle tracks, the fighting was going to be harder. For D Company, with tanks in support, had only just begun to advance along the road on August 30 when they came under fire from Point 5860 on the right of the road. A Company was sent to outflank this feature from the west but, after forcing their way through thick undergrowth, they found the enemy well dug in. Tanks came up along the road and succeeded in silencing a Japanese gun which was firing directly down it; but even with this aid A and D Companies' attempts to take the objective were unsuccessful. Casualties were five killed and twenty-six wounded. A ration party, which came up at dusk, took the wounded back.

Next morning B Company moved farther to the right through A Company to occupy positions in rear of the enemy. While this move was going on A and D Companies, supported by mortars and tanks, engaged the enemy frontally. The Japanese suffered many casualties. By dusk B Company had hacked its way slowly through a mass of fallen trees and creeper and had reached the road at Milestone 96. Still the enemy showed no signs of withdrawing. So at first light on September 1, B Company established a block astride the road in rear of them. At 11.30 a.m. the mortars laid a smoke screen over Point 5860, and under cover of it A Company attacked and occupied the feature without opposition. The enemy, realising that the smoke screen was the prelude to an attack, had used it to cover their own retirement. Small parties of Japanese, attempting to escape through B Company, were killed. It is probable that many more remained hidden in the dense jungle.

The Punjabis then took the lead on the road. By September 5 they had reached a bridge over a stream at Milestone 110 and had found it to be demolished. This caused a check. While bridging material was brought forward, the 4th Battalion protected Brigade Headquarters and the transport in the area of Milestone 105. This continued until September 10, when orders were received for the crossing of the Manipur River.

But 161st Brigade was not to reach the Manipur without another engagement. On September 11 the 4th Battalion moved forward to pass through the Rajputs at Milestone 119, where they were in contact with the enemy. B Company was sent to outflank the Japanese and, while climbing a steep spur which overlooked the enemy positions, they suffered some casualties, including Major Winstanley who was wounded in the leg. Next morning the battalion began a wider 'hook' and by the evening had reached a spur which overlooked the road at Milestone 122. There the troops spent a dismal night of rain which soaked them thoroughly. The enemy had now finally withdrawn from all prominent high ground north of the river, however, and by midday on the 14th the battalion was established about Milestone 124, with patrols on high ground overlooking the Manipur River. Our casualties in this engagement had been two officers wounded, one other rank killed and ten wounded.

*   *   *

In order to assist the crossing of the Manipur, 123rd Brigade was at this time advancing down the east bank of the river to rejoin the Tiddim road in the area of the crossing place. They were then to form a firm base on the high ground south-east of the river and make a bridgehead for 161st Brigade. This plan worked admirably, and the Japanese were thus prevented from dominating the vital river crossing from the south.

The Manipur River was 110 yards wide at the crossing place, with a fall of fifteen feet per mile. It was now in spate, and the torrent swirled rapidly between its banks. Waves and eddies broke up the surface and presented a frightening spectacle. No 'Fantails' were available as the 5th Battalion had had for the crossing of the Po, and even an elephant which the Punjabis had captured was of little use—though they painted the number 68 on its back to identify it as one of their vehicles. It seemed that no boat would be able to cross without being smashed on the half-submerged boulders. But eventually, on September 16, the initial crossing was made in a folding boat. A cable attached to a 3-inch mortar bomb was then fired across the river, and this line was caught by the men on the other bank. A 'flying ferry' was then rigged up, using the folding boat as a ferry. The Japanese offered no resistance, other than a little inaccurate shelling, owing to the presence of patrols from 123rd Brigade on the south bank.

The 4th Battalion moved down to the river on September 17 but, owing to the first boat capsizing and subsequent single crossings taking about two hours each, only D and A Companies crossed that day. A Company formed a bridgehead immediately covering the crossing. D Company went forward five miles south along the road, where they gained touch with troops of 123rd Brigade. No jeeps or mules were ferried across, and D Company had an uncomfortable night without bivouacs or blankets. The remainder of the battalion, except B Company, crossed on the following day; on the 19th, B Company was ferried over with three jeeps and their trailers.

161st Brigade concentrated near Milestone 137 and formed a firm base while the remainder of 5th Indian Division crossed the river. The lines of communication of the division now stretched 126 miles down the road from Imphal to the Manipur, and it was no longer possible to keep the road open without an exorbitant amount of labour. So the necessary operational requirements of the division were brought forward, and the bare minimum number of vehicles was ferried across the Manipur on rafts. The road was then closed. From now onwards no reinforcements would be received, and all supplies would be brought forward by air. Later on an airstrip would be made at Saizang for the evacuation of sick and wounded.

*   *   *

After 5th Indian Division had crossed the Manipur River, 123rd Brigade took the lead in the advance to Tiddim, and it was not for three weeks that the 4th Battalion moved forward again to the battle area. During this quiet period the troops were issued with their first clean clothes since leaving Milestone 77. Bathing was possible in the numerous streams which ran down the hillsides, and a Mobile Bath Unit was available for a few days. The battalion was now very much under strength. Battle casualties had not been replaced since the pursuit from Imphal had begun, some men were on leave, and scrub typhus, jaundice and dysentery had all taken their toll. Some casualties had also occurred from malaria, in spite of the strict routine of shirt-sleeves being rolled down at dusk and mepacrine tablets being swallowed every evening. The small final draft of 36 reinforcements and fifteen men from hospital, who joined at Milestone 137, did little to ease the shortage of personnel, and the battalion was reorganised into two rifle companies. A and C Companies were combined to form No. 1 Company under Major Williams, and B and D formed No. 2 Company under Captain Collett. At about this time also Brigadier Warren assumed command of the division. He was replaced in command of 161st Brigade by Brigadier R. G. C. Poole.

Meanwhile 123rd Brigade had continued its slow advance. By October 11 it was nearly in sight of Tiddim. It had climbed the steep hill, known as the 'Chocolate Staircase' from the colour of the road surface, and there had met strong opposition. The 4th Battalion was sent forward on the 12th to reinforce this brigade. That day the troops climbed the 'Chocolate Staircase' with all their kit on their backs in the heat of the day. They were not needed in the battle but remained in reserve.

It was during this pause that the remnants of the 2nd Battalion The West Yorkshire Regiment came from 9th Brigade to join the battalion. They had suffered very heavy casualties and were at this stage only able to raise enough troops to make up one full-strength company. This composite company, under Majors J. F. Newman and J. B. Miller, was attached for all purposes and became known as X Company. The mixed battalion settled down well. Various titles were suggested for it, such as 'The Western Brothers,' but none was adopted.

Tiddim was occupied by 123rd Brigade on October 19, and the period of rest at the top of the 'Chocolate Staircase' was prolonged. The air there was clear at 5,000 feet, the monsoon was ending, there was less rain, and the cold nights and sunny days made life attractive once more. It was with renewed vigour that the reorganised battalion returned to the battle.

9. *Fort White and Stockade 3*

Fourteen miles south-east of Tiddim a dominant feature rears up from the plains. This is Kennedy Peak. Farther south lies Fort White, named after Sir George White, defender of Ladysmith. These two obstacles now stood in the way of the advance to Kalemyo. While 9th Brigade drove for Kennedy Peak, 161st Brigade, less the Punjabis, was to make a wide right hook across country through Mualbem to come in at Fort White from the south. Accordingly, on October 29 the composite 4th Battalion moved up in daylight to Milestone 3 (from Tiddim) on the Tiddim–Kalemyo road. The Rajputs had gone ahead to reconnoitre and cover the route, for the Japanese were thought to be still in the area. The success of the operation depended largely on concealment, as the route was visible from Kennedy Peak, and all subsequent moves were to be by night.

The start was delayed by a landslide which blocked the track, but by midnight on the 29th the long column was on its way in bright moonlight along the narrow track which twisted through the jungle and crossed open grassland. Near Saizang the column passed close to the airstrip which was being built to enable casualties to be evacuated. To the right could be heard the roar of the Manipur River. There was a long check as the battalion walked man by man across a swaying and bouncing suspension bridge over a stream and each mule was led individually by its muleteer over the fifty yards' span. When all the battalion was across, the climb up to Mualbem began. The troops completed the first stage of the march as daylight broke.

After two days' rest at the pleasant village of Mualbem the battalion resumed its march on the evening of November 1. At first the track was good and ran along the side of a cliff, but when it turned downhill it became lost in landslides. Boulders overhung the track and at times mules were forced off it. As the sun rose, however the tail of the column reached the bivouac area. At sunset on the 2nd the battalion moved off on its climb up to the Falam road. Reaching this at midnight, a firm base was established with two companies, X Company having been left behind with the rear elements of the Brigade. The Rajputs were still ahead and were now established on a feature to the north towards Fort White. The 4th Battalion was ordered to swing north-east to cut the Fort White–Kalemyo road.

On the morning of November 3 a platoon of No. 2 Company was sent ahead to reconnoitre. This platoon, advancing stealthily, made its way up a sugar-loaf feature and suddenly came upon a large bunker. Inside it a Japanese working party was enjoying its 'elevenses.' The platoon quickly broke up the party with Tommy-gun fire and grenades, and withdrew when fire was opened on them from all sides. They had no casualties. The remainder of the company then moved up and established a position south of the enemy. That night No. 1 Company joined No. 2 in its forward position.

Probing attacks on November 4 showed that the Japanese occupied a strong and extensive position astride a track, and on the following day operations to encircle the enemy began. These were slow and arduous. Only No. 1 Company made contact with the Japanese, losing one man killed and three wounded. On the morning of the 6th, X Company rejoined the battalion. Detailed plans for a full-scale attack were then made, including air-strikes and artillery support. This attack, due to begin at first light on the 7th, was delayed by a heavy mist, and in the middle of the morning, when patrols were sent forward, it was found that the enemy had abandoned the whole area. Once again the Japanese had withdrawn in their uncanny way in the nick of time.

*   *   *

By this time Kennedy Peak had been captured, and the Rajputs had joined up with patrols of our 9th Brigade near Fort White. The enemy had gone right back. Ahead lay Kalemyo, and the division was ordered to press on with all speed. 161st Brigade took the lead. At the head of the brigade marched the 4th Battalion towards Stockade 3 and the plains.

A slight check occurred when X Company bumped a Japanese rearguard on November 8, but that night the enemy withdrew. No. 2 Company took the lead on the road next morning while No. 1 moved across country to a spur which overlooked Stockade 3. By the evening both companies had met opposition. No. 2 had bumped the enemy near Stockade 3; No. 1 had found them well dug in along a steep ridge. Patrols confirmed the enemy's positions next morning, and a mountain gun was man-handled up a hillside to deal with them. By the evening two enemy bunkers had been destroyed and much havoc caused amongst the Japanese. At first light on the 11th patrols found the way clear, and the battalion occupied Stockade 3. This was not a wooden palisade with rifle slits, but a clearing in the jungle where vehicles could be dispersed off the road and water was easy to find. Many dumps of enemy equipment and ammunition were captured there.

After this success the 4th Battalion went into reserve while the Rajputs took the lead. By November 16, Kalemyo had been entered and cleared. On the 18th the battalion moved down into that area. The Japanese had withdrawn to the hills well clear of Kalemyo, and the stay there was uneventful. The battalion had now been continuously in action for over a year, but its long saga was over for a time. On November 27 and 28 the troops flew to Imphal and thence moved north by road to Maram, on the Imphal–Kohima road, where a camp was taken over from a unit of 2nd Division. A long rest of three months followed.

At Kalemyo the company of the West Yorkshire Regiment had departed to rejoin 9th Brigade. This brought to an end a very happy and valued association between the two regiments.

10. *Objective Rangoon*

At Maram the 4th Battalion was far from the battle zone, and the troops recovered quickly from their gruelling campaign. Christmas 1944 was memorable for its good cheer, the Padre's rum punch and a battalion concert. Nor were those who had lost their lives forgotten, for a memorial stone was erected at Kohima. Several V.I.P.s visited the battalion, including Lord Louis Mountbatten and General Sir William Slim. The former invested the C.O. with the D.S.O. he had won at Kohima. A leave party was sent off to England, and with it went Captain Collett, who was to give a series of lectures there and in America. Others to leave the battalion were Colonel Laverty, who went to Dehra Dun as chief instructor, and Captain Short, the Adjutant, who went to Brigade Headquarters. Major Franklin stepped up to command, with Major Webster as second-in-command.

Soon after Christmas the battalion moved north to Jorhat, beside the Brahmaputra River. Tents were pitched in green fields, and training began in river crossings and operations in open country. Reinforcements arrived, and the battalion reorganised into four rifle companies on a motorised transport basis, with 15-cwt trucks and jeeps with trailers. These all had to be driven by the battalion's own men. The transport officer, Captain Hawkes, somehow managed to find and train sufficient drivers.

* * *

While the 4th Battalion was resting, the British advance into Burma had continued rapidly. By the third week in February 1945, four divisions and a tank brigade had crossed the Irrawaddy in readiness for a drive on Mandalay.[1] 17th Indian Division then drove straight for Meiktila, seventy miles south of Mandalay, and captured and held on to this strategic railway junction. This division was later reinforced by 9th Brigade of 5th Indian Division, which was flown in from Palel airstrip (south of Imphal). The intention was to follow up this success by clearing the ground between Mandalay and Meiktila. For this operation the remainder of 5th Indian Division (now commanded by Major-General E. C. Mansergh) was required.

The 4th Battalion left Jorhat by road on March 5, 1945. It was a long and monotonous journey in convoy over rough and dusty roads. East of Kalemyo the road was unspeakable, and the teak trees at the roadside gave but little shade from the blazing sun. After eight days of unbroken travel the battalion arrived at Monywa, headquarters of General Slim's 14th Army. There the Chindwin was crossed in ferry boats. On March 16 the more swiftly-flowing Irrawaddy was crossed in the same way, and a short distance farther on the battalion took over positions at Taungtha from a unit of 7th Indian Division.

The battalion was the first unit of 5th Indian Division to arrive. Most of the troops were in positions controlling the entrances to Taungtha, but B Company (Major Smith) was on a hill about a mile in front of it. The country was flat and open, and cover was to be found only in dry and broken river-beds. Occasionally, isolated hills reared up, steep-sided and bare of cover, affording positions ideal for defence.

Colonel Franklin's orders were to patrol ahead and locate the Japanese positions, while the remainder of 161st Brigade (now commanded by Brigadier E. H. W. Grimshaw) arrived and resources were built up. The clearing of the adjoining area would then

[1] See map 'Burma.'

begin. Patrols were therefore sent out in all directions, and the main Japanese position was definitely located about Point 1788 to the north-east. On March 22, C Company (Major Coath), with some tanks and artillery, made a reconnaissance in force down the road towards Meiktila. Enemy posts were encountered astride the road four miles out of Taungtha. The tanks damaged these, killing several Japanese, but the attack was not pressed home. Air and mortar strikes were also brought down on the few villages in the area in order to force the enemy into the open.

By March 27, 5th Indian Division was ready for the attack. 33rd Brigade of 7th Indian Division had begun to move round to the east of Point 1788, and 161st Brigade was to assault it from the west. The 4th Battalion, assisted by tanks, was directed on to three villages below the hill. When these had been captured, it was to cross a *chaung* and go on to an enemy gun area. B Company would remain on its hill until required in the battle.

A Company (Major Watts) led the attack and entered the southern village. The clearing of it took some time, but by midday C Company had moved through to the northern village. At the same time D Company (Captain King) attempted to cross the *chaung*. This they were unable to do, and sporadic fighting continued here and in the villages until the evening. By this time the forward troops and tanks of 33rd Brigade had concluded their encircling move and had made contact with A and C Companies. Enemy parties were still in the area, however, and difficulty was found in evacuating casualties and in getting up supplies that night. Early next morning A and C Companies began to move through the villages. It then became apparent that the enemy had withdrawn during the night. Point 1788 was occupied without further opposition.

On March 29 the C.O. and his R Group drove forward in a jeep to reconnoitre a new site for Battalion Headquarters. As they were returning the jeep struck a mine, and Colonel Franklin, Captain E. C. F. Brown (HQ Company) and Corporal Varney (acting Signal Officer) were badly wounded, the last mortally. This was a severe loss at one stroke. Major Webster assumed command temporarily.

At dawn on March 31 the move of 5th Indian Division along the good metalled road to Meiktila began, the battalion acting as advance guard with A Company and two troops of tanks in the van. There was a slight check about eleven miles from Meiktila when mines were discovered in a dry river-bed, but by evening the whole division was settled in the southern part of the town.

*   *   *

The battle had spread southwards, and preparations for the pursuit of the Japanese to Rangoon were hastened. Rangoon was 384 miles ahead, and the monsoon was expected to break at the end of April. Speed was therefore the first essential. No attention was to be paid to parties of enemy on the flanks. Every unit was to be responsible for its own protection and was to keep going as long as the road was clear. 161st Brigade was to be in reserve in the early stages, and the 4th Battalion was given the task of protecting the rear echelons of the division.

The move began on April 10. The journey was slow and tedious. The group of units under the command of the battalion amassed a total of 528 vehicles, most of them administrative lorries, and their control and protection, even with only ten yards between them, might have been difficult. But no Japanese molested the bivouac areas at night, and no emergencies arose except that on the morning of the 12th a few Japanese aircraft sneaked in at first light and attacked some vehicles ahead. As a result burning trucks blocked the road and made progress slower than ever.

After a day's rest in the area of Pyawbwe, caused by some resistance from the enemy, 161st Brigade went to the head of the column, and the battalion was relieved of its unenviable task. On April 17 an enemy rearguard was encountered, and a patrol of C Company, sent out to investigate a neighbouring village, killed six Japanese whom they found asleep. The next night was much disturbed by a skirmish with a small party of the enemy. Nine Japanese were killed. On the 20th, while the Rajputs cleared a village, C Company with tanks went on to Lewe, which was occupied by the whole battalion on the following day. 123rd Brigade then took the lead.

With the vital Lewe airfield in our hands the pursuit became even more rapid. The enemy became bewildered by the speed of the advance. Even then, weary and exhausted as they were and unable to hold up our tanks, the Japanese would not surrender. Those parties that were encountered consequently had to be killed. Sometimes these pockets of resistance were left for the troops in rear to destroy, and sometimes parties of enemy harassed our men in their bivouacs at night. In daylight both sides used aircraft to shoot up convoys and vehicles that were halted on the road.

On the afternoon of April 22, C and D Companies were detached to protect a ferry on the Sittang River, while the remainder of the battalion was ordered forward to Toungoo to assist 123rd Brigade to clear that town. The situation in Toungoo was still very confused, and traffic blocked the road. The battalion at last managed to enter the town and occupied positions on the bank of the Sittang, covering

DD

the ruins of a bridge. The night was quiet, and before morning the town had been cleared. C and D Companies then rejoined.

Rangoon now lay 166 miles ahead, and fighter aircraft from Toungoo airstrip were able to cover that distance. Nor was there any place until Pegu was reached where the Japanese could make an effectual stand. The column therefore hurried on. It was the turn of 161st Brigade to lead the pursuit, and on April 24 the 4th Battalion became the leading unit of the division with a squadron of tanks in support. Twenty-three miles were covered before the column reached a *chaung* near the village of Pyu. Here the tanks were held up by the swollen stream and by enemy anti-tank guns, and the battalion established a bridgehead south of the *chaung* while a diversion was constructed.

An advance still being impossible next day, it was decided to search a village which, it was reported, was occupied by the enemy. When our leading troops advanced into the open they were fired on by guns and machine-guns. So an air-strike and an artillery concentration were called for. As soon as these ended our troops entered the village unopposed. The enemy had withdrawn, leaving numerous corpses and two anti-aircraft guns, two mountain guns, one anti-tank gun and one machine gun abandoned. Many other parties of enemy were reported to be in the vicinity, but only one approached the bridgehead and this was quickly disposed of. The anti-tank gun that was captured is now in the Regimental Museum at the Depot.

On the 26th, 17th Indian Division went through and took the lead on the road. Pegu was cleared on May 1. South of that town the road to Rangoon forks, and it was arranged that 17th Indian Division should take one road and 5th Indian Division the other. A race to Rangoon did not materialise, however, for 26th Indian Division landed from the sea unopposed at the mouth of the Rangoon River, and on May 3 Rangoon was in our hands. Abandoned by the Japanese, the city thronged with Burmese crowds, who welcomed the liberating troops with elation.

11. *The End of the War*

Burma was now virtually ours, and the Japanese Army in the Irrawaddy valley had to make its escape eastwards across the Sittang River. This was difficult, for in doing so these troops had to traverse thick jungle, where the few good tracks were now water-logged by heavy rains, and to cross the Mandalay–Rangoon road.

To prevent this, 5th Indian Division was ordered to consolidate its hold on the main road by spreading outwards in depth. With this in view the 4th Battalion moved to an area near Waw, whence the companies continuously patrolled the countryside. Although no contact was made with parties of the enemy, it was a period of intense activity for the troops.

On May 14 the battalion was withdrawn to the Pegu area for rest. The troops were accommodated in buildings—an important amenity now that the rains had come. Because of the rapid advance and the long lines of communication the rations had been small since leaving Meiktila. Bully beef and biscuits had been the staple diet. At the best of times this is not particularly appetising; in a hot climate it can become positively distasteful. The P.R.I. was now able to supplement the rations by local purchases, and eggs and fresh food were eagerly welcomed by the troops.

When, at the beginning of June, the battalion resumed the task of blocking the escape of the Japanese, 161st Brigade was deployed along the main road at key points, with detachments operating in the thick jungle to the west of it. While two companies remained near the road as a firm base, the remainder of the battalion moved to Mokshitwa, ten miles from the road. The track was impassable for vehicles and, as no mules were available, all stores had to be taken to Mokshitwa on bullock carts. After strenuous efforts the normal stores were taken up; but more ammunition and wire were still required to make the position secure, when it was heavily attacked by a Japanese force attempting to break through to the Sittang.

This attack began soon after midnight on June 3, when a party of Japanese, approaching the position from the west, was driven off. A little later the main attack came in down a track from the north. The initial rush was broken up, but the Japanese, estimated at a hundred, took cover in some scrub. Re-forming there, the enemy then made a determined assault on a small feature and captured it. This feature overlooked Battalion Headquarters, and the situation became more critical when the Command Post itself was attacked. The assault was beaten off with difficulty, but the enemy still clung to positions which dominated Battalion Headquarters. Serjeant Hayman, who commanded a section of the Mortar Platoon, was then ordered to fire his mortars on to the enemy at the very short range of 100 yards. This he did, using only primary charges, from a forward observation post which was fully exposed to enemy fire. In face of this accurate mortar fire the Japanese withdrew, leaving thirty-six dead, three light machine guns and many rifles behind them. Our casualties were one officer and eight other ranks killed, and one officer and eleven other ranks wounded. The evacuation of the wounded was slow and difficult. It was nearly thirty-six hours before they reached the main road.

Next morning the new Commanding Officer, Lieutenant-Colonel I. G. Moon (S.W.B.), arrived in the battalion from 33rd Brigade of 7th Indian Division, of which he had been Brigade Major. There was talk of following up the enemy as they withdrew, but, although it was known that there must be many more Japanese in the locality, the policy was to destroy them as they attempted to cross the main road and not to search for them in the thick jungle. No move was therefore made.

The battalion was withdrawn from Mokshitwa on June 10, and for the next five weeks it was spread out along five miles of the road. Companies or platoons were accommodated in villages, and every man had a roof over his head when he was not out on patrol. The battalion's task was to patrol over a vast area, although the inclusion in it of a large lake cut down the amount of country that was patrollable. The task was difficult. To the east lay flooded paddy fields as far as the Sittang River, and only banked tracks were above water. To the west the thick jungle was intersected by swollen streams, many of which had to be waded neck-high. Wherever enemy parties or outposts were found they were engaged by mortar and artillery fire, but many long patrols yielded no result at all.

On June 25 the battalion came for the second time under command of 7th Indian Division. As the war in Europe was now over, the tour of duty overseas had been reduced to three years and four months, and before long nearly all the key personnel in the battalion would be due for repatriation. Consequently, when 5th Indian Division was withdrawn to Rangoon to prepare for the invasion of the Malay Peninsula, it was decided that the battalion must leave it. This decision was greatly regretted by all ranks, for the *esprit de corps* in 5th Indian Division had been very high.

*   *   *

There is very little more to tell of the war-time activities of the 4th Battalion. After a spell of duty at two stations on the railway line between Pegu and Rangoon, it moved into Government House, Rangoon, on August 7. On August 15 came the first hint that the atom bombs which had devastated the two Japanese cities of Hiroshima and Nagasaki had caused the enemy to surrender unconditionally.

To many in Rangoon this news was incredible, and for some hours it was thought to be merely a rumour. When the news was confirmed, those troops who were not on duty displayed their relief and surprise by firing Very lights and by other mild forms of celebration. But for most of them there was no undue rejoicing. Victory had been won, but the more important matter was to get home as soon as possible to the fields of Kent.

CHAPTER 24

The Affiliated and Allied Regiments

1. 569 (*The Queen's Own*) (*M*) *L.A.A./S.L. Regiment, Royal Artillery* (*T.A.*)

THE history of the 569 (The Queen's Own) (M) L.A.A./S.L. Regiment can be traced back to a Greenwich Volunteer unit which fought during the Civil War and was present at the Battle of Newbury in 1643. When, in 1859, each county was authorised to form its own Volunteer units, the following corps of Kent Rifle Volunteers were raised in the Greenwich and Blackheath area:—the 3rd at Lee, the 13th at Greenwich, the 21st at Lewisham, the 25th at Blackheath, the 27th at Deptford, the 28th at Charlton and the 34th at St. Johns (or Deptford New Town). In 1880 these corps, together with one from Dartford and one from Bromley, became companies in the 3rd Battalion West Kent Rifle Volunteers, which, in the autumn of 1881, was renamed 2nd Volunteer Battalion The Queen's Own (Royal West Kent Regiment). The 3rd Volunteer Battalion of The Queen's Own was formed from the 4th (Woolwich Town) and the 26th (Woolwich Arsenal) Kent Rifle Volunteers.

During the Boer War, 1899–1902, the 2nd and 3rd Volunteer Battalions of The Queen's Own supplied approximately two composite Volunteer Service Companies for service in South Africa. These companies gained the battle honour 'South Africa, 1900–02.'

In 1908 the Territorial Force was constituted to replace the County Volunteers. Some companies of the 2nd Volunteer Battalion were incorporated in the 5th Battalion The Queen's Own (Royal West Kent Regiment), but the other companies of the 2nd and the headquarter companies of the 3rd Volunteer Battalion were linked together and became the 20th (County of London) Battalion, The London Regiment (Blackheath and Woolwich) with headquarters at Holly Hedge House, Blackheath. Although this battalion did not retain the name of its parent regiment it was authorised still to wear the uniform of The Queen's Own,[1] with some modifications, and to play '*A Hundred Pipers*' as its Regimental March.

[1] The Corps Warrant of August 1916 shows the 20th London Regiment as part of the corps of The Queen's Own (Royal West Kent Regiment).

The war with Germany started on August 4, 1914, and the Territorial Force was embodied at midnight on that day. The 20th Battalion The London Regiment took over guard duties on Plumstead Marshes on August 5 and subsequently marched to Hatfield and St. Albans to train, while a 2nd Battalion was formed at Blackheath. The 1/20th proceeded to France in 1915, fought at Festubert, Loos, Somme 1916, Ypres, Cambrai, Messines, Bapaume, Albert and the Hindenburg Line and was demobilised in 1919. The 2/20th proceeded to France in 1916, moved to Salonika and later to Palestine, returned again to France in 1918 and formed part of the Army of Occupation in Germany. It was disbanded in March 1919. Its Battle Honours were: Macedonia 1916–17, Palestine 1917–18, Jerusalem, Jordan, Jericho, Nebi Samwil, Gaza and Doiran. A 3rd or Reserve Battalion, which was formed during the war, remained in England to supply drafts for the two battalions overseas. Altogether the two active service battalions won 260 decorations.

When the Territorial Army was constituted in 1920 the name of the battalion's parent regiment was once more incorporated in its title, for it was renamed the 20th London Regiment (The Queen's Own). For fifteen more years it retained its place as one of the Territorial Battalions of The Queen's Own, and its story is told in Chapters 1, 2 and 3 of this History. But in the autumn of 1935 the 20th London Regiment was converted to a Searchlight Battalion, with the title 34th (The Queen's Own Royal West Kent) Anti-Aircraft Battalion, Royal Engineers. It remained affiliated to the Regiment and retained the Cap Badge. The relevant extract from a War Office letter dated October 30, 1935, stated:

'The Army Council has decided that on the 15th December, 1935, certain Infantry Units of the Territorial Army in the Eastern Command and the London District will be converted into Anti-Aircraft Brigades, Royal Artillery, Territorial Army, each of two batteries, or into Anti-Aircraft Searchlight Battalions, Royal Engineers, Territorial Army, each of two companies, with probable ultimate expansion to three or four batteries and four companies respectively . .

'The units on conversion will form part of the Corps of Royal Artillery and Royal Engineers respectively; but will at the same time be affiliated to the regular infantry corps to which they have belonged in the past.'

The battalion did in fact expand to four companies. By 1937 there were two companies at Blackheath, one at Greenwich and one in a fine new drill hall at Eltham; and when it embodied in August 1939, shortly before the outbreak of war, it was approximately 2,450 strong. The four companies were scattered in small searchlight detachments over Kent and Sussex. Battalion Headquarters were at Staplehurst. A Z Section, based on Sheerness and Chatham, was formed to man such pleasure steamers as the *Royal Eagle*, *Crested Eagle* and *Golden Eagle*, with the role of anti-minelaying patrols. These ships took part in the evacuation of the Expeditionary Force from Dunkirk in May 1940, and personnel of the battalion were awarded a D.C.M. and an M.M. for gallantry while serving in them.

The battalion then became—as did the other searchlight battalions of the Territorial Army—part of the Corps of the Royal Regiment of Artillery. But its role remained the same and so did its affiliation to The Queen's Own.

During August and September 1940, while the Battle of Britain was being fought, many of the battalion's searchlight detachments were attacked, and their small arms shot down seven enemy aircraft and probably destroyed one other. From then until June 1944, the battalion remained deployed in the Kent and Sussex area to aid the R.A.F. fighters to locate and attack enemy raiders at night; though the pattern of deployment was constantly changed to comply with new plans for the spacing of searchlights and new ideas for the employment of radar and other devices for locating hostile aircraft.

The Flying Bomb attacks on London began on June 13, 1944, one week after the invasion of Normandy by the Allies. These bombs were called V.1 by Hitler, after the German word *Vergeltung*, meaning Retaliation. Although the red flames of their exhausts made these bombs easy to see at night, the searchlights played their part in aiding the guns to shoot them down as they flew along 'Bomb Alley,' as parts of Kent and Sussex had come to be called. When the direction of the attack was changed to the East Coast the battalion was taken off its normal searchlight duties, and the troops were employed on constructional work for the Royal Artillery in East Anglia.

Early in 1945 the battalion became a Garrison Regiment, Royal Artillery, and moved to Newport, Monmouthshire, as the 633rd Garrison Regiment, R.A. It soon became redundant. More infantry were required with the Army in France, and the Regiment was converted to a 'B' type infantry battalion, although it retained its Gunner title. In April 1945, it embarked at Tilbury and proceeded to Fallinbostel, where it became responsible for motor-boat patrols by day and river-bank patrols by night along a section of the River Elbe. When the war ended the Regiment was withdrawn to Luneburg. It was disbanded in the autumn of 1945.

The Regiment has now been re-constituted as a mixed light anti-aircraft gun and searchlight unit with the title 569 (The Queen's Own) (M) L.A.A./S.L. Regiment, Royal Artillery (T.A.). Its Headquarters are once more at Holly Hedge House, Blackheath, and the officers and men still wear The Queen's Own cap badge and march past to '*A Hundred Pipers*.'

2. *The Canterbury Regiment of New Zealand*

Three regiments of the Dominions are allied to The Queen's Own. The first of these alliances was with The Canterbury Regiment of New Zealand.

The history of The Canterbury Regiment goes back to 1866, when the Christchurch City Guards were accepted for service under a Volunteer Act. Christchurch, the third largest city in New Zealand, is situated on the Canterbury Plain in South Island. In 1886 the district was split into two military areas, and the Volunteer infantry in it were reorganised into two battalions. These units were later called the North Canterbury Battalion and the South Canterbury Battalion. When the New Zealand Territorial Force was constituted in 1910, these titles were changed to the 1st (Canterbury) Regiment, with headquarters at Christchurch, and the 2nd (South Canterbury) Regiment, with headquarters at Timaru.

During the Boer War, New Zealand 'Contingents' were specially raised for service in South Africa, and none of the Volunteer battalions served as units. But the Canterbury battalions supplied many men for the Contingents and were granted the Battle Honour 'South Africa, 1900–02.'

In 1913 the 1st (Canterbury) Regiment became allied to The Queen's Own. The 2nd (South Canterbury) Regiment was allied to The Durham Light Infantry. Both alliances still continue.

Three Canterbury battalions served overseas in the Great War, 1914–1918. The 1st Battalion took part in the Gallipoli campaign and then proceeded to France, where it was joined by the 2nd and 3rd Battalions. In France and Flanders these three battalions fought in most of the battles during 1916, 1917 and 1918—such as the Somme, Messines, Ypres, Cambrai, Hindenburg Line and the Sambre—and the following decorations were won: V.C.s 1, D.S.O.s 9, M.C.s 54, D.C.M.s 38, and M.M.s 247. A truly magnificent record.

On June 1, 1921, the 1st (Canterbury) Regiment and the 2nd (South Canterbury) Regiment were amalgamated to form the present Canterbury Regiment. By virtue of its early connection with the Christchurch City Guards, it became the senior regiment in the Royal New Zealand Infantry. '*A Hundred Pipers*' was adopted as its Regimental March.

Territorial titles were not used by units proceeding overseas from New Zealand during the Second World War. Numerical titles were used instead. But the Canterbury Regiment was represented in the New Zealand Expeditionary Force by 'A' Company of each of the 20th, 23rd and 26th Infantry Battalions. For Home Defence the Regiment raised six battalions, none of which saw any action, though at one time the Japanese menace was very close.

The 20th New Zealand Battalion was formed on October 5, 1939, under the command of Lieutenant-Colonel H. K. Kippenberger, who was commanding the 1st Battalion The Canterbury Regiment when war was declared. Colonel Kippenberger later commanded an infantry brigade in Crete, Libya and Italy and was awarded the D.S.O. and bar. He then commanded the New Zealand Division until he was seriously wounded in 1944. Major-General Kippenberger was then appointed to command the 2nd New Zealand P.O.W. Reception Group in the United Kingdom. He became a C.B. in 1945 and a Knight Commander of the British Empire in 1948. It was under his command that the 20th Battalion arrived in Egypt in February 1940. After training in the Western Desert, the battalion fought in the Greek campaign and in the ill-fated defence of Crete, where Captain C. H. Upham, then a 2nd Lieutenant, won the first of his V.C.s. On returning to Egypt the battalion took part in most of the fighting until, in July 1942, it lost 50 per cent casualties in the capture of Ruweisat Ridge. In this action Captain Upham was awarded a bar to his Victoria Cross[1] and thus became the third man to win a double V.C. The battalion's next battle was as an armoured regiment at the River Sangro in Italy. At Cassino one squadron of its tanks nearly reached the Monastery in the famous New Zealand attack in March 1944. The regiment then took part in the pursuit to Florence, the thrust from Rimini to Faenza, and the final battles in Italy. It was disbanded at the end of 1945.

The 23rd New Zealand Battalion was originally destined for Egypt, but it was diverted on account of the fall of France and in June 1940 arrived in the United Kingdom, where it immediately adopted an anti-invasion role. It was stationed at various places in Kent, Sussex and Hampshire. Early in 1941 the battalion embarked for Egypt, and from then until September 1942, it fought in Greece, Crete and the Western Desert, where it was joined by the 26th Battalion. After taking part in the Battle of Alamein both battalions were in the pursuit of Rommel to Tripoli, assisted in the break-through at Mareth and Enfidaville and joined in the defeat of the Germans in Tunisia.

[1] The citations for both of Captain Upham's V.C.s can be found in the *Queen's Own Gazette* for September 1949.

Their movements in Italy conformed closely to those of the 20th Battalion. The 23rd Battalion was finally disbanded at Florence in December 1945, while the 26th Battalion was disbanded near Lake Trasimene.

After the war the New Zealand Government was a long time making its defence plans. It was not until October 1948 that the reorganised Territorial Force was gazetted. The Canterbury Regiment remains unchanged, and Major-General Sir Howard K. Kippenberger, K.B.E., C.B., D.S.O., has been appointed Colonel of the Regiment. The motto still is *Ake, Ake Kia Kaha*, which means 'We shall fight on for ever and ever.'

N.B. Further information about The Canterbury Regiment can be obtained from articles which appeared in the *Queen's Own Gazette* for May, August, September and October 1949.

3. *The Carleton and York Regiment of Canada*

Before the Confederation of Canada the Carleton County Militia in the Province of New Brunswick existed chiefly on paper. During the American Civil War, however, owing to the closeness of Carleton County to the American State of Maine, the 1st Battalion Carleton County Militia[1] was reorganised at Woodstock in the autumn of 1862 and was knocked into shape by instructors from the 15th Regiment of the British Army (now the East Yorkshire Regiment), which was quartered in New Brunswick at the time. On July 1, 1867, the Provinces of Canada were confederated into one Dominion. The defence of the Dominion became a Federal concern, and the Carleton County Militia ceased to be. But the Militia elements were regrouped on September 10, 1869, to form the 67th Battalion, 'Carleton Light Infantry.'

With Confederation there opened a new era for the Canadian Militia. The men were issued with uniform and were paid when called out to camp, which usually occurred once in every two years. The 67th Battalion invariably went to camp with the 71st York Battalion, and a close union between these two battalions began.

When the Boer War broke out in the autumn of 1899 the 67th was at camp. Only a comparatively small Expeditionary Force, made up of Volunteers from all units, was sent from Canada, but several N.C.O.s and men of the Carleton Light Infantry were in its ranks.

On the outbreak of the Great War in 1914 the services of the

---

[1] An 'Historical Sketch of The Carleton Light Infantry' was published in the *Queen's Own Gazette* in December 1935.

Carleton Light Infantry were offered as a whole unit. This offer was declined by the Department of National Defence, as it had been decided to form new units for overseas service. Recruiting was started at once in Woodstock for these new battalions. The officers of the Carleton Light Infantry became scattered, but many of the other ranks who volunteered were swept into the 12th Battalion Canadian Expeditionary Force.

After the Armistice in 1918 the 67th Regiment lay dormant until June 1, 1920, when the battalion was re-formed by a General Order with the title of 1st Battalion The Carleton Light Infantry and headquarters at Woodstock. To it was assigned the duty of perpetuating the memory of two famous battalions of the Canadian Expeditionary Force, the 44th and the 104th.

In order to keep alive the spirit of comradeship which had grown during the war, alliances between Canadian Militia Battalions and Regiments of the British Army were made in 1925. The Queen's Own was selected to be allied with The Carleton Light Infantry. When the amalgamation of the Carleton Light Infantry with their old friends the York Regiment took place in 1937 and the title was changed to The Carleton and York Regiment, this alliance continued, although it is now shared with the East Yorkshire Regiment. The badge of The Carleton and York Regiment is the White Horse of Kent superimposed on the Star of Brunswick.

When war was declared in 1939 The Carleton and York Regiment mobilised with the 3rd Brigade of 1st Canadian Division and arrived on December 17, 1939, in Scotland, whence it moved to Delville Barracks at Cove, near Aldershot. After the fall of France its anti-invasion role took the battalion to Northampton, Woodstock and Caterham before it became responsible for the defence of a beach sector in the Brighton-Seaford area. Combined operations training in Scotland followed until, in July 1943, the battalion landed in Sicily and fought its way through that campaign. The first Canadian soldiers to cross the Straits of Messina to the mainland of Italy were men of The Carleton and York Regiment. They then thrust forward up the Adriatic Coast with the 8th Army and took part in that Army's victories at Cassino[1] and the Gothic Line from Rimini to Faenza. In March 1945, the battalion sailed from Leghorn to Marseilles and moved up the Rhone Valley to Lille in France. It went into action at Emmerich in Germany and finally fought in the battle for Holland.

The battalion returned to Canada when the war ended and, after demobilisation, has since been reorganised in New Brunswick with

[1] The Carleton and York Regiment actually relieved the 5th Battalion of The Queen's Own near Evangelista on May 16, 1944.

headquarters at Fredericton and companies at Woodstock, Grand Falls, Edmundston and Saint Stephen.

4. *The Kent Regiment of Canada*

In Kent County in the Province of Ontario, Canada, no Militia Units seem to have existed until a year or so before the Confederation, for the first Regiment to be raised was the 24th 'Kent' Battalion in 1866. Owing, apparently, to the impossibility of keeping it up to strength, this battalion was disbanded in 1892.

The existing battalion was first raised as a 'new regiment' in 1914 with the title 186th Battalion Canadian Expeditionary Force. This battalion arrived in the United Kingdom in April 1917, when it became a draft-finding unit for the 1st, 18th and 47th Battalions of the Canadian Corps. But after the war the battalion was re-formed on February 15, 1921, and was given the title The Kent Regiment with headquarters at Chatham, Ontario. To it was assigned the duty of perpetuating the memory of 186th Battalion Canadian Expeditionary Force.

In 1925, at the same time as the Carleton Light Infantry, The Kent Regiment became allied to The Queen's Own.

When the active Militia of Canada was reorganised in December 1936, the regiment was converted into a machine-gun battalion and re-designated The Kent Regiment (M.G.), a title it retained until it resumed the role of a rifle battalion in April 1941. In December 1937, the battalion won the Vickers Gun Competition at the Canadian Rifle Association Meeting.

During the Second World War the battalion was called out on active service on May 24, 1940, and remained at Chatham, Ontario, until January 15, 1941, when it moved to London, Ontario. In July of that year it took over the defence of a sector of the coast near Halifax, Nova Scotia, but moved back to Ontario in December to the Niagara Peninsula for protective duties along the Welland Canal. The Japanese victories now began to cause apprehension in British Columbia, and in March 1942, the battalion crossed the Dominion and came under Pacific Command, where it remained until the end of the war, supplying large numbers of men for the reinforcement stream.

After the war the battalion was demobilised at Niagara Camp, Ontario, on March 30, 1946. It has now been re-formed at Chatham, Ontario. The Regimental March of The Kent Regiment is '*A Hundred Pipers.*'

PART FOUR

AFTER THE WAR

1945–1950

CHAPTER 25

Release and Disbandment
1945-1948

1. *Regimental*

As soon as the war with Germany was over, a start was made on the gradual reduction of the Army to peace-time requirements. In order to avoid the widespread discontent which had occurred after the 1914–18 War, a methodical and impartial system of release from the forces was evolved. This system was based on the 'first in, first out' principle, but there was also a proviso that the older men should be released first. Every individual was placed in a Release Group according to his age and length of service, and a time-table, showing the rate at which it was hoped the releases would be carried out, was published. The release of key personnel could be deferred on the grounds that they were operationally vital. These were called D.O.V.s, but there were very few of them. On the other hand, men could volunteer to defer their release for periods of one or two years or until general demobilisation. These were called D.V.s.

When the personnel of The Queen's Own due for release arrived in England, they were sent to 13th Holding Battalion at Gravesend. This battalion was the holding unit for the linked Regiments, The Queen's and The Queen's Own. It was commanded by Lieutenant-Colonel Knatchbull, who had been second-in-command of the 6th Battalion in 1942. Its task was to 'hold' personnel until they were posted to other appointments or were released from the service, and practically every officer and other rank of the entire Regiment passed through its hands during this period.

At the same time the call up of young men for National Service under the Conscription Act was continued. This was essential because it would be a long time, probably many years, before British commitments overseas would permit a reduction to the pre-war strength of the Forces, and units had to be kept approximately up to strength. In order to train these National Service Men, as they were now called, the Infantry Training Centres were retained at Home; and 13th I.T.C. remained intact at 'Invicta Lines,' Maidstone.

EE

As the Army was gradually reduced, and as the number of immediate post-war commitments became less, units were disbanded one by one. In order to adhere strictly to the Release Regulations this meant that those men who were in the later Release Groups had to change their units and stations not once but often several times. Consequently the lives of most individuals became very unsettled. This unhappy state of affairs continued until General Demobilisation occurred on May 12, 1948, by which time the Army had been reshaped to its peace-time organisation.

* * *

The end of the war was a fitting moment for Sir Charles Bonham-Carter to retire as Colonel of the Regiment. He relinquished the appointment on September 30, 1946, after holding it for almost exactly ten years. No one who has read these pages can fail to realise how valuable he had been to the Regiment during a most difficult period of its history, and how well he had served his country while he was Governor and Commander-in-Chief of Malta. On October 11, 1946, Sir Charles paid his official farewell visit to the Depot. His successor, Brigadier N. I. Whitty, was present at the same time.

One of the greatest honours which had been bestowed upon the Regiment while Sir Charles was Colonel was the Freedom of the Borough of Maidstone. The certificate conferring this honour reads:

Borough of Maidstone.
Certificate of Honorary Freedom.
Be it remembered that on the 30th day
of August, 1944, by vote of the Town
Council passed in conformity with the
law, the Honorary Freedom of the
Borough was conferred on The Queen's
Own Royal West Kent Regiment in
consideration of the eminent services
rendered by the Regiment to our
Country and Empire

2. *The 1st Battalion*

The history of the 1st Battalion during this transition period is for the most part one of peace-time duties. The Artillery Barracks at Larissa in Greece, which the battalion occupied in August 1945, required a great deal of renovation and cleaning, and two companies laboured at these domestic tasks. Another company was employed in felling trees and building log cabins at a lumber camp; the fourth company was away acting as instructors and staff at a Greek Battle School, of which Major Raisin was the Commandant. The battalion was also responsible for the training of the Greek National Guard in the vicinity of Larissa.

As soon as shipping was available and the French railways had been sufficiently repaired, troops for release and leave were taken to and from England by way of the 'Medloc' route. This journey was by ship from Athens to Toulon, train from Toulon to Calais and boat from Calais to Dover. There was a constant stream of men travelling from Larissa to Athens for release and leave, and an equally large number of reinforcements and men returning from leave coming in the opposite direction. As this journey between Larissa and Athens was too long to be made in one day, a staging camp was established at Amphiklia. It was a small tented camp administered by C.S.M. Worsley and a small staff of nine, and went by the name of 'The White Horse.'

Release groups occupied most of the time at Larissa, though Cadre Courses, under R.S.M. Hayley, were held for those junior N.C.O.s who were to replace the senior N.C.O.s about to be released. For entertainment in the evenings the troops had regular cinema shows; an ENSA Concert Party came occasionally; and there were several Welfare wireless sets on which they could listen to the programmes of the Army Broadcasting Service from Radio Athens. In October an expedition of ten other ranks under Captain Upton and the Padre, Rev. T. D. Clatworthy, set out to climb Mount Olympus; but only the Padre, Corporal O'Connor and Private Kill (formerly a boy in the 2nd Battalion) succeeded in reaching the summit.

In November the lumber camp stopped work for the winter, the Greek Battle School closed down, and 'The White Horse' staging camp was replaced by a 4th Division camp, called 'Peter's Corner,' at Levadeia. The whole of the battalion was then concentrated in the barracks at Larissa. This concentration was short-lived, however, for detachments were soon sent away to neighbouring villages to supervise the distribution of Red Cross food and clothing. Although local leave had to be cancelled during this period, most of the battalion was able to enjoy its Christmas Dinner in barracks under near peace-time conditions.

*　　*　　*

The battalion moved on January 28, 1946, by road to Salonika, where it relieved an Indian unit which was returning to India. It was accommodated in the Technical Barracks, and was fully occupied with Garrison Guards and Duties. The Greek elections, which were held on March 31, passed off quietly and placed in power a government which had a reasonable measure of popular support. The need for British troops to remain in Greece was therefore greatly diminished. Lieutenant-General Sir Ronald Scobie handed over command of Land Forces Greece to Lieutenant-General K. N. Crawford, and in his Special Order of the Day he wrote:

'Since the British Forces re-entered this country nearly eighteen months ago you have achieved much in your task of helping Greece to recover from the ravages of war. Ports, roads and communications have been re-established. For seven months you have carried food, clothing and medical supplies even to the most inaccessible villages, but for which aid thousands of Greeks would inevitably have died. Until the Greek Gendarmerie had been re-formed it was due to the presence of British troops all over Greece that there was order and security in a country recently divided by bitter civil strife. Thanks to your help, and still more to the example you have set by your discipline and turnout and unfailing cheerfulness, the formation of the new Greek Army has made much progress in the past year.'

The battalion had been closely connected with the relief work and the training of the Greek Army, and as a token of appreciation the C.O. was awarded the Royal Order of George I with Swords by the Greek Government.

After that the days passed peacefully enough, and the process of despatching groups for release and welcoming drafts of reinforcements continued smoothly. In April the Colours arrived from the Depot and were taken into use at a Ceremonial Parade held on the 22nd. The Divisional Commander, now Major-General C. B. Callander, inspected the parade, and the Corps of Drums of the 2nd Royal Fusiliers (by kind permission of Lieutenant-Colonel C. A. L. Shipley) played for the march past. A few weeks later Colonel Braithwaite, who had been with the battalion since he was first commissioned in September 1940, and had commanded it since May 1944, left to be released from the Army. Lieutenant-Colonel P. H. Macklin came from commanding 13th I.T.C. to relieve him.

*   *   *

The battalion left Greece on August 18, 1946, embarking in the *Empire Anvil* 14 officers and 380 other ranks strong, and arriving at

Port Said on the 20th. The following day the journey was completed by train to Suez, where the battalion came under the command of 3rd Division. Two companies were stationed in Abbassia Barracks, Cairo, and found guards over certain buildings there, including the British Embassy and the Residence of the C.-in-C. These companies returned to Suez on November 6. Reinforcements of both officers and other ranks had been arriving in large numbers, and the strength of the battalion gradually increased. In January 1947, a large draft of over 100 joined from the 5th Battalion, then disbanding, and for several months a strength of 900 was maintained.

Early in March 1947, the battalion moved to Cairo, where it was engaged in internal security duties. It was the last British battalion in Cairo and took part in the final evacuation of the city by the British on March 29, when it handed over Kasr-El-Nil Barracks to a unit of the Egyptian Army—the barracks which had first been occupied by the battalion in 1882.

Meanwhile one company had been preparing a new camp at Connaught Lines, Moascar, near Ismailia in the Suez Canal Zone, and the whole battalion concentrated there after the evacuation of Cairo. For the first two months companies were moved from place to place to fulfil various commitments, but by the beginning of June the last outside duty had been handed over. By this time a Training Camp, to which companies could go one at a time for periods of three or four weeks, had been opened at East Bank on the shores of Lake Timsah. Excellent bathing was available, and this did much to maintain the morale of the troops and keep them happy during a somewhat dull period. Colonel Macklin proceeded on leave to England and was then transferred to the 2nd Battalion. Major H. B. H. Waring assumed command temporarily.

*   *   *

On September 3, 1947, the battalion embarked at Port Said in the *Clan Lamont* and arrived at Liverpool on the 13th. The band, under Bandmaster McKenna, was there to meet it and played on the quay while the Colonel of the Regiment, now Brigadier N. I. Whitty, and the new C.O., Lieutenant-Colonel C. A. de B. Brounlie, went on board. Next day the battalion disembarked and went by rail to Shudy Camp, Cambridge, whence the majority of the troops were sent on disembarkation leave.

On returning from leave the battalion made a short move to Gosfield, near Great Dunmow, in Essex, where it was accommodated in a camp on a war-time airfield. Two companies were employed on the maintenance of some thousands of vehicles at 21st Vehicle

Reception Depot at Great Dunmow, but the others gradually dwindled as more and more groups were released. In December a detachment, commanded by Major Harris, went to Harwich in order to administer a transit camp for troops travelling to and from the British Army of Occupation in Germany. The remainder of the battalion still struggled on with its task at Great Dunmow. Eventually all that was left of the battalion was accommodated at the V.R.D.

Finally, on April 24, 1948, a cadre of three officers and ten other ranks proceeded to the Depot at Maidstone with the property and the Colours and began to make preparations for placing the battalion in suspended animation.

3. *The 2nd Battalion*

When the war in Europe ended the 2nd Battalion was at Hastings carrying out the duties of a draft-finding unit. On June 11, 1945, the battalion moved to Broome Park, Barham, near Canterbury, where it formed part of 61st Division. This formation was intended to become a light air-portable division on an all-Jeep basis for operations against the Japanese, and training exercises were carried out with this in view. On June 19 there was a change of C.O.s, Colonel Macklin going to command 13th I.T.C. and Colonel Talbot, who returned to the Regiment from commanding 7th Royal Hampshires, replacing him. Major Martyn rejoined from the Staff to be second-in-command.

The quick victory over Japan was celebrated with due rejoicing on August 15 (known as V.J. or Victory over Japan Day), but there was no news of a change of role until October 5, when orders to mobilise were received. On the same day the battalion moved to Grandshaft Barracks, Dover. It was from there that those eligible for service overseas proceeded on embarkation leave. The process of mobilisation proceeded smoothly, and the battalion was brought up to strength in personnel. On November 22 Sir Charles Bonham-Carter paid a farewell visit, and on December 13 the battalion embarked at Dover to join the Army of Occupation in Germany. History was thus repeated, for in March 1920, nearly twenty-six years before, the 2nd Battalion had left Dover for duty with the B.A.O.R.

The first and temporary station was the Cathedral city of Malines in Belgium, where the battalion was accommodated in Cathedral Barracks. Carriers and wheeled vehicles were drawn from Ghent and Hamburg during January, and preparations were made for the move into Germany. On February 17, 1946, the main body of the battalion left by rail for Hardegsen. On arrival, companies went straight out to Uslar, Northeim and Adelebsen. This was the area in which the Regiment had first seen action in Europe during the Seven Years' War.

In this sector, which was practically untouched by war, the battalion was in 5th Division (Major-General R. A. Hull, and later Major-General P. G. S. Gregson-Ellis). A curfew was strictly enforced, and checks were carried out in the neighbouring villages. Any civilians found out after curfew or without identity documents were handed over to the civil police. There were many Displaced Persons (D.P.s) in these villages, and tact and sometimes even a display of force had to be used in order to avoid trouble between them and the German inhabitants. Efforts had also to be made to expose black market transactions and to prevent burglaries and looting of crops and livestock by these D.P.s.

On June 5 the battalion moved 100 miles north to Brunswick, where it was accommodated in Pontefract and Wiltshire Barracks. It provided the garrison troops for the Brunswick area, and the guards which had to be supplied included those for the Military Prison and the British General Hospital. In addition a Mobile Force stood-by in readiness to mount extra guards on vulnerable points in case of an emergency. Every village in the area had to be visited at least once a month at night in order to carry out curfew patrols. Several large-scale checks on the inhabitants were organised. One of these, in August, was a raid on the houses of civilians employed at the Ordnance Depot in Brunswick. Fifteen houses were searched simultaneously, and five persons were arrested for being in possession of Ordnance equipment.

In general the relations between the troops and the German civilians were friendly and correct, and discipline was good. The amenities and entertainments provided in bomb-battered Brunswick were much appreciated, but there was a shortage of playing fields. Towards the end of September the married families began to arrive from England, and later the band, newly formed under Bandmaster Jackson, arrived from the Depot. It appeared, in fact, that Brunswick was officially regarded as the battalion's permanent station.

Lieutenant-Colonel E. W. D. Western assumed command on August 23, Dennis Talbot having previously departed to the Royal Naval Staff College at Greenwich. 'Tank' Western returned to the Regiment after an absence of over twelve years, during which he had been seconded to the Royal West African Frontier Force. During the war he had been awarded the D.S.O. when in command of the

3rd Battalion The Gold Coast Regiment in the Abyssinian campaign in 1941; had risen to the rank of Brigadier; and had commanded the 2nd (West African) Brigade in Burma.

The feeling of permanency was short lived, for in December the battalion moved to Berlin. It was accommodated in Wavell Barracks, Spandau, in the British Zone. The battalion was mainly occupied in finding guards for various British Headquarters and residences of Military Commanders, but there were also a number of internal security duties to perform. It was responsible for the Tiergarten and Wilmersdorf areas, near the junction of the British, American and Russian sectors, and shooting affrays were not uncommon. One company was attached to the headquarters of Tiergarten District.

Berlin was not a comfortable place at that time. The town had been badly damaged by bombing, and entertainments were few. In addition the heating system in Wavell Barracks had broken down and could not be repaired for some time owing to lack of piping, and the Tiergarten detachment found that the coal ration was too small for that unusually severe winter. It was with some relief therefore that, after three months, the battalion returned to Brunswick at the end of March 1947, and resumed its duties there. 'Tank' Western had left to command 129th Brigade (T.A.) at Oxford early in February, so it was Major Martyn who organised the move. He was later appointed C.O.

At the beginning of April the battalion was called upon to quell a civil disturbance in Brunswick. This was a demonstration against the small rations. After rioters had smashed the windows of a Dutch unit and a Jewish club and had broken into the Married Families' Shop, the situation got beyond the control of the Civil Police, and command of the town was handed over to Tony Martyn as Military Commander. D Company, under Major M. G. M. Archer, was immediately dispatched to the scene of the disturbance. The crowds were soon dispersed. Picquets were placed on military installations, and control was then handed back to the Civil Police. The only casualties were one civilian killed, one British driver admitted to hospital with bruises, one 3-ton truck burnt out and several police cars overturned.

About a month after the return to Brunswick the battalion moved out for Brigade Training to a tented camp at Soltau, near Belsen. Another of these Brigade Camps was held in August. The battalion then became responsible for providing guards on the supply trains to Berlin and for sending internal security patrols to detect thefts of crops and livestock in the Watenstedt-Salzgitter area, south-west of

Brunswick. This area contained the extensive Reichwerke steel plant as well as thirty-four camps. These camps held some 17,000 D.P.s, and several major raids were made on them in co-operation with the Civil Police. At the same time the strength of the battalion was decreasing as men were released; one company had to be disbanded.

Another change in Commanding Officers occurred on September 7, when Colonel Macklin was transferred from the 1st Battalion in Egypt. Soon after this Tony Martyn was posted to a Staff appointment at Headquarters Rhine Army; Major Heygate became second-in-command. Towards the end of October the Colonel of the Regiment, Brigadier N. I. Whitty, visited the battalion for four days. During the visit he inspected the battalion on parade, when the Colours were carried for the first time since the war, and met some of the families at a Families' Tea Party. Next day a Regimental Luncheon, to which all officers of the Regiment serving in the B.A.O.R. and their wives were invited, was held at the Officers' Club, Brunswick. This was something of a Regimental Reunion.

* * *

Unexpectedly the battalion, after a tour of only two years in the Rhine Army, embarked at the Hook of Holland for Harwich in the *Biarritz* on November 15, 1947, and returned to England, where it was stationed at West Camp, Crowborough. A detachment of company strength under Major Heygate was away at Sevenoaks guarding 52nd Vehicle Reception Depot, a task similar to that being carried out by the 1st Battalion at Great Dunmow during the same period. The battalion was now gradually allowed to run down in strength, no drafts being received, until only Regulars remained. Many of these Regulars were either N.C.O.s or potential N.C.O.s, and Cadre Courses were held to prepare them for courses at Army Schools of Instruction. This suited them well, for it meant that most of them could spend Christmas at their homes, a privilege which some of them had not enjoyed since 1938.

Early in February the battalion, less the guard over 52 V.R.D. at Sevenoaks, moved to Shorncliffe, where it occupied Ross Barracks. It was to become the Training Unit for the National Servicemen of the Home Counties area, and many of the N.C.O.s were sent off on their various courses. The change in role actually took place on March 4, 1948, when the staff of the Home Counties Group Training Centre, together with the National Servicemen under training, were absorbed. So large was this establishment that four barracks were required to accommodate it. The new title was: 2nd Battalion

The Queen's Own Royal West Kent Regiment (Home Counties Training Battalion).

4. *The 4th Battalion*

When the Japanese surrendered on August 15, 1945, the 4th Battalion was at Rangoon, with Headquarters in Government House and the companies in billets in the vicinity. The battalion came under No. 1 Area for operational control and was responsible for finding many guards in the town, including one over Japanese prisoners in the Central Jail and another at the British General Hospital. Rangoon had not yet returned to normal. There was much looting in the streets, and in addition to its other duties the battalion had to be prepared to provide anti-riot guards and mobile patrols. Another task was to find the guard for the supply train from Rangoon to Prome. With all these duties to be done it was not possible to hold any large celebration on V.J. Day, but Colonel Moon arranged that every man should have at least one day's leave during the ensuing week.

On August 23 the battalion was ordered to provide an officers' escort and a guard for the Japanese envoys who were coming to Rangoon to sign the Treaty of Surrender. The second-in-command, Major Webster, Major Coath and Captain Webb were warned as the escort and Lieutenant Faulkner and twelve of his Mortar Platoon as the guard. The envoys failed to arrive, however, and it was not until three days later, at six in the morning, that a hurried order was received for the party to go at once to Mingaladon airfield to meet them. A guard was required, in addition, at Army Head-quarters for a Japanese wireless detachment, which had also arrived. The negotiations began at Government House at 11.30 the same morning, the 26th, and continued till 7.15 that evening, when the escort accompanied the envoys to their living quarters. Negotiations were resumed next day at 8.15 a.m. and continued until 1.4 a.m. on the 28th, when the Treaty of Surrender of all the Japanese forces in South-East Asia was signed. An hour later the envoys were escorted back to their quarters, and at 9.30 a.m. their aircraft took off from Mingaladon airfield. This was a unique and historic occasion for the officers of the Regiment who formed the escort.

The Japanese envoys came again on the evening of September 4. The same escort met them at Mingaladon. Further negotiations began at Government House next morning, and the envoys were escorted back to their quarters that evening. This procedure continued for three more days until the Japanese envoys again departed from the airfield at 1 p.m. on the 8th. When they returned two days later only the guard of other ranks was required for them.

More than half of the personnel was now due for immediate repatriation on account of length of service overseas, and the battalion was reorganised, those due for repatriation being assembled together into two companies and the remainder being placed in the other two companies.

No sooner had this reorganisation been completed than trouble broke out. On the evening of September 13 a raid occurred on a store at the Lammadaw Dock, and an S.I.B. officer was attacked and a sentry was threatened with a knife. These incidents required severe counter-action. Early the next morning the battalion moved off to form a cordon round the dock area, and nobody was allowed to go either in or out of the docks until permitted to do so by the S.I.B. It was explained to the troops that they were only to fire in self-defence. At 6.30 a.m. the S.I.B. began a search of the dock workers, and this continued for nearly two hours. By that time twenty-five arrests had been made and some stores had been found. There were no other incidents, and the battalion marched back to its normal routine duties.

At the end of September, Battalion Headquarters and two companies moved to the area of Bassein in the Irrawaddy Delta, the two companies containing the men due for repatriation remaining in Rangoon. The move was carried out in river craft. On arrival, the battalion came under 26th Brigade for internal security duties. Battalion Headquarters were established at My Aungmya and detachments were sent out to Maubin and Pyapon. All rations and stores had to be conveyed by storm boats and *sampans*. The main troubles in this area were caused by dacoits, but their crimes were investigated by the Civil Police, and the troops were not required to take any action.

The 'Python' men, that is the personnel with long service overseas, left Rangoon for England in October. The party was 277 strong and included Major Robins and Captain Wiles. Before the end of the month four officers and some 120 other ranks arrived as reinforcements, but men soon began to depart for release. The battalion never approached full strength again. Its stay in the Delta area was therefore cut short, and at the end of November the companies began to return to Rangoon.

In Rangoon the battalion was this time responsible for guards and duties in the Sule Pagoda, Ball Street, Lammadaw and Ahlone Docks. In addition, a Mobile Column stood by whenever political meetings or other assemblies occurred; but there was no trouble. The battalion was still running down in numbers, and on January 31, 1946, all commitments had to be handed over. The remaining personnel were then quickly posted away to other units, and in February the battalion passed into suspended animation.

Thus ended the war-time existence of the 4th Battalion, though it was later to be re-formed as a unit of the Territorial Army. Its record in the Second World War was almost unique, for it was one of the few battalions which fought in all of the three continents of Europe, Africa and Asia. But it can claim a greater distinction than that. It saved India at Kohima.

5. *The 5th Battalion*

As soon as the 5th Battalion arrived home in July 1945, the whole unit proceeded on leave for a month. On return the battalion assembled at Duncombe Park, Helmsley. The nearest town was York, fourteen miles away, and the surrounding countryside, though excellent training ground on which to prepare for a return to active service, contained few amenities for the troops. The intended embarkation for the Far East did not take place, for on August 15 the Japanese surrendered unconditionally.

The battalion had little chance of settling down. At first it was earmarked for home service, and the fit men left and were replaced by others of a lower category. Then the release scheme began to take the older men away group by group. With one of the earlier groups Jack Malcolmson went, and Lieutenant-Colonel Kerr, now recovered from his wounds received at Alam Halfa, returned from commanding a battalion of the Loyal Regiment in Germany. Finally the role of the battalion was changed once more, and 'Tim' Kerr was ordered to mobilise the unit for foreign service. In December 1945, the battalion—now just a collection of drafts thrown together—sailed in the *Duchess of Richmond* for garrison duty at Gibraltar. Of those who sailed only one, a corporal, had been with the battalion right through the campaigns in Egypt and Italy. Major Heygate was second-in-command.

At first Gibraltar seemed very attractive. The shops were full of goods unseen in England since before the war, and the sun shone. It was not till later that the troops began to realise how small 'The Rock' was and how confined they were. The battalion was divided into three detachments—at Moorish Castle, Casemates Barracks and Four Corners. Four Corners was on the frontier, and a guard was found on the frontier gates, our sentry being on one side of the gate and a Spanish soldier on the other. The Spaniard always wore a greatcoat no matter how hot it was, and our troops firmly believed that in summer he had nothing on underneath. The ceremony of 'The Keys' took place weekly at Casemates Barracks. This ceremony dates back to the time of the Great Siege of 1779–1783, when the Governor himself always locked the Water Gate which adjoins the barracks. Even in 1946 the Governor (Lieutenant-General Sir Ralph Eastwood) usually attended the ceremony, which involved a complete platoon and a band and required many rehearsals.

Any form of field training was impossible, and the longest route march was five miles along the road which runs round the Rock, partly through tunnels. The main preoccupations were therefore shooting on the indifferent range, educational training, drill, and 'waiting for my release group.' Gibraltar was not the easiest of places to see this period through. There was only one adequate football ground—the park, racecourse and playing fields in the neutral zone of pre-war days had all become an airstrip during the war—and leave home had not yet started. Visits to Spain were permissible but were restricted and made difficult by many regulations; plain clothes had to be worn, and a number of suits were kept for that purpose.

Just before Christmas 1946, when the battalion had been on The Rock for a year, orders were received that it was to be relieved by the 2nd Royal Northumberland Fusiliers from Greece and would then return to England for disbandment. In fact most of the officers and men were drafted direct to the Middle East, a large draft for the 1st Battalion in Egypt leaving Gibraltar on the night of December 31. The remainder—a small cadre with the Colours—embarked in the *Arundel Castle* a few days later and arrived at the Depot on a bitterly cold and foggy night in January 1947.

There the battalion's long journey came to an end, only a day's march from where it had begun. Since setting out from the Drill Halls of Bromley, Penge, Chatham and Dartford in September 1939, it had fought in France and Belgium; been evacuated at Dunkirk; taken part in the unhappy battle of Alam Halfa and the victory of Alamein; sojourned for a space in Iraq; and had then fought right through the campaign in Italy with its many river crossings and its grim mountain warfare. A truly remarkable record of fortitude, courage and endurance!

6. *The 6th Battalion*

The 6th Battalion remained at Griefenburg in Austria until October 1945, when it moved across a small range of mountains to Hermagor. This was an attractive village close to the Italian and Yugoslav borders and was actually in the Frontier Zone. Consequently the troops were occupied with frontier patrols to prevent unauthorised movement in and out of the zone, until these duties were taken over by the Austrian Frontier Police.

The battalion then embarked on a programme of tree-felling for the benefit of the troops as well as the inhabitants of Vienna, who were without reserve stocks of fuel. Thoughts also turned to Christmas, and a cloak-and-dagger expedition left for Italy in a 3-ton truck. Having made use of methods other than those laid down in King's Regulations, this party returned ten days later with sixty-two live turkeys and one which had succumbed on the journey. The Austrians joined merrily in the first peace-time Christmas, and the battalion organised three parties for over a thousand children between the ages of six and twelve.

After nearly a week of celebrations, the troops embussed and drove to Vienna to carry out garrison duties in the centre of the city. By this time the temperature had dropped considerably, and Schonbrun Barracks were cold and cheerless after the billets of Hermagor. The city itself was not at its best. The Opera House, St. Stephen's Church and other large buildings stood half-destroyed in piles of rubble. In one great square the Russians had erected a massive memorial to the Russian soldier. Flanked by a semi-circular colonnade, a twelve-foot Tommy-gunner glowered down from a fifty-foot column. Russians were everywhere, and armed soldiers and badly-dressed labour units slouched about in the international zone. Nor had the unhappy Viennese much to cheer about. They were faced with a winter without fuel and on short rations, and they huddled at street corners selling their valuables to buy bread and coffee at fabulous prices. Even so there were many consoling features about life in the city; the Viennese were invariably hospitable and friendly, and the troops were fairly content.

After two months in Vienna the battalion returned to Hermagor, where news of impending disbandment was received. The British occupational forces were rapidly being reduced, and several units had already been disbanded. Men, weapons and stores began to leave the battalion. The Divisional and Brigade Commanders said farewell. A guard of the 8th Argylls exchanged compliments with the quarter guard and took over responsibility for the town of

Hermagor. Finally, in March 1946, the Army Commander, General Sir R. L. McCreery, presented American decorations to two members of the battalion on the last small Ceremonial Parade.

Thus ended a battalion which, in less than seven years of life, had become famous with 78th Division as the spearhead of the British Army in North-West Africa; the victors at Longstop Hill; the vital reserve in Sicily; the first across the Sangro River; and the leaders of the advance through the Argenta Gap.

CHAPTER 26

The New Organisation
1948-1950

1. *Regimental*

WHEN the war ended in August 1945, the strength of the Army was some three million all ranks. The first essential was to reduce that strength as rapidly as possible to peace-time requirements. The process adopted has been outlined in the previous chapter.

The next step was to fix the general organisation of the peace-time Army. The aim was a balanced Field Army, consisting of Regulars and National Servicemen, and a Territorial Army into which the National Servicemen would go on completion of their full-time service. It was soon apparent that certain fundamental changes would have to be made in the organisation of the Infantry. The war had proved conclusively that it was impossible always to reinforce a particular battalion with men from the same Regiment. To overcome this difficulty it was decided to group Infantry Regiments geographically so that, if cross-postings were necessary, they would take place between Regiments from the same part of the country and with a common regional pride.

The Regiment was placed in the Home Counties Group, which consisted of:—

> The Queen's Royal Regiment (West Surrey).
> The Buffs (Royal East Kent Regiment).
> The Royal Fusiliers (City of London Regiment).
> The East Surrey Regiment.
> The Royal Sussex Regiment.
> The Queen's Own Royal West Kent Regiment.

Later on The Middlesex Regiment was added. The possible loss of morale and Regimental spirit inherent in this system was fully realised, and the need for preserving Regimental traditions was stressed.

In November 1946 the reorganisation to the Group System began with the establishment of the Home Counties Group Training Centre. The Infantry Training Centres at Maidstone, Canterbury and Hounslow and the Holding Battalions at Gravesend, Colchester and Chichester were all closed down, and these six establishments were concentrated in one mammoth organisation at Shorncliffe. The Commanding Officer was Lieutenant-Colonel M. P. D. Dewar (The Buffs).

The training of the National Servicemen was then divided into two parts. Enlistment into the General Service Corps and the basic training of recruits of all arms were carried out at County Primary Training Centres situated in or near Regimental Depots; the more advanced training was carried out at Corps or Infantry Group Training Centres, where, after their training had been completed, recruits were 'held' until they were drafted to one of the Regiments in the Group. For The Queen's Own the primary training was carried out at 50th Primary Training Centre, which was at 'Invicta Lines,' Maidstone. Lieutenant-Colonel Scott was the Commanding Officer.

In 1948 this system was modified because County Primary Training Centres had proved to be too expensive. It was decided to close them down and to carry out the basic training of recruits at the Group Training Centres instead. At the same time the designation of these Group Centres was changed to Arms Basic Training Units. Moreover, for financial reasons and because of a reduction in manpower, it was decided that one battalion in each Infantry Group should take over the training of the National Servicemen in the Group. For the Home Counties Group this was to be the 2nd Battalion of the Regiment, and it was for this purpose that the battalion was moved from Germany to Shorncliffe. At first sight this seemed to be a severe blow; but worse was to follow.

* * *

Before the war there had been 136 battalions of Infantry in the Army. In 1948 this number could no longer be maintained with the manpower allotted, if there was to be a balanced Army with the proper proportion of air-borne and armoured divisions. In order to achieve this balance it was necessary to reduce the number of infantry battalions by about half. So, as manpower dropped below the requirements of two battalions in each regiment, one battalion was placed in suspended animation. In The Queen's Own the battalion to be so treated was the 1st Battalion, after 192 years of unbroken service.

On June 1, 1948, the amalgamation of the Cadre of the 1st Battalion with the 2nd Battalion was completed, and the new designation '1st Battalion The Queen's Own Royal West Kent Regiment (Home Counties Training Battalion)' was officially adopted. The new battalion remained at Shorncliffe as the Basic Training Unit for the Home Counties Group. Colonel Macklin remained as its C.O. The Silver and other property of both battalions continued in use at Shorncliffe, and the reserve funds of both battalions were placed in the hands of a Committee of Trustees. The Colours of the former 2nd Battalion were later sent to the Regimental Depot for safe-keeping.

One other calamity befell the Regiment. When, on May 1, 1947, the Territorial Army was reconstituted, it was with a reduced establishment for the Infantry. There was to be one battalion only instead of two in The Queen's Own. The 4th Battalion was re-formed with its Headquarters at Tonbridge but with a recruiting area[1] which included much of that of the former 5th Battalion as well as its own. Lieutenant-Colonel Defrates, late C.O. of the 6th, was appointed Commanding Officer; Jack Malcolmson, late C.O. of the 5th, was second-in-command. Several more of the war-time officers rejoined, and men soon began to enlist. Colonel W. Nash, who had commanded the 6th at Doullens, was appointed Honorary Colonel. Later on, the designation was changed to 4/5th Battalion The Queen's Own.

* * *

In spite of these setbacks the Regimental spirit prevailed. One by one, all of the Regimental functions were revived. The Regimental Reunion, which had been resumed in 1946, was attended by ever-increasing numbers. The Past and Present Association, under the chairmanship of Colonel W. V. Palmer, continued with renewed vigour, and new branches were formed at Sevenoaks, Catford and Guernsey. The Regimental Museum at the Depot took on a new lease of life in larger premises. Presided over by Major Love, its collection of Regimental relics was much increased. The *Queen's Own Gazette*, which had been published only once a quarter during the latter part of the war, returned to its erstwhile thickness each month under the editorship of Colonel Eason, now retired and performing the duties of Administrative Officer at Regimental Headquarters.

The greatest factor in maintaining the morale of the Regiment was the appointment of Her Royal Highness The Duchess of Kent

[1] The companies were at Maidstone, St. Mary Cray, Sevenoaks and Penge.

MAJOR-GENERAL W. P. OLIVER, C.B., O.B.E.
WHO WAS APPOINTED COLONEL OF THE REGIMENT ON JANUARY 17, 1949

as Colonel-in-Chief in May 1947. The Duchess also graciously consented to become the patron of the Past and Present Association. These signal honours were deeply appreciated, not only by the older members of the Regiment, but also by the young National Servicemen. Her Royal Highness paid her first visit to the 1st Battalion at Shorncliffe on June 8, 1948, and to the Depot on November 25th of the same year. During the first of these visits she accepted a replica of the badge of the Regiment made into a brooch.

Brigadier N. I. Whitty relinquished the appointment of Colonel of the Regiment in January 1949, on taking up residence in Southern Rhodesia. His successor was Major-General W. P. Oliver, who, at the beginning of the war, had been an instructor at the Senior Officers' School. In 1941 he assumed command of the Young Soldiers' Battalion of the Welch Regiment, and in 1942 he was appointed Deputy Director of Military Operations at the War Office. His next appointment was in Syria, where he was B.G.S. 9th Army. At the end of the war he was Chief of the General Staff, Middle East. In 1946 he was given command of 31st Independent Infantry Brigade in Germany and, at the time of his appointment as Colonel, was Chief Army Instructor at the Imperial Defence College.

2. *The 1st Battalion at Shorncliffe*

The 1st Battalion trained recruits at Shorncliffe for the Home Counties Group for over two years. This Group, with its complement of seven Regiments, was the second largest in the Army, and the battalion was of greater numerical strength than any other Infantry Training Battalion. It was organised into Battalion Headquarters and Headquarter Company, which included the Band and Drums, four Training Companies and two Holding and Drafting Companies. The whole establishment occupied four barracks—Moore, Ross, Somerset and Napier. The permanent members of the battalion wore the uniform of The Queen's Own, although many of them belonged to other Regiments in the Group. Each fortnightly intake of recruits was posted to one of the Training Companies, and the men were placed into platoons according to the Regiment for which they were 'badged.'

On October 8, 1948, Lieutenant-Colonel A. Martyn was appointed to command. Major Pond bore the heavy burden of Quartermaster. These two were imbued with the traditions of the Regiment, in which their fathers had served, and, while satisfying the military needs of all Regiments in the Group, they yet maintained the morale of the battalion at a high level. Among the successes won were the Army Rifle Association Young Soldiers' Competition, the Eastern Command Inter-Unit Team Cross-country Race and the Eastern Command Inter-Unit Team Athletic Competition. Guards of Honour mounted by the battalion for the President of France at Dover and H.R.H. Princess Margaret at Ramsgate maintained the reputation of the Regiment for smartness and drill. Last, but by no means least, in May 1949, and again in 1950, the battalion boxing team gained magnificent victories in the Army Inter-Unit Team Boxing Competition. On both occasions the team captain was Captain Abrams and the instructor was Serjeant Connolly. The teams were :—

1949	*1950*
Sjt. J. Connolly	Cpl. A. Rodmell
Sjt. J. Watson	L/Cpl. L. Bardall
Cpl. J. Moran	Cpl. J. Moran
L/Cpl. G. W. Lilly	L/Cpl. G. W. Lilly
L/Cpl. J. Lucy	L/Cpl. J. Lucy
L/Cpl. G. Osmond	Cpl. G. Osmond
L/Cpl. R. Fuller	L/Cpl. C. Munro
L/Cpl. R. Ritchie	L/Cpl. S. Lee
Pte. E. Fossey	Pte. E. Fossey
Pte. A. Bernasconi	Pte. A. Bernasconi
Pte. P. Kelly	Pte. S. Lisbon

The passing-out parades of the National Servicemen became quite important events at Shorncliffe. They were supported by the Band and Drums and, whenever possible, the Colonel of one of the Regiments in the Group or the Mayor of one of the neighbouring towns was invited to take the salute, address the men and present the prizes. The families of the men flocked to these parades, and adverse parental comments about National Service were conspicuous by their absence.

There were other notable events. The battalion paraded to say farewell to Brigadier Whitty and to welcome Major-General Oliver on his appointment as Colonel of the Regiment. One of the holding companies assisted the Kent Constabulary in their search for the victim of a suspected murder. There was the visit to London to replace the stevedores and dockers during one of their strikes. In 1950 an extra company had to be formed to deal with the training of men bound for the war in Korea, which had just started, and to handle the large number of potential officers. Some of the latter came from the Guards Depot at Caterham and were the cause of an amicable disagreement as to the number of stripes a Lance-Corporal should wear. It seems that the Guards put two on them, but these embellishments take longer to earn in a County Regiment.

In the autumn of 1950 the tour of duty at Shorncliffe was over. It became known that the battalion was to proceed to Malaya, where the struggle against the Communist terrorists was at its height, and preparations began for a reversion to the traditional role as a Battalion of the Line. A Cadre Company was hastily formed to receive Regulars, to carry out the training of specialists and to take in trained National Servicemen. The battalion finally gave up its training role on November 20 and assembled in St. Martin's Plain Camp, Shorncliffe. This collection of First World War huts was pleasant enough for a summer camp, but in winter it was by no means a haven of comfort. Administrative preparations and 'jungle training' went ahead against an unrealistically arctic background.

One very notable event occurred before the battalion sailed. On January 10, 1951, Her Royal Highness The Duchess of Kent honoured the battalion by a farewell visit. The Lord Lieutenant of Kent and Lady Cornwallis were present on this occasion. After visiting the warrant officers and serjeants and their wives in the Serjeants' Mess, the Duchess lunched with the officers and then received a party of other ranks and their wives. Afterwards, she inspected the battalion on parade and took the salute during the march past. A detachment of the Past and Present Association, under Colonel Palmer, was on parade. Portions of the ceremony, including the address of Her Royal Highness, were broadcast by the B.B.C. The Duchess won the hearts of all ranks, and it was significant that, although embarkation leave had been delayed until the last possible moment to allow for her visit, embarkation was carried out without a single absentee.

After an all-night train journey from Shorncliffe the battalion embarked at Liverpool on February 2, 1951, in the troopship *Devonshire*. The Colonel of the Regiment went on board to say farewell. The Commanding Officer, still Tony Martyn, having seen the battalion away from Shorncliffe, left London by air on the 3rd to fly on ahead to Malaya. The detailed story of the battalion's tour of duty there will have to be told in a subsequent volume of the history of The Queen's Own; but, from the brief account of the first nine months which appears in Appendix F, it is apparent that the present generation of the Regiment is proving itself to be every whit as staunch as those which fought in the First and Second World Wars.

3. *The Regimental Depot*

This history ends, as is fitting, at the Regimental Depot, the home of the Regiment. After the move of the I.T.C. to Shorncliffe in 1946 it was a forlorn sight. It was still the Headquarters of the Regiment, but its barrack rooms were empty and no recruits drilled on the barrack square. A small maintenance party kept the precincts clean, and the Officers' and Serjeants' Messes remained open mainly to accommodate members of the Regiment who came to attend Regimental functions.

By 1950 it had become clear that one of the reasons why recruiting for the Regular Army was low was that the Infantryman had lost his life-line—he had no Regimental Depot which could be looked upon as his home. It was therefore decided to revert to the system by which Infantry Regiments were responsible for the enlistment and the basic training of their recruits at their own Depots. At Maidstone the Commanding Officer was Major Keenlyside, whose father also served in the Regiment, and he had the pleasure of receiving the first intake of recruits in June 1951. Once again the Regimental Depot assumed its proper place in the life of the Regiment.

4. *Conclusion*

The Regiment suffered many vicissitudes of fortune between 1945 and 1950. One by one its battalions were disbanded or placed in suspended animation, until only one Regular and one Territorial battalion and the Depot remained; and that Regular battalion was a non-operational unit and the Depot but an empty shell. In these circumstances none could have blamed the officers and other ranks if an atmosphere of despondency had clouded the scene.

But, thanks to the refusal of all ranks to be daunted by events, the morale of the Regiment remained high. This optimism was rewarded. Suddenly, in a few months, as we have seen, the whole prospect changed. The 1st Battalion reverted to its traditional role and proceeded overseas; and the Depot took up again the task of training the Regiment's own recruits. There can thus surely be no doubt that the Regiment is as virile to-day as it ever has been, and that all members of The Queen's Own are still ready to march 'Where Right and Glory Lead' in the service of the Queen.

Bibliography

1836. J. MacCarthy, late 50th Regiment. *Recollections of the Storming of the Castle of Badajos.*

1837. Maj. J. Patterson. *Adventures of Capt. John Patterson, with Notices of the Officers of the 50th, or Queen's Own Regiment, 1807–21.*

1840. Maj. J. Patterson. *Camp and Quarters, Scenes and Impressions of Military Life.* 2 vols.

1856. Catherine M. Marsh. *Memorials of Capt. Hedley Vicars, 97th Regiment.*

1857. Lt.-Gen. Sir Wm. Napier. *The Life and Opinions of Gen. Sir Charles James Napier.* 4 vols. 'Lives' of this distinguished 50th officer were also written by W. N. Bruce in 1885 and Gen. Sir Wm. Butler in 1890.

1875. *The Queen's Own Gazette.* Purely a 50th paper up till 1881. Published monthly at Maidstone.

1892–1895. *The Queen's Own Gazette Almanack.* Copies are still preserved in the British Museum Library.

1895. Col. A. E. Fyler. *The History of the 50th or (The Queen's Own) Regiment to 1881.*

1899. Anon. Articles in *Navy and Army Illustrated*, 11th March and 5th August.

1903. John Stirling. Chapter on the 2nd Battalion in *Our Regiments in South Africa, 1899–1902.*

1905. R. de M. Rudolf. Pamphlet outlining the Regiment's Services. (H.M.S.O.)

1906. Walter Wood (as told to). Chapter in *Survivors' Tales of Great Events* relating to Sikh War experiences.

1909. Col. J. Bonhote. *Historical Records of the West Kent Militia.* Relates to 3rd and 4th Battalions of the Regiment.

1913. Lt.-Col. J. J. Anderson, C.B., K.H. *Recollections of a Peninsular Veteran.*

1921. H. J. Wenyon and H. S. Brown. *The History of the 8th Bn., The Queen's Own Royal West Kent Regiment, 1914–19.* Printed for private circulation.

1923. Maj. C. V. Molony. *'Invicta.' With the 1st Bn., The Queen's Own Royal West Kent Regiment in the Great War.*

1924. C. T. Atkinson. *The Queen's Own Royal West Kent Regiment, 1914–19.*

1928. Lieut. H. N. Edwards. Medal Roll Part I 1793–1881. Part II 1882–1902 is published in *The Queen's Own Gazette*, Jan.–Dec. 1933.

1930. *A Short History of The Queen's Own Royal West Kent Regiment.* (Maidstone).

1933. Capt. H. N. EDWARDS. 'A Short Record of the Colours of The Queen's Own Royal West Kent Regiment.' Reprinted from *The Queen's Own Gazette.* (Maidstone).

1934. Capt. R. O. RUSSELL. *History of the 11th (Lewisham) Bn., The Queen's Own Royal West Kent Regiment, 1914–18.*

1937–1938. Capt. H. N. EDWARDS. Articles on 'The Clothing, Equipment and Arms of the Queen's Own, 1756–1936,' printed in *The Queen's Own Gazette.*

1942. MICHAEL JOSEPH. *The Sword in the Scabbard.* Author served in the 9th Battalion in 1940–41.

APPENDICES

Appendices

Honours and Awards
1940–1950

(The ranks and decorations shown are those held at the time of the recommendation)

(Members of other Regiments, who won awards while serving with The Queen's Own, are not included in this list.)

VICTORIA CROSS
Harman, J. P., 295822, L/Cpl.

ORDER OF THE BATH
Knight Grand Cross
Bonham-Carter, Sir Charles, K.C.B., C.M.G., D.S.O., General
Companion
Oliver, W. P., O.B.E., T/Maj.-General

ROYAL VICTORIAN ORDER
Dame Grand Cross
Kent, H.R.H., The Duchess of, C.I., G.B.E.

ORDER OF THE BRITISH EMPIRE
(Military Division)
Commander
Riddell, R. A., O.B.E., A/Maj.-General
Rome, F. D., D.S.O., T/Brig.
Waddington, T. T., M.C., T/Brig.
Wingfield-Stratford, G. E., M.C., Colonel

Order of the British Empire (Military Division)—*continued*

Officer

Brooke, H. J. S., T/Lt-Col.
Carr, J. M., T/Lt-Col.
Craven, C. E. P., T/Lt-Col.
Crook, P. E., T/Lt-Col.
Durtnell, C. S., T/Lt-Col.
Harris, F. A., T/Lt-Col.
Hicks, P. R., T/Lt-Col.
Hinton, H. O., T/Lt-Col.
Hudson, G. E., M.C., T.D.,
   T/Lt-Col.
Knox, H. M. O., T/Lt-Col.
Macklin, P. H., T/Lt-Col.

Moulton-Barrett, E. F., M.C.,
   Lt-Col.
Oliver, W. P., T/Brig.
Pulverman, R. O., T/Lt-Col.
Riddell, R. A., T/Brig.
Stapleton, D. G. H., T/Lt-Col.
Thomas, R. C. W., A/Lt-Col.
Thrift, K. G., T/Lt-Col.
Tong, R. P., T/Lt-Col.
Wilkin, H., M.B.E., M.C., local
   Lt-Col.

Member

Bayntun, T. F., T/Maj.
Benbow, R., Lt. (Q.M.)
Blake, A. G., Lt. (Q.M.)
Butler, R., T/Capt.
Christofas, K. C., T/Maj.
Clitherow-Smith, D., T/Maj.
Cobb, A. G. S., T/Maj.
Courtney, G. B., T/Capt.
Craddock, C. W., T.D., Maj.(Q.M.)
Creed, E. H., W.O.I (R.S.M.)
Edwards, H. N., A/Lt-Col.
Edwards, W. E., Capt.
Flint, A. J. M., A/Capt.
Flood, E. P., T/Capt.
Goddin, P. R., T/Maj.
James, H. B., T/Maj.
Lavington, R. H., 2nd Lt.
Le Cocq, F. B., T/Maj.

Mines, R. C. E., Capt. (Q.M.)
Pardington, G. E. L., T.D., Maj.
Pearson, W. F., T/Capt.
Pond, B. A., Capt. (Q.M.)
Pugh, P. D. S., M.C., Lt.
Rawcliffe, J., W.O.II
Ryder, R. R., T/Capt.
Sibree, J. H. D., M.C., T/Maj.
Thatcher, A. J., T/Maj.
Thornton, A. S., T/Maj.
Walker, A. W., Capt. (Q.M.)
Watts, A. E., Lt. (Q.M.)
Weymouth, G. U., Lt.
Wheater, J. D., T/Capt.
Whitehead, J. C., Capt.
Wilkins, H. D., W.O.II (R.Q.M.S.)
Wonnall, M. H., T/Maj.

(Civil Division)

Officer

Edlmann, F. J., D.S.O., Col.
Jackson, R. D., Lt-Col.

BAR TO THE DISTINGUISHED SERVICE ORDER

Howlett, B., D.S.O.   A/Brigadier   36th Bde.   Sicily. Centuripe and Bronte.

THE DISTINGUISHED SERVICE ORDER

Bowers, J. H.	Lieut.	2/4 Hamps.	Italy. River Gari.
Braithwaite, H. P.	T/Lt-Col.	1st Bn.	Italy. San Pancrazio.
Bryan, P. E. O., M.C.	A/Lt-Col.	6th Bn.	Sicily. Mt. Rivoglia.
Chitty, A. A. E.	A/Lt-Col.	4th Bn.	B.E.F. Oudenarde.
Defrates, G. K., M.C.	T/Lt-Col.	6th Bn.	Italy. Acqua Salata.
Elliott, G. G.	T/Lt-Col.	2 Essex	N.W. Europe. Periodic.
Grimsey, J. E.	T/Maj.	5th Bn.	Italy. Monte Romano.
Hazelton, B. E., M.C.	T/Lt-Col.	1 Gold Coast	Burma. Shaubin Taung.
Howlett, B.	A/Brigadier	36th Bde.	N. W. Africa. Longstop.
Talbot, D. E. B., M.C.	T/Lt-Col.	7th Hamps.	N.W. Europe. Periodic.
Western, E. W. D.	T/Lt-Col.	3 Gold Coast	Mid. East. Italian East Africa.
Whitty, J. H. H., M.C.	T/Lt-Col.	5th Bn.	Italy. Romagnoli.

SECOND BAR TO THE MILITARY CROSS

Stewart, S., M.C.   A/Major   6th Bn.   Italy. Boccaleone.

BAR TO THE MILITARY CROSS

Callf, L. S., M.C.	T/Capt.	Commando	Italy. Anzio.
Defrates, G. K., M.C.	A/Maj.	6th Bn.	Sicily. Centuripe.
Rooke, D. B., M.C.	T/Maj.	7th Hamps.	N.W. Europe. Waldenrath.
Stewart, S., M.C.	T/Capt.	36th Bde.	Italy. Termoli.

THE MILITARY CROSS

Allen, R. H. D.	Lieut.	4th Bn.	B.E.F. Foret de Nieppe.
Andrews, D. H.	Capt.	4th Bn.	B.E.F. Foret de Nieppe.
Archdeacon, T. C.	Lieut.	1st Bn.	Italy. River Ausa.
Archer, D. H.	A/Capt.	1st Bn.	B.E.F. Oudenarde.
Archer, M. G. M.	A/Capt.	7th Bn.	B.E.F. Albert.
Balbernie, R. W.	T/Maj.	4/6 Gurkha	Burma. Mindegon.
Beall, P.	A/Capt.	6th Bn.	Italy. Termoli.
Benge, R. C., M.M.	Lieut.	5th Buffs.	Italy. Cassino Station.
Brounlie, C. A. de B.	A/Maj.	3rd Nigeria	Mid. East. Italian East Africa.
Browne, J. B.	Lieut.	2nd Bn.	Aegean. Leros.
Bryan, P. E. O.	T/Maj.	6th Bn.	N.W. Africa. Longstop.
Butler, R., M.B.E.	T/Maj.	2nd Bn.	Aegean. Leros.
Callf, L. S.	A/Capt.	9 Commando	Italy. Anzio.
Cammiade, T. B.	Lieut.	1st R.Ir.F.	Sicily. R. Simeto.
Clark, C. A. L.	Lieut.	2nd Bn.	Mid. East. Malta.
Clarke, R. L.	A/Maj.	6th Bn.	Sicily. Mt. Rivoglia.
Cooke, D. D. B.	2nd Lt.	1/3 K.A.R.	Mid. East. Italian East Africa.
Cooke, K. H. N.	Lieut.	6th Bn.	Italy. Boccaleone.
Cooke, R. R.	Lieut.	11 Commando	N. Africa. Cyrene.
Courtney, G. B., M.B.E.	A/Maj.	S. Boat Sec.	Sardinia. Periodic.
Defrates, G. K.	T/Capt.	6th Bn.	N.W. Africa. Longstop.
Dixon, F. M.	W.O.II	6th Bn.	Italy. Periodic.
Doresa, P. C.	2nd Lt.	4th Bn.	Burma. Kohima.
Dunmall, L. S. C.	A/Capt.	1st Bn.	Italy. Cesena.
Dyas, G. M.	T/Capt.	5th Bn.	Mid. East. Alam Halfa.
Easten, D. F.	T/Capt.	4th Bn.	Burma. Kohima.
Faulkner, J. B.	2nd Lt.	4th Bn.	Burma. Kohima.
Flood, E. P., M.B.E.	T/Capt.	2nd Bn.	Aegean. Leros.
Gale, M. S.	A/Maj.	1st Hereford	N.W. Europe. Rottorf.
Grainger, B.	T/Capt.	1st Queen's	Burma. Periodic.
Hansen-Raae, H. W.	A/Capt.	1st Bn.	N.W. Africa. Peter's Corner.
Harmer, F. A.	T/Capt.	5th Bn.	Italy. Piedimonte.
Hazelton, B. E.	Capt.	1st Gold Coast	Mid. East. Italian East Africa.
Heffer, R.	Lieut.	3 Gold Coast	Burma. Letmauk-An Rd.
Heygate, E. S.	A/Maj.	5th Bn.	B.E.F. Foret de Nieppe.
Howard, D. S. de C.	Lieut.	6th Bn.	N.W. Africa. Green Hill.
Hoyle, R. H.	Lieut.	1 D.W.R.	Italy. Monte Cece.
James, R. A.	Lieut.	2nd Bn.	Aegean. Leros.
Jarrett, T.	T/Maj.	6th Bn.	Italy. Periodic.
Jode, A. E.	Lieut.	2nd Bn.	Aegean. Leros.
Jones, W. P.	Lieut.	2/7 Queen's	Italy. Menate Beach head.
King, V. T.	Lieut.	4th. Bn.	Burma. Western Tunnel.
McAvoy, R.	Lieut.	1st R. Berks.	Burma. Panywa.
McNair, J. McC.	Lieut.	7th Seaforth	N.W. Europe. Hasselt.
Maling, J. A.	Lieut.	6th Bn.	N. W. Africa. Djebel Abiod.
Mills, E. L.,	T/Capt.	1st Hereford	N.W. Europe. Zomeren.
Miskin, A. H.	T/Maj.	6th Bn.	N.W. Africa. Djebel Bou Diss.
Morson, G. T.	Lieut.	10 D.L.I.	N.W. Europe. Tilly.
Newbald, E. E.	T/Capt.	2nd Bn.	Aegean. Leros.
Nixon, J. R.	T/Capt.	6th Bn.	Italy. Periodic.
Phillips, B. C.	Lieut.	7th Bn.	B.E.F. Albert.

The Military Cross—*continued*

Pugh, P. D. S.	Lieut.	6th Bn.	B.E.F. Doullens.
Roper, I. H.	T/Maj.	6th Bn.	Italy. Cassino Castle.
Rooke, C. K.	Lieut.	3/6 Gurkha	Burma. Periodic.
Scott, K. B.	T/Capt.	6th Bn.	N.W. Africa. Djebel Bou Diss.
Sibree, J. H. D.	T/Capt.	36th Bde.	N.W. Africa. Periodic.
Smith, F. M. H.	2nd Lt.	4th Bn.	B.E.F. Oudenarde.
Smith, S. B.	2nd Lt.	1st Bn.	Italy. Garigliano.
Stevens, V. C.	Lieut.	7 D.W.R.	N.W. Europe. Arnhem.
Stewart, S.	Lieut.	6th Bn.	N.W. Africa. Djebel Abiod.
Stocker, J. D.	T/Maj.	5th Bn.	Italy. Romagnoli.
Talbot, D. E. B.	Capt.	30th Bde.	B.E.F. Calais.
Taylor, A. H.	Capt.	4th Bn.	B.E.F. Foret de Nieppe.
Turpin, J. E. M.	Lieut.	Spec. Recce Unit	Burma. Myittha.
Valentine, B. H.	T/Capt.	6th Bn.	N.W. Africa. Djebel Abiod.
Van Beek, T. R.	T/Capt.	5th Bn.	Italy. Periodic.
Wakefield, D. J.	Maj.	6th Bn.	Italy. Cassino Castle.
Warner, J. K.	2nd Lt.	4th Bn.	B.E.F. Oudenarde.
Warr, V. C.	Capt.	1st Bn.	B.E.F. Oudenarde.
Waters, A. J.	Lieut.	6th Bn.	B.E.F. Doullens.
Watts, P. E.	Lieut.	4th Bn.	Mid. East. Alam Halfa.
White, H. W. P.	Lieut.	5th Bn.	Italy. Colombella.
Winstanley, J. H.	T/Maj.	4th Bn.	Burma. Western Tunnel.
Young, E. G.	Capt.	5th Bn.	B.E.F. Oudenarde.

BAR TO THE DISTINGUISHED CONDUCT MEDAL

Obbard, A. S., D.C.M., M.M.	Sjt.	6th Bn.	Italy. Casone.

THE DISTINGUISHED CONDUCT MEDAL

Atkins, H. J.	W.O.II (C.S.M.)	5th Bn.	Italy. Lanciano.
Austin, G. A.	A/Sjt.	1st Bn.	Italy. River Ausa.
Bennett, S. L.	A/Sjt.	4th Bn.	Burma. Kohima.
Bryant, W. J.	Sjt.	6th Bn.	N.W. Africa. Djebel Bou Diss.
Byrne, P.	W.O.I (R.S.M.)	6th Bn.	Italy. Cassino Castle.
Catchpole, R. A.	W.O.II (C.S.M.)	4th Bn.	B.E.F. Foret de Nieppe.
Chapman, A. E.	W.O.III (P.S.M.)	4th Bn.	B.E.F. Oudenarde.
Dean, H. S.	W.O.II (C.S.M.)	6th Bn.	N.W. Africa. Djebel Bou Diss.
Gilligan, A. E.	W.O.III (P.S.M.)	4th Bn.	B.E.F. Foret de Nieppe.
Greenyer, W. R.	W.O.II (C.S.M.)	7th Hamps.	N.W. Europe. River Wurm.
Groves, L.	W.O.II (C.S.M.)	6th Bn.	Italy. Conselice.
Kendall, L. A., M.M.	Sjt.	6th Bn.	N.W. Africa. Green Hill.
King, R. J.	Sjt.	4th Bn.	Burma. Kohima.
Napier, W. J.	C.S.M.	4th Bn.	B.E.F. Foret de Nieppe.
Obbard, A. S., M.M.	L/Sjt.	6th Bn.	Italy. Sangro.
Povey, F. R.	L/Sjt.	6th Bn.	N.W. Africa. Djebel Abiod.
Tacon, S. J.	Sjt.	4th Bn.	Burma. Kohima.
White, E. G.	Cpl.	3 Commando	Norway. Vaagso.
Worsley, A. R.	W.O.II (C.S.M.)	1st Bn.	Italy. Cesena.

BAR TO THE MILITARY MEDAL

Cull, W. F., M.M.	L/Cpl.	6th Bn.	Italy. Acqua Salata.

THE MILITARY MEDAL

Andrews, J.	L/Cpl.	6th Bn.	Italy. Sangro.
Archer, G. H. T.	Pte.	4th Bn.	Burma. Kohima.
Armstead, R.	Cpl.	6th Bn.	Sicily. Mt. Rivoglia.
Banks, R. D.	Pte.	3 Commando	France. Dieppe.
Bell, B.	Cpl.	4th Bn.	B.E.F. See p. 150
Benge, R. C.	L/Sjt.	6th Bn.	N.W. Africa. Djebel Bou Diss.
Berwick, A. J. J.	Cpl.	6th Bn.	B.E.F. Doullens.
Bidmead, A. E.	L/Sjt.	2nd Bn.	Mid. East. Malta.
Boarer, R. G.	Cpl.	6th Bn.	N.W. Africa. Tabarka Bridge.
Bourne, A. H.	Sjt.	6th Bn.	N.W. Africa. Longstop.
Brindley, A. K.	Sjt.	6th Bn.	Italy. Cassino Castle.
Brooke, V. A.	Pte.	4th Bn.	B.E.F. Oudenarde.
Brooks, G. W.	L/Cpl.	4th Bn.	B.E.F. Oudenarde.
Brophy, T. J.	L/Sjt.	6th Bn.	Italy. Casoli.
Brown, A. L.	Drummer	2nd Bn.	Aegean. Leros.
Bucksey, L. E.	L/Sjt.	6th Bn.	N.W. Africa. Djebel Abiod.
Bullock, L. H.	Pte.	6th Bn.	N.W. Africa. Djebel Bou Diss.
Burden, L. A.	A/Cpl.	1st Bn.	N.W. Africa. Peter's Corner.
Carson, T.	Pte.	5th Bn.	Italy. Monte Romano.
Cockle, W. J.	Pte.	5th Bn.	Italy. Colombella.
Coker, J. T.	Pte.	1 Commando	Burma. Kangaw.
Coleman, C. B.	Pte.	6th Bn.	Italy. Acqua Salata.
Cooper, J.	Pte.	6th Bn.	N.W. Africa. Longstop.
Crosby, M. J.	A/Sjt.	6th Bn.	Italy. 'Vineyard Hill.'
Cull, W. F.	Pte.	6th Bn.	Italy. Lake Trasimene.
Culmer, E. F.	L/Cpl.	4th Bn.	B.E.F. Oudenarde.
Davies, W. G.	Pte.	2/5 Queen's	Italy. Lake Comacchio.
Degens, H. J.	A/Sjt.	5th Bn.	Italy. River Moro.
Dexter, I. J.	A/Cpl.	1st Bn.	Italy. Liri Valley.
Dickenson, H. W.	Cpl.	6th Bn.	Italy. Lake Trasimene.
Donnelly, W. F.	L/Cpl.	6th Bn.	N.W. Africa. Djebel Abiod.
Drew, C. V. T.	Pte.	5th Bn.	Italy. Lanciano.
Dyer, S. C.	Pte.	6th Bn.	Italy. Acqua Salata.
Dyke, R. C.	Sjt.	6th Bn.	Italy. Cassino Castle.
Eakins, J.	L/Cpl.	5th Bn.	Mid. East. Alam Halfa.
Edmeads, J.	Sjt.	6th Bn.	Italy. Casoli.
Enever, W. P.	L/Cpl.	5th Bn.	Italy. Lanciano.
England, A. R.	A/Sjt.	6th Bn.	Italy. Lake Trasimene.
Evans, D.	L/Sjt.	7th Bn.	B.E.F. Albert.
Eves, J. W. H.	C/Sjt.	4th Bn.	Burma. Kohima.
Ford, A. I.	L/Sjt.	6th Bn.	B.E.F. Doullens.
Fry, A. C.	Pte.	5th Bn.	Italy. Monte Romano.
Gallon, J. I.	A/Cpl.	4th Bn.	Mid. East. Alam Halfa.
Gibbons, J. H.	Sjt.	47 Light A/A	Italy. South of R. Arno.
Gilbert, A. J.	C.Q.M.S.	6th Bn.	Italy. Periodic.
Gilbert, F.	Cpl.	4th Bn.	Mid. East. Himeimat.
Godden, E. F.	Pte.	5th Bn.	Italy. Lanciano.
Goffee, W. A.	Pte.	1st Bn.	Italy. River Ausa.
Goude, A. J.	Sjt.	Att. Sierra Leone Regt.	Burma. Kyingri.
Greenyer, W. R.	W.O.II (C.S.M.)	2nd Bn.	Aegean. Leros.
Gridgeman, C.	Pte.	1st Bn.	Italy. Liri Valley.
Groves, J.	Pte.	1st Bn.	Italy. Cesena.
Haigh, G.	A/Cpl.	5th Bn.	Italy. Colombella.
Haines, W. F.	A/Sjt.	44th Recce Regt.	Mid. East. Himeimat.
Handley, W. S.	Pte.	1st Bn.	B.E.F. Foret de Nieppe.
Harris, I. W.	L/Cpl.	45 R.M. Commando	N.W. Europe. R. Weser.
Hay, A.	Cpl.	4th Bn.	Burma. Razabil.
Hayler, W. G. N.	Cpl.	6th Bn.	B.E.F. Doullens.
Hayman, W. H.	A/Sjt.	4th Bn.	Burma. Mokshitwa.
Healing, W. E.	A/Sjt.	5th Bn.	Italy. Colombella.

The Military Medal—*continued*

Hearn, S. E.	L/Sjt.	2/5 Queen's	Italy. R. Adige.
Hermitage, F.	L/Cpl.	1st Bn.	Italy. Forli.
Howard, A. J.	Pte.	4th Bn.	B.E.F. Oudenarde.
Hughes, O. G.	Pte.	1st Bn.	B.E.F. Oudenarde.
Hunt, W. A.	L/Cpl.	6th Bn.	Italy. Montecilfone.
Ingram, A.	A/Cpl.	6th Bn.	Italy. Casoli.
Jarvis, A. F.	Cpl.	4th Bn.	B.E.F. Oudenarde.
Jenkinson, S.	A/Sjt.	4th Bn.	Mid. East. Alam Halfa.
Jennings, D. W.	Pte.	1st Bn.	Italy. Liri Valley.
Jones, E. G.	Sjt.	6th Bn.	Italy. Acqua Salata.
Kench, G. H.	L/Cpl.	6th Bn.	N.W. Africa. Green Hill.
Kendall, L. A.	Sjt.	6th Bn.	N.W. Africa. Djebel Bou Diss.
Knight, R. A.	Sjt.	6th Bn.	Italy. Sangro.
Lambourne, A. J. R.	L/Sjt.	6th Bn.	Italy. Lake Trasimene.
Lancelotte, H.	Sjt.	6th Bn.	Italy. Periodic.
Lawry, E.	L/Cpl.	1st Bn.	Italy. Garigliano.
Lee, T. R.	A/Sjt.	6th Bn.	Italy. Acqua Salata.
Lenihan, D.	Sjt.	6th Bn.	N.W. Africa. Djebel Bou Diss.
Lingham, R. N. G.	L/Cpl.	6th Bn.	N.W. Africa. Longstop.
Lipscombe, G. A. W.	Pte.	6th Bn.	N.W. Africa. Djebel Abiod.
Longhurst, H. J.	L/Cpl.	5th Bn.	Italy. Romagnoli.
Lovering, F.	L/Cpl.	C.M.P. 8 Ind. Div. Pro. Coy.	Italy. Forello.
March, L. T.	Sjt.	5th Bn.	Mid. East. Alam Halfa.
Marchant, A. J.	L/Cpl.	1st Bn.	Italy. Cesena.
Marsh, J.	Sjt.	5th Bn.	Italy. Colombella.
Meade, E. R. J.	Sjt.	6th Bn.	Italy. Periodic.
Mitchell, D. J.	L/Cpl.	2nd Bn.	Mid. East. Malta.
Mitchell, E. A.	L/Cpl.	6th Bn.	Italy. Frosinone.
Moore, J. H.	A/Sjt.	5th Bn.	Italy. Monte Romano.
Mott, D. H.	W.O.II (C.S.M.)	5th Bn.	Italy. Cassino Station.
Munday, R. A. A.	Cpl.	5th Bn.	Italy. River Senio.
Murrell, W. G.	Pte.	4th Bn.	Burma. Western Tunnel.
Nelson, G.	Pte.	4th Bn.	Burma. Western Tunnel.
Nicholls, R. G.	Sjt.	1st Bn.	Italy. Forli.
Norman, C. F.	A/Sjt.	6th Bn.	Italy. Cassino Castle.
North, W.	Cpl.	2nd Bn.	Mid. East. Malta.
Obbard, A. S.	A/Sjt.	6th Bn.	Sicily. Centuripe.
O'Flynn, A.	L/Sjt.	6th Bn.	Italy. Ripi.
Parsons, W.	Pte.	1st Bn.	B.E.F. Oudenarde.
Pickford, J. J.	Cpl.	6th Bn.	Italy. Sangro.
Powell, D. A. E.	Pte.	5th Bn.	Italy. Piedimonte.
Reynolds, A.	Pte.	2nd Bn.	Aegean. Leros.
Richardson, W. J.	Sjt.	6th Bn.	Sicily, Mt. Rivoglia.
Rogan, M.	Pte.	6th Bn.	N.W. Africa. Djebel Bou Diss.
Roriston, R. S.	Sjt.	4th Bn.	B.E.F. Oudenarde.
Sharp, W. H.	L/Cpl.	6th Bn.	Italy. Boccaleone.
Shepherd, W. A.	L/Sjt.	1st Bn.	Italy. River Ausa.
Shiplee, A. E.	Pte.	6th Bn.	Italy. Cassino Castle.
Sisley, H. F.	Sjt.	6th Bn.	Italy. Lake Trasimene.
Sivers, A. E.	W.O.I (R.S.M.)	7th Bn.	B.E.F. Albert.
Smith, L. E. S.	Sjt.	Special Engineering Unit	Italy. Genoa.
Smith, L. G.	Pte.	7th Bn.	B.E.F. Albert.
Smith, S. G. P.	A/Sjt.	6th Bn.	Italy. Termoli.
Smith, W. G. T.	C.Q.M.S.	6th Bn.	Italy. Acqua Salata.
Stammers, C. F.	A/Sjt.	4th Bn.	Burma. Kohima.
Statham, A. V.	L/Sjt.	6th Bn.	Italy. Boccaleone.
Sullivan, M.	Pte.	6th Bn.	N.W. Africa. Longstop.
Veron, F. R.	A/Cpl.	6th Bn.	Italy. Acqua Salata.

The Military Medal—*continued*

Villette, A. L.	Sjt.	6th Bn.	Italy. Lake Trasimene.
Waller, W. J.	Pte.	1st Bn.	B.E.F. Foret de Nieppe.
Wallington, J. J.	Sjt.	2nd Bn.	Aegean. Leros.
Waterhouse, E. J.	Sjt.	6th Bn.	Italy. Acqua Salata.
Watts, B.	Cpl.	132 Bde.	B.E.F. Oudenarde.
Wearn, J.	Pte.	6th Bn.	Italy. 'Vineyard Hill.'
Webb, A. W.	Sjt.	1st Bn.	Italy. Monte Scalari.
Webb, G. H.	Pte.	1 Commando	Burma. Kangaw.
Webb, L. J.	Pte.	5th Bn.	Italy. Romagnoli.
Whittick, J. E.	L/Sjt.	1st Bn.	Italy. San Tome.
Williams, G. H.	Sjt.	4th Bn.	Burma. Kohima.
Woollaston, A.	Pte.	132 Bde.	B.E.F. Oudenarde.
Wrycraft, R. E.	Sjt.	5th Bn.	Italy. River Senio.
Wynne, J.	Pte.	2nd Bn.	Mid. East. Malta.

THE GEORGE MEDAL

Backhurst, H., Pte.   Chick, W., Sjt

THE BRITISH EMPIRE MEDAL

Austin, G. F., Sjt.   Harris, T. E., Sjt.
Chilcott, R. A., Sjt.   King, H. J., Sjt.
Chitty, A. C., A/W.O.II (R.Q.M.S.)   Moss, E. J., L/Cpl
Cowell, G. A., L/Cpl.   Perryman, R., Sjt.
Forester, C. G., C/Sjt.   Shaw, H. J., Sjt.

Foreign Orders and Decorations

Belgium

ORDER OF THE CROWN WITH PALM

Chevalier
Hinton, H. O., O.B.E., T/Lt-Col.

ORDER OF LEOPOLD II WITH PALM

Officer
Holland, J. R., T/Maj.

Chevalier
Waring, A. R. H., Capt.

CROIX DE GUERRE 1940 WITH PALM

Hinton, H. O., O.B.E., T/Lt-Col.
Holland, J. R., T/Maj.
Waring, A. R. H., Capt.

Greece

ROYAL ORDER OF GEORGE I WITH SWORDS

Officer
Braithwaite, H. P., D.S.O., T/Lt-Col.

ROYAL ORDER OF THE PHOENIX

Grand Cross
Oliver, W. P., C.B., O.B.E., T/Maj-Gen.

DISTINGUISHED SERVICE MEDAL

Henson, S. W., 6022345, A/Cpl.

Netherlands

ORDER OF ORANGE NASSAU WITH SWORDS

Officer
Brown, H. S., M.C., Col.
Edwards, H. N., M.B.E., Maj.

BRONZE CROSS

Gray, F., T/Capt.

United States of America

DISTINGUISHED SERVICE CROSS
Stewart, S., M.C., T/Maj.

LEGION OF MERIT

Commander
Oliver, W. P., C.B., O.B.E., T/Maj-Gen.

Officer
Stapleton, D. G. H., O.B.E., A/Col.

SILVER STAR MEDAL
Brock, J. H., T/Maj.
Groves, L., D.C.M., 6348538, W.O.II
Jarrett, T., M.C., T/Maj.

BRONZE STAR MEDAL
Crook, P. E., T/Lt-Col.
Riddell, R. A., C.B.E., T/Maj-Gen.
Sibree, J. H. D., M.B.E., M.C., T/Maj.

Mentioned in Despatches

Three Times
Jefferis, F. T., T/Maj.   Short, J. D. K., T/Maj.

Twice

Armitage, J. P., T/Capt.
Bernard, C. M., T/Capt.
Clarke, L. G. H., Sjt.
Clay, B. L., O.B.E., T/Lt-Col.
Cowan, M., Sjt.
Crook, P. E., T/Lt-Col.
Gore, N., Sjt.
Hales, N., A/W.O.II
Harris, R., Sjt.
Henley, D. O., T/Capt.
Howlett, B., D.S.O., T/Brig.
Jupp, M. F., T/Capt.
Marsh, G. C., Pte.

Mines, R. C. E., M.B.E., Capt. (Q.M.)
Nixon, J. R., T/Capt.
Shaw, P. E. M., T/Maj.
Taylor, F. W. P., T/Maj.
Turner, P. R. H., Maj.
Veall, C. J., Sjt.
Wainwright, R., Pte.
Wells, R. P., Sjt.
West, F. W., Cpl.
Western, E. W. D., D.S.O., T/Brig.
Young, G. R., T/Maj.

Once

Ady, C. E., Lt.
Aitken, H., L/Cpl.
Alder, F. D., Pte.
Allan, C. T. W., A/W.O.I (R.S.M.)
Allum, P. W., W.O.II (C.S.M.)
Allum, R. H., A/Sjt.
Atkins, H., L/Cpl.
Atkins, J., Sjt.
Austin, P. H., T/Maj.
Balbernie, R. W., A/Maj.
Balcam, R., Pte.
Barnard, W. P., Pte.
Barnes, G. L., Pte.
Barry, T., Sjt.

Bates, S. J., Lt.
Bayntun, T. F., T/Maj.
Beall, P., 2nd Lt.
Benge, R. C., M.M., L/Sjt.
Bethune, J., L/Cpl.
Bewley, F. J., Lt.
Bishop, J. E., L/Cpl.
Bishop, S. J., Pte.
Bloom, N., T/Capt.
Bloomfield, J. W., Cpl.
Bones, F., Pte.
Bowditch, K., Cpl.
Bowles, S. D., Lt.
Boxwell, G. F., Sjt.

Mentioned in Despatches (once)—*continued*

Bett, F., Pte.
Bradford, F., Pte.
Brand, E. F., Lt.
Brindley, A. K., M.M., Sjt.
Bristow-Jones, L. J., T/Capt.
Broadway, J. F., Cpl.
Brooks, S. H., L/Sjt.
Brophy, T. J., L/Sjt.
Brown, J. T., Cpl.
Brown, R. F. G., Pte.
Brown, R. W. H., 2nd Lt.
Bryan, P. E. O., M.C., T/Maj.
Bryant, W. J., D.C.M., Sjt.
Buckingham, B. O., Lt.
Buckle, P. C. M., T/Capt.
Bull, F. W., Sjt.
Bunday, T., L/Cpl.
Burke, M. A. T., 2nd Lt.
Burrows, J. H., T/Maj.
Caller, A. F. H. E., Lt.
Cammiade, T. B., M.C., T/Capt.
Carey, L. A., T/Maj.
Carpenter, R. W., Cpl.
Carr, J. M., A/Capt.
Carwardine, F. C., L/Sjt.
Caswell, R., Sjt.
Catchpole, R., Cpl.
Chambers, F. L. R., W.O.II
Chaplin, J., Pte.
Checketts, W. E., Sjt.
Chick, W. H., G.M., Col/Sjt.
Chitty, A. A. E., D.S.O., A/Lt-Col.
Chuter, D. A., T/Maj.
Clark, J. W., W.O.II (C.S.M.)
Clarke, E. B. S., Capt.
Clarke, J., L/Sjt.
Clarke, P., A/W.O.II
Clinch, R. C., Sjt.
Clout, C. W., M.B.E., Maj.
Collard, C. A., Capt.
Collins, G. C., Pte.
Combe, H. J. D., Capt.
Cook, E. S., Lt. (Q.M.)
Cook, T. C., Pte.
Cooper, D. J., Lt.
Cooper, G. F., C.Q.M.S.
Cooper, H., Cpl.
Copp, G. B. C., Pte.
Copper, C. G., W.O.II
Cottenham, C. V., Sjt.
Cotty, F., Pte.
Court, D. N., T/Capt.
Coussins, J., Sjt.
Craddock, C. W., T.D., Maj. (Q.M.)
Cronk, B. G., C.Q.M.S.
Cropper, D. J., T/Capt.
Culyer, T. R., T/Capt.
Cunnell, T., W.O.II
D'Avigdor-Goldsmid, Sir Henry J.,
  Bart., 2nd Lt.
Davies, E., C.Q.M.S.
Davies, W. E., Pte.

Davis, E. F. B., T/Maj.
Deed, E. A., Lt.
Dendy, R. W., Sjt.
Dillaway, A. A. J., Cpl.
Dinwiddy, G. D., Lt.
Dixon, F. M., W.O.II
Dorset, C. P., L/Cpl.
Drew, S. J., Pte.
Drummond, A. E., Sjt.
Duffield, G. W., T/Capt.
Duff, H. E., Capt.
Duffy, J., Pte.
Dunmall, E. C., A/W.O.I (R.S.M.)
Durance, F. F., L/Cpl.
Eason, J. A., T/Capt.
Easten, D. F., M.C., A/Maj.
Easton, A. P., Pte.
Easton, J. E. A., Sjt.
Edwards, W. J., Pte.
Elliott, G. G., Capt.
England, A. R., Cpl.
Evenden, G. C., Pte.
Farley, J., Pte.
Fearon, M., L/Cpl.
Fenwick, R. P., Sjt.
Firman, E. D. H., Lt.
Fleming, I. D. K., T/Capt.
Foot, H. F., Cpl.
Forsberg, G., L/Cpl.
Forster, C. A., Cpl.
Forster, H. F., Cpl.
Franklin, C. E., L/Sjt.
Gamman, S. E., Pte.
Gardner, D., L/Cpl.
Garland, F. D., Pte.
Gibbs, S. L., Capt.
Gibson, J. M., Capt.[1]
Gilbert, C. H., T/Lt-Col.
Glover, W., Pte.
Goodenough, B. J., T/Capt.
Gordon, C. T. R., Lt.
Granville, A., Cpl.
Groom, H. D. T., Lt.
Groves, L., D.C.M., W.O.II
Gwilliam, D. H., T/Maj.
Hall, H. W., A/W.O.I
Hall, J. R. J., Pte.
Hall, R. E., Sjt.
Hallett, F. G., Sjt.
Hammond, E., Cpl.
Hammond, V. G., Pte.
Hanks, J. G., Pte.
Harris, L. G., Pte.
Hay, A., Pte.
Hayley, A. J., W.O.I
Hazelton, B. E., Capt.
Healey, D., L/Cpl.
Heaslewood, E. W., Sjt.
Heskett, D., W.O.II
Hewitson, S. C., W.O.II
Heygate, E. S., M.C., T/Lt-Col.

[1] Killed in action in Malaya in 1950.

Mentioned in Despatches (once)—*continued*

Hicks, P. R., A/Lt-Col.
Hinton, H. O., A/Lt-Col.
Holland, J. E., Cpl.
Holland, J. R., 2nd Lt.
Hughes, J. S., T/Maj.
Iddenden, A. J., L/Cpl.
Ingham, G., Maj.
Inman, J., Sjt.
James, R. A., Lt.
Jarrett, T., Capt.
Jeffrey, F. F. S., L/Cpl.
Jenkins, H W., Pte.
Johnson, J. M., Lt.
Johnson, F. C., Col/Sjt.
Jones, W., Pte.
Keenlyside, C. H., A/Maj.
Kenny, J. H., Sjt.
Ker, K. R. W., T/Capt.
Key, J. W., Cpl.
King, F. W. G., Sjt.
King, H. J., Sjt.
King, R. J., D.C.M., Sjt.
King, S. A., L/Cpl.
King, W. G., W.O.I
Knight, R. A., M.M., 2nd Lt.
Knox, H. M. O., T/Lt-Col.
Lacey, N., Pte.
Landman, T. J., Lt.
Lawrence, F. J., T/Maj.
Leddell, E. H., Cpl.
Lee, T. E., Cpl.
Lenihan, D., M.M., Sjt.
Lewis-Barned, De S. H., M.C., T/Maj.
Lovell, H. O., T/Maj.
Lyons, G. E., W.O.II
MacAskie, I. B., Lt.
McDonald, A. G., L/Cpl.
McFarland, E. A., Lt.,
Maclean, N. G., T/Maj.
Maddock, J. W., L/Cpl.
Makins, A. W., Pte.
Mannell, F., Pte.
Martell, L. F. W., Col/Sjt. (O.R.S.)
Mason, J., Pte. 6340940
Mason, J., Pte. 6347207
Matthews, A. L., Pte.
Matthews, E. R. C., T/Maj.
Matthews, G. W., Lt.
Mayo, R. H., L/Cpl.
Mead, C. H., Pte.
Meade, E. R. J., Sjt.
Mitchell, A. G. F., Lt.
Mills, J., Sjt.
Miskin, A. H., M.C., T/Maj.
Mitchell, E. A., Pte.
Mitchem, R. A. J., Pte.
Montgomery, E. E., T/Capt.
Morris, G. W., Pte.
Mulhall, E. M., Lt.
Munro, J., Pte.
Murray, E., C.Q.M.S.

Nash, W., M.B.E., T.D., Lt-Col.
Neal, A. G., A/Sjt.
Newbery, G. F. O'B., Capt.
Newdick, D., Cpl.
Nicholson, J. W., L/Cpl.
Norgate, H. P., Lt.
Norrell, A. J., Cpl.
O'Brien, T. J., W.O.II (C.S.M.)
Orr, A. A., A/Sjt.
Packer, J. F., W.O.II
Palmer, R. V. D., 2nd Lt.
Parker, G. E., A/Col/Sjt.
Patfield, A. W., Pte.
Payne, J. C., Pte.
Peacock, H., W.O.II (C.S.M.)
Pearse, R. J., Pte.
Peirson, G. H., Lt.
Percy, F. H. G., T/Capt.
Perkins, D. G., A/Maj.
Perrin, R., Pte.
Phillips, C. W., Pte.
Pike, J. A., Lt.
Planel, J. M. C., T/Capt.
Potter, J. P. L., Pte.
Prescott, W. H., Cpl.
Preston, E., W.O.II
Price, F. C., W.O.II
Price, R., A/W.O.II
Purll, S. R. W., W.O.II
Rayner, E., Cpl.
Read, M. R., M.C., T/Capt.
Reid, N. T., T/Maj.
Richards, J., Cpl.
Rickcord, M. B., T/Capt.
Riley, D. H., Sjt.
Robinson, T., Pte.
Rogers, G. E., Cpl.
Romain, H. A., Lt.
Rooke, D. B., M.C., T/Maj.
Roper, I. H., T/Maj.
Roriston, R. S., M.M., T/Maj.
Rouse, W., W.O.II
Rowe, P. J., Pte.
Royal-Dawson, B. I., T/Capt.
Ruff, W. E., Sjt.
Sayle, L. R. E., T/Maj.
Scott, K. B., M.C., T/Capt.
Scull, G. A., Pte.
Sharp, R., Pte.
Sharpe, T., W.O.I
Sharpin, E. A., T/Lt-Col.
Sherratt, W. A., Sjt.
Sherwood, E. C., Lt.
Shobbrook, R. E., Pte.
Smith, C. F., C.Q.M.S.
Smith, F. E., A/Sjt.
Smith, H., Sjt.
Smith, H. C., T/Maj.
Smith, R. J. A., Lt.
Snowling, S. J., L/Cpl.
Stanyon, T. T. W., T/Capt.
Stapleton, D. G. H., T/Maj.

Mentioned in Despatches (once)—*continued*

Steddy, C. G., T/Maj.
Steptoe, J., L/Cpl.
Stevens, A., Sjt.
Stewart, R. A., Sgt.
Stoker, J. A., L/Cpl.
Stooke, P. C. I., A/Capt.
Strand, R. A., A/Maj.
Stray, R. M., Cpl.
Styles, W. J., Cpl.
Swift, C. M., Pte.
Talbot, D. E. B., Capt.
Thatcher, A. J., T/Capt.
Thomas, G. A., W.O.II
Thomas, P. C., Lt.
Thomas, P. C., Pte.
Thomas, R. C. W., O.B.E.,
  A/Lt-Col.
Thrift, A. C., Sjt.
Tillott, A. T., T/Capt.
Tong, R. P., T/Maj.
Tuffill, W. E. F., T/Maj.
Tullet, L. R. C., Col/Sjt.
Underdown, C. H., Pte.
Van Beek, T. R., T/Capt.
Vine, R. J., Pte.
Wakefield, D. J., M.C., T/Maj.
Wallace, H. H., Pte.
Wallace, M. B., T/Capt.

Ward, P. S., Sjt.
Waring, H. B. H., T/Maj.
Waterhouse, L. J., Pte.
Waterman, A., W.O.II
Watkins, L. C., W.O.II
Webb, J. J., Cpl.
Wells, S. H., W.O.II
Went, E. E., Pte.
West, A. J. C., Sjt.
Weston, E. F., M.C., A/Capt.
Whetstone, F. J., Pte.
Wheater, J. D., T/Capt.
Whiffen, E. V., Pte.
White, C. W., Cpl.
Whitty, J. H. H., M.C., Capt.
Wiles, A. J., A/Capt.
Wilkins, H. D., W.O.II (R.Q.M.S.)
Williams, L. M. C., A/Capt.
Winsper, E. T., L/Cpl.
Winstanley, J., 2nd Lt.
Wintgens, L. H., T/Capt.
Wollaston, J. McC., T/Maj.
Wonnall, M. H., T/Maj.
Wood, D. W. J., T/Capt.
Woodhouse, O. G., Maj.
Worth, W. H., Pte.
Wyatt, C. J., Sjt.
Wylie, D. V. J., Cpl.

Lists of Officers in Campaigns

1ST BATTALION, FRANCE

May 1940

Comd. Offr.	Lieut.-Colonel	E. A. Sharpin
2 i/c.	Major	I. R. Lovell
Adj.	Captain	J. H. H. Whitty, M.C.
I.O.	2/Lieutenant	K. C. Christofas
Q.M.	Lieutenant	R. C. E. Mines
R.S.M.	W.O.I	R. Benbow
R.Q.M.S.	W.O.II	J. G. Hammond

H.Q. Coy.

Coy. Com.	Major	H. J. S. Brooke
Signals	2/Lieutenant	D. O. Faulkner
A.A.	W.O.III	J. Hayward
Mortars	W.O.III	H. D. Wilkins
Carriers	Lieutenant	R. A. Axford
Pioneers	W.O.III	A. Brock
M.T.O.	Captain	R. E. Moss
C.S.M.	W.O.II	E. Bonwick

A Coy.

Coy. Com.	Captain	J. H. Burrows
2 i/c.*		
Pl. Com.	2/Lieutenant	M. A. Causbrook
Pl. Com.	2/Lieutenant	M. A. J. Burke
Pl. Com.	2/Lieutenant	P. N. Elgood
C.S.M.	W.O.II	G. White

B Coy.

Coy. Com.	Captain	E. G. Elliott
2 i/c.	Captain	V. C. Warr
Pl. Com.	2/Lieutenant	H. J. Child
Pl. Com.	2/Lieutenant	R. K. J. Fraser
Pl. Com.	2/Lieutenant	V. Dover
C.S.M.	W.O.II	A. Bennett

C Coy

Coy. Com.	Major	O. G. Woodhouse
2 i/c.	2/Lieutenant	M. H. Ensor
Pl. Com.	2/Lieutenant	J. D. C. Churchill
Pl. Com.	2/Lieutenant	E. Dann
Pl. Com.	W.O.III	G. Johnson
C.S.M.	W.O.II	A. E. Orchard

D Coy.

Coy. Com.	Captain	D. H. Archer
2 i/c.	Lieutenant	J. D. B. Bailey
Pl. Com.	2/Lieutenant	D. C. J. Manners
Pl. Com.	2/Lieutenant	H. J. Thompson
Pl. Com.	2/Lieutenant	D. W. A. Peach
C.S.M.	W.O.II	L. C. Watkins

1st Battalion, France—*continued*

Attached

M.O.	Lieutenant	T. P. H. McKelvey (R.A.M.C.)
Padre	Captain	E. W. Funnell (R.A.Ch.D.)

Detached

Major	A. A. Eason	Town Major, Armentières
Captain	P. D. Scott*	} On leave; rejoined about
Captain	J. C. Whitehead	} May 25
2/Lieutenant	R. V. D. Palmer	Brigade A/T Coy.
O.R.Q.M.S.	A. Waterman	} At the Base
W.O.III	H. Dumbrell	}

1ST BATTALION, TUNISIA

April 1943

Comd. Offr.	Lieut.-Colonel	J. M. Haycraft
2 i/c.	Major	D. H. Archer, M.C.
Adjt.	Captain	B. I. Royal-Dawson
I.O.	Lieutenant	C. M. S. Turner
Q.M.	Captain	R. C. E. Mines
R.S.M.	W.O.I	A. J. Hayley
R.Q.M.S.	W.O.II	H. D. Wilkins

H.Q. Coy.

Coy. Com.	Captain	E. G. Reeves
Signals	Lieutenant	N. H. Barber
Anti-Tank	Lieutenant	A. A. Merry
Mortars	Lieutenant	S. F. H. Glynn
Carriers	Captain	W. B. Coleman
	Lieutenant	D. J. Smethurst
Pioneers	Lieutenant	M. B. Wallace
M.T.O.	Captain	H. G. Manwaring
	Lieutenant	C. E. Reinstein
C.S.M.	W.O.II	H. W. Hall

A Coy.

Coy. Com.	Captain	M. H. Ensor
2 i/c	Captain	J. H. Brock
Pl. Com.	Lieutenant	L. H. Sharpe
Pl. Com.	Lieutenant	D. H. N. Whitty
Pl. Com.		
C.S.M.	W.O.II	J. J. Chattenton

B Coy.

Coy. Com.	Major	E. R. Dann
2 i/c.	Captain	H. W. Hansen-Raae
Pl. Com.	Lieutenant	R. C. Ashton
Pl. Com.	Lieutenant	C. Besley
Pl. Com.	Lieutenant	E. C. Bulford
C.S.M.	W.O.II	E. E. Preston

C Coy.

Coy. Com.	Major	H. P. Braithwaite
2 i/c.	Captain	E. W. Sutcliffe
Pl. Com.	Lieutenant	S. K. Keyes
Pl. Com.	Lieutenant	T. J. L. Farrell
Pl. Com.		
C.S.M.	W.O.II	F. J. Beadle

1st Battalion, Tunisia—*continued*

D Coy.

Coy. Com.	Captain	W. R. Follit
2 i/c.	Lieutenant	A. E. G. White
Pl. Com.	Lieutenant	B. H. Casson
Pl. Com.	Lieutenant	L. J. Lendon-Smith
Pl. Com.		
C.S.M.	W.O.II	F. Wilmshurst

Attached

M.O.	Captain	L. M. Reid (R.A.M.C.)
Padre	Captain	A. E. Beaumont (R.A.Ch.D.)

In Hospital

	Major	A. R. H. Waring

1ST BATTALION, ITALY

March 1944

Comd. Offr.	Lieut.-Colonel	J. M. Haycraft
2 i/c.	Major	H. P. Braithwaite
Adjt.	Captain	B. I. Royal-Dawson
I.O.	Lieutenant	M. B. Wallace
Q.M.	Captain	R. C. E. Mines
R.S.M.	W.O.I	A. J. Hayley
R.Q.M.S.	W.O.II	H. D. Wilkins

H.Q. Coy.

Coy. Com.	Major	E. G. Reeves
M.T.O.	Captain	H. G. Manwaring
	Lieutenant	E. A. MacFarland
C.S.M.	W.O.II	H. W. Hall

A Coy.

Coy. Com.	Captain	P. H. N. Jeffery (R. Hamps.)
2 i/c.	Captain	L. H. Sharpe
Pl. Com.	Lieutenant	J. N. McDowell
Pl. Com.	Lieutenant	J. Meade
Pl. Com.	Lieutenant	R. H. Harding
	Lieutenant	W. Ault
C.S.M.	W.O.II	C. G. Copper

B Coy.

Coy. Com.	Major	H. W. Hansen-Raae, M.C.
2 i/c.	Captain	R. G. Bosanquet
Pl. Com.	Lieutenant	J. H. Hyde
Pl. Com.	Lieutenant	K. Clarke
Pl. Com.	Lieutenant	P. J. Matthewman
	Lieutenant	J. E. Robson (R. Berks.)
C.S.M.	W.O.II	H. Peacock

C Coy.

Coy. Com.	Major	J. H. Brock
2 i/c.	Captain	H. P. Towers-Minors
Pl. Com.	Lieutenant	R. T. Hird
Pl. Com.	Lieutenant	A. H. Matthews
Pl. Com.	Lieutenant	G. S. Huckle
C.S.M.	W.O.II	F. J. Beadle

1st Battalion, Italy—*continued*

D Coy.

Coy. Com.	Major	W. B. Coleman
2 i/c.	Captain	H. N. Raisin
Pl. Com.	Lieutenant	D. O. Hogg
Pl. Com.	2/Lieutenant	T. C. Archdeacon
Pl. Com.	2/Lieutenant	S. B. Smith
	2/Lieutenant	D. A. Noall
C.S.M.	W.O.II	A. Worsley

Support Coy.

Coy. Com.	Captain	S. F. H. Glynn
2 i/c.	Lieutenant	R. L. Reeves
Mortars	Lieutenant	G. A. Batsford
Carriers	Lieutenant	C. M. King
Pioneers	Lieutenant	L. S. C. Dunmall
Anti-Tank	2/Lieutenant	S. F. Hall
C.S.M.	W.O.II	A Waters

Attached

M.O.	Captain	L. M. Reid (R.A.M.C.)
Padre	Captain	A. E. Beaumont (R.A.Ch.D.)

2ND BATTALION, MALTA

June 1940

(This list may contain some inaccuracies)

Comd. Offr.	Lieut.-Colonel	V. S. Clarke, M.C.
2 i/c.	Major	W. H. G. Goater, D.S.O., M.C.
Adjt.	Captain	W. E. F. Tuffill
I.O.	2/Lieutenant	P. R. H. Turner
Q.M.	Major	A. J. Coe
R.S.M.	W.O.I	E. P. Flood
R.Q.M.S.	W.O.II	E. Payne

H.Q. Coy.

Coy. Com.	Captain	H. E. Scott
	Captain	T. H. Holliday
Signals	2/Lieutenant	E. E. Newbald
A.A.	W.O.III	C. Clapson
Mortars	W.O.III	W. G. Grimshaw
Carriers	2/Lieutenant	M. B. Rickcord
	W.O.III	E. T. Bushell
Pioneers	W.O.III	J. Smith
M.T.O.	Captain	M. R. Read, M.C.
C.S.M.	W.O.II	H. D. T. Groom

A Coy.

Coy. Com.	Captain	R. M. Allfrey
2 i/c.	Lieutenant	G. W. Duffield
Pl. Com.	2/Lieutenant	A. White
Pl. Com.	W.O.III	W. Woodcock
Pl. Com.	W.O.III	C. G. Botting
C.S.M.	W.O.II	F. C. Spooner

B Coy.

Coy. Com.	Major	J. M. D. Booth-Tucker
2 i/c.	Lieutenant	B. A. Pond
Pl. Com.	2/Lieutenant	R. H. Lavington
Pl. Com.	W.O.III	C. R. Hallett
Pl. Com.	W.O.III	F. W. Grant
C.S.M.	W.O.II	A. Swann

2nd Battalion, Malta—*continued*

C Coy.

Coy. Com.	Captain	R. Butler
2 i/c.	2/Lieutenant	G. E. F. Turner
Pl. Com.	2/Lieutenant	C. M. Bernard
Pl. Com.		
Pl. Com.	W.O.III	E. A. Jode
C.S.M.	W.O.II	R. Silvester

D Coy.

Coy. Com.	Major	H. D. Chaplin
2 i/c.	Captain	P. C. M. Buckle
Pl. Com.	2/Lieutenant	P. Mackie
Pl. Com.	W.O.III	D. J. Cropper
Pl. Com.	W.O.III	W. R. Greenyer
C.S.M.	W.O.II	A. J. Thatcher

Detached

Captain	F. B. Le Cocq	Camp Comdt. Pembroke
2/Lieutenant	D. W. Jackson	Brigade H.Q.
2/Lieutenant	J. H. Marshall	Command H.Q.

2ND BATTALION, LEROS

November 1943

Comd. Offr.	Lieut.-Colonel	B. D. Tarleton (R.N.F.)
2 i/c.	Major	G. V. Shaw, O.B.E. (Welch)
Adjt.	Captain	D. J. Cropper
I.O.	Lieutenant	R. A. James
Q.M.	Captain	B. A. Pond
R.S.M.	W.O.I	F. W. Grant
R.Q.M.S.	W.O.II	A. Stone

H.Q. Coy.

Coy. Com.	Major	H. E. Scott
Signals	Captain	A. J. Thatcher
A.A.	Captain	M. B. Rickcord
Mortars	Lieutenant	D. A. Cruickshank
T.O.	Captain	C. M. Bernard
C.S.M.	W.O.II	H. Butcher

A Coy.

Coy. Com.	Major	R. Butler, M.B.E.
2 i/c.	Captain	W. G. Grimshaw
Pl. Com.	Lieutenant	V. H. Hewett
Pl. Com.	Lieutenant	C. John (R. Warwick.)
Pl. Com.	Lieutenant	H. D. T. Groom
C.S.M.	W.O.II	F. C. Spooner

B Coy.

Coy. Com.	Captain	E. P. Flood, M.B.E.
2 i/c.	Lieutenant	C. A. L. Clark, M.C.
Pl. Com.	Lieutenant	G. S. Huckle
Pl. Com.	Lieutenant	A. F. H. Caller
Pl. Com.	Lieutenant	F. R. Usher (R. Norfolk)
C.S.M.	W.O.II	W. R. Greenyer

2nd Battalion, Leros—*continued*

C Coy.

Coy. Com.	Major	M. R. Read, M.C.
2 i/c.	Captain	E. E. Newbald
Pl. Com.	Lieutenant	J. B. Browne
Pl. Com.	Lieutenant	A. E. Jode
Pl. Com.	Lieutenant	R. Norris (Bed. & Herts.)
	Lieutenant	W. Woodward (Glouc.)
C.S.M.	W.O.II	E. T. Bushell

D Coy.

Coy. Com.	Major	A. J. M. Flint, M.B.E.
2 i/c.	Captain	P. R. H. Turner
Pl. Com.	Lieutenant	J. A. Myers
Pl. Com.	Lieutenant	T. O. N. Fogg (Leics.)
Pl. Com.	Lieutenant	I. R. Reid (King's)
	Lieutenant	C. J. Underhill (Leics.)
C.S.M.	W.O.II	C. G. Botting

Attached

M.O.	Captain	J. C. Seddon (R.A.M.C.)
Padre	Captain	G. M. Young (R.A.Ch.D.)

4TH BATTALION, FRANCE

May 1940

Comd. Offr.	Lieut.-Colonel	A. A. E. Chitty
2 i/c.	Major	M. M. Ffinch
Adjt.	Captain	E. B. S. Clarke
Q.M.	Lieutenant	F. G. W. Lambkin
R.S.M.	W.O.I	A. Hennessey
R.Q.M.S.	W.O.II	J. C. Breaden

H.Q. Coy.

Coy. Com.	Major	M. H. Keane
2 i/c.	2/Lieutenant	J. W. F. Hay-Drummond-Hay
Signals	2/Lieutenant	J. C. Reitchel
A.A.	W.O.III	F. Boughton
Mortars	W.O. III	E. Oaten
Carriers	Lieutenant	J. K. Warner
Pioneers	W.O.III	A. Chapman
M.T.O.	2/Lieutenant	V. C. de St. Croix
C.S.M.	W.O.II	S. Law

A Coy.

Coy. Com.	Captain	D. H. Andrews
2 i/c.	Lieutenant	C. I. Haxell
No. 7 Pl.	2/Lieutenant	R. G. Bensted
No. 8 Pl.	2/Lieutenant	E. F. Brand
No. 9 Pl.	W.O.III	C. Earl
C.S.M.	W.O.II	W. J. Napier

B Coy.

Coy. Com.	Major	N. S. C. Elmslie
2 i/c.	Captain	M. H. Marnham
No. 10 Pl.	2/Lieutenant	J. H. Winstanley
No. 11 Pl.	2/Lieutenant	R. H. D. Allen
No. 12 Pl.	W.O. III	A. White
C.S.M.	W.O.II	R. A. Catchpole

4th Battalion, France—*continued*

C Coy.

Coy. Com.	Captain	A. H. Taylor
2 i/c.	Captain	J. B. W. Ash, M.C.
No. 13 Pl.	2/Lieutenant	C. D. Yarrow
No. 14 Pl.	2/Lieutenant	H. M. O. Knox
No. 15 Pl.	W.O.III	A. E. Gilligan
C.S.M.	W.O.II	P. Seal

D Coy.

Coy. Com.	Captain	P. F. Haynes
2 i/c.	Lieutenant	A. R. H. Waring
No. 16 Pl.	2/Lieutenant	F. M. H. Smith
No. 17 Pl.	2/Lieutenant	A. G. M. Cheale
No. 18 Pl.	W.O.III	T. Thomas
C.S.M.	W.O.II	E. Sutcliffe

Attached

M.O.	Captain	P. T. Cooper (R.A.M.C.)
Padre	Captain	A. A. Chapman (R.A.Ch.D.)

Detached

Captain	Sir D. W. Watson	Bde. A/T. Coy.
2/Lieutenant	H. M. Robinson	Bde A/T. Coy.
Captain	D. V. Bassett	
2/Lieutenant	I. B. MacAskie	
2/Lieutenant	T. E. Sampson	} At the Base
2/Lieutenant	H. B. Samuelson	

4TH BATTALION, EGYPT

August 1942

Comd. Offr.	Lieut.-Colonel	C. G. S. McAlester (K.O.S.B.)
2 i/c.	Major	J. A. E. Mulgan (Oxf. Bucks.)
Adjt.	Captain	H. B. H. Waring
I.O.	Lieutenant	H. H. J. Bishop-Williams
Q.M.	Captain	F. G. W. Lambkin
R.S.M.	W.O.I	W. Bowler

H.Q. Coy.

Coy. Com.	Major	T. Kenyon
Signals	Lieutenant	J. N. O. Topham
Anti-Tank	Captain	W. M. Ferguson (Middx.)
	Lieutenant	T. C. Coath
Mortars	Lieutenant	C. G. Steddy
Carriers	Captain	L. A. Carey
	Lieutenant	J. D. K. Short
M.T.O.	Lieutenant	J. P. Armitage
Battle Patrol	Lieutenant	P. E. Watts

A Coy.

Coy. Com.	Captain	C. B. E. Williams
2 i/c.	Captain	H. C. Smith
Pl. Com.	2/Lieutenant	P. P. Power
Pl. Com.	2/Lieutenant	C. E. B. Bouck-Standen
Pl. Com.	2/Lieutenant	B. Dungay

4th Battalion, Egypt—*continued*

B Coy.

Coy. Com.	Captain	J. H. Winstanley
2 i/c.	Captain	J. R. L. Potter
Pl. Com.	2/Lieutenant	T. D. Bell
Pl. Com.	2/Lieutenant	N. A. Yeo
Pl. Com.	2/Lieutenant	T. R. C. Facey

C Coy.

Coy. Com.	Major	P. E. M. Shaw
2 i/c.	Captain	J. E. Wyand-Brooks
Pl. Com.	Lieutenant	R. W. K. Hinton
Pl. Com.	2/Lieutenant	C. H. Watney
Pl. Com.	2/Lieutenant	G. E. H. Inglis

D Coy.

Coy. Com.	Captain	S. H. J. Roth (R. Sussex)
2 i/c.	Captain	H. P. Towers-Minors
Pl. Com.	Lieutenant	C. Windiate
Pl. Com.	2/Lieutenant	E. R. Bottle
Pl. Com.	2/Lieutenant	B. B. Brook

Reinforcement Coy.

Coy. Com.	Captain	J. C. Reitchel
	2/Lieutenant	C. S. A. Duncan
	2/Lieutenant	C. R. Gower
	2/Lieutenant	A. J. Wiles

Attached

M.O.	Captain	M. Herman (R.A.M.C.)
Padre	Captain	J. T. Bulbert (R.A.Ch.D.)

4TH BATTALION, BURMA

March 1944

Comd. Offr.	Lieut.-Colonel	H. J. Laverty, M.C. (Essex)
2 i/c.	Major	P. H. A. L. Franklin (Essex)
Adjt.	Captain	J. D. K. Short
I.O.	Lieutenant	B. Dungay

H.Q. Coy.

Coy. Com.	Captain	H. C. Smith
Signals	Captain	J. N. O. Topham
Mortars	Lieutenant	A. J. Wiles
Carriers	Lieutenant	C. S. A. Duncan (Leics.)
Pioneers	Lieutenant	E. C. Dunkley

Admin. Coy.

Coy. Com.	Major	C. B. E. Williams
M.T.O.	Captain	L. A. Carey
Q.M.	Lieutenant	J. C. Breaden

A Coy.

Coy. Com.	Major	T. Kenyon
2 i/c.	Captain	C. G. Steddy
No. 7 Pl.	Lieutenant	R. W. K. Hinton
No. 8 Pl.	2/Lieutenant	J. B. Faulkner
No. 9 Pl.	Lieutenant	J. D. Kaye

4th Battalion, Burma—*continued*

B Coy.

Coy. Com.	Major	J. H. Winstanley
2 i/c.	Captain	T. C. Coath
No. 10 Pl.	Lieutenant	T. Hogg (Worcs.)
No. 11 Pl.	Lieutenant	V. T. King
No. 12 Pl.	Lieutenant	G. F. H. Inglis

C Coy.

Coy. Com.	Major	P. E. M. Shaw
2 i/c.	Captain	P. E. Watts, M.C.
No. 13 Pl.		
No. 14 Pl.	2/Lieutenant	E. G. Leon
No. 15 Pl.	Lieutenant	K. Phythian (L.F.)

D Coy.

Coy. Com.	Captain	D. F. Easten
2 i/c.	Captain	F. J. Collett (L.F.)
No. 16 Pl.		
No. 17 Pl.	2/Lieutenant	A. W. Button (Sussex)
No. 18 Pl.	2/Lieutenant	P. C. Doresa

Attached

M.O.	Captain	A. Wattison (R.A.M.C.)
Padre	Captain	R. B. Randolph (R.A.Ch.D.)

Detached

M.T. Pool	Lieutenant	G. M. W. Smith (Border)
Leave Centre	Lieutenant	H. H. J. Bishop-Williams
Hospital	Lieutenant	A. F. Irvine
Hospital	Lieutenant	D. Watkins
Battle Casualties	{ Lieutenant	J. Clayton
	{ Lieutenant	D. I. Rogers

5TH BATTALION, FRANCE

May 1940

Comd. Offr.	Lieut.-Colonel	H. S. Brown, M.C.
2 i/c.	Major	E. B. Loveless
Adjt.	Captain	F. K. Theobald
I.O.	2/Lieutenant	D. E. Ryland
Q.M.	Major	C. W. Craddock
R.S.M.	W.O.I	S. J. Terry
R.Q.M.S.	W.O.II	C. S. Atkinson

H.Q. Coy.

Coy. Com.	Major	E. S. Heygate
2 i/c.	2/Lieutenant	G. M. Dyas
Signals	2/Lieutenant	C. G. Lupson
A.A.	W.O.III	R. W. Price
Mortars*		
Carriers	2/Lieutenant	E. F. B. Davies
Pioneers	W.O.III	W. Brewster
M.T.O.	Captain	M. H. Wonnall
C.S.M.	W.O.II	E. H. Creed

A Coy.

Coy. Com.	Captain	H. J. D. Combe
2 i/c.	Lieutenant	H. O. Hinton
Pl. Com.	2/Lieutenant	P. E. M. Shaw
Pl. Com.	W.O.III	H. Latham
Pl. Com.†		
C.S.M.	W.O.II	C. Page

5th Battalion, France—*continued*

B Coy.

Coy. Com.	Captain	E. G. Young
2 i/c.	Lieutenant	A. B. Thomson
Pl. Com.	2/Lieutenant	J. D. Stocker
Pl. Com.	2/Lieutenant	F. J. Dearing
Pl. Com.	W.O.III	F. H. Deakins
C.S.M.	W.O.II	C. V. M. Inward

C Coy.

Coy. Com.	Captain	T. Kenyon
2 i/c.‡		
Pl. Com.	2/Lieutenant	A. H. Coombes
Pl. Com.	2/Lieutenant	F. E. Tynan
Pl. Com.	W.O.III	H. R. Luke
C.S.M.	W.O.II	R. J. M. Phillips

D Coy.

Coy. Com.	Major	G. B. Knight
2 i/c.	Captain	D. A. Chuter
Pl. Com.	2/Lieutenant	J. R. Holland
Pl. Com.	2/Lieutenant	P. J. Willmett
Pl. Com.	W.O.III	R. J. Mathewson
C.S.M.	W.O.II	W. H. Loader

Attached

M.O.	Lieutenant	W. W. Deane (R.A.M.C.)
Padre	Captain	E. Ketley (R.A.Ch.D.)

Detached

‡Captain	L. M. C. Williams	Bde. Liaison Officer
*2/Lieutenant	A. G. Martin	Intelligence Course
†2/Lieutenant	A. T. V. Pine	Sick. Field Ambulance
2/Lieutenant	N. H. Coyle	Bde. A/T. Coy.
Lieutenant	G. E. Combe	} At the Base; rejoined about
2/Lieutenant	J. A. Eason	} May 25.

5TH BATTALION, EGYPT

August 1942

Comd. Offr.	Lieut.-Colonel	E. S. Kerr
2 i/c.	Major	J. H. H. Whitty, M.C.
Adj.	Captain	A. A. Faulkner
I.O.	2/Lieutenant	E. V. Chalk
Q.M.	Lieutenant	A. G. Blake
R.S.M.	W.O.I	E. H. Creed

H.Q. Coy.

Coy. Com.	Major	L. M. C. Williams
	Lieutenant	K. F. Fuller
Signals	Lieutenant	G. L. Upton
Anti-Tank	Captain	R. E. Spiller
	Lieutenant	P. M. Bishop
	Lieutenant	F. A. Harmer
Mortars	Lieutenant	A. C. Aylward-Marchant
Carriers	Captain	D. W. J. Wood
	Lieutenant	R. Veitch
M.T.O.	Captain	M. H. Wonnall
Battle Patrol	Lieutenant	J. R. L. Leslie

5th Battalion, Egypt—*continued*

A Coy.

Coy. Com.	Captain	J. D. Stocker
2 i/c.	Captain	C. G. Lupson
Pl. Com.	Lieutenant	T. R. Van Beek
Pl. Com.	Lieutenant	W. T. Rose
Pl. Com.	Lieutenant	C. N. Marley

B Coy.

Coy. Com.	Major	E. G. Young, M.C.
2 i/c.	Captain	J. M. Wollaston
Pl. Com.	Lieutenant	D. H. Robins
Pl. Com.	2/Lieutenant	C. T. E. Ewart Biggs
Pl. Com.		

C Coy.

Coy. Com.	Captain	G. M. Dyas
2 i/c.	Captain	F. N. Huckson
Pl. Com.	Lieutenant	F. H. Balleine
Pl. Com.	Lieutenant	L. D. Conolly
Pl. Com.	2/Lieutenant	S. B. Chandler

D Coy.

Coy. Com.	Captain	R. J. M. Phillips
2 i/c.		
Pl. Com.	Lieutenant	M. J. H. Washbourne
Pl. Com.	2/Lieutenant	I. S. Marshall
Pl. Com.		

Attached

M.O.	Lieutenant	H. D. Venning (R.A.M.C.)
Padre	Captain	H. P. Hansen (R.A.Ch.D.)

Detached

Captain	J. E. Grimsey	Instructor at a S. of I.
Lieutenant	R. A. Abbott	
Lieutenant	R. de C. Allen	⎫
Lieutenant	P. C. Thomas	⎬ 1st Reinforcements
Lieutenant	H. G. Henley	⎭

5TH BATTALION, ITALY

October 1943

Comd. Offr.	Lieut.-Colonel	J. H. H. Whitty, M.C.
2 i/c.	Major	D. W. Jackson
Adjt.	Captain	J. M. Wollaston
I.O.	Lieutenant	I. S. Marshall
Q.M.	Lieutenant	A. G. Blake
R.S.M.	W.O.I	E. H. Creed

H.Q. Coy.

Coy. Com.	Major	M. H. Wonnall
2 i/c.	Captain	F. N. Huckson
Signals	Lieutenant	B. O. Buckingham
M.T.O.	Lieutenant	R. G. Henley

HH

5th Battalion, Italy—*continued*

A Coy.

Coy. Com.	Captain	R. A. Abbott (Devon)
2 i/c.	Captain	D. G. Perkins
Pl. Com.	Lieutenant	J. R. L. Leslie
Pl. Com.	Lieutenant	F. W. O. Rundell (R. Warwick)*
Pl. Com.	Lieutenant	V. R. Reeves

B Coy.

Coy. Com.	Major	J. D. Stocker
2 i/c.	Captain	T. R. Van Beek
Pl. Com.	Lieutenant	R. F. Bland
Pl. Com.	Lieutenant	G. J. J. Watermeyer (Un. Def. For.)
Pl. Com.		

C Coy.

Coy. Com.	Captain	D. H. Gwilliam
2 i/c.	Captain	F. H. Balleine
Pl. Com.	Lieutenant	P. C. Thomas
Pl. Com.	Lieutenant	H. W. P. White
Pl. Com.		

D Coy.

Coy. Com.	Captain	E. L. Hill (Wilts.)
2 i/c.	Captain	A. W. Pease
Pl. Com.	Lieutenant	I. G. W. Ferguson (R. Berks.)
Pl. Com.		
Pl. Com.		

Support Coy.

Coy. Com.	Captain	D. W. J. Wood
Mortars	Lieutenant	E. H. Robson (R. Berks.)
Carriers		
Pioneers		
Anti-Tank	Captain	F. A. Harmer
,, ,,	Lieutenant	M. J. H. Washbourne
,, ,,	Lieutenant	J. F. Pearce

Attached

M.O.	Captain	R. A. S. Gibb (R.A.M.C.)
Padre	Captain	H. P. Hansen (R.A.Ch.D.)

* This officer may have been in B Company

6TH BATTALION, FRANCE

May 1940

Comd. Offr.	Lieut.-Colonel	W. Nash, M.B.E., T.D.
2 i/c.	Major	I. Pilditch
Adj.	Captain	T. T. W. Stanyon
I.O.	2/Lieutenant	E. L. Windsor
Q.M.	Lieutenant	E. R. Tadman
R.S.M.	W.O.I	F. G. Farrington

H.Q. Coy.

Coy. Com.	Captain	P. Scott-Martin, M.C.
Signals	2/Lieutenant	L. D. Lee
	2/Lieutenant	P. D. S. Pugh
M.T.O.	Captain	J. R. Nixon

6th Battalion, France—*continued*

A Coy.

Coy. Com.	Captain	H. E. Duff
Pl. Com.	2/Lieutenant	B. Henchie
Pl. Com.	2/Lieutenant	P. A. T. Campbell
Pl. Com.	2/Lieutenant	L. Waterhouse

B Coy.

Coy. Com.	Captain	C. H. Keenlyside
Pl. Com.	2/Lieutenant	C. F. Willis
Pl. Com.	2/Lieutenant	J. A. Bunce

C Coy.

Coy. Com.	Captain	J. M. Carr
Pl. Com.	2/Lieutenant	A. J. Waters
Pl. Com.	2/Lieutenant	B. Y. Watson

D Coy.

Coy. Com.	Captain	R. D. Ranking
Pl. Com.	2/Lieutenant	H. R. D. Langley
Pl. Com.	2/Lieutenant	I. S. Buckland

Attached

M.O.	Lieutenant	D. G. Sheffield (R.A.M.C.)
Padre	Captain	M. Roche (R.A.Ch.D.)

Detached

2/Lieutenant	P. E. O. Bryan	On a Course
2/Lieutenant	J. A. Culham	Rear Party
2/Lieutenant	J. C. W. Adams	In Hospital

6TH BATTALION, N.W. AFRICA

November 1942

Comd. Offr.	Lieut.-Colonel	B. Howlett
2 i/c.	Major	H. O. Lovell
Adj.	Captain	D. B. Burne
I.O.	Lieutenant	M. S. Gale
Q.M.	Lieutenant	H. E. Huskisson (Bed. & Hert.)
R.S.M.	W.O.I	W. J. Napier

H.Q. Coy.

Coy. Com.	Captain	A. J. Green (S.L.I.)
Signals	Lieutenant	P. M. Peerless
Anti-Tank	Captain	B. H. Valentine
	Lieutenant	J. S. Hughes
Mortars	Lieutenant	B. J. Goodenough
Carriers	Captain	I. H. Roper
Pioneers	Lieutenant	R. J. M. Bernau
M.T.O.	Captain	J. R. Nixon

A Coy.

Coy. Com.	Captain	B. E. Harvey
2 i/c.	Lieutenant	W. M. Kerr
Pl. Com.	Lieutenant	N. H. Edden
Pl. Com.	Lieutenant	C. J. Akehurst
Pl. Com.	Lieutenant	J. A. Maling

6th Battalion, N.W. Africa—*continued*

B Coy.

Coy. Com.	Major	A. H. Miskin
2 i/c.	Captain	K. B. Scott
Pl. Com.	Lieutenant	A. C. W. Adkins
Pl. Com.	Lieutenant	M. C. Wood
Pl. Com.	2/Lieutenant	W. J. Palmer

C Coy.

Coy. Com.	Captain	R. K. Murphy
2 i/c.	Captain	R. L. Crook
Pl. Com.	Lieutenant	G. K. Defrates
Pl. Com.	Lieutenant	G. U. Weymouth
Pl. Com.	Lieutenant	E. M. Mulhall

D Coy.

Coy. Com.	Major	P. E. O. Bryan
2 i/c.	Lieutenant	F. W. P. Taylor
Pl. Com.	Lieutenant	S. Stewart
Pl. Com.	Lieutenant	D. S. de C. Howard
Pl. Com.	2/Lieutenant	R. H. Palmer

Attached

M.O.	Captain	D. G. Sheffield (R.A.M.C.)
Padre	Captain	J. R. Lloyd Thomas (R.A.Ch.D.)

6TH BATTALION, ITALY

October 1943

Comd. Offr.	Lieut.-Colonel	P. E. O. Bryan, D.S.O., M.C.
2 i/c.	Major	W. L. R. Benyon (R.W.F.)
O.C. A Coy.	Major	R. L. Clarke, M.C.
O.C. C Coy.	Major	I. H. Roper
M.T.O.	Captain	J. R. Nixon
	Captain	R. K. Dowse
O.C. B Coy.	Captain	P. H. Austin
	Captain	P. M. Peerless
Adj.	Captain	B. J. Goodenough
	Captain	J. S. Hughes
O.C. Support Coy.	Captain	J. L. Williams (D.L.I.)
O.C. D Coy.	Captain	D. J. Wakefield
	Captain	P. Beall
O.C. H.Q. Coy.	Captain	W. R. A. Birch (King's)
I.O.	Lieutenant	R. J. M. Bernau
	Lieutenant	B. T. Wilkinson
	Lieutenant	J. M. Mackenzie (R. Norfolk)
	Lieutenant	T. Austin
	Lieutenant	J. R. Morris (Queen's)
	Lieutenant	M. Desmond
	Lieutenant	N. H. Delves (Buffs)
	Lieutenant	W. Kennedy (Buffs)
	Lieutenant	E. A. Lovejoy (Buffs)
Signals	Lieutenant	W. G. Mealing (Welch)
Q.M.	Lieutenant	T. J. Landman
	2/Lieutenant	T. J. Jarrett
	2/Lieutenant	C. Garner (Buffs)

6th Battalion, Italy—*continued*

Attached

M.O.	Captain	D. G. Sheffield (R.A.M.C.)
Padre	Captain	C. Lucas (R.A.Ch.D.)

7TH BATTALION, FRANCE

May 1940

Comd. Offr.	Lieut.-Colonel	B. L. Clay, O.B.E.
2 i/c.	Major	C. W. Clout, M.B.E.
Adj.	2/Lieutenant	R. W. H. Brown
Q.M.	Lieutenant	A. E. Watts
R.S.M.	W.O.I	A. E. Sivers

H.Q. Coy.

Coy. Com.	Captain	H. J. Langdon
	Captain	M. G. M. Archer

A Coy.

Coy. Com.	Captain	G. F. O'B. Newbery
2 i/c.	Captain	N. K. Denham
Pl. Com.	2/Lieutenant	J. M. O. Turner

B Coy.

Coy. Com.	Captain	C. B. Selby-Boothroyd
2 i/c.	Captain	W. E. Edwards
Pl. Com.	2/Lieutenant	I. Kennedy

C Coy.

Coy. Com.	Captain	S. L. Gibbs
Pl. Com.	2/Lieutenant	R. G. Aldrich
Pl. Com.	2/Lieutenant	T. Thorpe-Woods

D Coy.

Coy. Com.	Captain	E. F. Hill
Pl. Com.	2/Lieutenant	B. C. Phillips
Pl. Com.	2/Lieutenant	R. S. Bristow-Jones

Attached

M.O.	Lieutenant	A. Taylor-Smith (R.A.M.C.)
Padre	Captain	W. A. Griffith (R.A.Ch.D.)

Detached

2/Lieutenant	J. W. Kerr	On a Course
2/Lieutenant	E. C. F. Brown	Rear Party

The Home Guard

THE Local Defence Volunteers were raised in May 1940 on the proposal of Mr. Anthony Eden, who was then Secretary of State for War. In June the Prime Minister, Mr. Winston Churchill, proposed that 'Home Guard' would be a more inspiring name, and the Force was renamed The Home Guard in July 1940.

The Home Guard 'stood down' after the King's Parade in Hyde Park on December 3, 1944.

The units which wore the badge of The Queen's Own were:—

11th Kent (Maidstone) Bn.	Lt.-Col. W. A. N. Baker, O.B.E., M.C.
12th Kent (Chatham) Bn.	Lt.-Col. H. Evans
	Lt.-Col. W. J. Bray
13th Kent (Rochester) Bn.	Lt.-Col. H. S. Picking, O.B.E.
14th Kent (Hoo) Bn.	Lt.-Col. M. O. Gill
15th Kent (Cobham) Bn.	Lt.-Col. F. C. Stigant
16th Kent (Gravesend) Bn.	Lt.-Col. H. J. Bretton
17th Kent (Northfleet) Bn.	Lt.-Col. F. B. Anwell
18th Kent (Dartford) Bn.	Lt.-Col. E. Harrison, O.B.E.
19th Kent (Farningham) Bn.	Lt.-Col. O. H. G. K. Moseley
20th Kent (Sevenoaks) Bn.	Lt.-Col. G. Shaw, M.C.
21st Kent (Tonbridge) Bn.	Lt.-Col. E. K. B. Peck, M.C.
22nd Kent (Tunbridge Wells) Bn.	Lt.-Col. W. R. G. Bye, D.S.O., O.B.E., M.C.
24th Kent (Malling) Bn.	Lt.-Col. R. H. V. Cavendish, M.V.O.
	Lt.-Col. B. W. Lazenby
25th Kent (G.P.O.) Bn.	Lt.-Col. G. Casemore
	Lt.-Col. G. W. Hinks
27th Kent (Kent Electric) Bn.	Lt.-Col. H. R. M. Spofforth
28th Kent (1st Southern Railway) Bn.	Lt.-Col. S. H. Isaac
	Lt.-Col. S. E. Illman, B.E.M.
29th Mid-Kent Bn.	Lt.-Col. H. B. Forbes
31st Kent (Dockyard) Bn.	Lt.-Col. A. A. Hawkes
32nd Kent (Edenbridge) Bn.	Lt.-Col. C. E. Thompson, D.S.O., M.C.
33rd Kent (Short Brothers) Bn.	Lt.-Col. J. M. Prower, D.S.O.

26th Kent (Bus) Bn. became West Kent H.G. Transport Column — Lt.-Col. H. O. Hallas, Lt.-Col. G. Colling

North Kent H.G. Transport Column — Lt.-Col. G. Rice

⎰ 178 (101 Kent H.G.) A.A. 'Z' Bty. — Major P. T. Rogers, M.B.E.
⎱ 232 (102 Kent H.G.) A.A. 'Z' Bty. — Major K. A. Haddacks
became — Major F. E. East

No. 5 H.G. A.A. Regt. — Lt.-Col. T. Gregory, M.C.

51st Kent (Bromley) Bn. — Lt.-Col. T. Etchells, D.S.O., M.C.
Lt.-Col. H. W. O'Brien, M.C., T.D.

52nd Kent Bn. — Lt.-Col. R. N. W. Larking, C.B.E.
H.Q. Farnborough, Kent — Lt.-Col. H. L. Lewis

53rd Kent Bn. — Lt.-Col. A. J. Shepherd
H.Q. Orpington — Lt.-Col. D. Filshill

54th Kent Bn. — Lt.-Col. C. R. B. Chiesman
H.Q. Chislehurst — Lt.-Col. R. Hodder-Williams, M.C.

55th Kent Bn. — Lt.-Col. A. F. Hooper, O.B.E., T.D.
H.Q. Beckenham

56th Kent Bn. — Lt.-Col. F. W. Briggs
H.Q. Erith — Lt.-Col. W. Tobin

57th Kent (Sidcup) Bn. — Lt.-Col. J. Kirtland
Lt.-Col. R. Hoskyn

19th County of London (South Suburban Gas Co.) Bn. — Lt.-Col. J. A. Gould, M.C.
H.Q. Sydenham

20th County of London (General Factory) Bn. — Lt.-Col. W. Brightman
H.Q. Forest Hill

21st County of London (Eltham) Bn. — Lt.-Col. S. H. Lewis
Lt.-Col. H. C. Peirce

22nd County of London (Royal Arsenal) Bn. — Lt.-Col. F. L. D. Shelford
Lt.-Col. L. G. Taffs

23rd County of London Bn. — Lt.-Col. B. C. Bennett, J.P.
H.Q. Deptford

24th County of London Bn. — Lt.-Col. S. C. Bullock, M.C.
H.Q. Erith — Lt.-Col. H. M. Gorringe, M.C.

25th County of London Bn. — Lt.-Col. H. A. H. Newington, D.S.O.
H.Q. Greenwich
Lt.-Col. F. Thorne

26th County of London Bn. — Lt.-Col. C. E. Rothery Moss
H.Q. Woolwich

34th County of London (London River South) Bn. — Lt.-Col. E. C. Heath, C.V.O., D.S.O.
H.Q. Greenwich
Lt.-Col. C. G. Sandall
Lt.-Col. F. R. Bellingham, T.D.

Roll of Colonels and Commanding Officers
1920–1952

Colonels of the Regiment

Maj.-Gen.	Sir Edmund Leach, K.C.B.	April 3, 1904
Lieut.-Gen.	Sir Edwin A. H. Alderson, K.C.B.	Nov. 11, 1921
Lieut.-Gen.	Sir James W. O'Dowda, K.C.B., C.S.I., C.M.G.	Dec. 15, 1927
General	Sir Charles Bonham-Carter, G.C.B., C.M.G., D.S.O.	Sept. 1, 1936
Brigadier	N. I. Whitty, D.S.O.	Oct. 1, 1946
Maj.-Gen.	W. P. Oliver, C.B., O.B.E.	Jan. 17, 1949

Regimental Depot

Major	G. D. Lister	1.10.18–9.8.20
Bt. Lt.-Col.	T. H. C. Nunn	10.8.20–8.12.20
Bt. Lt.-Col.	J. T. Twisleton-Wykeham-Fiennes	17.12.20–16.12.23
Major	O. Y. Hibbert, D.S.O., M.C.	17.12.23–25.11.25
Major	N. I. Whitty, D.S.O.	26.11.25–26.11.28
Major	E. F. Moulton-Barrett, M.C.	27.11.28–20. 1.32
Major	W. V. Palmer	21. 1.32–20. 1.35
Major	A. A. E. Chitty	21. 1.35–21. 1.38
Major[1]	E. S. Kerr	22. 1.38–12. 5.41
Lieut.-Col.	A. A. Eason	13. 5.41–28. 9.41

Became 13th Infantry Training Centre

Major	A. A. Eason	2.11.45– 6. 7.48
Major	C. H. Keenlyside	7. 7.48–31. 3.52
Major	R. E. Moss	1. 4.52–

1st Battalion

Lieut.-Col.	P. M. Robinson, C.B., C.M.G.	29. 6.19–20. 3.20
Major	J. C. Parker (Acting)	21. 3.20– 9. 8.20
Lieut.-Col.	G. D. Lister	10. 8.20–23.11.21
Lieut.-Col.	H. D. Buchanan-Dunlop, C.M.G., D.S.O.	24.11.21–23.11.25
Lieut.-Col.	A. K. Grant, D.S.O.	24.11.25–23.11.29
Lieut.-Col.	O. Y. Hibbert, D.S.O., M.C.	24.11.29–23.11.33
Lieut.-Col.	G. E. Wingfield-Stratford, M.C.	24.11.33–23.11.37

[1] Promoted to Lieut.-Col. when the Depot expanded to 224 Infantry Training Centre on the outbreak of war.

1st Battalion—*continued*

Lieut.-Col.	P. N. Anstruther, D.S.O., M.C.	24.11.37–29. 9.39
Lieut.-Col.	E. A. Sharpin	30. 9.39–29. 5.40
Major	I. R. Lovell (Acting)	30. 5.40–20. 6.40
Lieut.-Col.	A. A. E. Chitty, D.S.O.	21. 6.40– 6. 4.41
Lieut.-Col.	J. M. Haycraft	7. 4.41– 8. 5.44
Lieut.-Col.	H. P. Braithwaite, D.S.O.	9. 5.44– 7. 5.46
Lieut.-Col.	P. H. Macklin, O.B.E.	8. 5.46–21. 8.47
Major	H. B. H. Waring (Acting)	22. 8.47–15. 9.47
Lieut.-Col.	C. A. de B. Brounlie, M.C.	16. 9.47–31. 5.48

Placed in Suspended Animation

2nd Battalion

Bt.-Col.	R. J. Woulfe-Flanagan, D.S.O.	14. 3.16–13. 3.20
Lieut.-Col.	C. E. Kitson, D.S.O.	14. 3.20–13. 3.24
Lieut.-Col.	J. T. Twisleton-Wykeham-Fiennes	14. 3.24–13. 3.28
Lieut.-Col.	E. H. Norman, D.S.O., O.B.E.	14. 3.28–13. 3.32
Lieut.-Col.	N. I. Whitty, D.S.O.	14. 3.32–13. 3.36
Lieut.-Col.	W. V. Palmer	14. 3.36–31. 7.39
Lieut.-Col.	V. S. Clarke, M.C.	1. 8.39–31.12.41
Major	H. D. Chaplin (Acting)	1. 1.42–14. 2.42
Lieut.-Col.	R. O. Pulverman, O.B.E.	15. 2.42– 8. 5.43
Lieut.-Col.	B. D. Tarleton (R.N.F.)	9. 5.43–17.11.43

Reforming after Leros

Lieut.-Col.	J. W. E. Blanch	3. 5.44–24. 8.44
Lieut.-Col.	P. H. Macklin	25. 8.44–18. 6.45
Lieut.-Col.	D. E. B. Talbot, D.S.O., M.C.	19. 6.45–22. 8.46
Lieut.-Col.	E. W. D. Western, D.S.O.	23. 8.46– 1. 2.47
Lieut.-Col.	A. Martyn	2. 2.47– 6. 9.47
Lieut.-Col.	P. H. Macklin, O.B.E.	7. 9.47–31. 5.48

↓

1st Battalion (*50th and 97th*)

Lieut.-Col.	P. H. Macklin, O.B.E.	1. 6.48– 7.10.48
Lieut.-Col.	A. Martyn, O.B.E.	8.10.48–19. 1.52
Lieut.-Col.	G. G. Elliott, D.S.O.	20. 1.52–

4th Battalion

Lieut.-Col.	A. R. Cheale	16. 2.20–18. 3.22
Lieut.-Col.	F. J. Henson, T. D.	19. 3.22–18. 3.26
Lieut.-Col.	H. I. Robinson, T.D.	19. 3.26–18. 3.31
Lieut.-Col.[1]	F. H. Hancock	19. 3.31–18. 3.36
Lieut.-Col.	G. E. L. Pardington, T.D.	19. 3.36– 3.12.39
Lieut.-Col.	A. A. E. Chitty	4.12.39–20. 6.40
Lieut.-Col.	M. M. Ffinch	21. 6.40–28. 3.42
Lieut.-Col.	C. G. S. McAlester, M.C. (K.O.S.B.)	29. 3.42–21. 9.42
Lieut.-Col.	W. H. Lambert (E. Lanc.)	22. 9.42–19. 2.43

[1] Later Brevet-Colonel.

4th Battalion—*continued*

Lieut.-Col.	S. F. Saville	20. 2.43–30. 9.43
Lieut.-Col.	H. J. Laverty, D.S.O., M.C. (Essex)	1.10.43–17.12.44
Lieut.-Col.	P. H. A. L. Franklin (Essex)	18.12.44–29. 3.45
Major	R. J. Webster (Acting)	30. 3.45– 3. 6.45
Lieut.-Col.	I. G. Moon, M.B.E. (S.W.B.)	4. 6.45–28. 2.46

Placed in Suspended Animation

↓

4/5th Battalion

Lieut.-Col.	G. K. Defrates, D.S.O., M.C.	1. 5.47– 8. 6.48
Lieut.-Col.	C. A. de B. Brounlie, M.C.	9. 6.48– 9. 5.51
Lieut.-Col.	L. F. W. Jackson	10. 5.51–

5th Battalion

Lieut.-Col.	A. E. Hills	16. 2.20–19. 8.22
Lieut.-Col.[1]	H. V. Combs, D.S.O., M.C., T.D.	20. 8.22–19. 8.28
Lieut.-Col.	A. F. Hooper, T.D.	20. 8.28–31. 1.31
Lieut.-Col.	T. T. Waddington, M.C.	1. 2.31–28. 6.36
Lieut.-Col.	H. S. Brown, M.C.	29. 6.36–12. 5.41
Lieut.-Col.	E. S. Kerr	13. 5.41– 4. 9.42
Lieut.-Col.	R. H. Senior (Queen's)	5. 9.42–27.10.42
Lieut.-Col.	J. H. H. Whitty, D.S.O., M.C.	28.10.42–23.10.44
Lieut.-Col.	B. J. F. Malcolmson	24.10.44–30. 8.45
Lieut.-Col.	E. S. Kerr	31. 8.45–15. 1.47

Disbanded

The 20th London Regiment (*The Queen's Own*)

Lieut.-Col.	E. Ball	16. 2.20–15. 2.24
Lieut.-Col.	G. D'U. Rodwell	16. 2.24–15. 2.28
Lieut.-Col.	P. S. Moore	16. 2.28–15. 2.32
Lieut.-Col.	E. Eton, D.S.O., T.D.	16. 2.32–20.12.35

Converted to a Searchlight Battalion, Royal Engineers

6th Battalion

Lieut.-Col.	W. Nash, M.B.E., T.D.	7. 9.39–20. 5.40

Reforming after Doullens

Lieut.-Col.	B. Howlett	7. 7.40–15.12.42
Major[2]	H. O. Lovell (Acting)	16.12.42–20. 2.43
Lieut.-Col.	E. S. Heygate, M.C.	21. 2.43–23. 4.43
Lieut.-Col.	H. O. Lovell	24. 4.43–10. 7.43
Lieut.-Col.	P. E. O. Bryan, D.S.O., M.C.	11. 7.43– 8. 5.44
Lieut.-Col.	R. A. Fyffe, M.C. (R.B.)	9. 5.44– 2. 7.44
Lieut.-Col.	G. K. Defrates, D.S.O., M.C.	3. 7.44–24. 3.46

Disbanded

[1] Later Brevet-Colonel.
[2] Granted the rank of Lieut.-Col. while in command.

7th Battalion

Lieut.-Col.	A. G. Fuller	13. 8.39–13.12.39
Lieut.-Col.	B. L. Clay, O.B.E.	14.12.39–20. 5.40
	Reforming after Albert	
Lieut.-Col.	D. C. S. Bryan, D.S.O.	8. 7.40– 5. 2.42
Lieut.-Col.	G. Ingham	6. 2.42– 5. 8.43
Lieut.-Col.	J. W. E. Blanch	6. 8.43– 2. 5.44
	Linked to 2nd Battalion	

8th (Home Defence) Battalion
(Later 30th Battalion)

Lieut.-Col.	A. Latham, D.S.O.	9.11.39–19. 7.40
Lieut.-Col.	O. M. Fry, M.C.	20. 7.40–26. 9.40
Lieut.-Col.	W. E. Hewett, M.C.	27. 9.40–26. 8.41
Lieut.-Col.	G. H. Sawyer, D.S.O. (Dorset)	27. 8.41– 1.11.41
Lieut.-Col.	E. A. Shipton, O.B.E., M.C. (R.B.)	2.11.41–10. 3.43
	Disbanded	

9th Battalion

| Lieut.-Col. | G. Ingham | 1. 7.40–12. 6.41 |
| Lieut.-Col. | P. H. Macklin | 13. 6.41–27. 7.42 |

Became 162nd Regiment, Royal Armoured Corps

10th Battalion
(Formed as 50th Holding Battalion)

Lieut.-Col.	R. H. Pigou	1. 6.40– 1. 9.41
Major[1]	E. G. Elliott (Acting)	2. 9.41– 7.12.41
Lieut.-Col.	C. E. P. Craven	8.12.41– 1. 2.42

Became 119th Light Anti-Aircraft Regiment, Royal Artillery

70th (Young Soldiers') Battalion

Lieut.-Col.	O. M. Fry, M.C.	19. 9.40–11. 4.41
Lieut.-Col.	A. A. E. Chitty, D.S.O.	12. 4.41–17. 5.42
Lieut.-Col.	E. S. Heygate, M.C.	18. 5.42–11.11.42

Became 28th Primary Training Centre

[1] Granted the rank of Lieut.-Col. while in command.

Escape of Captain D. E. B. Talbot
after the Fall of Calais

W HEN Calais was finally captured on the evening of May 26, 1940, Captain Talbot, who was Brigade Major of 30th Infantry Brigade, was in the Citadel with the advanced headquarters. The Citadel was enclosed and there was no opportunity for escape. Next morning all the prisoners were marched off with the few British officers and other ranks leading, followed by the French. The column, 1,000 strong, was controlled by several Germans on bicycles and motor-cycles. The party spent the night in a village church. The British, in particular, were very tired, having had little sleep since leaving England on May 21.

On May 28 the marching column was controlled in a different manner. It was led by a lorry on which was mounted a light automatic gun facing backwards. There was a similar lorry between the officers and the troops, and another behind the troops. The column had begun to straggle because of the tiredness of the men, thus presenting opportunities for escape. It was decided to keep on for the time being, however, because the prisoners were moving in a southerly direction, which was the only feasible direction for escape. That night was spent in a barracks at Hesdin.

Early next morning the prisoners found that they were marching eastwards towards Germany, and three officers—Captain Talbot, Captain E. A. W. Williams (K.R.R.C.) and Lieutenant W. Millett (R.C. of S.) —determined to get away that day. The column was already beginning to straggle, and they made every effort to disorganise it further. Williams had managed to retain his map, so it was possible to tell when they were approaching a suitable spot for escape. At a bend in the road the three of them slipped through a gap in the hedge and into a wood. Passing through water to throw off any scent, they halted on marshland and took cover till nightfall.

Their plan was to make for the coast and try to pick up a boat. They decided to move by night and to rest by day, and, optimistically, they hoped to reach the coast after three or four nights. Williams, who spoke French well, was appointed leader of the party. Between them they had managed to keep a good supply of French money. For food they had a few biscuits, a little cheese, one tin of meat, a few soup cubes and one emergency ration complete. This might well be eked out to last three days.

The three officers gladly left their marsh at about 10 p.m. on May 30, intending to march due west across country. It was a bright and starlight night, and Williams led the way with both hands free to explore wire fences and other obstacles. Millett followed, carrying most of the stores. Talbot brought up the rear and attempted to check the route. After five hours' march across very enclosed country which contained many wire fences, they lay up in a wood. At dawn they found that they had moved almost due south and were clean off the map! This was a great disappointment. The next night they had to march almost due north in order to get back on to the map again. They decided to keep to tracks and side roads in future.

On June 1 food was very short, and Williams cautiously approached a farm, after he and Talbot had watched it for two hours for signs of the enemy. While he was in the farm kitchen procuring some bread, boiled eggs and salted pork, some Germans arrived in a lorry. The farmer kept his head magnificently, and Williams made a successful though undignified retreat via the dung heap.

The march then continued for six more nights, until the vicinity of the mouth of the River Authie was reached shortly before dawn on June 7. The Hesdin–Abbéville road had been crossed on the night of June 2, and further supplies of food had been obtained next day from a very frightened lady on a farm. On another occasion provisions, including cognac and champagne, had been obtained from an invitingly empty shooting lodge. The ease with which an entry was effected was highly suspicious.

*   *   *

The coast had at last been reached, and the party lay up in the grounds of a château. Two painful and tormented days and nights were spent there, fighting a losing battle against mosquitoes of incredible size, while Williams crossed the Le Touquet–Abbéville road in order to search the sand dunes for a boat. The dunes and scrubby woods were thronged with Belgian refugees, but the only Germans encountered were two medical orderlies paddling in two inches of water and an officer enjoying a cigar in the shade of a bush. There was not a boat to be seen. The Germans had seized them all.

On the night of June 8, camp was moved to the sand dunes, and the whole of the sea front was reconnoitred without finding even an empty mooring. On the following night therefore the party crossed the River Authie and lay up in a wood on the south bank. The luck then changed. While obtaining food from a house they learned of a party of French soldiers who had a motor boat laid up in a creek nearby. This French party consisted of three officers and four other ranks and, although they had no knowledge of boats or the sea, they fully intended to make a voyage on their own. After some persuasion the three Englishmen were accepted as passengers in the already rather crowded cabin cruiser.

Water and as much food as possible were collected and loaded into the boat, and an attempt was made to get away on the night of June 11. The boat was rowed by Talbot and Williams—the only two who could row—to the mouth of the creek, where it was anchored while the French, who were in charge of the engine, tried to start it. The more the engine refused to start the more excited they became until, finally, they broke the starting gear. By this time it was becoming light and there was no alternative but to row back into the creek.

A mechanic was obtained from a garage, and it took him four days to repair the engine. During the wait the French were persuaded to make for England rather than a port farther south on the French coast. Command was gracefully handed over to Williams, and he and Millett took charge of the engine while Talbot was appointed navigator and helmsman.

*   *   *

At 9.30 p.m. on June 16, on the ebb tide, the moorings were finally cast off and the voyage began. With a scratch four at the oars the river was reached safely, but the boat ran ashore on a sandbank. The three British officers jumped overboard to lighten the load at once, but it took some time before the Frenchmen could be induced to remove their clothes and jump in. Eventually the boat was pushed off, and the open sea was reached, mainly by rowing but assisted by occasional signs of life from the engine. The Frenchmen had all been laid low by an attack of sea-sickness by midnight.

A westerly course was set to clear the coast. When about five miles out Talbot altered course to the north. The wind was off land, and Williams gradually persuaded the engine to run for minutes at a time instead of seconds. The boat soon started to take water, and the French-men were roused sufficiently to start bailing. At sunrise they were only off Le Touquet, but the engine was now running for periods of fifteen to thirty minutes at a time. When off Boulogne Talbot set course for Folke-stone, with one hand on the tiller and the other holding a flickering compass (which belonged to one of the Frenchmen) as far from the engine as possible.

About midday the engine stopped once again, and the boat was moored to a mid-channel buoy after energetic rowing. Lunch was then taken.

In the afternoon the engine took on a new lease of life and ran for nearly two hours without stopping. After avoiding a floating mine, tea was taken—without losing speed—and at about 5 p.m. Dungeness was sighted. More and more land then appeared until Dover Castle was discerned. The engine had now run out of oil, and it was only Williams's genius that kept it going; while Talbot had navigated and steered without pause for twenty-three hours. Some eight miles from Folkestone the engine finally stopped, and a towel was hoisted on an oar as a distress signal. At about 8 p.m. the destroyer *Vesper* took the Allied party on board and landed them at Dover soon afterwards.

When the exploit became known, the three British officers had the great honour of being received in audience by His Majesty King George VI at Buckingham Palace and of being interviewed by Mr. Eden (S. of S. for War), Sir John Dill (C.I.G.S.) and Lord Gort (C. in C. of the B.E.F.).

Brief Report on the 1st Battalion in Malaya

April to December 1951

(Shortened from an account by Lieutenant-Colonel A. Martyn,
O.B.E.)

THE 1st Battalion disembarked at Singapore on March 3, 1951, and moved into a tented camp at Nee Soon in the middle of the island. The advance party under Major Flint was awaiting them. This party included an officer and several N.C.O.s from each company, who had attended a short course of jungle training at the Far East Training Centre. Everybody then got down to intensive training with a will.

The battalion moved up to North Selangor at the end of March and was deployed and fully operational on April 1. H.Q. Company was organised in the normal way except that the transport included some fully armoured 3-ton vehicles, some trucks with armoured cabs and, in particular, ten armoured Scout Cars. No carriers were held. The rifle companies were organised on a 'patrol' basis, a patrol consisting of ten men divided into a Reconnaissance Group, Commander, Bren Group and Reserve Group. Silent control was achieved in the patrol by a series of hand signals.

The operational area extended from a point on the main trunk road eleven miles north of Kuala Lumpur (K.L.) to another point seventy miles farther north. In breadth it extended up to about twenty miles on either side of the road, which was flanked mainly by rubber estates. Behind the estates was the jungle. Planters' bungalows dotted the area between the main road and the jungle on each side. They were usually in isolated positions on cleared mounds, surrounded by barbed wire and guarded by special constables.

The terrorist organisation was divided into the Malayan Races Liberation Army (M.R.L.A.) and the Min Yuen. The M.R.L.A. boasted a loose military organisation, the strength of the platoons being up to about forty. The personnel wore khaki or jungle-green uniform with red-starred caps. Numbers 8 and 10 Platoons, which operated in the battalion's area, were both well-led and well-armed with at least two Bren guns each. The Min Yuen were everywhere and it was safe to trust nobody. They normally wore civilian clothes, and some were armed and some were not. They extorted money and food from the population, carried out political and other murders often by the most brutal means, and collected information about the Security Forces from agents in telephone exchanges and other official places.

On first deployment the battalion (less two companies) was at Kuala Kubu Bahru (K.K.B.), with A Company (Major Flint) as stand-by company and Major Buckle's Support Company (which was organised as a rifle company) in reserve. C Company (Major Crook) was on a rubber estate at Trolak in the extreme north of the area in support of the Tanjong Malim police. B Company (Major Rickcord) was at Kerling on another rubber estate in support of the K.K.B. police. Shortage of reinforcements had prevented D Company from being formed. The battalion had eighteen little Iban trackers from Borneo attached to it.

Routine patrols might be from twenty-four hours to eight days or more. Everything had to be carried, including hard rations. Four days' rations was the limit for one lift and, for a longer period, patrols had to be maintained by air supply to jungle bases. Water was plentiful, and sterilising tablets were carried. The terrain was full of water courses, precipitous slopes, leeches, monkeys and insects, and movement in the jungle by night was impossible. In the more difficult country hacking a way through the jungle would be necessary, and 500 yards to the hour was a fair rate of progress. Navigation was by map, compass and pro-tractor, and the youthful patrol leader had to rely very much on himself. Under these conditions the resourcefulness and adaptability of the National Servicemen were impressive.

Rations had to be brought up four times a week from K.L. and then distributed. This was a heavy burden on transport and escorts, and the danger of ambush was great. The chief problem was to give the troops enough fresh rations before the hot climate made the food go bad. About two thirds of the battalion were out on patrol at any one time and had to eat hard rations, and their health demanded that they should have as much fresh food as possible when they were resting at base.

* * *

The successes of the battalion began on the second night. On April 2, 1951, acting on police information, a platoon of A Company commanded by 2nd Lieutenant Beale laid an ambush on Sungei Kalong estate. Soon after dark heavy firing was heard, and at about 10 p.m. the platoon returned to K.K.B. with the bodies of two terrorists and their rifles and ammunition. A few days later another ambush was laid in the same area, and two more bandits were killed. On this occasion more of the enemy were thought to be lurking in the area, and all available troops hastily surrounded it. A Company then moved through the area and found another dead bandit. These early successes were great morale-raisers.

B Company then came into the picture with a successful ambush on the Ulu Selangor estate on May 16. Three bandits walked into it and, in the words of Major Rickcord's signal, 'were instantly destroyed.' Apart from the arms recovered, one of the deceased was a terrorist of

II

considerable note. On June 1, S Company relieved B Company at Kerling, and B came into reserve at K.K.B. From then onwards companies changed over frequently.

C Company's turn came on June 4, when 7 Platoon killed a bandit in a *kampong*, 2nd Lieutenant G. H. W. Howlett (son of Brigadier 'Swifty' Howlett) having a lucky escape when a grenade landed at his feet and failed to explode. This, in fact, was a very good effort because this company had a large area to look after and were a long way from their associated police H.Q.

By June 26 the battalion had received sufficient reinforcements to enable D Company to be formed under Captain Upton. Each draft on arrival had carried out four weeks' jungle training at K.K.B., and it was from these and their training cadres that the company had been built up. This increase in strength enabled parties to go regularly on leave, Penang being the most popular leave-centre. On August 21 the newly-formed D Company moved to Kerling in relief of S Company.

The battalion suffered its first battle casualties on August 22 when a road patrol sent out by B Company came under brief automatic fire. Two of the patrol were wounded (one mortally). The remainder debussed and returned the fire, but no known casualties were inflicted on the bandits. Shortly after this, four men of B Company under 2nd Lieutenant Wilson fought an engagement with about twenty terrorists. The result was inconclusive, but the enemy were forced into rapid flight.

On September 6 a platoon of D Company were moving through overgrown rubber in the Tanjong Malim district when they had head-on contact with a gang of about ten bandits, who had evidently seen them first. The leading scout was killed instantly and another man was wounded. The platoon immediately attacked the terrorists, who withdrew with no known casualties. During subsequent operations the platoon exacted some retribution by killing a member of the gang.

More terrorists were killed by the battalion in September and during the early days of October, and with eighteen bandits to their credit in the first six months the battalion could look back on an excellent start. Sombre events were about to follow.

*   *   *

On October 6 the battalion received the shattering news that the High Commissioner for Malaya, Sir Henry Gurney, had been ambushed and killed by terrorists at a steep bend on the Fraser's Hill road about a mile inside the battalion's boundary. Nobody in the battalion or at Brigade Headquarters had any knowledge of the journey Sir Henry was to make that day. Colonel Martyn was ordered to take charge of the situation, and all available troops in the area were placed under his command. When he arrived at the scene, he found that a gang of some forty terrorists with light machine guns had crossed the battalion boundary to lay the ambush. They were, in consequence, almost certain to have withdrawn into thick jungle which the troops did not know. A cordon was thrown round an extensive area, which was bombed by the R.A.F. and then searched by the troops, but no contact was made. After ten days the search was relaxed, and the battalion returned to routine patrolling.

This disaster was quickly followed by another. On October 22, having completed a forty-eight hours' patrol, 11 Platoon of D Company was picked up at the Ulu Caledonia Estate buildings by transport, which had been brought there by Captain Deed, and started on the return journey to Kerling. After travelling about two miles the convoy came under a withering fire from some forty terrorists entrenched in irrigation ditches on hillocks on the side of the track. Captain Deed, the Platoon Serjeant and three men were killed in the leading vehicle by the first bursts. 2nd Lieutenant Gregson, the Platoon Commander, was seriously wounded. Within a few moments L/Cpl. Martin was the only officer or N.C.O. alive or unwounded. The escorting Scout Car engaged one of the two main enemy positions, but its guns were put out of action by a hit on the mounting.

The object of the terrorists was the capture of arms. But the troops were not found wanting. They quickly took up the best positions they could find and fought back. All efforts of the bandits to charge were halted and, unable to subdue the troops by fire, they rolled grenades down the hillocks and resorted to weird yells and calls to surrender. L/Cpl. Martin was badly wounded, and Pte. Pannell assumed command. By moving about with complete disregard for his own safety, he inspired his comrades to beat back rush after rush. Finally, after about an hour, the terrorists withdrew, leaving three of their weapons in our hands. Pte. Pannell, who had been hit four times, then walked back with one other man to the estate for help.

When help arrived the signs of the desperate and gallantly-fought engagement could still be seen. A 3-ton lorry, a scout car and a 15-cwt truck were spaced over some 100 yards of track. All had tyres punctured and glass smashed, and the unarmoured vehicles were riddled with bullets. In the leading vehicle and in positions from which they had been firing on the ground were one officer, ten other ranks and three Iban trackers dead. There was not a single uninjured soldier. Lying amongst them were four terrorists dead, brought down as they charged. In the search and follow-up operations which followed two more bandits were killed.

Pte. Pannell and L/Cpl. Martin received immediate awards of the D.C.M. and M.M., though all who fought that day had contributed to the defeat of the enemy. If that thin jungle-green line had given way, five Bren guns, as well as the normal complement of weapons of a platoon, would have fallen into the hands of the terrorists. This would have been a disaster of the first magnitude. Once again the tradition of the Regiment had been upheld.

*   *   *

There is no space to record in detail the remaining engagements and successes of the battalion during the waning of 1951. When Lieutenant-Colonel A. Martyn handed over command in January 1952, the number of terrorists killed by the battalion had reached forty-one. This compared very favourably with other units.

Index

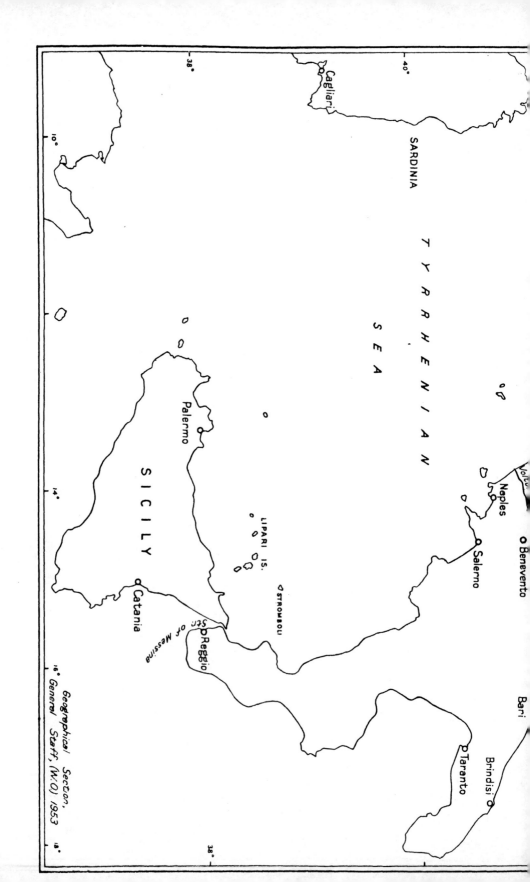

SARDINIA

Cagliari

T Y R R H E N I A N

S E A

Palermo

S I C I L Y

LIPARI IS.

STROMBOLI

Catania

Str. of Messina

Reggio

Naples

Salerno

Benevento

Bari

Brindisi

Taranto

Geographical Section,
General Staff, (W.O) 1953

40°

38°

10°

14°

16°

18°

38°

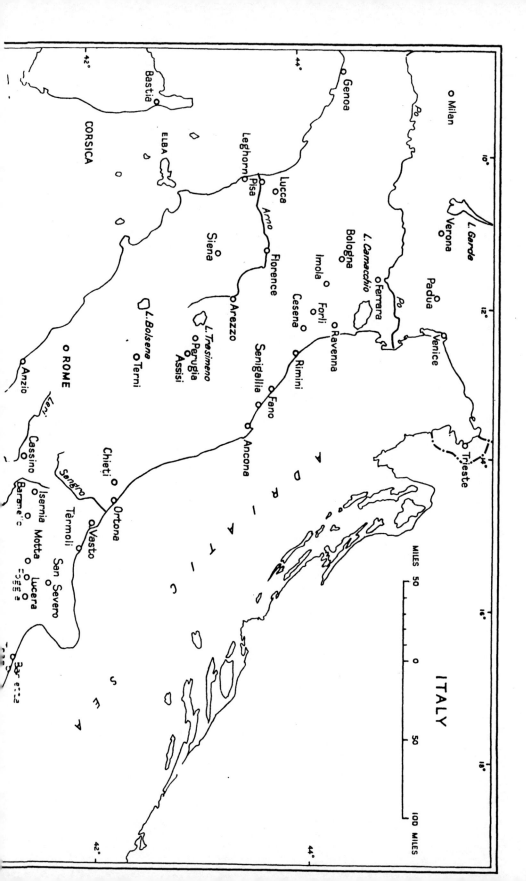